Baseball America

2000 DIRECTORY

The Complete Pocket Baseball Guide

Major, Minor and Independent League
Names, Addresses, Schedules,
Phone and FAX Numbers

Detailed Information
On International, College and
Amateur Baseball

PUBLISHED BY
BASEBALL AMERICA

Baseball America

2000 DIRECTORY

Published By Baseball America

EDITOR
Allan Simpson

ASSOCIATE EDITOR
Geoff Wilson

ASSISTANT EDITORS
Mark Derewicz
John Royster

PRODUCTION DIRECTOR
Phillip Daquila

PRODUCTION ASSISTANTS
Pattie Keckeisen
Alex Ladd

SERVICE DIRECTORY MANAGER
Stephanie Larkin

BaseBall america

PUBLISHER
Lee Folger

EDITOR
Allan Simpson

MANAGING EDITOR
Will Lingo

DESIGN & PRODUCTION DIRECTOR
Phillip Daquila

TABLEOFCONTENTS

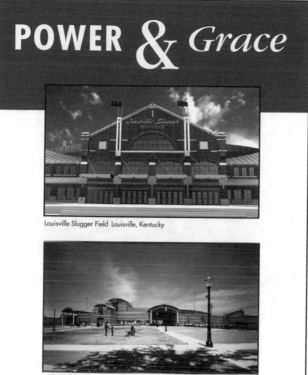

2000-2001 CALENDAR

March 2000

Sun	Mon	Tue	Wed	Thu	Fri	Sat
			1	2	3	4
5	6	7	8	9	10	11
12	13	14	15	16	17	18
19	20	21	22	23	24	25
26	27	28	29	30	31	

April 2000

Sun	Mon	Tue	Wed	Thu	Fri	Sat
						1
2	3	4	5	6	7	8
9	10	11	12	13	14	15
16	17	18	19	20	21	22
23	24	25	26	27	28	29
30						

May 2000

Sun	Mon	Tue	Wed	Thu	Fri	Sat
	1	2	3	4	5	6
7	8	9	10	11	12	13
14	15	16	17	18	19	20
21	22	23	24	25	26	27
28	29	30	31			

June 2000

Sun	Mon	Tue	Wed	Thu	Fri	Sat
				1	2	3
4	5	6	7	8	9	10
11	12	13	14	15	16	17
18	19	20	21	22	23	24
25	26	27	28	29	30	

July 2000

Sun	Mon	Tues	Wed	Thur	Fri	Sat
						1
2	3	4	5	6	7	8
9	10	11	12	13	14	15
16	17	18	19	20	21	22
23	24	25	26	27	28	29
30	31					

August 2000

Sun	Mon	Tue	Wed	Thu	Fri	Sat
		1	2	3	4	5
6	7	8	9	10	11	12
13	14	15	16	17	18	19
20	21	22	23	24	25	26
27	28	29	30	31		

September 2000

Sun	Mon	Tue	Wed	Thu	Fri	Sat
					1	2
3	4	5	6	7	8	9
10	11	12	13	14	15	16
17	18	19	20	21	22	23
24	25	26	27	28	29	30

October 2000

Sun	Mon	Tue	Wed	Thu	Fri	Sat
1	2	3	4	5	6	7
8	9	10	11	12	13	14
15	16	17	18	19	20	21
22	23	24	25	26	27	28
29	30	31				

November 2000

Sun	Mon	Tue	Wed	Thu	Fri	Sat
			1	2	3	4
5	6	7	8	9	10	11
12	13	14	15	16	17	18
19	20	21	22	23	24	25
26	27	28	29	30		

December 2000

Sun	Mon	Tue	Wed	Thu	Fri	Sat
					1	2
3	4	5	6	7	8	9
10	11	12	13	14	15	16
17	18	19	20	21	22	23
24	25	26	27	28	29	30
31						

January 2001

Sun	Mon	Tue	Wed	Thu	Fri	Sat
	1	2	3	4	5	6
7	8	9	10	11	12	13
14	15	16	17	18	19	20
21	22	23	24	25	26	27
28	29	30	31			

February 2001

Sun	Mon	Tue	Wed	Thu	Fri	Sat
				1	2	3
4	5	6	7	8	9	10
11	12	13	14	15	16	17
18	19	20	21	22	23	24
25	26	27	28			

March 2001

Sun	Mon	Tue	Wed	Thu	Fri	Sat
				1	2	3
4	5	6	7	8	9	10
11	12	13	14	15	16	17
18	19	20	21	22	23	24
25	26	27	28	29	30	31

April 2001

Sun	Mon	Tue	Wed	Thu	Fri	Sat
1	2	3	4	5	6	7
8	9	10	11	12	13	14
15	16	17	18	19	20	21
22	23	24	25	26	27	28
29	30					

EVENTSCALENDAR

March 2000-February 2001

March

31—Opening Day: Japan.

April

3—Opening Day: American League (Detroit at Oakland, Yankees at Anaheim, White Sox at Texas, Tampa Bay at Minnesota, Kansas City at Toronto, Cleveland at Baltimore).

3—Opening Day: National League (Los Angeles at Montreal, San Diego at Mets, Colorado at Atlanta, San Francisco at Florida, Houston at Pittsburgh, Milwaukee at Cincinnati, Cubs at St. Louis).

4—Opening Day: American League (Boston at Seattle).

4—Opening Day: National League (Philadelphia at Arizona).

5—Opening Day: Mexican League.

6—Opening Day: International League, Pacific Coast League, Southern League, Texas League, California League, Carolina League, Florida State League, Midwest League, South Atlantic League.

7—Opening Day: Eastern League.

17—National Classic High School Tournament at Orange County, Calif. (thru April 20).

28—Opening Day: Atlantic League.

May

4—Opening Day: Texas-Louisiana League.

18—Opening Day: Western League.

20—Junior College Division III World Series at Batavia, N.Y. (thru May 26).

26—Opening Day: Northern League.

26—NCAA Division I Regionals at campus sites (thru May 28).

26—NCAA Division III World Series at Appleton, Wis. (thru May 30).

26—NAIA World Series at Lewiston, Idaho (thru June 2).

27—NCAA Division II World Series at Montgomery, Ala. (thru June 3).

27—Junior College Division II World Series at Millington, Tenn. (thru June 3).

27—Junior College World Series at Grand Junction, Colo. (thru June 3).

31—Opening Day: Frontier League.

June

1—Opening Day: Atlantic Collegiate League, California Coastal Collegiate League, Coastal Plain League, Eastern Collegiate League, Pacific International League.

2—First Interleague Games (EAST—Baltimore at Montreal, Tampa Bay at Mets, Boston at Philadelphia, Yankees at Atlanta, Toronto at Florida. CENTRAL—Kansas City at Pittsburgh, Minnesota at Cincinnati, Detroit at Cubs, Cleveland at St. Louis, White Sox at Houston. WEST—San Diego at Seattle, San Francisco at Oakland, Los Angeles at Anaheim, Arizona at Texas).

2—NCAA Division I Super Regionals at campus sites (thru June 4).

2—Opening Day: Clark Griffith League, Coastal Plain League, Jayhawk League, Northwoods League, Shenandoah Valley League.

4—Opening Day: New England Collegiate League.

5—Amateur free agent draft (thru June 6).

6—Opening Day: Central Illinois Collegiate League.

8—Opening Day: Alaska League, Jayhawk League.

9—54th College World Series at Omaha (thru June 17).

9—Opening Day: Northeastern Collegiate League.

13—Opening Day: Cape Cod League.

16—Opening Day: Pioneer League.

16—USA Junior Olympic Championship at Tucson (thru June 24).

17—Florida State League all-star game at Jupiter, Fla.

18—Texas League all-stars vs. Mexican League all-stars at El Paso.

20—Opening Day: New York-Penn League, Northwest League.

20—Southern League All-Star Game at Greenville, S.C.

20—Texas League all-stars vs. Mexican League all-stars at Monterrey, Mexico.

20—California League/Carolina League all-star game at Kinston, N.C.

20—Midwest League all-star game at Geneva, Ill.

20—South Atlantic League all-star game at Charleston, S.C.

22—Team One National Showcase at Tempe, Ariz. (thru June 24).

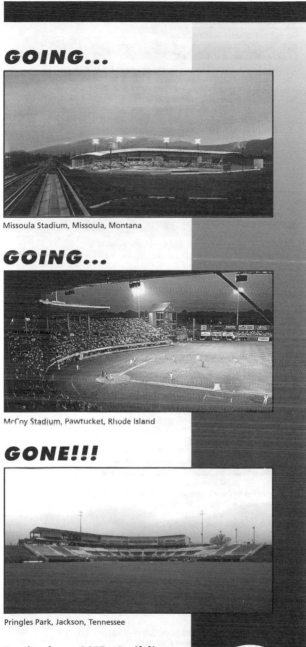

22—Sunbelt Classic Baseball Series at Shawnee/Tecumseh, Okla. (thru June 26)
23—Opening Day: Appalachian League.
23—Opening Day: Arizona League.

July

9—2nd Major League Futures Game at Turner Field, Atlanta.
10—Western League All-Star Game at Chico, Calif.
11—71st Major League All-Star Game at Turner Field, Atlanta.
12—Triple-A All-Star Game at Rochester, N.Y.
12—Double-A All-Star Game at Bowie, Md.
12—Atlantic League All-Star Game at Somerset, N.J.
12—Frontier League All-Star Game at O'Fallon, Mo.
13—Team USA junior national team trials at Joplin, Mo. (thru July 22).
22—Cape Cod League All-Star Game at Brewster, Mass.
22—Japan All-Star Game I at Tokyo Dome.
23—Japan All-Star Game II at Green Stadium, Kobe.
23—Hall of Fame induction ceremonies, Cooperstown.
24—Hall of Fame Game, Arizona vs. Cleveland at Cooperstown.
25—Japan All-Star Game III at Nagasaki Stadium.
29—National Baseball Congress World Series at Wichita (thru Aug. 12).

August

1—Northern League All-Star Game at Little Falls, N.J.
1—End of major league trading period without waivers.
1—East Coast Professional Baseball Showcase at Wilmington, N.C. (thru Aug. 5).
3—IBA World Junior Championship at Edmonton, Alberta (thru Aug. 14).
4—Connie Mack World Series at Farmington, N.M. (thru Aug. 11).
6—Area Code Games at Long Beach (thru Aug. 12).
12—Pony League World Series at Washington, Pa. (thru Aug. 19).
12—Babe Ruth 16-18 World Series at Concord, N.H. (thru Aug. 19).
18—American Legion World Series at Alton, Ill. (thru Aug. 22).
19—Babe Ruth 13-15 World Series at Jamestown, N.Y. (thru Aug. 26).
20—Little League World Series at Williamsport, Pa. (thru Aug. 26).
31—Postseason major league roster eligibility frozen.

September

1—Major league roster limits expanded from 25 to 40.
15—Opening ceremonies, Sydney Olympics.
17—Olympic baseball competition begins.
18—Triple-A World Series at Las Vegas, International League vs. Pacific Coast League (thru Sept. 22).
27—Gold and bronze medal games, Sydney Olympics.

October

1—Major league season ends.
2—Beginning of major league trading period without waivers.
3—Major league Division Series begin.
4—Opening Day: Arizona Fall League.
10—Major League Championship Series begin.
21—World Series begins at home of American League champion.
21—Japan Series begins at home of Central League champion.

November

20—Forty-man major league winter rosters must be filed.

December

1—National High School Baseball Coaches Association convention at Knoxville (thru Dec. 3).
8—98th annual Winter Meetings at Dallas (thru Dec. 11).
11—Rule 5 major league/minor league drafts.

January 2001

4—American Baseball Coaches Association convention at Nashville (thru Jan. 7)
6—NCAA Convention at Lake Buena Vista, Fla. (thru Jan. 9)

February 2001

2—Caribbean World Series at Culiacan, Mexico (thru Feb. 7).

BASEBALL AMERICA

ESTABLISHED 1981

PUBLISHER: Lee Folger

EDITOR: Allan Simpson

MANAGING EDITOR: Will Lingo
SENIOR EDITOR: John Royster
ASSOCIATE EDITOR: James Bailey
ASSOCIATE EDITOR: Lacy Lusk
ASSOCIATE EDITOR: John Manuel
SENIOR WRITER: Alan Schwarz
NATIONAL CORRESPONDENT: David Rawnsley
ASSISTANT EDITOR: Mark Derewicz
ASSISTANT EDITOR: Geoff Wilson

DESIGN AND PRODUCTION DIRECTOR: Phillip Daquila
PRODUCTION ASSISTANT: Pattie Keckeisen
PRODUCTION ASSISTANT: Alex Ladd

CUSTOMER SERVICE: Ronnie McCabe, Maxine Tillman
E-Mail Address: customerservice@baseballamerica.com

RECEPTIONIST: Linda Jackson

ADVERTISING SALES
Stephanie Larkin, MarketPlace Manager
P.O. Box 2089, Durham, NC 27702
Phone 800-845-2726; FAX: 919-682-2880

NATIONAL NEWSSTAND CONSULTANT
John Blassingame, Linden, NJ

BASEBALL AMERICA, Inc.

CHAIRMAN: Miles Wolff
Mailing Address: P.O. Box 2089, Durham, NC 27702
Street Address: 600 S. Duke St., Durham, NC 27701
Phone: 919-682-9635 • **Toll-Free:** 800-845-2726
FAX: 919-682-2880
Website: www.baseballamerica.com

BASEBALL AMERICA, the nation's most complete all-baseball newspaper, publishes 26 issues a year. Subscription rates are $48.95 for one year, payable in U.S. funds.

BASEBALL AMERICA PUBLICATIONS

2000 Almanac: A comprehensive look at the 1999 season, featuring major and minor league statistics and commentary. **$12.95** ($15.95 spiral bound)

2000 Directory: Names, addresses, phone numbers, major, minor and independent league schedules—vital to baseball insiders and fans. **$13.95** ($16.95 spiral bound)

2000 Super Register: A complete record, with biographical information, of every player who played professional baseball in 1999. **$39.95**

2000 Great Parks: The Baseball America Calendar **$10.95**

Encyclopedia of Minor League Baseball: The first total compilation of the teams and standings in the 90-year history of minor league baseball. The ultimate research tool. **$48.95** hardcover, **$39.95** softcover

The Minor League Register: An updated compilation of SABR's The Minor League Stars with more than 200 new entries, minor league milestones. **$39.95** softcover

BASEBALLAMERICA

1999 AWARD WINNERS

MAJOR LEAGUES

Player of the Year
Pedro Martinez, rhp, Boston

Position Player of the Year
Chipper Jones, 3b, Atlanta

Pitcher of the Year
Pedro Martinez, rhp, Boston

Rookie of the Year
Carlos Beltran, of, Kansas City

Manager of the Year
Jimy Williams, Boston

Executive of the Year
Jim Bowden, Cincinnati

MINOR LEAGUES

Organization of the Year
Oakland Athletics

Player of the Year (overall)
Rick Ankiel, lhp, Arkansas (Texas)/Memphis (Pacific Coast)

Manager of the Year
John Mizerock, Wichita (Texas)

Team of the Year
Trenton Thunder (Eastern)

Players of the Year
Triple-A: Steve Cox, 1b, Durham
Double-A: Adam Piatt, 3b, Midland
Class A: Chin-Feng Chen, of, San Bernardino
Short-Season: Lyle Overbay, 1b, Missoula

Freitas Awards
Triple-A: Louisville RiverBats (International)
Double-A: Portland Sea Dogs (Eastern)
Class A: Wilmington Blue Rocks (Carolina)
Short-Season: Portland Rockies (Northwest)

INDEPENDENT BASEBALL

Player of the Year
Carmine Cappuccio, of, New Jersey (Northern)

WINTER BASEBALL

Player of the Year
Morgan Burkhardt, 1b, Navojoa (Mexican Pacific)

COLLEGE BASEBALL

Player of the Year
Jason Jennings, rhp/dh, Baylor

Coach of the Year
Wayne Graham, Rice

Freshman of the Year
James Jurries, 2b, Tulane

AMATEUR BASEBALL

Summer Player of the Year
Xavier Nady, 3b, Team USA

HIGH SCHOOL BASEBALL

Player of the Year
Josh Hamilton, of/lhp, Athens Drive HS, Raleigh, N.C.

TOLLFREENUMBERS

Airlines

Aeromexico	800-237-6639
Air Canada	800-776-3000
Alaska Airlines	800-426-0333
Aloha Airlines	800-227-4900
America West	800-235-9292
American Airlines	800-433-7300
Canadian Air	800-282-4751
Continental Airlines	800-525-0280
Delta Air Lines	800-221-1212
Japan Air Lines	800-525-3663
Korean Air	800-438-5000
Midway Airlines	800-446-4392
Northwest Airlines	800-225-2525
Olympic Airways	800-223-1226
Qantas Airways	800-227-4500
Southwest Airlines	800-435-9792
Trans World Airlines	800-221-2000
United Airlines	800-631-1500
U.S. Airways	800-428-4322

Car Rentals

Alamo (except Florida)	800-327-9633
Alamo (Florida only)	800-732-3232
Avis	800-331-1212
Avis International	800-331-1084
Budget	800-527-0700
Dollar	800-800-4000
Enterprise	800-325-8007
Hertz	800-654-3131
Hertz International	800-654-3001
National	800-227-7368
Thrifty	800-367-2277

Hotels/Motels

Best Western	800-528-1234
Choice Hotels	800-424-6423
Comfort Inn	800-221-2222
Courtyard by Marriott	800-321-2211
Days Inn	800-325-2525
Doubletree Hotels/Guest Suites	800-424-2900
Econo Lodge	800-424-4777
Embassy Suites	800-362-2779
Hampton Inns	800-426-7866
Hilton Hotels	800-445-8667
Holiday Inns	800-465-4329
Howard Johnsons Motor Lodges	800-654-2000
Hyatt Hotels	800-228-9000
La Quinta	800-531-5900
Marriott Hotels	800-228-9290
Omni Hotels	800-843-6664
Radisson Hotels	800-333-3333
Ramada Inns	800-228-2828
Red Roof Inns	800-843-7663
Residence Inn (Marriott)	800-331-3131
Sheraton Hotels	800-325-3535
Renaissance Hotels/Resorts	800-468-3571
TraveLodge	800-578-7878
Westin Hotels	800-228-3000

Rail

Amtrak	800-872-7245

WHAT'S NEW IN '00

MAJOR LEAGUE BASEBALL

■ **BALLPARKS**
Detroit: Comerica Park.
Houston: Enron Field.
San Francisco: Pacific Bell Park.

MINOR LEAGUES

Triple-A

■ Vancouver (Pacific Coast) relocated to Sacramento.
■ **BALLPARKS**
Louisville: Louisville Slugger Field.
Memphis: AutoZone Park.
Sacramento: Raley Field.
■ **AFFILIATION CHANGES**
Cincinnati from Indianapolis to Louisville.
Milwaukee from Louisville to Indianapolis.

Double-A

■ Jackson (Texas) relocated to Round Rock.
■ **BALLPARKS**
Chattanooga: BellSouth Park.
Orlando: Disney Complex.
Round Rock: Dell Diamond.
Tennessee: Smokies Park.
■ **NAME CHANGE**
Knoxville (Southern) to Tennessee.

Class A

■ Rockford (Midwest) relocated to Dayton.
■ **BALLPARK**
Dayton: Fifth Third Field.
■ **NAME CHANGE**
Stockton Ports (California) to Mudville Nine.

Short-Season

■ St. Catharines (New York-Penn) relocated to Brooklyn.
■ Southern Oregon (Northwest) relocated to Vancouver, B.C.
■ **AFFILIATION CHANGES**
New York (NL) drops Gulf Coast League team.
San Francisco adds Arizona League team.

INDEPENDENT LEAGUES

■ Expansion franchises granted to Jackson (Texas-Louisiana), Long Island (Atlantic), Maryland (Atlantic), San Angelo (Texas-Louisiana), Valley/Scottsdale (Western) and Yuma (Western).
■ Abilene (Texas-Louisiana) folded.
■ Catskill (Northern) resumed operations.
■ Massachusetts (Northern) dormant, will relocate to Hartford in 2001.
■ Reno (Western) relocated to Feather River.
■ Sacramento (Western) relocated to Solano.

NICKNAMES

■ None.

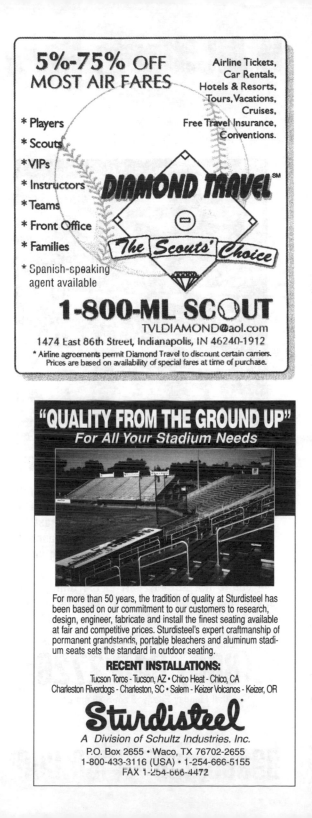

It All Starts Here

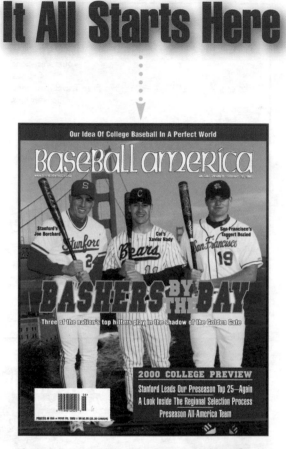

Long before the Directory or the Super Register, there was Baseball America–The Magazine. We've been around for almost 20 years and we're still bringing you the baseball news you can't get anywhere else, from youth baseball to the big leagues.

If you're not already part of the team, start saving today with a one-year subscription for only $48.95 (26 issues) or two years for $87.95 (52 issues).

(800) 845-2726

Call Monday-Friday, 9 am-5:30 pm ET

Come Visit Us At

baseballamerica.com

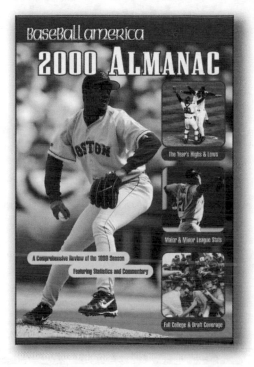

Opportunity doesn't knock anymore, it double-clicks.

Putting your business on the Web doesn't have to be a painful process. MindSpring Biz can help you do everything from reserve your domain name to design and publish your site on the Web. We can even provide high-speed access for your office. Once you're with MindSpring Biz, you'll be asking us "Why did I wait so long to get my business on the Web?"

Call MindSpring Biz today at 1-888-MSPRING - we'll waive your start-up fee and you'll get your first month of hosting free.*

MAJOR LEAGUES

MAJOR LEAGUE BASEBALL

Mailing Address: 245 Park Ave., New York, NY 10167. Telephone: (212) 931-7800. Website: www.majorleaguebaseball.com.

Commissioner: Allan H. "Bud" Selig.

Senior Executive Assistant to Commissioner: Lori Keck. Administrative Assistant to Commissioner: Sandy Ronback.

Chief Operating Officer: Paul Beeston.

Bud Selig

Baseball Operations

Executive Vice President: Sandy Alderson.

Executive Director: Bill Murray. Director: Roy Krasik. Supervisor: Jeff Pfeifer. Administrator, Latin America: George Moreira. Special Assistant: Ralph Nelson.

Executive Director, Minor League Operations: Jimmie Lee Solomon. Supervisor, Minor League Operations: Sylvia Galindo. Administrator, Minor League Operations: Pat Vixama.

General Administration

Executive Vice President, Administration: Robert DuPuy.

Executive VP, Labor Relations/Human Resources: Robert Manfred.

Paul Beeston

General Counsel, Office of the Commissioner: Thomas Ostertag. General Labor Counsel: Francis Coonelly. General Counsel, MLB Enterprises: Ethan Orlinsky.

Vice President, Finance: Thomas Duffy. Chief Financial Officer: Jeffrey White.

Executive Director, Security/Facilities Management: Kevin Hallinan.

Senior VP, Domestic and International Licensing: Tim Brosnan. Senior Vice President, MLB Productions: Stephen Hellmuth. Vice President, Broadcasting/New Media: Leslie Sullivan.

Vice President, Marketing: Kathy Francis. Vice President, Team Services: Mark Gorris. Vice President, Events: Marla Miller. Vice President, Licensing: Howard Smith Executive Director, Human Resources/Office Services: Wendy Lewis. Executive Director, Baseball Assistance Team: James Martin.

Public Relations

Telephone: (212) 931-7878. FAX: (212) 949-5654.

Executive Director: Richard Levin.

Managers: Carole Coleman, Pat Courtney, Derrick Johnson.

Manager, Baseball Information System: Rob Doelger. Supervisor: Kathleen Fineout. Administrators: Matt Gould, Lisa Quinn. Assistant, Public Relations: Blakely Blum. Assistant,

Sandy Alderson

Public Relations/Baseball Information System: John Blundell. Administrative Assistants: Heather Flock, Nelvie Henry.

Major League Baseball International

Mailing Address: 245 Park Ave., 30th Floor, New York, NY 10167. Telephone: (212) 931-7500. FAX: (212) 949-5795.

VP, International Business Operations: Paul Archey. VP, International Licensing: Shawn Lawson Cummings. International Licensing Manager, Latin America: Deidra Varona.

Manager, Sponsorship/Broadcasting Promotions: Sara Loarte. Supervisor, Client Services: Michael Luscher.

VP, Market Development: Jim Small. Manager, Business Affairs: Peter Carton. Coordinator, Market Development: Chris Tobias.

VP, International Production/Television Operations: Russell Gabay. Field Production Supervisor, International Broadcasting: Margie O'Neill. Coordinator, Broadcasting/Television: Marcia Price. Director, European Operations: Clive Russell. Director, Australian Operations: Simon Gray.

Events

2000 Major League All-Star Game: July 11 at Turner Field, Atlanta.

2000 World Series: Begins Oct. 21 at home of American League champion.

AMERICAN LEAGUE

AMERICAN LEAGUE

Mailing Address: 245 Park Ave., 28th Floor, New York, NY 10167.
Telephone: (212) 931-7600. **FAX:** (212) 949-5405.
Years League Active: 1901-.
Vice President: Carl Pohlad (Minnesota).
Board of Directors: Boston, Chicago, Cleveland, Detroit, Kansas City, Seattle.
Executive Director, Umpiring: Marty Springstead. **Coordinator, Umpire Operations:** Philip Janssen. **Administrator, Umpire Travel:** Tess Marino.
Senior Vice President: Phyllis Merhige.
Director, Waiver and Player Records: Brian Small. **Coordinator, Media and Waivers:** Jason Carr.
Administrative Assistant, Secretary to President: Carolyn Coen.
Administrative Assistant, Secretary to Vice Presidents: Angelica Cintron.
Receptionist: Nancy Navarro.
2000 Opening Date: April 3. **Closing Date:** Oct. 1.
Regular Season: 162 games.
Division Structure: East—Baltimore, Boston, New York, Tampa Bay, Toronto. **Central**—Chicago, Cleveland, Detroit, Kansas City, Minnesota. **West**—Anaheim, Oakland, Seattle, Texas.
Playoff Format: Three division champions and second-place team with best record meet in best-of-5 Division Series. Winners meet in best-of-7 League Championship Series.
All-Star Game: July 11 at Atlanta (National League vs. American League).
Roster Limit: 25, through Aug. 31 when rosters expand to 40.
Brand of Baseball: Rawlings.
Statistician: Elias Sports Bureau, 500 Fifth Ave., New York, NY 10110.
Umpires: Unavailable.

Stadium Information

| City | Stadium | Dimensions | | | | |
		LF	CF	RF	Capacity	'99 Att.
Anaheim	Edison International	365	406	365	45,050	2,253,040
Baltimore	Camden Yards	333	410	318	48,876	3,432,099
Boston	Fenway Park	310	390	302	33,871	2,446,277
Chicago	Comiskey Park	347	400	347	44,321	1,338,851
Cleveland	Jacobs Field	325	405	325	43,863	3,468,436
Detroit	Comerica Park	346	422	330	40,000	*2,026,491
Kansas City	Kauffman Stadium	330	400	330	40,529	1,501,292
Minnesota	Humphrey Metrodome	343	408	327	48,678	1,202,829
New York	Yankee Stadium	318	408	314	57,545	3,293,259
Oakland	Network Assoc. Coliseum	330	400	367	43,662	1,434,632
Seattle	Safeco Field	331	405	326	45,600	2,915,828
Tampa Bay	Tropicana Field	315	407	322	45,200	1,749,557
Texas	Ballpark in Arlington	334	400	325	49,166	2,774,501
Toronto	SkyDome	328	400	328	50,516	2,163,486

*Attendance figure for Tiger Stadium

ANAHEIM

Telephone, Address
Office Address: Edison International Field of Anaheim, 2000 Gene Autry Way, Anaheim, CA 92806. Mailing Address: P.O. Box 2000, Anaheim, CA 92803. Telephone: (714) 940-2000. FAX: (714) 940-2001. Website: www.angelsbaseball.com.

Ownership
Operated by: The Walt Disney Company. Chairman/Chief Executive Officer: Michael Eisner. President: Tony Tavares.

BUSINESS OPERATIONS
Vice President, Finance/Administration: Andy Roundtree.

Michael Eisner

Vice President, Business/Legal Affairs: Rick Schlesinger. Manager, Human Resources: Jenny Price. Assistant, Human Resources: Alex Oftelie. Administrative Assistant: Cindy Williams.

Finance/Administration
Director, Finance: John Rinehart. Senior Financial Analyst: Amy Langdale. Senior Business Development Analyst: Marc Kolin. Manager, Information Systems: Al Castro. Senior Network Engineer: Neil Farris. Senior Travel Consultant: Chantelle Ball.

Marketing, Sales
Vice President, Sales/Marketing: Ron Minegar.
Vice President, Advertising Sales/Broadcasting: Bob Wagner.
Director, Advertising Sales/Broadcasting: Lawrence Cohen. Manager, Sponsorship Services/Synergy: Sue O'Shea. Manager, Broadcasting: Dan Patin. Manager, Broadcast Advertising Sales: Annemarie de LeBohn. Sponsorship Services Representative: Jennifer Guran. Coordinator, Advertising Sales: Sheila Tavares.
Director, Marketing/Promotions: Lisa Manning. Manager, Group Sales: Steve Shiffman. Manager, Suites/Guest Relations: Robin Perches. Director, Entertainment: Rod Murray.

Public Relations, Communications
Telephone: (714) 940-2014. FAX: (714) 940-2205.
Vice President, Communications: Tim Mead.
Manager, Baseball Information: Larry Babcock. Manager, Media Services: Nancy Mazmanian. Manager, Publications: Doug Ward. Manager, Civic Affairs: Marie Moreno.
Media Services Representatives: Eric Kay, Aaron Tom.
Speakers' Bureau: Clyde Wright.

Stadium Operations
Vice President, Ballpark Operations: Kevin Uhlich.
Manager, Facility Services: Mike McKay. Manager, Event Services: John Drum. Manager, Security: Keith Cleary. Manager, Field/Ground Maintenance: Barney Lopas.
PA Announcer: David Courtney. Official Scorer: Ed Munson.

Ticketing
Director, Ticket Sales/Customer Service: Andy Silverman. Manager, Ticket Operations: Sheila Brazelton. Assistant Ticket Manager: Susan Weiss. Supervisor, Ticketing: Kevin Dart.

Travel, Clubhouse
Equipment Manager: Ken Higdon. Assistant Equipment Manager: Keith Tarter. Visiting Clubhouse: Brian Harkins.
Senior Video Coordinator: Diego Lopez. Video Coordinator: Ruben Montano.

General Information
Home Dugout: Third Base. Playing Surface: Grass.
Stadium Location: Highway 57 (Orange Freeway) to Katella Avenue exit, west on Katella, stadium on west side of Orange Freeway. Standard Game Times: 7:05 p.m., Sun. (April-June 25) 1:05, (July 2-Sept.) 5:05.
Player Representative: Troy Percival.

ANGELS

BASEBALL OPERATIONS

Vice President/General Manager: Bill Stoneman.

Assistant General Manager: Ken Forsch. Special Assistants to GM: Preston Gomez (Yorba Linda, CA), Gary Sutherland (Monrovia, CA). Administrative Assistant to GM: Cathy Caroy.

Manager, Baseball Operations: Tony Reagins.

Major League Staff

Manager: Mike Scioscia.

Coaches: Dugout—Joe Maddon; Pitching—Bud Black; Batting—Mickey Hatcher; First Base—Alfredo Griffin; Third Base—Ron Roenicke; Bullpen—Orlando Mercado.

Bill Stoneman

Mike Scioscia

Medical, Training

Medical Director: Dr. Lewis Yocum. Club Physician: Dr. Craig Milhouse. Head Trainer: Ned Bergert. Assistant Trainer: Rick Smith. Strength and Conditioning Specialist: Brian Grapes.

Player Development

Telephone: (714) 940-2031. FAX: (714) 940-2205.

Director, Player Development/Field Coordinator: Darrell Miller. Administrative Assistant: Laura Fazioli.

Roving Instructors: Bob Clear (special assignment), Mike Couchee (pitching), Trent Clark (strength/conditioning), Bruce Hines (defense), John McNamara (catching), Gene Richards (hitting).

Farm System

Class	Farm Team	Manager	Coach	Pitching Coach
AAA	Edmonton	Garry Templeton	Leon Durham	Greg Minton
AA	Erie	Don Wakamatsu	Bill Lachemann	Howie Gershberg
A	Lake Elsinore	Mario Mendoza	John Orton	Kernan Ronan
A	Cedar Rapids	Mitch Seoane	Tyrone Boykin	Randy Kramer
A	Boise	Tom Kotchman	Todd Claus	Zeke Zimmerman
R	Butte	Joe Urso	Jose Monzon	Mike Butcher
R	DSL	Unavailable	Unavailable	Unavailable

Scouting

Telephone: (714) 940-2038. FAX: (714) 940-2203.

Director, Scouting: Donny Rowland. Assistant to Director: Janet Mitchell.

Advance Scout: John Van Ornum (Bass Lake, CA). Major League Scouts: Jay Hankins (Greenwood, MO), Jon Neiderer (Johnstown, PA), Rich Schlenker (Walnut Creek, CA), Moose Stubing (Villa Park, CA), Dale Sutherland (La Crescenta, CA).

National Crosschecker: Rick Ingalls (Belmont Shores, CA). Free-Agent Supervisors: East—Clay Daniel (Jacksonville, FL), West Coast—Tom Davis (Ripon, CA), Midwest—Paul Robinson (Fort Worth, TX), North—Guy Mader (Tewksbury, MA).

Don Rowland

Area Scouts: Don Archer (Surrey, British Columbia), John Burden (Fairfield, OH), Tom Burns (Harrisburg, PA), Todd Claus (Tamarac, FL), Pete Coachman (Cottonwood, AL), Tim Corcoran (La Verne, CA), Jeff Crane (Huntsville, AL), Ed Crosby (Garden Grove, CA), David Crowson (College Station, TX), Steve Gruwell (West Covina, CA), Kevin Ham (Grand Prairie, TX), Al Hammell (Poughkeepsie, NY), Tim Kelly (Carlsbad, CA), Tom Kotchman (Seminole, FL), Bill Lachemann Jr. (Great Falls, MT), Ron Marigny (Lake Charles, LA), Tom Osowski (Milwaukee, WI), Michael Powers (Missouri City, TX), Jeff Scholzen (Hurricane, UT), Rick Schroeder (San Jose, CA), Jack Uhey (Vancouver, WA).

Coordinator, Latin America: George Lauzerique (Wellington, FL).

BALTIMORE

Telephone, Address
Office Address: 333 W Camden St., Baltimore, MD 21201. Telephone: (410) 685-9800. FAX: (410) 547-6272. E-Mail Address: fanservi@opacy.com. Website: www.theorioles.com.

Ownership
Operated by: Baltimore Orioles LP.
Principal Owner/Chairman: Peter Angelos. Executive Vice President: John Angelos. VP/Special Liaison to Chairman: Lou Kousouris.

BUSINESS OPERATIONS
Vice Chairman/Chief Operating Officer: Joe Foss. General Counsel: Russell Smouse.
Director, Human Resources: Martena Clinton.

Peter Angelos

Finance
Vice President/Chief Financial Officer: Robert Ames. Controller: Edward Kabernagel. Director, Information Systems: Jim Kline. Senior Staff Accountant: Mike Hopper.

Marketing, Sales
Vice President, Marketing/Broadcasting: Mike Lehr.
Manager, Advertising/Promotions: Jim Brylewski. Director, Sales: Matt Dryer. Manager, Corporate Marketing: Jim Hawes. Director, Publishing/Advertising: Christina Palmisano.

Public Relations, Communications
Telephone: (410) 547-6150. FAX: (410) 547-6272.
Director, Public Relations: Bill Stetka. Administrative Assistant, Public Relations: Kevin Behan.
Director, Community Relations: Julie Wagner. Manager, Community Relations: Stephani Lewis. Coordinator, Community Relations: Jennifer Steier.

Ballpark Operations
Director, Ballpark Operations: Roger Hayden. Manager, Event Operations: Doug Rosenberger.
Head Groundskeeper: Paul Zwaska.
PA Announcer: Dave McGowan. Official Scorers: Jim Henneman, Dave Hughes, Marc Jacobson.

Ticketing
Telephone: (410) 685-9800. FAX: (410) 547-6277.
Director, Fan/Ticket Services: Don Grove. Manager, Ticket Office: Audrey Brown. Manager, Ticket Operations: Steve Kowalski.

Travel, Clubhouse
Traveling Secretary: Phil Itzoe.
Manager, Home Clubhouse: Jim Tyler. Manager, Visitors Clubhouse: Fred Tyler.

General Information
Home Dugout: First Base. Playing Surface: Grass.
Stadium Location: From the north and east on I-95, take I-395 (exit 53), downtown to Russell Street; from the south or west on I-95, take exit 52 to Russell Street North. Standard Game Times: 7:35 p.m., 7:05 (April-May, September); Sat. 7:05, (April-May, September) 1:35; Sun. 1:35.
Player Representative: Mike Mussina.

ORIOLES

BASEBALL OPERATIONS
Telephone: (410) 547-6128. FAX: (410) 547-6271.
Executive VP, Baseball Operations: Syd Thrift.
Special Assistants to VP, Baseball Operations:
Danny Garcia, Bruce Manno, Bob Schaefer (Fort
Myers, FL). Executive Assistant to GM: Ann Lange.

Major League Staff
Manager: Mike Hargrove.
Coaches: Dugout—Jeff Newman; Pitching—
Sammy Elis; Batting—Terry Crowley; First Base—
Brian Graham; Third Base—Sam Perlozzo;
Bullpen—Elrod Hendricks, Eddie Murray.

Medical, Training
Club Physicians: Dr. William Goldiner, Dr.
Michael Jacobs.
Head Trainer: Richie Bancells. Assistant Trainer: Brian Ebel.
Strength/Conditioning Coach: Tim Bishop.

Syd Thrift

Mike Hargrove

Minor Leagues
Telephone: (410) 547 6120. FAX: (410) 547-6298.
Director, Minor League Operations: Don
Buford. Assistant Director, Minor League
Operations: Tripp Norton. Administrative Assis-
tant: Gabi Tapkas.
Director, Organizational Instruction: Tom
Trebelhorn. Camp Coordinator: Len Johnston.
Roving Instructors: Pat Hedge (strength/condi-
tioning), Bo McLaughlin (pitching), Dave Stockstill
(hitting), Denny Walling (infield/outfield/baserunning).
Coordinator, Latin America: Carlos Bernhardt.
Medical Coordinator: Mitch Bibb. Strength/
Conditioning Coordinator: Chris Dunaway.
Facilities Coordinator: Jaime Rodriguez.

Farm System

Class	Farm Team	Manager	Coach	Pitching Coach
AAA	Rochester	Marv Foley	Dave Cash	Larry McCall
AA	Bowie	Andy Etchebarren	Butch Davis	Dave Schmidt
A	Frederick	Dave Machemer	Dien Figueroa	Larry Jaster
A	Delmarva	Joe Ferguson	Bobby Rodriguez	Dave Schuler
R	Bluefield	Duffy Dyer	Len Johnston	Bob Lacey
R	Sarasota	Jesus Alfaro	Joe Tanner	Moe Drabowsky
R	DSL	Miguel Jabalara	Salvador Ramirez	

Scouting
Telephone: (410) 547-6187. FAX: (410) 547-6298.
Director, Scouting: Tony DeMacio.
Administrative Assistants: Brian Hopkins,
Marcy Zerhusen.
Advance Scout: Deacon Jones (Sugar Land,
TX). Professional Scouts: Cal Emery (Lake
Forest, CA), Curt Motton (Baltimore, MD), Tim
Thompson (Lewistown, PA), Fred Uhlman Sr.
(Baltimore, MD).
National Crosscheckers: Mike Ledna (Arlington
Heights, IL), Shawn Pender (Droxel Hill, PA).
Regional Crosscheckers: East—Dean Decillis
(Tamarac, FL); West—Logan White (Phoenix, AZ).

Tony DeMacio

Area Scouts: John Gillette (Kirkland, WA), Troy Hoerner (Minneapolis,
MN), Jim Howard (Clifton Park, NY), Gary Kendall (Baltimore, MD), Ray
Krawczyk (Lake Forest, CA), Gil Kubski (Huntington Beach, CA), Jeff Morris
(Tucson, AZ), Lamar North (Rossville, GA), Deron Rombach (Arlington, TX),
Harry Shelton (Ocoee, FL), Ed Sprague (Lodi, CA), Marc Tramuta
(Germantown, MD), Mike Tullier (New Orleans, LA), Dominic Viola
(Pittsburgh, PA), Marc Ziegler (Canal Winchester, OH).
Director, Latin American Scouting: Carlos Bernhardt (San Pedro de
Macoris, DR). Supervisor, Central/South America, Lesser Antilles:
Jesus Halabi (Aruba).

BOSTON

Telephone, Address
Office Address: Fenway Park, 4 Yawkey Way, Boston, MA 02215. **Telephone:** (617) 267-9440. **FAX:** (617) 375-0944. **Website:** www.redsox.com.

John Harrington

Ownership
Operated by: Boston Red Sox Baseball Club.
General Partner: Jean R. Yawkey Trust (Trustees: John Harrington, William Gutfarb).
Limited Partners: ARAMARK Corporation (Chairman: Joseph Neubauer); Dexter Group (Principal: Harold Alfond); Jean R. Yawkey Trust; Dr. Arthur Pappas; Samuel Tamposi Trust; Thomas DiBenedetto; John Harrington; John Kaneb.
Chief Executive Officer: John Harrington.

BUSINESS OPERATIONS
Executive Vice President, Administration: John Buckley. **Executive Administrative Assistant:** Jeanne Bill.
Director, Human Resources/Office Management: Michele Julian. **Administrative Assistant, Human Resources:** Adis Benitez.

Finance
Vice President, Chief Financial Officer: Robert Furbush.
Controller: Stanley Tran. **Assistant Controller:** Robin Yeingst.

Sales, Marketing
Vice President, Sales/Marketing: Larry Cancro.
Marketing Administrator: Deborah McIntyre. **Director, Advertising/Sponsorships:** Jeffrey Goldenberg.
Director, Sales: Michael Schetzel. **Manager, Promotions/Special Events:** Marcita Thompson. **Manager, Group Sales:** Corey Bowdre. **Manager, Season Tickets:** Joseph Matthews.
Vice President, Broadcasting/Technology: Jim Healey. **Manager, Broadcasting:** James Shannahan. **Manager, Information Technology:** Clay Rendon.

Public Affairs, Community Relations
Vice President, Public Affairs: Dick Bresciani.
Executive Consultant, Public Affairs: Lou Gorman. **Administrator, Public Affairs:** Mary Jane Ryan. **Manager, Publications:** Debra Matson. **Manager, Community Relations:** Ron Burton. **Manager, Public Affairs:** Fred Seymour. **Manager, Customer Relations:** Ann Marie Starzyk.

Stadium Operations
Vice President, Stadium Operations: Joe McDermott.
Superintendent, Grounds/Maintenance: Joe Mooney. **Manager, Ground Crew:** Casey Erven. **Stadium Operations:** Greg Arrington, Albert Forester. **Director, Facilities Management:** Thomas Queenan Jr.
PA Announcer: Ed Brickley. **Official Scorers:** Bruce Guindon, Dave O'Hara, Charles Scoggins.

Ticketing
Telephone: (617) 267-1700. **24-Hour Touchtone:** (617) 482-4769. **FAX:** (617) 236-6640.
Director, Ticket Operations: Joe Helyar. **Manager, Ticket Office:** Rich Beaton.

Travel, Clubhouse
Traveling Secretary: Jack McCormick. **Administrative Assistant:** Jean MacDougall.
Equipment Manager/Clubhouse Operations: Joe Cochran. **Visiting Clubhouse:** Tom McLaughlin.

General Information
Home Dugout: First Base. **Playing Surface:** Grass.
Directions to Stadium: Massachusetts Turnpike (I-90) to Prudential exit (stay left), right at first set of lights, right on Dalton Street, left on Boylston Street, right on Ipswich Street. **Standard Games Times:** 7:05 p.m.; Sat. 1:05, 5:05; Sun. 1:05.
Player Representative: Tim Wakefield.

RED SOX

BASEBALL OPERATIONS
Telephone: (617) 267-9440. FAX: (617) 236-6649.
Executive Vice President/General Manager: Dan Duquette.

Vice President, Baseball Operations: Mike Port. Vice President, Assistant GM/Legal Counsel: Elaine Steward. Assistant General Manager: Ed Kenney. Special Assistants to GM: Carlton Fisk, Lee Thomas. Executive Administrative Assistant: Lorraine Leong.

Director, Communications/Baseball Information: Kevin Shea. Coordinator, Baseball Information: Glenn Wilburn.

Dan Duquette

Major League Staff
Manager: Jimy Williams.
Coaches: Pitching—Joe Kerrigan; Batting—Jim Rice; First Base—Buddy Bailey; Third Base—Wendell Kim; Bullpen—John Cumberland; Outfield/Baserunning—Tommy Harper.

Medical, Training
Medical Director: Dr. Arthur Pappas.
Team Physician: Dr. William Morgan. Trainer: Jim Rowe. Coordinator, Strength/Conditioning: B.J. Baker. Physical Therapist: Rich Zawackl.

Player Development
Telephone: (617) 267-9440. FAX: (617) 236-6695.
Director, Player Development: Kent Qualls.
Special Assistant, Player Development: Johnny Pesky. Administrative Assistant, Minor Leagues/Scouting: Raquel Ferreira. Coordinator, Baseball Administration: Marci Blacker.

Jimy Williams

Field Coordinator: Dave Jauss. Assistant Field Coordinator: Dick Berardino. Coordinator, Florida Operations: Ryan Richeal.

Roving Instructors/Coordinators: Luis Aguayo (infield), Tommy Barrett (computer), Greg Biagini (hitting coordinator), Chris Correnti (rehabilitation), Bobby Mitchell (outfield/baserunning), Herm Starrette (rehab pitching), Gene Tenace (catching), Ralph Treuel (pitching coordinator).

Farm System

Class	Farm Team	Manager	Coach	Pitching Coach
AAA	Pawtucket	Gary Jones	Arnie Beyeler	Rich Bombard
AA	Trenton	Billy Gardner	Steve Braun	Mike Griffin
A	Sarasota	Ron Johnson	Ino Guerrero	Larry Pierson
A	Augusta	Mike Boulanger	Victor Rodriguez	Bob Kipper
A	Lowell	Arnie Beyeler	Steve Alonzo	Dave Tomlin
R	GCL	John Sanders	Gomer Hodge	W. Miranda/H. Starrette
R	DSL	Nelson Norman	Guadalupe Jabalera	Milciades Olivo

Scouting
Vice President, Scouting: Wayne Britton. Assistant Director, Scouting: Tom Moore.

Major League Scouts: Frank Malzone (Needham, MA), Eddie Robinson (Fort Worth, TX), Jerry Stephenson (Fullerton, CA), Lee Thomas (St. Louis, MO). Special Assignment Scout: Eddie Haas (Paducah, KY).

National Crosscheckers: Kevin Burrell (Sharpsburg, GA), Ray Crone Jr. (Cedar Hill, TX).

Area Scouts: Ben Cherington (Meriden, NH), Ray Fagnant (Manchester, CT), Matt Haas (Cincinnati, OH), Ernie Jacobs (Wichita, KS), Steve McAllister (Chillicothe, IL), Gary Rajsich (Lake Oswego, OR), Jim Robinson (Mansfield, TX), Ed Roebuck (Lakewood, CA), Matt Sczesny (Deer Park, NY), Fay Thompson (Vallejo, CA), Jeff Zona (Mechanicsville, VA).

Wayne Britton

Executive Director, International Operations: Ray Poitevint (Shadow Hills, CA). Director, Latin America Scouting: Levy Ochoa (Venezuela).

CHICAGO

Telephone, Address
Office Address: 333 W. 35th St., Chicago, IL 60616. **Telephone:** (312) 674-1000. **FAX:** (312) 674-5116. **Website:** www.chisox.com.

Ownership
Operated by: Chicago White Sox, Ltd.
Chairman: Jerry Reinsdorf. **Vice Chairman:** Eddie Einhorn.
Board of Directors: Fred Brzozowski, Jack Gould, Robert Judelson, Judd Malkin, Robert Mazer, Allan Muchin, Jay Pinsky, Larry Pogofsky, Lee Stern, Sanford Takiff, Burton Ury, Charles Walsh.
General Counsel: Allan Muchin.

Jerry Reinsdorf

BUSINESS OPERATIONS
Executive Vice President: Howard Pizer.
Director, Information Services: Don Brown. **Director, Human Resources:** Moira Foy. **Assistant to Chairman:** Anita Fasano. **Administrator, Human Resources:** Leslie Gaggiano.

Finance
Vice President, Administration/Finance: Tim Buzard.
Director, Finance: Bill Waters. **Accounting Manager:** Julie O'Shea.

Marketing, Sales
Senior Vice President, Marketing/Broadcasting: Rob Gallas.
Director, Marketing/Broadcasting: Bob Grim. **Manager, Promotions/ Marketing Services:** Sharon Sreniawski.
Manager, Scoreboard Operations/Production: Jeff Szynal. **Manager, Broadcasting/Marketing Services:** Jo Simmons. **Manager, Sponsorship Sales:** Dave Eck. **Marketing Account Executives:** Rob Louthain, Pam Malchow, Dale Song. **Coordinator, Sponsorship Sales:** Gail Tucker. **Coordinator, Promotions/Marketing Services:** Elizabeth Hoag.
Director, Ticket Sales: Jim Muno. **Manager, Suiteholder Relations:** Martha Black. **Manager, Ticket Sales:** Tom Sheridan.
Director, Advertising/Community Relations: Christine Makowski. **Director, Marketing Communications:** Amy Kress. **Manager, Design Services:** David Ortega. **Coordinator, Charitable Programs:** Dionne Smith. **Coordinator, Community Relations:** Amber Simons. **Coordinator, Publications:** Kyle White.

Public Relations
Telephone: (312) 674-5300. **FAX:** (312) 674-5116.
Director, Public Relations: Scott Reifert. **Manager, Public Relations:** Bob Beghtol. **Coordinator, Baseball Information:** Eric Phillips. **Coordinator, Public Relations:** Vivian Stalling.

Stadium Operations
Vice President, Stadium Operations: Terry Savarise.
Director, Park Operations: David Schaffer. **Director, Guest Services/Diamond Suite Operations:** Julie Taylor.
Head Groundskeeper: Roger Bossard.
PA Announcer: Gene Honda. **Official Scorer:** Bob Rosenberg.

Ticketing
Telephone: (312) 674-1000. **FAX:** (312) 674-5102.
Director, Ticket Operations: Bob Devoy.
Manager, Ticket Operations: Mike Mazza. **Manager, Ticket Accounting Administration:** Ken Wisz.

Travel, Clubhouse
Manager, Team Travel: Ed Cassin.
Equipment Manager/Clubhouse Operations: Vince Fresso. **Visiting Clubhouse:** Gabe Morell. **Umpires Clubhouse:** Joey McNamara.

General Information
Home Dugout: Third Base. **Playing Surface:** Grass.
Stadium Location: 35th Street exit off Dan Ryan Expressway (I-90/94).
Standard Game Times: 7:05 p.m., Sat. 6:05, Sun. 1:05.
Player Representative: James Baldwin.

WHITE SOX

BASEBALL OPERATIONS

Senior Vice President, Major League Operations: Ron Schueler. **Senior VP, Baseball:** Jack Gould.

Director, Baseball Operations/Assistant General Manager: Dan Evans. **Assistants, Baseball Operations:** J.J. Lally, Brian Porter.

Special Assistants to Senior VP/Major League Operations: Ed Brinkman, Dave Yoakum.

Computer Scouting Analyst: Mike Gellinger. **Technical Director:** Joe Inzerillo. **Video Coordinator:** Andrew Pinter.

Ron Schueler

Major League Staff

Manager: Jerry Manuel.

Coaches: Dugout—Joe Nossek; Pitching—Nardi Contreras; Batting—Von Joshua; First Base—Bryan Little; Third Base—Wallace Johnson; Bullpen—Art Kusnyer.

Jerry Manuel

Medical, Training

Senior Team Physician: Dr. James Boscardin. **Head Trainer:** Herm Schneider. **Assistant Trainer:** Mark Anderson. **Director, Conditioning:** Steve Odgers.

Player Development

Telephone: (312) 674-1000. **FAX:** (312) 674-5105.

Vice President, Player Development: Ken Williams. **Director, Minor League Administration:** Grace Zwit. **Coordinator, Minor League Administration:** Kathy Potoski.

Manager, Clubhouse/Equipment: Dan Flood. **Coordinator, Instruction:** Jim Snyder.

Roving Instructors/Coordinators: Mike Brumley (bunting), Trung Cao (conditioning), Don Cooper (pitching), Mike Lum (hitting), Gary Pettis (outfield), Rafael Santana (infield), Tommy Thompson (catching).

Farm System

Class	Farm Team	Manager	Coach	Pitching Coach
AAA	Charlotte	Nick Leyva	Gary Ward	Kirk Champion
AA	Birmingham	Nick Capra	Steve Whitaker	Curt Hasler
A	Winston-Salem	Brian Dayett	Daryl Boston	Juan Nieves
A	Burlington	Jerry Terrell	Greg Ritchie	J.R. Perdew
R	Bristol	R.J. Reynolds	Orsino Hill	Sean Snedeker
R	Tucson	Jerry Hairston	Chet DiEmidio	Chris Sinacori
R	DSL	Denny Gonzalez	Ruben Rodriguez	Unavailable

Scouting

Telephone: (312) 674-1000. **FAX:** (312) 451-5105.

Vice President, Free Agent/Major League Scouting: Larry Monroe.

Director, Scouting: Duane Shaffer.

Assistant Director, Scouting/Minor League Operations: Dan Fabian.

Special Assignment Scouts: Ed Brinkman (Cincinnati, OH), Bob Fontaine (Chico Hills, CA), Mike Pazik (Bethoeda, MD), Dave Yoakum (Orlando, FL). **Professional Scouts:** George Bradley (Tampa, FL), Gary Pellant (Chandler, AZ).

National Crosschecker: Doug Laumann (Florence, KY). **Regional Supervisors:** West Coast—Ed Pebley (Brigham City, UT), Midwest—Ken Stauffer (Katy, TX).

Duane Shaffer

Full-Time Area Scouts: Joe Butler (Long Beach, CA), Hernan Cortes (Tampa, FL), Alex Cosmidis (Raleigh, NC), Nathan Durst (Chicago, IL), Larry Grefer (Park Hills, KY), Warren Hughes (Mobile, AL), George Kashigian (Coronado, CA), John Kazanas (Phoenix, AZ), Jose Ortega (Fort Lauderdale, FL), Paul Provas (Arlington, TX), Mark Salas (Fullerton, CA), John Tumminia (Newburgh, NY).

Latin America Coordinator: Mike Sgobba (Scottsdale, AZ).

CLEVELAND

Telephone, Address
Office Address: Jacobs Field, 2401 Ontario St., Cleveland, OH 44115. **Telephone:** (216) 420-4200. **FAX:** (216) 420-4396. **Website:** www.indians.com.

Larry Dolan

Ownership
President/Chief Executive Officer: Lawrence Dolan.
Vice President/General Counsel: Paul Dolan

BUSINESS OPERATIONS
Executive Vice President, Business: Dennis Lehman. **Director, Human Resources:** Sara Lehrke.
Manager, Spring Training: Jerry Crabb.

Finance
Vice President, Finance: Ken Stefanov.
Manager, SEC Reporting: Rich Dorffer. **Controller:** Sarah Taylor. **Director, Information Systems:** Dave Powell. **Manager, Accounting:** Karen Menzing. **Network Manager:** Kelly Janda.

Marketing, Sales
Vice President, Marketing/Communications: Jeff Overton.
Senior Director, Corporate Marketing/Broadcasting: Jon Starrett. **Manager, Corporate Marketing:** Chris Previte. **Director, Advertising/Publications:** Valerie Arcuri. **Manager, Advertising/Publications:** Bernadette Repko.
Senior Director, Merchandising/Licensing: Jayne Churchmack. **Manager, Merchandise:** Michael Thom. **Manager, Operations:** Marie Patten. **Manager, Broadcasting/Special Events:** Nadine Glinski.

Public Relations, Communications
Telephone: (216) 420-4350. **FAX:** (216) 420-4396.
Vice President, Public Relations: Bob DiBiasio.
Director, Media Relations: Bart Swain. **Manager, Media Relations/Administration:** Susie Giuliano. **Coordinator, Media Relations:** Curtis Danburg. **Press Box Supervisor:** John Krepop.
Coordinator, Public Relations: Angela Brdar.
Director, Community Relations: Allen Davis. **Manager, Community Relations:** Melissa Zapanta.

Stadium Operations
Senior Director, Ballpark Operations: Jim Folk. **Manager, Ballpark Operations:** Mike DeCore. **Manager, Building Maintenance:** Chris Donahoe. **Manager, Field Maintenance:** Brandon Koehnke.
PA Announcer: Unavailable. **Official Scorers:** Hank Kosloski, Bill Nichols, Rick Rembielak.

Ticketing
Telephone: (216) 420-4240. **FAX:** (216) 420-4481.
Director, Ticket Services: John Schulze. **Manager, Box Office:** Gail Liebenguth. **Controller, Box Office:** Carolyne Villao. **Director, Ticket Sales:** Scott Sterneckert. **Manager, Ticket Sales:** Larry Abel. **Senior Account Executive:** Dick Sapara.

Travel, Clubhouse
Director, Team Travel: Mike Seghi.
Home Clubhouse/Equipment Manager: Ted Walsh. **Visiting Clubhouse Manager:** Cy Buynak.

General Information
Home Dugout: Third Base. **Playing Surface:** Grass.
Stadium Location: From south, I-77 North to East Ninth Street exit, to Ontario Street; From east, I-90/Route 2 west to downtown, remain on Route 2 to East Ninth Street, left to stadium. **Standard Game Times:** 7:05 p.m., Sat-Sun. 1:05.
Player Representative: Charles Nagy.

INDIANS

BASEBALL OPERATIONS
Telephone: (216) 420-4200. **FAX:** (216) 420-4321.
Executive Vice President, General Manager: John Hart. **Vice President, Baseball Operations/ Assistant General Manager:** Mark Shapiro.
Special Assistant to GM/Professional Player Procurement: Jay Robertson (Citrus Heights, CA). **Special Assistant to GM/Professional and Advanced Scouting:** Dom Chiti (Bartlett, TN).
Administrator, Player Personnel: Wendy Hughes. **Executive Administrative Assistant, Baseball Operations:** Ethel LaRue. **Assistant, Baseball Operations:** Chris Antonetti.

John Hart

Charlie Manuel

Major League Staff
Manager: Charlie Manuel.
Coaches: Bench—Grady Little; Pitching—Dick Pole; Batting—Clarence Jones; First Base—Ted Uhlaender; Third Base—Jim Riggleman; Bullpen—Luis Isaac.

Medical, Training
Medical Director: Dr. William Wilder.
Head Trainer: Paul Spicuzza. **Assistant Trainer:** Jim Warfield. **Strength and Conditioning Coach:** Fernando Montes. **Director, Rehabilitation:** Jim Mehalik.

Player Development
Telephone: (216) 420-4308. **FAX:** (216) 420-4321.
Director, Player Development: Neal Huntington. **Assistant Director:** Mike Brown. **Assistant, Player Development:** Jon Darsky. **Administrative Assistant:** Joan Pachinger.
Field Coordinator: Jeff Datz. **Roving Instructors:** Mike Brown (pitching), Al Bumbry (outfield/baserunning), Johnny Goryl (defense), Dave Keller (hitting), Joe Hughes (strength/conditioning).

Farm System
Class	Farm Team	Manager	Coach	Pitching Coach
AAA	Buffalo	Joel Skinner	Mario Diaz	Ken Rowe
AA	Akron	Eric Wedge	Mike Sarbaugh	Carl Willis
A	Kinston	Brad Komminsk	Luis Rivera	Steve Lyons
A	Columbus	Rick Gutierrez	Lou Frazier	Sam Militello
A	Mahoning Valley	Ted Kubiak	Willie Aviles	Terry Clark
R	Burlington	Dave Turgeon	Jack Mull	Tony Arnold
R	DSL	Felix Fermin	J. Urena/V. Veras	Juan Jimenez

Scouting
Telephone: (216) 420-4309. **FAX:** (216) 420-4321.
Director, Scouting: John Mirabelli.
Assistant Director, Scouting: Brad Grant. **Assistant, Scouting Operations:** Scott Meaney.
Major League Scouts: Dan Carnevale (Buffalo, NY), Tom Giordano (Amityville, NY), Bill Werle (San Mateo, CA). **Professional Scouts:** Scott Cerny (Rocklin, CA), Bob Gardner (Oviedo, FL), Tom McDevitt (Charleston, IL), Kevin Murphy (Studio City, CA), Gary Tuck (Spring, TX).
Free-Agent Supervisors: East Coast—Jerry Jordan (Wise, VA). Midwest—Bob Mayer (Somerset, PA). West Coast—Jesse Flores (Sacramento, CA).

John Mirabelli

Full-Time Area Scouts: Steve Abney (Lawrence, KS), Scott Anderson (Lake Oswego, OR), Doug Baker (Carlsbad, CA), Keith Boeck (Chandler, AZ), Jim Bretz (South Windsor, CT), Paul Cogan (Rocklin, CA), Henry Cruz (Fajardo, PR), Dan Durst (Rockford, IL), Jim Gabella (Deltona, FL), Rene Gayo (Alvin, TX), Mark Germann (Chattanooga, TN), Chris Jefts (Redondo Beach, CA), Tim Kissner (Pensacola, FL), Chad MacDonald (Arlington, TX), Dave Miller (Wilmington, NC), Chuck Ricci (Myersville, MD), Bill Schudlich (Dearborn, MI).

DETROIT

Telephone, Address
Office Address: 2100 Woodward Ave., Detroit, MI 48201. Telephone: (313) 962-4000. FAX: (313) 471-2138. Website: www.detroittigers.com.

Ownership
Operated by: Detroit Tigers, Inc.
Principal Owner/Chairman: Mike Ilitch.
President, Chief Executive Officer: John McHale Jr. Senior Director/Special Assistant to President: Gary Vitto.

John McHale Jr.

BUSINESS OPERATIONS
Vice President, Business Operations: David Glazier. VP, Planning/Research: Elaine Lewis. Director, Human Resources: Lara Baremor.

Finance
VP, Finance/Chief Financial Officer: Steve Quinn. Director, Finance: Jennifer Marroso. Director, Information Systems: Cole Stewart. Corporate Accountant: Steve Dady. Payroll Administrator: Lori Nowak. Supervisor, Accounts Payable: Christine Edwards.

Marketing, Sales
Manager, Marketing: Ellen Hill. Marketing Coordinator: Kelley Behrendt.
Director, Promotions: Joel Scott. Director, Corporate Sales: Dan Sinagoga. Senior Account Executives: Earle Fisher, Bob Raymond. Manager, Group Sales: Tammie Weis. Coordinator, Corporate Sales: Jim Spadafore.

Media, Community Relations
Telephone: (313) 471-2114. FAX: (313) 471-2138.
Senior Director, Marketing/Communications: Tyler Barnes. Manager, Public Relations: Jim Anderson. Coordinator, Public Relations: Melanie Waters. Administrative Assistant, Public Relations: Hunter Logan.
Director, Community Relations: Celia Bobrowsky. Manager, Community Relations: Fred Feliciano. Coordinator, Community Relations: Masico Brown.

Park Operations
Vice President, Park Operations: Tom Folk.
Manager, Park Operations: Mary Lehnert. Senior Manager, Guest Services: Jodi Engler. Coordinator, Event Operations: Brian Kutz. Coordinator, Guest Services: Sue Gerten. Managers, Ballpark Services: Dushawn Brandy, Allan Carisse, Ed Goward.
Head Groundskeeper: Heather Nabozny.
PA Announcer: Unavailable. Official Scorers: Chuck Klonke, Rich Shook.

Ticketing
Telephone: (313) 471-2255.
Senior Director, Ticket Services: Ken Marchetti. Director, Ticket Sales: Barry Gibson. Assistant Director, Ticket Services: Bob Palmisano. Coordinator, Ticket Sales: David Krakower.

Travel, Clubhouse
Traveling Secretary: Bill Brown.
Manager, Tiger Clubhouse: Jim Schmakel. Manager, Visitors Clubhouse: John Nelson. Baseball Video Operations: Tom Progar.

General Information
Home Dugout: Third Base. Playing Surface: Grass.
Stadium Directions: Take I-75 to Grand River exit, follow service drive east to stadium, located off Woodward Avenue. Standard Game Times: 7:05 p.m., Sat. 5:05, Sun. 1:05.
Player Representative: Damion Easley.

TIGERS

BASEBALL OPERATIONS

Telephone: (313) 471-2096. **FAX:** (313) 471-2099.
**Vice President, Baseball Operations/General
Manager:** Randy Smith.

Special Assistants to GM: Al Hargesheimer
(Chicago, IL), Randy Johnson (Plymouth, MI).
Assistant to GM: Gwen Keating. **Assistant,
Baseball Operations:** Ricky Bennett. **Assistant,
Baseball Operations/Foreign Affairs:** Ramon
Pena. **Administrator, Baseball Operations:** Hiroshi
Yoshimura. **Liaison, Latin America:** Luis Mayoral.

Randy Smith

Major League Staff

Manager: Phil Garner.
Coaches: Dugout—Bob Melvin; Pitching—Dan
Warthen; Batting—Bill Madlock; First Base—Juan Samuel; Third Base—
Doug Mansolino; Bullpen—Lance Parrish.

Phil Garner

Medical, Training

Team Physicians: Dr. Kyle Anderson, Dr. David
Collon, Dr. Terry Lock, Dr. Michael Workings.
Medical Director/Head Trainer: Russ Miller.
Strength Conditioning Coach: Dennie Taft.

Player Development

Telephone, Detroit: (313) 471-2096. **FAX:** (313)
471-2099. **Telephone, Florida Operations:** (863)
686-8075. **FAX:** (863) 688-9589.
Assistant General Manager/Player Devel-
opment: Steve Lubratich.
Director, Minor League Operations: Dave
Miller. **Administrative Assistant, Minor Leagues:**
Audrey Zielincki.

Field Coordinator: Steve Boros. **Roving Instructors:** Clarence
Cockrell (strength/conditioning), Glenn Ezell (catching), Mike Humphreys
(outfield/baserunning), Rafael Landestoy (infield), Jon Matlack (pitching),
Tom Runnells (hitting).

Farm System

Class	Farm Team	Manager	Coach	Pitching Coach
AAA	Toledo	Dave Anderson	Mark Meleski	Jeff Jones
AA	Jacksonville	Gene Roof	Matt Martin	Steve McCatty
A	Lakeland	Skeeter Barnes	Basilio Cabrera	Joe Boever
A	West Michigan	Bruce Fields	Brian Saltzgaber	Joe Georger
A	Oneonta	Kevin Bradshaw	Liliano Castro	Bill Monbouquette
R	Lakeland	Gary Green	Unavailable	Greg Sabat
R	DSL	Max Diaz	Felix Nivar	Jose Tapia

Scouting

Director, Player Development/Scouting: Greg
Smith. **Administrative Assistant, Scouting:**
Gwen Keating.

Advance Scout: Scott Bream (Phoenix, AZ).
Major League Scout: Larry Parrish (Haines City,
FL).

National Crosschecker: Rob Guzik (Latrobe,
PA). **Regional Supervisors:** Midwest—Steven
Williams (Raleigh, NC), Northeast—Pat Murtaugh
(Lafayette, IN), Southeast—Jeff Wetherby (Tampa,
FL), West—Jeff Malinoff (Lopez, WA).

Area Scouts: Bill Buck (Manassas, VA), Jerome
Cochran (New Orleans, LA), Tim Grieve (Katy, TX),
Jack Hays (Lake Oswego, OR), Lou Laslo

Greg Smith

(Pemberville, OH), Dennis Lieberthal (Westlake Village, CA), Steve Nichols
(Mount Dora, FL), Jim Olander (Tucson, AZ), Buddy Paine (Scarsdale, NY),
Derrick Ross (Manchester, CT), Steve Taylor (Shawnee, OK), Rob Wilfong
(West Covina, CA), Gary York (Rome, GA), Harold Zonder (Louisville, KY).
Director, International Scouting: Ramon Pena (Dominican Republic).

Telephone, Address

Office Address: One Royal Way, Kansas City, MO 64129. **Mailing Address:** P.O. Box 419969, Kansas City, MO 64141. **Telephone:** (816) 921-8000. **FAX:** (816) 921-1366. **Website:** www.kcroyals.com.

Ownership

Operated by: Kansas City Royals Baseball Club, Inc. **Principal Owner:** Greater Kansas City Community Foundation.

Chairman, Chief Executive Officer: David Glass. **President:** Mike Herman.

Board of Directors: Richard Green, Mike Herman, Julia Kauffman, Janice Kreamer, Joe McGuff, Louis Smith.

David Glass

General Counsel/Assistant Secretary: Jay Newcom.

BUSINESS OPERATIONS

Senior Vice President, Business Operations/Administration: Art Chaudry. **Senior Director, Operations/Administration:** Jay Hinrichs. **Executive Administrative Assistant:** Cindy Hamilton. **Administrator, Human Resouces:** Lynne Elder.

Finance

Vice President, Finance/Information Systems: Dale Rohr.

Senior Director/Controller: John Luther. **Director, Payroll/Benefits Accounting:** Tom Pfannenstiel. **Manager, Accounting:** Scott Stamp.

Director, Information Systems: Jim Edwards. **Manager, Client Services:** Scott Novak. **Manager, Programming:** Becky Randall.

Marketing, Sales

Vice President, Marketing/Communications: Mike Levy.

Director, Marketing: Tonya Mangels. **Coordinator, Marketing:** Kim Hillix. **Director, Corporate Sponsorships:** Kevin Battle. **Director, Event Operations/Revenue Development:** Chris Richardson.

Public Relations, Communications

Telephone: (816) 921-8000. **FAX:** (816) 921-5775.

Senior Director, Communications: Jim Lachimia.

Director, Media Relations: Steve Fink. **Coordinator, Media Relations:** Chris Stathos. **Manager, Community Relations/Special Markets:** Shani Tate. **Coordinator, Publications/Internet:** Chad Rader.

Stadium Operations

Director, Stadium Operations: Rodney Lewallen. **Coordinator, Stadium Operations:** Judy VanMeter.

Director, Groundskeeping/Landscaping: Trevor Vance. **Manager, Groundskeeping:** Jonnie Reed. **Manager, Stadium Engineering:** Chris Frank. **Supervisor, Stadium Services:** Johnny Williams.

PA Announcer: Dan Hurst. **Official Scorers:** Del Black, Sid Bordman, Lou Spry.

Ticketing

Telephone: (816) 921-8000. **FAX:** (816) 504-4144.

Director, Ticket Services: Christine Burgeson. **Director, Group Sales:** Michelle Kammerer. **Manager, Group Sales:** Mandee Schaaf. **Account Executive:** Paul Frederick. **Director, Lancer Program:** Larry Sherrard. **Director, Season Ticket Services:** Joe Grigoli.

Travel, Clubhouse

Director, Team Travel: David Witty.

Equipment Manager: Mike Burkhalter. **Visiting Clubhouse Manager:** Chuck Hawke.

General Information

Home Dugout: First Base. **Playing Surface:** Grass.

Stadium Location: From north or south, take I-435 to stadium exits. From east or west, take I-70 to stadium exits. **Standard Game Times:** 7:05 p.m.; Sun. 1:05.

Player Representative: Johnny Damon.

ROYALS

BASEBALL OPERATIONS
Telephone: (816) 921-8000. **FAX:** (816) 924-0347.
Executive Vice President/General Manager: Herk Robinson.
Vice President, Baseball Operations: George Brett. **Vice President/Assistant GM, Baseball Operations:** Allard Baird. **Assistant GM, Baseball Administration:** Muzzy Jackson.
Senior Special Assistant to GM: Art Stewart. **Senior Administrative Assistant:** Karol Kyte. **Executive Administrative Assistant:** Joanne Snow.

Herk Robinson

Major League Staff
Manager: Tony Muser.
Coaches: Bench—Jamie Quirk; Pitching—Mark Wiley; Batting—Lamar Johnson; First Base—Frank White; Third Base—Rich Dauer; Bullpen—Tom Burgmeier.

Medical, Training
Team Physician: Dr. Steve Joyce.

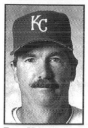

Head Trainer: Nick Swartz. **Assistant Trainer:** Lee Kuntz. **Coordinator, Strength and Conditioning:** Tim Maxey. **Rehabilitation Coordinator:** Frank Kyte.

Minor Leagues
Telephone: (816) 921-8000. **FAX:** (816) 924-0347.
Senior Director, Minor League Operations: Bob Hegman. **Coordinator, Minor League Operations:** Shaun McGinn.
Coordinator, Instruction: Mike Jirschele. **Roving Instructors:** Juan Agosto (pitching/Latin America), Andre David (hitting), Mike Mason (pitching), Brian Poldberg (catching), Luis Silverio (outfield).
Coordinator, Equipment: Mike Crouse.

Tony Muser

Farm System
Class	Farm Team	Manager	Coach	Pitching Coach
AAA	Omaha	John Mizerock	Scott Leius	Rick Mahler
AA	Wichita	Keith Bodie	Kevin Long	Steve Crawford
A	Wilmington	Jeff Garber	Steve Balboni	Larry Carter
A	Charleston, W.Va.	Joe Szekely	Terry Bradshaw	Jaime Garcia
A	Spokane	Tom Poquette	Unavailable	Randy Smith
R	Baseball City	Ron Karkovice	Jose Tartabull	Juan Agosto
R	DSL	Oscar Martinez	P. Paredes	Unavailable

Scouting
Senior Director, Scouting: Terry Wetzel.
Coordinator, Scouting Operations: Jin Wong. **Administrative Assistant:** Laura Bokenkroger.
Advance Scout: Ron Clark (Largo, FL). **Major League Scout:** Gail Henley (La Verne, CA).
Special Assignment Scouts: Carlos Pascual (Miami, FL), John Wathan (Blue Springs, MO).
National Crosscheckers: Pat Jones (Coconut Creek, FL), Jeff McKay (Walterville, OR), Earl Winn (Bowling Green, KY).
Area Scouts: Frank Baez (Los Angeles, CA), Bob Bishop (San Dimas, CA), Jason Bryans

Terry Wetzel

(Detroit, MI), Dave Herrera (Danville, CA), Keith Hughes (Berwyn, PA), Phil Huttmann (Overland Park, KS), Gary Johnson (Costa Mesa, CA), Cliff Pastornicky (Venice, FL), Bill Price (Austin, TX), Johnny Ramos (Carolina, PR), Sean Rooney (Morristown, NJ), Chet Sergo (Houston, TX), Greg Smith (Harrington, WA), Craig Struss (Grand Island, NE), Gerald Turner (Euless, TX), Junior Vizcaino (Wake Forest, NC), Mark Willoughby (Hammond, LA), Dennis Woody (Pensacola, FL).
Coordinator, Dominican Operations: Luis Silverio. **Coordinator, Latin America:** Albert Gonzalez (Pembroke Pines, FL).

MINNESOTA

Telephone, Address
Office Address: 34 Kirby Puckett Place, Minneapolis, MN 55415. Telephone: (612) 375-1366. FAX: (612) 375-7480. Website: www.twins baseball.com.

Ownership
Operated by: The Minnesota Twins.
Owner: Carl Pohlad. Chairman, Executive Committee: Howard Fox.
Executive Board: Jerry Bell, Chris Clouser, Carl Pohlad, Eloise Pohlad, James Pohlad, Robert Pohlad, William Pohlad, Kirby Puckett.
President: Jerry Bell.

Carl Pohlad

BUSINESS OPERATIONS
Senior Vice President, Business Affairs: Dave St. Peter. VP, Operations: Matt Hoy. VP, Human Resources/Diversity: Raenell Dorn. Coordinator, Human Resources: Leticia Fuentes. Administrative Assistant to President/Office Manager: Joan Boeser.

Finance
Chief Financial Officer: Kip Elliott.
Assistant Controller: Angela Meagher. Payroll Manager: Lori Beasley. Accountant: Jerry McLaughlin. Accounts Payable: Amy Fong.
Director, Information Systems: Wade Navratil. Director, Network/Baseball Information Systems: Jon Avenson.

Marketing, Sales
Vice President, Sales: Jim Denn.
Director, Marketing: Patrick Klinger. Account Sales Executives: Jack Blesi, Dan Craighead, Jeff Hibicke, Rob Malec, Chris Malek, Heather Proskey, Wayne Sorensen. Marketing Manager, Advertising: Nikki White. Marketing Manager, Boradcasting/Events: Wayne Petersen. Manager, Sales Administration: Beth Vail. Corporate Sales Managers: Cory Howerton, Chad Jackson, Lori Schurman, Dick Schultz. Manager, Client Services: Bodie Rykken.

Public Relations, Communications
Telephone: (612) 375-7471. FAX: (612) 375-7473.
Manager, Media Relations: Sean Harlin. Assistant Manager, Media Relations: Brad Smith. Coordinator, Media Relations: Denise Johnson.
Manager, Community Affairs: Darrell Cunningham. Coordinator, Community Affairs: Gloria Westerdahl. Coordinator, Community Affairs (Youth Baseball): Ron Belvin.

Stadium Operations
Manager, Stadium Operations: Ric Johnson. Manager, Event Services: Dave Horsman. Manager, Special Events: Heidi Sammon. Manager, Security: Scott Larson.
PA Announcer: Bob Casey. Official Scorer: Tom Mee.

Ticketing
Telephone: (612) 338-9467, (800) 338-9467. FAX: (612) 375-7464.
Director, Ticket Sales: Scott O'Connell.
Director, Ticket Operations: Paul Froehle. Manager, Box Office: Mike Stiles. Supervisor, Ticket Office: Karl Dedenbach. Coordinator, Ticket Office: Mike Johnson. Manager, Telemarketing: Patrick Forsland.

Travel, Clubhouse
Traveling Secretary: Remzi Kiratli.
Equipment Manager: Jim Dunn. Visitors Clubhouse: Troy Matchan. Internal Video Specialist: Nyal Peterson.

General Information
Home Dugout: Third Base. Playing Surface: Artificial turf.
Stadium Directions: I-35W south to Washington Avenue exit or I-35W north to Third Street exit. I-94 East to I-35W north to Third Street exit or I-94 West to Fifth Street exit. Standard Game Times: 12:15 p.m., 7:05, Sun. 1:05.
Player Representative: Denny Hocking.

TWINS

BASEBALL OPERATIONS
Telephone: (612) 375-7484. **FAX:** (612) 375-7417.
Vice President/General Manager: Terry Ryan.
Executive VP, Baseball: Kirby Puckett.
VP/Assistant General Manager: Bill Smith.
Assistant GM: Wayne Krivsky. **Special Assistants to GM:** Larry Corrigan, Joe McIlvaine.
Director, Baseball Operations: Rob Antony.
Administrative Assistant, Major League Operations: Juanita Lagos-Benson.

Major League Staff
Manager: Tom Kelly.
Coaches: Dugout—Paul Molitor; Pitching—Dick Such; Batting—Scott Ullger; First Base—Jerry White; Third Base—Ron Gardenhire; Bullpen—Rick Stelmaszek.

Terry Ryan

Tom Kelly

Medical, Training
Club Physicians: Dr. Dan Buss, Dr. Veejay Eyunni, Dr. Tom Jetzer, Dr. John Steubs.
Head Trainer: Dick Martin. **Assistant Trainer:** Jim Kahmann. **Strength/Conditioning Coach:** Randy Popple.

Player Development
Telephone: (612) 375-7477. **FAX:** (612) 375-7417.
Director, Minor Leagues: Jim Rantz.
Administrative Assistant, Minor Leagues: Colleen Schroeder.
Field Coordinator: Steve Liddle. **Roving Instructors:** Jim Dwyer (hitting), Rick Knapp (pitching).

Farm System

Class	Farm Team	Manager	Coach	Pitching Coach
AAA	Salt Lake	Phil Roof	Bill Springman	Rick Anderson
AA	New Britain	John Russell	Jarvis Brown	Stu Cliburn
A	Fort Myers	Jose Marzan	Riccardo Ingram	Eric Rasmussen
A	Quad City	Stan Cliburn	Floyd Rayford	Gary Lucas
R	Elizabethton	Jeff Carter	Ray Smith	Jim Shellenback
R	Fort Myers	Al Newman	Brad Weitzel	Reno Aragon
R	DSL	Frank Valdez	Gino Fernandez	Unavailable

Scouting
Telephone: (612) 375-7488. **FAX:** (612) 375-7417.
Director, Scouting: Mike Radcliff (Overland Park, KS).
Administrative Assistant, Scouting: Alison Walk.
Special Assignment Scouts: Larry Corrigan (Fort Myers, FL), Cal Ermer (Chattanooga, TN).
Major League Scout: Bill Harford (Chicago, IL).
Coordinator, Professional Scouting: Vern Followell (Buena Park, CA).
Scouting Supervisors: East—Earl Frishman (Tampa, FL); West—Deron Johnson (Antioch, CA); Midwest—Mike Ruth (Lee's Summit, MO).

Mike Radcliff

Area Scouts: Kevin Bootay (Sacramento, CA), Ellsworth Brown (Beason, IL), Marty Esposito (Hewitt, TX), John Leavitt (Garden Grove, CA), Joel Lepel (Plato, MN), Bill Lohr (Centralia, WA), Lee MacPhail (Tempe, AZ), Bill Mele (El Segundo, CA), Gregg Miller (Pratt, KS), Billy Milos (South Holland, IL), Tim O'Neil (Lexington, KY), Hector Otero (Guaynabo, PR), Mark Quimuyog (Lynn Haven, FL), Ricky Taylor (Hickory, NC), Brad Weitzel (Haines City, FL), Jay Weitzel (Salamanca, NY), John Wilson (Blairstown, NJ).
Director, International Scouting: Joe McIlvaine (Tuckahoe, NY).
International Scouts: Rudy Hernandez (Venezuela), David Kim (South Korea), Howard Norsetter (Australia, Canada), Yoshi Okamoto (Japan), Johnny Sierra (Dominican Republic).

Telephone, Address

Office Address: Yankee Stadium, 161st Street and River Avenue, Bronx, NY 10451. **Telephone:** (718) 293-4300. **FAX:** (718) 293-8431. **Website:** www.yankees.com.

Ownership

Operated by: New York Yankees.

Principal Owner: George Steinbrenner. **General Partners:** Stephen Swindal, Hal Steinbrenner.

Limited Partners: Daniel Crown, James Crown, Lester Crown, Michael Friedman, Marvin Goldklang, Barry Halper, Daniel McCarthy, Jessica Molloy, Harry Nederlander, James Nederlander, Robert Nederlander, William Rose Jr., Edward Rosenthal, Jack Satter, Henry Steinbrenner, Joan Steinbrenner, Jennifer Swindal, Charlotte Witkind, Richard Witkind.

George Steinbrenner

BUSINESS OPERATIONS

Executive Vice President, General Counsel: Lonn Trost. **Vice President:** Ed Weaver. **Vice President, Administration:** Sonny Hight. **Director, Human Resources:** Mike Ferrentino.

Finance

Vice President, Chief Financial Officer: Marty Greenspan. **Controller:** Robert Brown.

Marketing, Community Relations

Director, Marketing: Deborah Tymon.

Director, Community Relations: Brian Smith. **Assistant Director, Community Relations:** Sean Sullivan. **Director, Concessions/Hospitality:** Joel White. **Assistant Director, Concessions/Hospitality:** David Bernstein. **Manager, Sponsorship Services:** Kristin Costello. **Manager, Promotions/Special Events:** Kristina Papa. **Director, Yankee Alumni Association:** Jim Ogle. **Director, Entertainment:** Stanley Kay. **Special Assistant:** Joe Pepitone.

Media Relations, Publications

Telephone: (718) 579-4460. **FAX:** (718) 293-8414.

Director, Media Relations/Publicity: Rick Cerrone. **Assistant Director, Media Relations:** Jason Zillo. **Senior Advisor:** Arthur Richman.

Director, Publications/Multimedia: Dan Cahalane. **Editor-in-Chief, Publications:** Mark Mandrake. **Editor-in-Chief, yankees.com:** Mike Henry.

Stadium Operations

Director, Stadium Operations: Kirk Randazzo. **Assistant Director, Stadium Operations:** Doug Behar. **Stadium Superintendent:** Bob Wilkinson. **Assistant, Stadium Operations:** Bob Pelegrino.

Manager, Scoreboard/Broadcasting: Joe Pullia.

PA Announcer: Bob Sheppard. **Official Scorer:** Red Foley.

Ticketing

Telephone: (718) 293-6000. **FAX:** (718) 293-4841.

Vice President, Ticket Operations: Frank Swaine. **Executive Director, Ticket Operations:** Jeff Kline. **Senior Ticket Director:** Ken Skrypek.

Travel, Clubhouse

Traveling Secretary: David Szen.

Equipment Manager/Home Clubhouse: Rob Cucuzza. **Visiting Clubhouse:** Lou Cucuzza.

General Information

Home Dugout: First Base. **Playing Surface:** Grass.

Stadium Directions: From I-95 North, George Washington Bridge to Cross Bronx Expressway to exit 1C; Major Deegan South (I-87) to exit G (161st Street); I-87 North to 149th or 155th Streets; I-87 South to 161st Street. **Standard Game Times:** 7:05 p.m., Weekends 1:05.

Player Representative: David Cone.

YANKEES

BASEBALL OPERATIONS

Telephone: (718) 293-4300. FAX: (718) 293-0015.
Vice President/General Manager: Brian Cashman.

Assistant General Manager: Kim Ng. Special Assistant to GM: Stump Merrill. Director, Baseball Operations: Dan Matheson. Assistant Director, Baseball Operations: Rigo Garcia. Special Advisory Group: Clyde King, Dick Williams.

Major League Staff

Manager: Joe Torre.
Coaches: Dugout—Don Zimmer; Pitching—Mel Stottlemyre; Batting—Chris Chambliss; First Base—Lee Mazzilli; Third Base—Willie Randolph; Bullpen—Tony Cloninger; Catching—Bob Didier.

Brian Cashman

Medical, Training

Team Physician: Dr. Stuart Hershon. Head Trainer: Gene Monahan. Assistant Trainer: Steve Donohue. Strength/Conditioning Coach: Jeff Mangold.

Player Development

Florida Complex: 3102 N Himes Ave., Tampa, FL 33607. Telephone: (813) 875-7569. FAX: (813) 873-2302.

VP, Baseball Operations: Mark Newman. Director, Player Personnel: Billy Connors. Director, Player Development: Rob Thomson. Director, Player Personnel: Damon Oppenheimer. Coordinator, Instruction: Steve Webber.

Joe Torre

Roving Instructors: Gary Denbo (hitting), Mick Kelleher (infield), Greg Pavlick (pitching).

Farm System

Class	Farm Team	Manager	Coach	Pitching Coach
AAA	Columbus	Trey Hillman	Bill Robinson	Rick Tomlin
AA	Norwich	Dan Radison	Ken Dominguez	Tom Filer
A	Tampa	Tom Nieto	Unavailable	Rich Monteleone
A	Greensboro	Stan Hough	Tony Perezchica	Gary Lavelle
A	Staten Island	Joe Arnold	Kevin Higgins	Neil Allen
R	GCL	Derek Shelton	Ty Hawkins	Steve Webber
R	DSL	Rafael Concepcion	Juan Castillo	Wilfredo Cordova

Scouting

Telephone: (813) 875-7569. FAX: (813) 348-9198.
VP/Director, Major League Scouting: Gene Michael.

Director, Scouting: Lin Garrett. Director, International/Professional Scouting: Gordon Blakeley. Assistant Director, Scouting: Tommy Larsen.

Advance Scouts: Jim Spencer, Wade Taylor (Orlando, FL). Major League Scouts: Ron Brand (Mesa, AZ), Ron Hansen (Baldwin, MD), Graig Nettles (San Diego, CA).

Professional Scouts: Ket Barber (Ocala, FL), Joe Caro (Tampa, FL), Bill Emslie (Safety Harbor, FL), Bob Miske (Amherst, NY).

Lin Garrett

Regional Crosscheckers: East—Joe Arnold (Lakeland, FL); Midwest—Tim Kelly (New Lenox, IL); West—Greg Orr (Sacramento, CA).

Area Scouts: Mike Baker (Cave Creek, AZ), Mark Batchko (Arlington, TX), Steve Boros (Kansas City, MO), Bobby DeJardin (Hidden Hills, CA), Dick Groch (Marysville, MI), Steve Lemke (Lincolnshire, IL), Scott Pleis (Tampa, FL), Cesar Presbott (Bronx, NY), Gus Quattlebaum (Kirkland, WA), Joe Robison (Dayton, TX), Phil Rossi (Jessup, PA), Steve Swail (Charlotte, NC), Leon Wurth (Nashville, TN), Bill Young (Long Beach, CA).

Coordinator, Pacific Rim Operations: John Cox (Redlands, CA). Director, Canadian Scouting: Dick Groch (Marysville, MI). Coordinator, Latin American Operations: Carlos Rios (Lake Worth, FL).

OAKLAND

Telephone, Address
Office Address: 7677 Oakport St., Suite 200, Oakland, CA 94621. **Telephone:** (510) 638-4900. **FAX:** (510) 562-1633. **Website:** www.oaklandath-letics.com.

Ownership
Operated by: Athletics Investment Group LLC (1996).

Co-Owner/Managing Partner: Steve Schott. **Partner/Owner:** Ken Hofmann.

President: Michael Crowley. **Executive Assistant to President:** Carolyn Jones.

Steve Schott

BUSINESS OPERATIONS

Finance, Administration
Controller: Paul Wong. **Assistant Controller:** Linda Rease. **Director, Human Resources:** Eleanor Yee. **Payroll Specialist:** Kathy Leviege-Bey. **Accounts Payable:** Lynell Roeber. **Senior Staff Accountant:** Isabelle Mahaffey. **Staff Accountant:** Helga Mahlmann.

Marketing, Sales
Senior Director, Sales/Marketing: David Alioto.

Director, Business Services: David Lozow. **Assistant, Business Services/Ticket Sales:** Johanna Hopper. **Director, Merchandising:** Drew Bruno. **Director, Corporate Advertising Sales:** Franklin Lowe. **Director, Promotions/Special Events:** Susan Weiglein. **Director, Marketing Communications:** Jim Bloom. **Director, Preferred Seating:** Nancy O'Brien.

Manager, Merchandising: Dayn Floyd. **Manager, Corporate Events:** Angela Rundles.

Public Relations, Communications
Telephone: (510) 563-2207. **FAX:** (510) 562-1633.

Senior Director, Broadcasting/Communications: Ken Pries.

Director, Public Relations: Jim Young. **Manager, Baseball Information:** Mike Selleck. **Manager, Broadcasting:** Robert Buan. **Coordinator, Media Services:** Debbie Gallas.

Manager, Community Relations: Matt Bennett. **Coordinator, Community Relations:** Detra Paige. **Assistant, Community Relations:** Page Pratt.

Director, Stadium Entertainment: Troy Smith. **Director, Multimedia Services:** David Don.

Stadium Operations
Senior Director, Stadium Operations: David Rinetti.

Event Manager, Game Day Services: David Avila. **Manager, Facility and Special Events:** Matt Fucile.

Head Groundskeeper: Clay Wood.

PA Announcer: Roy Steele. **Official Scorer:** Chuck Dybdal.

Ticketing
Director, Ticket Sales: Dennis Murphy. **Manager, Box Office/Customer Service:** Steve Fanelli. **Manager, Inside Sales:** Parker Newton. **Manager, Season Tickets:** Michael Ono. **Manager, Premium Seating Sales:** Tom VanEss. **Manager, Premium Seating Services:** Joshua England. **Coordinator, Premum Seating:** Amy Shapiro.

Travel, Clubhouse
Director, Team Travel: Mickey Morabito.

Equipment Manager: Steve Vucinich. **Visitors Clubhouse:** Mike Thalblum. **Assistant Equipment Manager:** Brian Davis. **Head Groundskeeper:** Clay Wood.

General Information
Home Dugout: Third Base. **Playing Surface:** Grass.

Location: From I-880, take either the 66th Avenue or Hegenberger Road exit. **Standard Game Times:** Weekday—12:35 p.m., 7:05, 7:35. Weekend—1:05, 6:05.

Player Representative: Matt Stairs.

ATHLETICS

BASEBALL OPERATIONS
General Manager: Billy Beane.
Assistant General Manager: Paul DePodesta.
Special Assistants to GM: Bob Johnson, J.P. Ricciardi, Bill Rigney.
Director, Baseball Administration: Pamela Pitts. **Assistant, Baseball Operations:** David Forst.

Major League Staff
Manager: Art Howe.
Coaches: Dugout—Ken Macha; Pitching—Rick Peterson; Batting—Mike Quade; First Base—Thad Bosley; Third Base—Ron Washington; Bullpen—Brad Fischer.

Billy Beane

Art Howe

Medical, Training
Team Physician: Dr. Allan Pont. **Team Orthopedist:** Dr. Jerrald Goldman.
Head Trainer: Larry Davis. **Assistant Trainer:** Steve Sayles. **Strength and Conditioning Coordinator:** Bob Alejo.

Player Development
Telephone, Oakland: (510) 638-4900. **FAX:** (510) 563-2376.
Arizona Complex: Papago Park Baseball Complex, 1802 N 64th St., Phoenix, AZ 85008. **Telephone:** (602) 949-5951. **FAX:** (602) 945-0557.
Director, Player Development: Keith Lieppman. **Assistant Director:** Dave Hudgens.
Assistant, Player Development and Scouting: Danny McCormack.
Director, Minor League Operations: Ted Polakowski.
Roving Instructors: Orv Franchuk (hitting), Ron Plaza (general), Ron Romanick (pitching).

Farm System
Class	Farm Team	Manager	Coach	Pitching Coach
AAA	Sacramento	Bob Geren	Roy White	Rick Rodriguez
AA	Midland	Tony DeFrancesco	Webster Garrison	Curt Young
A	Modesto	Greg Sparks	Brian McArn	Glenn Abbott
A	Visalia	Juan Navarrete	Steve Hosey	Jim Bennett
A	Vancouver	Dave Joppie	Billy Owens	Unavailable
R	Phoenix	John Kuehl	Ruben Escalera	Fernando Arroyo
R	DSL I	Evaristo Lantigua	Luis Martinez	Unavailable
R	DSL II	Tomas Silverio	Luis Gomez	Nasusel Cabrera

Scouting
Telephone: (510) 638-4900, ext. 2213. **FAX:** (510) 563-2376.
Director, Scouting: Grady Fuson.
Special Assignment Scout: Dick Bogard (La Palma, CA). **Advance/Major League Scout:** Bob Johnson (Rockaway, NJ).
National Crosscheckers: Ron Hopkins (Seattle, WA), Chris Pittaro (Hamilton, NJ).
Area Scouts: Steve Bowden (Houston, TX), Tom Clark (Worcester, MA), Ruben Escalera (Villa Carolina, PR), Kelly Heath (Crystal Beach, FL), Tim Holt (Plano, TX), John Kuehl (Fountain Hills, AZ), Rick Magnante (Van Nuys, CA), Gary McGraw (Newberg, OR), Billy Owens (Raleigh, NC), John

Grady Fuson

Poloni (Tarpon Springs, FL), Jim Pransky (Bettendorf, IA), Will Schock (Oakland, CA), Rich Sparks (Hazel Park, MI), Ron Vaughn (Corona, CA).
International Scouting Supervisor: Eric Kubota (Oakland, CA).
Dominican Republic Coordinator: Raymond Abreu (Santo Domingo, DR).
International Scouts: Ruben Barradas (Venezuela), Juan Carlos de la Cruz (Dominican Republic), Angel Eusebio (Dominican Republic), Julio Franco (Venezuela), Fausto Pena (Dominican Republic), Luis Perez (Dominican Republic), Bernardino Rosario (Dominican Republic), Oswaldo Troconis (Venezuela).

SEATTLE

Telephone, Address
Office Address: 1250 First Avenue S, Seattle, WA 98104. Mailing Address: P.O. Box 4100, Seattle, WA 98104. Telephone: (206) 346-4000. FAX: (206) 346-4400. E-Mail Address: mariners@mariners.org. Website: www.mariners.org.

Chuck Armstrong

Ownership
Operated by: Baseball Club of Seattle, LP.
Board of Directors: Minoru Arakawa, John Ellis, Chris Larson, Howard Lincoln, John McCaw, Frank Shrontz, Craig Watjen.
Chairman/Chief Executive Officer: Howard Lincoln. President/Chief Operating Officer: Chuck Armstrong.

BUSINESS OPERATIONS

Finance
Executive Vice President, Finance/Ballpark Operations: Kevin Mather.
Controller: Tim Kornegay. Assistant Controller: Greg Massey. Director, Human Resources: Marianne Short. Director, Information Systems: Larry Witherspoon.

Marketing, Sales
Executive Vice President, Business/Sales: Bob Aylward.
Director, Corporate Business/Community Relations: Joe Chard. Director, Marketing: Kevin Martinez. Manager, Marketing: Jon Schuller. Director, Retail Operations: Jim La Shell. Manager, Retail Operations: Jeff Ibach. New Ballpark Suite Sales: Moose Clausen. Manager, Merchandise Marketing: Cheryl Kotschevar.

Public Relations, Communications
Telephone: (206) 346-4000. FAX: (206) 346-4400.
VP, Communications: Randy Adamack.
Director, Baseball Information: Tim Hevly. Director, Public Information: Rebecca Hale. Assistant Director, Baseball Information: Matt Roebuck. Manager, Graphic Design: Carl Morton.
Coordinator, Community Relations: Gina Hasson. Assistant, Communications: Dan Wartelle. Assistant, Community Relations: Jennifer Sullivan. Webmaster: Sonja Rassmussen.

Ticketing
Telephone: (206) 346-4001. FAX: (206) 346-4100.
Director, Ticket Services: Kristin Fortier. Manager, Ticket Operations: Connie McKay. Coordinator, Group Tickets: Steve Belling. Coordinator, Ticket Sales: Mike Aceto. Senior Account Executive, Ticket Sales: Bob Hellinger.

Stadium Operations
VP, Ballpark Operations: Neil Campbell. VP, Ballpark Planning/Development: John Palmer. Director, Ballpark Operations: Tony Pereira. Manager, Event Services: Kameron Durham. Director, Engineering/Maintenance: Ben Barton. Head Groundskeeper: Steve Peeler.
PA Announcer: Tom Hutyler. Official Scorer: Unavailable.

Travel, Clubhouse
Director, Team Travel: Ron Spellecy.
Clubhouse Manager: Scott Gilbert. Visiting Clubhouse Manager: Henry Genzale. Video Coordinator: Carl Hamilton.

General Information
Home Dugout: First Base. Playing Surface: Grass.
Stadium Location: I-5 or I-90 to Fourth Avenue South exit. Standard Game Times: 7:05 p.m., Sat. 1:05, Sun. 1:35.
Player Representative: Dan Wilson.

MARINERS

BASEBALL OPERATIONS

Executive VP, Baseball Operations/General Manager: Pat Gillick. VP, Baseball Administration: Lee Pelekoudas. VP, Scouting/Player Development: Roger Jongewaard.

Special Assignments: Woody Woodward. Administrator, Baseball Operations: Debbie Larsen. Coordinator, Baseball Technical Information: Mike Kuharich.

Major League Staff

Manager: Lou Piniella.

Coaches: Dugout—John McLaren; Pitching—Bryan Price; Batting—Gerald Perry; First Base—John Moses; Third Base—Larry Bowa; Bullpen—Matt Sinatro.

Pat Gillick

Lou Piniella

Medical, Training

Medical Director: Dr. Larry Pedegana. Club Physician: Dr. Mitchel Storey.

Head Trainer: Rick Griffin. Assistant Trainer: Tom Newberg. Strength/Conditioning Coach: Allen Wirtala.

Player Development

Director, Player Development: Benny Looper. Assistant Director, Player Development: Greg Hunter. Administrator, Player Development: Jan Plein.

Coordinator, Instruction: Mike Goff. Roving Instructors: James Clifford (strength/conditioning), Darnell Coles (hitting), Pat Rice (pitching), Steve Roadcap (catching).

Farm System

Class	Farm Team	Manager	Coach	Pitching Coach
AAA	Tacoma	Dave Myers	Dave Brundage	Jim Slaton
AA	New Haven	Dan Rohn	Henry Cotto	Steve Peck
A	Lancaster	Mark Parent	Dana Williams	Scott Budner
A	Wisconsin	Gary Thurman	Scott Steinmann	Rafael Chaves
A	Everett	Terry Pollreisz	D. Garner/A. Bottin	Marcos Garcia
R	Peoria	Omer Munoz	Tommy Cruz	Gary Wheelock
R	DSL	Ramon de los Santos	Alvarez/Martinez	Raul Santana

Scouting

Director, Scouting: Frank Mattox (Long Beach, CA). Administrator, Scouting: Hallie Larson.

Advance Scout: Stan Williams (Lakewood, CA).

Director, Professional Scouting: Ken Compton (Cypress, CA).

Major League Scouts: Bob Harrison (Long Beach, CA), Bill Kearns (Milton, MA), Steve Pope (Asheville, NC).

National Crosschecker: Steve Jongewaard (Huntington Beach, CA).

Regional Supervisors: West—Curtis Dishman (San Juan Capistrano, CA); East—John McMichen (Treasure Island, FL); Midwest—Carroll Sembera (Shiner, TX); Canada—Wayne Norton (Port Moody, British Columbia).

Frank Mattox

Full-Time Scouts: Dave Alexander (Lafayette, IN), Rodney Davis (Glendale, AZ), Phil Geisler (Portland, OR), Larry Harper (South San Francisco, CA), Mark Lummus (Cleburne, TX), Ken Madeja (Novi, MI), John Martin (Tampa, FL), Tom McNamara (Bronx, NY), Steve Rath (Newport Beach, CA), Eric Robinson (Hiram, GA), Matt Schafer (Charlotte, NC), Alex Smith (Abingdon, MD), Derek Valenzuela (Lakewood, CA), Kyle Van Hook (Brenham, TX).

Director, Pacific Rim Operations: Jim Colborn (Ventura, CA). Assistant, Pacific Rim Operations: Hide Sueyoshi (Bellevue, WA). Supervisors, Latin America: Mike Cadahia (Miami, FL), Bob Engle (Tampa, FL).

Telephone, Address

Office Address: Tropicana Field, One Tropicana Dr., St. Petersburg, FL 33705. **Telephone:** (727) 825-3137. **FAX:** (727) 825-3111. **Website:** www.devilray.com.

Ownership

Operated by: Tampa Bay Devil Rays, Ltd.

Ownership: Robert Basham, P.J. Benton, Mark Bostick, Mel Danker, Daniel Doyle, Florida Progress Corporation, Claude Focardi, Griffin Family Trust, Robert Kleinert, Gary Markel, Vincent Naimoli, Lance Ringhaver, Gus Stavros, Chris Sullivan.

Managing General Partner/Chief Executive Officer: Vincent Naimoli.

Vince Naimoli

BUSINESS OPERATIONS

Senior Vice President, Administration/General Counsel: John Higgins. **Director, Human Resources:** Jeep Weber. **Administrator, Human Resources:** Jennifer Thayer.

Finance

Controller: Patrick Smith. **Supervisor, Accounting:** Sandra Faulkner. **Payroll:** Debbie Clement. **Payables:** Debbie Brooks.

Marketing, Sales

Vice President, Sales/Marketing: John Browne. **Administrative Assistant:** Kim Phoenix. **Senior Director, Corporate Sales/Broadcasting:** Larry McCabe.

Manager, Broadcast Operations: Joe Ciaravino. **Director, Corporate Sales:** Tom Whaley. **Coordinator, Merchandise:** Tim Osterhout. **Managers, Sponsorship Coordination:** Tammy Atmore, Kelly Davis, Sean McHale. **Manager, Promotions/Special Events:** Christopher Dean.

Public Relations, Communications

Telephone: (727) 825-3242. **FAX:** (727) 825-3111.

Vice President, Public Relations: Rick Vaughn. **Assistant to Vice President, Public Relations:** Carmen Molina. **Manager, Media Relations:** Chris Costello. **Assistant, Media Relations:** Greg Landy.

Director, Publications: Matt Lorenz. **Assistant Director, Publications:** Charles Parker. **Manager, Internet:** Eric Helmer.

Manager, Community Relations: Liz-Beth Lauck. **Executive Director, Community Development:** Dick Crippen.

Director, Event Productions/Entertainment: John Franzone.

Stadium Operations

Vice President, Operations/Facilities: Rick Nafe. **Administrative Assistant, Facilities:** Tom Buscemi.

General Manager, Tropicana Field: Bob Leighton. **Event Manager:** Tom Karac. **Event Coordinator:** Scott Kelyman. **Head Groundskeeper:** Mike Williams. **Director, Audio Visual Services:** Todd Schirmer.

PA Announcer: Bill Couch. **Official Scorers:** Jim Ferguson, Allen Lewis, Rick Martin.

Ticketing

Telephone: (727) 825-3250. **FAX:** (727) 825-3294.

Director, Ticket Operations: Robert Bennett. **Assistant Director, Ticket Operations:** Ken Mallory. **Director, Ticket Sales:** Carola Ross.

Ticket Operations: Karen Smith, Curtis Brown. **Coordinator, Ticket Sales:** Shawn Haverfield. **Coordinator, Devil Rays Express:** T.J. McElaney.

Travel, Clubhouse

Traveling Secretary: Jeff Ziegler. **Equipment Manager/Home Clubhouse:** Carlos Ledezma. **Visitors Clubhouse:** Guy Gallagher.

General Information

Home Dugout: First Base. **Playing Surface:** Artificial Turf.

Directions to Stadium: I-275 South to St. Petersburg, exit 11, left onto Fifth Avenue, right onto 16th Street. **Standard Games Times:** 7:15 p.m., Sat. 4:15, Sun. 1:15.

Player Representative: Mike Difelice.

DEVIL RAYS

BASEBALL OPERATIONS
Senior Vice President, Baseball Operations/ General Manager: Chuck LaMar.

Assistant GM, Baseball Operations: Bart Braun. Assistant GM, Administration: Scott Proefrock. Executive Assistant to GM: Sandy Dengler.

Special Assistants to GM: Eddie Bane (Carlsbad, CA), Wade Boggs (Tampa, FL), Bill Livesey (St. Petersburg Beach, FL). Special Advisor, Baseball Operations: Frank Howard. Video Coordinator: Chris Fernandez.

Major League Staff
Manager: Larry Rothschild.
Coaches: Bench—Bill Russell; Pitching—Rick Williams; Batting—Leon Roberts; First Base—Jose Cardenal; Third Base— Billy Hatcher; Bullpen—Orlando Gomez.

Chuck LaMar

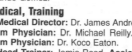

Medical, Training
Medical Director: Dr. James Andrews. Medical Team Physician: Dr. Michael Reilly. Orthopedic Team Physician: Dr. Koco Eaton.

Head Trainer: Jamie Reed. Assistant Trainer: Ken Crenshaw. Strength and Conditioning/ Coordinator, Rehabilitation: Kevin Harmon.

Minor Leagues
Telephone: (727) 825-3267. FAX: (727) 825-3493.
Director, Minor League Operations/Coordinator, Instruction: Tom Foley. Assistant, Player Development: Mitch Lukevics. Administrative Assistant, Player Development: Denise Vega-Smith.

Larry Rothschild

Minor League Coordinators: Buddy Biancalana (infield), Steve Henderson (hitting), Chuck Hernandez (pitching), Tom Mohr (strength/conditioning), Ron Porterfield (medical/rehabilitation).

Farm System
Class	Farm Team	Manager	Coach	Pitching Coach
AAA	Durham	Bill Evers	Max Oliveras	Joe Coleman
AA	Orlando	Mike Ramsey	Steve Livesey	Ray Searage
A	St. Petersburg	Julio Garcia	Mike Compton	Bryan Kelly
A	Charleston, S.C.	Charlie Montoyo	Dwight Smith	Milt Hill
A	Hudson Valley	Dave Silvestri	Ramon Ortiz	John Duffy
R	Princeton	Edwin Rodriguez	Jamie Nelson	Unavailable
R	DSL	Manny Castillo	Hector Del Pozo	Marcos Matos

Scouting
Telephone: (727) 825-3137. FAX: (727) 825-3300.
Director, Scouting: Dan Jennings. Assistant Director, Scouting: Sherard Clinkscales. Administrative Assistant, Scouting: Silvia Bynes.

Major League Scouts: Jerry Gardner (Los Alamitos, CA), Bart Johnson (Bridgeview, IL), Matt Keough (Coto de Caza, CA), Al LaMacchia (San Antonio, TX), Don Lindeberg (Anaheim, CA), Don Williams (Paragould, AR).

National Crosscheckers: Jack Gillis (Sarasota, FL), R.J. Harrison (Phoenix, AZ), Stan Meek (Norman, OK).

Dan Jennings

Area Scouts: Fernando Arango (Oklahoma City, OK), Jonathan Bonifay (Winston-Salem, NC), Skip Bundy (Birmingham, AL), Matt Dodd (Boston, MA), Kevin Elfering (Wesley Chapel, FL), Steve Foster (Weston, WI), Doug Gassaway (Blum, TX), Matt Kinzer (Fort Wayne, IN), Paul Kirsch (Tigard, OR), Fred Repke (Upland, CA), Edwin Rodriguez (Trujillo Alto, PR), Charles Scott (Novato, CA), Mac Seibert (Molino, FL), Craig Weissmann (LaCosta, CA), Doug Witt (St. Petersburg, FL).

Director, International Scouting: Rudy Santin (Miami, FL).

Telephone, Address

Office Address: 1000 Ballpark Way, Arlington, TX 76011. **Mailing Address:** P.O. Box 90111, Arlington, TX 76004. **Telephone:** (817) 273-5222. **FAX:** (817) 273-5206.

Website: www.texasrangers.com.

Ownership

Owner/Chairman: Tom Hicks.

President: James Lites. **Assistant to President:** Cheryl Hocker.

BUSINESS OPERATIONS

Executive Vice President, Finance/Operations: John McMichael. **VP, Diversified Operations:** Rick McLaughlin. **VP, Business Operations:** Geoff Moore.

Tom Schieffer

Assistant VP, Human Resources: Terry Turner. **Corporate Counsel:** Lance Lankford. **Assistant to Executive VP:** Judy Southworth.

Finance

Vice President, Finance: Chip Sawicki. **Controller:** Kellie Fischer. **Director, Purchasing:** Millicent Van Wie.

Marketing, Sales

Executive Vice President, Broadcasting/Sales: Bill Strong. **Executive VP, Marketing/Communications:** Jeff Cogen. **VP, Corporate Sales:** Charlie Seraphin. **Assistant VP, Corporate Sales:** Jill Cogen. **Assistant VP, Marketing:** Christy Martinez.

Director, Sponsorship Sales: Tom Fireoved. **Director, Corporate Sales:** Mike Phillips. **Manager, Broadcast/Sales Services:** Hilary Roberts. **Coordinator, Corporate Sales:** Ginger Reed.

Senior Director, Events: Lee Gleiser. **Senior Director, Entertainment:** Chuck Morgan.

Public Relations, Communications

Telephone: (817) 273-5203. **FAX:** (817) 273-5206.

Senior Vice President, Communications: John Blake.

Director, Media Relations: Kurt Daniels. **Assistant Director, Media Relations:** Brad Horn.

Vice President, Community Development/Relations: Norm Lyons. **Director, Community Relations:** Taunee Taylor. **Director, Community Development:** Rhonda Houston. **Assistant Director, Communications:** Dana Wilcox. **Coordinator, Community Relations:** Gretchen Rivera.

Stadium Operations

Vice President, Facilities/Construction: Billy Ray Johnson.

Director, Facilities/Special Events Operations: Kevin Jimison. **Director, Maintenance:** Gib Searight. **Director, Grounds:** Tom Burns. **Youth Ballpark Groundskeeper:** Andrew St. Julian. **Coordinator, Facility Services:** Duane Arber. **Coordinator, Complex Grounds:** Tom Jones.

PA Announcer: Chuck Morgan. **Official Scorers:** Kurt Iverson, John Mocek, Steve Weller.

Ticketing

Telephone: (817) 273-5100. **FAX:** (817) 273-5190.

Assistant VP, Ticket Operations: Augie Manfredo. **Assistant VP, Ticket Sales:** Brian Byrnes. **Director, Ticket Operations:** Michael Wood. **Assistant Director, Ticket Operations:** Mike Lentz.

Travel, Clubhouse

Director, Travel: Chris Lyngos.

Equipment/Home Clubhouse Manager: Zack Minasian. **Visiting Clubhouse Manager:** Joe Macko.

General Information

Home Dugout: First Base. **Playing Surface:** Grass.

Directions to Stadium: From I-30, take Ballpark Way exit, south on Ballpark Way; From Route 360, take Randol Mill exit, west on Randol Mill. **Game Times:** 7:35 p.m.; Sun. (April-May, Sept.) 2:05, (June-Aug.) 7:05.

Player Representative: Tim Crabtree.

RANGERS

BASEBALL OPERATIONS
Telephone: (817) 273-5222. **FAX:** (817) 273-5285.
Executive Vice President/General Manager: Doug Melvin.
Assistant GM: Dan O'Brien. **Director, Major League Administration:** Judy Johns. **Administrative Assistant:** Margaret Bales.

Major League Staff
Manager: Johnny Oates.
Coaches: Dugout—Bucky Dent; Pitching—Dick Bosman; Batting—Rudy Jaramillo; First Base—Ed Napoleon; Third Base—Jerry Narron; Bullpen—Larry Hardy.

Doug Melvin

Johnny Oates

Medical, Training
Medical Director: Dr. John Conway. **Team Internist:** Dr. David Hunter.
Head Trainer: Danny Wheat. **Assistant Trainer:** Ray Ramirez. **Director, Strength/Conditioning:** Mike Arndt.

Player Development
Telephone: (817) 273-5222. **FAX:** (817) 273-5285.
Director, Player Development: Reid Nichols.
Assistant Director, Player Development: John Lombardo.
Coordinator, Instruction: Bob Miscik (infield).
Roving Instructors: Dick McLaughlin (outfield/baserunning), Al Nipper (pitching), Frank Velazquez (conditioning), Butch Wynegar (hitting/catching).
Equipment Manager: Kent Brown. **Sports Psychologist:** Tom Hanson.

Farm System

Class	Farm Team	Manager	Coach	Pitching Coach
AAA	Oklahoma	DeMarlo Hale	Bruce Crabbe	Lee Tunnell
AA	Tulsa	Bobby Jones	Moe Hill	Mark Brewer
A	Charlotte	James Byrd	Edgar Caceres	Aris Tirado
A	Savannah	Paul Carey	Unavailable	Fred Dabney
R	Pulaski	Bruce Crabbe	Unavailable	Jonathan Jenkins
R	Port Charlotte	Darryl Kennedy	Carlos Subero	John O'Donoghue
R	DSL	Pedro Gonzalez	Unavailable	Unavailable

Scouting
Telephone: (817) 273-5277. **FAX:** (817) 273-5243.
Director, Scouting: Chuck McMichael. **Assistant to Director, Scouting:** Debbie Bent.
Assistant Director, Professional/International Scouting: Monty Clegg.
Advance Scout: Mike Paul (Tucson, AZ).
Professional Scouts: Ray Coley (Tucson, AZ), Toney Howell (Country Club Hills, IL), Bob Reasonover (Smyrna, TN), Rudy Terrasas (Santa Fe, TX), Bill Wood (Coppell, TX).
National Crosscheckers: Tim Hallgren (Chandler, AZ), Dave Klipstein (McAllen, TX), Jeff Taylor (Newark, DE).

Chuck McMichael

Area Scouts: Dave Birecki (Peoria, AZ), Mike Daughtry (St. Charles, IL), Jay Eddings (Sperry, OK), Kip Fagg (Manteca, CA), Jim Fairey (Clemson, SC), Tim Fortugno (Huntington Beach, CA), Mark Giegler (Fenton, MI), Joel Grampietro (Shrewsbury, MA), Mike Grouse (Independence, MO), Todd Guggiana (Garden Grove, CA), Doug Harris (Carlisle, PA), Zachary Hoyrst (Tallahassee, FL), Ray Jackson (Birmingham, AL), Jim Lentine (San Clemente, CA), Sammy Melendez (Vega Alta, PR), Randy Taylor (Katy, TX), Greg Whitworth (Mill Creek, WA), Jeff Wren (Ridge Manor, FL).
Latin Coordinator: Manny Batista (Vega Alta, PR).

TORONTO

Telephone, Address
Office/Mailing Address: 1 Blue Jays Way, Suite 3200, Toronto, Ontario M5V 1J1. **Telephone:** (416) 341-1000. **FAX:** (416) 341-1250. **E-Mail Address:** bluejay@bluejays.ca. **Website:** www.bluejays.ca.

Ownership
Operated by: Toronto Blue Jays Baseball Club. **Principal Owner:** Interbrew SA.
Board of Directors: John Barnes, Derek Hayes, Don Kitchen, Hugo Powell, George Taylor.
Senior Chairman: Sam Pollock. **Chairman:** Allan Chapin.

Sam Pollock

BUSINESS OPERATIONS
Senior Vice President, Finance/Operations: Stu Hutcheson.

Finance
Vice President, Finance/Administration: Susan Brioux.
Controller: Cathy McNamara-MacKay. **Manager, Employee Compensation:** Perry Nicoletta. **Office Manager:** Anne Fulford. **Consultant, Human Resources:** Linda Alexander. **Manager, Information Systems:** Peter Ferwerda.

Marketing, Sales
Senior Vice President, Marketing/Sales: Terry Zuk.
Director, Marketing: Peter Cosentino. **Manager, Marketing/Player Relations:** Laurel Lindsay. **Manager, Promotions:** Julian Franklin.
Director, Corporate Partnerships: Mark Lemmon. **Senior Account Executive:** Robert MacKay. **Service Coordinator:** Jon Lalonde.
Director, Sales: Greg McNamara. **Administrator, Ticket Sales:** Doug Barr. **Executive Assistant, Sales:** Darla McKeen.
General Manager, TBJ Merchandising: Michael Andrejek.

Media Relations, Communications
Telephone: (416) 341-1301/1303. **FAX:** (416) 341-1250.
Vice President, Media Relations: Howard Starkman.
Assistant Director, Media Relations: Jay Stenhouse. **Coordinator, Media Relations:** Mike Shaw. **Supervisor, Media Relations:** Laura Ammendolia.
Manager, Game Entertainment/Productions: Bart Given. **Manager, Community Relations:** Jennifer Santamaria.

Stadium Operations
Director, Operations: Mario Coutinho. **Game Security:** John Booth. **Supervisor, Office Services:** Mick Bazinet.
Grounds Supervisor: Tom Farrell.
PA Announcer: Murray Eldon. **Official Scorers:** Joe Sawchuk, Doug Hobbs, Neil MacCarl, Louis Cauz.

Ticketing
Telephone: (416) 341-1280. **FAX:** (416) 341-1177.
Director, Ticket Operations: Randy Low. **Manager, Ticket Vault Services:** Paul Goodyear. **Manager, Mail Order Services:** Sandra Wilbur. **Manager, Special Ticket Services:** Sheila Cantarutti. **Manager, Telephone Order Services:** Jan Marshall.

Travel, Clubhouse
Manager, Team Travel: John Brioux.
Equipment Manager: Jeff Ross. **Clubhouse Manager:** Kevin Malloy. **Visitors Video Operations:** Robert Baumander.

General Information
Home Dugout: Third Base. **Playing Surface:** Artificial turf.
Stadium Location: From west, take QEW/Gardiner Expressway eastbound and exit at Spadina Avenue, go north on Spadina one block, right on Bremner Boulevard. From east, take Gardiner Expressway westbound and exit at Spadina Avenue, north on Spadina one block, right on Bremner Boulevard. **Standard Game Times:** 7:05 p.m.; Sat. 4:05; Sun. 1:05.
Player Representative: Darrin Fletcher.

BLUE JAYS

BASEBALL OPERATIONS

President, Baseball Operations/General Manager: Gord Ash. Vice President, Baseball Operations/Assistant GM: Tim McCleary. Vice President, Baseball: Bob Mattick.

Assistant GM/Director, Player Personnel: Dave Stewart. Special Assistant to President and GM/Director, International Operations: Wayne Morgan. Special Assistants to President/GM: Mel Queen, Al Widmar.

Director, Florida Operations: Ken Carson. Manager, Amateur Baseball: Kevin Briand. Executive Administrative Assistant: Fran Brown. Baseball Assistant, Major League Operations: Heather Connolly.

Gord Ash

Major League Staff

Manager: Jim Fregosi.

Coaches: Bench—Lee Elia; Pitching—Rick Langford; Batting—Cito Gaston; First Base—Bobby Knoop; Third Base—Terry Bevington; Bullpen—Roly de Armas.

Medical, Training

Team Physician: Dr. Ron Taylor.

Head Trainer: Scott Shannon. Assistant Trainer: George Poulis. Strength/Conditioning Coordinator: Jeff Krushell.

Jim Fregosi

Player Development

Director, Minor League Operations: Bob Nelson. Administrative Assistants: Donna Kuzoff, Angie Van Evera.

Director, Player Development: Jim Hoff. Assistant Director, Player Development: Jim Lett. Pitching Coordinator: Bruce Walton. Hitting/Catching Coordinator: Ernie Whitt. Roving Instructors: George Boll (hitting), Garth Iorg (defense/baserunning), Eddie Rodriguez (infield).

Farm System

Class	Farm Team	Manager	Coach	Pitching Coach
AAA	Syracuse	Pat Kelly	Omar Malave	Gary Lance
AA	Tennessee	Rocket Wheeler	Hector Torres	Craig Lefferts
A	Dunedin	Marty Pevey	Dennis Holmberg	Scott Breeden
A	Hagerstown	Rolando Pino	Ken Landreaux	Hector Berrios
A	Brooklyn	Eddie Rodriguez	Unavailable	Jim Rooney
R	Medicine Hat	Paul Elliott	Geovany Miranda	Dane Johnson
R	DSL	Unavailable	Melvin Gomez	Antonio Caceres

Scouting

Director, Scouting: Tim Wilken. Assistant Director, Scouting: Chris Buckley. Coordinator, Scouting Operations: Marteese Robinson. Assistant, Scouting: Charlie Wilson.

Advance Scout: Sal Butera. Special Assignment Scouts: Chris Bourjos (Scottsdale, AZ), Mike Cadahia (Miami Springs, FL), Duane Larson (Knoxville, TN), Ted Lekas (Worcester, MA).

National Crosschecker: Mark Snipp (Granbury, TX). Regional Supervisors: West—Bill Moore (Alta Loma, CA); East—Mike Mangan (Clermont, FL); Central—Jeff Cornell (Lee's Summit, MO).

Scouting Supervisors: Charles Aliano (Columbia, SC), Jaymie Bane (Lexington, KY), Andy

Tim Wilken

Beene (Center Point, TX), Dave Blume (Elk Grove, CA), Joey Davis (Bridgeport, CT), Ellis Dungan (Pensacola, FL), Tom Hinkle (Atascadero, CA), Tim Huff (Cave Creek, AZ), Edwin Lawrence (Silver Spring, MD), Marty Miller (Chicago, IL), Ty Nichols (Riverbank, CA), Demerius Pittman (Chino, CA), Jorge Rivera (Puerto Nuevo, PR), Jim Rooney (St. Petersburg, FL), Joe Siers (Orlando, FL), Ron Tostenson (Issaquah, WA).

Director, Latin America Operations: Tony Arias (Miami Lakes, FL).
Director, Canadian Scouting: Bill Byckowski.

NATIONAL LEAGUE

NATIONAL LEAGUE

Mailing Address: 245 Park Ave., New York, NY 10167. **Telephone:** (212) 931-7700. **Fax:** (212) 935-5069.

Years League Active: 1876-.

Executive Committee: Montreal, San Diego, San Francisco.

Senior Vice President, Secretary: Katy Feeney.

Administrator, Umpires: Cathy Davis. **Supervisor, Umpires:** Tom Lepperd.

Vice President, Public Relations/Market Development: Ricky Clemons.

Executive Director, Player Records: Nancy Crofts. **Assistant, Media Relations/Player Records:** Moises Rodriguez.

Executive Secretary: Rita Aughavin.

2000 Opening Date: April 3. **Closing Date:** Oct. 1.

Regular Season: 162 games.

Division Structure: East—Atlanta, Florida, Montreal, New York, Philadelphia. **Central**—Chicago, Cincinnati, Houston, Milwaukee, Pittsburgh, St. Louis. **West**—Arizona, Colorado, Los Angeles, San Diego, San Francisco.

Playoff Format: Three division champions and second-place team with best record meet in best-of-5 Division Series. Winners meet in best-of-7 League Championship Series.

All-Star Game: July 11 at Atlanta (National League vs. American League).

Roster Limit: 25, through Aug. 31 when rosters expand to 40.

Brand of Baseball: Rawlings.

Statistician: Elias Sports Bureau, 500 Fifth Ave., New York, NY 10110.

Umpires: Unavailable.

Stadium Information

City	Stadium	Dimensions			Capacity	'99 Att.
		LF	CF	RF		
Arizona	Bank One Ballpark	330	407	334	48,500	3,019,654
Atlanta	Turner Field	335	401	330	50,528	3,284,897
Chicago	Wrigley Field	355	400	353	38,884	2,813,854
Cincinnati	Cinergy Field	330	404	330	52,953	2,061,222
Colorado	Coors Field	347	415	350	50,200	3,481,065
Florida	Pro Player Stadium	335	410	345	40,585	1,369,421
Houston	Enron Field	315	435	326	42,000	*2,706,017
Los Angeles	Dodger Stadium	330	395	330	56,000	3,095,346
Milwaukee	County Stadium	315	402	315	53,192	1,701,796
Montreal	Olympic Stadium	325	404	325	46,500	773,277
New York	Shea Stadium	338	410	338	55,777	2,725,668
Philadelphia	Veterans Stadium	330	408	330	62,363	1,825,337
Pittsburgh	Three Rivers Stadium	335	400	335	48,044	1,638,023
St. Louis	Busch Stadium	330	402	330	49,676	3,225,334
San Diego	Qualcomm Stadium	327	405	327	46,510	2,523,538
San Francisco	Pacific Bell Park	335	404	307	40,800	#1,925,634

*Attendance figure for Astrodome.
#Attendance figure for 3Com Park.

ARIZONA

Telephone, Address
Office Address: Bank One Ballpark, 401 E Jefferson St., Phoenix, AZ 85004. **Mailing Address:** P.O. Box 2095, Phoenix, AZ 85001. Telephone: (602) 462-6500. **FAX:** (602) 462-6599. Website: www.azdiamondbacks.com.

Ownership
Operated by: AZPB Limited Partnership.
Chairman: Jerry Colangelo.
Advisory Committee: George Getz, Dale Jensen, Bob Lavinia, Jerry Moyes, Rich Stephan.

Jerry Colangelo

BUSINESS OPERATIONS
President: Richard Dozer. **Assistant to President:** Michelle Avella.
General Counsel: Tom O'Malley.
Vice President, Human Resources: Cheryl Naumann.

Finance
Vice President, Finance: Tom Harris. **Vice President, Accounting:** Larry White. **Director, Management Information Systems:** Bill Bolt. **Controller:** Michelle Johnson. **Manager, Accounting:** Barbara Ragsdale. **Office Manager:** Pat Perez.

Marketing, Sales
Senior Vice President, Sales/Marketing: Scott Brubaker. **Vice President, Sales:** Blake Edwards. **Vice President, Broadcasting:** Scott Geyer.
Director, Hispanic Marketing: Richard Saenz. **Director, Tucson Operations:** Rich Tomey. **Director, Marketing:** Gina Giallonardo. **Manager, Broadcast Services:** Leo Gilmartin. **Manager, Internet Development:** Steve Gilbert. **Assistant, Marketing:** Kelly Wilson.

Community Affairs
Vice President, Community Affairs: Mark Fernandez. **Director, Youth Development:** Craig Pletenik. **Managers, Community Affairs:** Veronica Zendejas, Susan Hirohata. **Coordinator, Community Affairs:** Maggie Horwitz.

Public Relations, Communications
Telephone: (602) 462-6519. **FAX:** (602) 462-6527.
Director, Public Relations: Mike Swanson. **Manager, Media Relations:** Bob Crawford. **Manager, Publications:** Joel Horn. **Media Coordinator:** Brenda Maxey. **Assistants, Media Relations:** Mike McNally, Jeff Munn, David Pape.

Stadium Operations
President: Bob Machen. **General Manager:** Paige Peterson.
Vice President, Facilities Management: Alvan Adams. **Vice President, Event Services:** Russ Amaral. **Vice President, Security:** George Bevans. **Director, Suite Services:** Diney Mahoney. **Director, Ballpark Attractions:** Charlene Vazquez-Inzunza. **Director, Guest Relations:** Kristin Kurtz. **Director, Event Operations:** Craig Machen.
Head Groundskeeper: Grant Trenbeath.
PA Announcer: Jeff Munn. **Official Scorers:** Bob Eger, Gary Rausch.

Ticketing
Telephone: (602) 514-8400. **FAX:** (602) 462-4141.
Vice President, Ticket Operations/Special Services: Dianne Aguilar.
Director, Sales: Rob Kiese. **Director, Ticket Operations:** Darrin Mitch.

Travel, Clubhouse
Director, Team Travel: Roger Riley.
Equipment Manager/Home Clubhouse: Chris Guth. **Vistitors Clubhouse:** Bob Doty.

General Information
Home Dugout: Third Base. **Playing Surface:** Grass.
Stadium Location: Exit at Seventh Street from I-10 and turn south, or I-17 and turn north. **Standard Game Times:** 7:05 p.m., Sun. 1:35 p.m.
Player Representative: Brian Anderson.

DIAMONDBACKS

BASEBALL OPERATIONS

Telephone: (602) 462-6500. **FAX:** (602) 462-6599.

Vice President, General Manager: Joe Garagiola Jr. **Senior Executive Vice President, Baseball Operations:** Roland Hemond. **Assistant GM:** Sandy Johnson. **Senior Assistant to GM:** Mel Didier. **Special Assistants to GM:** Shooty Babitt, Ron Hassey, Bryan Lambe.

Director, Pacific Rim Operations: Jim Marshall. **Coordinator, Spring Training:** Ethan Blackaby. **Business Manager, Baseball Operations:** Craig Bradley. **Assistant to GM:** Shirena Smith.

Joe Garagiola Jr.

Major League Staff

Manager: Buck Showalter.

Coaches: Bench—Carlos Tosca; Pitching—Mark Connor; Batting—Jim Presley; First Base—Dwayne Murphy; Third Base—Brian Butterfield; Bullpen—Glenn Sherlock.

Medical, Training

Club Physicians: Dr. David Zeman, Dr. Roger McCoy.

Head Trainer: Paul Lessard. **Assistant Trainer:** Dave Edwards. **Strength/Conditioning Coach:** David Page.

Minor Leagues

Telephone: (602) 462-4400. **FAX:** (602) 462-6425.

Director, Minor League Operations: Tommy Jones. **Administrative Assistant, Player Development/Scouting:** Lisa Ventresca. **Assistant, Baseball Operations:** Tyler Agenter.

Buck Showalter

Roving Instructors: Derek Bryant (out field/baserunning), Ron Hassey (catching), Bob Mariano (hitting), Gil Patterson (pitching), Keith Wilson (strength/conditioning).

Farm System

Class	Farm Team	Manager	Coach	Pitching Coach
AAA	Tucson	Tom Spencer	Mike Barnett	Chuck Kniffin
AA	El Paso	Bobby Dickerson	Ty Van Burkleo	Dennis Lewallyn
A	High Desert	Scott Coolbaugh	Rick Schu	Mike Parrott
A	South Bend	Dave Jorn	Rodney Lofton	Royal Clayton
R	Missoula	Chip Hale	Aurelio Rodriguez	James Keller
R	Tucson	Bob Mariano	Carlos Mota	Mark Davis
R	DSL	Audo Vicente	Bernardo Brito	Pablo Frias

Scouting

Telephone: (602) 462-6520. **FAX:** (602) 462-6421.

Director, Scouting: Mike Rizzo. **Assistant Director, Scouting:** Bob Miller.

Major League Advance Scout: Dick Scott.

Professional Scouts: Bill Earnhart (Point Clear, AL), Mike Piatnik (Winter Haven, FL).

National Coordinator: Kendall Carter. **National Supervisors:** East—Ed Durkin (Safety Harbor, FL); Central—Kris Kline (Scottsdale, AZ); West— Steve Springer (Huntington Beach, CA).

Area Supervisors: Ray Blanco (Miami, FL), Ray Corbett (College Station, TX), Jason Goligoski (Vancouver, WA), Brian Guinn (Richmond, CA), Scott

Mike Rizzo

Jaster (Midland, MI), James Keller (Long Beach, CA), Chris Knabenshue (Edmond, OK), Hal Kurtzman (Van Nuys, CA), Greg Lonigro (Connellsville, PA), Howard McCullough (Greenville, NC), Louie Medina (Phoenix, AZ), Matt Merullo (Madison, CT), Phil Rizzo (Rolling Meadows, IL), Mike Valarezo (Jacksonville, FL), Brad Vaughn (Griffithville, AR), Luke Wrenn (Lakeland, FL).

Area Scouts: John Cole (Lake Forest, CA), Tony Levato (Peotone, IL), David May (Newark, DE), Mark Smelko (La Mesa, CA), Bob Sullivan (Grand Rapids, MI), Doyle Wilson (Chandler, AZ), John Wright (Chantilly, VA).

Latin American Coordinator: Junior Noboa (Santo Domingo, D.R.). **Coordinator, Mexico:** Derek Bryant (Hermosillo, Mexico).

ATLANTA

Telephone, Address
Office Address: 755 Hank Aaron Dr., Atlanta, GA 30315. Mailing Address: P.O. Box 4064, Atlanta, GA 30302. Telephone: (404) 522-7630. FAX: (404) 614-1391. Website: www.atlantabraves.com.

Ownership
Operated by: Atlanta National League Baseball Club, Inc.

Principal Owner: Ted Turner. Chairman: Bill Bartholomay.

Board of Directors: Henry Aaron, Bill Bartholomay, Bobby Cox, Stan Kasten, Rubye Lucas, Terry McGuirk, John Schuerholz, M.B. Seretean, Ted Turner.

Stan Kasten

President: Stan Kasten.

Senior Vice President, Assistant to President: Henry Aaron.

BUSINESS OPERATIONS
Senior VP, Administration: Bob Wolfe. Team Counsel: David Payne. Director, Human Resources: Michelle Thomas.

Finance
VP/Controller: Chip Moore.

Marketing, Sales
VP, Marketing/Broadcasting: Wayne Long.

Senior Director, Promotions/Civic Affairs: Miles McRea. Director, Ticket Sales: Paul Adams. Director, Community Relations: Cara Maglione. Director, Corporate Sales: Jim Allen.

Public Relations, Communications
Telephone: (404) 614-1456. FAX: (404) 614-1391.

Director, Public Relations: Jim Schultz.

Manager, Media Relations: Glen Serra. Assistants, Public Relations: Steve Copses, Robert Gahagan, Kim Ziegler.

Stadium Operations
Director, Stadium Operations/Security: Larry Bowman. Field Director: Ed Mangan.

PA Announcer: Bill Bowers. Official Scorers: Mark Frederickson, Mike Stamus.

Director, Audio-Video Operations: Jennifer Berger.

Ticketing
Telephone: (800) 326-4000. FAX: (404) 614-1391.

Director, Ticket Operations: Ed Newman.

Travel, Clubhouse
Director, Team Travel/Equipment Manager: Bill Acree. Visiting Clubhouse Manager: John Holland.

General Information
Home Dugout: First Base. Playing Surface: Grass.

Directions to Stadium: I-75/85 northbound/southbound, take exit 91 (Fulton Street); I-20 westbound, take exit 24 (Capitol Avenue); I-20 eastbound, take exit 22 (Windsor Street), right on Windsor Street, left on Fulton Street. Standard Game Times: 7:40 p.m.; Sat. 7:10, Sun. 1:10.

Player Representative: Tom Glavine.

BRAVES

BASEBALL OPERATIONS
Telephone: (404) 522-7630. **FAX:** (404) 523-3962.
Executive VP/General Manager: John Schuerholz.
VP/Assistant General Manager: Frank Wren.
Special Assistant to GM/Player Development: Jose Martinez. **Executive Assistant:** Melissa Hill. **Administrative Coordinator:** Linda Smith.

Major League Staff
Manager: Bobby Cox.
Coaches: Dugout—Pat Corrales; Pitching—Leo Mazzone; Batting—Merv Rettenmund; First Base—Glenn Hubbard; Third Base—Ned Yost; Bullpen—Bobby Dews.

John Schuerholz

Bobby Cox

Medical, Training
Team Physician: Dr. David Watson. **Trainer:** Dave Pursley. **Assistant Trainer:** Jeff Porter. **Strength/Conditioning Coach:** Frank Fultz.

Player Development
Telephone: (404) 614-7630. **FAX:** (404) 614-1350.
Director, Player Development: Dick Balderson.
Assistant Director, Player Development/Scouting: Dayton Moore. **Administrative Assistant:** Chris Rice.
Coordinator, Instruction: Chino Cadahia.
Roving Instructors: Rick Adair (pitching), Jim Beauchamp (outfield), Rafael Belliard (infield), Franklin Stubbs (hitting).

Farm System

Class	Farm Team	Manager	Coach	Pitching Coach
AAA	Richmond	Randy Ingle	Mel Roberts	Bill Fischer
AA	Greenville	Paul Runge	Bobby Moore	Mike Alvarez
A	Myrtle Beach	Brian Snitker	Sixto Lezcano	Bruce Dal Canton
A	Macon	Jeff Treadway	Tommy Gregg	Kent Willis
A	Jamestown	Jim Saul	Manny Jimenez	Jerry Nyman
R	Danville	J.J. Cannon	Edinson Renteria	Bill Champion
R	Kissimmee	Rick Albert	Ralph Henriquez	M. Perez/E. Watt
R	DSL	Dario Paulino	Thomas Vasquez	Unavailable

Scouting
Director, Scouting: Roy Clark. **Administrative Assistant:** Bobbie Cranford.
Advance Scout: Bobby Wine (Norristown, PA).
Major League Scouts: Deric Ladnier (Newnan, GA), Scott Nethery (Houston, TX).
Special Assignment Scouts: Bill Lajoie (Osprey, FL), Brian Murphy (Sarasota, FL), Paul Snyder (Lilburn, GA).
National Crosschecker: Tony LaCava (Oakmont, PA).
Regional Supervisors: Hep Cronin (Cincinnati, OH), Paul Faulk (Raleigh, NC), John Flannery (Austin, TX), Bob Wadsworth (Westminster, CA).

Roy Clark

Area Supervisors: Mike Baker (Santa Ana, CA), Daniel Rates (Oklahoma City, OK), Stu Cann (Bradley, IL), Rob English (Duluth, GA), Ralph Garr (Missouri City, TX), Rod Gilbreath (Lilburn, GA), John Hagemann (Staten Island, NY), J. Harrison (Sacramento, CA), Kurt Kemp (Eugene OR), Brian Kohlscheen (Norman, OK), Robert Lucas (Atlanta, GA), Jim Martz (Lima, OH), Marco Paddy (Palm Coast, FL), J.J. Picollo (Centreville, VA), Don Poplin (Norwood, VA), John Ramey (Murrieta, CA), Charlie Smith (Austin, TX), John Stewart (Granville, NY), Fernando Villaescusa (San Luis, AZ), Gene Watson (Georgetown, TX).
International Supervisors: Phil Dale (Victoria, Australia), Rene Francisco (West Palm Beach, FL), Julian Perez (Levittown, PR).
International Scouts: Amado Dinzey (Dominican Republic), Felix Francisco (Dominican Republic), Andres Lopez (Dominican Republic), Rolando Petit (Venezuela).

CHICAGO

Telephone, Address
Office Address: Wrigley Field, 1060 W Addison St., Chicago, IL 60613. **Telephone:** (773) 404-2827. **FAX:** (773) 404-4129. **E-Mail Address:** cubs@cubs.com. **Website:** www.cubs.com.

Ownership
Operated by: Chicago National League Ball Club, Inc. **Owner:** Tribune Company.

Board of Directors: Dennis Fitzsimmons, Andy MacPhail, Andrew McKenna.

President/Chief Executive Officer: Andy MacPhail.

Andy MacPhail

BUSINESS OPERATIONS
Executive Vice President, Business Operations: Mark McGuire.

Manager, Information Systems: Carl Rice.

PC Systems Analyst: Kyle Hoker. **Senior Legal Counsel/Corporate Secretary:** Crane Kenney. **Executive Secretary, Business Operations:** Annette Hannah. **Director, Human Resources:** Jenifer Surma.

Finance
Controller: Jodi Norman. **Manager, Accounting:** Terri Lynn. **Payroll Administrator:** Mary Jane Iorio. **Senior Accountant:** Angela Boone.

Marketing, Broadcasting
VP, Marketing/Broadcasting: John McDonough.

Director, Promotions/Advertising: Jay Blunk. **Manager, Cubs Care/Community Relations:** Rebecca Polihronis. **Coordinator, Marketing/Community Affairs:** Mary Dosek. **Manager, Mezzanine Suites:** Louis Artiaga. **Manager, Sponsorship Sales:** Susan Otolski.

Media Relations, Publications
Telephone: (773) 404-4191. **FAX:** (773) 404-4129.

Director, Media Relations: Sharon Pannozzo. **Manager, Media Information:** Chuck Wasserstrom. **Assistant, Media Relations:** Benjamin de la Fuente.

Director, Publications: Lena McDonagh. **Manager, Publications:** Jay Rand. **Editorial Specialist, Publications:** Jim McArdle. **Graphic Design Specialists:** Joaquin Castillo, Juan Alberto Castillo. **Coordinator, Internet:** John Davila. **Photographer:** Stephen Green.

Stadium Operations
Director, Stadium Operations: Paul Rathje.

Manager, Event Operations/Security: Mike Hill. **Coordinator, Event Operations/Security:** Julius Farrell. **Head Groundskeeper:** Roger Baird. **Facility Supervisor:** Bill Scott. **Coordinator, Office Services:** Randy Skocz. **Coordinator, Stadium Operations:** Danielle Alexa. **Switchboard Operator:** Brenda Morgan.

PA Announcer: Paul Friedman. **Official Scorers:** Bob Rosenberg, Don Friske.

Ticketing
Telephone: (773) 404-2827. **FAX:** (773) 404-4014.

Director, Ticket Operations: Frank Maloney. **Assistant Director, Ticket Sales:** Brian Garza. **Assistant Director, Ticket Services:** Joe Kirchen. **Vault Room Supervisor:** Cherie Blake.

Travel, Clubhouse
Traveling Secretary: Jimmy Bank.

Home Clubhouse Manager: Tom Hellmann. **Visiting Clubhouse Manager:** Dana Noeltner.

General Information
Home Dugout: Third Base. **Playing Surface:** Grass.

Stadium Location: From I-90/94 take Addison Street exit, follow Addison five miles to ballpark. One mile west of Lakeshore Drive, exit at Belmont going northbound, exit at Irving Park going southbound. **Standard Game Times:** 1:20 p.m., 7:05; Fri. 2:20; Sat. 12:15, 1:20, 3:05; Sun. 1:20.

Player Representative: Joe Girardi.

CUBS

BASEBALL OPERATIONS

Telephone: (773) 404-2827. **FAX:** (773) 404-4111.
Vice President/General Manager: Ed Lynch.
Director, Baseball Operations: Scott Nelson.
Special Assistants to GM: Keith Champion (Ballwin, MO), Larry Himes (Mesa, AZ), Ken Kravec (Sarasota, FL). **Executive Assistant to President/GM:** Arlene Gill.

Ed Lynch

Major League Staff

Manager: Don Baylor.
Coaches: Bench—Rene Lachemann; Pitching—Oscar Acosta; Batting—Jeff Pentland; First Base—Billy Williams; Third Base—Gene Glynn; Bullpen—Sandy Alomar Sr.

Don Baylor

Medical, Training

Team Physicians: Dr. Stephen Adams, Dr. Michael Schafer.
Head Trainer: David Tumbas. **Assistant Trainer:** Steve Melendez. **Strength/Conditioning Coordinator:** Mark Wilbert.

Player Development

Telephone: (773) 404 4035. **FAX:** (773) 404-4147.
Director, Player Development/Scouting: Jim Hendry. **Assistant, Player Development:** Patti Kargakis.
Field Coordinator: Terry Kennedy.
Roving Instructors: John Cangelosi (outfield/baserunning), Bruce Hammel (strength/conditioning), Nate Oliver (infield), John Pierson (hitting), Lester Strode (pitching).
Equipment Manager: Michael Burkhart.

Farm System

Class	Farm Team	Manager	Coach	Pitching Coach
AAA	Iowa	Dave Trembley	Glenn Adams	Rick Tronerud
AA	West Tenn	Dave Bialas	Tack Wilson	Alan Dunn
A	Daytona	Richie Zisk	Joey Cora	Tom Pratt
A	Lansing	Steve McFarland	Pat Listach	Stan Kyles
A	Eugene	Danny Sheaffer	Tom Beyers	Mike Anderson
R	Mesa	Carmelo Martinez	Trey Forkerway	David Haas
R	DSL	Julio Valdez	Leo Hernandez	Unavailable

Scouting

Telephone: (773) 404-2827. **FAX:** (773) 404-4117.
Director, Scouting: Jim Hendry. **Coordinator, Scouting:** John Stockstill (Lees Summit, MO).
Administrative Assistant: Patricia Honzik.
Major League Advance Scout: Terry Collins (St. Petersburg, FL). **Special Player Consultant:** Hugh Alexander (Spring Hill, FL).
Major League Scout: Bill Harford (Chicago, IL).
Special Assignment Scout: Glen Van Proyen (Lisle, IL).
Regional Supervisors: East—Joe Housey (Hollywood, FL); Central—Brad Kelley (Glendale, AZ); West—Larry Maxie (Upland, CA).

Jim Hendry

Full-Time Scouts: Mark Adair (Hazelwood, MO), Billy Blitzer (Brooklyn, NY), Jim Crawford (Columbia, TN), Steve Fuller (Brea, CA), Al Geddes (Canby, OR), John Gracio (Chandler, AZ), Gene Handley (Huntington Beach, CA), Steve Hinton (Sacramento, CA), Sam Hughes (Marietta, GA), Spider Jorgensen (Cucamonga, CA), Buzzy Keller (Seguin, TX), Scott May (Wonder Lake, IL), Brian Milner (Edgecliff Village, TX), Fred Petersen (Long Beach, CA), Marc Russo (Mooresville, NC), Mark Servais (La Crosse, WI), Tom Shafer (Hartford, CT), Mike Soper (Tampa, FL), Billy Swoope (Norfolk, VA).
Director, Latin American Operations: Oneri Fleita (Omaha, NE).
Coordinator, Pacific Rim: Leon Lee (Folsom, CA).
International Scouts: Hector Ortega (Venezuela), Jose Serra (Dominican Republic), Jose Trujillo (Puerto Rico).

CINCINNATI

Telephone, Address
Office Address: 100 Cinergy Field, Cincinnati, OH 45202. **Telephone:** (513) 421-4510. **FAX:** (513) 421-7342. **Website:** www.cincinnatireds.com.

Ownership
Operated by: The Cincinnati Reds, Inc.

Limited Partners: Gannett Co., Inc.; Carl Kroch estate; Mrs. Louis Nippert; William Reik; Marge Schott; George Strike.

Chief Executive Officer: Carl Lindner. **Chief Operating Officer:** John Allen.

John Allen

BUSINESS OPERATIONS
General Counsel: Robert Martin.

Executive Assistant, Administrative Offices: Joyce Pfarr.

Finance
Controller: Anthony Ward. **Systems Analyst:** Kelly Gronotte. **Payroll Supervisor:** Cathy Secor. **Accounts Payable/Receivable:** JoAnne Ludmann. **Administrative Assistant, Accounting:** Lois Wingo. **Administrator, Business/Broadcasting:** Ginny Kamp.

Marketing, Sales
Marketing Consultant: Cal Levy. **Assistants, Marketing:** Jen Black, Molly Mott.

Director, Season Ticket/Group Sales: Pat McCaffrey. **Manager, Group Sales:** Brad Callahan. **Assistant, Season/Group Sales:** Ryan Niemeyer. **Account Executives:** Brad Blettner, Chris Herrell, Stuart King.

Manager, Merchandise: Jill Perrin.

Public Relations, Communications
Telephone: (513) 421-2990. **FAX:** (513) 421-7342.

Director, Media Relations: Rob Butcher. **Assistant Director, Media Relations:** Michael Vassallo. **Assistant, Public Relations:** Larry Herms.

Director, Communications: Mike Ringering. **Assistant Director, Communications:** Ralph Mitchell. **Communications:** Emily Dixon.

Stadium Operations
Director, New Stadium Development: Jenny Gardner.

Director, Stadium Operations: Jody Pettyjohn. **Superintendents, Stadium Operations:** Bob Harrison, Steve Sears. **Field Superintendent:** Jeff Guilkey. **Administrative Assistant, Stadium Operations:** Mitzi Harmeyer. **Switchboard Supervisor:** Lauren Gaghan.

PA Announcer: John Walton. **Official Scorers:** Ron Roth, Glenn Sample.

Ticketing
Telephone: (513) 421-4510. **FAX:** (513) 421-7342.

Director, Ticket Operations: John O'Brien. **Assistant Ticket Director:** Ken Ayer. **Administrator, Ticket Office:** Hallie Kinney. **Manager, Season Sales:** Cyndi Strzynski. **Administrative Assistant, Season Tickets:** Shannon Bohman. **Administrative Assistant, Ticket Office:** Colleen Brown.

Travel, Clubhouse
Traveling Secretary: Gary Wahoff.

Senior Clubhouse/Equipment Manager: Bernie Stowe. **Equipment Manager/Home Clubhouse:** Rick Stowe. **Visitors Clubhouse:** Mark Stowe.

General Information
Home Dugout: First Base. **Playing Surface:** Artificial turf.

Stadium Location (subject to daily construction changes)**:** From I-75 South, exit onto I-71 North, exit at Pete Rose Way (exit 1B), left off ramp; From I-71 South, go left at Vine Street/Covington (exit 1C), right off ramp onto Third Street, right on Broadway, right onto Mehring Way. From I-75/I-71 North, cross over Brent Spence Bridge, exit at Pete Rose Way (exit 1B), left off ramp. **Standard Game Times:** 7:05 p.m., Sun. 1:15 p.m..

Player Representative: Unavailable.

BASEBALL OPERATIONS
Telephone: (513) 421-4510. **FAX:** (513) 579-9145.

General Manager: Jim Bowden.

Assistant General Manager: Darrell "Doc" Rodgers. **Senior Assistants to GM:** Al Goldis, Gary Hughes. **Special Assistants to General Manager:** Larry Barton, Gene Bennett, Bob Boone, Johnny Bench, Tim Naehring. **Executive Assistant to GM:** Lois Schneider.

Director, Baseball Administration: Brad Kullman.

Major League Staff
Manager: Jack McKeon.

Jim Bowden

Coaches: Dugout—Ken Griffey Sr.; Pitching—Don Gullett; Batting—Denis Menke; First Base—Dave Collins. Third Base—Ron Oester; Bullpen—Tom Hume.

Medical, Training
Medical Director: Dr. Tim Kremchek.

Head Trainer: Greg Lynn. **Assistant Trainer:** Mark Mann. **Director, Strength/Conditioning:** Lance Sewell.

Player Development
Senior Director, Player Development/Scouting: Leland Maddox. **Director, Player Development:** Bill Doran. **Senior Advisor:** Chief Bender. **Assistant, Player Development/Scouting:** Paul Pierson.

Administrative Assistant, Player Development: Lois Hudson.

Jack McKeon

Camp Coordinator: Donnie Scott. **Roving Instructors:** Joe Hall (baserunning), Jim Hickman (hitting), Brook Jacoby (hitting), Brian Koelling (infield), Rodney McCray (outfield).

Farm System

Class	Farm Team	Manager	Coach	Pitching Coach
AAA	Louisville	Dave Miley	Phillip Wellman	Grant Jackson
AA	Chattanooga	Mike Rojas	Jamie Dismuke	Mack Jenkins
A	Dayton	Fred Benavides	Brian Conley	Don Alexander
A	Clinton	Jay Sorg	Greg Grall	Derek Botelho
R	Billings	Russ Nixon	Brian Wilson	Ted Power
R	Sarasota	Luis Quinones	Lino Diaz	Jeff Gray
R	DSL	Roberto Valdez	Leo Perez	Jose Duran

Scouting
Telephone: (513) 421-4510. **FAX:** (513) 579-9145.
Director, Scouting: DeJon Watson. **Director, Pro Scouting:** Gary Hughes. **Senior Advisor, Scouting:** Bob Zuk (Redlands, CA). **Director, Scouting Administration:** Wilma Mann.

National Crosscheckers: Kasey McKeon (Stoney Creek, NC), Jeff Barton (Higley, AZ).

Regional Crosscheckers: Latin America/Mexico—Johnny Almaraz (Spring Branch, TX); East—Bill Scherrer (Buffalo, NY); West—Ross Sapp (Cherry Valley, CA); Central—Alvin Rittman (Memphis, TN).

DeJon Watson

Scouting Supervisors: Terry Abbott (Orlando, FL), Butch Baccala (Windsor, CA), Howard Bowens (Tacoma, WA), John Brickley (Melrose, MA), Mark Corey (Highlands Ranch, CO), Robert Filotei (Wilmer, AL), Jerry Flowers (Dolton, IL), Jimmy Gonzales (San Antonio, TX), David Jennings (St. Charles, MO), Robert Koontz (McConnellsburg, PA), Craig Kornfeld (Rancho Santa Margarita, CA), Steve Kring (Charlotte, NC), Brian Mejia (Miami, FL), Cotton Nye (Edmond, OK), Tom Severtson (Denver, CO), Perry Smith (Charlotte, NC), Brian Wilson (Albany, TX), Greg Zunino (Cape Coral, FL).

Director, International Scouting: Jorge Oquendo (Aguadilla, PR).

COLORADO

Telephone, Address
Office Address: 2001 Blake St., Denver, CO 80205. Telephone: (303) 292-0200. FAX: (303) 312-2116. Website: www.coloradorockies.com.

Ownership
Operated by: Colorado Rockies Baseball Club, Ltd.

Chairman/Chief Executive Officer: Jerry McMorris. Vice Chairmen: Charles Monfort, Richard Monfort. Executive Assistant to Chairman: Adele Armagost. Executive Assistant to Vice Chairmen: Patricia Penfold.

Jerry McMorris

BUSINESS OPERATIONS
Executive Vice President, Business Operations: Keli McGregor. Assistant to Executive Vice President: Terry Douglass.

Senior Vice President, Corporate Counsel: Clark Weaver. Assistant to Senior VP: Nancy Kilpatrick. Senior Director, Personnel/Administration: Elizabeth Stecklein. Director, Information Systems: Mary Burns.

Finance
Senior Vice President/Chief Financial Officer: Hal Roth.

Vice President, Finance: Michael Kent. Director, Accounting: Gary Lawrence. Senior Accountant: Phil Emerson.

Marketing, Sales
Vice President, Sales/Marketing: Greg Feasel. Assistant to VP: Marcia McGovern. Senior Director, Corporate Sales: Marcy English Glasser. Assistant Director, Sales/Marketing: Dave Madsen.

Director, Promotions/Special Events: Alan Bossart. Coordinator, Promotions: Michael Thumim. Director, Broadcasting: Eric Brummond. Director, Merchandising: Jim Kellogg.

Public Relations, Communications
Telephone: (303) 312-2325. FAX: (303) 312-2319.

Senior Director, Communications/Public Relations: Jay Alves. Assistant to Director, Public Relations: Zak Gilbert. Coordinator, Public Relations: Charity Stowell.

Director, Community Affairs: Roger Kinney. Assistant to Director, Community Affairs: Hollie Casson. Coordinator, Community Affairs: Stacy Schafer.

Stadium Operations
Senior Director, Coors Field Operations: Kevin Kahn. Director, Coors Field Administration/Development: Dave Moore. Coordinator, Stadium Services: Mary Beth Benner. Director, Guest Services: Mike Rock. Managers, Guest Services: Steven Burke, Todd Zeo.

Head Groundskeeper: Mark Razum. Assistant Head Groundskeeper: Jose Gonzalez. Assistant, Groundskeeping: Javier Rivera.

PA Announcer: Kelly Burnham. Official Scorers: Dave Einspahr, Jack Rose.

Ticketing
Telephone: (303) ROCKIES, (800) 388-ROCK. FAX: (303) 312-2115.

Vice President, Ticket Operations/Sales: Sue Ann McClaren. Assistant to VP: LaTanya Hamilton. Director, Ticket Sales: Jill Roberts.

Director, Ticket Operations/Development: Kevin Fenton. Assistant Director, Ticket Operations/Finances: Kent Hakes.

Travel, Clubhouse
Director, Team Travel: Brandy Lay.

Clubhouse/Equipment Manager: Dan McGinn. Visiting Clubhouse Manager: Keith Schulz. Video Coordinator: Mike Hamilton.

General Information
Hometown Dugout: First Base. Playing Surface: Grass.

Stadium Location: From I-70 to I-25 South to exit 213 (Park Avenue) or 212C (20th Street); I-25 to 20th Street, east to park. Standard Game Times: 7:05 p.m., 1:05; Sat. 1:05, 6:05; Sun. 1:05.

Player Representative: Todd Helton.

ROCKIES

BASEBALL OPERATIONS

Executive Vice President/General Manager: Dan O'Dowd. Senior Director, Baseball Operations/Assistant GM: Josh Byrnes. Administrator, Major Leagues: Thad Levine.

Special Assistant to GM: Pat Daugherty.

Senior Director, Player Personnel: Mark Wiley.

Director, Baseball Administration: Tony Siegle.

Major League Staff

Manager: Buddy Bell.

Coaches: Bench—Toby Harrah; Pitching—Marcel Lachemann; Batting—Clint Hurdle; First Base—Dallas Williams; Third Base—Rich Donnelly; Bullpen—Fred Kendall; Strength—Brad Andress. Senior Advisor: Dave Garcia.

Dan O'Dowd

Buddy Bell

Medical, Training

Medical Director: Dr. Richard Hawkins.

Head Trainer: Tom Probst. Assistant Trainer: Keith Dugger. Rehabilitation Coordinator: Scott Gehret. Strength/Conditioning Coordinator: Brian Jordan.

Player Development

Director, Player Development: Michael Hill. Administrator, Player Development: Marc Gustafson. Administrative Assistant: Jody Ross.

Director, Minor League Operations: Paul Egins. Field Coordinator: Boyd Coffie. Roving Instructors: Lorenzo Bundy (outfield/baserunning), Mike Gallego (infield), Greg Gross (hitting), Rick Mathews (pitching), Rolando Fernandez (Latin American coordinator).

Farm System

Class	Farm Team	Manager	Coach	Pitching Coach
AAA	Colo. Springs	Chris Cron	Jim Eppard	Jim Wright
AA	Carolina	Ron Gideon	Theron Todd	Jerry Cram
A	Salem	Alan Cockrell	Joe Marchese	Bob McClure
A	Asheville	Joe Mikulik	Javier Gonzalez	Tom Edens
A	Portland	Billy White	Stu Cole	Richard Palacios
R	Tucson	P.J. Carey	Fred Ocasio	Unavailable
R	DSL	Unavailable	Edison Lora	Unavailable

Scouting

Director, Scouting: Bill Schmidt.

Assistant Directors, Scouting: Coley Brannon, Paul Herfurth. Administrative Assistant: Holly Burkett.

Major League Scouts: Jim Fregosi Jr. (Murrieta, CA), Dave Garcia (El Cajon, CA), Will George (Woolwich Township, NJ), Milt May (Bradenton, FL), Mark Wiley (Boca Raton, FL). Professional Scouts: Joe McDonald (Lakeland, FL), Art Pontarelli (Cranston, RI), Steve Schryver (Williams Bay, WI).

National Crosscheckers: Bill Gayton (Houston, TX), Dave Holliday (Coalgate, OK). Regional Crosscheckers: West—Danny Montgomery (Union City, CA); Midwest—Jay Darnell (Plano, TX); East—Robyn Lynch (Coral Springs, FL).

Bill Schmidt

Full-Time Area Scouts: John Cedarburg (Fort Myers, FL), Ty Coslow (Louisville, KY), Dar Cox (Frisco, TX), Mike Ericson (Glendale, AZ), Abe Flores (Huntington Beach, CA), Mike Garlatti (Edison, NJ), Bert Holt (Visalia, CA), Greg Hopkins (Beaverton, OR), Bo Hughes (Sherman Oaks, CA), Damon Iannelli (Brandon, MS), Eric Johnson (Houston, TX), Bill MacKenzie (Ottawa, Ontario), Jay Matthews (Asheville, NC), Lance Nichols (Dodge City, KS), Sean O'Conner (Milford, MA), Jorge de Posada (Rio Piedras, PR), Brooks Roybal (Tallahassee, FL), Ed Santa (Powell, OH), Nick Venuto (Boardman, OH), Tom Wheeler (Pleasant Hill, CA).

Director, Pacific Rim Scouting: Tim Ireland (Pleasanton, CA).

FLORIDA

Telephone, Address
Office Address: Pro Player Stadium, 2267 NW 199th St., Miami, FL 33056. Telephone: (305) 626-7400. FAX: (305) 626-7428. Website: www.floridamarlins.com.

Ownership
Operated by: Florida Marlins Baseball Club, Inc.
Chairman: John Henry. Vice Chairman: David Ginsberg.
Executive Assistant to Chairman: Patty Sweeney.

BUSINESS OPERATIONS

John Henry

Finance
Executive VP/Chief Financial Officer: Jonathan Mariner.
Director, Finance/Controller: Susan Jaison. Director, Information Technology: Esther Fleming. Director, Administration: Mike Whittle. Director, Legal Affairs: Lucinda Treat. Director, Public Affairs: Susan Budd.

Marketing, Sales
Vice President, Sales/Communications: Julio Rebul. VP, Sales: Lou DePaoli.
Director, Marketing: John Pierce. Director, Creative Services/In-Game Entertainment: Leslie Riguero. Director, Marketing Partnerships: Jim Frevola. Executive Director, Marlins Community Foundation: Nancy Olson. Manager, Community Affairs: Israel Negron.

Media Relations, Communications
Telephone: (305) 626-7429. FAX: (305) 626-7302.
VP, Communications/Broadcasting: Ron Colangelo.
Director, Media Relations: Eric Carrington. Coordinator, Media Relations: Jonathan Jensen. Secretary, Media Relations: Susu Rodriguez.
Manager, Broadcasting: Sandra van Meek.

Stadium Operations
President, Stadium Operations: Bruce Schulze. Assistant General Manager: Steve Froot. Director, Event Operations/Security: Todd Ellzey. Director, Team Security: Dan Vaniman. Head Groundskeeper: Alan Sigwardt.
PA Announcer: Unavailable. Official Scorer: Doug Pett.

Ticketing
Telephone: (305) 930-4487. FAX: (305) 626-7432.
VP, Ticket Operations: Bill Galante. Director, Season Tickets/Group Sales: Pat McNamara.

Travel, Clubhouse
Director, Team Travel: Bill Beck.
Equipment Manager/Home Clubhouse: Mike Wallace. Visitors Clubhouse: Matt Rosenthal. Video Coordinator: Cullen McRae.

General Information
Home Dugout: First Base. Playing Surface: Grass.
Standard Game Times: 7:05 p.m.; Sun. 4:05.
Stadium Location: From south, Florida Turnpike extension to stadium exit; From north, I-95 to I-595 West to Florida Turnpike to stadium exit; From west, I-75 to I-595 to Florida Turnpike to stadium exit; From east, Highway 826 West to NW 27th Avenue, north to 199th Street, right to stadium.
Player Representative: Mark Kotsay.

MARLINS

BASEBALL OPERATIONS
Telephone: (305) 626-7400. FAX: (305) 626-7433.
Executive Vice President/General Manager: Dave Dombrowski.
Vice President/Assistant General Manager: Dave Littlefield. Director, Major League Administration: Dan Lunetta. Assistant to GM: Scott Reid. Special Assistants to GM: Andre Dawson, Orrin Freeman (La Jolla, CA), Tony Perez. Assistant, Baseball Operations: Rob McDonald. Director, Brevard Operations: Andy Dunn.

Dave Dombrowski

Major League Staff
Manager: John Boles.
Coaches: Dugout—Joe Breeden; Pitching—Rich Dubee; Batting—Jack Maloof; First Base—Rusty Kuntz; Third Base—Fredi Gonzalez; Infield—Tony Taylor.

Medical, Training
Club Physician: Dr. Dan Kanell. Head Trainer: Larry Starr. Assistant Trainer: Kevin Rand. Director, Strength/Conditioning: Rick Slate.

John Boles

Player Development
Office Address: 5600 Stadium Parkway, Melbourne, FL 32940. Telephone: (321) 633-8119. FAX: (321) 633-9216.

Director, Field Operations: Rob Leary. Manager, Minor League Operations: Mike Parkinson. Manager, Minor League Administration: Kim-Lee Carkeek Luchs. Assistant, Minor League Operations: Andrew Lobpries.
Coordinator, Trainers/Equipment: John Spinosa. Coordinator, Rehabilitation: Mike McGowan. Coordinator, Strength/Fitness: Toby Oldham. Coordinator, Player Program Development: Laurie Soltman.
Roving Instructors: Britt Burns (pitching), Manny Crespo (infield), Adrian Garrett (hitting), Bob Natal (catching), Dave Nelson (baserunning), Brian Peterson (performance enhancement), Pookie Wilson (outfield).

Farm System
Class	Farm Team	Manager	Coach	Pitching Coach
AAA	Calgary	Lynn Jones	Sal Rende	Randy Hennis
AA	Portland	Rick Renteria	Jose Castro	Steve Luebber
A	Brevard County	Dave Huppert	Frank Cacciatore	Euclides Rojas
A	Kane County	Russ Morman	Matt Winters	Jeff Andrews
A	Utica	Jon Deeble	Joe Aversa	Bill Sizemore
R	Melbourne	Kevin Boles	Hayward Cook	Jeff Schwarz
R	DSL	Nelson Silverio	Joselyn Feliz	Pablo Blanco

Scouting
Telephone: (305) 626-7400. FAX: (305) 626-7294.
Director, Scouting/Latin American Operations: Al Avila. Manager, Scouting Administration: Cheryl Evans. Assistant, Scouting: James Orr.
Professional Scouts: Dick Egan (Phoenix, AZ), Manny Estrada (Brandon, FL), Jax Robertson (Cary, NC).
National Crosscheckers: Murray Cook (Washington, DC), Bill Singer (Decatur, AL). Regional Crosscheckers: East—Mike Russell (Gulf Breeze, FL); Midwest—David Chadd (Wichita, KS); West—Tim Schmidt (San Bernardino, CA).

Al Avila

Area Scouts: John Booher (Las Vegas, NV), Ty Brown (Ruther Glen, VA), John Castleberry (High Point, NC), Brad Del Barba (Taylor Mill, KY), David Finley (San Diego, CA), Larry Keller (Memphis, TN), Bob Laurie (Plano, TX), Steve Minor (Long Beach, CA), Steve Mondile (Wenonah, NJ), Cucho Rodriguez (San Juan, PR), Doug Rogalski (Jacksonville, FL), Jim Rough (Wichita, KS), Dennis Sheehan (Glasco, NY), Keith Snider (Stockton, CA), Stan Zielinski (Winfield, IL).
Coordinator, Latin American Scouting: Louie Eljaua (Pembroke Pines, FL). International Scout: Jon Deeble (Australia).

HOUSTON

Telephone, Address
Office Address: Union Station at Enron Field, 501 Crawford, Suite 200, Houston, TX 77002. **Mailing Address:** P.O. Box 288, Houston, TX 77001. **Telephone:** (713) 259-8000. **FAX:** (713) 259-8915. **E-Mail Address:** twinspin@astros.com. **Website:** www.astros.com.

Ownership
Operated by: McLane Group, LP.
Chairman/Chief Executive Officer: Drayton McLane.
Board of Directors: Drayton McLane, Bob McClaren, Sandy Sanford, Webb Stickney.

Drayton McLane

BUSINESS OPERATIONS
President, Business Operations: Bob McClaren. **Vice President, Human Resources:** Mike Anders. **VP, Information Systems:** Teresa Palanne. **Executive Assistant:** Tracy Faucette.

Finance
Vice President, Finance: Robert McBurnett.
Accounts Receivable: Mary Ann Bell. **Accounts Payabale:** Irene Dumenil. **Manager, General Accounting:** Mary Duvernay. **Manager, Payroll:** Ruth Kelly. **Accounting Clerk:** Chang Rooker.

Marketing, Sales
Senior VP, Sales/Marketing: Pam Gardner. **VP, Market Development:** Rosi Hernandez. **VP, Sales/Broadcasting:** Jamie Hildreth. **Manager, Advertising:** Duone Byars. **Manager, Marketing:** Kelly Makimaa. **Assistant Director, Advertising Sales/Promotions:** Jim Ballweg. **Coordinator, Broadcast Network Traffic:** Christine Alford.

Public Relations, Communications
Telephone: (713) 259-8000. **FAX:** (713) 799-9881.
Vice President, Communications: Rob Matwick. **Director, Media Relations:** Warren Miller. **Assistant Director, Media Relations:** Alyson Footer. **Manager, Communcations:** Todd Fedewa. **Coordinator, Media Services:** Desta Kimmel. **Manager, Marketing Operations:** Phoenix Mak.
VP, Community Development: Marian Harper. **Coordinator, Community Development:** Rita Suchma.

Stadium Operations
Senior VP, Non-Baseball Events: Mike Puryear. **VP, Customer Service:** Bob Brubaker. **VP, Traffic Operations:** Don Collins. **VP, Engineering:** Rob Harris.
Head Groundskeeper: Luke Jenkins.
PA Announcer: Bob Ford. **Official Scorers:** Rick Blount, Fred Duckett, Ivy McLemore.

Ticketing
VP, Ticket Sales/Services: John Sorrentino.
Director, Ticket Sales: Tina Cash. **Ticket Manager:** Marcia Coronado. **Manager, Premium Sales:** Shannon Sawyer. **Enron Field Tour Manager:** Jill McCormick.

Clubhouse
Equipment Manager: Dennis Liborio. **Assistant Equipment Manager:** Carl Schneider. **Visiting Clubhouse:** Steve Perry.

General Information
Home Dugout: First Base. **Playing Surface:** Grass.
Stadium Location: From I-10 East: take Smith Street (exit 769A), 0.3 miles to Texas Ave. left, 0.6 miles to park at corner of Texas Ave. and Crawford St.; from I-10 West: take San Jacinto St. (exit 769B), 0.4 miles then bear right on Fannin St., left on Texas Ave., 0.3 miles to park; from Hwy. 59 North: take Gray Ave./Pierce Ave. exit, 0.3 miles on Gray to Crawford St., 1.0 miles to park. **Standard Game Times:** 7:05 p.m., Sun. 2:05.
Player Representative: Shane Reynolds.

BASEBALL OPERATIONS
Telephone: (713) 259-8000. **FAX:** (713) 799-9562.
President, Baseball Operations: Tal Smith.
General Manager: Gerry Hunsicker.
Director, Baseball Administration: Barry Waters. **Administrative Assistant:** Beverly Rains. **Assistant, Baseball Operations:** David Gottfried.

Major League Staff
Manager: Larry Dierker.
Coaches: Dugout—Matt Galante; Pitching—Vern Ruhle; Batting—Tom McCraw; First Base—Jose Cruz Sr.; Third Base—Mike Cubbage; Bullpen—John Tamargo.

Gerry Hunsicker

Medical, Training
Medical Director: Dr. David Lintner.
Head Trainer: Dave Labossiere. **Assistant Trainer:** Rex Jones. **Strength/Conditioning Coach:** Dr. Gene Coleman.

Player Development
Telephone: (713) 259-8922. **FAX:** (713) 259-8915.
Assistant GM/Director, Player Development: Tim Purpura. **Administrator, Minor Leagues:** Jay Edmiston. **Administrative Assistant:** Carol Wogsland.
Field Coordinator: Harry Spilman. **Assistant Field Coordinator:** Gordy MacKenzie. **Roving Instructors:** Johnny Lewis (hitting), Jim Pankovits (infield), Dewey Robinson (pitching).

Larry Dierker

Farm System

Class	Farm Team	Manager	Coach	Pitching Coach
AAA	New Orleans	Tony Pena	T. Torchia/G. Langbehn	Jim Hickey
AA	Round Rock	Jackie Moore	Mark Bailey	Burt Hooton
A	Kissimmee	Manny Acta	Ivan DeJesus	Jack Billingham
A	Michigan	Al Pedrique	John Massarelli	Charley Taylor
A	Auburn	Unavailable	Jorge Orta	Bill Ballou
R	Martinsville	Brad Wellman	Scott Makarewicz	Stan Boroski
R	DSL	Rafael Ramirez	Miguel de la Cruz	Rick Aponte

Scouting
Director, Scouting: David Lakey.
Assistant Director, Scouting: Pat Murphy.
Administrative Assistant, Scouting: Traci Dearing.
Coordinator, Professional Scouting: Paul Ricciarini (Pittsfield, MA). **Advance Scout:** Fred Nelson (Richmond, TX). **Special Assignment Scout:** Tom Wiedenbauer (Ormond Beach, FL).
Major League Scouts: Stan Benjamin (Port Charlotte, FL), Walt Matthews (Texarkana, TX), Tom Mooney (Pittsfield, MA), Bob Skinner (San Diego, CA), Paul Weaver (Phoenix, AZ).
Professional Scouts: Kimball Crossley (Providence, RI), Gene DeBoer (Brandon, WI), Leo Labossiere (Lincoln, RI), Joe Pittman (Columbus, GA), Tom Romenesko (Santee, CA), Scipio Spinks (Houston, TX).

David Lakey

National Supervisor: Bill Kelso (Fort Worth, TX).
Regional Supervisors: East—Gerry Craft (St. Clairsville, OH); West—Bob King (La Mesa, CA); Central—Tad Slowik (Arlington Heights, IL).
Area Scouts: Bob Blair (Commack, NY), Joe Bogar (Carmel, IN), Ralph Bratton (Dripping Springs, TX), Chuck Carlson (Orlando, FL), Doug Deutsch (Costa Mesa, CA), James Farrar (Shreveport, LA), David Henderson (Edmond, OK), Dan Huston (Bellevue, WA), Mark Johnson (Englewood, CO), Brian Keegan (Charlotte, NC), Mike Maggart (Penn Yan, NY), Jerry Marik (Chicago, IL), Tom McCormack (University City, MO), Mel Nelson (Highland, CA), Bob Poole (Redwood City, CA), Joe Robinson (Burlington, IA), Frankie Thon (Guaynabo, PR), Tim Tolman (Tucson, AZ), Danny Watkins (Humble, TX), Gene Wellman (Danville, CA).

LOS ANGELES

Telephone, Address
Office Address: 1000 Elysian Park Ave., Los Angeles, CA 90012. Telephone: (323) 224-1500. FAX: (323) 224-1269. Website: www.dodgers.com.

Ownership
Operated by: Los Angeles Dodgers, Inc. Principal Owner: News Corp.

Managing Partner/Chairman/Chief Executive Officer: Bob Daly. President/Chief Operating Officer: Bob Graziano.

Board of Directors: Chase Carey, Sam Fernandez, Bob Graziano.

Senior Vice President: Tommy Lasorda.

Bob Daly

BUSINESS OPERATIONS
Senior VP/General Counsel: Santiago Fernandez. Director, Business Development: Fred Coons.

Director, Human Resources/Administration: Gina Galasso. Administrator, Human Resources: Leonor Romero. Assistant, Human Resources: Silvia Camacho. Manager, Administrative Services: Linda Cohen. Assistant, Administrative Services: George Barajas.

Managing Director, Dodgertown: Craig Callan.

Finance
Chief Financial Officer: Cristine Hurley. Manager, Accounting: Bobby Crisostomo. Manager, Finance/Financial Reporting: Amanda Shearer. Director, Management Information Systems: Mike Mularky.

Marketing, Sales
Executive Vice President/Chief Marketing Officer: Kris Rone. Director, Ticket Marketing: Bob Wymbs. Manager, Group Sales: Lisa Johnson. Manager, Youth Marketing: Steve Everett.

Media Relations, Public Affairs
Telephone: (323) 224-1301. FAX: (323) 224-1459.

Senior Vice President, Communications: Derrick Hall.

Director, Media Relations/Publicity: Julio Sarmiento. Office Coordinator, Media Relations: Barbara Conway. Assistant, Baseball Information: David Tuttle.

Director, Broadcasting/Publications: Brent Shyer. Supervisor, Broadcast/Publications: Paul Gomez. Assistants, Broadcast/Publications: Donna Carter, Mark Langill, Jorge Valencia.

VP, Communications: Tommy Hawkins. Director, Community Relations: Don Newcombe. Director, Public Affairs: Monique Brandon.

Stadium Operations
VP, Stadium Operations: Doug Duennes. Assistant Director, Stadium Operations: Chris Fighera. Manager, Stadium Operations: David Born. Superintendent, Turf and Grounds: Eric Hansen.

PA Announcer: Mike Carlucci. Official Scorers: Don Hartack, Terry Johnson, Gordie Verrell.

Ticketing
Telephone: (323) 224-1471. FAX: (323) 224-2609.

Director, Ticket Operations: Billy Hunter. Managers, Ticket Operations: Gary Barbee, Chris Furmento, Mike Rodriguez.

Travel, Clubhouse
Traveling Secretary: Billy DeLury. Assistant Director, Team Travel: Shaun Rachau.

Home Clubhouse Manager: Dave Wright. Visiting Clubhouse Manager: Jerry Turner.

General Information
Home Dugout: Third Base. Playing Surface: Grass.

Stadium Location: I-5 to Stadium Way exit, left on Stadium Way, right on Academy Road, left to Stadium Way to Elysian Park Avenue, left to stadium; I-110 to Dodger Stadium exit, left on Stadium Way, right on Elysian Park Avenue; U.S. 101 to Alvarado exit, right on Sunset, left on Elysian Park. Standard Game Times: 7:10 p.m., 1:05 ; Wed. 7:05.

Player Representative: Devon White.

DODGERS

BASEBALL OPERATIONS
Telephone: (323) 224-1500. **FAX:** (323) 224-1269.
Executive Vice President/General Manager: Kevin Malone. **Assistant GM:** Bill Geivett. **Special Assistant to GM:** Jeff Schugel. **Administrator:** Luchy Guerra.

Major League Staff
Manager: Davey Johnson.
Coaches: Bench—Jim Tracy; Pitching—Claude Osteen; Batting—Rick Down; First Base—John Shelby; Third Base—Rick Dempsey; Bullpen—Glenn Hoffman.

Kevin Malone

Medical, Training
Team Physicians: Dr. Herndon Harding, Dr. Frank Jobe, Dr. Michael Mellman.
Head Trainer: Stan Johnston. **Assistant Trainer:** Matt Wilson. **Physical Therapist:** Pat Screnar. **Strength/Conditioning Coach:** Todd Clausen.

Player Development
Telephone: (323) 224-1431. **FAX:** (323) 224-1359.
Director, Player Development: Jerry Weinstein.
Project Coordinator: Joe Bohringer.
Administrative Assistant: Chris Haydock. **Field Coordinator:** Rick Sofield. **Roving Instructors:** Jim Benedict (pitching), Alvaro Espinoza (infield), Chris Mihlfeld (strength/conditioning), Jimmy Johnson (hitting), Joe Vavra (baserunning).

Davey Johnson

Farm System
Class	Farm Team	Manager	Coach	Pitching Coach
AAA	Albuquerque	Tom Gamboa	Ron Jackson	Dean Treanor
AA	San Antonio	Rick Burleson	U.L. Washington	Mark Littell
A	San Bernardino	Dino Ebel	Jack Clark	Shawn Barton
A	Vero Beach	John Shoemaker	Tony Harris	Marty Reed
A	Yakima	Butch Hughes	Damon Farmar	Fred Corral
R	Great Falls	Juan Bustabad	Quinn Mack	Greg Gohr
R	DSL	Unavailable	Unavailable	Unavailable

Scouting
Assistant to General Manager/Scouting: Ed Creech.
Assistant Director, Scouting: Matt Slater. **Project Coordinator, Scouting:** Tasha Noriega. **Assistant, Scouting:** Bill McLaughlin.
Senior Scouting Advisor: Don Welke.
Advance Scout: Mark Weidemaier (Tierre Verde, FL). **Major League Scouts:** Phil Favia (Pasadena, TX), Carl Loewenstine (Hamilton, OH).
Coordinator, Minor League Scouting: Terry Reynolds (Altadena, CA). **Professional Scouts:** Dan Freed (Lexington, IL), Marty Maier (Piedmont, CA), Ron Rizzi (Joppa, MD).

Ed Creech

National Crosscheckers: Gib Bodet (San Clemente, CA), Jimmy Lester (Columbus, GA).
Regional Supervisors: East—John Barr (Palm City, FL); Midwest—Mike Hankins (Lee's Summit, MO); West Coast—Joe Ferrone (Santa Clarita, CA).
Area Scouts: Doug Carpenter (Jupiter, FL), Jim Chapman (Delta, British Columbia), Bobby Darwin (Cerritos, CA), Scott Groot (Mission Viejo, CA), Hank Jones (Vancouver, WA), Lon Joyce (Spartanburg, SC), John Kosciak (Milford, MA), Marty Lamb (Lexington, KY), Mike Leuzinger (Mansfield, TX), Bump Merriweather (Los Angeles, CA), Bill Pleis (Parrish, FL), Willie Powell (Pensacola, FL), Scott Sharp (Finksburg, MD), Mark Sheehy (Sacramento, CA), Chris Smith (Montgomery, TX), Bob Szymkowski (Chicago, IL), Tom Thomas (Phoenix, AZ), Mitch Webster (Great Bend, KS).
Director, Asian Relations: Acey Kohrogi.

MILWAUKEE

Telephone, Address
Office Address: County Stadium, 201 S 46th St., Milwaukee, WI 53214. **Mailing Address:** P.O. Box 3099, Milwaukee, WI 53201. **Telephone:** (414) 933-4114. **FAX:** (414) 933-3251. **Website:** www.milwaukeebrewers.com.

Ownership
Operated by: Milwaukee Brewers Baseball Club.

Board of Directors: John Canning, Mitchell Fromstein, Michael Grebe, Charles Krause, Richard Strup, Wendy Selig-Prieb.

President, Chief Executive Officer: Wendy Selig-Prieb. **Special Assistant to President:** Sal Bando. **Executive Assistant to President:** Mary Burns.

Wendy Selig-Prieb

Vice President, General Counsel: Tom Gausden. **Assistant General Counsel:** Eugene Randolph.

BUSINESS OPERATIONS
Vice President, New Ballpark Development: Michael Bucek. **Director, Suite Sales/Advertising:** Geoff Campion.

Administrator, Human Resources: Mariela Garcia.

Finance
Vice President, Finance: Paul Baniel. **Director, Purchasing:** Charlotte Tisdale. **Director, Management Information Systems:** Dan Krautkramer.

Corporate Affairs, Sales/Marketing
Vice President, Corporate Affairs: Laurel Prieb.

Director, Sponsorships/Promotions: Dean Rennicke. **Directors, Corporate Sales:** Matt Groniger, Amy Welch. **Manager, Corporate Affairs/Internet:** Cathy Bradley. **Manager, Corporate Sales:** Nicole Clark.

Public Relations, Communications
Telephone: (414) 933-6975. **FAX:** (414) 933-3251.

Director, Publications: Mario Ziino.

Director, Community Relations: Michael Downs. **Manager, Community Relations:** Marquette Baylor.

Director, Media Relations: Jon Greenberg. **Manager, Media Relations:** Amy Abramczyk. **Manager, Baseball Information:** Jason Parry. **Team Photographer:** Joe Picciolo.

Director, Broadcasting: Tim Van Wagoner. **Manager, Broadcasting:** Aleta Mercer.

Stadium Operations
Vice President, Stadium Operations: Scott Jenkins.

Director, Event Services: Steve Ethier. **Director, Grounds:** Gary Vanden Berg. **Assistant Director, Grounds:** David Mellor.

PA Announcer: Robb Edwards. **Official Scorers:** Tim O'Driscoll, Wayne Franke.

Ticketing
Vice President, Ticket Operations: Bob Voight.

Director, Season Ticket/Group Sales: Jim Bathey. **Director, Ticket Operations:** John Barnes. **Administrative Assistants, Ticket Operations:** Irene Bolton, Nancy Jorgensen. **Operations Manager, Ticketing:** Scott Parsons. **Manager, Outbound Ticket Sales:** Chris Barlow.

Travel, Clubhouse
Traveling Secretary: Dan Larrea.

Director, Clubhouse Operations: Tony Migliaccio. **Coordinator, Visiting Clubhouse:** Phil Rozewicz. **Assistant, Home Clubhouse:** Meshach Belle. **Assistant, Visiting Clubhouse:** Darnell Bowden.

General Information
Home Dugout: First Base. **Playing Surface:** Grass.

Stadium Location: From airport/south, I-94 West to Madison exit, to stadium. **Standard Game Times:** 7:05 p.m., (April) 6:05; Day, Sun. 1:05.

Player Representative: Unavailable.

BREWERS

BASEBALL OPERATIONS

Senior Vice President, Baseball Operations/ General Manager: Dean Taylor.

Vice President, Player Personnel: David Wilder. Senior Special Assistant to GM: Larry Haney. Special Assistant to GM: Cecil Cooper. Special Assistant, Baseball Operations: Chuck Tanner. Coordinator, Baseball Information: Tom Flanagan. Senior Administrator, Baseball Operations: Barb Stark. Administrative Assistant, Baseball Operations: Adela Martinez.

Major League Staff

Manager: Davey Lopes.

Dean Taylor

Coaches: Bench—Jerry Royster; Pitching—Bob Apodaca; Batting—Rod Carew; First Base—Gary Allenson; Third Base—Chris Speier; Bullpen—Bill Castro.

Medical, Training

Team Physician: Dr. Angelo Mattalino.

Head Trainer: John Adam. Assistant Trainer: Roger Caplinger. Strength/Conditioning Coach: Phil Falco.

Player Development

Director, Player Development: Greg Riddoch. Assistant Director, Player Development/Scouting: Scott Martens. Administrator, Minor League Operations: Kate Geenen.

Dave Lopes

Field Coordinator: Ralph Dickenson. Roving Instructors: Tim Blackwell (catching), Guy Hansen (pitching), Ed Romero (infield), Jim Skaalen (hitting), Herm Winningham (outfield/baserunning).

Farm System

Class	Farm Team	Manager	Coach	Pitching Coach
AAA	Indianapolis	Steve Smith	Luis Salazar	Dwight Bernard
AA	Huntsville	Carlos Lezcano	John Mallee	Mike Caldwell
A	Mudville	Barry Moss	George McPherson	Lonnie Keeter
A	Beloit	Don Money	Rich Morales	R.C. Lichtenstein
R	Helena	Dan Norman	Frank Kremblas	Gil Rondon
R	Ogden	Ed Sedar	Jorge Brito	Steve Cline
DSL	DSL	Mike Guerrero	Alberto Morillo	Unavailable

Scouting

Director, Scouting: Jack Zduriencik.

Major League Scouts: Russ Bove (Apopka, FL), Ken Califano (Brookfield, WI), Larry Haney (Barboursville, VA), Tim Johnson, Al Monchak (Bradenton, FL), Chuck Tanner (New Castle, PA), Dick Wiencek (Rancho Mirage, CA).

Professional Scouts: Carl Blando (Sarasota, FL), Alan Regier (Gilbert, AZ), Daraka Shaheed (Vallejo, CA), Elanis Westbrooks (Houston, TX).

National Crosscheckers: Midwest—Tom Allison (Scottsdale, AZ); East Coast—Bobby Heck (Altamonte Springs, FL); West Coast—Ric Wilson (Chandler, AZ).

Jack Zduriencik

Scouts: Lary Aaron (Atlanta, GA), Fred Beene (Oakhurst, TX), Jeff Brookens (Chambersburg, PA), Kevin Christman (Elk Grove, CA), Steve Connelly (Durham, NC), Mike Farrell (Carmel, IN), Dick Foster (Otis, OR), Mike Gibbons (Liberty Township, OH), Brian Johnson (Phoenix, AZ), Harvey Kuenn Jr. (New Berlin, WI), Demie Mainieri (Tamarac, FL), Justin McCray (Alameda, Calif.), Alex Morales (Lake Worth, FL), Doug Reynolds (Tallahassee, FL), Corey Rodriguez (Hermosa Beach, CA), Bruce Seid (Laguna Niguel, CA), Jonathan Story (Gulfport, MS), Tom Tanous (Swansea, MA), Red Whitsett (Villa Rica, GA), Walter Youse (Sykesville, MD).

Director, International Scouting: Epy Guerrero (Santo Domingo, D.R.). International Scouts: Felix Delgado (Rio Piedras, PR), Manny Hernandez (Moca, DR), Elvio Jimenez (Dominican Republic), John Viney (Australia).

MONTREAL

Telephone, Address

Office Address: 4549 Pierre-de-Coubertin Ave., Montreal, Quebec H1V 3N7. **Mailing Address:** P.O. Box 500, Station M, Montreal, Quebec H1V 3P2. **Telephone:** (514) 253-3434. **Fax:** (514) 253-8282.**Website:** www.montrealexpos.com.

Ownership

Operated by: Montreal Baseball Club, Inc.

Chairman/Chief Operating Officer/Managing General Partner: Jeffrey Loria.

Executive Vice President: David Samson. **Executive Assistant:** Monique Chibok.

Jeff Loria

BUSINESS OPERATIONS

Finance

Vice President, Finance/Treasurer: Michel Bussiere. **Risk Manager:** Marlene Auclair.

Sales, Marketing

Directors, Advertising Sales: Luigi Carola, John Di Terlizzi, Danielle La Roche. **Director, Promotions/Special Events:** Gina Hackl. **Director, Adminstration, Sales/Marketing:** Stephany Peschlow.

Coordinator, Broadcast Services: Marc Griffin. **Producer, Scoreboard Operations:** Louis Simard. **Coordinator, Entertainment:** Jean-Simon Bibeau. **Coordinator, Promotions/Special Events:** Denis Boucher.

Media Relations, Communications

Director, Media Relations: P.J. Loyello. **Director, Media Services:** Monique Giroux. **Coordinator, Media Relations:** Francois Boutin. **Administrative Assistant:** Sina Gabrielli.

Stadium Operations

Vice President, Stadium Operations: Claude Delorme. **General Manager, Jupiter Stadium Limited:** Rob Rabenecker. **Director, Stadium Operations:** Denis Pare. **Director, Management Information System:** Yves Poulin. **Manager, Souvenirs:** Peggy O'Leary.

PA Announcer: Marc Leveille. **Official Scorer:** Mike Spinelli.

Ticketing

Director, Season Ticket Sales: Gilles Beauregard. **Director, Business Development:** Real Sureau. **Director, Downtown Ballpark Ticket Office:** Chantal Dalpe. **Director, Olympic Stadium Ticket Office:** Hubert Richard. **Assistant Director, Ticket Office:** Frederique Brault.

Travel, Clubhouse

Coordinator, Team Travel/Conditioning: Sean Cunningham.

Equipment Manager: John Silverman. **Visiting Clubhouse:** Bryan Greenberg.

General Information

Home Dugout: First Base. **Playing Surface:** Artificial turf.

Stadium Location: From New England, take I-87 North from Vermont to Quebec Highway 15 to the Jacques Cartier Bridge, exit left, right on Sherbrooke. From upstate New York, take I-81 North to Trans Canada Highway 401, east to Quebec Highway 20, north to Highway 40 to Boulevard Pie IX exit south to stadium. Access by subway from downtown Montreal to Pie IX Metro station. **Standard Game Times:** Day 1:35 p.m.; Night 7:35.

Player Representative: Anthony Telford.

EXPOS

BASEBALL OPERATIONS

Vice President/General Manager: Jim Beattie.
Assistant GM: Larry Beinfest. **Assistant to GM:** Mike Berger.
Administrative Assistant: Marcia Schnaar.

Major League Staff

Manager: Felipe Alou.
Coaches: Dugout—Luis Pujols; Pitching—Bobby Cuellar; Batting—Pat Roessler; First Base/Infield—Perry Hill; Third Base—Pete Mackanin; Bullpen—Pierre Arsenault (coordinator), Brad Arnsberg (coach).

Jim Beattie

Medical, Training

Team Physician: Dr. Michael Thomassin. **Team Orthopedist:** Dr. Larry Coughlin.
Head Trainer: Ron McClain. **Assistant Trainer:** Mike Kozak. **Coordinator, Conditioning:** Sean Cunningham.

Player Development

Felipe Alou

Office Address: Roger Dean Stadium, 4657 Main St., Jupiter, FL 33458. **Mailing Address:** P.O. Box 8978, Jupiter, FL 33468. **Telephone:** (561) 775-1818. **FAX:** (561) 775-9935.
Director, Player Development: Don Reynolds.
Assistant Director, Player Development: Adam Wogan. **Administrative Assistant:** Maria Arellano.
Field Coordinator: Rick Sweet.
Roving Instructors: Jim Bowie (hitting), Paul Fournier (conditioning/rehabilitation), Wayne Rosenthal (pitching), Craig Shipley (infield/baserunning).

Farm System

Class	Farm Team	Manager	Coach	Pitching Coach
AAA	Ottawa	Jeff Cox	Eric Fox	Randy St. Claire
AA	Harrisburg	Doug Sisson	Tony Barbone	Jerry Reuss
A	Jupiter	Luis Dorante	Mike Felder	Ace Adams
A	Cape Fear	Bill Masse	Johnny Rodriguez	Tom Signore
A	Vermont	Tim Leiper	Keke Ayo	Gil Lopez
R	Jupiter	Steve Phillips	Mo Blakeney	Craig Bjornson
R	DSL	Arturo DeFreites	Solomon Torres	Jose Zapata

Scouting

Telephone: (561) 775-1818. **FAX:** (561) 775-9935.
Director, Scouting: Jim Fleming (Purcell, OK).
Assistant Director, Scouting: Gregg Leonard.
Administrative Assistant, Scouting: Mike Wickham.
Major League Scouts: Mike Berger (Pittsburgh, PA), Bob Cluck (La Mesa, CA).
National Crosschecker: Len Strelitz (Temple City, CA). **Regional Supervisors:** East—Marc DelPiano (Auburn, NY); West—Dave Malpass (Huntington Beach, CA).
Area Scouts: Alex Agostino (St. Bruno, Quebec), Matt Anderson (Montoursville, PA), Mark Baca (Temecula, CA), Carlos Berroa (San Juan, PR), Dennis Cardoza (Denton, TX), Robby Corsaro (Adelanto, CA), Dave Dangler (Birmingham, AL), Scot Engler (Jupiter, FL), Scott Goldby (Vancouver, WA), John Hughes (Walnut Creek, CA), Joe Jordan (Blanchard, OK), Mark Leavitt (Fern Park, FL), Darryl Monroe (Marietta, GA), Bob Oldis (Iowa City, IA) Steve Payne (Cherry Hill, NJ), Scott Stanley (Peoria, AZ), Tommy Thompson (Greenville, NC).
Vice President/Director, International Operations: Fred Ferreira (Fort Lauderdale, FL). **Assistant Director, International Scouting:** Randy Kierce.

Jim Fleming

NEW YORK

Fred Wilpon

Telephone, Address
Office Address: 123-01 Roosevelt Ave., Flushing, NY 11368. **Telephone:** (718) 507-6387. **FAX:** (718) 507-6395. **Website:** www.mets.com.

Ownership
Operated by: Sterling Doubleday Enterprises, LP.
Board of Directors: Richard Cummings, Nelson Doubleday, Saul Katz, Steve Phillips, Marvin Tepper, Fred Wilpon.
Chairman: Nelson Doubleday. **President/Chief Executive Officer:** Fred Wilpon.

BUSINESS OPERATIONS
Senior Vice President, Business Operations: David Howard.
General Counsel: David Cohen.

Finance
Senior Vice President/Treasurer: Harold O'Shaughnessy.
Vice President, Purchasing/Special Projects: Bob Mandt. **Controller:** Lenny Labita. **Director, Information Systems:** Russ Richardson. **Senior Staff Accountant:** Alon Kindler.

Marketing, Sales
Senior Vice President, Marketing/Broadcasting: Mark Bingham.
Director, Marketing: Kit Geis. **Director, Marketing Productions:** Tim Gunkel. **Director, Corporate Sales:** Paul Danforth. **Director, Promotions:** Jim Plummer. **Director, Group Sales:** Tom Fersch.
Manager, Publications: Jill Grabill.
Director, Community Outreach: Jill Knee. **Assistant Director, Community Outreach:** Jonathan Rosenberg.

Media Relations, Community Relations
Telephone: (718) 565-4330. **FAX:** (718) 639-3619.
Director, Media Relations: Jay Horwitz. **Media Relations Specialists:** Shannon Dalton, Stella Fiore, Ethan Wilson.

Stadium Operations
Director, Stadium Operations: Kevin McCarthy. **Assistant Director:** Sue Lucchi. **Head Groundskeeper:** Pete Flynn.
PA Announcer: Del DeMontreux. **Official Scorers:** Joe Donnelly, Red Foley, Bill Shannon.

Ticketing
Telephone: (718) 507-8499. **FAX:** (718) 507-6396.
Vice President, Ticket Sales/Services: Bill Ianniciello.
Director, Group/Ticket Sales Services: Thomas Fersch. **Director, Ticket Operations:** Dan DeMato. **Manager, Ticket Sales Development:** Robert Livingston.

Travel, Clubhouse
Equipment Manager/Associate Travel Director: Charlie Samuels.
Assistant Equipment Manager: Vinny Greco. **Visiting Clubhouse Manager:** Tony Carullo. **Video Editor:** Joe Scarola.

General Information
Home Dugout: First Base. **Playing Surface:** Grass.
Stadium Location: From Bronx and Westchester, take Cross Bronx Expressway to Bronx-Whitestone Bridge, then take bridge to Whitestone Expressway to Northern Boulevard/Shea Stadium exit. From Brooklyn, take Eastbound BQE to Eastbound Grand Central Parkway. From Long Island, take either Northern State Parkway or LIE to Westbound Grand Central Parkway. From northern New Jersey, take George Washington Bridge to Cross Bronx Expressway. From Southern New Jersey, take any of bridge crossings to Verazzano Bridge, and then take either Belt Parkway or BQE to Grand Central Parkway. **Standard Game Times:** 7:10 p.m.; Sat.-Sun. 1:10.
Player Representative: Al Leiter.

METS

BASEBALL OPERATIONS

Senior Vice President/General Manager: Steve Phillips.

Senior Assistant General Manager/International Scouting: Omar Minaya. **Special Assistants to GM:** Larry Doughty, Darrell Johnson, Harry Minor. **Executive Assistant:** Denise Morris.

Major League Staff

Manager: Bobby Valentine.

Coaches: Batting—Tom Robson; Pitching—Dave Wallace; First Base/Outfield—Mookie Wilson; Third Base—Cookie Rojas; Bullpen—Al Jackson; Catching—John Stearns.

Steve Phillips

Bobby Valentine

Medical, Training

Team Physicians: Dr. David Altchek, Dr. John Olichney.

Head Trainer: Fred Hina. **Assistant Trainer:** Scott Lawrenson. **Fitness Coach:** Barry Heyden.

Player Development

Assistant GM/Director, Player Development: Jim Duquette. **Assistant Director:** Kevin Morgan. **Coordinator, Minor League Administration:** Maureen Cooke.

Latin American Coordinator: Juan Lopez. **Advisor, Minor Leagues:** Chuck Hiller. **Training Coordinator:** Michael Herbst.

Field Coordinator: Bob Floyd. **Roving Instructors:** Mickey Brantley (hitting), Jason Craig (strength/conditioning), Tim Foli (infield/baserunning), Rich Miller (outfield/baserunning), Randy Niemann (pitching), Ray Rippelmeyer (assistant pitching).

Farm System

Class	Farm Team	Manager	Coach	Pitching Coach
AAA	Norfolk	John Gibbons	Howie Freiling	Rick Waits
AA	Binghamton	Doug Davis	Luis Natera	Guy Conti
A	St. Lucie	Dave Engle	Roger LaFrancois	Buzz Capra
A	Capital City	John Stephenson	Donovan Mitchell	Doug Simons
A	Pittsfield	Tony Tijerina	Ken Berry	Bob Stanley
R	Kingsport	Edgar Alfonzo	Juan Lopez	Unavailable
R	DSL 1	Miguel Dilone	Jose Guillen	Unavailable
R	DSL 2	Unavailable	Herminio Toribio	Unavailable

Scouting

Telephone: (718) 565-4311 (amateur), (718) 803-4013 (professional). **FAX:** (718) 205-7920.

Assistant GM/Professional Scouting: Carmen Fusco. **Assistant GM/Amateur Scouting:** Gary LaRocque. **Assistant Directors, Amateur Scouting:** Jack Bowen (Bethel Park, PA), Fred Wright.

Advance Scout: Bruce Benedict (Atlanta, GA).

Professional Scouts: Erwin Bryant (Lexington, KY), Dick Gernert (Reading, PA), Howard Johnson (Poway, CA), Roland Johnson (Newington, CT), Bill Latham (Trussville, AL), Harry Minor (Long Beach, CA), Tim Teufel (Poway, CA), Mike Toomey (Gaithersburg, MD).

Gary LaRocque

Regional Supervisors: West—Paul Fryer (Calabasas, CA), East—Gene Kerns (Hagerstown, MD); Midwest—Terry Tripp (Harrisburg, IL).

Area Supervisors: Kevin Blankenship (Rocklin, CA), Quincy Boyd (Plainfield, IL), Larry Chase (Pearcy, AR), Joe Delli Carri (Longwood, FL), Kevin Frady (Mesa, AZ), Chuck Hensley (Oxnard, CA), Dave Lottsfeldt (Richardson, TX), Fred Mazuca (Tustin, CA), Marlin McPhail (Irmo, SC), Randy Milligan (Owings Mills, MD), Bob Minor (Garden Grove, CA), Greg Morhardt (Enfield, CT), Joe Morlan (New Albany, OH), Joe Nigro (Staten Island, NY), Jim Reeves (Camas, WA), Junior Roman (San Sebastian, PR), Bob Rossi (Baton Rouge, LA), Joe Salerno (Miami Lakes, FL), Greg Tubbs (Cookeville, TN).

PHILADELPHIA

Telephone, Address
Office Address: Veterans Stadium, 3501 S Broad St., Philadelphia, PA 19148. **Mailing Address:** P.O. Box 7575, Philadelphia, PA 19101. **Telephone:** (215) 463-6000. **FAX:** (215) 389-3050. **Website:** www.phillies.com.

Ownership
Operated by: The Phillies.
General Partner: David Montgomery.
Partners: Claire Betz, Fitz Eugene Dixon, Double Play Inc. (John Middleton), Giles Limited Partnership (Bill Giles), Tri-Play Associates (Alexander Buck, Mahlon Buck, William Buck).
President/Chief Executive Officer: David Montgomery. **Chairman:** Bill Giles.

David Montgomery

BUSINESS OPERATIONS
Vice President/General Counsel: Bill Webb. **Special Assistant to President:** Sharon Swainson. **Director, Business Development:** Joe Giles. **Manager, Human Resources:** Terry DeRugeriis. **Executive Administrator:** Nancy Nolan.

Finance
Senior VP/Chief Financial Officer: Jerry Clothier. **Controller:** John Fusco. **Staff Accountant:** Reeny Samara. **Director, Information Systems:** Brian Lamoreaux.

Marketing, Promotions
Vice President, Advertising Sales: David Buck.
Manager, Client Services: Debbie Nocito. **Manager, National Sales:** Rob MacPherson. **Director, Events:** Kurt Funk. **Director, Entertainment:** Chris Long.
Director, Broadcasting/Video Services: Rory McNeil. **Manager, Advertising/Internet Services:** Jo-Anne Levy-Lamoreaux.

Public Relations, Communications
Telephone: (215) 463-6000. **FAX:** (215) 389-3050.
Vice President, Public Relations: Larry Shenk.
Manager, Print/Creative Services: Tina Urban. **Manager, Publicity:** Leigh Tobin. **Manager, Media Relations:** Gene Dias. **Administrator, Public Relations:** Christine Negley.
Director, Community Relations: Regina Castellani. **Speakers' Bureau Representative:** Maje McDonnell. **Community/Fan Development Representative:** Dick Allen.

Stadium Operations
Director, Stadium Operations: Mike DiMuzio. **Assistant Director, Stadium Operations:** Eric Tobin. **Secretary, Stadium Operations:** Bernie Mansi. **Operations Assistant/Concessionaire Liaison:** Bruce Leith.
Supervisor, Field/Maintenance Operations: Ralph Frangipani.
PA Announcer: Dan Baker. **Official Scorers:** Jay Dunn, Bob Kenney, John McAdams.

Ticketing
Telephone: (215) 463-1000. **FAX:** (215) 463-9878.
Vice President, Ticket Operations: Richard Deats.
Director, Ticket Department: Dan Goroff. **Director, Sales:** John Weber. **Director, Group Sales:** Kathy Killian.

Travel, Clubhouse
Traveling Secretary: Eddie Ferenz.
Manager, Equipment/Team Travel: Frank Coppenbarger. **Assistant Equipment Manager:** Joe Dunn. **Manager, Visiting Clubhouse:** Kevin Steinhour. **Assistant, Home Clubhouse:** Phil Sheridan.

General Information
Home Dugout: First Base. **Playing Surface:** Artificial turf.
Stadium Location: I-95 or I-76 to Broad Street exit. **Standard Game Times:** 7:05 p.m.; (June-Aug.) 7:35; Sat. 7:05; Sun. 1:35.
Player Representative: Curt Schilling.

PHILLIES

BASEBALL OPERATIONS

Vice President/General Manager: Ed Wade.
Assistant General Manager: Ruben Amaro Jr.
Executive Assistant to GM: Susan Ingersoll.
Computer Analysis: Jay McLaughlin. **Senior Advisors to GM:** Dallas Green, Paul Owens.

Major League Staff

Manager: Terry Francona.
Coaches: Dugout—Chuck Cottier; Pitching—Galen Cisco; Batting—Hal McRae; First Base—Brad Mills; Third Base—John Vukovich; Bullpen—Ramon Henderson.

Ed Wade

Medical, Training

Director, Medical Services: Dr. Michael Ciccotti. **Assistant Director, Medical Services:** Dr. John McShane. **Head Trainer:** Jeff Cooper. **Assistant Trainer:** Mark Andersen. **Conditioning Coordinator:** Scott Hoffman.

Player Development

Telephone: (215) 463-6000. **FAX:** (215) 755-9324.
Director, Minor League Operations: Steve Noworyta. **Director, Minor League Personnel/Instruction:** Gary Ruby. **Assistant to Director, Minor League Operations/Scouting:** Rob Holiday.
Director, Latin America Operations: Sal Artiaga.
Director, Florida Operations: John Timberlake.
Secretary, Minor Leagues/Scouting: Karen Nocella. **Administrative Assistant, Minor Leagues/Scouting:** Mike Ondo.
Coordinator, Instruction: Ruben Amaro Sr. (defense). **Roving Instructors:** Mick Billmeyer (catching), Bill Dancy (infield), Glenn Gregson (pitching), Don Long (hitting).

Terry Francona

Farm System

Class	Farm Team	Manager	Coach	Pitching Coach
AAA	Scranton/W-B	Marc Bombard	Tony Scott	Gorman Heimueller
AA	Reading	Gary Varsho	Milt Thompson	Carlos Arroyo
A	Clearwater	Ken Oberkfell	Al LeBoeuf	Warren Brusstar
A	Piedmont	Greg Legg	Jerry Martin	Rod Nichols
A	Batavia	Frank Klebe	Alberto Fana	Ken Westray
R	Clearwater	Ramon Aviles	Manny Trillo	Darold Knowles
R	DSL	Sammy Mejias	Domingo Brito	Cesar Mejia

Scouting

Telephone: (215) 952-8204. **FAX:** (215) 755-9324.
Director, Scouting: Mike Arbuckle.
Director, Major League Scouts: Gordon Lakey (Barker, TX). **Major League Scout:** Jimmy Stewart (Odessa, FL). **Advance Scout:** Hank King (Limerick, PA).
Coordinator, Professional Coverage: Dick Lawlor (Windsor, CT). **Professional Scouts:** Larry Rojas (Clearwater, FL), Del Unser (Dove Canyon, CA). **Special Assignment Scout:** Dean Jongewaard (Fountain Valley, CA).
National Supervisor: Marti Wolever (Papillion, NE). **Regional Supervisors:** Central—Sonny

Mike Arbuckle

Bowers (Waco, TX); West—Mitch Sokol (Phoenix, AZ); East—Scott (Hobart, IN).
Area Scouts: Emil Belich (West Allis, WI), Darrell Conner (CA), Steve Gillispie (Helena, AL), Bill Harper (Corvallis, Hultzapple (Newport, PA), Marlin Jones (Ocala, FL), Jerry Laffe MO), Matt Lundin (Santa Ana, CA), Miguel Machado (Miam Lloyd Merritt (Franklin, TN), Venice Murray (Merrillville, IN (Cleburne, TX), Scott Ramsay (Rocklin, CA), Paul Scott (Tanner (Charleston, SC).
International Supervisor: Sal Agostinelli (Deer Park **Supervisor:** Doug Takaragawa (Fountain Valley, CA).

PITTSBURGH

Telephone, Address
Office Address: 600 Stadium Circle, Pittsburgh, PA 15212. **Mailing Address:** P.O. Box 7000, Pittsburgh, PA 15212. **Telephone:** (412) 323-5000. **FAX:** (412) 323-5024. **Website:** www.pirateball.com.

Kevin McClatchy

Ownership
Operated by: Pittsburgh Pirates Acquisition, Inc. **Principal Owner:** Kevin McClatchy.
Board of Directors: William Allen, Don Beaver, Frank Brenner, Chip Ganassi, Kevin McClatchy, Thomas Murphy Jr., Ogden Nutting.

BUSINESS OPERATIONS
Executive Vice President/Chief Operating Officer: Dick Freeman. **Director, Human Resources:** Sarah Tarosky.

Finance
Vice President, Finance: Jim Plake.
Controller: David Bowman. **Director, Finance:** Patti Mistick. **Director, Information Systems:** Terry Zeigler.

Marketing, Sales
Vice President, Marketing/Broadcasting: Vic Gregovits.
Director, Sales: Jim Alexander. **Director, Merchandising:** Joe Billetdeaux.
Director, Promotions: Rick Orienza. **Director, Broadcasting/Corporate Sales:** Mark Ferraco. **Coordinator, Broadcasting:** Marc Garda.

Communications
Telephone: (412) 323-5031. **FAX:** (412) 323-5009.
Vice President, Communications/New Ballpark Development: Steven Greenberg.
Director, Media Relations: Jim Trdinich. **Assistant Director, Media Relations:** Ben Bouma. **Assistant, Media Relations:** Dan Hart. **Assistants, Public Relations:** Sherry Rusiski, Christine Serkoch.
Director, Player Relations: Kathy Guy.
Director, Marketing Communications: Michael Gordon.
VP, Special Events: Nelson Briles. **Alumni Liaison:** Sally O'Leary.

Stadium Operations
Vice President, Stadium Operations: Dennis DaPra.
Assistant Director, Stadium Operations: Chris Hunter.
Coordinator, In-Game Entertainment: Eric Wolff.
Head Groundskeeper: Tony LaPia.
PA Announcer: Tim DeBacco. **Official Scorers:** Tony Krizmanich, Evan Pattak, Bob Webb.

Ticketing
Telephone: (412) 321-2827. **FAX:** (412) 323-9133.
Director, Ticket Operations: Ryan Meyer. **Manager, Ticket Sales:** Susy Pavone. **Director, Premium Sales:** Susan Smith. **Director, Season Ticket Services:** Gary Remlinger.

ravel, Clubhouse
Traveling Secretary: Greg Johnson.
quipment Manager/Home Clubhouse Operations: Roger Wilson.
rs Clubhouse Operations: Kevin Conrad.

ral Information
Dugout: First Base. **Playing Surface:** Artificial Turf.
Directions: From south, I-279 through Fort Pitt Tunnel, make
to Fort Duquesne Bridge, cross Fort Duquesne Bridge, follow
Rivers Stadium, make left to stadium parking at light. From
hree Rivers Stadium exit (exit 12, left lane), follow directions
ard Game Times: 7:05 p.m., Sun. 1:35.
entative: Al Martin.

PIRATES

BASEBALL OPERATIONS

Cam Bonifay

Telephone: (412) 323-5012. **FAX:** (412) 323-5024.

Senior Vice President/General Manager: Cam Bonifay.

Assistant General Managers: John Sirignano, Roy Smith. **Assistant to GM:** George Zuraw. **Senior Advisor, Player Personnel:** Lenny Yochim. **Special Assistants to GM:** Chet Montgomery, Kenny Parker, Willie Stargell. **Administrative Assistant, Baseball Operations:** Jeannie Donatelli.

Major League Staff

Manager: Gene Lamont.

Coaches: Bench—Rick Renick; Pitching—Pete Vuckovich; Batting—Lloyd McClendon; First Base—Joe Jones; Third Base—Jack Lind; Bullpen—Spin Williams.

Gene Lamont

Medical, Training

Team Physicians: Dr. Joe Coroso, Dr. Jack Failla. **Head Trainer:** Kent Biggerstaff. **Assistant Trainer:** Bill Henry. **Strength/Conditioning Coach:** Dr. Warren Sipp.

Minor Leagues

Telephone: (412) 323-5033. **FAX:** (412) 323-5024.

Director, Player Development: Paul Tinnell. **Coordinator, Minor League Player Personnel:** John Green. **Administrator, Minor Leagues:** Diane Grimaldi.

Coordinator, Instruction: Steve Demeter. **Roving Instructors:** Marty DeMerritt (pitching), Marc Hill (catching), Scott Little (outfield), Bobby Meacham (infield/baserunning).

Farm System

Class	Farm Team	Manager	Coach	Pitching Coach
AAA	Nashville	Trent Jewett	Richie Hebner	Jim Bibby
AA	Altoona	Marty Brown	Jeff Livesey	Bruce Tanner
A	Lynchburg	Tracy Woodson	Tony Beasley	Scott Lovekamp
A	Hickory	Jay Loviglio	Greg Briley	Blaine Beatty
A	Williamsport	Curtis Wilkerson	Eric Chavez	Miguel Bonilla
R	Bradenton	Woody Huyke	Ramon Sambo	Steve Watson
R	DSL	Ramon Zapata	Leandro Mejia	Unavailable

Scouting

Mickey White

Telephone: (412) 323-5035. **FAX:** (412) 323-5024.

Director, Scouting: Mickey White.

Assistant Director, Scouting: Steve Fleming. **Assistant to Scouting/Director, Amateur Development:** Jon Mercurio. **Coordinator, Scouting Systems:** Sandy Deutsch.

Advance Scout: Chris Lein (Boca Raton, FL).

Special Assignment Scouts: Jack Bloomfield (McAllen, TX), Brannon Bonifay (Okeechobee, FL), Jim Guinn (Fairfield, CA), Chet Montgomery, George Swain (Raleigh, NC).

National Crosschecker: Mark McKnight (Atlanta, GA). **Regional Coordinators:** Midwest—Tom Barnard (Houston, TX); East—Dana Brown (Somerset, NJ); West—Scott Littlefield (Long Beach, CA).

Area Supervisors: Russell Bowen (Charlotte, NC), Gran (Oklahoma City, OK), Duane Gustavson (Columbus, OH), Ja (Seattle, WA), Mike Kendall (Manhattan Beach, CA), Hank Kr IA), Greg McClain (Chandler, AZ), Jack Powell (Sweetwate Russell (Monroe, LA), Delvy Santiago (Vega Alta, PR (Windermere, FL), Charlie Sullivan (Latham, NY), Mike W CA), Ted Williams (Glendale, AZ).

Latin America Coordinators: Pablo Cruz (Dominic Luna (Miami, FL).

ST. LOUIS

Mark Lamping

Telephone, Address
Office Address: 250 Stadium Plaza, St. Louis, MO 63102. **Telephone:** (314) 421-3060. **FAX:** (314) 425-0640. **Website:** www.stlcardinals.com.

Ownership
Operated by: St. Louis Cardinals, LP.
General Partner: Bill DeWitt Jr. **Chairman:** Fred Hanser. **Secretary/Treasurer:** Andrew Baur.
President: Mark Lamping.

BUSINESS OPERATIONS
Vice President, Business Development: Bill DeWitt III. **Director, Human Resources:** Marian Rhodes. **Manager, Office Administration/Human Resources Specialist:** Karen Brown.

Finance
Vice President, Controller: Brad Wood.
Director, Information Systems: Sally Lemons. **Director, Accounting:** Deborah Pfaff. **Senior Accountant:** Michelle Flach.

Marketing, Sales
Senior Vice President, Sales/Marketing: Dan Farrell.
Director, Corporate Sales: Thane van Breusegen. **Director, Target Marketing:** Ted Savage. **Corporate Sales Representatives:** Matt Gifford, Theron Morgan, Tony Simokaitis.
Director, Group Sales: Joe Strohm. **Coordinator, Sales:** Angie Jerome.

Public Relations, Community Relations
Telephone: (314) 425-0604. **FAX:** (314) 982-7399.
Director, Media Relations: Brian Bartow. **Assistant to Director, Media Relations:** Brad Hainje. **Assistant, Media Relations:** Melody Yount.
Manager, Publications/Media Relations: Steve Zesch.
Vice President, Community Relations: Marty Hendin. **Associate Manager, Community Relations:** Shawn Bertani.

Stadium Operations
Vice President, Stadium Operations: Joe Abernathy. **Administrative Assistant:** Nan Bommarito.
Director, Stadium Operations: Mike Bertani. **Director, Security/Special Services:** Joe Walsh. **Administrative Assistant, Security:** Hope Baker.
Director, Quality Assurance/Guest Services: Mike Ball. **Coordinator, Operations:** Cindy Richards.
Director, Event Services: Vicki Bryant. **Coordinator, Event Services:** Lori Jones. **Administrative Assistant, Event Services:** Bernie Fassler.
Head Groundskeeper: Bill Findley. **Assistant Head Groundskeeper:** Chad Casella.

Ticketing
Telephone: (314) 421-2400. **FAX:** (314) 425-0649.
Vice President, Ticket Operations: Josie Arnold.
Vice President, Ticket Sales: Kevin Wade. **Manager, Box Office:** Julie Baker. **Manager, Ticket Sales:** Mark Murray. **Manager, Customer Service/Telephone Operations:** Patti McCormick. **Supervisor, Customer Service:** Marilyn Mathews. **Deluxe Suite Services:** Dennis Dolan.

el, Clubhouse
veling Secretary: C.J. Cherre.
ment Manager: Buddy Bates. **Assistant Equipment Manager:**
n. **Visiting Clubhouse Manager:** Jerry Risch.

Information
out: First Base. **Playing Surface:** Grass.
me Times: Weekdays 12:10 p.m., 7:10.
tions: From Illinois, take I-55 South, I-64 West, I-70 West
across the Mississippi River (Poplar Street Bridge) to
In Missouri, take I-55 North, I-64 East, I-70 East, I-44
to downtown St. Louis and Busch Stadium exit.
ive: Alan Benes.

CARDINALS

BASEBALL OPERATIONS
Telephone: (314) 425-0687. **FAX:** (314) 425-0648.
Vice President/General Manager: Walt Jocketty. **Special Assistants to GM:** Bob Gebhard, Red Schoendienst.
Vice President, Player Personnel: Jerry Walker. **Director, Baseball Administration/International Operations:** Tim Hanser. **Senior Executive Assistant to GM:** Judy Carpenter-Barada.

Walt Jocketty

Major League Staff
Manager: Tony La Russa.
Coaches: Bench—Mark DeJohn; Pitching—Dave Duncan; Batting—Mike Easler; First Base—Jose Oquendo; Third Base—Dave McKay; Bullpen—Marty Mason.

Tony La Russa

Medical, Training
Senior Medical Advisor: Dr. Stan London. **Club Physician:** Dr. George Paletta.
Head Trainer: Barry Weinberg. **Assistant Trainer:** Brad Henderson. **Coordinator, Medical/Rehabilitation:** Mark O'Neal.

Player Development
Telephone: (314) 425-0628. **FAX:** (314) 425-0638.
Director, Player Development: Mike Jorgensen.
Administrative Assistant: Judy Francis.
Director, Minor League Operations: Scott Smulczenski. **Manager, Baseball Information/Assistant, Player Development:** John Vuch.
Senior Field Coordinator: George Kissell. **Field Coordinator:** Joe Pettini. **Pitching Coordinator:** Mark Riggins. **Hitting Coordinator:** Mitchell Page. **Roving Instructors:** Ray Burris (pitching), Dyar Miller (pitching), Dave Ricketts (catching).
Supervisor, Latin American Development: Marty Martinez.

Farm System
Class	Farm Team	Manager	Coach	Pitching Coach
AAA	Memphis	Gaylen Pitts	Boots Day	Bill Campbell
AA	Arkansas	Chris Maloney	Brian Rupp	Dave LaPoint
A	Potomac	Joe Cunningham	Glen Brummer	Mark Grater
A	Peoria	Tom Lawless	Todd Steverson	Sid Monge
A	New Jersey	Jeff Shireman	None	Gary Buckels
R	Johnson City	Luis Melendez	None	Elias Sosa
R	DSL	Unavailable	Unavailable	Unavailable

Scouting
Telephone: (314) 516-0152. **FAX:** (314) 425-0638.
Director, Player Procurement: Jeff Scott. **Director, Scouting:** John Mozeliak. **Administrative Assistant, Scouting:** Linda Brauer.
Advance Scout: Joe Sparks (Phoenix, AZ).
Major League/Special Assignment Scouts: Bing Devine, Marty Keough (Scottsdale, AZ), Fred McAlister (Katy, TX), Mike Squires (Kalamazoo, MI). **Professional Scouts:** Chuck Fick (Newbury Park, CA), Jim Leyland (Pittsburgh, PA), Joe Rigoli (Parsippany, NJ).
National Crosschecker: Mike Roberts (Kansas City, MO). **Regional Crosscheckers:** East—Tim Conroy (Monroeville, PA); West—Clark Crist (Tucson, AZ).

John Moze

Area Supervisors: Randy Benson (Salisbury, NC), Chuck F
Park, CA), Ben Galante (Houston, TX), Steve Grilli (Bald
Manny Guerra (Las Vegas, NV), Dave Karaff (Lee's Sum
Melvin (Quincy, IL), Scott Nichols (Richland, MS), Jay Nort
Dan Ontiveros (Santa Clara, CA), Tommy Shields (Lititz.
(Eastman, GA), Steve Turco (Largo, FL), Dane Walker (

SAN DIEGO

Telephone, Address
Office Address: 8880 Rio San Diego Dr., Suite 400, San Diego, CA 92108. **Mailing Address:** P.O. Box 122000, San Diego, CA 92112. **Telephone:** (619) 881-6500. **FAX:** (619) 497-5339. **E-Mail Address:** comments@padres.com. **Website:** www.padres.com.

Ownership
Operated by: Padres, LP.
Principal Owners: John Moores, Larry Lucchino.
Chairman: John Moores. **President, Chief Executive Officer:** Larry Lucchino.

John Moores

BUSINESS OPERATIONS
Executive Vice President/Chief Operating Officer: Jack McGrory.
Special Counsel: Bob Vizas. **Director, Human Resources:** Lucy Freeman.

Finance
Vice President/Chief Financial Officer: Bob Wells.
Controller: Steve Fitch. **Director, Information Systems:** Joe Lewis. **Senior Staff Accountant:** Duane Wright.

Marketing, Sales
Senior Vice President, Corporate Marketing: Mike Dee.
Director, Marketing: Sam Kennedy. **Director, Promotions:** Cheryl Smith. **Director, Season Ticket/Group Sales:** Mark Tilson.

Public Relations, Community Relations
Telephone: (619) 881-6510. **FAX:** (619) 497-5454.
Executive Vice President, Public Affairs: Dr. Charles Steinberg.
Director, Public Relations: Glenn Geffner. **Director, Publications:** John Schlegel. **Assistants, Public Relations:** John Dever, Karen Slaton.
VP, Community Relations: Michele Anderson. **Manager, Community Relations:** Veronica Delgado.

Stadium Operations
Director, Stadium Operations: Mark Guglielmo. **Assistant, Stadium Operations:** Ken Kawachi. **Head Groundskeeper:** Steve Wightman.
PA Announcer: Unavailable. **Official Scorer:** Phil Collier.

Ticketing
Telephone: (619) 283-4494. **FAX:** (619) 280-6239.
Executive Director, Ticket Operations/Services: Dave Gilmore.

Travel, Clubhouse
Director, Team Travel/Equipment Manager: Brian Prilaman. **Home Clubhouse Operations:** Tony Petricca. **Visitors Clubhouse Operations:** David Bacharach.

General Information
Home Dugout: First Base. **Playing Surface:** Grass.
Stadium Location: From downtown, Route 163 North to Friars Road, ast to stadium. From north, I-15 South to Friars Road, west to stadium, or 05 South to Route 163 South to Friars Road, west to stadium. From east, West to I-15 North to Friars Road, west to stadium. From west, I-8 East ute 163 North to Friars Road, east to stadium. **Standard Game** 7:05 p.m.; Thurs. 2:05; Sat. 7:05; Sun. (April-May, Sept.-Oct.) 1:05, g.) 4:05.
Representative: Brian Boehringer.

PADRES

BASEBALL OPERATIONS
Telephone: (619) 881-6526. **FAX:** (619) 497-5338.
Senior Vice President/General Manager: Kevin Towers.
Assistant General Manager: Fred Uhlman Jr. **Special Assistant to GM:** Ken Bracey. **Director, Baseball Operations:** Theo Epstein. **Administrative Assistant:** Herta Bingham.

Major League Staff
Manager: Bruce Bochy.
Coaches: Bench—Rob Picciolo; Pitching—Dave Smith; Batting—Ben Oglivie; First Base—Alan Trammell; Third Base—Tim Flannery; Bullpen—Greg Booker.

Kevin Towers

Bruce Bochy

Medical, Training
Club Physician: Scripps Clinic medical staff.
Head Trainer: Todd Hutcheson. **Assistant Trainer:** Jim Daniel. **Strength/Conditioning Coach:** Sam Gannelli.

Player Development
Telephone: (619) 881-6512. **FAX:** (619) 497-5338.
Vice President, Minor Leagues/Scouting: Ted Simmons. **Director, Player Development:** Tye Waller. **Assistant Director, Player Development:** Jason McLeod.
Director, Minor League Operations: Priscilla Oppenheimer. **Administrative Support:** Melissa Garcia. **International Baseball Consultant:** Tom House.
Special Assistant to GM/Field Coordinator: Bill Bryk. **Roving Instructors:** Ben Bethea (strength/conditioning), Tom Brown (pitching), Doug Dascenzo (outfield/baserunning), Mike Epstein (hitting), Tony Franklin (infield), Jack Lamabe (pitching), Don Werner (catching).

Farm System
Class	Farm Team	Manager	Coach	Pitching Coach
AAA	Las Vegas	Duane Espy	Randy Whisler	Darrel Akerfelds
AA	Mobile	Mike Basso	George Hendrick	Dave Rajsich
A	R. Cucamonga	Tom LeVasseur	Eric Bullock	Mike Harkey
A	Fort Wayne	Craig Colbert	Brian Giles	Darren Balsley
R	Idaho Falls	Don Werner	Jake Molina	Darryl Milne
R	Peoria	Howard Bushong	Tom Tomincasa	Urbano Lugo

Scouting
Director, Scouting: Brad Sloan (Brimfield, IL).
Director, Professional Scouting: Gary Nickels (Naperville, IL).
Major League Scouts: Ken Bracey (Morton, IL), Ray Crone (Waxahachie, TX), Moose Johnson (Arvada, CO). **Advance Scout:** Jeff Gardner (Newport Beach, CA).
Professional Scouts: Chas Bolton (San Diego, CA), Rich Hacker (Belleville, IL), Ben McLure (Hummelstown, PA), Gary Roenicke (Nevada City, CA), Van Smith (Belleville, IL).
Full-Time Scouts: Joe Bochy (Plant City, FL), Rich Bordi (Rohnert Park, CA), Bob Cummings (Oak Lawn, IL), Lane Decker (Piedmont, OK), Jimmy Dreyer (Keller, TX), Leroy Dreyer (Brenham, TX), Robert Gutie (Carol City, FL), Chris Gwynn (Alta Loma, CA), Andy Hancock (Tryon Mike Keenan (Chicago, IL), William Killian (Stanwood, MI), Steve (Huntington Beach, CA), Don Lyle (Sacramento, CA), Jose Martinez NY), Tim McWilliam (San Diego, CA), Darryl Milne (Denver, CO), Re (Manchester, NH), Chuck Pierce (Bakersfield, CA), Gene (Scottsdale, AZ), Mark Wasinger (El Paso, TX), Jim Woodward CA).

Brad Sloan

International Supervisor: Bill Clark (Columbia, MO).

Telephone, Address
Office Address: 24 Willie Mays Plaza, San Francisco, CA 94107. **Telephone:** (415) 972-2000. **FAX:** (415) 947-2800. **Website:** www.sfgiants.com.

Ownership
Operated by: San Francisco Baseball Associates, LP.

President/Managing General Partner: Peter Magowan. **Senior General Partner:** Harmon Burns. **Special Assistant:** Willie Mays. **Special Advisor:** Willie McCovey.

Peter Magowan

BUSINESS OPERATIONS
Executive Vice President, Chief Operating Officer: Larry Baer. **Senior VP/General Counsel:** Jack Bair.
Director, Human Resources: Joyce Thomas.

Finance
Senior VP/Chief Financial Officer: John Yee. **VP/Chief Information Officer:** Bill Schlough. **Director, Information Systems:** Jerry Drobny.
VP, Finance: Robert J. Quinn.

Marketing, Sales
Senior VP, Corporate Marketing: Mario Alioto. **Director, Corporate Sponsorship:** Jason Pearl. **Promotions Manager:** Valerie McGuire.
Senior VP, Consumer Marketing: Tom McDonald.
Director, Client Relations: Annemarie Hastings. **Director, Sales:** Rob Sullivan. **Director, Group Sales:** Jeff Tucker. **Manager, Season Ticket Sales:** Craig Solomon.

Public Relations, Community Relations
Telephone: (415) 972-2440. **FAX:** (415) 947-2800.
VP, Communications: Bob Rose.
Manager, Media Relations: Jim Moorehead. **Manager, Media Services/Broadcasting:** Maria Jacinto. **Manager, Baseball Information:** Blake Rhodes. **Assistant, Media Relations:** Dan Martinez. **VP, Public Affairs:** Staci Slaughter. **Manager, Community Relations:** Kerry Mar.

Stadium Operations
Senior VP, Ballpark Operations: Jorge Costa. **VP, Guest Services:** Rick Mears.
Director, Ballpark Operations: Gene Telucci. **Director, Maintenance:** Tito Guzman. **Supervisor, Ballpark Operations:** Bob DeAntoni.
Head Groundskeeper: Scott MacVicar.
PA Announcer: Renel Brooks-Moon. **Official Scorers:** Chuck Dybdal, Dick O'Connor, Art Santo Domingo, Bob Stevens.

Ticketing
Telephone: (415) 467-8000. **FAX:** (415) 330-2572.
Vice President, Ticket Services/Client Relations: Russ Stanley. **Manager, Ticket Services:** Bob Bisio.

Travel, Clubhouse
Director, Travel: Reggie Younger Jr.
Equipment Manager: Miguel Murphy. **Visitors Clubhouse:** Harvey Hodgerney. **Assistant Equipment Manager:** Richard Cacace.

General Information
Home Dugout: Third Base. **Playing Surface:** Grass.
Stadium Location: From Peninsula/South Bay, take I-280 north (or U.S. 101 ___ to I-280 north) to Mariposa Street exit, right on Mariposa Street, left on Third ___. From East Bay (Bay Bridge), take I-80/Bay Bridge to Fifth Street exit, right on ___reet, right on Folsom Street, right on Fourth Street, continue on Fourth Street ___arking lots (across bridge). From North Bay (Golden Gate Bridge), take U.S. ___/Golden Gate Bridge to Downtown/Lombard Street exit, right on Van Ness ___ on Golden Gate Ave., right on Hyde Street and across Market Street to ___t, left on Bryant Street, right on Fourth Street. **Standard Game Times:** ___:05, 7:15, 7:35; Sat.-Sun. 1:05.
___presentative: Jeff Kent.

GIANTS

BASEBALL OPERATIONS
Telephone: (415) 468-3700. **FAX:** (415) 330-2691.
Senior Vice President/General Manager: Brian Sabean.

VP/Assistant General Manager: Ned Colletti. **Special Assistant to GM:** Ron Perranoski. **Senior Advisor/Director, Arizona Operations:** Robert E. Quinn. **Executive Assistant, Baseball Operations:** Karen Sweeney. **Assistant, Baseball Operations:** Jeremy Shelley.

Brian Sabean

Major League Staff
Manager: Dusty Baker.
Coaches: Bench—Ron Wotus; Pitching—Dave Righetti; Batting—Gene Clines; First Base—Robby Thompson; Third Base—Sonny Jackson; Bullpen—Juan Lopez.

Dusty Baker

Medical, Training
Team Physicians: Dr. William Montgomery, Dr. Robert Murray.
Medical Director/Head Trainer: Stan Conte. **Assistant Trainer:** Barney Nugent. **Director, Strength/Conditioning:** Dave Groeschner.

Player Development
Vice President/Player Personnel: Dick Tidrow. **Director, Player Development:** Jack Hiatt. **Special Assistant, Player Development:** Joe Amalfitano. **Director, Minor League Administration:** Bobby Evans. **Special Assistant, Player Personnel:** Bobby Bonds.
Coordinator, Hitting: Joe Lefebvre. **Roving Instructor:** Jim Davenport.

Farm System
Class	Farm Team	Manager	Coach	Pitching Coach
AAA	Fresno	Shane Turner	Mike Hart	Pete Richert
AA	Shreveport	Bill Hayes	None	Ross Grimsley
A	Bakersfield	Lenn Sakata	None	Steve Renko
A	San Jose	Keith Comstock	None	Bert Bradley
A	Salem-Keizer	Fred Stanley	Bert Hunter	Trevor Wilson
R	Scottsdale	Unavailable	Unavailable	Unavailable
R	DSL	Fausto Sosa	Jesus Lazos	Unavailable

Scouting
Telephone: (415) 330-2538. **FAX:** (415) 330-2691.
Coordinator, Scouting: Matt Nerland.
Major League Scouts: Joe DiCarlo (Ringwood, NJ), Pat Dobson (San Diego, CA), Randy Waddill (Valrico, FL).
Special Assignment Scouts: Bo Osborne (Woodstock, GA), Tom Zimmer (St. Petersburg, FL).
Regional Crosscheckers: West—Doug Mapson (Phoenix, AZ); North—Stan Saleski (Dayton, OH); South—Paul Turco (Sarasota, FL).
Area Scouts: Steve Arnieri (Palatine, IL), Dick Cole (Costa Mesa, CA), John DiCarlo (Glenwood, NJ), Lee Elder (Martinez, GA), Charlie Gonzales (Davie, FL), Tom Korenek (Houston, TX), Alan Marr (Sarasota, FL), Doug McMillan (Shingle Springs, CA), Bobby Myrick (C[...] Heights, VA), John Shafer (Portland, OR), Joe Strain (Englewood, CO[...] Thomas (Dallas, TX), Glenn Tufts (Bridgewater, MA), Darren Wittcke [...] Niguel, CA).

Dick Tidrow

Coordinator, International Operations: Rick Ragazzo (Le[...] CA). **Coordinator, Latin Operations:** John Dipuglia. **Special A[...] Scout:** Matty Alou (Dominican Republic).
International Scouts: Jose Cassino (Panama), Bien[...] (Dominican Republic), Luis Pena (Mexico), Carlos Rami[...] Republic), Alex Torres (Nicaragua), Ciro Villalobos (Venez[...] Lee (South Korea).

MAJOR LEAGUE SCHEDULES

1999 Standings • Spring Training

AMERICAN LEAGUE

1999 STANDINGS

EAST	W	L	PCT	GB	Manager
New York Yankees	98	64	.605	—	Joe Torre
Boston Red Sox*	94	68	.580	4	Jimy Williams
Toronto Blue Jays	84	78	.519	14	Jim Fregosi
Baltimore Orioles	78	84	.481	20	Ray Miller
Tampa Bay Devil Rays	69	93	.426	29	Larry Rothschild

CENTRAL	W	L	PCT	GB	Manager
Cleveland Indians	97	65	.599	—	Mike Hargrove
Chicago White Sox	75	86	.466	21½	Jerry Manuel
Detroit Tigers	69	92	.429	27½	Larry Parrish
Kansas City Royals	64	97	.398	32½	Tony Muser
Minnesota Twins	63	97	.394	33	Tom Kelly

WEST	W	L	PCT	GB	Manager
Texas Rangers	95	67	.586	—	Johnny Oates
Oakland Athletics	87	75	.537	8	Art Howe
Seattle Mariners	79	83	.488	16	Lou Piniella
Anaheim Angels	70	92	.432	25	Terry Collins/Joe Maddon

*Won wild-card playoff berth

PLAYOFFS: Division Series (best-of-5)—New York defeated Texas 3-0; Boston defeated Cleveland 3-2. **League Championship Series** (best-of-7)—New York defeated Boston 4-1.

NATIONAL LEAGUE

1999 STANDINGS

EAST	W	L	PCT	GB	Manager
Atlanta Braves	103	59	.636	—	Bobby Cox
New York Mets#	97	66	.595	6½	Bobby Valentine
Philadelphia Phillies	77	85	.475	26	Terry Francona
Montreal Expos	68	94	.420	35	Felipe Alou
Florida Marlins	64	98	.395	39	John Boles

CENTRAL	W	L	PCT	GB	Manager
Houston Astros	97	65	.599	—	Larry Dierker
Cincinnati Reds	96	67	.589	1½	Jack McKeon
Pittsburgh Pirates	78	83	.484	18½	Gene Lamont
St. Louis Cardinals	75	86	.466	21½	Tony La Russa
Milwaukee Brewers	74	87	.460	22½	P. Garner/J. Lefebvre
Chicago Cubs	67	95	.414	30	Jim Riggleman

WEST	W	L	PCT	GB	Manager
Arizona Diamondbacks	100	62	.617	—	Buck Showalter
San Francisco Giants	86	76	.531	14	Dusty Baker
Los Angeles Dodgers	77	85	.475	23	Davey Johnson
San Diego Padres	74	88	.457	26	Bruce Bochy
Colorado Rockies	72	90	.444	28	Jim Leyland

#Defeated Cincinnati in one-game playoff to win wild-card playoff berth

PLAYOFFS: Division Series (best-of-5)—Atlanta defeated Houston 3-1; New York defeated Arizona 3-1. **League Championship Series** (best-of-7)—Atlanta defeated New York 4-2.

WORLD SERIES
(Best-of-7)
New York defeated Atlanta 4-0

AMERICANLEAGUE

ANAHEIM ANGELS
Edison International Field

APRIL
3-4-5 .... Yankees
7-8-**9** .... Boston
10-11-12 .... Toronto
14-**15-16** ... at White Sox
17-18-19-20 .. at Toronto
21-**22-23** . at Tampa Bay
24-25-26 .... Detroit
27-28-29-**30** Tampa Bay

MAY
2-3-**4** ...... at Baltimore
5-**6-7** .... at Seattle
8-9-10 .... Oakland
11-12-**13-14** .... Texas
16-17 .... Baltimore
19-20-**21** .... Kansas City
23-24-**25** ... at Minnesota
26-27-**28** at Kansas City
29-30-31 ... at Cleveland

JUNE
2-**3-4** .... Los Angeles*

5-6-7 ..... San Francisco*
9-**10-11** .... at Arizona*
13-14-15 . at Tampa Bay
16-17-**18** ... at Baltimore
20-21-22 .... Kansas City
23-24-25-**26**.. Minnesota
27-28-**29** .... at Seattle
30 .... Oakland

JULY
1-2 .... Oakland
3-4-5-6 .... Seattle
7-**8**-9 .... Cororado*
13-14-**15** .... at L.A.*
16-17-18 . at San Diego*
19-20 .... Texas
21-**22-23** .... at Oakland
24-25-26 .... at Texas
27-28-**29**-30 .. White Sox
31 .... Detroit

AUGUST
1-**2** .... Detroit

4-**5-6** .... at Cleveland
7-8-9 .... Boston
11-12-13 .... Yankees
15-**16** .... at Toronto
17-18-**19-20**. at Yankees
21-22-23 ...... at Boston
25-26-27 .... Cleveland
28-29-30 .... Toronto

SEPTEMBER
1-2-**3** .... at White Sox
4-5-6-**7** .... at Detroit
8-9-10-11 .... Baltimore
12-13 .... Tampa Bay
15-16-**17** ... at Minnesota
19-20-21 at Kansas City
22-23-**24** .... at Texas
25-26-**27-28**. at Oakland
29-30 .... Seattle

OCTOBER
1 .... Seattle

BALTIMORE ORIOLES
Oriole Park at Camden Yards

APRIL
3-5-6 .... Cleveland
7-**8-9** .... Detroit
11-12-**13** at Kansas City
14-15-**16** ... at Minnesota
17-18-19 ..... Tampa Bay
21-**22-23** ...... at Oakland
24-25-26-**27**. at White Sox
28-**29-30** .... Texas

MAY
2-3-**4** .... Anaheim
5-**6-7** .... at Yankees
8-9-10 .... at Toronto
11-12-**13-14** .... Boston
16-17 .... at Anaheim
18-19-20-21 ... at Texas
23-24-25 .... Seattle
26-27-**28** .... Oakland
29-30-31 . at Tampa Bay

JUNE
1 .... at Tampa Bay
2-3-**4** .... at Montreal*

5-6-7 .... at Mets*
9-10-**11** ..... Philadelphia*
13-14-15 .... Texas
16-17-**18**.......... Anaheim
19-**20**-21 ...... at Oakland
22-23-**24-25** ... at Seattle
27-28-29 .... at Boston
30 .... Toronto

JULY
1-2-**3** .... Toronto
4-5-**6** .... at Yankees
7-8-**9** .... at Philadelphia*
13-14-**15** .... Atlanta*
16-17-18 .... Florida*
19-20 .... Boston
21-**22-23**.... at Toronto
24-25-26 .... Yankees
28-**29-30**....... Cleveland
31 .... Minnesota

AUGUST
1-**2** .... Minnesota
4-**5-6** .... at Tampa Bay

7-8-9-**10**.......... at Detroit
11-12-**13** at Kansas City
14-15-16-**17**.. White Sox
18-19-**20**-21 .... K.C.
23-**24** ...... at White Sox
25-26-**27**...... Tampa Bay
29-30-31 .... Detroit

SEPTEMBER
1-2-3 .... at Cleveland
4-5-6 .... at Minnesota
8-9-10-11..... at Anaheim
12-13 .... at Texas
15-16-**17** .... Seattle
18-19-20 .... Oakland
22-23-**24** .... at Boston
26-27-28............ Toronto
29-30 .... Yankees

OCTOBER
1 .... Yankees

NOTE: Dates in **bold** indicate afternoon games.
*Interleague Series

BOSTON RED SOX
Fenway Park

APRIL
4-5-6 .... at Seattle
7-8-9 .... at Anaheim
11-12-13 .... Minnesota
14-15-16-17 .... Oakland
18-19-20 .... at Detroit
21-22-23 .... Cleveland
24-25-26 .... at Texas
28-29-30 .... at Cleveland

MAY
1-2-3 .... Detroit
5-6-7 .... Tampa Bay
8-9-10 .... White Sox
11-12-13-14 .... at Toronto
15-16-17 .... at Toronto
19-20-21 .... Detroit
23-24-25 .... Toronto
26-27-28 .... at Yankees
30-31 .... Kansas City

JUNE
1 .... Kansas City
2-3-4 .... at Philadelphia*

5-6-7 .... at Florida*
9-10-11 .... at Atlanta*
12-13-14 .... at Yankees
16-17-18 .... Toronto
19-20-21-22 .... Yankees
23-24-25 .... at Toronto
27-28-29 .... Baltimore
30 .... at White Sox

JULY
1-2 .... at White Sox
3-4-5 .... at Minnesota
7-8-9 .... Atlanta*
13-14-15 .... Montreal*
16-17-18 .... Montreal*
19-20 .... at Baltimore
21-22-... .... White Sox
24-25-26 .... Minnesota
27-28-29-30 .... at Cub.
31 .... at Seattle

AUGUST
1-2 .... at Seattle
4-5-6 .... Kansas City

7-8-9 .... at Anaheim
11-12-13 .... at Texas
14-15-16 .... Tampa Bay
17-18-19-20 .... Texas
21-22-23 .... Anaheim
24-25-26-27 .... at K.C.
28-29-30 ... at Tampa Bay

SEPTEMBER
1-2-3-4 .... Seattle
5-6 .... Oakland
8-9-10 .... Yankees
12-13-14 .... at Cleveland
15-16-17 .... at Detroit
19-20-21 .... Cleveland
22-23-24 .... Baltimore
26-27-... .. at White Sox
29-30 .... Tampa Bay

OCTOBER
1 .... at Tampa Bay

CHICAGO WHITE SOX
Comiskey Park

APRIL
3-4 .... at Texas
7-8-9 .... at Oakland
11-12-13 .... at Tampa Bay
14-15-16 .... Anaheim
17-18-19 .... Seattle
21-22-23 .... Detroit
24-25-26-27 .... Baltimore
28-29-30 .... at Detroit

MAY
1-2-3 .... Toronto
5-6-7 .... at Kansas City
8-9-10 .... at Boston
12-13-14 .... Minnesota
16-17 .... at Yankees
19-20-21-22 .... at Toronto
23-24-25 .... Yankees
26-27-28 .... Cleveland
29-30-31 .... at Seattle

JUNE
2-3-4 .... at Houston*

5-6-7 .... at Cincinnati*
9-10-11 .... Cubs
12-13-14 .... at Cleveland
15-16-17-18 .... at Yankees
19-20-21-22 .... Cleveland
23-24-25 .... Yankees
27-28-29 .... Minnesota
30 .... Boston

JULY
1-2 .... Boston
3-4-5 .... at Kansas City
7-8-9 .... at Cub*
13-14-15 .... St. Louis*
16-17-18 .... Milwaukee*
19-20 .... at Minnesota
21-22-23 .... Boston
24-25-26 .... Kansas City
27-28-29-30 .... at Anaheim

AUGUST
1-2 .... at Texas
4-5-6 .... Oakland

8-9-10 .... Seattle
11-12-13 .... at Tampa Bay
14-15-16-17 .... at Balt.
18-19-20-21 .... T.B.
23-24 .... Baltimore
25-26-27 .... at Seattle
28-29-30 .... at Oakland

SEPTEMBER
1-2-3 .... Anaheim
4-5-6-7 .... Texas
8-9-10 .... at Cleveland
11-12-13 .... Detroit
15-16-17 .... Toronto
18-19-20 .... at Detroit
21-22-23-24 .... at Minn.
26-27-28 .... Boston
29-30 .... Kansas City

OCTOBER
1 .... Kansas City

CLEVELAND INDIANS
Jacobs Field

APRIL
3-5-6 .... at Baltimore
7-8-9 .... at Tampa Bay
10-11-12 .... at Oakland
14-15-16 .... Texas
18-19-20 .... Oakland
21-22-23 .... at Boston
24-25-26 .... at Seattle
28-29-30 .... Boston

MAY
1-2-3 .... Yankees
4-5-6-7 .... at Toronto
8-9-10 .... at Minnesota
11-12-13-14 .... K.C.
16-17-18 .... Detroit
19-20-21 .... Yankees
23-24-25 .... at Detroit
26-27-28 .... at White Sox
29-30-31 .... Anaheim

JUNE
2-3-4 .... at St. Louis*

5-6-7 .... at Milwaukee*
9-10-11 .... Cincinnati*
12-13-14 .... White Sox
16-17-18 .... at Detroit
19-20-21-22 .... at Wh. Sox
23-24-25-26 .... Detroit
27-28-29 .... at K.C.
30 .... Minnesota

JULY
1-2 .... Minnesota
4-5-6 .... Toronto
7-8-9 .... at Cincinnati*
13-14-15 .... Pittsburgh*
16-17-18 .... Houston*
19-20 .... Kansas City
21-22-23 .... at Minn.
25-26 .... at Toronto
28-29-30 .... at Balt.

AUGUST
1-2-3 .... at Tampa Bay
4-5-6 .... Anaheim

7-8-9 .... Texas
11-12-13 .... at Seattle
14-15-16 .... at Oakland
18-19-20 .... Seattle
22-23-24 .... Oakland
25-26-27 .... at Anaheim
28-29-30-31 ..... at Texas

SEPTEMBER
1-2-3 .... Baltim
4-5-6-7 .... Tampa
8-9-10 .... Wh
12-13-14 ....
15-16-17-18 . a
19-20-21 ....
22-23-24 ....
25-26-27-2
29-30

OCTOBER
1 .....

DETROIT TIGERS
Comerica Park

APRIL
3-4-**5** .... at Oakland
7-**8**-**9** .... at Baltimore
11-12-13............. Seattle
14-**15**-16...... Tampa Bay
18-19-20 .... Boston
21-**22**-**23** .. at White Sox
24-25-26 ...... at Anaheim
28-**29**-**30** ...... White Sox

MAY
1-2-3 .... at Boston
4-5-6-**7**...... at Minnesota
8-9-**10** .... Kansas City
12-**13**-**14** .... Yankees
16-17-18 .... at Cleveland
19-**20**-**21** ...... at Boston
23-24-25....... Cleveland
26-27-**28**........... Toronto
29-30-31 .... Texas

JUNE
2-3-4................ at Cubs*

5-6-7........ at Pittsburgh*
9-10-**11** ...... St. Louis*
12-13-14............. Toronto
16-**17**-**18**...... Cleveland
20-21-22..... at Cleveland
23-24-**25**-26 . at Cleveland
27-28-29 .... Yankees
30............ at Kansas City

JULY
1-**2** .... at Kansas City
3-4-5 ...... at Tampa Bay
7-**8**-**9** ...... at Milwaukee*
13-14-**15**.......... Houston*
16-17-18 ...... Cincinnati*
19-**20** .... at Yankees
21-22-**23** .... Kansas City
24-25-26...... Tampa Bay
27-28-29-30 ..... at Texas
31 .... at Anaheim

AUGUST
1-**2**.............. at Anaheim

4-5-**6** .... Minnesota
7-8-9-**10** .... Baltimore
11-**12**-**13** .... at Oakland
14-15-**16** .... at Seattle
18-19-20-21 ..... Oakland
22-23-**24** .... Seattle
25-26-**27** .... at Minn.
29-30-31 .... at Balt.

SEPTEMBER
1-**2**-**3** .... Texas
4-5-6-7 .... Anaheim
8-9-**10** .... at Toronto
11-12-13 ...... at Wh. Sox
15-16-**17** .... Boston
18-19-20 ...... White Sox
22-**23**-**24**-25. at Yankees
26-27-28 .... at K.C.
29-30 .... Minnesota

OCTOBER
1 .... Minnesota

KANSAS CITY ROYALS
Kauffman Stadium

APRIL
3-4-5-**6** .... at Toronto
7-**8**-**9**-**10**........ Minnesota
11-12-**13**........... Baltimore
14-**15**-**16**..... at Yankees
18-19-**20**.... at Minnesota
21-**22**-**23** .... at Seattle
25-26 .... Tampa Bay
28-29-**30** .... Seattle

MAY
1-2-3 .... Oakland
5-6-**7** .... White Sox
8-9-**10**......... at Detroit
11-12-**13**-**14** ... at Cleve.
15-**16**-**17** ...... at Oakland
19-20-21 ..... at Anaheim
23-24-25 .... Texas
26-27-**28** ..... at Anaheim
30-31 .... at Boston

JUNE
1...................... at Boston

2-3-**4**........ at Pittsburgh*
5-6-7 .... at St. Louis*
9-10-**11** ...... Pittsburgh*
12-13-**14** .... Seattle
16-17-**18** .... Oakland
20-21-22 ..... at Anaheim
23-**24**-**25**........ at Oakland
27-28-29........ Cleveland
30 .... Detroit

JULY
1-**2** .... Detroit
3-4-5 .... White Sox
7-**8**-**9** .... at Houston*
13-14-15 ...... Milwaukee*
16-17-18............. Cubs*
19-20.......... at Cleveland
21-22-**23** .... at Detroit
24-25-**26** ... at White Sox
27-28-29-**30** .... T.B.

AUGUST
1-**2**-**3** .... at Yankees

4-**5**-**6** .... at Boston
7-8-9-**10** .... Toronto
11-12-**13**........... Baltimore
15-16-**17**.......... at Minn.
18-19-**20**-21 ..... at Balt.
22-23........... at Toronto
24-25-26-**27** .... Boston
29-**30** .... Minnesota
31 .... at Tampa Bay

SEPTEMBER
1-**2**-**3** ...... at Tampa Bay
4-5-6-7.............. Yankees
8-9-**10** .... Texas
11-12-13........ at Seattle
14-15-16-**17** ..... at Texas
18-19-20-21 ...... Anaheim
22-23-**24**........ Cleveland
26-27-28 .... Detroit
29-30 .... at White Sox

OCTOBER
1 .... at White Sox

MINNESOTA TWINS
Hubert H. Humphrey Metrodome

APRIL
3-4-5-**6** .... Tampa Bay
7-**8**-**9**-**10** .... at K.C.
11-12-13 .... at Boston
14-15-16 .... Baltimore
18-19-**20** .... Kansas City
1-22-**23** .... at Texas
5-26 ...... at Yankees
9-**30** .... Oakland

MAY
.... Seattle
.... Detroit
.... Cleveland
at White Sox
at Seattle
t Oakland
Anaheim
Texas
ronto

5-6-**7**....... at Houston*
9-10-**11** ...... Milwaukee*
12-13-14 .... Oakland
16-17-**18** .... Seattle
20-21-22 .... at Texas
23-24-25-**26** at Anaheim
27-28-**29** ... at White Sox
30 .... at Cleveland

JULY
1-**2** .... at Cleveland
3-4-5-**6** .... Boston
7-**8**-**9** .... at Pittsburgh*
13-14-15.............. Cubs*
16-17-18 .... St. Louis*
19-**20** .... White Sox
21-22-**23**........ Cleveland
24-25-**26** .... at Boston
27-28-29-**30**..... Yankees
31 .... at Baltimore

AUGUST
1-**2** .... at Baltimore
4-5-**6**................. at Detroit

7-8-9-**10** .. at Tampa Bay
11-12-**13**............. Toronto
15-16-**17** ...... Kansas City
18-**19**-**20**........ at Toronto
22-23 .... Tampa Bay
25-26-**27** .... Detroit
29-**30** ..... at Kansas City

SEPTEMBER
1-**2**-**3** .... at Yankees
4-5-6 .... Baltimore
8-9-**10** .... at Seattle
12-**13** .... at Oakland
15-16-**17**......... Anaheim
18-19-20 .... Texas
21-22-23-**24** .. White Sox
25-26-27-28 ... at Cleve.
29-30 .... at Detroit

OCTOBER
1 .... at Detroit

NEW YORK YANKEES
Yankee Stadium

APRIL
3-4-5 ...... at Anaheim
7-8-9 ...... at Seattle
11-12-13 ...... Texas
14-15-16 ...... Anaheim
17-18-19 ...... at Texas
21-22-23 ...... at Toronto
24-25-26 ...... Minnesota
28-29-30 ...... Toronto

MAY
1-2-3 ...... at Cleveland
5-6-7 ...... Baltimore
8-9-10 ...... Tampa Bay
12-13-14 ...... at Detroit
16-17 ...... White Sox
19-20-21 ...... Cleveland
23-24-25 ...... at White Sox
26-27-28 ...... Boston
29-30-31 ...... Oakland

JUNE
2-3-4 ...... at Atlanta*

5-6-7 ...... at Montreal*
9-10-11 ...... Mets*
12-13-14 ...... Boston
15-16-17-18 .. White Sox
19-20-21-22 ... at Boston
23-24-25 ...... at White Sox
27-28-29 ...... at Detroit
30 ...... at Tampa Bay

JULY
1-2 ...... Tampa Bay
4-5-6 ...... Baltimore
7-8-9 ...... at Mets*
13-14-15 ...... Florida
16-17-18 .. Philadelphia*
19-20 ...... Detroit
21-22-23 .... Tampa Bay
24-25-26 .... at Baltimore
27-28-29-30 ... at Minn.

AUGUST
1-2-3 ...... Kansas City
4-5-6-7 ...... Seattle

8-9-10 ...... Oakland
11-12-13 ...... at Anaheim
14-15-16 ...... at Texas
17-18-19-20 .... Anaheim
22-23-24 ...... Texas
25-26-27 ...... at Oakland
28-29-30 ...... at Seattle

SEPTEMBER
1-2-3 ...... Minnesota
4-5-6-7 ... at Kansas City
8-9-10 ...... at Boston
12-13-14 ...... Toronto
15-16-17-18 .. Cleveland
19-20-21 ...... at Toronto
22-23-24-25 ...... Detroit
26-27 ...... at T.B.
29-30 ...... at Baltimore

OCTOBER
1 ...... at Baltimore

OAKLAND ATHLETICS
Oakland-Alameda County Coliseum

APRIL
3-4-5 ...... Detroit
7-8-9 ...... White Sox
10-11-12 ...... Cleveland
14-15-16-17 .. at Boston
18-19-20 ... at Cleveland
21-22-23 ...... Baltimore
24-25-26 ...... Toronto
28-29-30 .. at Minnesota

MAY
1-2-3 ...... at Kansas City
5-6-7 ...... at Texas
8-9-10 ...... at Anaheim
11-12-13-14 ...... Seattle
15-16-17 .... Kansas City
18-19-20-21 .... Minnesota
23-24-25 . at Tampa Bay
26-27-28 ...... at Baltimore
29-30-31 ...... at Yankees

JUNE
2-3-4 ..... San Francisco*

5-6-7 ...... San Diego*
9-10-11. at Los Angeles*
12-13-14 .. at Minnesota
16-17-18 ...... at K.C.
19-20-21 ...... Baltimore
23-24-25 .... Kansas City
27-28-29 ...... Texas
30 ...... at Anaheim

JULY
1-2 ...... at Anaheim
3-4-5 ...... at Texas
7-8-9 ...... Arizona*
13-14-15 ... at San Fran.*
16-17-18 ... at Colorado*
19-20 ...... Seattle
21-22-23 ...... Anaheim
24-25-26 ...... at Seattle
27-28-29-30 ...... Boston
31 ...... Toronto

AUGUST
1-2 ...... Toronto

4-5-6 ...... at White Sox
8-9-10 ...... at Yankees
11-12-13 ...... Detroit
14-15-16 ...... Cleveland
18-19-20-21 ... at Detroit
22-23-24 ... at Cleveland
25-26-27 ...... Yankees
28-29-30 .... White Sox

SEPTEMBER
1-2-3-4 ...... at Toronto
5-6 ...... at Boston
8-9-10-11 .... Tampa Bay
12-13 ...... Minnesota
15-16-17 . at Tampa Bay
19-20 ...... at Baltimore
21-22-23-24 ... at Seattle
25-26-27-28 ... Anaheim
29-30 ...... Texas

OCTOBER
1 ...... Texas

SEATTLE MARINERS
Safeco Field

APRIL
4-5-6 ...... Boston
7-8-9 ...... Yankees
11-12-13 ...... at Detroit
14-15-16 ...... at Toronto
17-18-19 .. at White Sox
21-22-23 .... Kansas City
24-25-26 ...... Cleveland
28-29-30 ...... at K.C.

MAY
1-2-3 ...... at Minnesota
5-6-7 ...... Anaheim
8-9-10 ...... at Texas
11-12-13-14 .. at Oakland
15-16-17 ...... Minnesota
19-20-21 ...... Tampa Bay
23-24-25 .. at Baltimore
26-27-28 ...... at T.B.
29-30-31 ...... White Sox

JUNE
2-3-4 ...... San Diego*

5-6-7 ...... Colorado*
9-10-11 ... at San Fran.*
12-13-14 .. at Kansas City
16-17-18 .... at Minnesota
19-20-21 ...... Tampa Bay
22-23-24-25 .. Baltimore
27-28-29 ...... Anaheim
30 ...... at Texas

JULY
1-2 ...... at Texas
3-4-5-6 ...... Anaheim
7-8-9 ...... Los Angeles*
13-14-15 .. at San Diego*
16-17-18 ...... at Arizona
19-20 ...... at Oakland
21-22-23 ...... Texas
24-25-26 ...... Oakland
27-28-29-30 ...... Toronto
31 ...... Boston

AUGUST
1-2 ...... Boston

4-5-6-7 ...... at Yankees
8-9-10 ...... at White Sox
11-12-13 ...... Cleveland
14-15-16 ...... Detroit
18-19-20 ... at Cleveland
22-23-24 ...... at Detroit
25-26-27 ...... White Sox
28-29-30 ...... Yankees

SEPTEMBER
1-2-3-4 ...... at
5-6-7 ......
8-9-10 ......
11-12-13 ...
15-16-17 ...
19-20 ......
21-
26-27-
29-3

TAMPA BAY DEVIL RAYS
Tropicana Field

APRIL
3-4-5-**6**...... at Minnesota
7-8-**9**.............. Cleveland
11-12-**13** ...... White Sox
14-**15-16** .... at Detroit
17-18-19 .... at Baltimore
21-**22-23**.......... Anaheim
25-26 ..... at Kansas City
27-28-29-**30** at Anaheim

MAY
2-3-4 .... Texas
5-**6-7** .... at Boston
8-9-10 ...... at Yankees
12-**13-14**.......... Toronto
15-16-**17** ...... at Texas
19-**20-21** .... at Seattle
23-24-25 .... Oakland
26-**27-28** .... Seattle
29-30-31 .... Baltimore

JUNE
1..................... Baltimore

2-3-**4** .... at Mets*
5-6-7 .... at Philadelphia*
9-**10-11** .... Florida*
13-14-15.......... Anaheim
16-17-18 .... Texas
19-20-21 .... at Seattle
23-24-25 .... at Texas
27-28-**29**............ Toronto
30 .... Yankees

JULY
1-2 .... Yankees
3-**4**-5 .... Detroit
7-8-**9** .... at Florida*
13-14-**15** ...... Montreal*
16-17-18 .... Atlanta*
19-20.......... at Toronto
21-**22-23**...... at Yankees
24-25-26 .... at Detroit
27-28-29-**30** .... at K.C.

AUGUST
1-2-3............. Cleveland

4-**5-6** .... Baltimore
7-8-9-**10**....... Minnesota
11-**12-13** .... White Sox
14-15-16 .... at Boston
18-19-**20**-21.. at Wh. Sox
22-23 .... at Minnesota
25-26-**27** .... at Baltimore
28-29-30 .... Boston
31 .... Kansas City

SEPTEMBER
1-**2-3** .... Kansas City
4-5-6-7 .... at Cleveland
8-**9-10**-11 .... at Oakland
12-13........... at Anaheim
15-**16-17** .... Oakland
18-19-20 .... Seattle
22-23-24-25 .. at Toronto
26-27-28 .... Yankees
29-30................. Boston

OCTOBER
1 .... Boston

TEXAS RANGERS
Ballpark in Arlington

APRIL
3-4-5-**6**.......... White Sox
7-8-**9**................. Toronto
11-12-13 .... at Yankees
14-15-16 ... at Cleveland
17-18-**19** .... Yankees
21-**22-23**...... Minnesota
24-25-**26** .... Boston
28-**29-30** .... at Baltimore

MAY
2-3-4 .... at Tampa Bay
5-6-**7** .... Oakland
8-9-**10** .... Anaheim
11-12-13-**14**. at Anaheim
15-16-**17**...... Tampa Bay
18-19-20-21.. Baltimore
23-24-25 .... at K.C.
26-27-**28**.......... at Minn.
29-30-31 ....at Detroit

JUNE
2-3-4 .... Arizona*

5-6-**7** .... Los Angeles*
9-10-**11**...... at Colorado*
13-14-15 ... at Baltimore
16-17-18 . at Tampa Bay
20-21-22 ...... Minnesota
23-24-25...... Tampa Bay
27-28-**29** ...... at Oakland
30 .... Seattle

JULY
1-2............... Seattle
3-4-5 .... Oakland
7-8-9 .... San Diego*
13-14-**15** ...... at Arizona*
16-17-18 .. at San Fran.*
19-20.......... at Anaheim
21-22-**23** ..... at Seattle
24-25-26......... Anaheim
27-28-29-30........ Detroit

AUGUST
1-2 .... White Sox
3-4-**5-6** .... at Toronto

7-8-9 .... at Cleveland
11-12-13.......... Boston
14-15-16 .... Yankees
17-18-**19-20**... at Boston
22-23-**24**....... at Yankees
25-26-27 .... Toronto
28-29-30-31 .. Cleveland

SEPTEMBER
1-2-**3** .... at Detroit
4-5-6-7 .... at White Sox
8-9-**10** .... at K.C.
12-13............ Baltimore
14-15-16-**17** .... K.C.
18-19-20........... at Minn.
22-23-**24**.......... Anaheim
26-27-**28** .... at Seattle
29-**30** .... at Oakland

OCTOBER
1 .... at Oakland

TORONTO BLUE JAYS
SkyDome

APRIL
3-4-5-**6** .... Kansas City
7-8-**9** .... at Texas
10-11-12...... at Anaheim
14-**15-16** .... Seattle
7-18-19-20 .... Anaheim
22-23 .... Yankees
5-**26** .... at Oakland
30 ...... at Yankees

MAY
...... at White Sox
.. Cleveland
. Baltimore
mpa Bay
Boston
te Sox
ston
roit

5-6-7 .... at Atlanta*
9-**10-11** .... Montreal*
12-13-14...... at Detroit
16-17-**18** .... at Boston
20-21-22 .... Detroit
23-**24-25** .... Boston
27-28-**29** .... at T.B.
30............... at Baltimore

JULY
1-**2-3** .... at Baltimore
4-5 .... at Cleveland
7-8-**9** .... at Montreal*
13-14-**15**... Philadelphia*
16-17-18 .... Mets*
19-20....... Tampa Bay
21-**22-23** .... Baltimore
25-**26**............ Cleveland
27-28-**29-30** ... at Seattle
31 .... at Oakland

AUGUST
1-2 .... at Oakland
3-4-**5-6** .... Texas

7-8-9-**10** .... at K.C.
11-12-**13** .... at Minn.
15-**16** .... Anaheim
18-**19-20** .... Minnesota
22-23 .... Kansas City
25-26-27 ...... at Texas
28-29-30 ... at Anaheim

SEPTEMBER
1-2-**3-4** .... Oakland
5-6-7 .... Seattle
8-**9-10** .... Detroit
12-13-14..... at Yankees
15-16-**17**..... at Wh. Sox
19-20-21........ Yankees
22-**23-24**-25 .... T.B.
26-27-28 ... at Baltimore
29-**30**............ at Cleveland

OCTOBER
1 .... at Cleveland

NATIONALLEAGUE

ARIZONA DIAMONDBACKS
Bank One Ballpark

APRIL
4-5-6 .... Philadelphia
7-8-9 .... Pittsburgh
10-11-12-13.. at San Diego
14-16-16.... at San Fran.
17-18-19-20,... Colorado
21-22-23 ...... San Fran.
24-26-27 ... ,.. at Phila.
28-29-30 .... at Cubs

MAY
2-3-4 ...... at Milwaukee
5-6-7 .... San Diego
8-9-10 .... Los Angeles
12-13-14.... at San Diego
16-17-18 ..... at Montreal
19-20-21 .... at Mets
23-24-25 ... ,. Milwaukee
26-27-28.... Milwaukee
29-30-31 .... St. Louis

JUNE
1 .... ,.. ,.... St. Louis

2-3-4 .... at Texas*
5-6-7 .... at Cubs
9-10-11 .... Anaheim*
12-13-14-15 .... at L.A.
16-17-18 ... ,.... at Colo.
19-20-21..... San Diego
23-24-25 .... Colorado
26-27-28-29.. , Houston
30 ,..... .... Cincinnati

JULY
1-2-3 ...... ,... Cincinnati
4-5-6 ... ,.. at Houston
7-8-9 .... at Oakland
13-14-15.. ,...... Texas*
16-17-18.. ... Seattle*
19-20.... ,.. St. Louis
21-22-23.... at Cincinnati
25-26-27 ... at St. Louis
28-29-30 .... at Florida

AUGUST
1-2-3 .... Atlanta

4-5-6 .... ,. Mets
7-8-9 .... Montreal
11-12-13............. at Pitt.
14-15-16 .... at Phila.
18-19-20 .... Cubs
21-22-23...... Milwaukee
25-26-27..... at Mets
28-29-30 ..... at Montreal

SEPTEMBER
1-2-3 ,............... Florida
5-6-7 .... ,... at Atlanta
8-9-10 .... at Florida
11-12-13 .. Los Angeles
15-16-17....... ,... Atlanta
18-19-20 .... at L.A.
21-22-23-24 .... at C.F.
26-27-28 ,..... at Colo.
29-30 .... San. Fran

OCTOBER
1 ...... ,.. San Francisco

ATLANTA BRAVES
Turner Field

APRIL
3-4-5 .... ,. Colorado
7-8-9 ,........... San Fran.
10-12-13 ...... at Cubs
14-15-16 .. at Milwaukee
18-19-20 ... Philadelphia
21-22-23 ...... Pittsburgh
25-26-27 .... Los Angeles
28-29-30... at San Diego

MAY
1-2-3 .... at Los Angeles
5-6-7 .... Philadelphia
8-9-10-11........ at Florida
12-13-14.. at Philadelphia
16-17-18....... San Fran.
19-20-21....... San Diego
23-24-25 .. at Milwaukee
26-27-28 ...... at Houston
29-30-31 .... at Cubs

JUNE
2-3-4 .... Yankees*

5-6-7 ,........... Toronto*
9-10-11 ,..... ,... Boston*
12-13-14-15,... ,.. at Pitt.
16-17-18-19 .... at Phila.
20-21-22 ,...... , Cubs
23-24-25 ... Milwaukee
27-28 ,..... at Montreal
29-30..... ,..... at Mets

JULY
1-2 .... ,......... at Mets
3-4-5-6 .... Montreal
7-8-9 .... at Boston*
13-14-15... at Baltimore*
16-17-18 at Tampa Bay*
19-20.............. at Florida
21-22-23............. Mets
25-26-27........... Florida
28-29-30 .... Houston

AUGUST
1-2-3 .... at Arizona
4-5-6 .... at St. Louis

7-8-9 .... at Cincinnati
11-12-13 .... Los Angeles
14-15-16 ,..... San Diego
18-19-20 ... at San Fran.
21-22-23 ... at Colorado
24-25-26-27 .... St. Louis
28-29-30-31... Cincinnati

SEPTEMBER
1-2-3 ... ,.. ,. at Houston
5-6-7 .... ,...... Arizona
8-9-10 ,...... ,. Montreal
12-13-14.. ,. ,.. Florida
15-16-17 ,..... at Arizona
18-19-20 ,..... ,...... Mets
22-23-24-25 .. Montreal
26-27-28 ,......... Mets
29-30 .... ,..... Colorado

OCTOBER
1 .... Colorado

NOTE: Dates in **bold** indicate afternoon games.
* Interleague Series

CHICAGO CUBS
Wrigley Field

MARCH
29-30.... Mets (in Japan)

APRIL
3-5-6 .... at St. Louis
7-8-9 .... at Cincinnati
10-12-13 .... Atlanta
14-15-16-17 .... Florida
18-19-20 ...... at Montreal
21-22-23 .... at Mets
25-26-27 ...... at Houston
28-29-30 .... Arizona

MAY
2-3-4 .... Houston
5-6-7 .... Pittsburgh
8-9-10-11 ..... Milwaukee
12-13-14 ..... at Montreal
16-17-18 ..... Los Angeles
19-20-21 .... Cincinnati
23-24-25 ...... at Colorado
26-27-28 ..... at San Fran.
29-30-31 .... Atlanta

JUNE
2-3-4 .... Detroit*
5-6-7 .... Arizona
9-10-11 .... at White Sox*
13-14 .... Mets
16-17-18 .... Montreal
20-21-22 .... at Atlanta
23-24-25 .... at Florida
27-28-29 .... at Pitt.
30 .... at Milwaukee

JULY
1-2 .... at Milwaukee
3-4-5 .... Pittsburgh
7-8-9 .... White Sox*
13-14-15 .... at Minn.*
16-17-18 .... at K.C.*
19-20 .... Philadelphia
21-22-23 .... Milwaukee
25-26-27 .... at Phila.
28-29-30 .... San Fran.
31 .... Colorado

AUGUST
1-2 .... Colorado
3-4-5-6 ..... at San Diego
7-8-9.... at Los Angeles
11-12-13 ... Cincinnati
14-15-16 .... St. Louis
18-19-20 ...... at Arizona
21-22-23 .... at Houston
25-26-27 .... Los Angeles
28-29-30-31 . San Diego

SEPTEMBER
1-2-3 .... at San Fran.
4-5-6 .... at Colorado
8-9-10 .... Houston
11-12-13 ... at Cincinnati
14-15-16-17 at St. Louis
18-19-20 .. at Milwaukee
22-23-24 .... St. Louis
25-26-27-28 .... Phila.
29-30 .... at Pittsburgh

OCTOBER
1 .... at Pittsburgh

CINCINNATI REDS
Cinergy Field

APRIL
3-5-6 .... Milwaukee
7-8-9 .... Cubs
10-11-12 ..... at Colorado
14-15-16 .... at L.A.
18-19-20 ...... San Fran.
21-22-23 .... Los Angeles
25-26-27 .... at Mets
28-29-30 .... at Pitt.

MAY
1 .... at Pittsburgh
2-3-4 ...... at Philadelphia
5-6-7 .... St. Louis
9-10-11 .... San Diego
12-13-14-15. at Houston
16-17-18 .... Pittsburgh
19-20-21 .... at Cubs
22-23-24 .... at L.A.
26-27-28............. Florida
30-31 .... Montreal

JUNE
1 .... Montreal

2-3-4........ Minnesota*
5-6-7 .... White Sox*
9-10-11 .... at Cleveland*
12-13-14.... at San Fran.
16-17-18... at San Diego
20-21-22 ...... Colorado
23-24-25....... San Diego
26-27-28-29 .... St. Louis
30 .... at Arizona

JULY
1-2-3 .... at Arizona
4-5-6 ...... at St. Louis
7-8-9 .... Cleveland*
13-14-15..... at Colorado
16-17-18 .... at Detroit*
19-20 .... at Houston
21-22-23 .... Arizona
24-25-26 .... Houston
28-29-30 ..... at Montreal
31 .... at Mets

AUGUST
1-2 .... at Mets

4-5-6 .... Florida
7-8-9 .... Atlanta
11-12-13 .... at Cubs
14-15-16 .. at Milwaukee
18-19-20 ...... Pittsburgh
21-22-23-24 .... Phila.
25-26-27 .... at Florida
28-29-30-31 .. at Atlanta

SEPTEMBER
1-2-3 .... Montreal
4-5-6 .... Mets
8-9-10 .... at Pittsburgh
11-12-13 .... Cubs
14-15-16-17 . Milwaukee
18-19-20 ... at San Fran.
22-23-24 .... Houston
26-27-28 .. at Milwaukee
29-30 .... at St. Louis

OCTOBER
1 .... at St. Louis

COLORADO ROCKIES
Coors Field

APRIL
3-4-5 .... at Atlanta
7-8-9 .... at Florida
10-11-12 .... Cincinnati
13-14-15-16 .... St. Louis
17-18-19-20 .. at Arizona
21-22-23-24 at St. Louis
25-26 .... at Montreal
29-30 .... Mets

MAY
.... Montreal
..... at San Fran.
..... at Houston
.... San Fran.
.... at Mets
.... at Phila.
.... Cubs
.....ttsburgh
...ouston

....kee

5-6-7 .... at Seattle*
9-10-11 .... Texas*
13-14-15 .... Houston
16-17-18 .... Arizona
20-21-22.... at Cincinnati
23-24-25 .... at Arizona
26-27-28-29 .. San Fran.
30 .... at San Diego

JULY
1-2-3 .... at San Diego
4-5-6 .... at San Fran.
7-8-9 .... at Anaheim*
13-14-15 ...... Cincinnati
16-17-18 .... Oakland*
19-20 .... at Los Angeles
21-22-23 ...... San Diego
24-25-26-27 .... L.A.
28-29-30 .. at Milwaukee
31 .... at Cubs

AUGUST
1-2 .... at Cubs

4-5-6 .... Philadelphia
7-8-9 .... Pittsburgh
11-12-13-14. at Montreal
15-16-17 .... at Mets
18-19-20 .... Florida
21-22-23 .... Atlanta
25-26-27 .... at Pittsburgh
28-29-30 .... at Phila.

SEPTEMBER
1-2-3 .... Milwaukee
4-5-6 .... Cubs
8-9-10 ...... Los Angeles
11-12-13 .. at San Diego
14-15-16-17 .... at L.A.
19-20-21 ...... San Diego
22-23-24 .... Florida
26-27-28 .... Arizona
29-30 .... at Atlanta

OCTOBER
1 .... at Atlanta

FLORIDA MARLINS
Pro Player Stadium

APRIL
3-4-5-**6** ... San Francisco
7-8-**9** .... Colorado
10-11-12... at Milwaukee
14-**15**-**16**-**17**..... at Cubs
18-19-20 .... Pittsburgh
21-22-**23**-24 .... Phila.
25-**26**...... San Francisco
28-29-**30** .... at L.A.

MAY
1-2-3..........at San Diego
5-6-**7**................... Mets
8-9-10-11.......... Atlanta
12-**13**-14.......... at Mets
16-17-18....... San Diego
19-20-**21**.... Los Angeles
23-24-**25** ...... at St. Louis
26-27-**28**.... at Cincinnati
29-30-31 ... at Pittsburgh

JUNE
2-3-**4** .... Toronto*

5-6-7 .... Boston*
9-**10**-11 .. at Tampa Bay*
12-13-14 at Philadelphia
16-17-**18** ... at Pittsburgh
19-20-21-22 . Milwaukee
23-24-**25** .... Cubs
26-27-28............ at Mets
30................ at Montreal

JULY
1-**2**.................. Montreal
3-4-5................... Mets
7-8-**9** .... Tampa Bay*
13-14-**15** ... at Yankees*
16-17-18 ... at Baltimore*
19-20................ Atlanta
21-22-**23**.......... Montreal
25-26-27 ...... at Atlanta
28-29-**30**......... Arizona
31.................... Houston

AUGUST
1-2-**3** .... Houston

4-5-**6**.......... at Cincinnati
7-8-**9** .... at St. Louis
11-12-**13**....... San Diego
14-15-16.... Los Angeles
18-19-**20**.... at Colorado
21-22-**23**..... at San Fran.
25-26-**27** ...... Cincinnati
28-29-30 ..... St. Louis

SEPTEMBER
1-2-**3** .... at Arizona
4-5-6-**7** .... at Houston
8-9-**10**.............. Arizona
12-13-**14** .... at Atlanta
15-16-**17** .... at Phila.
18-19-20-**21** at Montreal
22-**23**-**24** ..... at Colorado
26-27-**28**....... Montreal
29-30 ...... Philadelphia

OCTOBER
1 .... Philadelphia

HOUSTON ASTROS
Enron Field

APRIL
3-5-**6** .... at Pittsburgh
7-**8**-**9** .... Philadelphia
10-11-12....... St. Louis
14-15-**16**... at San Diego
17-18-19 .... at L.A.
21-**22**-**23**...... San Diego
25-26-**27** .... Cubs
28-**29**-**30** .. at Milwaukee

MAY
1 .... at Milwaukee
2-**3**-**4** .... at Cubs
5-6-**7**.... at Los Angeles
8-9-10 .... Colorado
12-**13**-14-15... Cincinnati
16-17-**18** .. at Milwaukee
19-20-**21** ..... at Montreal
23-24-25 ...... Philadelphia
26-**27**-**28**............. Atlanta
29-30-31.... at Colorado

JUNE
2-**3**-**4**........... White Sox*

5-6-7............ Minnesota*
9-10-**11**.... at San Diego
13-14-15.... at Colorado
16-**17**-**18**.... at San Fran.
20-21-22.... Los Angeles
23-**24**-**25** ...... at San Fran.
26-27-28-29 .. at Arizona
30................ at St. Louis

JULY
1-**2** .... at St. Louis
4-5-6................. Arizona
7-8-**9** .... Kansas City*
13-14-**15** ...... at Detroit*
16-17-18 .. at Cleveland*
19-20 .... Cincinnati
21-**22**-**23** .... St. Louis
24-25-**26**.... at Cincinnati
28-**29**-**30** .... at Atlanta
31............... at Florida

AUGUST
1-2-**3** .... at Florida
4-5-**6**.............. Montreal

7-8-9-**10**................. Mets
11-**12**-**13**........... at Phila.
14-15-16 ...... Pittsburgh
18-19-**20**........ Milwaukee
21-22-23 .... Cubs
25-26-27 .... at Montreal
28-29-30........... at Mets

SEPTEMBER
1-2-3.................. Atlanta
4-5-6-**7** .... Florida
8-**9**-10 .... at Cubs
11-12-13 .... San Fran.
14-15-16-**17** .. Pittsburgh
19-20-**21** .... at St. Louis
22-**23**-**24**..... at Cincinnati
26-27-28 .... at Pittsburgh
29-30 .... Milwaukee

OCTOBER
1 .... Milwaukee

LOS ANGELES DODGERS
Dodger Stadium

APRIL
3-4-5-6 .... at Montreal
7-**8**-**9**.................. at Mets
11-12-13.... at San Fran.
14-15-16....... Cincinnati
17-18-19 .... Houston
21-**22**-**23**.... at Cincinnati
25-26-**27** .... at Atlanta
28-29-**30**.......... Florida

MAY
1-2-3.................. Atlanta
5-6-**7**............... Houston
8-9-10 .... at Arizona
12-13-**14** .... at St. Louis
16-**17**-18 .... at Cubs
19-20-**21** .... at Florida
22-23-24....... Cincinnati
26-27-**28** .... Philadelphia
29-30-31 .... Mets

JUNE
2-**3**-**4** .... at Anaheim*

5-6-**7**.............. at Texas*
9-10-**11** .... Oakland*
12-13-14-15 .... Arizona
16-**17**-18 .... St. Louis
20-21-22.... at Houston
23-**24**-**25** ..... at St. Louis
26-27-28-29 . San Diego
30 .... at San Fran.

JULY
1-**2**............ at San Fran.
4-5-**6**......... at San Diego
7-8-**9** .... at Seattle*
13-14-**15** .... Anaheim*
16-17-**18** .... Pittsburgh
19-20 .... Colorado
21-**22**-23........ San Fran.
24-25-26-**27** ...... at Colo.
28-29-**30** .... at Phila.
31............... at Pittsburgh

AUGUST
1-2 .... at Pittsburgh

4-5-6............. Milwaukee
7-8-9 .... Cubs
11-**12**-**13**......... at Atlanta
14-15-16 .... at Florida
18-**19**-**20**............. Mets
21-22-23-**24** ..... Montreal
25-**26**-**27** .... at Cubs
28-29-30-**31**.... at Mi

SEPTEMBER
1-2-3 .... Philade
4-5-6 .... Pitts
8-**9**-**10**.... at C
11-12-13....... a
14-15-16-**17**...
18-19-20..
22-23-**24**..
26-27-28
29-30...

1 ...

MILWAUKEE BREWERS
County Stadium

APRIL
3-5-6 .... at Cincinnati
7-8-9 .... at St. Louis
10-12-13 .... Florida
14-15-16 .... Atlanta
18-19-20 .... at Mets
21-22-23 .... at Montreal
25-26-27 ...... at St. Louis
28-29-30 .... Houston
MAY
1 .... Houston
2-3-4 .... Arizona
5-6-7 .... Montreal
8-9-10-11 .... at Cubs
12-13-14 ... at Pittsburgh
16-17-18 .... Houston
19-20-21 ...... San Fran.
23-24-25 .... Atlanta
26-27-28 ...... at Arizona
29-30-31 ... at San Diego
JUNE
2-3-4 .... Colorado

5-6-7 .... Cleveland*
9-10-11 .... at Minnesota*
12-13-14 .... Montreal
16-17-18 .... Mets
19-20-21-22 ... at Florida
23-24-25 .... at Atlanta
27-28-29 .... at Phila.
30 .... Cubs
JULY
1-2 .... Cubs
3-4-5-6 ...... Philadelphia
7-8-9 .... Detroit*
13-14-15 .... at K.C.*
16-17-18.. at White Sox*
19-20 .... Pittsburgh
21-22-23 .... at Cubs
25-26-27 .... at Pittsburgh
28-29-30 .... Colorado
31 .... San Fran.
AUGUST
1-2 .... San Francisco
4-5-6 ..... at Los Angeles

7-8-9 .... at San Fran.
11-12-13 .... St. Louis
14-15-16 .... Cincinnati
18-19-20 ...... at Houston
21-22-23 ...... at Arizona
25-26-27 ...... San Diego
28-29-30-31 .... L.A.
SEPTEMBER
1-2-3 .... at Colorado
4-5-6 ...... at San Diego
8-9-10 .... St. Louis
11-12-13 .... at Mets
14-15-16-17 ..... at Cinc.
18-19-20 .... Cubs
21-22-23-24 .. Pittsburgh
26-27-28 .... Cincinnati
29-30 .... at Houston
OCTOBER
1 .... at Houston

MONTREAL EXPOS
Olympic Stadium

APRIL
3-4-5-6 ...... Los Angeles
7-8-9 .... San Diego
11-12-13 ... at Pittsburgh
14-15-16-17 ..... at Phila.
18-19-20 .... Cubs
21-22-23 ...... Milwaukee
25-26 .... Colorado
28-29-30 ... at San Fran.
MAY
1-2-3 .... at Colorado
5-6-7 ...... at Milwaukee
8-9-10 ...... Philadelphia
12-13-14 .... Cubs
16-17-18 .... Arizona
19-20-21 .... Houston
23-24-25 .... at San Fran.
26-27-28 ... at San Diego
30-31 ...... at Cincinnati
JUNE
1 .... at Cincinnati
2-3-4 .... Baltimore*

5-6-7 .... Yankees*
9-10-11 .... at Toronto*
12-13-14 .. at Milwaukee
16-17-18 .... at Cubs
19-20-21-22 .. Pittsburgh
23-24-25 .... Philadelphia
27-28 .... Atlanta
30 .... Florida
JULY
1-2 .... Florida
3-4-5-6 .... at Atlanta
7-8-9 .... Toronto*
13-14-15 at Tampa Bay*
16-17-18 ...... at Boston*
19-20 .... Mets
21-22-23 .... at Florida
25-26-27 .... at Mets
28-29-30 .... Cincinnati
31 .... St. Louis
AUGUST
1-2 .... St. Louis
4-5-6 .... at Houston

7-8-9 .... at Arizona
11-12-13-14 .... Colorado
15-16-17 .... San Fran.
18-19-20 .... at San Diego
21-22-23-24 .... at L.A.
25-26-27 .... Houston
28-29-30 .... Arizona
SEPTEMBER
1-2-3 .... at Cincinnati
4-5-6-7 ...... at St. Louis
8-9-10 .... at Atlanta
12-13 ...... at Philadelphia
14-15-16-17 .... Mets
18-19-20-21 .... Florida
22-23-24-25 .... Atlanta
26-27-28 .... at Florida
29-30 .... at Mets
OCTOBER
1 .... at Mets

NEW YORK METS
Shea Stadium

MARCH
29-30 ... Cubs (in Japan)
APRIL
3-5-6 .... San Diego
7-8-9 .... Los Angeles
10-12-13 at Philadelphia
14-15-16 .... at Pittsburgh
19-20 .... Milwaukee
2-23 .... Cubs
27 .... Cincinnati
0 .... at Colorado
MAY
at San Fran.
.. at Florida
Pittsburgh
Florida
olorado
izona
iego
uis

5-6-7 .... Baltimore*
9-10-11 .... at Yankees*
13-14 .... at Cubs
16-17-18 .. at Milwaukee
20-21-22 ...... Philadelphia
23-24-25 .... Pittsburgh
26-27-28 .... Florida
29-30 .... Atlanta
JULY
1-2 .... Atlanta
3-4-5 .... at Florida
7-8-9 .... Yankees*
13-14-15 ...... at Boston*
16-17-18 .... at Toronto*
19-20 .... at Montreal
21-22-23 .... at Atlanta
25-26-27 .... Montreal
28-29-30 .... St. Louis
31 .... Cincinnati
AUGUST
1-2 .... Cincinnati
4-5-6 .... at Arizona
7-8-9-10 .... at Houston

11-12-13-14 ... San Fran.
15-16-17 .... Colorado
18-19-20 .... at L.A.
21-22-23 .. at San Diego
25-26-27 .... Arizona
28-29-30 .... Houston
SEPTEMBER
1-2-3 .... at St. Louis
4-5-6 ...... at Cincinnati
8-9-10 ...... Philadelphia
11-12-13 .... Milwaukee
14-15-16-17 at Montreal
18-19-20 .... at Atlanta
21-22-23-24 .... at Phila.
26-27-28 .... Atlanta
29-30 .... Montreal
OCTOBER
1 .... Montreal

PHILADELPHIA PHILLIES
Veterans Stadium

APRIL
4-5-6 .... at Arizona
7-8-9 .... at Houston
10-12-13 .... Mets
14-15-16-17 .... Montreal
18-19-20 .... at Atlanta
21-22-23-24 .. at Florida
25-26-27 .... Arizona
28-29-30 .... St. Louis
MAY
2-3-4 .... Cincinnati
5-6-7 .... at Atlanta
8-9-10 .... at Montreal
12-13-14 .... Atlanta
16-17-18 ...... St. Louis
19-20-21 .... Colorado
23-24-25 ...... at Houston
26-27-28 .... at L.A.
29-30-31.. at San Fran.
JUNE
2-3-4 .... Boston*

5-6-7 .... Tampa Bay*
9-10-11 ... at Baltimore*
12-13-14............. Florida
16-17-18-19 ...... Atlanta
20-21-22............ at Mets
23-24-25 ..... at Montreal
27-28-29...... Milwaukee
30 .... Pittsburgh
JULY
1-2................. Pittsburgh
3-4-5-6 .... at Milwaukee
7-8-9 .... Baltimore*
13-14-15 ...... at Toronto*
16-17-18 ... at Yankees*
19-20 .... at Cubs
21-22-23 .. at Pittsburgh
25-26-27 .... Cubs
28-29-30.... Los Angeles
31 .... at San Diego
AUGUST
1-2............. at San Diego

4-5-6 .... at Colorado
7-8-9-10 .... San Diego
11-12-13 .... Houston
14-15-16 .... Arizona
18-19-20 ... at St. Louis
21-22-23-24 ...... at Cinc.
25-26-27 .... San Fran.
28-29-30 .... Colorado
SEPTEMBER
1-2-3..... at Los Angeles
4-5-6 .... at San Fran.
8-9-10 .... at Mets
12-13 .... Montreal
15-16-17 .... Florida
18-19-20 .... Pittsburgh
21-22-23-24 .... Mets
25-26-27-28 ...... at Cubs
29-30 .... at Florida
OCTOBER
1 .... at Florida

PITTSBURGH PIRATES
Three Rivers Stadium

APRIL
3-5-6 .... Houston
7-8-9 .... at Arizona
11-12-13 .... Montreal
14-15-16 .... Mets
18-19-20 ...... at Florida
21-22-23 ..... at Atlanta
25-26-27 ...... San Diego
28-29-30 .... Cincinnati
MAY
1 .... Cincinnati
2-3-4 .... at St. Louis
5-6-7 .... at Cubs
9-10-11 .... Mets
12-13-14.... Milwaukee
16-17-18.... at Cincinnati
19-20-21 .... St. Louis
23-24-25 ...... at Arizona
26-27-28 ..... at Colorado
29-30-31 .... Florida
JUNE
2-3-4 .... Kansas City*

5-6-7 .... Detroit*
9-10-11 .... at K.C.*
12-13-14-15 .... Atlanta
16-17-18............. Florida
19-20-21-22 at Montreal
23-24-25.......... at Mets
27-28-29 .... Cubs
30 .... at Philadelphia
JULY
1-2 .... at Philadelphia
3-4-5 .... at Cubs
7-8-9............ Minnesota*
13-14-15 .. at Cleveland*
16-17-18.... Los Angeles
19-20.......... at Milwaukee
21-22-23 .... Philadelphia
25-26-27.... Milwaukee
28-29-30...... San Diego
31 .... Los Angeles
AUGUST
1-2 .... Los Angeles
3-4-5-6 ...... at San Fran.

7-8-9........... at Colorado
11-12-13............ Arizona
14-15-16 ..... at Houston
18-19-20... at Cincinnati
21-22-23 ..... at St. Louis
25-26-27 .... Colorado
28-29-30-31 .. San Fran.
SEPTEMBER
1-2-3......... at San Diego
4-5-6.... at Los Angeles
8-9-10............ Cincinnati
11-12-13.......... St. Louis
14-15-16-17. at Houston
18-19-20 .... at Phila.
21-22-23-24 ...... at Mil.
26-27-28 .... Houston
29-30 .... Cubs
OCTOBER
1............................ Cubs

ST. LOUIS CARDINALS
Busch Stadium

APRIL
3-5-6 .... Cubs
7-8-9............ Milwaukee
10-11-12 ...... at Houston
13-14-15-16 .... at Colo.
18-19-20....... San Diego
21-22-23-24 ..... Colorado
25-26-27....... Milwaukee
28-29-30 .... at Phila.
MAY
2-3-4 .... Pittsburgh
5-6-7......... at Cincinnati
8-9-10...... at San Fran.
12-13-14.... Los Angeles
16-17-18 at Philadelphia
19-20-21 ... at Pittsburgh
23-24-25............. Florida
26-27-28.............. Mets
29-30-31 .... at Arizona
JUNE
1.................... at Arizona
2-3-4 .... Cleveland*

5-6-7......... Kansas City*
9-10-11.......... at Detroit*
12-13-14... at San Diego
16-17-18 .... at L.A.
20-21-22....... San Fran.
23-24-25.... Los Angeles
26-27-28-29...... at Cinc.
30..................... Houston
JULY
1-2 .... Houston
4-5-6.............. Cincinnati
7-8-9.............. San Fran.
13-14-15... at White Sox*
16-17-18 .... at Minn.*
19-20............. at Arizona
21-22-23 ...... at Houston
25-26-27........... Arizona
28-29-30............ at Mets
31 .... at Montreal
AUGUST
1-2............. at Montreal
4-5-6.................. Atlanta

7-8-9................... Florida
11-12-13... at Milwaukee
14-15-16 .... at Cubs
18-19-20 ... Philadelphia
21-22-23 .... Pittsburgh
24-25-26-27 ... at Atlanta
28-29-30 ...... at Florida
SEPTEMBER
1-2-3..................... M
4-5-6-7 .... Mo
8-9-10 ..... at Milw
11-12-13... at Pi
14-15-16-17
19-20-21
22-23-24
26-27-28
29-30
O
1

SAN DIEGO PADRES
Qualcomm Stadium

APRIL
3-5-6	at Mets
7-8-9	at Montreal
10-11-12-13	Arizona
14-15-16	Houston
18-19-20	at St. Louis
21-22-23	at Houston
25-26-27	at Pittsburgh
28-29-30	Atlanta

MAY
1-2-3	Florida
5-6-7	at Arizona
9-10-11	at Cincinnati
12-13-14	Arizona
16-17-18	at Florida
19-20-21	at Atlanta
22-23-24	Mets
26-27-28	Montreal
29-30-31	Milwaukee

JUNE
2-3-4	at Seattle*
5-6-7	at Oakland*
9-10-11	Houston
12-13-14	St. Louis
16-17-18	Cincinnati
19-20-21	at Arizona
23-24-25	at Cincinnati
26-27-28-29	at L.A.
30	Colorado

JULY
1-2-3	Colorado
4-5-6	Los Angeles
7-8-9	at Texas*
13-14-15	Seattle*
16-17-18	Anaheim*
19-20	at San Fran.
21-22-23	at Colorado
24-25-26	San Fran.
28-29-30	at Pittsburgh
31	Philadelphia

AUGUST
1-2	Philadelphia
3-4-5-6	Cubs
7-8-9-10	at Philadelphia
11-12-13	at Florida
14-15-16	at Atlanta
18-19-20	Montreal
21-22-23	Mets
25-26-27	at Milwaukee
28-29-30-31	at Cubs

SEPTEMBER
1-2-3	Pittsburgh
4-5-6	Milwaukee
7-8-9-10	at San Fran.
11-12-13	Colorado
15-16-17	San Fran.
19-20-21	at Colorado
22-23-24	at L.A.
26-27-28	St. Louis
29-30	Los Angeles

OCTOBER
1	Los Angeles

SAN FRANCISCO GIANTS
Pacific Bell Park

APRIL
3-4-5-6	at Florida
7-8-9	at Atlanta
11-12-13	Los Angeles
14-15-16	Arizona
18-19-20	at Cincinnati
21-22-23	at Arizona
25-26	at Florida
28-29-30	Montreal

MAY
1-2-3-4	Mets
5-6-7	Colorado
8-9-10	St. Louis
12-13-14	at Colorado
16-17-18	at Atlanta
19-20-21	at Milwaukee
23-24-25	Montreal
26-27-28	Cubs
29-30-31	Philadelphia

JUNE
2-3-4	at Oakland*
5-6-7	at Anaheim*
9-10-11	Seattle*
12-13-14	Cincinnati
16-17-18	Houston
20-21-22	St. Louis
23-24-25	at Houston
26-27-28-29	at Colo.
30	Los Angeles

JULY
1-2	Los Angeles
4-5-6	Colorado
7-8-9	at St. Louis
13-14-15	Oakland*
16-17-18	Texas*
19-20	San Diego
21-22-23	at L.A.
24-25-26	at San Diego
28-29-30	at Cubs
31	at Milwaukee

AUGUST
1-2	at Milwaukee
3-4-5-6	Pittsburgh
7-8-9	Milwaukee
11-12-13-14	at Mets
15-16-17	at Montreal
18-19-20	Atlanta
21-22-23	Florida
25-26-27	at Phila.
28-29-30-31	at Pitt.

SEPTEMBER
1-2-3	Cubs
4-5-6	Philadelphia
7-8-9-10	San Diego
11-12-13	at Houston
15-16-17	at San Diego
18-19-20	Cincinnati
21-22-23-24	Arizona
26-27-28	at L.A.
29-30	at Arizona

OCTOBER
1	at Arizona

INTERLEAGUE SCHEDULE

JUNE 2

Baltimore at Montreal
Tampa Bay at Mets
Boston at Philadelphia
Yankees at Atlanta
Toronto at Florida
Kansas City at Pittsburgh
Minnesota at Cincinnati

Detroit at Cubs
Cleveland at St. Louis
White Sox at Houston
San Diego at Seattle
San Francisco at Oakland
Los Angeles at Anaheim
Arizona at Texas

JUNE 3

Baltimore at Montreal
Tampa Bay at Mets
Boston at Philadelphia
Yankees at Atlanta
Toronto at Florida
Kansas City at Pittsburgh
Minnesota at Cincinnati

Detroit at Cubs
Cleveland at St. Louis
White Sox at Houston
San Diego at Seattle
San Francisco at Oakland
Los Angeles at Anaheim
Arizona at Texas

JUNE 4

Baltimore at Montreal
Tampa Bay at Mets
Boston at Philadelphia
Yankees at Atlanta
Toronto at Florida
Kansas City at Pittsburgh
Minnesota at Cincinnati

Detroit at Cubs
Cleveland at St. Louis
White Sox at Houston
San Diego at Seattle
San Francisco at Oakland
Los Angeles at Anaheim
Arizona at Texas

JUNE 5

Yankees at Montreal
Baltimore at Mets
Tampa Bay at Philadelphia
Toronto at Atlanta
Boston at Florida
Detroit at Pittsburgh
White Sox at Cincinnati

Cleveland at Milwaukee
Kansas City at St. Louis
Minnesota at Houston
Colorado at Seattle
San Diego at Oakland
San Francisco at Anaheim
Los Angeles at Texas

JUNE 6

Yankees at Montreal
Baltimore at Mets
Tampa Bay at Philadelphia
Toronto at Atlanta
Boston at Florida
Detroit at Pittsburgh
White Sox at Cincinnati

Cleveland at Milwaukee
Kansas City at St. Louis
Minnesota at Houston
Colorado at Seattle
San Diego at Oakland
San Francisco at Anaheim
Los Angeles at Texas

JUNE 7

Yankees at Montreal
Baltimore at Mets
Tampa Bay at Philadelphia
Toronto at Atlanta
Boston at Florida
Detroit at Pittsburgh
White Sox at Cincinnati

Cleveland at Milwaukee
Kansas City at St. Louis
Minnesota at Houston
Colorado at Seattle
San Diego at Oakland
San Francisco at Anaheim
Los Angeles at Texas

JUNE 9

Boston at Atlanta
Texas at Colorado
Anaheim at Arizona
Oakland at Los Angeles
Houston at San Diego
Seattle at San Francisco
Pittsburgh at Kansas City
Milwaukee at Minnesota

Cubs at White Sox
St. Louis at Detroit
Cincinnati at Cleveland
Montreal at Toronto
Florida at Tampa Bay
Philadelphia at Baltimore
Mets at Yankees

JUNE 10

Boston at Atlanta
Texas at Colorado
Anaheim at Arizona
Oakland at Los Angeles
Houston at San Diego
Seattle at San Francisco
Pittsburgh at Kansas City
Milwaukee at Minnesota

Cubs at White Sox
St. Louis at Detroit
Cincinnati at Cleveland
Montreal at Toronto
Florida at Tampa Bay
Philadelphia at Baltimore
Mets at Yankees

JUNE 11

Boston at Atlanta
Texas at Colorado
Anaheim at Arizona
Oakland at Los Angeles
Houston at San Diego

Seattle at San Francis
Pittsburgh at Kansas
Milwaukee at Minne
Cubs at White Sox
St. Louis at Detroi

Cincinnati at Cleveland
Montreal at Toronto
Florida at Tampa Bay

Philadelphia at Baltimore
Mets at Yankees

JULY 7

Toronto at Montreal
Yankees at Mets
Baltimore at Philadelphia
Tampa Bay at Florida
Minnesota at Pittsburgh
Cleveland at Cincinnati
White Sox at Cubs

Detroit at Milwaukee
Kansas City at Houston
Los Angeles at Seattle
Arizona at Oakland
Colorado at Anaheim
San Diego at Texas
Atlanta at Boston

JULY 8

Toronto at Montreal
Yankees at Mets
Baltimore at Philadelphia
Tampa Bay at Florida
Minnesota at Pittsburgh
Cleveland at Cincinnati
White Sox at Cubs

Detroit at Milwaukee
Kansas City at Houston
Los Angeles at Seattle
Arizona at Oakland
Colorado at Anaheim
San Diego at Texas
Atlanta at Boston

JULY 9

Toronto at Montreal
Yankees at Mets
Baltimore at Philadelphia
Tampa Bay at Florida
Minnesota at Pittsburgh
Cleveland at Cincinnati
White Sox at Cubs

Detroit at Milwaukee
Kansas City at Houston
Los Angeles at Seattle
Arizona at Oakland
Colorado at Anaheim
San Diego at Texas
Atlanta at Boston

JULY 13

Texas at Arizona
Anaheim at Los Angeles
Seattle at San Diego
Oakland at San Francisco
Milwaukee at Kansas City
Cubs at Minnesota
St. Louis at White Sox

Houston at Detroit
Pittsburgh at Cleveland
Philadelphia at Toronto
Montreal at Tampa Bay
Atlanta at Baltimore
Florida at Yankees
Mets at Boston

JULY 14

Texas at Arizona
Anaheim at Los Angeles
Seattle at San Diego
Oakland at San Francisco
Milwaukee at Kansas City
Cubs at Minnesota
St. Louis at White Sox

Houston at Detroit
Pittsburgh at Cleveland
Philadelphia at Toronto
Montreal at Tampa Bay
Atlanta at Baltimore
Florida at Yankees
Mets at Boston

JULY 15

Texas at Arizona
Anaheim at Los Angeles
Seattle at San Diego
Oakland at San Francisco
Milwaukee at Kansas City
Cubs at Minnesota
St. Louis at White Sox

Houston at Detroit
Pittsburgh at Cleveland
Philadelphia at Toronto
Montreal at Tampa Bay
Atlanta at Baltimore
Florida at Yankees
Mets at Boston

JULY 16

Oakland at Colorado
Seattle at Arizona
Anaheim at San Diego
Texas at San Francisco
Cubs at Kansas City
St. Louis at Minnesota
Milwaukee at White Sox

Cincinnati at Detroit
Houston at Cleveland
Mets at Toronto
Atlanta at Tampa Bay
Florida at Baltimore
Philadelphia at Yankees
Montreal at Boston

JULY 17

Oakland at Colorado
Seattle at Arizona
Anaheim at San Diego
Texas at San Francisco
Cubs at Kansas City
St. Louis at Minnesota
Milwaukee at White Sox

Cincinnati at Detroit
Houston at Cleveland
Mets at Toronto
Atlanta at Tampa Bay
Florida at Baltimore
Philadelphia at Yankees
Montreal at Boston

JULY 18

d at Colorado
t Arizona
at San Diego
an Francisco
sas City
Minnesota
White Sox

Cincinnati at Detroit
Houston at Cleveland
Mets at Toronto
Atlanta at Tampa Bay
Florida at Baltimore
Philadelphia at Yankees
Montreal at Boston

SPRINGTRAINING

ANAHEIM ANGELS
Major League Club
Complex Address (first year): Diablo Stadium (1993), 2200 W Alameda, Tempe, AZ 85282. Telephone: (602) 438-4300. FAX: (602) 438-7950. **Seating Capacity:** 9,785.

Hotel Address: Fiesta Inn, 2100 S Priest Dr., Tempe, AZ 85282. Telephone: (602) 967-1441.

Minor League Clubs
Complex Address: Gene Autry Park, 4125 E McKellips, Mesa, AZ 85205. Telephone: (480) 830-4137. FAX: (480) 438-7950. **Hotel Address:** Lindsay Palms, 2855 E Broadway, Mesa, AZ 85204.

ARIZONA DIAMONDBACKS
Major League Club
Complex Address (first year): Tucson Electric Park (1998), 2500 Ajo Way, Tucson, AZ 85713. Telephone: (520) 434-1400. FAX: (520) 434-1443. **Seating Capacity:** 11,000.

Hotel Address: Doubletree Suites, 6555 E Speedway, Tucson, AZ 85710. Telephone: (520) 721-7100.

Minor League Clubs
Complex Address: Kino Veterans Memorial Sportspark, 3600 S Country Club, Tucson, AZ 85713. Telephone: (520) 434-1400. FAX: (520) 434-1443. **Hotel Address:** Holiday Inn, 181 W Broadway, Tucson, AZ 85701. Telephone: (520) 624-8711.

CHICAGO CUBS
Major League Club
Complex Address (first year): HoHoKam Park (1979), 1235 N Center St., Mesa, AZ 85201. Telephone: (480) 668-0500. FAX: (480) 668-4541. Seating Capacity: 8,963.

Hotel Address: Best Western Dobson Ranch Inn, 1666 S Dobson Rd., Mesa, AZ 85202. Telephone: (480) 831-7000.

Minor League Clubs
Complex Address: Fitch Park, 160 E Sixth Pl., Mesa, AZ 85201. Telephone: (480) 668-0500. FAX: (480) 668-4501. **Hotel Address:** Best Western Mezona, 250 W Main St., Mesa, AZ 85201. Telephone: (480) 834-9233.

CHICAGO WHITE SOX
Major League Club
Complex Address (first year): Tucson Electric Park (1998), 2500 Way, Tucson, AZ 85713. Telephone: (520) 434-1300. FAX: (52 1151. **Seating Capacity:** 11,000.

Hotel Address: Doubletree Guest Suites, 6555 E Speedw Tucson, AZ 85710. Telephone: (520) 721-7100.

Minor League Clubs
Complex Address: Same as major league club. **Ho** Ramada Palo Verde, 5251 S Julian Dr., Tucson, AZ 8570 (520) 294-5250.

COLORADO ROCKIES
Major League Club
Complex Address (first year): U.S. West Sports Complex at Hi Corbett Field (1993), 3400 E Camino Campestre, Tucson, AZ 85716. Telephone: (520) 322-4500. **Seating Capacity:** 9,500.
Hotel Address: Tucson Inn Suites, 475 N Granada, Tucson, AZ 85701. Telephone: (520) 622-3000.
Minor League Clubs
Complex Address: Same as major league club.
Hotel Address: Holiday Inn-Palo Verde, 4550 S Palo Verde Blvd., Tucson, AZ 85714. Telephone: (520) 746-1161.

MILWAUKEE BREWERS
Major League Club
Complex Address (first year): Maryvale Baseball Park (1998), 3600 N 51st Ave., Phoeniz, AZ 85031. Telephone: (623) 245-5555. FAX: (623) 247-7404.
Hotel Address: Wyndham Metro Center, 10220 N Metro Parkway East, Phoenix, AZ 85051. Telephone: (602) 997-5900.
Minor League Clubs
Complex Address: Maryvale Baseball Complex, 3805 N 53rd Ave., Phoenix, AZ 85031. Telephone: (602) 245-5600. FAX: (602) 849-8941.
Hotel Address: Red Roof Inn, 17222 N Black Canyon Fwy., Phoenix, AZ 85023. Telephone: (602) 866-1049.

OAKLAND ATHLETICS
Major League Club
Complex Address (first year): Phoenix Municipal Stadium (1982), 5999 E Van Buren, Phoenix, AZ 85008. Telephone: (602) 225-9400. FAX: (602) 225-9473. **Seating Capacity:** 8,500.
Hotel Address: Doubletree Suites Hotel, 320 N 44th St., Phoenix, AZ 85008. Telephone: (602) 225-0500.
Minor League Clubs
Complex Address: Papago Park Baseball Complex, 1802 N 64th St., Phoenix, AZ 85008. Telephone: (480) 949-5951. FAX: (480) 945-0557. **Hotel Address:** Fairfield Inn, 5101 N Scottsdale Rd., Scottsdale, AZ 85251. Telephone: (480) 945-4392.

SAN DIEGO PADRES
Major League Club
Complex Address (first year): Peoria Sports Complex (1994), 8131 W Paradise Ln., Peoria, AZ 85382. Telephone: (623) 486-7000. FAX: (623) 412-9382. **Seating Capacity:** 10,000.
Hotel Address: Crowne Plaza, 2352 W Peoria Ave., Peoria, AZ 85382. Telephone: (623) 943-2341.
Minor League Clubs
Complex Address: Same as major league club. **Hotel Address:** Premier Inns, 10402 Black Canyon Hwy., Phoenix, AZ 85051. Telephone: (602) 943-2371.

SAN FRANCISCO GIANTS
Major League Club
Complex Address (first year): Scottsdale Stadium (1981), 7408 E Osborn Rd., Scottsdale, AZ 85251. Telephone: (480) 990-7972. FAX: (480) 990-2643. **Seating Capacity:** 10,500.
Hotel Address: Courtyard by Marriott, 3311 N Scottsdale Rd., Scottsdale, AZ 85251. Telephone: (480) 429-7785.
Minor League Clubs
Complex Address: Indian School Park, 4289 N Hayden Road at Camelback Road, Scottsdale, AZ 85251. Telephone: (480) 990-0052. FAX: (480) 990-2349. **Hotel Address:** Days Inn, 4710 N Scottsdale Rd., cottsdale, AZ 85351. Telephone: (480) 947-5411.

SEATTLE MARINERS
Major League Club
mplex Address (first year): Peoria Sports Complex (1993), 15707 Ave., Peoria, AZ 85382. Telephone: (602) 412-9000. FAX: (602) 2. **Seating Capacity:** 10,000.
Address: Wyndham Metrocenter, 10220 N Metro Parkway, Z 85051. Telephone: (602) 997-5900.
Minor League Clubs
Address: Same as major league club. **Hotel Address:** 711 W Bell Rd., Phoenix, AZ 85023. Telephone: (602) 866-

ATLANTA BRAVES
Major League Club
Stadium Address (first year): Disney's Wide World of Sports Complex (1998), 700 S Victory Way, Kissimmee, FL 34747. Telephone: (407) 939-2200. **Seating Capacity:** 9,100.

Hotel Address: World Center Marriott, World Center Dr., Orlando, FL 32821. Telephone: (407) 239-4200.
Minor League Clubs
Complex Address: Same as major league club. Telephone: (407) 939-8630. FAX: (407) 939-8236. **Hotel Address:** Quality Inn Suites, 5820 W Irlo Bronson Memorial Hwy., Kissimmee, FL 34746. Telephone: (407) 396-7900.

BALTIMORE ORIOLES
Major League Club
Complex Address (first year): Fort Lauderdale Stadium (1996), 5301 NW 12th Ave., Fort Lauderdale, FL 33309. Telephone: (954) 776-1921. FAX: (954) 776-9116. **Seating Capacity:** 8,340.

Hotel Address: Sheraton Suites, 555 NW 62nd St., Fort Lauderdale, FL 33309. Telephone: (954) 772-5400.
Minor League Clubs
Complex Address: Twin Lakes Park, 6700 Clark Rd., Sarasota, FL 34241. Telephone: (941) 923-1996. FAX: (941) 922-3751. **Hotel Address:** Ramada Inn Osprey, 1660 S Tamiami Trail, Osprey, FL 34229. Telephone: (941) 966-2121.

BOSTON RED SOX
Major League Club
Complex Address (first year): City of Palms Park (1993), 2201 Edison Ave., Fort Myers, FL 33901. Telephone: (941) 334-4799. FAX: (941) 334-6060. **Seating Capacity:** 6,850.

Hotel Address: Holiday Inn Select, 13501 Bell Tower Dr., Fort Myers, FL 33901. Telephone: (941) 482-2900.
Minor League Clubs
Complex Address: Red Sox Minor League Complex, 4301 Edison Ave., Fort Myers, FL 33916. Telephone: (941) 332-8106. FAX: (941) 332-8107. **Hotel Address:** Amtel Marina Hotel, 2500 Edwards Dr., Fort Myers, FL 33901. Telephone: (941) 337-0300.

CINCINNATI REDS
Major League Club
Complex Address (first year): Ed Smith Stadium (1998), 12th S Tuttle Ave., Sarasota, FL 34237. Telephone: (941) 955-6501. FA 955-6365. **Seating Capacity:** 7,500.

Hotel Address: Marriott Residence Inn, 1040 Universi Sarasota, FL 34234. Telephone: (941) 358-1468. FAX: (941) 3
Minor League Clubs
Complex Address: Same as major league club. Ho Wellesley Inn, 1803 N. Tamiami Trail, Sarasota, FL 342 (941) 366-5128.

CLEVELAND INDIANS
Major League Club
Complex Address (first year): Chain O' Lakes Park (1993), Cypress Gardens Blvd. at U.S. 17, Winter Haven, FL 33880. Telephone: (863) 293-5405. FAX: (863) 291-5772. **Seating Capacity:** 7,000.

Hotel Address: Holiday Inn, 1150 Third St. SW, Winter Haven, FL 33880. Telephone: (863) 294-4451.

Minor League Clubs
Complex/Hotel Address: Same as major league club.

DETROIT TIGERS
Major League Club
Complex Address (first year): Joker Marchant Stadium (1946), 2301 Lakeland Hills Blvd., Lakeland, FL 33805. Telephone: (863) 686-8075. FAX: (863) 688-9589. **Seating Capacity:** 7,027.

Hotel Address: Wellesley Inn, 3520 Hwy. 98 N, Lakeland, FL 33805. Telephone: (863) 859-3399.

Minor League Clubs
Complex/Hotel Address: Tigertown, 2125 N Lake Ave., Lakeland, FL 33805. Telephone: (863) 686-8075. FAX: (863) 688-9589.

FLORIDA MARLINS
Major League Club
Complex Address (first year): Space Coast Stadium (1993), 5800 Stadium Pkwy., Viera, FL 32940. Telephone: (321) 633-9200. FAX: (321) 633-9210. **Seating Capacity:** 7,200.

Hotel Address: Melbourne Airport Hilton, 200 Rialto Pl., Melbourne, FL 32901. Telephone: (321) 768-0200.

Minor League Clubs
Complex Address: Carl Barger Baseball Complex, 5600 Stadium Pkwy., Viera, FL 32940. Telephone: (321) 633-8119. FAX: (321) 633-9216. **Hotel Address:** Holiday Inn Cocoa Beach Resort, 1300 N Atlantic Ave., Cocoa Beach, FL 32931. Telephone: (407) 783-2271.

HOUSTON ASTROS
Major League Club
Complex Address (first year): Osceola County Stadium (1985), 1000 Bill Beck Blvd., Kissimmee, FL 34744. Telephone: (407) 933-6500. FAX: (407) 933-0385. **Seating Capacity:** 5,130.

Minor League Clubs
Complex Address: Same as major league club. Telephone: (407) 933-5500. FAX: (407) 847-6237. **Hotel Address:** Holiday Inn-Kissimmee, 2009 West Vine St. (U.S. 192), Kissimmee, FL 34741. Telephone: (407) 846-2713.

KANSAS CITY ROYALS
Major League Club
Complex Address (first year): Baseball City Sports Complex (1988), 300 Stadium Way, Davenport, FL 33837. Telephone: (941) 424-7211. FAX: (941) 424-5611. **Seating Capacity:** 8,000.

Hotel Address: Hampton Inn, 5530 U.S. Hwy. 27 N, Davenport, FL 33837. Telephone: (941) 420-9898.

Minor League Clubs
Complex/Hotel Address: Same as major league club.

LOS ANGELES DODGERS
Major League Club
Complex Address (first year): Holman Stadium (1948). **Seating Capacity:** 6,500.

Hotel Address: Dodgertown, 4001 26th St., Vero Beach, FL 32960. Telephone: (561) 569-4900. FAX: (561) 567-0819.

Minor League Clubs
Complex/Hotel Address: Same as major league club.

MINNESOTA TWINS
Major League Club
...plex Address (first year): Lee County Sports Complex/Hammond ... (1991), 14100 Six Mile Cypress Pkwy., Fort Myers, FL 33912. ...: (941) 768-4282. FAX: (941) 768-4211. **Seating Capacity:** 7,500. ...ddress: Radisson Inn, 12635 Cleveland Ave., Fort Myers, FL ...phone: (941) 936-4300.

Minor League Clubs
...ddress: Lee County Sports Complex, 14200 Six Mile ... Fort Myers, FL 33912. Telephone: (941) 768-4282. FAX: ...Hotel Address:** Same as major league club.

MONTREAL EXPOS
Major League Club
Complex Address (first year): Roger Dean Stadium (1998), 4657 Main St., Jupiter, FL 33458. Telephone: (561) 775-1818. **Seating Capacity:** 7,000.

Hotel Address: Doubletree Hotel, 4431 PGA Blvd. at I-95, Palm Beach Gardens, FL 33403. Telephone: (561) 622-2260.
Minor League Clubs
Complex Address: Same as major league club. **Hotel Address:** Holiday Inn Express, 13950 U.S. Hwy. 1, Juno Beach, FL 33409. Telephone: (561) 622-4366.

NEW YORK METS
Major League Club
Complex Address (first year): St. Lucie Sports Complex (1987), 525 NW Peacock Blvd., Port St. Lucie, FL 34986. Telephone: (561) 871-2100. FAX: (561) 878-9802. **Seating Capacity:** 7,347.

Hotel Address: Holiday Inn, 10120 S Federal Hwy., Port St. Lucie, FL 34952. Telephone: (561) 337-2200.
Minor League Clubs
Complex/Hotel Address: Same as major league club. Telephone: (561) 871-2152.

NEW YORK YANKEES
Major League Club
Complex Address (first year): Legends Field (1996), One Steinbrenner Dr., Tampa, FL 33614. Telephone: (813) 875-7753. FAX: (813) 673-3199. **Seating Capacity:** 10,000.

Hotel Address: Radisson Bay Harbor Inn, 770 Courtney Campbell Causeway, Tampa, FL 33607. Telephone: (813) 281-8900.
Minor League Clubs
Complex Address: Yankees Minor League Complex, 3102 N Himes Ave., Tampa, FL 33607. Telephone: (813) 875-7569. FAX: (813) 873-2302. **Hotel Address:** Holiday Inn Express, 4732 N Dale Mabry, Tampa, FL 33614.

PHILADELPHIA PHILLIES
Major League Club
Complex Address (first year): Jack Russell Memorial Stadium (1955), 800 Phillies Dr., Clearwater, FL 33755. Telephone: (727) 441-9941. FAX: (727) 461-7768. **Seating Capacity:** 6,917.

Hotel: None.
Minor League Clubs
Complex Address: Carpenter Complex, 651 Old Coachman Rd., Clearwater, FL 33765. Telephone: (727) 799-0503. FAX: (727) 726-1793. **Hotel Addresses:** Hampton Inn, 21030 U.S. Highway 19 North, Clearwater, FL 34625. Telephone: (727) 797-8173; Econolodge, 21252 U.S. Highway 19, Clearwater, FL 34625. Telephone: (727) 799-1569.

PITTSBURGH PIRATES
Major League Club
Stadium Address (first year): McKechnie Field (1969), 17th Ave. W and Ninth St. W, Bradenton, FL 34205. **Seating Capacity:** 6,562.

Complex/Hotel Address: Pirate City, Roberto Clemente Memorial Drive, 1701 27th St. E, Bradenton, FL 34208. Telephone: (941) 747-3031. FAX: (941) 747-9549.
Minor League Clubs
Complex/Hotel Address: Same as major league club.

ST. LOUIS CARDINALS
Major League Club
Stadium Address (first year): Roger Dean Stadium (1998), 4751 Main St., Jupiter, FL 33458. **Seating Capacity:** 6,871. **Complex Address:** Cardinals Complex, 4795 Main St., Jupiter, FL 33458. Telephone: (561) 775-1818. FAX: (561) 630-1830.

Hotel Address: Palm Beach Gardens Marriott, 4000 RCA Blvd., Palm Beach Gardens, FL 33410. Telephone: (561) 622-8888.
Minor League Clubs
Complex: Same as major league club. **Hotel:** Doubletree Hotel, PGA Blvd., Palm Beach Gardens, FL 33410. Telephone: (561) 622-

TAMPA BAY DEVIL RAYS
Major League Club
Stadium Address (first year): Florida Power Park, Al L (1998), 180 Second Ave. SE, St. Petersburg, FL 33701. Teleph 344-1306. FAX: (813) 334-1905. **Seating Capacity:** 6,436

Address: Devil Rays Spring Training Complex, 7901 30th Ave. N, St. Petersburg, FL 33710. Telephone: (727) 825-3042.

Hotel Address: St. Petersburg Bayfront Hilton, 333 First St. S, St. Petersburg, FL 33705. Telephone: (727) 894-5000.

Minor League Clubs

Complex/Hotel Address: Same as major league club.

TEXAS RANGERS
Major League Club

Complex Address (first year): Charlotte County Stadium (1987), 2300 El Jobean Rd., Port Charlotte, FL 33948. Telephone: (941) 625-9500. FAX: (941) 624-5168. **Seating Capacity:** 6,026.

Hotel Address: Days Inn, 1941 Tamiami Trail, Murdock, FL 33938. Telephone: (941) 627-8900.

Minor League Clubs

Complex/Hotel Address: Same as major league club.

TORONTO BLUE JAYS
Major League Club

Stadium Address (first year): Dunedin Stadium (1977), 373 Douglas Ave., Dunedin, FL 34697. Telephone: (727) 933-9302. **Seating Capacity:** 6,106. **Complex Address:** Englebert Complex, 1700 Solon Ave., Dunedin, FL 34697. Telephone: (727) 733-3339. FAX: (727) 733-9389.

Hotel: None.

Minor League Clubs

Complex Address: Same as major league club. **Hotel Address:** Red Roof Inn, 3200 U.S. 19 N, Clearwater, FL 34684. Telephone: (727) 786-2529.

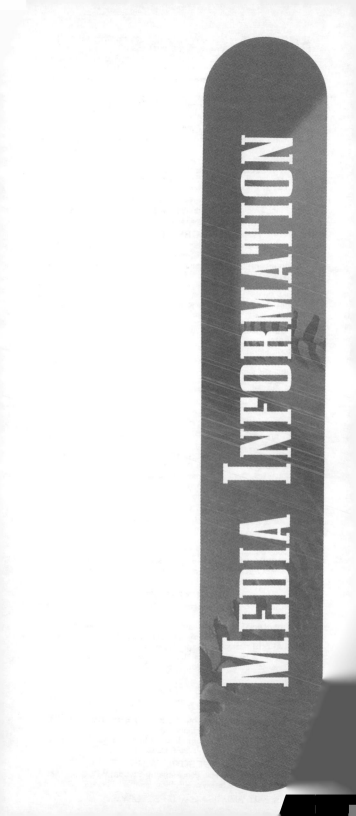

MEDIA INFORMATION

MEDIA INFORMATION

American League

ANAHEIM ANGELS

Radio Announcers: Mario Impemba, Daron Sutton. **Flagship Station:** KLAC 570-AM.

TV Announcers: Rex Hudler, Steve Physioc. **Flagship Stations:** KCAL Channel 9, Fox Sports Net (regional cable).

NEWSPAPERS, Daily Coverage (beat writers): Long Beach Press Telegram, Los Angeles Times (Tim Brown, Mike DiGiovanna, Ross Newhan, Bill Shaikin), Orange County Register (Earl Bloom, Cheryl Rosenberg), Riverside Press Enterprise (Gordon Wittenmyer), San Gabriel Valley Tribune (Joe Haakenson), Inland Valley Daily Bulletin (Lance Pugmire).

BALTIMORE ORIOLES

Radio Announcers: Jim Hunter, Fred Manfra. **Flagship Station:** WBAL 1090-AM.

TV Announcers: Mike Flanagan, Jim Palmer, Michael Reghi. **Flagship Stations:** WJZ-TV, WNUV-TV, Home Team Sports (regional cable).

NEWSPAPERS, Daily Coverage (beat writers): Baltimore Sun (Roch Kubatko, Joe Strauss), Washington Post (Dave Sheinin), Washington Times (Brooke Tunstall), York (Pa.) Daily Record (Dave Buscema).

BOSTON RED SOX

Radio Announcers: Joe Castiglione, Jerry Trupiano. **Flagship Station:** WEEI 850-AM.

TV Announcers: Fox—Sean McDonough, Jerry Remy; NESN—Bob Kurtz, Jerry Remy. **Flagship Stations:** FOX-25, New England Sports Network (regional cable).

NEWSPAPERS, Daily Coverage (beat writers): Boston Globe (Gordon Edes), Boston Herald (Tony Massarotti), Providence Journal (Steve Krasner, Sean McAdam), Worcester Telegram (Bill Ballou, Phil O'Neill), Hartford Courant (Paul Doyle, Dave Heuschkel).

CHICAGO WHITE SOX

Radio Announcers: John Rooney, Ed Farmer. **Flagship Station:** WMVP/ESPN Radio 1000-AM.

TV Announcers: Ken Harrelson, Darrin Jackson. **Flagship Stations:** WGN TV-9, WCIU-TV, Fox Sports Chicago (regional cable).

NEWSPAPERS, Daily Coverage (beat writers): Chicago Sun-Times (Joe Goddard), Chicago Tribune (Paul Sullivan), Arlington Heights Daily Herald (Scot Gregor), Daily Southtown (Joe Cowley).

CLEVELAND INDIANS

Radio Announcers: Tom Hamilton, Mike Hegan, Matt Underwood. **Flagship Station:** WTAM 1100-AM.

TV Announcers: WUAB—Jack Corrigan, Mike Hegan. FOX—Rick Manning, John Sanders. **Flagship Stations:** WUAB-TV 43, Fox Sports Net.

NEWSPAPERS, Daily Coverage (beat writers): Cleveland Plain Dealer (Paul Hoynes), Lake County News-Herald (Jim Ingraham), Akron Beacon-Journal (Sheldon Ocker).

DETROIT TIGERS

Radio Announcers: Ernie Harwell, Jim Price, Dan Dickerson. **Flagship Station:** WJR 760-AM.

TV Announcers: Frank Beckmann, Al Kaline, Kirk Gibson, Josh Lewin. **Flagship Stations:** WKBD 50, Fox Sports Net Detroit (regional cable).

NEWSPAPERS, Daily Coverage (beat writers): Detroit Free Press (John Lowe, Gene Guidi), Detroit News (Tom Gage), Oakland Press (Pat Caputo, Steve Kornacki), Booth Newspapers (Danny Knobler), Windsor Star (Dave Hall).

KANSAS CITY ROYALS

Radio Announcers: Ryan Lefebvre, Denny Matthews. **Flagship Station:** KMBZ 980-AM.

TV Announcers: Bob Davis, Paul Splittorff. **Flagship Stations:** KMBC-CWE-29, Fox Sports Net (regional cable).

NEWSPAPERS, Daily Coverage (beat writers): Kansas City Star (Dick), Topeka Capital Journal (Alan Eskew).

MINNESOTA TWINS

Announcer: John Gordon. **Flagship Station:** WCCO 830-AM. **Announcers:** Bert Blyleven, Dick Bremer. **Flagship Stations:**

KMSP-TV, Midwest SportsChannel (regional cable).

NEWSPAPERS, Daily Coverage (beat writers): St. Paul Pioneer Press, Star Tribune (La Velle Neal).

NEW YORK YANKEES

Radio Announcers: Michael Kay, John Sterling. **Flagship Station:** WABC 770-AM.

TV Announcers: Tim McCarver, Jim Kaat, Michael Kay, Bobby Murcer, Ken Singleton, Al Trautwig, Suzyn Waldman. **Flagship Stations:** WNYW-TV, Madison Square Garden Network (regional cable).

NEWSPAPERS, Daily Coverage (beat writers): New York Daily News (Anthony McCarron), New York Post (George King), New York Times (Buster Olney), Newark Star-Ledger (Dan Graziano), The Bergen Record (Ken Davidoff), Newsday (Larry Rocca), Hartford Courant (Dom Amore), The Journal News (John Delcos).

OAKLAND ATHLETICS

Radio Announcers: Bill King, Ray Fosse, Ken Korach. **Flagship Station:** KABL 960-AM.

TV Announcers: Ray Fosse, Greg Papa. **Flagship Stations:** KICU, Fox Sports Net (regional cable).

NEWSPAPERS, Daily Coverage (beat writers): San Francisco Chronicle (Susan Slusser), Oakland Tribune (Mark Saxon), Contra Costa Times (Gary Washburn), Sacramento Bee, San Francisco Examiner (Brian Murphy), San Jose Mercury-News (Howard Bryant).

SEATTLE MARINERS

TV/Radio Announcers: Dave Henderson, Dave Niehaus, Ron Fairly, Rick Rizzs, Dave Valle. **Flagship Stations (radio):** KIRO 710-AM, **(TV):** KIRO Channel 7, Fox Sports Net Northwest (regional cable).

NEWSPAPERS, Daily Coverage (beat writers): Seattle Times (Bob Finnegan), Seattle Post-Intelligencer (John Hickey), Tacoma News Tribune (Larry LaRue).

TAMPA BAY DEVIL RAYS

Radio Announcers: Paul Olden, Charlie Slowes. **Flagship Station:** WFLA 970-AM.

TV Announcer: DeWayne Staats. **Flagship Stations:** WWWB-TV 32, WTSP-TV 10, SportsChannel Florida (regional cable).

NEWSPAPERS, Daily Coverage (beat writers): St. Petersburg Times (Marc Topkin), Tampa Tribune (Bill Chastain), Bradenton Herald (Roger Mooney), Charlotte Sun-Herald (Pat Obig), Lakeland Ledger (Pat Zier), Sarasota Herald Tribune (Chris Anderson).

TEXAS RANGERS

Radio Announcers: Eric Nadel, Vince Cotroneo. **Flagship Station:** KRLD 1080-AM. **TV Announcers:** Bill Jones, Tom Grieve. **Flagship Stations:** KXAS, KXTX, Fox Sports Southwest (regional cable)

NEWSPAPERS, Daily Coverage (beat writers): Dallas Morning News (Gerry Fraley, Evan Grant), Fort Worth Star-Telegram (T.R. Sullivan), Arlington Morning News (Todd Wills).

TORONTO BLUE JAYS

Radio Announcers: Tom Cheek, Jerry Howarth, Gary Matthews. **Flagship Station:** CHUM 1050-AM.

TV Announcers: CBC—Brian Williams, John Cerutti; TSN—Buck Martinez, Dan Shulman; CTV—Rod Black, Joe Carter. **Flagship Stations:** CBC, The Sports Network (cable), CTV Sports Net (cable).

NEWSPAPERS, Daily Coverage (beat writers): Toronto Sun (Mike Rutsey, Bob Elliott, Mike Ganter), Toronto Star (Geoff Baker, Richard Griffin, Alan Ryan), Globe and Mail (Larry Millson), Southam News (Tom Maloney).

National League

ARIZONA DIAMONDBACKS

Radio Announcers: English—Thom Brennaman, Greg Schulte, Rod Allen; Spanish—Miguel Quintana, Oscar Soria. **Flagship Stations:** KTAR 620-AM, KPHX 1480-AM (Spanish).

TV Announcers: Thom Brennaman, Greg Schulte, Bob Brenly. **Flagship Stations:** KTVK-TV 3, Fox Sports Arizona (regional cable). **Spanish TV Announcers:** Miguel Quintana, Oscar Soria. **Spanish Flagship Station:** KDR-TV 64.

Newspapers, Daily Coverage (beat writers): Arizona Republic (Mark Gonzales), Tribune Newspapers (Ed Price), Arizona Star (Jack Magruder), Tucson Citizen (Chris Walsh).

ATLANTA BRAVES

Radio Announcers: Skip Caray, Don Sutton, Joe Simpson, Pete Wieren. **Flagship Station:** WSB 750-AM.

TV Announcers: TBS—Skip Caray, Pete Van Wieren, Don Sutton, Joe Simpson. Fox Sports Net—Bob Rathbun. **Flagship Stations:** TBS Channel 17 (national cable), Fox Sports Net, Turner South (regional cable).

NEWSPAPERS, Daily Coverage (beat writers): Atlanta Journal-Constitution (Carroll Rogers), Morris News Service (Bill Zack).

CHICAGO CUBS

Radio Announcers: Pat Hughes, Ron Santo. **Flagship Station:** WGN 720-AM.

TV Announcers: Chip Caray, Steve Stone. **Flagship Stations:** WGN Channel 9 (national cable), Fox Sports Net Chicago (regional cable), WCIU-TV Channel 26 (local).

NEWSPAPERS, Daily Coverage (beat writers): Chicago Tribune (Teddy Greenstein, Phil Rogers), Chicago Sun-Times (Mike Kiley, Dave Van Dyck), Arlington Heights Daily Herald (Bruce Miles).

CINCINNATI REDS

Radio Announcers: Marty Brennaman, Joe Nuxhall. **Flagship Station:** WLW 700-AM.

TV Announcers: George Grande, Chris Welsh. **Flagship Station:** Fox Sports Ohio (regional cable).

Newspapers, Daily Coverage (beat writers): Cincinnati Enquirer (Chris Haft), Cincinnati Post (Jeff Horrigan), Dayton Daily News (Hal McCoy).

COLORADO ROCKIES

Radio Announcers: Wayne Hagin, Jeff Kingery. **Flagship Station:** KOA 850-AM.

TV Announcers: Dave Armstrong, George Frazier. **Flagship Station:** KWGN-TV Channel 2, Fox Sports Net (regional cable).

NEWSPAPERS, Daily Coverage (beat writers): Rocky Mountain News (Tracy Ringolsby, Jack Etkin), Denver Post (Mike Klis, John Henderson), Boulder Daily Camera (Barney Hutchinson), Colorado Springs Gazette (Ray McNulty).

FLORIDA MARLINS

Radio Announcers: Joe Angel, Dave O'Brien, Jon Sciambi, Felo Ramirez (Spanish). **Flagship Stations:** WQAM 560-AM, WQBA 1140-AM (Spanish).

TV Announcers: Joe Angel, Dave O'Brien, Tommy Hutton. **Flagship Stations:** WAMI Channel 69, Fox Sports Net (regional cable).

NEWSPAPERS, Daily Coverage (beat writers): Miami Herald (Mike Phillips, Clark Spencer), Fort Lauderdale Sun-Sentinel (Mike Berardino, David O'Brien), Palm Beach Post (Joe Capozzi), Florida Today. Spanish—El Nuevo Herald (Aurelio Moreno).

HOUSTON ASTROS

Radio Announcers: Alan Ashby, Bill Brown, Milo Hamilton. **Flagship Station:** KTRH 740-AM.

TV Announcers: Bill Brown, Jim Deshaies, Milo Hamilton, Bill Worrell. **Flagship Stations:** KNWS, Fox Sports Net (regional cable).

NEWSPAPERS, Daily Coverage (beat writers): Houston Chronicle (Joseph Duarte, Carlton Thompson), Beaumont Enterprise (Kenton Brooks).

LOS ANGELES DODGERS

Radio Announcers: English—Vin Scully, Rick Monday, Ross Porter; Spanish—Jaime Jarrin, Pepe Yniguez. **Flagship Stations:** XTRA 1150-AM, KWKW 1330-AM (Spanish).

TV Announcers: Vin Scully, Rick Monday, Ross Porter. **Flagship Station:** KTLA Channel 5, Fox Sports Net 2 (regional cable).

NEWSPAPERS, Daily Coverage (beat writers): Los Angeles Times (Ross Newhan, Jason Reid), South Bay Daily Breeze (Bill Cizek), Los Angeles Daily News (Brian Dohn), Orange County Register (Robert Kuwada), Riverside Press Enterprise (Joe Christensen).

MILWAUKEE BREWERS

Radio Announcers: Bob Uecker, Jim Powell. **Flagship Station:** WTMJ 620-AM.

TV Announcers: Bill Schroeder, Matt Vasgersian. **Flagship Station:** WCGV Channel 24, Midwest Sports Channel (regional cable).

NEWSPAPERS, Daily Coverage (beat writers): Milwaukee Journal Sentinel (Tom Haudricourt, Drew Olson).

MONTREAL EXPOS

Radio Announcers: English—Dave Van Horne, Elliott Price, Joe ᴣnnon; French—Jacques Doucet, Rodger Brulotte, Alain Chantelois. **ᴣʰip Stations:** CIQC 600-AM, CKAC 730-AM (French).

ᵛ Announcers: Dave Van Horne, Gary Carter; SRC/French—Rene ᵉr, Claude Raymond; RDS/French—Denis Casavant, Rodger Brulotte.

Flagship Stations: The Sports Network (national cable); French—Societe Radio Canada.

NEWSPAPERS, Daily Coverage (beat writers): English—Montreal Gazette (Stephanie Myles, Jack Todd, Pat Hickey). French—Canadian Press (Michel Lajeunesse, Richard Milo), La Presse (Alexandre Pratt, Pierre Ladouceur), Le Journal de Montreal (Serge Touchette, Daniel Cloutier).

NEW YORK METS

Radio Announcers: Gary Cohen, Ed Coleman, Bob Murphy. **Flagship Station:** WFAN 660-AM.

TV Announcers: Fran Healy, Ralph Kiner, Matt Loughlin, Howie Rose, Tom Seaver, Gary Thorne. **Flagship Stations:** WPIX-TV, Fox Sports New York (regional cable).

NEWSPAPERS, Daily Coverage (beat writers): New York Times (Tyler Kepner), New York Daily News (Rafael Hermoso), New York Post (Dave Waldstein), Newsday (Marty Noble), Newark Star-Ledger (Jose Ortiz), The Bergen Record (T.J. Quinn), The News Journal (Kit Stier).

PHILADELPHIA PHILLIES

Radio Announcers: Larry Andersen, Scott Graham, Harry Kalas, Andy Musser, Chris Wheeler. **Flagship Station:** WPHT 1210-AM.

TV Announcers: Larry Andersen, Harry Kalas, Chris Wheeler. **Flagship Stations:** WPSG UPN Channel 57, Comcast SportsNet (regional cable).

NEWSPAPERS, Daily Coverage (beat writer): Philadelphia Inquirer (Jim Salisbury, Jayson Stark), Philadelphia Daily News (Paul Hagen), Bucks County Courier-Times (Randy Miller), Camden Courier Post (Kevin Roberts), Delaware County Times (Bob Brookover), Wilmington News-Journal (Doug Lesmerises), Trenton Times (Chris Edwards).

PITTSBURGH PIRATES

Radio Announcers: Steve Blass, Greg Brown, Lanny Frattare, Bob Walk. **Flagship Station:** KDKA 1020-AM.

TV Announcers: Steve Blass, Greg Brown, Lanny Frattare, Bob Walk. **Flagship Station:** Fox Sports Net Pittsburgh (regional cable).

NEWSPAPERS, Daily Coverage (beat writers): Pittsburgh Post-Gazette (Paul Meyer), Pittsburgh Tribune-Review (Joe Rutter), Beaver County Times (John Perrotto).

ST. LOUIS CARDINALS

Radio Announcers: Jack Buck, Joe Buck, Mike Shannon. **Flagship Station:** KMOX 1120-AM.

TV Announcers: Bob Carpenter, Al Hrabosky, Ozzie Smith. **Flagship Stations:** KPLR Channel 11, Fox Sports Midwest (regional cable).

NEWSPAPER, Daily Coverage (beat writers): St. Louis Post-Dispatch (Rick Hummel).

SAN DIEGO PADRES

Radio Announcers: Jerry Coleman, Ted Leitner. **Flagship Stations:** KOGO 600-AM.

TV Announcers: Mel Proctor, Rick Sutcliffe, Mark Grant. **Flagship Stations:** KUSI TV-9/51, Channel 4 Padres (regional cable).

NEWSPAPERS, Daily Coverage (beat writers): San Diego Union-Tribune (Bill Center, Tom Krasovic), North County Times (Shaun O'Neill, John Maffei).

SAN FRANCISCO GIANTS

Radio Announcers: Mike Krukow, Duane Kuiper, Jon Miller, Ted Robinson, Lon Simmons. **Flagship Station:** KNBR 680-AM.

TV Announcers: Fox—Jon Miller, Duane Kuiper. KTVU—Mike Krukow, Ted Robinson, Lon Simmons, Jon Miller. **Flagship Stations:** KTVU-TV 2, Fox Sports Net (regional cable).

NEWSPAPERS, Daily Coverage (beat writers): San Francisco Chronicle (Henry Schulman), San Francisco Examiner (John Shea), San Jose Mercury News, Contra Costa Times (Joe Roderick), Sacramento Bee (Nick Peters), Oakland Tribune (Mark Saxon), Santa Rosa Press Democrat (Jeff Fletcher).

GENERALINFORMATION

BASEBALL STATISTICS

ELIAS SPORTS BUREAU INC.
Official Major League Statistician

Mailing Address: 500 Fifth Ave., New York, NY 10110. **Telephone:** (212) 869-1530. **FAX:** (212) 354-0980.

President: Seymour Siwoff.

Executive Vice President: Steve Hirdt. **Vice President:** Peter Hirdt. **Data Processing Manager:** Chris Thorn.

HOWE SPORTSDATA
(A service of SportsTicker, LP)
Official Minor League Statistician

Mailing Address: Boston Fish Pier, West Bldg. #1, Suite 302, Boston, MA 02210. **Telephone:** (617) 951-0070. **Stats Service:** (617) 951-1379. **FAX:** (617) 737-9960.

President/General Manager: Jay Virshbo.

Assistant General Manager: Jim Keller. **Programmer/Analysts:** John Foley, Walter Kent, Vin Vitro. **Senior Bureau Managers:** Brian Joura, Paul LaRocca, Michael Walczak. **Bureau Managers:** Bob Chaban, Tom Graham. **Associate Bureau Managers:** Joe Barbieri, Matt Bruce, Don Goss, Matt Santillo, Marshall Wright.

Historical Consultant: Bill Weiss.

STATS, Inc.

Mailing Address: 8130 Lehigh Ave., Morton Grove, IL 60053. **Telephone:** (847) 677-3322. **FAX:** (847) 470-9160. **Website:** www.stats.com.

Chief Executive Officer: John Dewan.

President: Alan Leib. **Vice President, Research/Development:** Susan Dewan. **Vice President, Special Projects:** Robert Meyerhoff. **Vice President, Commercial Products:** Vincent Smith. **Vice President, Publishing Products:** Don Zminda. **Vice President, Interactive Products:** Michael Canter. **Vice President, Fantasy Sports:** Steve Byrd. **Vice President, Sports Operations:** Allan Spear. **Senior Vice President, Sales:** Jim Capuano. **Vice President, Systems:** Arthur Ashley. **Director, Major League Operations:** Craig Wright.

TELEVISION NETWORKS

ESPN/ESPN2

- Baseball Tonight
- Sunday Night Baseball
- Wednesday Night Doubleheaders
- Division Series

Mailing Address, Connecticut Office: ESPN Plaza, Bristol, CT 06010. **Telephone:** (860) 766-2000. **FAX:** (860) 766-2213.

Mailing Address, New York Office: 605 Third Ave., New York, NY 10158. **Telephone:** (212) 916-9200. **FAX:** (212) 916-9312. **Executive Offices:** 77 W 66th St., New York, NY 10023. **Telephone:** (212) 456-7777. **FAX:** (212) 456-2930.

Website: www.espn.go.com.

President: George Bodenheimer.

Executive Vice President, Administration: Ed Durso. **Executive Vice President, Production/Technical Operations:** Steve Anderson. **Senior Vice President/Executive Editor:** John Walsh. **Senior Vice President, Programming:** John Wildhack. **Vice President, Programming:** Steve Risser. **Manager, Programming:** Mike Ryan. **Vice President, Remote Production:** Jed Drake. **Coordinating Producer:** Tim Scanlan. **Vice President, Managing Editor/Studio Production:** Bob Eaton. **Assistant Managing Editor/News Director:** Norby Williamson. **Coordinating Producer, Baseball Tonight/Studio:** Jeff Schneider. **Executive Editor, espn.com.:** John Marvel.

Senior Vice President, Communications: Rosa Gatti. **Vice President, Communications:** Chris LaPlaca. **Manager, Communications:** Diane Lamb. **Senior Publicist:** Dave Nagle.

Sunday Night Telecasts: Play-by-play—Jon Miller. Analyst—Joe Morgan.

Studio Hosts: Chris Berman, Karl Ravech. **Studio Analysts:** Peter Gammons, Ray Knight, Tim Kurkjian, Harold Reynolds, Jayson Stark.

Play-by-Play Announcers: Dave Barnett, Bob Carpenter, Dan Shulman, Charley Steiner, Gary Thorne. **Analysts:** Dave Campbell, Rob Dibble, Buck Martinez, Rick Sutcliffe.

ESPN Classic
Vice President, General Manager: Mark Shapiro. **Executive Producer:** Vince Doria.

ESPN International
Senior Vice President, Managing Director: Willy Burkhardt. **Senior Vice President:** Minard Hamilton.

FOX SPORTS

- *Saturday Game of the Week*
- *Division Series*
- *National League Championship Series*
- *World Series*

Mailing Address, Los Angeles: Fox Nework Center, Building 101, 10201 W Pico Blvd., Los Angeles, CA 90035. **Telephone:** (310) 369-6000. **FAX:** (310) 969-6192.

Mailing Address, New York: 1211 Avenue of the Americas, 2nd Floor, New York, NY 10036. **Telephone:** (212) 556-2500. **FAX:** (212) 354-6902.

President: David Hill. **Executive Producer:** Ed Goren. **Senior Coordinating Producer, Major League Baseball:** John Filippelli. **Senior Producer:** Bill Brown. **Vice President, Media Relations:** Lou D'Ermilio. **Manager, Media Relations:** Dan Bell.

Play-by-Play Announcers (Analysts): Thom Brennaman (Bob Brenly), Joe Buck (Tim McCarver), Kenny Albert (Jeff Torborg), Josh Lewin (George Brett/Frank Robinson).

FOX SPORTS NET

- *Baseball Thursday (Game of the Week)*

Mailing Address: 10201 W Pico Blvd., Building 101, Los Angeles, CA 90035. **Telephone:** (310) 369-6000. **FAX:** (310) 969-6122.

Chairman, Chief Executive Officer: David Hill.
Chief Operating Officer: Tracy Dolgin. **Executive Vice President, Programming/Production:** Arthur Smith. **Executive Vice President/Chief Executive Officer, Regional Networks:** Bob Thompson.

Managers, Media Relations: Dennis Johnson, Greg Phillips.

FX

- *Saturday Night Game of the Week*

Mailing Address: 1440 S Sepulveda Blvd., Suite 398, Los Angeles, CA 90025. **Telephone:** (310) 444-8183. **FAX:** (310) 235-2853.

President: Peter Liquori. **Vice President:** Steve Webster.

NBC SPORTS

- *All-Star Game*
- *Division Series*
- *American League Championship Series*

Mailing Address: 30 Rockefeller Plaza, Suite 1558, New York, NY 10112. **Telephone:** (212) 664-4444. **FAX:** (212) 664-3602.

Chairman, NBC Sports: Dick Ebersol. **President, NBC Sports:** Ken Schanzer.

Vice President, Sports Information/Special Projects: Ed Markey.
Play-by-Play Announcer: Bob Costas. **Analyst:** Joe Morgan.

Other Television Networks

ABC SPORTS

Mailing Address: 47 West 66th St., New York, NY 10023. **Telephone:** (212) 456-7777. **FAX:** (212) 456-2877. **Website:** www.abcsports.com.

President, ABC Sports: Steve Bornstein. **Executive Vice President/General Manager:** Brian McAndrews. **Vice President, Media Relations:** Mark Mandel.

CBS SPORTS

Mailing Address: 51 W 52nd St., New York, NY 10019. **Telephone:** (212) 975-5230. **FAX:** (212) 975-4063.

President, CBS Sports: Sean McManus. **Executive Producer:** Terry Ewart. **Vice President, Communications:** Leslie Anne Wade.

CNN/SPORTS ILLUSTRATED

Mailing Address: One CNN Center, 3 North Tower, Atlanta, GA 30303. **Telephone:** (404) 878-1600. **FAX:** (404) 878-0011. **Website:** www.cnnsi.com.

President: Jim Walton.
Managing Editor: Steve Robinson. **Coordinating Producers:** Greg Agvent, Tony Florkowski, Bill Galvin, Gus Lalone, Sandy Malcolm, Howar

Sappington. **Assignment Manager:** Tony Lamb. **Publicist:** Amy Sasser.

CTV and CTV Sportsnet (Canada)

Mailing Address: 9 Channel Nine Court, Scarborough, Ontario M1S 4B5. **Telephone:** (416) 332-5600. **FAX:** (416) 332-5629.

Senior Vice President/General Manager: Suzanne Steeves. **Vice President/Managing Director:** Doug Beeforth. **Vice President, Production:** Scott Moore. **Manager, Communications:** David Rashford.

Play-by-Play Announcers: Rod Black, Rob Faulds.

THE SPORTS NETWORK (Canada)

Mailing Address: 2225 Sheppard Ave. E, Suite 100, North York, Ontario M2J 5C2. **Telephone:** (416) 494-1212. **FAX:** (416) 490-7010. **Website:** www.tsn.ca. **Telephone, Sports Desk:** (416) 490-7380. **FAX, Sports Desk:** (416) 490-7032.

President/General Manager: Rick Brace. **Senior Vice President, Programming/Production:** Keith Pelley. **Executive Producer, Baseball:** Rick Briggs-Jude. **Executive Producer, News/Information:** Mike Day.

Commentators: Dan Shulman (Blue Jays), Dave Van Horne (Expos). **Analysts:** Buck Martinez (Blue Jays), Gary Carter (Expos).

Baseball Today/Tonight: Dave Hodge/Vic Rauter (hosts), Pat Tabler (analyst).

Superstations

TBS

(Atlanta Braves)

Mailing Address: 1050 Techwood Dr. NW, Atlanta, GA 30318. **Telephone:** (404) 827-1700. **FAX:** (404) 827-1593. **Website:** www.tbssuperstation.com.

Executive Producer: Glenn Diamond.

WGN

(Chicago Cubs, Chicago White Sox)

Mailing Address: 2501 W Bradley Pl., Chicago, IL 60618. **Telephone:** (773) 528-2311. **FAX:** (773) 528-6050. **Website:** www.wgntv.com.

RADIO NETWORKS

ESPN RADIO

- ■ *All-Star Game*
- ■ *All postseason games*
- ■ *Sunday Night Game of the Week*

Mailing Address: ESPN Plaza, Bristol, CT 06010. **Telephone:** (860) 766-2661. **FAX:** (860) 766-5523.

General Manager: Eric Schoenfeld. **Assistant General Manager/Program Director:** Len Weiner. **Executive Producer:** John Martin.

ABC RADIO NETWORK SPORTS

Mailing Address: 125 West End Ave., 6th Floor, New York, NY 10023. **Telephone:** (212) 456-5185. **FAX:** (212) 456-5405. **Website:** www.abcradio.com.

Vice Presidents: Bernard Gershon, Chris Berry. **Director, Sports/Executive Producer:** Mike Rizzo.

ONE-ON-ONE SPORTS RADIO NETWORK

Mailing Address: 1935 Techny Rd., Suite 18, Northbrook, IL 60062. **Telephone:** (847) 509-1661. **Guest Line:** (800) 224-2004. **FAX:** (847) 509-8149. **Website:** www.oneononesports.com.

President: Chris Brennan. **Chief Financial Officer:** John Drain. **Vice President, Programming:** Mark Gentzkow.

SPORTS BYLINE USA

Mailing Address: 300 Broadway, Suite 8, San Francisco, CA 94133. **Telephone:** (415) 434-8300. **Guest Line:** (800) 878-7529. **Studio Line:** (800) 358-4457. **FAX:** (415) 391-2569. **E-Mail Address:** byline@pacbell.net. **Website:** www.sportsbyline.com.

President: Darren Peck. **Executive Producer:** Ed Gorelick. **Senior Producer:** Alex Murillo.

SPORTSFAN RADIO NETWORK

Mailing Address: 1455 E Tropicana Ave., Suite 250, Las Vegas, NV 89119. **Telephone:** (800) 895-1022, (702) 740-4240. **FAX:** (702) 740-4171. **Website:** www.sportsfanradio.com.

Program Director: Ryan Williams. **Producers:** Nick Pavlatos, John Thornquist.

ASSOCIATED PRESS

Mailing Address: 50 Rockefeller Plaza, New York, NY 10020. **Telephone:** (212) 621-1630. **FAX:** (212) 621-1639. **Website:** www.ap.org.
Sports Editor: Terry Taylor. **Deputy Sports Editor:** Brian Friedman. **Assistant Sports Editor:** Aaron Watson. **Agate Editor:** Paul Montella. **Sports Photo Editor:** Brian Horton. **Baseball Writers:** Ron Blum, Josh Dubow, Ben Walker.

BLOOMBERG SPORTS NEWS

Mailing Address: P.O. Box 888, Princeton, NJ 08542. **Telephone:** (609) 279-4058. **FAX:** (609) 279-5878.
Sports Editor: Jay Beberman. **Deputy Sports Editor:** Mike Sillup. **National Baseball Writer:** Jerry Crasnick.

ESPN/SPORTSTICKER

Mailing Address: Harborside Financial Center, 800 Plaza Two, 8th Floor, Jersey City, NJ 07311. **Telephone:** (201) 309-1200. **FAX:** (800) 336-0383, (201) 860-9742. **E-Mail Address:** newsroom@sportsticker.com.
Vice President, General Manager: Rick Alessandri. **Executive Director:** Jim Morganthaler. **General Manager, News:** John Mastroberardino. **Senior Editor, Major League Baseball:** Doug Mittler. **Director, Publicity/Marketing/Newsroom Services:** Lou Monaco.

CANADIAN PRESS

Mailing Address: 36 King St. East, Toronto, Ontario M5C 2L9. **Telephone:** (416) 507-2154. **FAX:** (416) 507-2074. **E-Mail Address:** sports @cp.org.
General Sports Editor: Neil Davidson. **Baseball Writers:** Glen Colbourn, Dan Ralph.

BASEBALL WRITERS ASSOCIATION OF AMERICA

Mailing Address: 78 Olive St., Lake Grove, NY 11755. **Telephone:** (631) 981-7938. **FAX:** (631) 585-4669. **E-Mail Address:** bbwaa@aol.com.
President: Charles Scoggins (Lowell, Mass., Sun). **Vice President:** Ian McDonald (Montreal Gazette).
Board of Directors: Bob Elliott (Toronto Sun), Jim Finnigan (Seattle Times), Gerry Fraley (Dallas Morning News), Jeff Horrigan (Cincinnati Post).
Secretary-Treasurer: Jack O'Connell (Hartford Courant). **Assistant Secretary:** Jack Lang (SportsTicker).

NATIONAL ASSOCIATION OF BASEBALL WRITERS AND BROADCASTERS

Mailing Address: P.O. Box A, St. Petersburg, FL 33731. **Telephone:** (727) 822-6937. **FAX:** (727) 821-5819.
Secretary-Treasurer: Jim Ferguson (Minor League Baseball).

NATIONAL COLLEGIATE BASEBALL WRITERS ASSOCIATION

Mailing Address: 35 E Wacker Dr., Suite 650, Chicago, IL 60601. **Telephone:** (312) 553-0483. **FAX:** (312) 553-0495.
Executive Director: Bo Carter (Big 12 Conference).
President: Charles Bloom (Southeastern Conference). **First Vice President:** Russ Anderson (Conference USA). **Second Vice President:** Barry Allen (Alabama). **Third Vice President:** Kip Carlson (Oregon State).
Newsletter Editor: John Askins, Sports Media Group. **Telephone:** (713) 686-0201. **E-Mail Address:** jaskins@sprynet.com.

USA TODAY

Mailing Address: 1000 Wilson Blvd., Arlington, VA 22229. **Telephone/Baseball Desk:** (703) 276-3731, 276-3744, 276-3725. **FAX:** (703) 558-3988. **Website:** www.usatoday.com
Publishing Frequency: Daily (Monday-Friday).
Baseball Editors: John Porter, Denise Tom, John Tkach. **Baseball Columnist:** Hal Bodley. **Baseball Writers:** Mel Antonen, Rod Beaton, Mike Dodd, Chuck Johnson.

THE SPORTING NEWS

Mailing Address: 10176 Corporate Square Dr., Suite 200, St. Louis, MO 63132. **Telephone:** (314) 997-7111. **FAX:** (314) 997-0765. **Website:** www.sportingnews.com.
Publishing Frequency: Weekly.
Editor: John Rawlings. **Executive Editor:** Steve Meyerhoff. **Managing**

Editor: Bob Hille. **Managing Editor/Online:** Barry Reeves. **Senior Writer:** Michael Knisley. **Photo Editor:** Paul Nisely.

SPORTS ILLUSTRATED

Mailing Address: Time & Life Building, 1271 Avenue of the Americas, New York, NY 10020. **Telephone:** (212) 522-1212. **FAX, Editorial:** (212) 522-4543. **FAX, Public Relations:** (212) 522-4832.

Publishing Frequency: Weekly.

Managing Editor: Bill Colson. **Senior Editors:** Dick Friedman, Richard O'Brien. **Senior Writers:** Michael Farber, Tom Verducci. **Staff Writer:** Jeff Pearlman. **Writer-Reporter:** Stephen Canella.

Vice President, Communications: Art Berke.

USA TODAY BASEBALL WEEKLY

Mailing Address: 1000 Wilson Blvd., 21st Floor, Arlington, VA 22229. **Telephone:** (703) 558-5630. **FAX:** (703) 558-4678. **Website:** bbw.usato day.com.

Publishing Frequency: Weekly.

Publisher: Keith Cutler. **Executive Editor:** Lee Ivory. **Deputy Editor:** Tim McQuay. **Deputy Editor/Operations:** Gary Kicinski. **Assignment Editor:** Margaret McCahill. **Editor:** Paul White.

STREET AND SMITH'S
SPORTS BUSINESS JOURNAL

Mailing Address: 120 W. Morehead St., Suite 310, Charlotte, NC 28202. **Telephone:** (704) 973-1400. **Fax:** (704) 973-1401. **Website:** www.sports businessjournal.com.

Publishing Frequency: Weekly.

Publisher: Richard Weiss. **Editor:** John Genzale.

ESPN THE MAGAZINE

Mailing Address: 19 E 34th St., 7th Floor, New York, NY 10016. **Telephone:** (212) 515-1000. **FAX:** (212) 515-1290.

Publishing Frequency: Bi-weekly.

Publisher: Michael Rooney. **Editor:** John Papanek. **Executive Editor:** Steve Wulf. **Senior Editor, Baseball:** Glen Waggoner. **General Editor:** Jeff Bradley. **Senior Writers:** Peter Gammons, Tim Kurkjian. **Senior Reporter:** Brendan O'Connor.

SPORT MAGAZINE

Mailing Address: 110 Fifth Ave., New York, NY 10011. **Telephone:** (212) 880-3600. **FAX:** (212) 229-4838. **E-Mail Address:** sport@ema pusa.com.

Publishing Frequency: Monthly.

Editor: Norb Garrett. **Writer:** David Scott.

BASEBALL DIGEST

Mailing Address: 990 Grove St., Evanston, IL 60201. **Telephone:** (847) 491-6440. **FAX:** (847) 491-6203. **E-Mail Address:** century@wwa.com.

Publishing Frequency: Monthly.

Publisher: Norman Jacobs. **Editor:** John Kuenster. **Managing Editor:** Bob Kuenster.

COLLEGIATE BASEBALL

Mailing Address: P.O. Box 50566, Tucson, AZ 85703. **Telephone:** (520) 623-4530. **FAX:** (520) 624-5501. **E-Mail Address:** editor@baseballnews. com. **Website:** www.baseballnews.com.

Publishing Frequency: Bi-weekly, January-June; September, October.

Publisher: Lou Pavlovich. **Editor:** Lou Pavlovich Jr.

JUNIOR BASEBALL MAGAZINE

Mailing Address: P.O. Box 9099, Canoga Park, CA 91309. **Telephone:** (818) 710-1234. **Customer Service:** (888) 487-2448. **FAX:** (818) 710-1877. **Website:** www.juniorbaseball.com.

Publishing Frequency: Bi-monthly.

Publisher/Editor: Dave Destler.

INTERNATIONAL BASEBALL RUNDOWN

Mailing Address: P.O. Box 608, Glen Ellyn, IL 60138. **Telephone:** (630) 668-8341. **FAX:** (630) 510-1154. **E-Mail Address:** ibrundown@aol.com.

Publishing Frequency: Nine times/year.

Editor: Jeff Elijah.

SPORTS ILLUSTRATED FOR KIDS

Mailing Address: Time & Life Building, Rockefeller Center, New York, NY 10020. **Telephone:** (212) 522-1212. **FAX:** (212) 522-0120. **Website:** www.sikids.com.

Publishing Frequency: Monthly.

Managing Editor: Neil Cohen. **Deputy Managing Editor:** Stephen

Malley.

BASEBALL PARENT
Mailing Address: 4437 Kingston Pike, Suite 2204, Knoxville, TN 37919. **Telephone:** (865) 523-1274. **FAX:** (865) 673-8926. **Website:** www.members.aol.com/baseparent.
   Publishing Frequency: Bi-monthly.
   Publisher/Editor: Wayne Christensen.

Baseball Annuals

ATHLON'S BASEBALL
Mailing Address: 220 25th Ave. N, Suite 200, Nashville, TN 37203. **Telephone:** (615) 327-0747. **FAX:** (615) 327-1149. **E-Mail Address:** athlon@nashville.net.
   Chief Executive Officer: Roger DiSilvestro. **President:** Charles Allen. **Managing Editor:** Charlie Miller. **Senior Editor:** Rob Doster.

STREET AND SMITH'S BASEBALL
Mailing Address: 342 Madison Ave., New York, NY 10017. **Telephone:** (212) 880-8698. **FAX:** (212) 880-4347. **Website:** www.streetandsmiths.com.
   Editor: Gerard Kavanagh.

THE SPORTING NEWS BASEBALL YEARBOOK
Mailing Address: 10176 Corporate Square Dr., Suite 200, St. Louis, MO 63132. **Telephone:** (314) 997-7111. **FAX:** (314) 997-0705.
   Editor: John Rawlings. **Executive Editor:** Steve Meyerhoff. **Managing Editor:** Bob Hille.

SPRING TRAINING BASEBALL YEARBOOK
Mailing Address: Vanguard Sports Publications, P.O. Box 667, Chapel Hill, NC 27514. **Telephone:** (919) 967-2420. **FAX:** (919) 967-6294. **E-Mail Address:** vanguard@interpath.com. **Website:** www.springtrainingmagazine.com.
   Publisher: Merle Thorpe. **Editor:** Myles Friedman.

ULTIMATE SPORTS BASEBALL
Mailing Address: Ultimate Sports Publishing, P.O. Box 75299, Seattle, WA 98125. **Telephone:** (206) 301-9466. **FAX:** (206) 301-9420. **Business Telephone:** (319) 322-8110. **Website:** www.ultsports.com.
   Publisher: Shane O'Neill. **Editor:** Nick Rousso.

Baseball Encyclopedias

TOTAL BASEBALL
The Official Encyclopedia of Major League Baseball
Mailing Address: 100 Enterprise Drive, Kingston, NY 12401. **Telephone:** (914) 382-6964. **FAX:** (914) 382-6037. **E-Mail Address:** info@totalsports.net. **Website:** www.totalbaseball.com.
   Co-Editors: Mike Gershman, John Thorn. **Statistician:** Pete Palmer.

BASEBALL WEBSITES

GENERAL SPORTS

CBS Sportsline	www.sportsline.com
CNN/Sports Illustrated	www.cnnsi.com
ESPN	www.espn.go.com
Nando Sports	www.sportserver.com
The Sporting News	www.sportingnews.com
Total Sports	www.totalsports.com
USA Today	www.usatoday.com

BASEBALL ONLY

Fastball	www.fastball.com
John Skilton's Baseball Links	www.baseball-links.com
Major League Baseball	www.majorleaguebaseball.com
Minor League Baseball	www.minorleaguebaseball.com
MLB Players Association	www.bigleaguers.com

HOBBY PUBLICATIONS

BECKETT PUBLICATIONS
Beckett Baseball Card Monthly
Mailing Address: 15850 Dallas Pkwy., Dallas, TX 75248. **Telephone:** (972) 991-6657. **FAX:** (972) 991-8930. **Website:** www.beckett.com.
   CEO/Publisher: James Beckett. **Editor:** Mike Payne.

KRAUSE PUBLICATIONS

Mailing Address: 700 E State St., Iola, WI 54990. **Telephone:** (715) 445-2214. **FAX:** (715) 445-4087. **Website:** www.krause.com.

Publisher: Hugh McAloon.

Editor, Fantasy Sports/Sports Cards Magazine: Greg Ambrosius. **Editor, Sports Collectors Digest:** Tom Mortenson. **Editor, Tuff Stuff:** Rocky Landsverk.

TEAM PUBLICATIONS

COMAN PUBLISHING

Diehard (Boston Red Sox), Mets Inside Pitch (New York Mets)

Mailing Address: P.O. Box 2331, Durham, NC 27702. **Telephone:** (919) 688-0218. **FAX:** (919) 682-1532. **Publisher:** Stuart Coman. **Managing Editor:** Kevin Bradford.

PINSTRIPES

(Philadelphia Phillies)

Mailing Address: P.O. Box 306, Whitehall, PA 18052. **Telephone:** (888) 409-2200. **Website:** www.phillyteams.com. **President/Editor:** Jeff Moeller.

VINE LINE

(Chicago Cubs)

Mailing Address: Chicago Cubs Publications, 1060 W. Addison St., Chicago, IL 60613. **Telephone:** (773) 404-2827. **FAX:** (773) 404-4129. **Managing Editor:** Lena McDonagh. **Editor:** Jay Rand.

YANKEES MAGAZINE

(New York Yankees)

Mailing Address: Yankee Stadium, Bronx, NY 10451. **Telephone:** (800) 469-2657. **Publisher:** Dan Cahalane. **Editor:** Stephanie Geosits.

JET MEDIA/INDIANS INK

(Cleveland Indians)

Mailing Address: P.O. Box 539, Mentor, OH 44061. **Telephone:** (440) 953-2200. **FAX:** (440) 953-2202. **Editor:** Frank Derry.

OUTSIDE PITCH

(Baltimore Orioles)

Mailing Address: P.O. Box 27143, Baltimore, MD 21230. **Telephone:** (410) 234-8888. **FAX:** (410) 234-1029. **Website:** www.outsidepitch.com. **Publisher:** David Simone. **Editor:** David Hill.

REDS REPORT

(Cincinnati Reds)

Mailing Address: Columbus Sports Publications, P.O. Box 12453, Columbus, OH 43212. **Telephone:** (614) 486-2202. **FAX:** (614) 486-3650. **Publisher:** Frank Moskowitz. **Editor:** Steve Helwagen.

FANTASY BASEBALL

DIAMOND LIBRARY PUBLICATIONS

Mailing Address: 15 Cannon Rd., Wilton, CT 06897. **Telephone:** (800) 707-9090, (203) 834-1231. **Website:** www.johnbenson.com.

Publisher: John Benson. **Managing Editor:** Douglas DelVecchio.

HAWES FANTASY BASEBALL GUIDE

Mailing Address: Ultimate Sports Publishing, P.O. Box 75299, Seattle, WA 98125. **Editorial Telephone:** (206) 301-9466. **FAX:** (206) 301-9420. **Business Telephone:** (319) 322-8110. **Website:** www.ultsports.com.

Publisher: Shane O'Neill. **Editor:** Nick Rousso.

THE SPORTING NEWS
FANTASY BASEBALL OWNERS MANUAL

Mailing Address: 10176 Corporate Square Dr., Suite 200, St. Louis, MO 63132. **Telephone:** (314) 997-7111. **FAX:** (314) 993-7726.

Managing Editor: Bob Hille.

MAJORS–OTHER INFORMATION

GENERAL INFORMATION

MAJOR LEAGUE BASEBALL
PLAYERS ASSOCIATION

Mailing Address: 12 E 49th St., 24th Floor, New York, NY 10017. **Telephone:** (212) 826-0808. **FAX:** (212) 752-4378. **Website:** www.bigleaguers.com.

Year Founded: 1966.

Executive Director, General Counsel: Donald Fehr.

Special Assistants: Tony Bernazard, Phil Bradley, Steve Rogers.

Associate General Counsel: Gene Orza. **Assistant General Counsel:** Robert Lenaghan, Doyle Pryor, Michael Weiner.

Director, Licensing: Judy Heeter. **General Manager:** Richard White. **Manager, Marketing Services:** Allyne Price. **Category Manager, Novelties:** Evan Kaplan. **Category Director, Interactive Games:** John Olshan. **Administrative Manager:** Tina Morris. **Editor, Website:** Chris Dahl. **Licensing Assistant:** Heather Saks.

Executive Board: Player representatives of the 30 major league clubs.

League Representatives: American League—David Cone; **National League**—Tom Glavine.

MAJOR LEAGUE BASEBALL PRODUCTIONS

Mailing Address: 245 Park Ave., New York, NY 10167. **Telephone:** (212) 931-7900. **FAX:** (212) 949-5795.

Senior Vice President, General Manager: Steve Hellmuth. **Executive Producer:** David Gavant. **Vice President, Programming/Sales:** James Scott. **Director, Home Videos/Marketing:** Chris Brande. **Director, Operations:** Michael Kusama.

SCOUTING

MAJOR LEAGUE SCOUTING BUREAU

Mailing Address: 3500 Porsche Way, Suite 100, Ontario, CA 91764. **Telephone:** (909) 980-1881. **FAX:** (909) 980-7794.

Year Founded: 1974.

Director: Frank Marcos. **Assistant Director:** Rick Oliver. **Administrator:** RoseMary Durgin. **Administrative Assistant:** Joanne Costanzo.

Board of Directors: Bill Murray, chairman; Dave Dombrowski (Marlins), Dan Duquette (Red Sox), Bob Gebhard (Rockies), Roland Hemond (Diamondbacks), Frank Marcos, Randy Smith (Tigers), Art Stewart (Royals), Kevin Towers (Padres).

Scouts: Rick Arnold (Northridge, CA), Mike Childers (Lexington, KY), Dick Colpaert (Utica, MI), Craig Conklin (Fresno, CA), Dan Dixon (Temecula, CA), J.D. Elliby (Richmond, VA), Jim Elliott (Mission, KS), Art Gardner (Walnut Grove, MS), Rusty Gerhardt (New London, TX), Doug Horning (Schererville, IN), Don Jacoby (Winter Haven, FL), Brad Kohler (Bethlehem, PA), Don Kohler (Asbury Park, NJ), Mike Larson (Waseca, MN), Jethro McIntyre (Pittsburg, CA), Bob Meisner (Golden, CO), Lenny Merullo (Reading, MA), Paul Mirocke (Lutz, FL), Carl Moesche (Gresham, OR), Tim Osborne (Woodstock, GA), Buddy Pritchard (Fullerton, CA), Gary Randall (Rock Hill, SC), Willie Romay (Miami, FL), Al Ronning (Sunnyvale, CA), Kevin Saucier (Pensacola, FL), Kirk Shrider (Long Beach, CA), Pat Shortt (South Hempstead, NY), Craig Smajstrla (Pearland, TX), Ed Sukla (Irvine, CA), Marv Thompson (Glendale, AZ), Tom Valcke (Fresno, CA), Jim Walton (Shattuck, OK).

Canadian Scouts: Walt Burrows (Brentwood Bay, B.C.), supervisor; Jim Baba (Saskatoon, Saskatchewan), Curtis Bailey (Red Deer, Alberta), Gerry Falk (Carman, Manitoba), Bill Green (Vancouver, B.C.), Sean Gulliver (St. John's, Newfoundland), Ian Jordan (Pointe-Claire, Quebec), Ken Lenihan (Bedford, N.S.), Dave McConnell (Kelowna, B.C.), Dan Mendham (London, Ontario), Jean Marc Mercier (Charlesbourg, Quebec), Greg O'Halloran (Guelph, Ontario), Tony Wylie (Anchorage, AK).

Supervisor, Puerto Rico: Pepito Centeno (Bayamon).

SCOUT OF THE YEAR FOUNDATION

Mailing Address: P.O. Box 211585, West Palm Beach, FL 33421. **Telephone:** (561) 798-5897.

President: Roberta Mazur. **Vice President:** David Rawnsley. **Secretary:** Joe Klein. **Treasurer:** Ron Mazur II.

Board of Advisors: Joe L. Brown, Bob Fontaine, Pat Gillick, Gary Hughes, Tracy Ringolsby, Ron Shapiro, Allan Simpson, Ted Spencer, Bob Watson.

WORLD UMPIRES ASSOCIATION
Mailing Address: 8730 Raintree Run, Poland, OH 44514. **Telephone:** (330) 757-7417.

Year Founded: 2000.

Organizing Committee Members: John Hirschbeck, Joe Brinkman.

MAJOR LEAGUE UMPIRES ASSOCIATION
Mailing Address: 1735 Market St., Suite 3420, Philadelphia, PA 19103. **Telephone:** (215) 979-3200. **FAX:** (215) 979-3201.

Year Founded: 1967.

General Counsel: Richie Phillips. **Associate General Counsel:** Pat Campbell.

PROFESSIONAL BASEBALL UMPIRE CORPORATION
Office Address: 201 Bayshore Dr. SE, St. Petersburg, FL 33701. **Mailing Address:** P.O. Box A, St. Petersburg, FL 33731. **Telephone:** (727) 822-6937. **FAX:** (727) 821-5819.

President: Mike Moore.

Treasurer/Vice President, Administration: Pat O'Conner. **Secretary/General Counsel:** Ben Hayes.

Administrator: Eric Krupa. **Assistant to Administrator:** Lillian Patterson.

Director, PBUC: Mike Fitzpatrick (Kalamazoo, MI).

Field Evaluators/Instructors: Dennis Cregg (Webster, MA), Mike Felt (Lansing, MI), Cris Jones (Wheat Ridge, CO).

UMPIRE DEVELOPMENT SCHOOLS
Harry Wendelstedt Umpire School
Mailing Address: 88 S St. Andrews Dr., Ormond Beach, FL 32174. **Telephone:** (904) 672-4879. **FAX:** (904) 672-3212. **E-Mail:** umpsch @aol.com. **Website:** www.umpireschool.com.

Operator: Harry Wendelstedt.

Jim Evans Academy of Professional Umpiring
Mailing Address: 12741 Research Blvd., Suite 401, Austin, TX 78759. **Telephone:** (512) 335-5959. **FAX:** (512) 335-5411. **E-Mail:** jimsacade my@earthlink.net. **Website:** www.umpireacademy.com.

Operator: Jim Evans.

PROFESSIONAL BASEBALL ATHLETIC TRAINERS SOCIETY
Mailing Address: 400 Colony Square, Suite 1750, 1201 Peachtree St., Atlanta, GA 30361. **Telephone:** (404) 875-4000. **FAX:** (404) 892-8560. **Website:** www.pbats.org.

Year Founded: 1983.

President: Russ Miller (Detroit Tigers). **Secretary:** Larry Starr (Florida Marlins). **Treasurer:** Paul Spicuzza (Cleveland Indians). **Immediate Past Preisdent:** Kent Biggerstaff (Pittsburgh Pirates). **American League Representative:** Ned Bergert (Anaheim Angels). **American League Assistant Trainer Representative:** Brian Ebel (Baltimore Orioles). **National League Representative:** John Adam (Milwaukee Brewers). **National League Assistant Trainer Representative:** Kevin Rand (Florida Marlins).

General Counsel: Rollin Mallernee.

BABE RUTH BIRTHPLACE and OFFICIAL ORIOLES MUSEUM
Office Address: 216 Emory St., Baltimore, MD 21230. **Telephone:** (410) 727-1539. **FAX:** (410) 727-1652. **Website:** www.baberuthmuseum. com.

Year Founded: 1973.

Executive Director: Mike Gibbons. **Curator:** Greg Schwalenberg.

Museum Hours: April-October, 10 a.m.-5 p.m. (10 a.m.-7 p.m. for Baltimore Orioles home games); November-March, 10 a.m.-4 p.m.

CANADIAN BASEBALL HALL OF FAME and MUSEUM
Museum Address: 386 Church St., St. Marys, Ontario N4X 1C **Mailing Address:** P.O. Box 1838, St. Marys, Ontario N4X 1C2. **Telephor**

(519) 284-1838. **FAX:** (519) 284-1234. **E-Mail Address:** baseball@quadro. net. **Website:** www.baseballhof.ca.

Year Founded: 1983.

Executive Director: John Harlton. **Curator:** Carl McCoomb.

Museum Hours: May 6-Oct. 8, Mon.-Sat. 10:30 a.m.-4:30 p.m.; Sun noon-4 p.m. Closed Wednesday. Weekends only in May and October.

FIELD OF DREAMS MOVIE SITE

Address: 28963 Lansing Rd., Dyersville, IA 52040. **Telephone:** (888) 875-8404. **FAX:** (319) 875-7253. **Website:** www.fieldofdreamsmoviesite. com.

Year Founded: 1989.

Manager, Business/Marketing: Betty Boeckenstedt.

Hours: April-November, 9 a.m.-6 p.m.

LITTLE LEAGUE BASEBALL MUSEUM

Office Address: Rte. 15 S, Williamsport, PA 17701. **Mailing Address:** P.O. Box 3485, Williamsport, PA 17701. **Telephone:** (570) 326-3607. **FAX:** (570) 326-2267. **Website:** www.littleleague.org/museum.

Year Founded: 1982.

Director: Cynthia Stearns. **Curator:** Michael Miller.

Museum Hours: Memorial Day-Labor Day, 9 a.m.-7 p.m., Sun. 12-7; September-May, 9 a.m.-5 p.m., Sun. 12-5. Open every day except Thanksgiving, Christmas Day, New Year's Day.

LOUISVILLE SLUGGER MUSEUM

Office Address: 800 W Main St., Louisville, KY 40202. **Telephone:** (502) 588-7228. **FAX:** (502) 585-1179. **Website:** www.slugger.com/museum.

Year Founded: 1996.

Executive Director: Bill Williams.

Museum Hours: Jan. 2-Dec. 23, 9 a.m.-5 p.m. Closed Sunday.

NATIONAL BASEBALL
HALL OF FAME AND MUSEUM

Office Address: 25 Main St., Cooperstown, NY 13326. **Mailing Address:** P.O. Box 590, Cooperstown, NY 13326. **Telephone:** (607) 547-7200. **FAX:** (607) 547-2044. **E-Mail Address:** info@baseballhalloffame.org. **Website:** www.baseballhalloffame.org.

Year Founded: 1939.

Chairman: Ed Stack. **Vice Chairman:** Jane Forbes Clark. **President:** Dale Petroskey. **Vice President, Communications and Education:** Jeff Idelson. **Vice President/ Chief Curator:** Ted Spencer. **Vice President, Business and Administration:** Frank Simio. **Executive Director, Communications and Museum Programs:** John Ralph. **Executive Director, Retail Marketing:** Barbara Shinn. **Curator of Collections:** Peter Clark. **Librarian:** Jim Gates. **Controller:** Fran Althiser.

Museum Hours: Oct. 1-April 30—9 a.m.-5 p.m.; May 1-Sept. 30—9 a.m.-9 p.m. Open every day except Thanksgiving, Christmas Day, New Year's Day.

2000 Hall of Fame Induction Ceremonies: July 23, 1:30 p.m., Cooperstown, NY. **Hall of Fame Game:** July 24, 2 p.m., Cleveland vs. Arizona.

NEGRO LEAGUES
BASEBALL MUSEUM

Office Address: 1616 E 18th St., Kansas City, MO 64108. **Mailing Address:** P.O. Box 414897, Kansas City, MO 64141. **Telephone:** (816) 221-1920. **FAX:** (816) 221-8424. **Website:** www.nlbm.com.

Year Founded: 1990.

Chairman: Buck O'Neil. **President:** Randall Ferguson.

Executive Director: Don Motley. **Director of Development:** Bob Kendrick. **Curator:** Raymond Doswell.

Museum Hours: Tues.-Sat. 9 a.m.-6 p.m., Sun. noon.-6 p.m. Closed Monday.

RESEARCH

SOCIETY FOR AMERICAN
BASEBALL RESEARCH

Mailing Address: 812 Huron Rd. E, Suite 719, Cleveland, OH 44115. **Telephone:** (216) 575-0500. **FAX:** (216) 575-0502. **Website:** www.sabr.org.

Year Founded: 1971.

President: Jim Riley. **Vice President:** Frederick Ivor-Campbell. **Secretary:** Dick Beverage. **Treasurer:** Len Levin. **Directors:** Rodney Johnson, Lois Nicholson, Norman Macht, Tom Shieber.

Manager, Membership Services: John Zajc. **Director, Publications:** rk Alvarez.

MLB PLAYERS ALUMNI ASSOCIATION

Mailing Address, National Headquarters: 1631 Mesa Ave., Suite C, Colorado Springs, CO 80906. **Telephone:** (719) 477-1870. **FAX:** (719) 477-1875.

Mailing Address, Florida Operations Center: 33 Sixth St. S, St. Petersburg, FL 33701. **Telephone:** (727) 892-6744. **FAX:** (727) 892-6771.

Year Founded: 1982.

President: Brooks Robinson.

Vice Presidents: Bob Boone, George Brett, Carl Erskine, Mike Hegan, Chuck Hinton, Al Kaline, Rusty Staub, Robin Yount.

Board of Directors: Paul Beeston, Nellie Briles, Darrel Chaney, Denny Doyle, Don Fehr, Jim "Mudcat" Grant, Rich Hand, Jim Hannan (chairman), Jerry Moses, Ken Sanders, Jose Valdivielso, Fred Valentine.

Legal Counsel: Sam Moore. **Executive Vice President:** Dan Foster. **Director, Special Events:** Chris Torgusen. **Coordinator, Special Events:** Geoff Hixson. **Coordinator, Youth Baseball:** Lance James. **Membership Coordinator:** Wade Den Hartog. **Office Manager:** Chandra Von Nostrand.

ASSOCIATION OF PROFESSIONAL BASEBALL PLAYERS OF AMERICA

Mailing Address: 12062 Valley View St., Suite 211, Garden Grove, CA 92845. **Telephone:** (714) 892-9900. **FAX:** (714) 897-0233. **E-mail:** apba@gte.net.

Year Founded: 1924.

President: John McHale. **Vice President:** Bob Kennedy. **Consultant:** Chuck Stevens. **Secretary-Treasurer:** Dick Beverage.

BASEBALL ASSISTANCE TEAM (BAT)

Mailing Address: 245 Park Ave., 31st Floor, New York, NY 10167. **Telephone:** (212) 931-7822. **FAX:** (212) 949-5652.

Year Founded: 1986.

Chairman: Ralph Branca. **President:** Joe Garagiola. **Vice Presidents:** Joe Black, Earl Wilson.

Executive Director: James Martin. **Secretary:** Thomas Ostertag. **Treasurer:** Jeff White. **Administrator:** Meredith Firmani. **Consultant:** Sam McDowell.

BASEBALL CHAPEL

Mailing Address: P.O. Box 1366, Ocean City, NJ 08226. **Telephone:** (609) 398-3505. **FAX:** (610) 586-4538. **E-Mail:** baseballchapel@juno.com.

Year Founded: 1972.

Executive Director: Vince Nauss.

BASEBALL FAMILY

(Minor Leagues)

Mailing Address: 8744 Warm Springs Way, Knoxville, TN 37923. **Telephone:** (865) 692-9291. **FAX:** (865) 769-4386. **E-Mail:** leen74@aol.com, donnakirby@juno.com.

Year Founded: 1991.

Coordinators: Colleen Endres, Donna Kirby.

THE BASEBALL TRADE SHOW

Mailing Address: P.O. Box A, St. Petersburg, FL 33731. **Telephone:** (727) 822-6937. **FAX:** (727) 821-5819.

Manager, Trade Show: Reghan Guptill.

2000 Convention: Dec. 8-11 at Dallas.

PROFESSIONAL BASEBALL EMPLOYMENT OPPORTUNITIES

Mailing Address: P.O. Box 310, Old Fort, NC 28762. **Telephone:** (800) 842-5618. **FAX:** (828) 668-4762.

Director: Ann Perkins.

MEN'S SENIOR BASEBALL LEAGUE

(30 and Over, 40 and Over)

Mailing Address: One Huntington Quadrangle, Suite 3N07, Mellville, NY 11747. **Telephone:** (631) 753-6725. **FAX:** (631) 753-4031.

President: Steve Sigler. **Vice President:** Gary D'Ambrisi.

Website: www.msblnational.com. **E-Mail:** info@msblnational.com.

2000 World Series: Oct. 23-Nov. 4, Phoenix; Oct. 30-Nov. 4, St. Petersburg, FL.

MEN'S ADULT BASEBALL LEAGUE
(18 and Over)

Mailing Address: One Huntington Quadrangle, Suite 3N07, Mellville, NY 11747. **Telephone:** (631) 753-6725. **FAX:** (631) 753-4031.
Website: www.msblnational.com. **E-Mail:** info@msblnational.com.
President: Steve Sigler. **Vice President:** Gary D'Ambrisi.
2000 World Series: Oct. 18-22, Phoenix; Oct. 27-30, St. Petersburg, FL.

NATIONAL ADULT BASEBALL ASSOCIATION
(18-65)

Mailing Address: 3900 E Mexico Ave., Suite GL-8, Denver, CO 80210. **Telephone:** (800) 621-6479. **FAX:** (303) 639-6605. **E-Mail:** nabanatl @aol.com. **Website:** www.dugout.org.
President/National Director: Shane Fugita. **Director of Baseball Operations:** J.D. Magee. **Director of League Development:** Lou Palmer.
2000 National Championship: 18 and over (three divisions)—Oct. 7-10, Phoenix. 30 and over (two divisions), 40 and over (two divisions), 50 and over—Oct. 9-14, Phoenix.

ROY HOBBS BASEBALL
(Open, 30-Over, 40-Over, Masters (48-Over), Classics (58-Over)

Mailing Address: 2224 Akron Peninsula Rd., Akron, OH 44313. **Telephone:** (888) 484-7422. **FAX:** (330) 923-1967. **E-Mail Address:** tom@royhobbs.com. **Website:** www.royhobbs.com.
President: Tom Giffen. **Vice President:** Ellen Giffen. **Director, Operations:** Todd Windhorst.
2000 World Series (all in Fort Myers, FL): Oct. 28-Nov. 4—Open Division, 30s (four divisions); Nov. 4-11—40s (four divisions); Nov. 11-18—Masters (two divisions), Classics; Nov. 15-19—Women's.

FANTASY CAMPS

LOS ANGELES DODGERS
ADULT BASEBALL CAMP

Mailing Address: Dodgertown, P.O. Box 2887, Vero Beach, FL 32961. **Telephone:** (407) 569-4900. **FAX:** (407) 770-2424. **E-Mail Address:** lad abc@aol.com.

RANDY HUNDLEY'S
FANTASY BASEBALL CAMPS

Mailing Address: 128 S Northwest Hwy., Palatine, IL 60067. **Telephone/FAX:** (847) 991-9595. **E-Mail:** rhundley@mediaone.net. **Website:** www.cubsfantasycamp.com.

BASEBALL CARD MANUFACTURERS

FLEER/SKYBOX INTERNATIONAL
Mailing Address: CSC Plaza, 1120 Route 73, Suite 300, Mount Laurel, NJ 08054. **Telephone:** (856) 231-6200. **FAX:** (856) 727-9460. **E-Mail:** info@flrsbx.com. **Website:** www.fleerskybox.com

GRANDSTAND CARDS
Mailing Address: 22647 Ventura Blvd., #192, Woodland Hills, CA 91364. **Telephone:** (818) 992-5642. **FAX:** (818) 348-9122.

PACIFIC TRADING CARDS
Mailing Address: 18424 Hwy. 99, Lynnwood, WA 98037. **Telephone:** (800) 551-2002. **Website:** www.pacifictradingcards.com.

PLAYOFF
Mailing Address: 1517 W North Carrier Pkwy., Suite 155, Grand Prairie, TX 75050. **Telephone:** (972) 595-1180. **FAX:** (972) 595-1190.

TEAM BEST
Mailing Address: 7115 Oak Ridge Pkwy., Suite 180, Austell, GA 30168. **Telephone:** (770) 745-3434. **FAX:** (770) 745-3433. **Website:** www. teambest.com.

TOPPS
Mailing Address: One Whitehall St., New York, NY 10004. **Telephone:** (212) 376-0300. **FAX:** (212) 376-0573. **E-Mail:** bparkinson@topps.com.

UPPER DECK
Mailing Address: 5909 Sea Otter Place, Carlsbad, CA 92008. **Telephone:** (760) 929-6500. **FAX:** (760) 929-6556. **Website:** www.upperdeck.com.

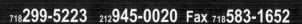

MINOR LEAGUE SCHEDULES

MINOR LEAGUE BASEBALL

NATIONAL ASSOCIATION OF PROFESSIONAL BASEBALL LEAGUES

Office Address: 201 Bayshore Dr. SE, St. Petersburg, FL 33701. **Mailing Address:** P.O. Box A, St. Petersburg, FL 33731. **Telephone:** (727) 822-6937. **FAX:** (727) 821-5819.

Year Founded: 1901.
President/Chief Executive Officer: Mike Moore.
Assistant to President: Carolyn Ashe.
Vice President: Stan Brand (Washington, DC).
Treasurer/Chief Operating Officer and VP, Administration: Pat O'Conner. **Assistant to VP, Administration:** Mary Wooters.
Secretary/General Counsel: Ben Hayes.
Assistant to General Counsel: Debbie Carlisle.

Mike Moore

Executive Director, Special Operations: Misann Ellmaker.
Director, Baseball Operations: Tim Brunswick.
Director, Media Relations: Jim Ferguson. **Assistant Director, Media Relations:** Steve Densa.
Director, Business/Finance: Eric Krupa. **Assistant to Director, Business/Finance:** Lillian Patterson.
Official Statistician: Howe Sportsdata, Boston Fish Pier, West Bldg. #1, Suite 302, Boston, MA 02210. Telephone: (617) 951-0070.
2000 Winter Meetings: Dec. 8-12, Dallas, TX.

Affiliated Members/Council of League Presidents

Class AAA

League	President	Telephone	FAX Number
International	Randy Mobley	(614) 791-9300	(614) 791-9009
Mexican	Jose Orozco Topete	(525) 557-1007	(525) 395-2454
Pacific Coast	Branch Rickey	(719) 636-3399	(719) 636-1199

Class AA

League	President	Telephone	FAX Number
Eastern	Bill Troubh	(207) 761-2700	(207) 761-7064
Southern	Unavailable	(770) 428-4749	(770) 428-4849
Texas	Tom Kayser	(210) 545-5297	(210) 545-5298

Class A Advanced

League	President	Telephone	FAX Number
California	Joe Gagliardi	(408) 369-8038	(408) 369-1409
Carolina	John Hopkins	(336) 691-9030	(336) 691-9070
Florida State	Chuck Murphy	(904) 252-7479	(904) 252-7406

Class A

League	President	Telephone	FAX Number
Midwest	George Spelius	(608) 364-1188	(608) 364-1913
South Atlantic	John Moss	(704) 739-3466	(704) 739-1974

Short-Season Class A

League	President	Telephone	FAX Number
New York-Penn	Bob Julian	(315) 733-8036	(315) 797-7403
Northwest	Bob Richmond	(208) 429-1511	(208) 429-1525

Rookie Advanced

League	President	Telephone	FAX Number
Appalachian	Lee Landers	(704) 873-5300	(704) 873-4333
Pioneer	Jim McCurdy	(509) 456-7615	(509) 456-0136

Rookie

League	President	Telephone	FAX Number
Arizona	Bob Richmond	(208) 429-1511	(208) 429-1525
Dominican Summer	Freddy Jana	(809) 563-3233	(809) 563-2455
Gulf Coast	Tom Saffell	(941) 966-6407	(941) 966-6872
Venez. Summer	Saul Gonzalez	(584) 354-4632	(584) 354-4134

National Association Board of Trustees

Class AAA (at-large)—Russ Parker (Calgary). **International League**—Ken Young (Norfolk). **Pacific Coast League**—Sam Bernabe (Iowa).

Eastern League—Joe Finley (Trenton). **Southern League**—Steve Bryant (Carolina). **Texas League**—Miles Prentice, chairman (Midland).

California League—Hank Stickney (Rancho Cucamonga). **Carolina League**—Kelvin Bowles (Salem). **Florida State League**—Ken Carson, secretary (Dunedin). **Midwest League**—Dave Walker (Burlington). **South Atlantic League**—Winston Blenckstone (Hagerstown).

New York-Penn League—Sam Nader (Oneonta). **Northwest League**—Bob Beban, vice chairman (Eugene).

Appalachian League—Bill Smith (Elizabethton). **Pioneer League**—Bob Wilson (Billings). **Gulf Coast League**—Cam Bonifay (Pirates).

PROFESSIONAL BASEBALL
PROMOTION CORPORATION

Office Address: 201 Bayshore Dr. SE, St. Petersburg, FL 33701. **Mailing Address:** P.O. Box A, St. Petersburg, FL 33731. **Telephone:** (727) 822-6937. **FAX/Marketing:** (727) 894-4227. **FAX/Licensing:** (727) 825-3785.

President/Chief Executive Officer: Mike Moore.

Treasurer/Chief Operating Officer and VP, Administration: Pat O'Conner. **Assistant to Chief Operating Officer:** Mary Wooters.

Executive Director, Special Operations: Misann Ellmaker. **Assistant Director, Special Operations:** Kelly Butler.

Director, Licensing: Brian Earle. **Assistant Director, Licensing:** Tina Gust.

Director, Marketing: Rod Meadows. **Club Coordinator, Marketing:** Jessica Bayer.

Director, Professional Baseball Employment Opportunities: Ann Perkins (Old Fort, NC). **Manager, Trade Show:** Unavailable. **Manager, Trademarks/Contracts:** Derek Johnson.

PROFESSIONAL BASEBALL
UMPIRE CORPORATION

Office Address: 201 Bayshore Dr. SE, St. Petersburg, FL 33701. **Mailing Address:** P.O. Box A, St. Petersburg, FL 33731. **Telephone:** (727) 822-6937. **FAX:** (727) 821-5819.

President: Mike Moore.

Treasurer/Vice President, Administration: Pat O'Conner. **Secretary/General Counsel:** Ben Hayes.

Administrator: Eric Krupa. **Assistant to Administrator:** Lillian Patterson.

Director, PBUC: Mike Fitzpatrick (Kalamazoo, MI).

Field Evaluators/Instructors: Dennis Cregg (Webster, MA), Mike Felt (Lansing, MI), Cris Jones (Wheat Ridge, CO).

MINORLEAGUES

1999 STANDINGS

Parent club in parentheses. *Split-season champion.

INTERNATIONAL LEAGUE   AAA

EAST	W	L	PCT	GB	Manager
Scranton/W-B (Phillies)	78	66	.542	—	Marc Bombard
Pawtucket (Red Sox)	76	68	.528	2	Gary Jones
Syracuse (Blue Jays)	73	71	.507	5	Pat Kelly
Buffalo (Indians)	72	72	.500	6	Jeff Datz
Rochester (Orioles)	61	83	.424	17	Dave Machemer
Ottawa (Expos)	59	85	.410	19	Jeff Cox
WEST	**W**	**L**	**PCT**	**GB**	**Manager**
Columbus (Yankees)	83	58	.589	—	Trey Hillman
Indianapolis (Reds)	75	69	.521	9½	Dave Miley
Louisville (Brewers)	63	81	.438	21½	Gary Allenson
Toledo (Tigers)	57	87	.396	27½	Gene Roof
SOUTH	**W**	**L**	**PCT**	**GB**	**Manager**
Durham (Devil Rays)	83	60	.580	—	Bill Evers
Charlotte (White Sox)	82	62	.569	1½	Tom Spencer
Norfolk (Mets)	77	63	.550	4½	John Gibbons
Richmond (Braves)	64	78	.451	18½	Randy Ingle

PLAYOFFS—Semifinals (best-of-5)—Durham def. Columbus 3-0; Charlotte def. Scranton 3-2. **Finals** (best-of-5)—Charlotte def. Durham 3-1.

PACIFIC COAST LEAGUE   AAA

AMERICAN/EAST	W	L	PCT	GB	Manager
Oklahoma (Rangers)	83	59	.585	—	Greg Biagini
Nashville (Pirates)	80	60	.571	2	Trent Jewett
Memphis (Cardinals)	74	64	.536	7	Gaylen Pitts
New Orleans (Astros)	55	85	.393	27	Tony Pena
AMERICAN/CENTRAL	**W**	**L**	**PCT**	**GB**	**Managers**
Omaha (Royals)	81	60	.574	—	Ron Johnson
Colorado Springs (Rockies)	66	73	.475	14	Bill Hayes
Albuquerque (Dodgers)	65	74	.468	15	Mike Scioscia
Iowa (Cubs)	65	76	.461	16	Terry Kennedy
PACIFIC/SOUTH	**W**	**L**	**PCT**	**GB**	**Manager**
Salt Lake (Twins)	73	68	.518	—	Phil Roof
Fresno (Giants)	73	69	.514	½	Ron Roenicke
Las Vegas (Padres)	67	75	.472	6½	Mike Ramsey
Tucson (Diamondbacks)	66	76	.465	7½	Chris Speier
PACIFIC/WEST	**W**	**L**	**PCT**	**GB**	**Manager**
Vancouver (Athletics)	84	58	.592	—	Mike Quade
Tacoma (Mariners)	69	70	.496	13½	Dave Myers
Edmonton (Angels)	65	74	.468	17½	Carney Lansford
Calgary (Marlins)	57	82	.410	25½	Lynn Jones

PLAYOFFS—Semifinals (best-of-5)—Oklahoma def. Omaha 3-1; Vancouver def. Salt Lake 3-2. **Finals** (best-of-5)—Vancouver def. Oklahoma 3-1.

EASTERN LEAGUE   AA

NORTH	W	L	PCT	GB	Manager
Trenton (Red Sox)	92	50	.648	—	DeMarlo Hale
Norwich (Yankees)	78	64	.549	14	Lee Mazzilli
Portland (Marlins)	65	77	.458	27	Frank Cacciatore
New Haven (Mariners)	65	77	.458	27	Dan Rohn
New Britain (Twins)	59	82	.418	32½	John Russell
Binghamton (Mets)	54	88	.380	38	Doug Davis
SOUTH	**W**	**L**	**PCT**	**GB**	**Manager(s)**
Erie (Angels)	81	61	.570	—	Garry Templeton
Harrisburg (Expos)	76	66	.535	5	Doug Sisson/Rick Sweet
Reading (Phillies)	73	69	.514	8	Gary Varsho
Bowie (Orioles)	70	71	.496	10½	Joe Ferguson
Akron (Indians)	69	71	.493	11	Joel Skinner
Altoona (Pirates)	64	73	.479	13	Marty Brown

PLAYOFFS—Semifinals (best-of-5)—Norwich def. Trenton 3-2; Harrisburg def. Erie 3-1. **Finals** (best-of-5)—Harrisburg def. Norwich 3-2.

SOUTHERN LEAGUE   AA

EAST	W	L	PCT	GB	Manager
Jacksonville (Tigers)	75	66	.532	—	Dave Anderson

*Orlando (Devil Rays)	70	68	.507	3½	Bill Russell
*Knoxville (Blue Jays)	71	69	.507	3½	Omar Malave
Carolina (Rockies)	60	80	.429	14½	Jay Loviglio
Greenville (Braves)	58	80	.420	15½	Paul Runge
WEST	**W**	**L**	**PCT**	**GB**	**Manager**
**West Tenn (Cubs)	84	57	.596	—	Dave Trembley
Chattanooga (Reds)	78	62	.557	5½	Phillip Wellman
Birmingham (White Sox)	73	67	.521	10½	Chris Cron
Mobile (Padres)	66	73	.475	17	Mike Basso
Huntsville (Brewers)	64	77	.454	20	Darrell Evans

PLAYOFFS—Semifinals (best-of-5)—West Tenn def.Chattanooga 3-1; Orlando def. Knoxville 3-1. **Finals** (best-of-5)—Orlando def. West Tenn 3-1.

TEXAS LEAGUE   AA

EAST	**W**	**L**	**PCT**	**GB**	**Manager**
*Tulsa (Rangers)	74	66	.529	—	Bobby Jones
*Shreveport (Giants)	71	69	.507	3	Shane Turner
Jackson (Astros)	68	72	.486	6	Jim Pankovits
Arkansas (Cardinals)	59	81	.421	15	Chris Maloney
WEST	**W**	**L**	**PCT**	**GB**	**Manager**
**Wichita (Royals)	83	57	.593	—	John Mizerock
Midland (Athletics)	74	66	.529	9	Tony DeFrancesco
San Antonio (Dodgers)	67	73	.479	16	Jimmy Johnson
El Paso (Diamondbacks)	64	76	.457	19	Don Wakamatsu

PLAYOFFS—Semifinals (best-of-5)—Tulsa def. Shreveport 3-1. **Finals** (best-of-7)—Wichita def. Tulsa 4-0.

CALIFORNIA LEAGUE   A ADVANCED

NORTH	**W**	**L**	**PCT**	**GB**	**Manager(s)**
**Modesto (Athletics)	88	52	.629	—	Bob Geren
Visalia (Athletics)	75	65	.536	13	Juan Navarrete
San Jose (Giants)	75	65	.536	13	Lenn Sakata
Bakersfield (Giants)	64	76	.457	24	Keith Comstock
Stockton (Brewers)	57	83	.407	31	BernieMoncallo/Carlos Ponce
SOUTH	**W**	**L**	**PCT**	**GB**	**Manager**
*San Bernardino (Dodgers)	80	61	.567	—	Rick Burleson
*Rancho Cuca. (Padres)	76	64	.543	3½	Tom LeVasseur
High Desert (Dbacks)	68	73	.482	12	Derek Bryant
Lake Elsinore (Angels)	63	77	.450	16½	Mario Mendoza
Lancaster (Mariners)	55	85	.393	24½	Darrin Garner

PLAYOFFS—First Round: (best-of-3)—San Bernardino def. High Deset 2-1; San Jose def. Visalia 2-1. **Semifinals:** (best-of-5)—San Bernardino def. Rancho Cucamonga 3-2; San Jose def. Modesto 3-2. **Finals:** (best-of-5)—San Bernardino def. San Jose 3-2.

CAROLINA LEAGUE   A ADVANCED

NORTH	**W**	**L**	**PCT**	**GB**	**Manager**
**Wilmington (Royals)	77	61	.558	—	Jeff Garber
Frederick (Orioles)	67	71	.486	10	Andy Etchebarren
Lynchburg (Pirates)	64	73	.467	12½	Scott Little
Potomac (Cardinals)	54	85	.388	23½	Joe Cunningham
SOUTH	**W**	**L**	**PCT**	**GB**	**Manager**
*Kinston (Indians)	78	58	.577	—	Eric Wedge
*Myrtle Beach (Braves)	79	60	.568	1	Brian Snitker
Salem (Rockies)	69	69	.500	10½	Ron Gideon
Winston-Salem (White Sox)	63	75	.457	16½	Jerry Terrell

PLAYOFFS—Semifinals (best-of-3)—Myrtle Beach def. Kinston 2-1. **Finals—**Final game of best-of-5 championship series cancelled due to Hurricane Floyd; Wilmington and Myrtle Beach declared co-champions.

FLORIDA STATE LEAGUE   A ADVANCED

EAST	**W**	**L**	**PCT**	**GB**	**Manager**
*Jupiter (Expos)	73	65	.529	—	Luis Dorante
*Kissimmee (Astros)	71	66	.518	1½	Manny Acta
St. Lucie (Mets)	68	70	.493	5	Howie Freiling
Daytona (Cubs)	63	75	.457	10	Nate Oliver
Brevard County (Marlins)	61	74	.452	10½	Dave Huppert
Vero Beach (Dodgers)	48	85	.361	22½	Alvaro Espinoza
SOUTH	**W**	**L**	**PCT**	**GB**	**Manager**
*Dunedin (Blue Jays)	86	51	.628	—	Rocket Wheeler
Tampa (Yankees)	78	58	.574	7½	Tom Nieto
*Clearwater (Phillies)	77	59	.566	8½	Bill Dancy
St. Petersburg (Devil Rays)	74	63	.540	12	Roy Silver

Charlotte (Rangers)	69	70	.496	18	James Byrd
Sarasota (Red Sox)	67	72	.482	20	Butch Hobson
Lakeland (Tigers)	65	73	.471	21½	Mark Meleski
Fort Myers (Twins)	60	79	.432	27	Mike Boulanger

PLAYOFFS—Semifinals (best-of-3)—Dunedin def. Clearwater 2-1; Kissimmee def. Jupiter 2-1. **Finals** (best-of-5)—Kissimmee def. Dunedin 3-1.

MIDWEST LEAGUE — A

EAST	W	L	PCT	GB	Manager
*Michigan (Astros)	76	62	.551	—	Al Pedrique
*Lansing (Cubs)	73	67	.521	4	Oscar Acosta
South Bend (Dbacks)	68	71	.489	8½	Mike Brumley
West Michigan (Tigers)	68	72	.486	9	Bruce Fields
Fort Wayne (Padres)	61	79	.436	16	Dan Simonds
CENTRAL	**W**	**L**	**PCT**	**GB**	**Manager**
Kane County (Marlins)	78	59	.569	—	Rick Renteria
*Rockford (Reds)	76	63	.547	3	Mike Rojas
*Wisconsin (Mariners)	72	66	.522	6½	Steve Roadcap
Peoria (Cardinals)	63	76	.453	16	Brian Rupp
Beloit (Brewers)	59	80	.424	20	Don Money
WEST	**W**	**L**	**PCT**	**GB**	**Manager**
Quad City (Twins)	77	62	.554	—	Jose Marzan
*Burlington (White Sox)	71	68	.511	6	Nick Capra
*Clinton (Reds)	68	69	.496	8	Freddie Benavides
Cedar Rapids (Angels)	61	77	.442	15½	Mitch Seoane

PLAYOFFS—Quarterfinals (best-of-3)—Kane County def. Quad City 2-1, Burlington def. Clinton 2-1, Lansing def. Michigan 2-0; Wisconsin def. Rockford 2-0. **Semifinals** (best-of-3)—Wisconsin def. Lansing 2-0; Burlington def. Kane County 2-1. **Finals** (best-of-5)—Burlington def. Wisconsin 3-2.

SOUTH ATLANTIC LEAGUE — A

NORTH	W	L	PCT	GB	Manager
*Hagerstown (Blue Jays)	84	56	.600	—	Rolando Pino
*Cape Fear (Expos)	75	65	.536	9	Frank Kremblas
Charleston, W.Va., (Royals)	61	80	.433	23½	Tom Poquette
Delmarva (Orioles)	58	80	.420	25	Butch Davis
CENTRAL	**W**	**L**	**PCT**	**GB**	**MANAGER**
*Capital City (Mets)	83	58	.589	—	Dave Engle
*Greensboro (Yankees)	77	64	.546	6	Stan Hough
Hickory (Pirates)	70	70	.500	12½	Tracy Woodson
Piedmont (Phillies)	69	71	.493	13½	Ken Oberkfell
Asheville (Rockies)	64	77	.454	19	Jim Eppard
Charleston, S.C. (Devil Rays)	66	77	.458	18½	Charlie Montoyo
SOUTH	**W**	**L**	**PCT**	**GB**	**Manager**
Macon (Braves)	74	64	.536	—	Jeff Treadway
*Columbus (Indians)	70	71	.496	5½	Brad Komminsk
*Augusta (Red Sox)	69	70	.496	5½	Billy Gardner Jr.
Savannah (Rangers)	62	78	.443	13	Paul Carey

PLAYOFFS—Quarterfinals (best-of-3)—Augusta def. Columbus 2-0, Hickory def. Macon 2-0, Capital City def. Greensboro 2-1, Cape Fear def. Hagerstown 2-0. **Semifinals** (best-of-3)—Augusta def. Hickory 2-1; Cape Fear def. Capital City 2-0. **Finals** (best-of-3)—Augusta def. Cape Fear 2-1.

NEW YORK-PENN LEAGUE — SHORT-SEASON A

McNAMARA	W	L	PCT	GB	Manager
Mahoning Valley (Indians)	43	33	.566	—	Ted Kubiak
Batavia (Phillies)	42	34	.553	1	Greg Legg
Auburn (Astros)	39	37	.513	4	Lyle Yates
Jamestown (Braves)	38	38	.500	5	Jim Saul
St. Catharines (Blue Jays)	34	42	.447	9	Eddie Rodriguez
Williamsport (Pirates)	32	44	.421	11	Curtis Wilkerson
STEDLER	**W**	**L**	**PCT**	**GB**	**Manager**
Utica (Marlins)	42	33	.560	—	Ken Joyce
Hudson Valley (Devil Rays)	42	34	.553	½	Edwin Rodriguez
Oneonta (Tigers)	41	34	.547	1	Kevin Bradshaw
Pittsfield (Mets)	41	35	.539	1½	Tony Tijerina
Staten Island (Yankees)	39	35	.527	2½	Joe Arnold
Lowell (Red Sox)	34	42	.447	8½	Luis Aguayo
Vermont (Expos)	33	43	.434	9½	Tony Barbone
New Jersey (Cardinals)	30	46	.395	12½	Jeff Shireman

PLAYOFFS—Semifinals (best-of-3)—Mahoning Valley def. Batavia 2-0, Hudson Valley def. Utica 2-1. **Finals** (best-of-3)—Hudson Valley def. Mahoning Valley 2-1.

NORTHWEST LEAGUE — SHORT-SEASON A

NORTH	W	L	PCT	GB	Manager
Spokane (Royals)	44	32	.579	—	Kevin Long
Boise (Angels)	43	33	.566	1	Tom Kotchman
Everett (Mariners)	41	35	.539	3	Terry Pollreisz
Yakima (Dodgers)	33	43	.434	11	Dino Ebel

SOUTH	W	L	PCT	GB	Manager
Portland (Rockies)	39	37	.513	—	Alan Cockrell
Southern Oregon (Athletics)	38	38	.500	1	Greg Sparks
Salem-Keizer (Giants)	37	39	.487	2	Frank Reberger
Eugene (Cubs)	29	47	.382	10	Bob Ralston

PLAYOFFS—Finals (best-of-5)—Spokane def. Portland 3-0.

APPALACHIAN LEAGUE — ROOKIE ADVANCED

EAST	W	L	PCT	GB	Manager
Martinsville (Astros)	41	29	.586	—	Brad Wellman
Danville (Braves)	38	31	.551	2½	J.J. Cannon
Bluefield (Orioles)	25	43	.368	15	Duffy Dyer
Princeton (Devil Rays)	25	45	.357	16	Bobby Ramos
Burlington (Indians)	21	49	.300	20	Jack Mull

WEST	W	L	PCT	GB	Manager
Pulaski (Rangers)	48	21	.696	—	Bruce Crabbe
Bristol (White Sox)	45	24	.652	3	Gary Pellant
Elizabethton (Twins)	40	30	.571	8½	Jon Mathews
Kingsport (Mets)	34	36	.486	14½	Guy Conti
Johnson City (Cardinals)	30	39	.435	18	Steve Turco

PLAYOFFS—Finals (best-of-3)—Martinsville def. Pulaski 2-0.

PIONEER LEAGUE — ROOKIE ADVANCED

NORTH	W	L	PCT	GB	Manager
*Helena (Brewers)	47	28	.627	—	Carlos Lezcano
*Missoula (Diamondbacks)	45	31	.592	2½	Joe Almaraz
Medicine Hat (Blue Jays)	33	43	.434	14½	Paul Elliott
Great Falls (Dodgers)	29	47	.382	18½	Tony Harris

SOUTH	W	L	PCT	GB	Manager(s)
**Idaho Falls (Padres)	48	27	.640	—	Don Werner
Billings (Reds)	42	33	.560	6	Russ Nixon
Butte (Angels)	32	43	.427	16	Joe Urso
Ogden (Brewers)	26	50	.342	22½	Jon Pont/Ed Sedar

PLAYOFFS—Semifinals (best-of-3)—Billings def. Idaho Falls 2-0; Missoula def. Helena 2-0. **Finals** (best-of-3)—Missoula def. Billings 2-0.

GULF COAST LEAGUE — ROOKIE

EAST	W	L	PCT	GB	Manager
Mets	39	21	.650	—	John Stephenson
Expos	29	31	.483	10	Bill Masse
Braves	27	33	.450	12	Rick Albert
Marlins	25	35	.417	14	Jon Deeble

NORTH	W	L	PCT	GB	Manager
Royals	33	27	.550	—	Andre David
Yankees	32	28	.533	1	Ken Dominguez
Tigers	29	31	.483	4	Gary Green
Phillies	26	34	.433	7	Ramon Aviles

WEST	W	L	PCT	GB	Manager
Rangers	37	23	.617	—	Darryl Kennedy
Twins	33	26	.559	3½	Al Newman
Orioles	31	28	.525	5½	Jesus Alfaro
Red Sox	30	29	.508	6½	John Sanders
Pirates	24	35	.407	12½	Woody Huyke
Reds	23	37	.383	14	Donnie Scott

PLAYOFFS—Semifinals— Twins def. Rangers, Mets def. Royals in one-game playoffs. **Finals** (best-of-3)—Mets def. Twins 2-0 .

ARIZONA LEAGUE — ROOKIE

Club	W	L	PCT	GB	Manager
Athletics	39	17	.696	—	John Kuehl
Mariners	32	24	.571	7	Gary Thurman
Padres	31	24	.564	7½	Randy Whisler
Rockies	28	28	.500	11	P.J. Carey
Mexican All-Stars	28	28	.500	11	—
Diamondbacks	24	32	.429	15	Roly de Armas
White Sox	23	33	.411	16	Jerry Hairston
Cubs	18	37	.327	20½	Carmelo Martinez

INTERNATIONAL LEAGUE

Class AAA

Office Address: 55 S High St., Suite 202, Dublin, OH 43017. **Telephone:** (614) 791-9300. **FAX:** (614) 791-9009. **E-Mail Address:** office@ilbaseball.com. **Website:** www.ilbaseball.com.

Years League Active: 1884-.

President/Treasurer: Randy Mobley.

Vice Presidents: Harold Cooper, Dave Rosenfield (Norfolk), Tex Simone (Syracuse), George Sisler Jr. **Corporate Secretary:** Max Schumacher (Indianapolis).

Directors: Bruce Baldwin (Richmond), Don Beaver (Charlotte), Gene Cook (Toledo), Howard Darwin (Ottawa), George Habel (Durham), Rick Muntean (Scranton/Wilkes-Barre), Bob Rich Jr. (Buffalo),

Randy Mobley

Dave Rosenfield (Norfolk), Ken Schnacke (Columbus), Max Schumacher (Indianapolis), Naomi Silver (Rochester), John Simone (Syracuse), Mike Tamburro (Pawtucket), Gary Ulmer (Louisville).

Office Manager: Toni Balcarel. **Assistant to President:** Nathan Blackmon.

2000 Opening Date: April 6. **Closing Date:** Sept. 4.

Regular Season: 144 games.

Division Structure: North—Buffalo, Ottawa, Pawtucket, Rochester, Scranton/Wilkes-Barre, Syracuse. **West**—Columbus, Indianapolis, Louisville, Toledo. **South**—Charlotte, Durham, Norfolk, Richmond.

Playoff Format: West champion plays South champion in best-of-5 series; wild-card club (non-division winner with best record) plays North champion in best-of-5 series. Winners meet in best-of-5 series for Governors' Cup championship. **Triple-A World Series:** Best-of-5 series vs. Pacific Coast League champion, Sept. 18-22 at Las Vegas.

All-Star Game: July 12 at Rochester (IL vs. Pacific Coast League).

Roster Limit: 23; 24 from April 6-May 5 and after Aug. 10. **Player Eligibility Rule:** No restrictions.

Brand of Baseball: Rawlings ROM-INT.

Statistician: Howe Sportsdata, Boston Fish Pier, West Bldg. #1, Suite 302, Boston MA 02210.

Umpires: Jorge Bauza (San Juan, PR), Mike Billings (Pembroke Pines, FL), Troy Blades (Dartmouth, Nova Scotia), Chris Boberg (Charlotte, NC), Robb Cook (Blacklick, OH), John Creek (Kalamazoo, MI), Cory Erickson (Independence, MO), Mark Facto (Ellicott City, MD), Michael Fichter (Lansing, IL), Jeff Head (Hoover, AL), Dan Iassogna (Smyrna, GA), Justin Klemm (Brentwood, NY), Jeff Kowalczyk (Bloomington, IL), Patrick McGinnis (Joliet, IL), Scott Nelson (Coshocton, OH), Stu Robertson (Gretna, VA), Willie Rodriguez (Bayamon, PR), Jeff Speodoske (Lansing, MI), Tim Timmons (Columbus, OH), Mike VanVleet (Battle Creek, MI), Roger Walling (Birmingham, AL).

Stadium Information

Club	Stadium	Dimensions LF	CF	RF	Capacity	'99 Att.
Buffalo	Dunn Tire Park	325	404	325	21,050	684,051
Charlotte	Knights	325	400	325	10,002	344,199
Columbus	Cooper	355	400	330	15,000	460,923
Durham	Durham Bulls Athletic	305	400	327	10,000	464,001
Indianapolis	Victory Field	320	402	320	15,500	658,250
Louisville	Louisville Slugger Field	325	400	340	13,200	*361,419
Norfolk	Harbor Park	333	410	338	12,069	486,727
Ottawa	JetForm Park	325	404	325	10,332	195,979
Pawtucket	McCoy	325	400	325	10,000	596,624
Richmond	The Diamond	330	402	330	12,134	523,670
Rochester	Frontier Field	335	402	325	10,840	481,039
Scranton	Lackawanna County	330	408	330	11,232	439,171
Syracuse	P&C	330	400	330	11,602	446,025
Toledo	Ned Skeldon	325	410	325	10,197	295,173

*Attendance figure for Cardinal Stadium

BUFFALO
Bisons

Office Address: 275 Washington St., Buffalo, NY 14203. **Mailing Address:** P.O. Box 450, Buffalo, NY 14205. **Telephone:** (716) 846-2000. **FAX:** (716) 852-6530. **E-Mail Address:** bisons@buffnet.net. **Website:** www.bisons.com.

Affiliation (first year): Cleveland Indians (1995). **Years in League:** 1886-98, 1901-70, 1998-.

Ownership, Management
Operated by: Rich Products Corp.

Principal Owner/President: Robert E. Rich Jr. **Chairman:** Robert E. Rich Sr. **President, Rich Entertainment Group:** Melinda Rich. **Executive Vice President, Rich Entertainment Group:** Jon Dandes. **Vice President/Treasurer:** David Rich. **Vice President/Secretary:** William Gisel Jr.

Vice President/General Manager: Mike Buczkowski. **Vice President, Sales/Marketing:** Marta Hiczewski. **Director, Finance:** Joe Segarra. **Corporate Counsel:** Jill Bond, William Grieshober. **Director, Public Relations/Marketing:** Tom Burns. **Coordinator, Public/Community Relations:** Matt Herring. **Stadium Operations Manager:** John Wiedeman. **Equipment Manager:** Ron Krauza. **Marketing/Game Day Manager:** Don Feldman. **Controller:** John Rupp. **Accounting Assistant:** Amy Drobits. **Accountants:** Jennifer Gallagher, Linda Gallagher, Aaron Leach. **Ticket Office Accounting Manager:** Rita Clark. **Ticket Operations Manager:** Mike Poreda. **Ticket/Sales Account Executives:** Carole Bogoniewski, Daniel Magee, Burt Mirti, Frank Mooney, Greg Grzebielucha, Carrie Eysaman, Jason Isbrandt. **Human Resources Manager:** Lynn Gauthier. **Visiting Clubhouse Manager:** Nick Birti. **Home Clubhouse Assistant:** Kevin Hodge.

Field Staff
Manager: Joel Skinner. **Coach:** Mario Diaz. **Pitching Coach:** Ken Rowe. **Trainer:** Rick Jameyson.

Game Information
Radio Announcers: Jim Rosenhaus, Duke McGuire. **No. of Games Broadcast:** Home-72, Away-72. **Flagship Station:** WWKB 1520-AM.

PA Announcer: Unavailable. **Official Scorers:** Kevin Lester, Mike Kelly.

Stadium Name (year opened): Dunn Tire Park (1988). **Location:** From north, take I-190 to Elm Street exit, left onto Swan Street. From east, take I-90 West to exit 51 (Route 33) to end, exit at Oak Street, right onto Swan Street. From west, take I-90 East, exit 53 to I-190 North, exit at Elm Street, left onto Swan Street. **Standard Game Times:** 7:05 p.m.; Wed 1:05; Sat. 4:05; Sun 2:05.

Visiting Club Hotel: Downtown Holiday Inn, 620 Delaware Ave., Buffalo, NY 14202. Telephone: (716) 886-2121.

CHARLOTTE
Knights

Office Address: 2280 Deerfield Dr., Fort Mill, SC 29715. **Telephone:** (704) 357-8071. **FAX:** (704) 329-2155. **E-Mail Address:** knights@ aaaknights.com. **Website:** www.aaaknights.com.

Affiliation (first year): Chicago White Sox (1999). **Years in League:** 1993-.

Ownership, Management
Operated by: Knights Baseball, LLC.

Principal Owners: Bill Allen, Don Beaver, Derick Close.

President: Don Beaver.

Vice President/General Manager: Tim Newman. **Assistant GM, Marketing/Promotions:** Mark Viniard. **Assistant GM, Stadium Operations:** Jon Percival. **Director, Ticket Operations:** Melissa Dudek. **Director, Media/Community Relations:** Shannon Motley. **Director, Group Sales:** R.J. Martino. **Assistant Director, Group Sales:** Erica Poag. **Group Event Coordinators:** Mac Chapman, Sean Owens, Mike Schline. **Director, Corporate Sales:** Anthony DeNino. **Corporate Account Manager:** Adam Deschenes. **Director, Broadcasting:** Matt Swierad. **Director, Community Relations:** Tommy John. **Stadium Operations Manager:** Brandon

Witherspoon. **Mascot Coordinator:** Billy Yandle. **Business Manager/Director, Team Travel:** Keta Stogner. **Head Groundskeeper:** Joey Simmons. **Assistant Groundskeeper:** John Krashner. **Office Manager:** Ronda Lessmeister. **Facility Maintenance Manager:** Joe Sistare. **Director, Merchandise:** Misty Gilbert. **Clubhouse Manager:** John Bare.

Field Staff

Manager: Nick Leyva. **Coach:** Gary Ward. **Pitching Coach:** Kirk Champion. **Trainer:** Scott Johnson.

Game Information

Radio Announcers: Matt Swierad, Tommy John. **No. of Games Broadcast:** Home-72, Away-72. **Flagship Station:** Unavailable.

PA Announcer: Unavailable. **Official Scorers:** Brent Stastny, Ed Walton.

Stadium Name (year opened): Knights Stadium (1990). **Location:** Exit 88 off I-77, east on Gold Hill Road. **Standard Game Times:** 7:15 p.m., (April, 6), Sun. 5.

Visiting Club Hotel: Charlotte Hilton Executive Park, 5624 W Park Dr., Charlotte, NC 28217. Telephone: (704) 527-8000.

COLUMBUS
Clippers

Office Address: 1155 W Mound St., Columbus, OH 43223. **Telephone:** (614) 462-5250. **FAX:** (614) 462-3271. **E-Mail Address:** colsclippers @earthlink.net. **Website:** www.clippersbaseball.com.

Affiliation (first year): New York Yankees (1979). **Years in League:** 1955-70, 1977-.

Ownership, Management

Operated by: Columbus Baseball Team, Inc.

Principal Owner: Franklin County, Ohio.

Chairman: Donald Borror. **President:** Richard Smith.

General Manager: Ken Schnacke. **Assistant General Manager:** Mark Warren. **Assistant GM/Park Supervisor:** Dick Fitzpatrick **Director, Stadium Operations:** Steve Dalin. **Director, Ticket Operations:** Scott Ziegler. **Director, Media Relations:** Chris Daugherty. **Director, Sales:** Mark Galuska. **Director, Marketing:** Shawne Beck. **Director, Broadcasting:** Terry Smith. **Director, Merchandising:** Kelly Ryther. **Director, Advertising:** Jamie Dato. **Director, Finance:** Chad Fetterhoff. **Director, Communications:** Ben Lewis. **Assistant Director, Media Relations:** Joe Hall. **Assistant Director, Marketing:** Kevin Morris. **Assistant Director, Sales:** Ty Sonagere. **Assistant to General Manager:** Judi Timmons. **Secretary:** Stephanie Pawluch. **Head Groundskeeper:** Jeffrey Limburg.

Field Staff

Manager: Trey Hillman. **Coaches:** Hop Cassady, Bill Robinson. **Pitching Coach:** Rick Tomlin. **Trainer:** Darren London.

Game Information

Radio Announcers: Terry Smith, Gary Richards. **No. of Games Broadcast:** Home-72, Away-72. **Flagship Station:** WSMZ 103.1-FM.

PA Announcer: Rich Hanchette. **Official Scorers:** Chuck Emmerling, Frank Fraas, Kris Hutchins, Joe Santry.

Stadium Name (year opened): Cooper Stadium (1977). **Location:** From north/south, I-71 to I-70 West, exit at Mound Street. From west, I-70 East, east at Broad Street, east to Glenwood, south to Mound Street. From east, I-70 West, exit at Mound Street. **Standard Game Times:** 7:15 p.m.; Sat. 6:15, 7:15, 7:35; Sun. 2:15, 6:15.

Visiting Club Hotels: Best Western-Columbus North, 888 E Dublin-Granville Rd., Columbus, OH 43229. Telephone: (614) 888-8230; Clarion Hotel, 7007 N High St., Columbus, OH 43085. Telephone: (614) 436-0700.

DURHAM
Bulls

Office Address: 409 Blackwell St., Durham, NC 27701. **Mailing Address:** P.O. Box 507, Durham, NC 27702. **Telephone:** (919) 687-6500. **FAX:** (919) 687-6560. **Website:** www.dbulls.com.

Affiliation (first year): Tampa Bay Devil Rays (1998). **Years in League:** 1998-.

Ownership, Management
Operated by: Capitol Broadcasting Co., Inc.
President/Chief Executive Officer: Jim Goodmon.
Vice President/General Manager: George Habel. **VP/Legal Counsel:** Mike Hill.
Assistant GM: Mike Birling. **Manager, Accounting:** Jolene Meyer. **Manager, Sales:** Matt West. **Account Executives, Sponsorship:** Mike Davis, Teresa Haley, Chip Hutchinson. **Coordinator, Promotions:** Brian Crichton. **Manager, Ticket Sales:** Jon Bishop. **Coordinator, Box Office:** Josh Levi. **Coordinator, Group Outings:** Melissa Kopp. **Manager, Merchandise:** Allan Long. **Manager, Concessions:** Jamie Jenkins. **Head Groundskeeper:** Kevin Robinson. **Supervisor, Operations:** Mike Tilly. **Manager, Office Systems:** Andrea Harris. **Director, Security:** Ed Sarvis. **Facility Superintendent:** Steve Banos. **Administrative Assistant:** Libby Hamilton. **Accounting Clerk:** Cheryl Clement. **Advertising Sales Administrator:** Janel Hopkins. **Receptionist/Secretary:** Barbara Goss.

Field Staff
Manager: Bill Evers. **Coach:** Max Oliveras. **Pitching Coach:** Joe Coleman. **Trainer:** Paul Harker.

Game Information
Radio Announcer: Steve Barnes. **No. of Games Broadcast:** Home-72, Away-72. **Flagship Station:** WDNC 620-AM.
PA Announcer: Bill Law. **Official Scorer:** Brent Belvin.
Stadium Name (year opened): Durham Bulls Athletic Park (1995). **Location:** From Raleigh, I-40 West to Highway 147 North, exit 12B to Willard, two blocks on Willard to stadium. From I-85, Gregson Street exit to downtown, left on Chapel Hill Street, right on Mangum Street. **Standard Game Times:** 7 p.m.; Sun. 5.
Visiting Club Hotel: Durham Marriott at the Civic Center, 201 Foster St., Durham, NC 27701. Telephone: (919) 768-6000.

INDIANAPOLIS
Indians

Office Address: 501 W Maryland St., Indianapolis, IN 46225. **Telephone:** (317) 269-3542. **FAX:** (317) 269-3541. **E-Mail Address:** indians@indyindians.com. **Website:** www.indyindians.com.
Affiliation (first year): Milwaukee Brewers (2000). **Years in League:** 1963, 1998-.

Ownership, Management
Operated by: Indians, Inc.
Chairman/President: Max Schumacher.
General Manager: Cal Burleson. **Director, Business Operations:** Brad Morris. **Director, Stadium Operations:** Randy Lewandowski. **Head Groundskeeper:** Mike Boekholder. **Director, Media/Public Relations:** Tim Harms. **Director, Sales/Marketing:** Daryle Keith. **Marketing Associate:** Scott Rubin. **Director, Community Relations:** Chris Herndon. **Director, Ticket Sales:** Mike Schneider. **Director, Group Sales:** Robin Ellet. **Director, Merchandising:** Mark Schumacher. **Director, Food Services:** Mike Moos. **Director, Special Projects:** Bruce Schumacher. **Clubhouse Operations:** J.R. Rinaldi. **Office Manager:** Traci Gilliland. **Facility Director:** Bill Sampson. **Director, Maintenance:** Tim Hughes. **Box Office Manager:** Matt Guay.

Field Staff
Manager: Steve Smith. **Coach:** Luis Salazar. **Pitching Coach:** Dwight Bernard. **Trainer:** Paul Anderson.

Game Information
Radio Announcers: Howard Kellman, Brian Griffin. **No. of Games Broadcast:** Home-62, Away-61. **Flagship Station:** WTLC-AM 1310.
PA Announcer: Bruce Schumacher. **Official Scorers:** Kim Rogers, Tom Akins, Mark Walpole.
Stadium Name (year opened): Victory Field (1996). **Location:** I-70 to West Street exit, north on West Street to ballpark; I-65 to Martin Luther King and West Street exit, south on West Street to ballpark. **Standard Game Times:** 7 p.m.; Sun. 2, 6.
Visiting Club Hotel: Comfort Inn, 530 S Capitol, Indianapolis, IN 46204. Telephone: (317) 631-9000.

LOUISVILLE
RiverBats

Office Address: Louisville Slugger Field, 401 E Main Street, Louisville, KY 40202. **Telephone:** (502) 212-2287. **FAX:** (502) 515-2255. **E-Mail Address:** info@batsbaseball.com.

Affiliation (first year): Cincinnati Reds (2000). **Years in League:** 1968-72, 1998-.

Ownership, Management
Operated by: Louisville Baseball Club, Inc.

Board of Directors: Dan Ulmer, Jack Hillerich, Dale Owens, Ed Glasscock, Kenny Huber, Jim Morrissey, Tom Musselman, Bob Stallings, Gary Ulmer.

Chairman: Dan Ulmer.

President: Gary Ulmer. **Vice President/General Manager:** Dale Owens. **Assistant GM/Director, Marketing:** Greg Galiette. **Assistant GM, Sales:** David Gardner. **Director, Baseball Operations:** Mary Barney. **Director, Stadium Operations:** Scott Shoemaker. **Director, Sales:** James Breeding. **Director, Broadcasting:** Jim Kelch. **Accounting Manager:** Michele Anderson. **Ticket Manager:** George Veith. **Group Sales Manager:** Colgan Tyler. **Suite Level Manager:** Ashley Saltsman. **Public Relations:** Matt Gorsky. **Account Executive/On Field Promotions:** Chris Subczyk. **Account Executive/PR Assistant:** Jeff Hollis. **Account Executives:** Joe Bryzinski, Mike Maddox, Chris Parker. **Sales Representatives:** Josh Bennett, Josh Eberenz, Sven Jansen. **Ticket Office Assistant:** Jeff Edwards. **Head Groundskeeper:** Tom Nielsen. **Clubhouse Manager:** Trey Hyberger.

Field Staff
Manager: Dave Miloy. **Coach:** Phillip Wellman. **Pitching Coach:** Grant Jackson. **Trainer:** John Young.

Game Information
Radio Announcers: Mark Gorsky, Jim Kelch. **No. of Games Broadcast:** Home-72, Away-72. **Flagship Station:** WLKY 970-AM.

PA Announcer: Charles Gazaway. **Official Scorer:** Unavailable.

Stadium Name (year opened): Louisville Slugger Field (2000). **Location:** I-64 and I-71 to I-65 South/North to Brook Street exit, right on Market Street, left on Jackson Street, stadium on Main Street between Jackson and Preston. **Standard Game Times:** 7:15 p.m.; Sat. 6:15; Sun. 1:15.

Visiting Club Hotel: Holiday Inn Downtown Louisville, 120 W Broadway, Louisville, KY 40202. **Telephone:** (502) 582-2241.

NORFOLK
Tides

Office Address: 150 Park Ave., Norfolk, VA 23510. **Telephone:** (757) 622-2222. **FAX:** (757) 624-9090. **E-Mail Address:** info@norfolktides.com. **Website:** www.norfolktides.com.

Affiliation (first year): New York Mets (1969). **Years in League:** 1969-.

Ownership, Management
Operated by: Tides Baseball Club, LP.

President: Ken Young.

General Manager: Dave Rosenfield. **Assistant General Manager:** Joe Gorza. **Director, Community Relations:** Susan Pinckney. **Director, Media Relations:** Shon Sbarra. **Director, Merchandising:** Mike Giedlin. **Director, Sales/Marketing:** Jay Richardson. **Director, Ticket Operations:** Glenn Riggs. **Director, Video Operations:** Mike Martine. **Director, Group Sales:** Dave Harrah. **Assistant, Group Sales:** Heather Harkins. **Accounting Manager:** Lew Schwartz. **Operations Manager:** Chris Vtipil. **Ticket Manager:** Linda Waisanen. **Receptionist:** Stephanie Brammer. **Clubhouse Manager:** Kevin Kierst. **Visiting Clubhouse Manager:** Stan Hunter. **Head Groundskeeper:** Ken Magner. **Assistant Groundskeeper:** Keith Collins.

Field Staff
Manager: John Gibbons. **Coach:** Howie Freiling. **Pitching Coach:** Rick Waits. **Trainer:** Joe Hawkins.

Game Information

Radio Announcers: Rob Evans, John Castleberry. **No. of Games Broadcast:** Home-72, Away-72. **Flagship Station:** WHKT-AM 1650.

PA Announcer: Frank Bennett. **Official Scorers:** Bob Moskowitz, Charlie Denn.

Stadium Name (year opened): Harbor Park (1993). **Location:** Exit 9, 11A or 11B off I-264, adjacent to the Elizabeth River in downtown Norfolk. **Standard Game Times:** 7:15 p.m.; Sun. (April-June) 1:15, (July-Sept.) 6:15.

Visiting Club Hotels: Sheraton Waterside, 777 Waterside Dr., Norfolk, VA 23510. Telephone: (757) 622-6664; Doubletree Club Hotel, 880 N Military Hwy., Norfolk, VA 23502. Telephone: (757) 461-9192.

OTTAWA
Lynx

Office Address: 300 Coventry Rd., Ottawa, Ontario K1K 4P5. **Telephone:** (613) 747-5969. **FAX:** (613) 747-0003. **E-Mail Address:** lynx@ottawalynx.com. **Website:** www.ottawalynx.com.

Affiliation (first year): Montreal Expos (1993). **Years in League:** 1898, 1951-54, 1993-.

Ownership, Management

Operated By: Ottawa Triple-A Baseball, Inc.
Principal Owner/President: Howard Darwin.
Director, Baseball Operations: Kevin Whalen. **Controller:** Richard Paulin. **Director, Stadium Operations:** Jack Darwin. **Head Groundskeepers:** Brad Keith, Pete Webb. **Director, Media/Public Relations:** Ian Mendes. **Director, Sales/Marketing:** Mark Sluban. **Director, Ticket Sales:** Joe Fagan. **Director, Merchandising:** Nancy Darwin. **Clubhouse Operations:** John Bryk. **Office Manager:** Lorraine Charrette.

Field Staff

Manager: Jeff Cox. **Coach:** Eric Fox. **Pitching Coach:** Randy St. Claire. **Trainer:** Sean Bearer.

Game Information

Radio: None.
PA Announcer: Gord Breen. **Official Scorer:** Frank Calamatas.
Stadium Name (year opened): JetForm Park (1993). **Location:** Highway 417 to Vanier Parkway exit, Vanier Parkway north to Coventry Road, right on Coventry to stadium. **Standard Game Times:** 7:05 p.m.; Sat., Sun. 2:05.

Visiting Club Hotel: Chimo Hotel, 1199 Joseph Cyr Rd., Gloucester, Ontario K1K 3P5. Telephone: (613) 744-1060.

PAWTUCKET
Red Sox

Office Address: One Ben Mondor Way, Pawtucket, RI 02860. **Mailing Address:** P.O. Box 2365, Pawtucket, RI 02861. **Telephone:** (401) 724-7300. **FAX:** (401) 724-2140. **E-Mail Address:** pawsox@worldnet.att.net. **Website:** www.pawsox.com.

Affiliation (first year): Boston Red Sox (1973). **Years in League:** 1973-.

Ownership, Management

Operated by: Pawtucket Red Sox Baseball Club, Inc.
Chairman: Ben Mondor. **President:** Mike Tamburro.
Vice President/General Manager: Ludwig Schwechheimer. **VP, Chief Financial Officer:** Kathy Crowley. **VP, Sales/Marketing:** Michael Gwynn. **VP, Stadium Operations:** Mick Tedesco. **VP, Public Relations:** Bill Wanless. **Assistant to General Manager:** Daryl Jasper. **Controller:** Matthew White. **Office Manager:** Kathy Davenport. **Director, Ticket Operations:** Keith Kuceris. **Ticket Operations:** Jeff Bradley. **Director, Community Relations:** Don Orsillo. **Media Services:** Jill Murphy. **Secretary:** Sandi Browne. **Clubhouse Manager:** Chris Parent. **Head Groundskeeper:** Larry DiVito. **Director, Stadium Services:** Derek Molhan. **Director, Concession Services:** Dave Johnson. **Director, Merchandising:** Steve Napolillo. **Account Executive:** Gordon Smith. **Director, Hospitality:** Kathy Walsh. **Game Day Operations:** Dave Lancaster.

Field Staff
Manager: Gary Jones. **Coach:** Unavailable. **Pitching Coach:** Rich Bombard. **Trainer:** Jim Young.

Game Information
Radio Announcers: Don Orsillo, Mike Logan. **No. of Games Broadcast:** Home-72, Away-72. **Flagship Station:** WSKO 790-AM

PA Announcer: Jim Martin. **Official Scorer:** Bruce Guindon.

Stadium Name (year opened): McCoy Stadium (1999). **Location:** I-95 North to exit 2B (School Street); I-95 South to exit 2A (Newport Avenue). **Standard Game Times:** 7 p.m.; Sat. 6; Sun. 1.

Visiting Club Hotel: Comfort Inn, 2 George St., Pawtucket, RI 02860. Telephone: (401) 723-6700.

RICHMOND
Braves

Office Address: 3001 N Boulevard, Richmond, VA 23230. **Mailing Address:** P.O. Box 6667, Richmond, VA 23230. **Telephone:** (804) 359-4444. **FAX:** (804) 359-0731. **E-Mail Address:** info@rbraves.com. **Website:** www.rbraves.com.

Affiliation (first year): Atlanta Braves (1966). **Years in League:** 1884, 1915 17, 1954 64, 1966-.

Ownership, Management
Operated by: Atlanta National League Baseball, Inc.

Principal Owner: Ted Turner. **President:** Stan Kasten.

General Manager: Bruce Baldwin. **Assistant General Manager:** Ken Clary. **Receptionist:** Janet Zimmerman. **Manager, Stadium Operations:** Nate Doughty. **Manager, Field Maintenance:** Chad Mulholland. **Manager, Public Relations:** Todd Feagans. **Assistant, Public/Community Relations:** Monica Pence. **Manager, Promotions:** Townley Goldsmith. **Manager, Ticket Operations:** Kelly Harris. **Assistant, Ticket Operations:** Bob Fasoldt. **Group Sales Manager:** Katie McFadden. **Assistant, Group Sales:** Jeremy Wells. **Office Manager:** Joanne Cornutt.

Field Staff
Manager: Randy Ingle. **Coach:** Mel Roberts. **Pitching Coach:** Bill Fischer. **Trainer:** Jim Lovell.

Game Information
Radio Announcers: Robert Fish, Rick Page. **No. of Games Broadcast:** Home-72, Away-72. **Flagship Station:** WHNL 910-AM.

PA Announcer: Mike Blacker. **Official Scorers:** Leonard Alley, Roscoe Puckett.

Stadium Name (year opened): The Diamond (1985). **Location:** Exit 78 (Boulevard) at junction of I-64 and I-95, follow signs to park. **Standard Game Times:** 7 p.m., Sun. 2.

Visiting Club Hotel: Quality Inn, 8008 W Broad St., Richmond, VA 23230. Telephone: (804) 346-0000.

ROCHESTER
Red Wings

Office Address: One Morrie Silver Way, Rochester, NY 14608. **Telephone:** (716) 454-1001. **FAX:** (716) 454-1056. **E-Mail Address:** redwings@frontiernet.net. **Website:** www.redwingsbaseball.com.

Affiliation (first year): Baltimore Orioles (1961). **Years in League:** 1885-89, 1891-92, 1895-.

Ownership, Management
Operated by: Rochester Community Baseball, Inc.

Chairman: Naomi Silver. **President:** Gary Larder.

General Manager: Dan Mason. **Assistant General Manager:** Will Rumbold. **Controller:** Darlene Giardina. **Operations Coordinator:** Mary Goldman. **Head Groundskeeper:** Gene Buonomo. **Director, Media/Public Relations:** Chuck Hinkel. **Director, Sales/Marketing:** Steve Salluzzo. **Senior Account Representatives:** Mike Ciavarri, Ryan Ginsberg, Brian Golding. **Director, Human Resources:** Paula LoVerde. **Director, Promotions:** Mike Lipani. **Director, Ticket Sales:** Joe Ferrigno. **Director, Group Sales:** Russ Ruter. **Director, Merchandising:** Josh Harris.

Director, Food Services: Jeff Dodge. **Manager, Suites/Catering:** Tracy DonVito. **Clubhouse Operations:** Kenny Slough. **Manager, Concessions:** Sue King. **Videographer:** Jeff Giarizzo. **Night Secretary:** Cathie Costello. **Business Manager, Concessions:** Dave Bills.

Field Staff
Manager: Marv Foley. **Coach:** Dave Cash. **Pitching Coach:** Larry McCall. **Trainer:** Al Price.

Game Information
Radio Announcers: Joe Castellano, Joe Altobelli. **No. of Games Broadcast:** Home-72, Away-72. **Flagship Stations:** WHTK 1280-AM, WHAM 1180-AM.

PA Announcer: Pete Kennedy. **Official Scorer:** Len Lustik.

Stadium Name (year opened): Frontier Field (1997). **Location:** I-490 East to exit 12 (Brown/Broad Street) and follow signs. I-490 West to Exit 14 (Plymouth Avenue) and follow signs. **Standard Game Times:** 7:15 p.m., Sun. 2:15.

Visiting Club Hotel: Crown Plaza, 70 State St., Rochester NY 14608. Telephone: (716) 546-3450.

SCRANTON/WILKES-BARRE
Red Barons

Office Address: 235 Montage Mountain Rd., Moosic, PA 18507. **Mailing Address:** P.O. Box 3449, Scranton, PA 18505. **Telephone:** (570) 969-2255. **FAX:** (570) 963-6564. **E-Mail Address:** barons@epix.net. **Website:** www.redbarons.com.

Affiliation (first year): Philadelphia Phillies (1989). **Years in League:** 1989-.

Ownership, Management
Operated by: Lackawanna County Stadium Authority.

Chairman: Bill Jenkins.

General Manager: Rick Muntean. **Director, Promotions/Executive Assistant:** Kelly Byron. **Director, Media/Public Relations:** Mike Cummings. **Director, Stadium Operations:** Jeremy Ruby. **Director, Sales/Marketing:** Ron Prislupski. **Senior Account Representatives:** Joe McConnon, Travis Spencer, Jack Gowron, Joe Shaughnessy, Steve Minner. **Director, Ticket Sales:** Ann Marie Nocera. **Director, Merchandising:** Ray Midura. **Director, Food Services:** Rich Sweeney. **Clubhouse Operations:** Red Brower, Rich Revta. **Director, Special Projects:** Karen Healey. **Office Manager:** Donna McDonald. **Controller:** Vicki Lamberton. **Head Groundskeeper:** Bill Casterline. **Directors, Community Relations:** John Hill, Bob Schmidt.

Field Staff
Manager: Marc Bombard. **Coach:** Tony Scott. **Pitching Coach:** Gorman Heimueller. **Trainer:** Clete Sigwart.

Game Information
Radio Announcer: Kent Westling. **No. of Games Broadcast:** Home-72, Away-72. **Flagship Station:** WICK 1400-AM.

PA Announcer: Johnny Davies. **Official Scorers:** Jeep Fanucci, Bob McGoff.

Stadium Name (year opened): Lackawanna County Stadium (1989). **Location:** I-81 to exit 51 (Davis Street/Montage Mountain Road). Take Montage Mountain Road. one mile to stadium. **Standard Game Times:** 7, 7:30 p.m.; Sun. 2, 6.

Visiting Club Hotel: Radisson at Lackawanna Station, 700 Lackawanna Ave., Scranton, PA 18503. Telephone: (570) 342-8300.

SYRACUSE
SkyChiefs

Office Address: P&C Stadium, One Tex Simone Dr., Syracuse, NY 13208. **Telephone:** (315) 474-7833. **FAX:** (315) 474-2658. **E-Mail Address:** baseball@skychiefs.com. **Website:** www.skychiefs.com.

Affiliation (first year): Toronto Blue Jays (1978). **Years in League:** 1885-89, 1891-92, 1894-1901, 1918, 1920-27, 1934-55, 1961-.

Ownership, Management
Operated by: Community Owned Baseball Club of Central New York, Inc. **Chairman:** Richard Ryan. **President:** Donald Waful. **Vice President/Chief Operating Officer:** Anthony "Tex" Simone.

General Manager: John Simone. **Assistant General Manager:** Tom Van Schaack. **Director, Business Operations:** Don Lehtonen. **Director, Stadium Operations:** Brian McManus. **Head Groundskeeper:** John Walters. **Director, Community Relations/Personnel:** Andy Gee. **Director, Ticket Sales:** H.J. Refici. **Director, Group Sales:** Vic Galucci. **Director, Merchandising:** Wendy Shoen. **Director, Food Services:** Kyle Rogers. **Clubhouse Operations:** Jody Puccello. **Receptionist:** Priscilla Venditti. **Assistant Ticket Manager/Group Sales:** Ed Holmes.

Field Staff
Manager: Pat Kelly. **Coach:** Omar Malave. **Pitching Coach:** Gary Lance. **Trainer:** Jon Woodworth.

Game Information
Radio Announcers: Ted DeLuca, Bob McElligot. **No. of Games Broadcast:** Home-72, Away-72. **Flagship Station:** WHEN 620-AM.

PA Announcer: Dave Perkins. **Official Scorers:** Tom Leo, Joel Marieniss.

Stadium Name (year opened): P&C Stadium (1997). **Location:** New York State Thruway to exit 36 (I-81 South), to 7th North Street exit, left on 7th North, right on Hiawatha Boulevard. **Standard Game Times:** 7 p.m.; Sun. 6.

Visiting Club Hotel: Ramada Inn, 1305 Buckley Rd., Syracuse, NY 13212. Telephone: (315) 457-8670.

TOLEDO
Mud Hens

Office Address: 2901 Key St., Maumee, OH 43537. **Telephone:** (419) 893-9483. **FAX:** (419) 893-5847. **E-Mail Address:** mudhens@mud hens.com. **Website:** www.mudhens.com.

Affiliation (first year): Detroit Tigers (1987). **Years in League:** 1889, 1965-.

Ownership, Management
Operated by: Toledo Mud Hens Baseball Club, Inc.

Chairman: Edwin Bergsmark. **President:** Michael Miller.

General Manager: Joseph Napoli. **Assistant GM/Director, Corporate Sales:** Scott Jeffer. **Assistant GM/Director, Marketing:** Neil Neukam. **Manager, Business Operations:** Dorothy Welniak. **Controller:** Bob Eldridge. **Manager, Stadium Operations:** Greg Elliott. **Head Groundskeeper:** L.C. Bates. **Manager, Media/Public Relations:** Brian Britten. **Manager, Promotions:** Kerri White. **Director, Ticket Sales/Group Sales:** Erik Ibsen. **Manager, Merchandising:** Alexander Gonzales. **Clubhouse Operations:** Gary Cook. **Office Manager:** Carol Hamilton. **Associates, Season Ticket/Group Sales:** Joe Barbarito, Andy Koester, Thom Townley. **Associate, Merchandising:** Greg Setola.

Field Staff
Manager: Dave Anderson. **Coach:** Mark Meleski. **Pitching Coach:** Jeff Jones. **Trainer:** Lon Pinhey.

Game Information
Radio Announcers: Jim Weber, Frank Gilhooley. **No. of Games Broadcast:** Home-72, Away-72. **Flagship Station:** Unavailable.

PA Announcer: Unavailable. **Official Scorer:** Unavailable.

Stadium Name (year opened): Ned Skeldon Stadium (1965). **Location:** From Ohio Turnpike 80/90, exit 59, north on Reynolds toward Toledo, right onto Heatherdowns Boulevard, right onto Key Street; From Detroit, I-75 South to exit 201A (Route 25), right onto Key Street; From Ann Arbor, Route 23 South to Route 475 South, exit 6, left at stoplight, follow Dussel Drive to stadium; From Dayton, I-75 via Route 475 to Maumee exit (Route 24), left onto Key Street. **Standard Game Times:** 7 p.m., Sun. 2.

Visiting Club Hotel: Holiday Inn Toledo West, 2340 S Reynolds Rd., Toledo, OH 43614. Telephone: (419) 865-1361.

PACIFICCOASTLEAGUE

Class AAA

Mailing Address: 1631 Mesa Ave., Colorado Springs, CO 80906. **Telephone:** (719) 636-3399. **FAX:** (719) 636-1199. **E-Mail Address:** pcloffice@earthlink.net. **Website:** www.pacificcoastleague.com.

Years League Active: 1903-.
President: Branch B. Rickey.
Vice President: Don Logan.
Directors: Joe Buzas (Salt Lake), Hugh Campbell (Edmonton), John Carbray (Fresno), Rob Couhig (New Orleans), Dave Elmore (Colorado Springs), Michael Gartner (Iowa), Al Gordon (Nashville), Rick Holtzman (Tucson), Dean Jernigan (Memphis), Rob Knight (Omaha), Pat McKernan (Albuquerque), Tim O'Toole (Oklahoma), Russ Parker (Calgary), Art Savage (Sacramento), Hank Stickney (Las Vegas), Mel Taylor (Tacoma).

Branch Rickey

Director, Operations: David Sheriff. **Secretary:** Christine Mazzei.
2000 Opening Date: April 6. **Closing Date:** Sept. 4.
Regular Season: 144 games.
Division Structure: American Conference—Central: Albuquerque, Colorado Springs, Iowa, Omaha. **East:** Memphis, Nashville, New Orleans, Oklahoma. **Pacific Conference—South:** Fresno, Las Vegas, Salt Lake, Tucson. **West:** Calgary, Edmonton, Sacramento, Tacoma.
Playoff Format: West champion plays South champion, and Central champion plays East champion in best-of-5 semifinal series. Winners meet in best-of-5 series for league championship. **Triple-A World Series:** Best-of-5 series vs. International League champion, Sept. 18-22 at Las Vegas.
All-Star Game: July 12 at Rochester, NY (International League vs. PCL).
Roster Limit: 23; 24 for first 30 days of season and after Aug. 24. **Player Eligibility Rule:** No restrictions.
Brand of Baseball: Rawlings ROM.
Umpires: Mike Alvarado (Moses Lake, WA), David Aschwege (Lincoln, NE), Lance Barksdale (Jackson, MS), David Brandt (San Antonio, TX), Fred Cannon (Brookhaven, MS), Robert Drake (Mesa, AZ), Joel Fincher (Arlington, TX), Dan Gnadt (Moorhead, MN), Chris Guccione (Salida, CO), Wes Hamilton (Edmond, OK), Billy Haze (Gilbert, AZ), Scott Higgins (Keizer, OR), Morris Hodges (Helena, AL), Heath Jones (Glendale, AZ), Travis Katzenmeier (Liberal, KS), Ian Lamplugh (Victoria, British Columbia), Brian McCraw (Nashville, TN), Ken Page (Phoenix, AZ), Timothy Pasch (Plant City, FL), Jack Samuels (Orange, CA), Kraig Sanders (Little Rock, AR), Patrick Spieler (Omaha, NE), Chris Taylor (Kansas City, MO), Jim Wolf (West Hills, CA).

Stadium Information

Club	Stadium	Dimensions LF	CF	RF	Capacity	'99 Att.
Albuquerque	Albuquerque Sports	360	410	340	10,510	319,339
Calgary	Burns	345	400	345	8,000	269,002
Colo. Springs	Sky Sox	350	400	350	9,000	202,724
Edmonton	TELUS Field	340	420	320	9,200	385,913
Fresno	Beiden Field	331	410	330	6,575	311,804
Iowa	Sec Taylor	335	400	335	10,800	416,804
Las Vegas	Cashman Field	328	433	323	9,334	339,702
Memphis	AutoZone Park	319	400	322	14,200	397,339
Nashville	Herschel Greer	327	400	327	10,700	335,901
New Orleans	Zephyr Field	333	405	332	11,000	472,665
Oklahoma	Southwestern Bell	325	400	325	13,066	471,722
Omaha	Rosenblatt	332	408	332	24,000	411,233
*Sacramento	Raley Field	330	405	335	11,200	241,461
Salt Lake	Franklin Covey	345	420	315	15,500	505,547
Tacoma	Cheney	325	425	325	9,600	271,026
Tucson	Tucson Electric	340	405	340	11,000	254,817

*Club operated in Vancouver, British Columbia, in 1999

ALBUQUERQUE
Dukes

Office Address: 1601 Avenida Cesar Chavez SE, Albuquerque, NM 87106. **Telephone:** (505) 243-1791. **FAX:** (505) 842-0561. **E-Mail Address:** coastdukes@aol.com.

Affiliation (first year): Los Angeles Dodgers (1972). **Years in League:** 1972-.

Ownership, Management
Operated by: Albuquerque Professional Baseball, Inc.

Principal Owner/Chairman: Bob Lozinak. **President/General Manager:** P. Patrick McKernan.

Assistant GM/Director, Merchandising: Patrick J. McKernan. **Director, Business Operations/Accounting:** Dawnene Shoup. **Director, Stadium Operations:** Mick Byers. **Head Groundskeeper:** Louie Garcia. **Director, Media Relations:** John Miller. **Director, Sales:** Jim Guscott. **Director, Community Relations:** Jay Butler. **Director, Ticket Sales:** Sam Roybal. **Director, Group Sales:** Alex Hamilton. **Director, Food Services:** Matthew McKernan. **Director, Marketing:** Emily Evans. **Home Clubhouse Operations:** Merced Garcia. **Visiting Clubhouse Operations:** Jason Sierra. **Mascot:** Tim McKernan.

Field Staff
Manager: Tom Gamboa. **Coach:** Ron Jackson. **Pitching Coach:** Dean Treanor. **Trainer:** Jason Mahnke.

Game Information
Radio Announcers: Russ Langer, Jim Lawwill. **No. of Games Broadcast:** Home-72, Away-72. **Flagship Station:** KDEF 1150-AM.

PA Announcer: Alex Hamilton. **Official Scorer:** Gary Herron.

Stadium Name (year opened): Albuquerque Sports Stadium (1969). **Location:** I-25 to Avenida Cesar Chavez exit, east to stadium. **Standard Game Times:** 7 p.m., Sun. 1.

Visiting Club Hotel: Plaza Inn Albuquerque, 900 Medical Arts NE, Albuquerque, NM 87102. Telephone: (505) 243-5693.

CALGARY
Cannons

Office Address: 2255 Crowchild Trail NW, Calgary, Alberta T2M 4S7. **Telephone:** (403) 284-1111. **FAX:** (403) 284-4343. **E-Mail Address:** cannons@telusplanet.net. **Website:** www.calgarycannons.com.

Affiliation (first year): Florida Marlins (1999). **Years in League:** 1985-.

Ownership, Management
Operated by: Braken Holdings Ltd.

President: Russ Parker. **Secretary/Treasurer:** Diane Parker.

Vice President, Baseball Operations: John Traub. **VP, Marketing:** Bill Cragg. **VP, Finance:** Chris Poffenroth.

Director, Ticketing: Greg Winthers. **Coordinator, Media Relations:** J.J. Hebert. **Coordinator, Group Sales:** Johnny Hribar. **Sales:** Doug DeNance, Garth Werschler. **Receptionist:** Roberta Siegel. **Administrative Assistant:** Dalyce Binette. **Head Groundskeeper:** Chris Howell. **Clubhouse Operations:** Blair McAusland, Brian Miettinen.

Field Staff
Manager: Lynn Jones. **Coach:** Sal Rende. **Pitching Coach:** Randy Hennis. **Trainer:** Tim Abraham.

Game Information
Radio: None.

PA Announcer: Bill Clapham. **Official Scorer:** Fred Collins.

Stadium Name (year opened): Burns Stadium (1966). **Location:** Crowchild Trail NW to 24th Avenue, adjacent to McMahon Stadium. **Standard Game Times:** 7:05 p.m., (April) 6:05; Sun. 1:35.

Visiting Club Hotel: The Coast Plaza Hotel, 1316 33rd St. NE, Calgary, Alberta T2A 6B6. Telephone: (403) 248-8888.

COLORADO SPRINGS Sky Sox

Office Address: 4385 Tutt Blvd., Colorado Springs, CO 80922.
Telephone: (719) 597-1449. **FAX:** (719) 597-2491. **E-Mail Address:**
info@skysox.com. **Website:** www.skysox.com.

Affiliation (first year): Colorado Rockies (1993). **Years in League:**
1988-.

Ownership, Management

Operated by: Colorado Springs Sky Sox, Inc.

Principal Owner: David G. Elmore.

President/General Manager: Bob Goughan. **Senior Vice President,
Administration:** Sam Polizzi. **Senior VP, Operations:** Dwight Hall. **Senior
VP, Marketing:** Rai Henniger. **Senior VP, Stadium Operations:** Mark
Leasure. **VP, Advertising:** Nick Sciarratta. **Coordinator, Special Events:**
Brien Smith. **Assistant GM, Merchandising:** Robert Stein. **Assistant GM,
Public Relations:** Michael Hirsch. **Director, Finance:** Craig Levin. **Director,
Broadcast Operations:** Dan Karcher. **Director, Community Relations:**
Jake Pierson. **Director, Clubhouse Operations/Marketing Representative:**
Murlin Whitten. **Director, Group Sales:** Michael Humphreys. **Group
Sales/Ticket Operations:** Chip Dreamer, Jeremy Tonniges. **Visiting
Clubhouse Manager:** Greg Grimaldo. **Marketing Representatives:** Sean
Aronson, Mike Brogden, Mike Daniels, Andrew Gassman, Dan Schaefer.

Field Staff

Manager: Chris Cron. **Coach:** Jim Eppard. **Pitching Coach:** Jim Wright.
Trainer: Dan DeVoe.

Game Information

Radio Announcers: Dick Chase, Norm Jones, Dan Karcher. **No. of
Games Broadcast:** Home-72, Away-72. **Flagship Station:** KRDO 1240-AM.

PA Announcer: Nick Sciarratta. **Official Scorer:** Marty Grantz.

Stadium Name (year opened): Sky Sox Stadium (1988). **Location:** I-25
South to Woodmen Road exit, east on Woodmen to Powers Boulevard,
right on Powers to Barnes Road. **Standard Game Times:** 7:05 p.m.; Sat.-
Sun. 1:35.

Visiting Club Hotel: Sheraton Colorado Springs, 2886 S Circle Dr.,
Colorado Springs, CO 80906. Telephone: (719) 576-5900.

EDMONTON Trappers

Office Address: 10233 96th Ave., Edmonton, Alberta T5K 0A5.
Telephone: (780) 414-4450. **FAX:** (780) 414-4475. **E-Mail Address:** trappers@trappersbaseball.com. **Website:** www.trappersbaseball.com.

Affiliation (first year): Anaheim Angels (1999). **Years in League:** 1981-.

Ownership, Management

Operated by: Edmonton Trapper Baseball Club.

Principal Owner: Edmonton Eskimos Football Club. **Chairman:** Hugh
Campbell.

President/General Manager: Mel Kowalchuk. **Assistant General
Manager:** Dennis Henke. **Accountant:** Gabrielle Hampel. **Stadium
Manager:** Don Benson. **Head Groundskeeper:** Luke Syme. **Manager,
Baseball Information:** Gary Tater. **Manager, Sales:** Ken Charuk. **Account
Executives:** Craig Leibel, Del Schjefte. **Manager, Marketing:** Trent Houg.
Manager, Tickets: Victor Liew. **Manager, Group Sales:** Jeff Ivanochko.
Manager, Merchandise: Darin Kowalchuk. **Manager, Special
Events/Assistant to GM:** Lauri Holomis. **Office Manager:** Debbie
Zaychuk. **Home Clubhouse Manager:** James Rosnau. **Visiting
Clubhouse Manager:** Ian Rose.

Field Staff

Manager: Garry Templeton. **Coach:** Leon Durham. **Pitching Coach:**
Greg Minton. **Trainer:** Doug Baker.

Game Information

Radio Announcer: Al Coates. **No. of Games Broadcast:** Unavailable.
Flagship Station: 930-AM The Light.

PA Announcer: Dean Parthenis. **Official Scorers:** Al Coates, Gary
Tater.

Stadium Name (year opened): TELUS Field (1995). Location: From north, 101st Street to 96th Avenue, left on 96th, one block east; From south, Calgary Trail North to Queen Elizabeth Hill, right across Walterdale Bridge, right on 96th Avenue. Standard Game Times: 7:05 p.m.; Sun. 2:05.

Visiting Club Hotel: Sheraton Grande, 10235 101st St., Edmonton, Alberta T5J 3E9. Telephone: (780) 428-7111.

FRESNO
Grizzlies

Office Address: 700 Van Ness Ave., Fresno, CA 93721. Telephone: (559) 442-1994. FAX: (559) 264-0795. Website: www.fresnogrizzlies.com. Affiliation (first year): San Francisco Giants (1998). Years in League: 1998-.

Ownership, Management

Operated by: Fresno Diamond Group.

Principal Owners: John Carbray, Dave Cates, Diane Engelken, Rick Roush. Chairman: William Connolly. President: John Carbray. Vice President, Special Projects: Tim Cullen.

General Manager: Joe Hart. Controller: Art Mehl. Director, Stadium Operations: Glenn Wolff. Director, Media/Public Relations: Brian Snider. Director, Sales/Marketing: David Martin. Senior Account Representatives: Al Balto, Mike Maiorana, Josh Phanco, Ron Thomas. Director, Community Relations: Gus Zernial. Director, Ticket Sales: Theresa Graham. Director, Merchandising: Sarah Jackson. Clubhouse Operations: Alan Lee. Executive Assistants: Sarrah Soza, Leticia Vazquez. Ticket Assistants: Nick Strait, Nicole Ullrich. Assistant, Public Relations: Jesse Molina.

Field Staff

Manager: Shane Turner. Coach: Mike Hart. Pitching Coach: Pete Richert. Trainer: Rick Lembo.

Game Information

Radio Announcers: Johnny Doskow, Jess Gonzalez. No. of Games Broadcast: Home-72, Away-72. Flagship Stations: KCBL 1340-AM, KGST 1600-AM.

PA Announcer: Brian Anthony. Official Scorer: Unavailable.

Stadium Name (year opened): Beiden Field (1987). Location: Highway 41 to Shaw Avenue, east to Cedar, left to stadium. Standard Game Times: 7:05 p.m.; Sun. 2:05.

Visiting Club Hotel: Doubletree Inn-Fresno, 1055 Van Ness Ave., Fresno, CA 93721. Telephone: (559) 485-9000.

IOWA
Cubs

Office Address: 350 SW First St., Des Moines, IA 50309. Telephone: (515) 243-6111. FAX: (515) 243-5152. E-Mail: sbernabe@iowacubs.com. Website: www.iowacubs.com.

Affiliation (first year): Chicago Cubs (1981). Years in League: 1998-.

Ownership, Management

Operated by: Greater Des Moines Baseball Co., Inc.

Majority Owner/Chairman: Michael Gartner.

President/General Manager: Sam Bernabe. Vice President/Assistant General Manager: Jim Nahas. VP/Chief Financial Officer: Sue Tollefson. VP/Director, Stadium Operations: Tom Greene. Director, Broadcasting: Deene Ehlis. Director, Media Relations: Brett Dolan. Director, Public Relations: Jeff Lantz. Director, Stadium Operations: Jeff Tilley. Ticket Manager: Scott Fuller. Director, Group Sales: Brent Conkel. Director, Community Relations/Special Projects: Scott Sailor. Director, Corporate Sales: Jeff Starr. Director, Corporate Relations: Red Hollis. Sales Executive: David Paugh. Head Groundskeeper: Luke Yoder. Office Manager: Peggy Ramsey.

Field Staff

Manager: Dave Trembley. Coach: Glenn Adams. Pitching Coach: Rick Tronerud. Trainer: Bob Grimes.

Game Information

Radio Announcers: Brett Dolan, Deene Ehlis. **No. of Games Broadcast:** Home-72, Away-72. **Flagship Station:** KXTK 940-AM.

PA Announcers: Mike McGuire, Chuck Shockley. **Official Scorer:** Dirk Brinkmeyer.

Stadium Name (year opened): Sec Taylor Stadium (1992). **Location:** I-80 or I-35 to I-235, to Third Street exit, south on Third Street, left on Tuttle Street. **Standard Game Times:** 7:05 p.m.; Sun. 1:35.

Visiting Club Hotel: Des Moines Marriott, 700 Grand Ave., Des Moines, IA 50309. Telephone: (515) 245-5500.

Office Address: 850 Las Vegas Blvd. N, Las Vegas, NV 89101. **Telephone:** (702) 386-7200. **FAX:** (702) 386-7214. **E-Mail Address:** lvstars@earthlink.net. **Website:** www.lasvegasstars.com.

Affiliation (first year): San Diego Padres (1982). **Years in League:** 1982-.

Ownership, Management

Operated by: Mandalay Sports Entertainment.

Chief Executive Officer: Henry Stickney. **Managing Director:** Ken Stickney.

Chairman: Peter Gruber. **Vice Chairman:** Paul Schaeffer.

President/General Manager: Don Logan. **Vice President, Corporate Sales:** Mark Grenier. **VP, Stadium Operations:** Nick Fitzenreider. **VP, Marketing/Broadcasting:** Jon Sandler. **VP, Ticket Sales:** Jeff Eiseman. **Controller:** Allen Taylor. **Manager, Public Relations:** Tracey Elikan. **Director, Merchandising:** Laurie Wanser. **Office Manager:** Denise Korach. **Manager, Marketing:** Tiffany Sanderson.

Field Staff

Manager: Duane Espy. **Coach:** Randy Whisler. **Pitching Coach:** Darrel Akerfelds. **Trainer:** Lance Cacanindin.

Game Information

Radio Announcer: Jon Sandler. **No. of Games Broadcast:** Home-72, Away-72. **Flagship Station:** KBAD 920-AM.

PA Announcer: Dan Bickmore. **Official Scorer:** Jim Gemma.

Stadium Name (year opened): Cashman Field (1983). **Location:** I-15 to U.S. 95 exit (Fremont Street), east on 95 to Las Vegas Boulevard North exit, north on Las Vegas Boulevard. **Standard Game Times:** 7:05 p.m., Sun. 1:05.

Visiting Club Hotel: Palace Station, 2411 W Sahara Ave., Las Vegas, NV 89102. Telephone: (702) 367-2411.

Office Address: 200 Union Ave., Memphis, TN 38103. **Telephone:** (901) 721-6050. **FAX:** (901) 721-6017. **Website:** www.memphisredbirds.com.

Affiliation (first year): St. Louis Cardinals (1998). **Years in League:** 1998-.

Ownership, Management

Operated By: Memphis Redbirds Baseball Foundation, Inc.

Principal Owners: Dean Jernigan, Kristi Jernigan. **Chairman:** Dr. Jesse McClure.

President/General Manager: Allie Prescott. **Assistant General Manager:** Dan Madden. **Assistant to President/Office Manager:** Kipp Williams. **Vice President, Finance:** Chris Jernigan. **Controller:** Don Heitner. **Staff Accountant:** Debbie Ross. **General Accountant:** Arnita Brooks. **Payroll Administrator:** Pam Abney. **VP, Marketing:** Kim Gaskill. **Manager, Marketing:** Beth Hammond. **Graphic Designer:** Iris Horne. **Mascot Coordinator:** Chris Pegg. **Director, Promotions:** Dakota Crow. **Coordinator, Promotions:** Amber Seidel. **Director, Broadcasting:** Tom Stocker. **Manager, Media Relations:** Jason Jones. **VP, Development:** Gwen Driscoll. **Manager, Special Events:** Kate Cannon. **VP, Sales:** Pete Rizzo. **Coordinator, Group Sales:** Paige Perkins. **Coordinator, Sales:** Jennifer Young. **Sales Executives:** Rob Edgerton, Velver Haynes. **VP,**

Community Relations: Reggie Williams. Coordinator, Community Relations: Marsean Bernard. Director, Retail Operations: Kerry Sewell. Director, Field Operations: Steve Horne. Assistant Groundskeeper: Ed Collins. Operations Manager: Steele Ford. Ticket Manager: Scott Gross. Ticketing: Phil McKay. Facilities Manager: Don Rovak. VP, Construction: Arthur Yeates. Director, Project Development: Ray Brown. Manager, Concessions: Robert Garcia.

Field Staff
Manager: Gaylen Pitts. Coach: Boots Day. Pitching Coach: Bill Campbell. Trainer: Pete Fagan.

Game Information
Radio Announcers: Tom Stocker, Reggie Williams. No. of Games Broadcast: Home-72, Away-72. Flagship Station: WHBQ 560-AM.
PA Announcer: Tim VanHorn. Official Scorer: J.J. Guinozzo.
Stadium Name (year opened): AutoZone Park (2000). Location: North on I-240, exit at Union Avenue West, approx. 1.5 miles to park. Standard Game Times: 7:05 p.m., Sat. 6:05, Sun. 2:05.
Visiting Club Hotel: Sleep Inn at Court Square, 40 N Front, Memphis, TN 38103. Telephone: (901) 522-9700.

NASHVILLE
Sounds

Office Address: 534 Chestnut St., Nashville, TN 37203. Telephone: (615) 242-4371. FAX: (615) 256-5684. Website: www.nashsounds.com.
Affiliation (first year): Pittsburgh Pirates (1998). Years in League: 1998-.

Ownership, Management
Operated by: Nashville Sounds Baseball Club, Inc./American Sports Enterprises, Inc.
President/Owner: Al Gordon.
General Manager: Tom Moncrief. Assistant GM/Director, Marketing: Jim Herllhy. Director, Resale/Baseball Operations: Jason Hise. Director, Stadium Operations: Dan Slayden. Director, Ticketing: Chris Snyder. Director, Accounting: Barb Walker. Manager, Public/Community Relations: Crystal Richardson. Manager, Resale: Gary Shephard. Manager, Broadcasting: Chuck Valenches. Office Manager: Sharon Ridley. Manager, Stadium Operations: Phil Laws. Support Coordinator: Ryan Christman. Coordinator, Ticketing Programs: Misha Joseph. Senior Account Executives: Jeff Lyman, Kristin Taylor. Account Executive: Jeremiah Bennett. Clubhouse Manager: Kevin Bryant. Head Groundskeeper: Kenny Franks.

Field Staff
Manager: Trent Jewett. Coach: Richie Hebner. Pitching Coach: Jim Bibby. Trainer: Sandy Krum.

Game Information
Radio Announcer: Chuck Valenches No. of Games Broadcast: Home-72, Away-72. Flagship Station: WNSR 560-AM.
PA Announcer: Unavailable. Official Scorer: Unavailable.
Stadium Name (year opened): Herschel Greer Stadium (1978). Location: I-65 to Wedgewood exit, west to Eighth Avenue, right on Eighth to Chestnut Street, right on Chestnut. Standard Game Times: 7 p.m., (April, Aug. 15-Sept. 2) 6; Sat. 6; Sun. 4 (April 2 p.m.).
Visiting Club Hotel: Unavailable.

NEW ORLEANS
Zephyrs

Office Address: 6000 Airline Dr., Metairie, LA 70003. Telephone: (504) 734-5155. FAX: (504) 734-5118. E-Mail Address: zephyrs@zephyrsbaseball.com. Website: www.zephyrsbaseball.com.
Affiliation (first year): Houston Astros (1997). Years in League: 1998-.

Ownership, Management
Vice President, General Manager: Dan Hanrahan. Assistant VP, Communications: Les East. Assistant VP, Sales/Marketing: Dawn Mentel. Controller: Stephanie Kleehammer. Director, Stadium

Operations: Steven O'Connor. Director, Community Relations/Group Sales: Aaron Lombard. Director, Ticket Sales: Kathy Kaleta. Account Representative: Rene Nadeau. Director, Merchandising: Heather Woods-Menendez. Director, Food Services: George Messina. Head Groundskeeper: Russell Brown. Clubhouse Operations: Richie Runnels. Office Manager: Angie Green. Corporate Sales: Jennifer Dupuy, Brian McGuinness. Assistant, Public Relations: Jamie Howard.

Field Staff
Manager: Tony Pena. Coach: Tony Torchia. Pitching Coach: Jim Hickey. Trainer: Mike Freer.

Game Information
Radio Announcer: Ken Trahan. No. of Games Broadcast: Home-72, Away-72. Flagship Stations: WSMB 1350-AM.

PA Announcer: Rene Nadeau. Official Scorer: J.L. Vangilder.

Stadium Name (year opened): Zephyr Field (1997). Location: I-10 to Clearview Parkway South exit, right on Airline Drive (Route 61) for 1 mile. Standard Game Times: 7:05 p.m.; Sun. (April-May) 2:05, (June-Sept.) 6:05.

Visiting Club Hotel: Best Western Landmark, 2601 Severn Ave., Metairie, LA 70002. Telephone: (504) 888-9500.

OKLAHOMA
Redhawks

Mailing Address: Southwestern Bell Bricktown Ballpark, 2 S Mickey Mantle Dr., Oklahoma City, OK 73104. Telephone: (405) 218-1000. FAX: (405) 218-1001. E-Mail Address: info@redhawksbaseball.com. Website: www.redhawksbaseball.com.

Affiliation (first year): Texas Rangers (1983). Years in League: 1963-1968, 1998-.

Ownership, Management
Operated by: OKC Athletic Club, LP.

Principal Owner: Gaylord Entertainment Co.

President/General Manager: Tim O'Toole. Controller: Steve McEwen. Director, Sales/Marketing: Dianna Bonfiglio. Director, Baseball Operations: John Allgood. Director, Facility Operations: Harlan Budde. Director, Merchandise/Guest Services: Mike Prange. Assistant Director, Sales/Marketing: Brad Tammen. Ticket Manager: Sarah Miller. Senior Accountant: Kristi Fairchild. Broadcaster/Account Manager: Jim Byers. Account Managers: Kristen Clifford, Royal Lewis, Mike Pomeroy, Amy Shreck. Head Groundskeeper: Monte McCoy. Clubhouse Manager: Mike Moulder. Operations Supervisor: Beth Stone. Administrative Assistant: Amy Farnsworth.

Field Staff
Manager: DeMarlo Hale. Coach: Bruce Crabbe. Pitching Coach: Lee Tunnell. Trainer: Greg Harrel.

Game Information
Radio Announcer: Jim Byers. No. of Games Broadcast: Home-72, Away-72. Flagship Station: Unavailable.

PA Announcer: Randy Kemp. Official Scorers: Max Nichols, Pat Petree.

Stadium Name (year opened): Southwestern Bell Bricktown Ballpark (1998). Location: At interchange of I-235 and I-40, take Reno exit, east on Reno. Standard Game Times: 7:05 p.m.; Sun. (April-June) 2:05.

Visiting Club Hotel: Westin Hotel, One N Broadway, Oklahoma City, OK 73102. Telephone: (405) 235-2780.

OMAHA
GoldenSpikes

Office Address: Rosenblatt Stadium, 1202 Bert Murphy Dr., Omaha, NE 68107. Telephone: (402) 734-2550. FAX: (402) 734-7166. E-Mail Address: omahabaseball@goldenspikes.com. Website: www.golden spikes.com.

Affiliation (first year): Kansas City Royals (1969). Years in League: 1998-.

Ownership, Management

Operated by: Omaha Royals, LP.

Principal Owners: Union Pacific Railroad, Warren Buffett, Walter Scott.
President: Rob Knight.

General Manager: Bill Gorman. **Assistant GM:** Terry Wendlandt.
Comptroller: Sue Nicholson. **Head Groundskeeper:** Jesse Cuevas.
Director, Media Relations: Mike Mashanic. **Director, Marketing:** Mike
Stephens. **Account Representatives:** Tony Duffek, Eric Tomb, Shane Tritz.
Director, Radio Broadcasts: Kevin McNabb. **Manager, Ticket Office:** Joe
Volquartsen. **Assistant to Ticket Manager:** Marlene Lee. **Assistant,
Ticket Office:** Bob Brown. **General Manager, Concessions:** Chris
Benevento. **Administrative Assistants:** Kay Besta, Lois Biggs.

Field Staff

Manager: John Mizerock. **Coach:** Scott Leius. **Pitching Coach:** Rick
Mahler. **Trainer:** Jeff Stevenson.

Game Information

Radio Announcer: Kevin McNabb. **No. of Games Broadcast:** Home-
72, Away-72. **Flagship Station:** KOSR 1490-AM.

PA Announcers: Walt Gibbs, Bill Jensen, Steve Roberts. **Official
Scorers:** Frank Adkisson, Steve Pivovar, Rob White.

Stadium Name (year opened): Rosenblatt Stadium (1948). **Location:** I-
80 to 13th Street South exit, south one block. **Standard Game Times:** 7:05
p.m.; Sun. 1:35.

Visiting Club Hotel: Ramada Hotel Central, 7007 Grover St., Omaha,
NE 68106. Telephone: (402) 397-7030.

Office Address: 1001 Second St., Old Sacramento, CA 95814.
Telephone: (916) 319-4700. FAX: (916) 319-4710. E-Mail Address:
info@rivercats.com. Website: www.rivercats.com.

Affiliation (first year): Oakland Athletics (1999). Years in League: 2000 .

Ownership, Management

Owned by: Sacramento River Cats, LLC.

Principal Owner/President: Art Savage. **Executive Vice Presidents:**
Bob Hemond, Warren Smith.

Vice President/General Manager: Gary Arthur. **VP, Sales/Marketing:**
Tom Glick. **VP, Stadium Operations:** Bob Herrfeldt. **VP,
Finance/Administration.** Dan Viotica. **Director, Media Relations:** Mike
Gazda. **Manager, Stadium Operations:** Matt LaRose. **General Manager,
Food/Merchandise:** Dale Haynes. **Director, Corporate Sales:** Darrin
Gross. **Director, Ticketing:** Dave Wolloch. **Executive Assistant:** Nina
Handen.

Field Staff

Manager: Bob Geren. **Coach:** Roy White. **Pitching Coach:** Rick
Rodriguez. **Trainer:** Walt Horn.

Game Information

Radio Announcer: Jeff Walker. **No. of Games Broadcast:** Home-72,
Away-72. **Flagship Station:** KCTC 1320-AM.

PA Announcer: Unavailable. **Official Scorer:** Unavailable.

Stadium Name (year opened): Raley Field (2000). **Location:** Hwy 275
South between Risk Lane and South River Rd. **Standard Game Times:**
7:05 p.m.; Sun. 1:05, 7:05.

Visiting Club Hotel: Holiday Inn Downtown Capitol Plaza, 300 J St.,
Sacramento, CA 95814. Telephone: (916) 446-0100.

Office Address: 77 West 1300 S, Salt Lake City, UT 84115. Mailing
Address: P.O. Box 4108, Salt Lake City, UT 84110. Telephone: (801) 485-
3800. FAX: (801) 485-6818. E-Mail Address: slbuzz@buzzbaseball.com.
Website: www.buzzbaseball.com.

Affiliation (first year): Minnesota Twins (1994). Years in League: 1915-
25, 1958-65, 1970-84, 1994-.

Ownership, Management
Operated by: Buzas Baseball, Inc.
President/General Manager: Joe Buzas. **Vice President:** Hilary Buzas-Drammis. **VP/Assistant GM:** Dorsena Picknell. **Director, Media/Public Relations:** Rob White. **Director, Ticket Sales:** Michael O'Conor. **Sales Manager:** Michael Begley. **Director, Marketing:** Jim Hochstrasser. **Director, Group Sales:** Emily Humphrey. **Administrative Assistant:** Kristin Kirkpatrick.

Field Staff
Manager: Phil Roof. **Coach:** Bill Springman. **Pitching Coach:** Rick Anderson. **Trainer:** Rick McWane.

Game Information
Radio Announcer: Steve Klauke. **No. of Games Broadcast:** Home-72, Away-72. **Flagship Station:** KFNZ 1320-AM.
PA Announcer: Jeff Reeves. **Official Scorers:** Bruce Hilton, Howard Nakagama.
Stadium Name (year opened): Franklin Covey Field (1994). **Location:** From I-15 North, take 2100 South exit, east at West Temple, north to 1300 South; from I-15 South, take the Beck Street exit, which becomes 300 West, continue south to 1300 South. **Standard Game Times:** 7 p.m., 6:15 (April-May); Sun. (April-June) 2, (July-Aug.) 5.
Visiting Club Hotel: Quality Inn City Center, 154 West 600 S, Salt Lake City, UT 84101. Telephone: (801) 521-2930.

TACOMA
Rainiers

Office Address: 2502 S Tyler, Tacoma, WA 98405. **Telephone:** (253) 752-7707. **FAX:** (253) 752-7135. **E-Mail Address:** tacomapcl@aol.com. **Website:** www.rainiers.com.
Affiliation (first year): Seattle Mariners (1995). **Years in League:** 1904-05, 1960-.

Ownership, Management
Operated by: George's Pastime, Inc.
President: George Foster.
Executive Vice President: Mel Taylor. **President, Community Fund:** Sue Foster. **Assistant General Manager:** Dave Lewis. **VP, Budget/Finance:** Laurie Yarbrough. **Director, Baseball Operations:** Kevin Kalal. **Director, Marketing/Public Relations:** Rachel Marcele. **Director, Media Sales/Special Events:** Renee Waltz. **Director, Broadcasting/Media Relations:** Mike Curto. **Director, Ticket Sales:** Tim Sexton. **Director, Food/Beverage:** Randy Yarger. **Assistant Director, Food/Beverage:** Twila Elrod. **Ticket Manager:** Philip Cowan. **Assistant Ticket Manager:** Dan Davidson. **Corporate Sales:** Connie Littlejohn-Rivers. **Staff Accountant:** Saundra Field. **Account Representative:** Jennie Van Ella. **Office Manager/Community Fund:** Mary Lanier. **Stadium Manager/Head Groundskeeper:** Bob Christofferson. **Clubhouse Manager:** Rob Reagle.

Field Staff
Manager: Dave Myers. **Coach:** Dave Brundage. **Pitching Coach:** Jim Slaton. **Trainer:** Randy Roetter.

Game Information
Radio Announcer: Mike Curto. **No. of Games Broadcast:** Home-72, Away-72. **Flagship Station:** KLAY 1180-AM.
PA Announcer: Jeff Randall. **Official Scorer:** Darin Padur.
Stadium Name (year opened): Cheney Stadium (1960). **Location:** From I-5, take exit 132 (Highway 16 West) for 1.2 miles to 19th Street East exit, right on Tyler Street for 1/3 mile. **Standard Game Times:** 7:05 p.m., 12:35; Sat. 1:35, 7:05; Sun. 1:35.
Visiting Club Hotel: La Quinta Inn, 1425 E 27th St., Tacoma, WA 98421. Telephone: (253) 383-0146.

TUCSON
Sidewinders

Office Address: 2500 E Ajo Way, Tucson, AZ 85713. **Mailing Address:** P.O. Box 27045, Tucson, AZ 85726. **Telephone:** (520) 434-1021. **FAX:** (520) 889-9477. **E-Mail Address:** tuffy@azstarnet.com. **Website:** www.tucsonsonsidewinders.com.

Affiliation (first year): Arizona Diamondbacks (1998). **Years in League:** 1969-.

Ownership, Management

Operated by: Tucson Baseball, LLC.

Principal Owner/President: Jay Zucker.

Vice President, Baseball Operations: Mike Feder. **VP, Business Development:** Jack Donovan. **Assistant General Manager:** Todd Woodford. **Controller:** DiAnne Brogna. **Head Groundskeeper:** Jamie Ruffle. **Director, Media/Public Relations:** Eric Thomae. **Director, Telemarketing:** Doug Leary. **Director, Group Sales:** Eric May. **Ticket Manager:** Darby Whitman. **Director, Food Services:** Bob Newman. **Marketing Assistant:** Nicole Strauss. **Clubhouse Operations:** Chad Chiffin.

Field Staff

Manager: Tom Spencer. **Coach:** Mike Barnett. **Pitching Coach:** Chuck Kniffin. **Trainer:** Greg Barber.

Game Information

Radio Announcer: Eric Thomae. **No. of Games Broadcast:** Home-72, Away-72. **Flagship Station:** KTKT 990-AM.

PA Announcer: Anthony DeFazio. **Official Scorer:** Unavailable.

Stadium Name (year opened): Tucson Electric Park (1998). **Location:** From southeast, I-10 to Palo Verde exit, north to Ajo, west to stadium; From northwest, I-10 to Ajo exit, east on Ajo to stadium. **Standard Game Times:** 7:30 p.m., (April-May) 7; Sun. 7, (April-May) 6.

Visiting Club Hotel: Viscount Suite Hotel, 4855 E Broadway, Tucson, AZ 85711. Telephone. (520) 745-6500.

EASTERN LEAGUE

Class AA

Office Address: 511 Congress St., 7th Floor, Portland, ME 04104. **Mailing Address:** P.O. Box 9711, Portland, ME 04104. **Telephone:** (207) 761-2700. **FAX:** (207) 761-7064. **E-Mail Address:** elpb@easternleague.com. **Website:** www.easternleague.com.

Years League Active: 1923-.

President/Treasurer: Bill Troubh.

Vice President/Corporate Secretary: Joe McEacharn. **Administrative Assistant:** William Cook.

Directors: Greg Agganis (Akron), William Dowling (New Britain), Charles Eshbach (Portland), Barry Gordon (Norwich), Alan Levin (Erie), Bob Lozinak (Altoona), Ed Massey (New Haven), Steve Resnick (Harrisburg), Dick Stanley (Trenton), Craig Stein (Reading), Mike Urda (Binghamton).

Bill Troubh

2000 Opening Date: April 7. **Closing Date:** Sept. 4.

Regular Season: 142 games.

Division Structure: North—Binghamton, New Britain, New Haven, Norwich, Portland, Trenton. **South**—Akron, Altoona, Bowie, Erie, Harrisburg, Reading.

Playoff Format: Top two teams in each division play best-of-5 series. Winners meet in best-of-5 series for league championship.

All-Star Game: July 12 at Bowie, MD (joint Double-A game).

Roster Limit: 23; 24 until 30th day of season and after Aug. 10. **Player Eligibility Rule:** No restrictions.

Brand of Baseball: Rawlings ROM-EL.

Statistician: Howe Sportsdata, Boston Fish Pier, West Bldg. #1, Suite 302, Boston MA 02210.

Umpires: Greg Ayers (Boulder, CO), Robert Bainter (Galesburg, IL), John Bennett (Shelbyville, KY), Adam Dowdy (Pontiac, IL), Robert Driskell (Panama City, FL), David Glass (Altanta, GA), Don Goller (East Aurora, NY), Matthew Hollowell (Whitehouse Station, NJ), James Hoye (North Olmsted, OH), Eric MacMillan (Chester, NJ), Scott Packard (Horseheads, NY), Brian Rayder (Morristown, NJ), Alexander Rea (Miami, FL), Andrew Shultz (Millersville, PA), Neil Taylor (St. Petersburg, FL), Scott Walendowski (St. Clair, MI), Mark Winters (Pleasant Plains, IL).

Stadium Information

Club	Stadium	Dimensions LF	CF	RF	Capacity	'99 Att.
Akron	Canal Park	331	400	337	9,297	522,459
Altoona	Altoona Ballpark	325	400	325	6,120	323,932
Binghamton	Binghamton Municipal	330	400	330	6,012	203,674
Bowie	Prince Georges	309	405	309	10,000	421,398
Erie	Jerry Uht Park	312	400	328	6,000	234,257
Harrisburg	RiverSide	335	400	335	6,302	253,399
New Britain	New Britain	330	400	330	6,146	177,026
New Haven	Yale Field	340	405	315	6,200	197,163
Norwich	Thomas J. Dodd	309	401	309	6,275	244,442
Portland	Hadlock Field	315	400	330	6,860	402,582
Reading	GPU	330	400	330	8,800	448,367
Trenton	Waterfront Park	330	407	330	6,440	440,033

AKRON
Aeros

Office Address: 300 S Main St., Akron, OH 44308. **Telephone:** (330) 253-5151. **FAX:** (330) 253-3300. **E-Mail Adress:** aaeros@neo.rr.com. **Website:** www.akronaeros.com.

Affiliation (first year): Cleveland Indians (1989). **Years in League:** 1997-.

Ownership, Management
Operated by: Akron Professional Baseball, Inc.
Principal Owners: Mike Agganis, Greg Agganis.
Chief Executive Officer: Greg Agganis. **Vice President:** Drew Cooke. **Chief Financial Officer:** Bob Larkins.
Executive Vice President/General Manager: Jeff Auman. **Senior Director, Ticket Operations:** Kurt Landes. **Director, Group Sales:** Kim Usselman. **Manager, Group Sales:** Matt Ippolito. **Manager, Ticket Sales:** Mark Yonker. **Senior Account Representative, Group Sales:** Thomas Craven. **Account Representative, Group Sales:** Mike Swope. **Group Sales Associate:** Arlene Vidumansky. **Director, Corporate Marketing/Communications:** Erin Wander. **Director, Media Relations:** James Carpenter. **Director, Community Relations:** Katie Dannemiller. **Director, Merchandising:** Kris Roukey. **Director, Field Maintenance:** Rick Izzo. **Director, Stadium Operations:** Scott Smith. **Receptionist:** Jean Dockus.

Field Staff
Manager: Eric Wedge. **Coach:** Mike Sarbaugh. **Pitching Coach:** Carl Willis. **Trainer:** Nick Paparesta.

Game Information
Radio Announcers: Todd Bell, Jim Clark. **No. of Games Broadcast:** Home-71, Away-71. **Flagship Station:** WTOU 1350-AM.
PA Announcer: Rob Brender. **Official Scorers:** Tom Liggett, Will Roleson.
Stadium Name (year opened): Canal Park (1997). **Location:** From I 76 East or I-77 South, exit onto Route 59 East, exit at Exchange/Cedar and turn right onto Cedar, go left at Main Street. From I 76 West or I 77 North, exit at Main Street/Downtown, follow exit onto Broadway Street, left onto Exchange Street, right at Main Street. **Standard Game Times:** 7:05 p.m., Sat. (April) 2:05; Sun. 2:05.
Visiting Club Hotel: Radisson Hotel Akron City Centre, 20 W Mill St., Akron, OH 44308. Telephone: (330) 384-1500.

ALTOONA
Curve

Office Address: 1000 Park Ave., Altoona, PA 16602. **Mailing Address:** P.O. Box 1029, Altoona, PA 16603. **Telephone:** (814) 943-5400. **FAX:** (814) 943-9050. **E-Mail Address:** curvekid@penn.com. **Website:** www.altoonacurve.com.

Affiliation (first year): Pittsburgh Pirates (1999). **Years in League:** 1999-.

Ownership, Management
Operated by: Altoona Baseball Properties, LLC.
Principal Owner: Bob Lozinak.
Senior Advisor, Baseball Operations: Sal Baglieri. **General Manager:** Jeff Parker. **Assistant GM:** Stephen Lozinak. **Director, Finance/Human Resources:** Mary McMullen. **Director, Marketing:** Jim Gregory. **Director, Media Relations/Events:** Robin Wentz. **Manager, Tickets:** Robert Greene. **Manager, Group Sales:** Shawn Hicks. **Co-Manager, Group Sales:** C.K. Egan. **Manager, Merchandising:** Rich McKeon. **Manager, Stadium Operations:** Ryan Donahue. **Manager, Customer Service:** Matt Fiochetta. **Assistant Ticket Manager:** Shawn Reimer. **Director, Broadcasting:** Rob Egan. **Sales Associate:** Judy Savine. **Head Groundskeeper:** Justin Spillman. **Assistant Groundskeeper:** Rusty Reese. **Clubhouse Operations:** Jake Hundt.

Field Staff
Manager: Marty Brown. **Coach:** Jeff Livesey. **Pitching Coach:** Bruce Tanner. **Trainer:** Mike Sandoval.

Game Information
Radio Announcer: Rob Egan. **No. of Games Broadcast:** Home-71,

Away-71. **Flagship Station:** WFBG 1290-AM.

PA Announcer: Rich Deleo. **Official Scorer:** Unavailable.

Stadium Name (year opened): Altoona Ballpark (1999). **Location:** I-99 to Frankstown Road exit. **Standard Game Times:** 7:05 p.m., (April-May) 6:35, Sun. 1:35.

Visiting Club Hotel: Days Inn, 3306 Pleasant Valley Blvd., Altoona, PA 16602. **Telephone:** (814) 944-9661.

 **Mets**

BINGHAMTON

Office Address: 211 Henry St., Binghamton, NY 13902. **Mailing Address:** P.O. Box 598, Binghamton, NY 13902. **Telephone:** (607) 723-6387. **FAX:** (607) 723-7779. **E-Mail Address:** bmets@bmets.com. **Website:** www.bmets.com.

Affiliation (first year): New York Mets (1992). **Years in League:** 1923-63, 1967-68, 1992-.

Ownership, Management

Operated by: Binghamton Mets Baseball Club, Inc.

Principal Owners: David Maines, William Maines, R.C. Reuteman, George Scherer, Christopher Urda, Michael Urda.

President: Michael Urda.

Vice President/General Manager: R.C. Reuteman. **Director, Business Operations:** Jim Weed. **Director, Stadium Operations:** Richard Tylicki. **Head Groundskeeper:** Scott Dobbins. **Director, Corporate Sales:** Kevin Mahoney. **Sales Representative:** Robert O'Brien. **Director, Community Relations:** Tracy Beskid. **Manager, Merchanding:** Greg Ronneburger. **Director, Food/Beverage:** Pete Brotherton. **Clubhouse Operations:** Craig Holly. **Bookkeeper:** Karen Micalizza.

Field Staff

Manager: Doug Davis. **Coach:** Luis Natera. **Pitching Coach:** Guy Conti. **Trainer:** Bill Wagner.

Game Information

Radio Announcer: Unavailable. **No. of Games Broadcast:** Home-71, Away-71. **Flagship Station:** WNBF 1290-AM.

PA Announcer: Roger Neel. **Official Scorer:** Steve Kraly.

Stadium Name (year opened): Binghamton Municipal (1992). **Location:** I-81 to exit 4S (Binghamton), Route 11 exit to Henry Street. **Standard Game Times:** 7 p.m., (April-May) 6; Sat. (April-May) 1:30; Sun. 1:30.

Visiting Club Hotel: Holiday Inn Arena, Vestal Parkway East, Vestal, NY 13850. **Telephone:** (607) 729-6371.

 Baysox

BOWIE

Office Address: 4101 NE Crain Hwy., Bowie, MD 20716. **Mailing Address:** P.O. Box 1661, Bowie, MD 20717. **Telephone:** (301) 805-6000. **FAX:** (301) 805-6008. **E-Mail Address:** info@baysox.com. **Website:** www.baysox.com.

Affiliation (first year): Baltimore Orioles (1993). **Years In League:** 1993-.

Ownership, Management

Operated by: Maryland Baseball, LLC.

Principal Owners: John Daskalakis, Peter Kirk, Frank Perdue, Hugh Schindel, Pete Simmons.

Maryland Baseball/Chairman: Peter Kirk. **President:** Pete Simmons. **Vice Chairman:** Hugh Schindel. **Senior Vice President, Club Operations:** Keith Lupton. **Executive Secretary:** Jan Varney. **Chief Financial Officer:** Tom Foard. **Director, Public Relations:** Charlie Vascellaro.

General Manager: Jon Danos. **Assistant GM, Ticket Operations:** Mike Munter. **Director, Stadium Operations:** Bill Staub. **Director, Sponsorship Sales:** Chuck Nagle. **Director, Broadcasting/Media Relations:** Dave Collins. **Director, Communications/Promotions:** Kerry Lang. **Group Sales:** Ann Hinsberg, Becci Velasco, Phillip Wrye. **Graphic Design:** Ryan MacMurray. **Account Managers:** Tom DeGroff, Gary Groll, Bill Snitcher. **Assistant Director, Ticket Operations:** Brad Sims. **Assistant Director, Ticket Management/Database Marketing:** Brooks Sears. **Office**

Manager: Margo Carpenter. **Receptionist:** Lynn Cloutier. **Public Relations Intern:** Andy Frankel. **Ticket Operations Intern:** Meghan O'Connell.

Field Staff

Manager: Andy Etchebarren. **Coach:** Butch Davis. **Pitching Coach:** Dave Schmidt. **Trainer:** Dave Walker.

Game Information

Radio Announcer: Dave Collins. **No. of Games Broadcast:** Home-71, Away-71. **Flagship Station:** WNAV 1430-AM.

PA Announcer: Unavailable. **Official Scorer:** Jeff Hertz.

Stadium Name (year opened): Prince Georges Stadium (1994). **Location:** U.S. 50 to U.S. 301 South, left at second light. **Standard Game Times:** 7:05 p.m.; Thurs. 6:35; Sun. 1:05.

Visiting Club Hotel: Radisson-Annapolis, 210 Holiday Court, Annapolis, MD 21401. Telephone: (410) 224-3150.

ERIE
SeaWolves

Office Address: 110 E 10th St., Erie, PA 16501. **Mailing Address:** P.O. Box 1776, Erie, PA 16507. **Telephone:** (814) 456-1300, (800) 456-1304. **FAX:** (814) 456-7520. **E-Mail Address:** seawolves@seawolves.com. **Website:** www.seawolves.com.

Affiliation (first year): Anaheim Angels (1999). **Years in League:** 1999-.

Ownership, Management

Operated by: Palisades Baseball Ltd.

Principal Owner: Alan Levin. **Executive Vice President:** Erik Haag. **VP, Sales:** Keith Hallal. **Director, Finance:** Andy Zmudzinski.

General Manager: John Frey. **Head Groundskeeper:** Pete Geddes. **Director, Corporate/Media Relations:** Steve Glenn. **Director, Marketing/Promotions:** Bill Murray. **Director, Ticket Operations:** Greg Milo. **Director, Group Sales:** Shawn Waskiewicz. **Director, Concessions:** Matt Broooo. **Director, Broadcasting:** Kale Beers. **Assistant Director, Marketing/Promotions:** Brad Schmitt. **Account Executive:** Mike Uden. **Accountant.** Bernadette Mulvihill. **Administrative Assistant:** Christine Brown.

Field Staff

Manager: Don Wakamatsu. **Coach:** Bill Lachemann. **Pitching Coach:** Howie Gershberg. **Trainer:** Geoff Hostetter.

Game Information

Radio Announcer: Kale Beers. **No. of Games Broadcast:** Home-71, Away-71. **Flagship Station:** WLKK 1400-AM.

PA Announcer: Unavailable. **Official Scorer:** Les Caldwell.

Stadium Name (year opened): Jerry Uht Park (1995). **Location:** U.S. 79 North to East 12th Street exit, left on State Street, right on 10th Street. **Standard Game Times:** 7 p.m.; (April-May) 6; Sat. (April-May) 2; Sun. 2.

Visiting Club Hotel: Avalon Hotel, 16 W 10th St., Erie, PA 16501. Telephone: (814) 459-2220.

HARRISBURG
Senators

Office Address: RiverSide Stadium, City Island, Harrisburg, PA 17101. **Mailing Address:** P.O. Box 15757, Harrisburg, PA 17105. **Telephone:** (717) 231-4444. **FAX:** (717) 231-4445. **E-Mail Address:** hbgsenator-@aol.com. **Website:** www.senatorsbaseball.com.

Affiliation (first year): Montreal Expos (1991). **Years in League:** 1924-35, 1987-.

Ownership, Management

Operated by: Harrisburg Senators Baseball Club, Inc.

Chairman: Greg Martini.

General Manager: Todd Vander Woude. **Assistant GM, Baseball Operations:** Mark Mattern. **Assistant GM, Business Operations:** Mark Clarke. **Director, Broadcasting/Media Relations:** Brad Sparesus. **Director, Facilities Operations:** Tim Foreman. **Director, Concessions Operations:** Steve Leininger. **Director, Ticket Sales:** Tom Wess. **Director, Group Sales:** Brian Egli. **Director, Picnic Operations:** Carol Baker.

Human Resources: Karen Coxson. **Director, Community Relations:** Richard House. **Coordinator, Community Relations:** Jocelyn Johnson. **Ticket Sales Associate:** Mark Brindle. **Clubhouse Operations:** Michael Diehl.

Field Staff
Manager: Doug Sisson. **Coach:** Tony Barbone. **Pitching Coach:** Jerry Reuss. **Trainer:** Dave Cohen.

Game Information
Radio Announcers: Brad Sparesus, Mark Mattern. **No. of Games Broadcast:** Home-71, Away-71. **Flagship Station:** WKBO 1230-AM.
PA Announcer: Chris Andree. **Official Scorer:** Gary Ritter.
Stadium Name (year opened): RiverSide Stadium (1987). **Location:** I-83, exit 23 (Second Street) to Market Street, bridge to City Island. **Standard Game Times:** 6:35 p.m.; Sat. 6:05; Sun. 1:05.
Visiting Club Hotel: Hilton Hotel, One N Second St., Harrisburg, PA 17101. Telephone: (717) 233-6000.

NEW BRITAIN
Rock Cats

Office Address: New Britain Stadium, 230 John Karbonic Way, New Britain, CT 06051. **Mailing Address:** P.O. Box 1718, New Britain, CT 06050. **Telephone:** (860) 224-8383. **FAX:** (860) 225-6267. **Website:** www.rockcats.com.
Affiliation (first year): Minnesota Twins (1995). **Years in League:** 1983-

Ownership, Management
Operated by: New Britain Baseball, Inc.
Principal Owners: William Dowling, Coleman Levy.
Chairman: Coleman Levy. **President/General Manager:** William Dowling.
Director, Stadium/Ticket Operations: Sebastian Thomas. **Director, Media Relations:** Chris McKibben. **Director, Marketing/Promotions:** Evan Levy. **Account Executives:** Peter Colon, Alexander Moore. **Director, Group Sales/Community Affairs:** Melinda Mayne. **Director, Merchandise/Internet Services:** John Willi. **Home Clubhouse Manager:** Rich Grajewski. **Visiting Clubhouse Manager:** Jack Josephs.

Field Staff
Manager: John Russell. **Coach:** Jarvis Brown. **Pitching Coach:** Stu Cliburn. **Trainer:** Dave Pruemer.

Game Information
Radio Announcer: Jeff Dooley. **No. of Games Broadcast:** Home-71, Away-71. **Flagship Station:** WMRD 1150-AM.
PA Announcer: Unavailable. **Official Scorers:** Bob Kirschner, Ken Lipshez.
Stadium Name (year opened): New Britain Stadium (1996). **Location:** From I-84, take Route 72 East (exit 35) or Route 9 South (exit 39A), left at Ellis Street (exit 25), left at South Main Street, stadium one mile on right; From Route 91 or Route 5, take Route 9 North to Route 71 (exit 24), first exit. **Standard Game Times:** 7 p.m.; (April-May) 6:35; Sun. 2.
Visiting Club Hotel: Super 8, 1 Industrial Park Rd., Cromwell, CT 06416. Telephone: (860) 632-8888.

NEW HAVEN
Ravens

Office Address: 252 Derby Ave., West Haven, CT 06516. **Telephone:** (203) 782-1666. **FAX:** (203) 782-3150. **E-Mail Address:** ravens@connix. com. **Website:** www.ravens.com.
Affiliation (first year): Seattle Mariners (1999). **Years in League:** 1916-32, 1994-.

Ownership, Management
Operated By: New Haven Baseball, LP.
Principal Owner: Edward Massey.
General Manager: Chris Canetti. **Assistant GM, Operations:** Greg Schmidt. **Assistant GM, Sales/Marketing:** Bill Berger. **Director, Group Sales:** Jay Eylward. **Director, Operations:** Ian Bethune. **Director, Merchandise/Community Relations:** Traci Culotta. **Director, Food

Services: Jason Matlock. **Controller:** Tamara Nolin. **Director, Broadcasting/Home Clubhouse:** Bill Schweizer. **Visiting Clubhouse:** Eric Del Ricci. **Manager, Accounts Receivable:** Barbara Prato. **Manager, Ticket Operations:** Jan Moffat. **Corporate Sales:** Lori McCarthy. **Group Sales Account Executives:** Chris Brown, Erin Scheuren. **Head Groundskeeper:** Rick Capacelatro. **Chief Marketing Officer:** Dave Dittman.

Field Staff

Manager: Dan Rohn. **Coach:** Henry Cotto. **Pitching Coach:** Steve Peck. **Trainer:** Rob Nadine.

Game Information

Radio Announcer: Bill Schweizer. **No. of Games Broadcast:** Home-71, Away-71. **Flagship Station:** WAVZ 1300-AM.

PA Announcer: Don Laviano. **Official Scorer:** Tim Bennett.

Stadium Name (year opened): Yale Field (1927). **Location:** From I-95, take eastbound exit 44 or westbound exit 45 to Route 10 and follow the Yale Bowl signs. From Merritt Parkway, take exit 57, follow to 34 East. **Standard Game Times:** 7 p.m.; Sun. 1.

Visiting Club Hotel: Best Western Executive Hotel, 490 Saw Mill Rd., West Haven, CT 06516. **Telephone:** (203) 933-0344.

Office Address: 14 Stott Ave., Norwich, CT 06360. **Mailing Address:** P.O. Box 6003, Yantic, CT 06389. **Telephone:** (860) 887-7962. **FAX:** (860) 886-5996. **E-Mail Address:** tater@gators.com. **Website:** www.gators.com.

Affiliation (first year): New York Yankees (1995). **Years in League:** 1995-.

Ownership, Management

Operated by: Minor League Sports Enterprises, LP.

Principal Owners: Bob Friedman, Neil Goldman, Barry Gordon, Marc Klee, Hank Smith.

Chairman: Barry Gordon. **President:** Hank Smith.

Vice President/General Manager: Brian Mahoney. **Assistant GM, Marketing/Sales:** Tom Hinsch. **Director, Finance:** Richard Darling. **Director, Stadium Operations:** Chris Fritz. **Director, Media/Broadcasting:** Shawn Holliday **Assistant Director, Broadcasting/Marketing:** Mark Leinweaver. **Manager, Marketing:** John Fleming. **Ticket Manager:** Chris Caulfield. **Director, Group Sales:** John Gilbert. **Manager, Group Sales:** Tom Gentile. **Director, Ticket Operations:** Lara Wroblewski. **Director, Merchandise:** Kara Infante. **Director, Food Services:** Rick Fitzpatrick. **Office Manager:** Michelle Sadowski. **Head Groundskeeper:** Chris Langley. **Stadium Superintendent:** Kevin Johns. **Merchandise Assistant:** Andy Revell. **Ticket Assistant:** Ben Master. **FanCard Assistant:** Craig Drilling.

Field Staff

Manager: Dan Radison. **Coach:** Ken Dominguez. **Pitching Coach:** Tom Filer. **Trainer:** Carl Randolph.

Game Information

Radio Announcers: Shawn Holliday, Mark Leinweaver. **No. of Games Broadcast:** Home-71, Away-71. **Flagship Station:** WSUB 980-AM.

PA Announcer: John Tuite. **Official Scorer:** Gene Gumbs.

Stadium Name (year opened): Senator Thomas J. Dodd Memorial Stadium (1995). **Location:** I-395 to exit 82, follow signs to Norwich Industrial Park, stadium is in back of industrial park. **Standard Game Times:** Mon.-Thur. (April-May) 6:05 p.m., (June-Sept.) 7:05; Fri. 7:05; Sat. (April-May) 1:05, (June-Sept.) 7:05; Sun. 1:05.

Visiting Club Hotel: Days Inn-Niantic, 265 Flanders Rd., Niantic, CT 06357. Telephone: (860) 739-6921.

Office Address: 271 Park Ave., Portland, ME 04102. **Mailing Address:** P.O. Box 636, Portland, ME 04104. **Telephone:** (207) 874-9300. **FAX:** (207) 780-0317. **E-Mail Address:** seadogs@portlandseadogs.com. **Website:** www.portlandseadogs.com.

Affiliation (first year): Florida Marlins (1994). **Years in League:** 1994-.

Ownership, Management
Operated By: Portland, Maine, Baseball, Inc.
Principal Owner/Chairman: Daniel Burke.
President/General Manager: Charles Eshbach. **Assistant General Manager:** John Kameisha. **Director, Sales/Marketing:** Michael Gillogly. **Director, Business Operations:** James Heffley. **Director, Group Sales:** James Beaudoin. **Director, Business Development:** Kelli Hoschtetler. **Director, Ticketing:** Chris Cameron. **Box Office Manager:** Jason Lemont. **Office Manager:** Judy Bray. **Associate Director, Food Services/ Merchandising:** Katie Harris. **Director, Broadcasting:** Andy Young. **Clubhouse Managers:** Craig Candage, Greg Goslin. **Administrative Assistants:** Jo Burgoon, Kathie Connelly, Matt Lefebvre, Sara Murray, Brendan Poutre, Wendy Sotos.

Field Staff
Manager: Rick Renteria. **Coach:** Jose Castro. **Pitching Coach:** Steve Luebber. **Trainer:** Shane Kennedy.

Game Information
Radio Announcers: Steve Pratt, Andy Young. **No. of Games Broadcast:** Home-71, Away-71. **Flagship Station:** WZAN 970-AM.
PA Announcer: Dean Rogers. **Official Scorer:** Leroy Rand.
Stadium Name (year opened): Hadlock Field (1994). **Location:** From south, I-295 to exit 5, merge onto Congress Street, left at St. John Street, merge right onto Park Avenue; From north, I-295 to exit 6A, right on Park Avenue. **Standard Game Times:** (First half) 6 p.m., (second half) 7; Sat. (first half) 1, (second half) 7; Sun. (first half) 1, (second half) 4.
Visiting Club Hotels: Suisse Chalet Inn, 340 Park Ave., Portland, ME 04102. Telephone: (207) 871-0611; Doubletree Hotel, 1230 Congress St., Portland, ME 04102. Telephone: (207) 774-5611.

READING
Phillies

Office Address: Rt. 61 South/1900 Centre Ave., Reading, PA 19601. **Mailing Address:** P.O. Box 15050, Reading, PA 19612. **Telephone:** (610) 375-8469. **FAX:** (610) 373-5868. **E-Mail Address:** info@reading phillies.com. **Website:** www.readingphillies.com.
Affiliation (first year): Philadelphia Phillies (1967). **Years in League:** 1933-35, 1952-61, 1963-65, 1967-.

Ownership, Management
Operated By: E&J Baseball Club, Inc.
Principal Owner/President: Craig Stein.
General Manager: Chuck Domino. **Assistant General Manager:** Scott Hunsicker. **Director, Stadium Operations/Concessions:** Andy Bortz. **Director, Facility Maintenance:** Jamie Keitsock. **Director, Game/Staff Operations:** Troy Pothoff. **Director, Communications/Community Development:** Mark Wallace. **Assistant Director, Communications/ Community Development:** Rob Hackash. **Director, Stadium Grounds:** Dan Douglas. **Director, Office Management:** Denise Haage. **Director, Tickets/Group Sales:** Joe Pew. **Director, Merchandising/Group Sales Associate:** Kevin Sklenarik. **Ticket Manager:** Mike Becker. **Group Sales Assistant:** Mike Hoyt. **Assistant, Tickets/Group Sales:** Bree Hagan. **Director, New Business Development:** Joe Bialek.

Field Staff
Manager: Gary Varsho. **Coach:** Milt Thompson. **Pitching Coach:** Carlos Arroyo. **Trainer:** Troy Hoffert.

Game Information
Radio Announcer: Steve Degler. **No. of Games Broadcast:** Home-71, Away-71. **Flagship Station:** WIOV 1240-AM.
PA Announcer: Dave Bauman. **Official Scorer:** John Lemcke.
Stadium Name (year opened): GPU Stadium (1950). **Location:** From east, take Pennsylvania Turnpike West to Morgantown exit, to 176 North, to 422 West, to Route 12 East, to Route 61 South exit. From west, take 422 East to Route 12 East, to Route 61 South exit. From north, take 222 South to Route 12 exit, to Route 61 South exit. From south, take 222 North to 422 West, to Route 12 East exit at Route 61 South. **Standard Game Times:** 7:05 p.m.; Mon.-Thurs. (April-May) 6:35; Sun. 1:05.
Visiting Club Hotel: Wellesley Inn, 910 Woodland Ave., Wyomissing, PA 19610. Telephone: (610) 374-1500.

TRENTON
Thunder

Office Address: One Thunder Rd., Trenton, NJ 08611. **Telephone:** (609) 394-3300. **FAX:** (609) 394-9666. **E-Mail Address:** office@trenton thunder.com. **Website:** www.trentonthunder.com.

Affiliation (first year): Boston Red Sox (1995). **Years in League:** 1994-.

Ownership, Management

Operated by: Garden State Baseball, LP.

General Manager/Chief Operating Officer: Wayne Hodes. **Assistant General Manager:** Rick Brenner. **Director, Marketing/Merchandising:** Eric Lipsman. **Director, Ticket Operations:** John Coletta. **Director, Media/Public Relations:** Andy Freed. **Director, Stadium Operations:** Adam Palant. **Controller:** Kelly Beach. **Office Manager:** Sue Chassen. **Manager, Group Sales:** Jeremy Fishman. **Manager, Media/Public Relations:** Chris Tobin. **Manager, Stadium Operations:** Josh Watson. **Manager, Merchandising:** Matt Armentano. **Director, Food Services:** Harry Smith. **Head Groundskeeper:** Jeff Migliaccio. **Assistants:** David Brown, Owen Duffy, Amy Volinski. **Interns:** Brian Cassidy, Hal Hansen, Rob McFadden, Matt Pentima, Ian Young. **Clubhouse Operations:** Scott Calabrese, Mike Stehlmac.

Field Staff

Manager: Billy GardnerJr. **Coach:** Steve Braun. **Pitching Coach:** Mike Griffin. **Trainer:** Bryan Jaquette.

Game Information

Radio Announcers: Andy Freed, Tom McCarthy. **No. of Games Broadcast:** Home-71, Away-71. **Flagship Station:** WTTM 1680-AM.

PA Announcer: Bill Bromberg. **Official Scorers:** Jay Dunn, Mike Maconi.

Stadium Name (year opened): Sam Plumeri Sr. Field at Mercer County Waterfront Park (1994). **Location:** Route 129 North, left at Cass Street; From I-95 take Route 29 South. **Standard Game Times:** 7:05 p.m.; Sat. (April-May) 1:05, (June) 4:05; Sun. 1:05.

Visiting Club Hotel: MacIntosh Hotel, 3270 Brunswick Pike, Lawrenceville, NJ 08648. Telephone: (609) 896-3700.

SOUTHERN LEAGUE

Class AA

Mailing Address: One Depot St., Suite 300, Marietta, GA 30060.
Telephone: (770) 428-4749. **FAX:** (770) 428-4849. **E-Mail Address:**
soleague@bellsouth.net. **Website:** www.southernleague.com.

Years League Active: 1964-.

Interim President: Don Mincher.

Directors: Don Beaver (Tennessee), Peter Bragan Sr. (Jacksonville),
Steve Bryant (Carolina), Frank Burke (Chattanooga), Steve DeSalvo
(Greenville), Dave Elmore (Birmingham), David Hersh (West Tenn), Chuck
LaMar (Orlando), Eric Margenau (Mobile), Don Mincher (Huntsville).

Executive Assistant: Lori Webb.

2000 Opening Date: April 6. **Closing Date:** Sept. 4.

Regular Season: 140 games (split schedule).

Division Structure: East—Carolina, Greenville, Jacksonville, Orlando,
Tennessee. **West**—Birmingham, Chattanooga, Huntsville, Mobile, West
Tenn.

Playoff Format: First-half division champions play second-half division
champions in best-of-5 series. Winners meet in best-of-5 series for league
championship.

All-Star Games: June 20 at Greenville; July 12 at Bowie, MD (joint
Double-A game).

Roster Limit: 23 active, until midnight Aug. 10 when roster can be
expanded to 24. **Player Eligibility Rule:** No restrictions.

Brand of Baseball: Rawlings.

Statistician: Howe Sportsdata, Boston Fish Pier, West Bldg. #1, Suite
302, Boston MA 02210.

Umpires: Damien Beal (Stone Mountain, GA), Robert Daly (Winter
Springs, FL), David Dunlevy (Tempe, AZ), Troy Fullwood (Hampton, VA),
Adonis Hill (Newberry, SC), Jimmy Horton (Louisville, MS), Jack Kennedy
(Frankfort, KY), Brian Knight (Helena, MT), Ricardo Losoya (Salinas, CA),
Olindo Mattia (Port St. Lucie, FL), Steven Mattingly (Phoenix, AZ), Darren
Spagnardi (Lexington, NC), James Thomas (Marietta, GA), Webb Turner
(Hope Mills, NC), Greg Williams (Fort Lauderdale, FL).

Stadium Information

Club	Stadium	Dimensions			Capacity	'99Att.
		LF	CF	RF		
Birmingham	Hoover Metropolitan	340	405	340	10,800	314,010
Carolina	Five County	330	400	330	6,500	238,002
Chattanooga	BellSouth Park	325	400	330	6,160	218,946
Greenville	Greenville Municipal	335	400	335	7,027	257,171
Huntsville	Davis Municipal	345	405	330	10,200	275,000
Jacksonville	Wolfson Park	323	401	323	8,200	233,630
Mobile	Hank Aaron	325	400	310	6,000	293,147
Orlando	Disney Complex	340	400	340	9,100	81,032
*Tennessee	Smokies Park	330	400	330	6,000	119,571
West Tenn	Pringles Park	310	395	320	6,000	302,203

*Known as Knoxville in 1999

BIRMINGHAM
Barons

Office Address: 100 Ben Chapman Dr., Hoover, AL 35244. **Mailing Address:** P.O. Box 360007, Birmingham, AL 35236. **Telephone:** (205) 988-3200. **FAX:** (205) 988-9698. **E-Mail Address:** barons@barons.com. **Website:** www.barons.com.

Affiliation (first year): Chicago White Sox (1986). **Years in League:** 1964-65, 1967-75, 1981-.

Ownership, Management
Operated by: Elmore Sports Group, Ltd.
Principal Owner: Dave Elmore.
President/General Manager: Tony Ensor. **Assistant General Manager:** Jonathan Nelson. **Director, Operations:** Chris Jenkins. **Director, Stadium Operations:** Joe Dorolek. **Head Groundskeeper:** Darren Seybold. **Director, Media Relations:** David Lee. **Director, Sales/Marketing:** George Dennis. **Director, Broadcasting:** Curt Bloom. **Director, Ticket Sales:** Joe Drake. **Group Sales:** Eric Crook, Brian Krueger, Enrico Tesio. **Director, Food Services:** Will Dvoranchik. **Director, Catering:** Janie Weyerbacher. **Clubhouse Operations:** Ken Dunlap. **Office Manager:** Norma Rosebrough. **Accounting Clerk:** Kecia Arnold. **Accounting:** Edwina Britton.

Field Staff
Manager: Nick Capra. **Coach:** Steve Whitaker. **Pitching Coach:** Curt Hasler. **Trainer:** Scott Takao.

Game Information
Radio Announcer: Curt Bloom. **No. of Games Broadcast:** Home-70, Away-70. **Flagship Station:** WAPI 1070-AM.
PA Announcer: Scott Stewart. **Official Scorer:** Bill Graham.
Stadium Name (year opened): Hoover Metropolitan Stadium (1988). **Location:** I-459 to Highway 150 (exit 10) in Hoover. **Standard Game Times:** 7 p.m.; Wed, 12:30; Sun. (April-June) 2, (July-Aug.) 6.
Visiting Club Hotel: Riverchase Inn, 1800 Riverchase Dr., Birmingham, AL 35244. Telephone: (205) 985-7500.

CAROLINA
Mudcats

Office Address: 1501 N.C. Highway 39, Zebulon, NC 27597. **Mailing Address:** P.O. Drawer 1218, Zebulon, NC 27597. **Telephone:** (919) 269-2287. **FAX:** (919) 269-4910. **E-Mail Address:** muddy@gomudcats.com. **Website:** www.gomudcats.com.
Affiliation (first year): Colorado Rockies (1999). **Years in League:** 1991-.

Ownership, Management
Operated by: Carolina Mudcats Professional Baseball Club, Inc.
Principal Owner: Steve Bryant.
General Manager: Joe Kremer. **Assistant General Manager:** Eric Gardner. **Director, Broadcasting:** Patrick Kinas. **Director, Corporate Sales:** Bill Gunger. **Director, Operations:** Aaron Banker. **Director, Sales:** Thomas Phelps. **Director, Group Sales:** Will Barfield. **Director, Media Relations/Webmaster:** Allison Lent. **Director, Community Relations:** Duke Sanders. **Director, Ticket Sales:** Bill Mize. **Director, Special Events:** Jim Tennison. **Head Groundskeeper:** Patrick Skunda. **Office Manager:** Jackie DiPrimo. **Corporate Sales Associates:** Meredith Morgan, Angela Wood. **Group Sales Associates:** Frederick Cook, Elizabeth Henderson.

Field Staff
Manager: Ron Gideon. **Coach:** Theron Todd. **Pitching Coach:** Jerry Cram. **Trainer:** Travis Anderson.

Game Information
Radio Announcer: Patrick Kinas. **No. of Games Broadcast:** Home-70, Away-70. **Flagship Station:** WSAY 98.5-FM.
PA Announcer: Duke Sanders. **Official Scorer:** John Hobgood.
Stadium Name (year opened): Five County Stadium (1991). **Location:** From Raleigh, U.S. 64 East to 264 East, exit at Highway 39 in Zebulon. **Standard Game Times:** 7:30 p.m.; Sun. (April-May, Sept.) 2:05, (June-Aug.) 5:05.

Visiting Club Hotel: Country Inn and Suites, 2715 Capital Blvd., Raleigh, NC 27604. Telephone: (919) 872-5000.

CHATTANOOGA
Lookouts

Office Address: 201 Power Alley, Chattanooga, TN 37402. Mailing Address: P.O. Box 11002, Chattanooga, TN 37401. Telephone: (423) 267-2208. FAX: (423) 267-4258. E-Mail Address: lomktg@bellsouth.net. Website: www.lookouts.com.

Affiliation (first year): Cincinnati Reds (1988). Years in League: 1964-65, 1976-.

Ownership, Management
Operated by: Chattanooga Baseball, LLC.
Principal Owners: Daniel Burke, Frank Burke, Charles Eshbach.
President: Frank Burke.
General Manager: Rich Mozingo. Director, Stadium Operations: Allen Key. Head Groundskeeper: Jake Witherspoon. Director, Public Relations/Group Sales: Jo Jo Freeman. Director, Marketing: Michelle Genia. Director, Community Relations: Stephanie Dawn. Director, Ticket Sales: Suzy Gannon. Director, Concessions: Brad Smith. Assistant Groundskeeper: Dave Clarke. Merchandising Intern: Caroline Grace. Concessions Intern: Ben Harden. Ticket Intern: Michael Williams.

Field Staff
Manager: Mike Rojas. Coach: Jamie Dismuke. Pitching Coach: Mack Jenkins. Trainer: John Finley.

Game Information
Radio Announcer: Larry Ward. No. of Games Broadcast: Home-70, Away-70. Flagship Station: WQMT 98.9-FM.
PA Announcer: Unavailable. Official Scorer: Wirt Gammon.
Stadium Name (year opened): BellSouth Park (2000). Location: From I-24, take U.S. 27 North to exit 1C (4th Street), first left onto Chestnut Street, left onto Third Street. Standard Game Times: 7 p.m.; Sun. 2, 5.
Visiting Club Hotel: Howard Johnson Plaza, 6700 Ringgold Rd., Chattanooga, TN 37412. Telephone: (423) 892-8100.

GREENVILLE
Braves

Office Address: One Braves Ave., Greenville, SC 29607. Mailing Address: P.O. Box 16683, Greenville, SC 29606. Telephone: (864) 299-3456. FAX: (864) 277-7369. Website: www.gbraves.com.
Affiliation (first year): Atlanta Braves (1984). Years in League: 1984-.

Ownership, Management
Operated by: Atlanta National League Baseball Club, Inc.
Principal Owner: Ted Turner. President: Stan Kasten.
General Manager: Steve DeSalvo. Assistant GM: Jim Bishop. Director, Media/Public Relations: Jed Anthony. Head Groundskeeper: Matt Taylor. Director, Community Relations: Brenda Yoder. Director, Ticket Sales: Hollye Edwards. Director, Food Services: Yetu Riley. Clubhouse Operations: Joey Gault, Brad Van Name. Office Manager: Leann Esmann.

Field Staff
Manager: Paul Runge. Coach: Bobby Moore. Pitching Coach: Mike Alvarez. Trainer: Jay Williams.

Game Information
Radio Announcer: Mark Hauser. No. of Games Broadcast: Home-70, Away-70. Flagship Station: WCCP 104.9-FM.
PA Announcer: Unavailable. Official Scorer: Jimmy Moore.
Stadium Name (year opened): Greenville Municipal Stadium (1984). Location: I-85 to exit 46 (Mauldin Road), east two miles. Standard Game Times: 7:15 p.m.; Sun. 6:15.
Visiting Club Hotel: Quality Inn, 50 Orchard Park Dr., Greenville, SC 29615. Telephone: (864) 297-9000.

HUNTSVILLE
Stars

Office Address: 3125 Leeman Ferry Rd., Huntsville, AL 35801. **Mailing Address:** P.O. Box 2769, Huntsville, AL 35804. **Telephone:** (256) 882-2562. **FAX:** (256) 880-0801. **E-Mail Address:** stars@traveller.com. Website: www.huntsvillestars.com.

Affiliation (first year): Milwaukee Brewers (1999). **Years In League:** 1985-.

Ownership, Management
Operated by: Huntsville Stars Baseball, LLC.

President/General Manager: Don Mincher. **Vice President/Executive Director:** Patrick Nichol. **Assistant GM:** Bryan Dingo. **Director, Business Operations:** Pat Mincher. **Director, Stadium Operations:** Jason Hawkins. **Director, Public Relations/Promotions:** Jim Riley. **Group Sales Representatives:** Frank Buccieri, Shawn Bulman, Mark Gorenc. **Director, Ticket Sales:** Cliff Pate. **Director, Food Services:** Jamie Crow. **Office Manager:** Sonya Crow. **Head Groundskeeper:** Craig Shaw.

Field Staff
Manager: Carlos Lezcano. **Coach:** John Mallee. **Pitching Coach:** Mike Caldwell. **Trainer:** Bryan Butz.

Game Information
Radio Announcer: Steve Kornya. **No. of Games Broadcast:** Home-70, Away-70. **Flagship Station:** WTKI 1450-AM.

PA Announcer: Tommy Hayes. **Official Scorer:** Larry Smith.

Stadium Name (year opened): Joe W. Davis Municipal Stadium (1985). **Location:** I-65 to I-565 East, south on Memorial Parkway to Drake Avenue exit. **Standard Game Times:** 7:05 p.m.; Sun. (April-June) 2:05, (July-Sept.) 6:05.

Visiting Club Hotel: La Quinta Inn, 3141 University Dr., Huntsville, AL 35805. Telephone: (256) 533-0756.

JACKSONVILLE
Suns

Office Address: 1201 E Duval St., Jacksonville, FL 32202. **Mailing Address:** P.O. Box 4756, Jacksonville, FL 32201. **Telephone:** (904) 358-2040. **FAX:** (904) 358-2045. **E-Mail Address:** jaxsuns@bellsouth.net. Website: www.jaxsuns.com.

Affiliation (first year): Detroit Tigers (1995). **Years in League:** 1970-.

Ownership, Management
Operated by: Baseball Jax, Inc.

Principal Owner/President: Peter Bragan Sr. **Assistant to President:** Jerry LeMoine.

Vice President/General Manager: Peter Bragan Jr. **Vice President:** Bonita Bragan. **Assistant GM:** Kirk Goodman. **Director, Ticket Operations:** Jamie Smith. **Director, Sales:** Jimmy Fessler. **Director, Community Relations:** Shannon Sharp. **Director, Group Sales:** Amy Howard. **Director, Food Services:** David Leathers. **Office Manager:** Cathy Wiggins. **Ticket Manager:** Jen Adkison. **Clubhouse Operations:** Tim Kendron. **Administrative Assistants:** Jennifer Daniels, Noir Fowler, Guy Garbarino, Jon Wells.

Field Staff
Manager: Gene Roof. **Coach:** Matt Martin. **Pitching Coach:** Steve McCatty. **Trainer:** Matt Lewis.

Game Information
Radio Announcer: Alan Garrett. **No. of Games Broadcast:** Home-70, Away-70. **Flagship Station:** WBWL 600-AM.

PA Announcer: John Leard. **Official Scorer:** Paul Ivice.

Stadium Name (year opened): Wolfson Park (1955). **Location:** From I-95 North to 20th Street East exit, take to end, turn right before Jacksonville Municipal Stadium; From I-95 South to Emerson Street exit, take right to Hart Bridge, take Sports Complex exit, left at light to stop sign, take right and quick left; From Mathews Bridge, take A. Phillip Randolph exit, right off ramp, right at stop sign, left at second light to stadium. **Standard Game Times:** 7:35 p.m, 12:35; Sun. 3, 6.

Visiting Club Hotel: La Quinta-Orange Park, 8555 Blanding Blvd., Jacksonville, FL 32244. Telephone: (904) 778-9539.

MOBILE
BayBears

Office Address: Hank Aaron Stadium, 755 Bolling Bros. Blvd., Mobile, AL 36606. **Telephone:** (334) 479-2327. **FAX:** (334) 476-1147. **E-Mail Address:** baybears@mobilebaybears.com. **Website:** www.mobilebay bears.com.

Affiliation (first year): San Diego Padres (1997). **Years in League:** 1966, 1970, 1997-.

Ownership, Management
Operated by: United Sports Ventures.
President: Eric Margenau.
Vice President/General Manager: Bill Shanahan. **General Sales Manager:** Travis Toth. **Assistant GM, Marketing/Sales:** Allen Jernigan. **Assistant GM, Stadium Operations:** Angelo Mazzella. **Assistant GM, Finance/Merchandise:** Betty Adams. **Assistant GM, Group Sales:** Dan Zusman. **Assistant GM, Ticket Operations:** Doug Stephens. **Assistant Director, Group Sales:** Deneen Owen. **Head Groundskeeper:** Garlon Rainey. **Assistant Director, Merchandising:** Kim Coleman. **Assistant Director, Facility Operations:** Scott Balzer. **Executive Secretary/Receptionist:** Karen Kinsey. **Sales Representatives/Customer Service:** Heather Quinn, La Toni Taylor. **Sales Representatives:** Grant Barnett, Charlie Norton. **Stadium Operations Assistants:** Matt Attaway, Wade Vadakin.

Field Staff
Manager: Mike Basso. **Coach:** George Hendrick. **Pitching Coach:** Dave Rajsich. **Trainer:** John Maxwell.

Game Information
Radio Announcer: Tom Nichols. **No. of Games Broadcast:** Home-70, Away-70. **Flagship Station:** WNSP 105.5-FM.
PA Announcer: John Finora. **Official Scorers:** Craig Gault, Tommie Pierce.
Stadium Name (year opened): Hank Aaron Stadium (1997). **Location:** I-65 to exit 1A (Government Street East), right at Satchel Paige Drive, right at Bolling Bros. Boulevard. **Standard Game Times:** 6:05 p.m.; Fri.-Sat. 7:05.
Visiting Club Hotel: Clarion Hotel, 3101 Airport Blvd., Mobile, AL 36606. Telephone: (334) 476-6400.

ORLANDO
Rays

Office Address: 700 S Victory Way, Kissimmee, FL 34747. **Mailing Address:** P.O. Box 10000, Lake Buena Vista, FL 32830. **Telephone:** (407) 938-3519. **FAX:** (407) 938-3442. **Website:** www.orlandorays.com.
Affiliation (first year): Tampa Bay Devil Rays (1999). **Years in League:** 1973-.

Ownership, Management
Operated by: Orlando Rays Baseball, Inc.
Principal Owner: Tampa Bay Devil Rays, Ltd.
President/Chief Executive Officer: Vincent Naimoli. **Vice President:** John Higgins.
General Manager/Tampa Bay: Mitch Lukevics. **Assistant GM/Disney Liaison:** Alex Vergara. **On-Site Manager/Tampa Bay:** Tom Tisdale. **Manager, Stadium/Operations:** Rich Gilrane. **Manager, Marketing/Public Relations:** Greg Otte. **Sponsorship Representatives:** Michael Benn, Shan Daniels. **Manager, Ticket Sales:** Pad McMeel. **Manager, Box Office:** Scott St. George. **Manager, Merchandise:** Dara Trujillo.

Field Staff
Manager: Mike Ramsey. **Coach:** Steve Livesey. **Pitching Coach:** Ray Searage. **Trainer:** Tom Tisdale.

Game Information
Radio: None.
PA Announcer: Unavailable. **Official Scorer:** Unavailable.
Stadium Name (year opened): Disney's Wide World of Sports Complex (1997). **Location:** I-4 to exit 25B, Hwy. 192 West, follow signs to Magic Kingdom/Wide World of Sports, right onto Victory Way. **Standard Game Time:** 7:35 p.m.
Visiting Club Hotel: The Diplomat Resort at Maingate, 7491 W Hwy. 192, Kissimmee, FL 34747. Telephone: (800) 669-6753, (407) 369-6000.

TENNESSEE
Smokies

Office Address: 3450 Line Drive, Kodak, TN 37764. **Telephone:** (865) 637-9494. **FAX:** (865) 523-9913. **E-Mail Address:** info@smokiesbaseball.com. **Website:** www.smokiesbaseball.com.

Affiliation (first year): Toronto Blue Jays (1980). **Years in League:** 1964-67, 1972-.

Ownership, Management
Operated by: Tennessee Smokies Baseball, Inc.
Principal Owner/President: Don Beaver.
Vice President/General Manager: Dan Rajkowski. **Assistant General Manager:** Brian Cox. **Executive Director, Marketing/Sales:** Mark Seaman. **Director, Community Relations:** Jeff Shoaf. **Director, Stadium Operations:** Justin Ewart. **Director, Broadcasting/Media Relations:** Tim Grubbs. **Director, Sales:** Jon Zeitz. **Director, Group Sales:** Kevin Hill. **Director, Ticket Operations:** Penelope Keller. **Director, Promotions:** Christa Derr. **Director, Field Operations:** Bob Shoemaker. **Business Manager:** Ed Morgan. **Senior Account Executives:** Greg Castelloe, Rob Durrant. **Account Executives:** Jennifer Hampton, Matt Martin. **Assistant, Media Relations:** Mike Newman. **Operations Assistant:** Brian Webster.

Field Staff
Manager: Rocket Wheeler. **Coach:** Hector Iorres. **Pitching Coach:** Craig Lefferts. **Trainer:** Mike Wirsta.

Game Information
Radio Announcer: Tim Grubbs. **No. of Games Broadcast:** Home-70, Away-70. **Flagship Station:** WSEV 930-AM.
PA Announcer: Mike Newman. **Official Scorer:** Unavailable.
Stadium Name (year opened): Smokies Park (2000). **Location:** I-40 to exit 407, Highway 66 North. **Standard Game Times:** 7:15 p.m., Sun. 5.
Visiting Club Hotel: Unavailable.

WEST TENN
Diamond Jaxx

Office Address: 4 Fun Place, Jackson, TN 38305. **Telephone:** (901) 664-2020. **FAX:** (901) 988-5246. **E-Mail Address:** baseball@diamondjaxx.com. **Website:** www.diamondjaxx.com.

Affiliation (first year): Chicago Cubs (1998). **Years in League:** 1998-.

Ownership, Management
Operated by: Professional Sports and Entertainment Associates of Tennessee, LP.
President/General Manager: David Hersh. **Assistant General Manager:** Brian Cheever. **Office Manager:** Terrie Hopper. **Accounting Manager:** Brian Bonecutter. **Director, Stadium Operations:** Steve Kaylor. **Head Groundskeeper:** Matt LaRose. **Director, Broadcasting:** Matt Park. **Director, Media Relations:** Travis Perry. **Director, Sales:** Martie Cordaro. **Director, Marketing:** Nicole Piersiak. **Box Office/Events Manager:** Steven Aldridge. **Director, Group Sales:** Dave Endress. **Regional Sales Managers:** Brandon Baker, Jeremy Johnson, Scott Williams. **Director, Merchandising:** Kelley Dunn. **Customer Service Specialist:** Amy Balthrop. **Director, Food Services:** Chuck Futrell. **Home Clubhouse Manager:** Brandon Tecklenburg. **Visiting Clubhouse Manager:** Casey Westenrieder.

Field Staff
Manager: Dave Bialas. **Coach:** Tack Wilson. **Pitching Coach:** Alan Dunn. **Trainer:** Jim O'Reilly.

Game Information
Radio Announcer: Matt Park. **No. of Games Broadcast:** Home-70, Away-70. **Flagship Station:** WNWS 101.5-FM.
PA Announcer: Brad McCoy. **Official Scorer:** Seaton Ennis.
Stadium Name (year opened): Pringles Park (1998). **Location:** From I-40, take exit 85 South to F.E. Wright Drive, left onto Ridgecrest Extended. **Standard Game Times:** 7:05 p.m.; Sun. (April-May) 2:05.
Visiting Club Hotel: Garden Plaza Hotel, 1770 Hwy. 45 Bypass, Jackson, TN 38305. Telephone: (901) 664-6900.

TEXASLEAGUE

Class AA

Mailing Address: 2442 Facet Oak, San Antonio, TX 78232. **Telephone:** (210) 545-5297. **FAX:** (210) 545-5298. **E-Mail Address:** tkayser@iamerica.net. **Website:** www.texas-league.com.

Years League Active: 1888-1890, 1892, 1895-1899, 1902-1942, 1946-.

President/Treasurer: Tom Kayser.

Vice President: Chuck Lamson (Tulsa). **Corporate Secretary:** Andrew Wheeler.

Directors: Chuck Lamson (Tulsa), Taylor Moore (Shreveport), Rick Parr (El Paso), Miles Prentice (Midland), Reid Ryan (Round Rock), Steve Shaad (Wichita), Bill Valentine (Arkansas), Burl Yarbrough (San Antonio).

Administrative Assistant: Ryan Forim.

2000 Opening Date: April 6. **Closing Date:** Sept. 3.

Tom Kayser

Regular Season: 140 games (split schedule).

Division Structure: East—Arkansas, Shreveport, Tulsa, Wichita. **West**—El Paso, Midland, Round Rock, San Antonio.

Playoff Format: First-half division champions play second-half division champions in best-of-5 series. Winners meet in best-of-7 series for league championship.

All-Star Games: June 18 at El Paso vs. Mexican League All-Stars; June 20 at Monterrey, Mexico vs. Mexican League All-Stars; July 12 at Bowie, MD (joint Double-A game).

Roster Limit: 23 active, until midnight Aug. 10 when roster can be expanded to 24. **Player Eligibility Rule:** No restrictions.

Brand of Baseball: Rawlings.

Statistician: Howe Sportsdata, Boston Fish Pier, West Bldg. #1, Suite 302, Boston, MA 02210.

Umpires: Ramon Armendariz (Oceanside, CA), Geoff Burr (San Diego, CA), Jared Heeter (Blandford, MA), Scott Hepinstall (Midland, MI), Alan Hoover (Tempe, AZ), Michael Jost (Modesto, CA), Kevin Kelley (Huntington Beach, CA), Jason Moore (San Bernardino, CA), Casey Moser (Iowa Park, TX), Pat Riley (Gilbert, AZ), Matt Schaeffer (Clearwater, FL).

Stadium Information

Club	Stadium	Dimensions			Capacity	'99 Att.
		LF	CF	RF		
Arkansas	Ray Winder Field	330	390	345	6,083	191,346
El Paso	Cohen	340	410	340	9,725	313,622
Midland	Christensen	333	398	333	5,000	176,369
Round Rock*	Dell Diamond	330	400	325	10,000	99,240
San Antonio	Wolff Municipal	310	402	340	6,200	318,590
Shreveport	Fair Grounds Field	330	400	330	6,200	155,416
Tulsa	Drillers	335	390	340	10,963	351,929
Wichita	Lawrence-Dumont	344	401	312	6,055	181,40

* Club operated in Jackson, Miss., in 1999

ARKANSAS
Travelers

Office Address: Ray Winder Field at War Memorial Park, Little Rock, AR 72205. Mailing Address: P.O. Box 55066, Little Rock, AR 72215. Telephone: (501) 664-1555. FAX: (501) 664-1834. E-Mail Address: travs@travs.com. Website: www.travs.com; www.travsfan.com.

Affiliation (first year): St. Louis Cardinals (1966). Years in League: 1966-.

Ownership, Management
Operated by: Arkansas Travelers Baseball Club, Inc.
President: Bert Parke.
Executive Vice President/General Manager: Bill Valentine. Assistant GM, Sales/Operations: Hap Seliga. Assistant GM, Concessions/Merchandising: John Evans. Assistant GM, Stadium Operations: Pete Laven. Park Superintendent: Greg Johnston. Assistant Park Superintendent: Reggie Temple. Bookkeeper: Nena Valentine. Community Relations Executive: Al Janssen. Office Manager: Treva Young.

Field Staff
Manager: Chris Maloney. Coach: Brian Rupp. Pitching Coach: Dave LaPoint. Trainer: Aaron Bruns.

Game Information
Radio Announcer: Bob Harrison. No. of Games Broadcast: Home-70. Flagship Station: KARN 920-AM.
PA Announcer: Bill Downs. Official Scorer: Mike Garrity.
Stadium Name (year opened): Ray Winder Field at War Memorial Park (1932). Location: I-630 to Fair Park Boulevard exit, go north from exit, turn right after zoo. Standard Game Times: 7:30 p.m.; Sat. DH 6:30, Sun. 2.
Visiting Club Hotel: Little Rock Hilton, 925 South University, Little Rock, AR 72204. Telephone: (501) 664-5020.

EL PASO
Diablos

Office Address: 9700 Gateway North Blvd., El Paso, TX 79924. Telephone: (915) 755-2000. FAX: (915) 757-0671. E-Mail Address: awheeler@elp.rr.com. Website: www.diablos.com.

Affiliation (first year): Arizona Diamondbacks (1999). Years in League: 1962-70, 1972-.

Ownership, Management
Operated by: Diamond Sports, Inc.
Principal Owners: Peter Gray, Bill Pereira.
President: Rick Parr. Vice President/General Manager: Andrew Wheeler. VP/Director, Sales and Marketing: Ken Schrom. Director, Ticket Sales: Bruce McKinney. Director, Hispanic Marketing: Larry Romero. Director, Group Sales: Corina Vasquez. Director, Broadcasting: Matt Hicks. Director, Media/Public Relations: Rose Lucero. Controller: Melissa Wachter. Ticket Manager: Mary Hill. Head Groundskeeper: Sergio Lopez. Assistant Operations Director/Manager, Merchandise: Heather Smith. Director, Stadium Operations: Jimmy Hicks. Account Representatives: Miguel Flores, Matt Hicks, Angela Nelson, Brett Pollock, Bernie Ricono.

Field Staff
Manager: Bobby Dickerson. Coach: Ty Van Burkleo. Pitching Coach: Dennis Lewallyn. Trainer: Dale Gilbert.

Game Information
Radio Announcers: Matt Hicks, Brett Pollock (English); Miguel Flores, Juan Gonzalez (Spanish). No. of Games Broadcast: Home-70, Away-70. Flagship Stations: KHEY 690-AM (English), KAMA 750-AM (Spanish).
PA Announcer: Unavailable. Official Scorer: Bernie Olivas.
Stadium Name (year opened): Cohen Stadium (1990). Location: I-10 to U.S. 54 (Patriot Freeway), east to Diana exit to Gateway North Boulevard. Standard Game Times: April-May 6:30 p.m., June-Aug. 7; Sun. 6:30.
Visiting Club Hotel: Ramada Inn-Executive Center, 500 Executive Center Blvd., El Paso, TX 79902. Telephone: (915) 532-8981.

MIDLAND
Rockhounds

Office Address: 4300 N Lamesa Rd., Midland, TX 79705. **Mailing Address:** P.O. Box 51187, Midland, TX 79710. **Telephone:** (915) 683-4251. **FAX:** (915) 683-0994. **Website:** www.midlandrockhounds.org.

Affiliation (first year): Oakland Athletics (1999). **Years in League:** 1972-.

Ownership, Management
Operated by: Midland Sports, Inc.

Principal Owners: Miles Prentice, Bob Richmond.

President: Miles Prentice. **Executive Vice President:** Bob Richmond.

General Manager: Monty Hoppel. **Director, Broadcasting:** Bob Hards. **Director, Sales/Corporate Development:** Harold Fuller. **Director, Operations:** Jeff Von Holle. **Director, Business Operations:** Eloisa Robledo. **Director, Merchandising:** Ray Fieldhouse. **Director, Marketing:** Jamie Richardson. **Office/Ticket Manager:** Stacy Fielding. **Director, Tickets:** Ryan Haskell. **Clubhouse Manager:** Joe Harrell. **Director, Community Relations:** Ryan Lovell.

Field Staff
Manager: Tony DeFrancesco. **Coach:** Webster Garrison. **Pitching Coach:** Curt Young. **Trainer:** Brian Thorson.

Game Information
Radio Announcer: Bob Hards. **No. of Games Broadcast:** Home-70, Away-70. **Flagship Station:** KCRS 550-AM.

PA Announcer: Barry Sykes. **Official Scorer:** Bobby Dunn.

Stadium Name (year opened): Christensen Stadium (1952). **Location:** From I-20, north on Rankin Highway/Big Spring exit to Loop 250, exit right on Lamesa Road. **Standard Game Times:** 7:11 p.m.; Sun. (April-May) 2, (June-Aug) 6.

Visiting Club Hotel: Holiday Inn Hotel and Suites, 4300 W Hwy. 80, Midland, TX 79703. Telephone: (915) 697-3181.

ROUND ROCK
Express

Office Address: 3400 Pal Valley Blvd., Round Rock, TX 78664. **Mailing Address:** P.O. Box 5309, Round Rock, TX 78683. **Telephone:** (512) 255-2255. **FAX:** (512) 255-1558. **Website:** www.roundrockexpress.com.

Affiliation (first year): Houston Astros (2000). **Years in League:** 2000-.

Ownership, Management
Operated by: Round Rock Baseball, Inc.

Principal Owners: Rich Hollander, Eddie Maloney, J. Con Maloney, Nolan Ryan, Reid Ryan, Don Sanders. **Chairman/President:** Reid Ryan.

Vice President/General Manager: Jay Miller. **Assistant GM, Stadium Operations:** R.D. Sneed. **Assistant GM, Sales/Marketing:** Dave Fendrick. **Controller:** Emily Merrill. **Director, Promotions/Stadium Entertainment:** Derrick Grubbs. **Director, Media/Public Relations:** J.J. Gottsch. **Director, Merchandising:** Mark Kay Schultz. **Director, Ticket Operations:** Tony Zefiretto. **Director, Convention Center/Special Events:** Scott Allen. **Director, Community Relations:** Wendy Ryan. **Director, Customer Relations:** George Smith. **Office Manager:** Laura Smith. **Head Groundskeeper:** Dennis Klein. **Community Relations Representative:** Spike Owen. **Clubhouse Manager:** Hugh Staple.

Field Staff
Manager: Jackie Moore. **Coach:** Mark Bailey. **Pitching Coach:** Burt Hooton. **Trainer:** Nathan Lucero.

Game Information
Radio Announcer: Mike Capps. **No. of Games Broadcast:** Home-70, Away-70. **Flagship Station:** The Zone 1300-AM.

PA Announcer: Derrick Grubbs. **Official Scorer:** Unavailable.

Stadium Name (year opened): The Dell Diamond (2000). **Location:** I-35 North to exit 253 (Hwy. 79 East/Taylor), stadium on left approx. 3½ miles. **Standard Game Times:** 7:05 p.m.; Sun. (April-May) 2:05, (June-Sept.) 6:05.

Visiting Club Hotel: Hilton Garden Inn, 2310 N IH-35, Round Rock, TX 78681. Telephone: (512) 341-8200.

SAN ANTONIO
Missions

Office Address: 5757 Hwy. 90 W, San Antonio, TX 78227. **Telephone:** (210) 675-7275. **FAX:** (210) 670-0001. **E-Mail Address:** sainfo@21stcenturyaccess.com. **Website:** www.samissions.com.

Affiliation (first year): Los Angeles Dodgers (1977). **Years In League:** 1888, 1892, 1895-99, 1907-42, 1946-64, 1968-.

Ownership, Management
Operated by: Elmore Sports Group.
Principal Owner: Dave Elmore.
President/General Manager: Burl Yarbrough. **Assistant General Managers:** Tom Davis, Jeff Long, Jimi Olsen. **Controller:** Marc Frey. **Head Groundskeeper:** Tom McAfee. **Director, Media/Public Relations:** Jim White. **Director, Community Relations:** Eric Von. **Director, Ticket Sales:** Ben Rivers. **Assistant Ticket Manager:** Chris Ross. **Director, Group Sales:** Jeff Windle. **Director, Merchandising:** Bill Gerlt.

Field Staff
Manager: Rick Burleson. **Coach:** U.L. Washington. **Pitching Coach:** Mark Littell. **Trainer:** Homer Zulaika.

Game Information
Radio Announcers: Roy Acuff, Eric Von. **No. of Games Broadcast:** Home-70, Away-70. **Flagship Station:** KKYX 680-AM.
PA Announcer: Stan Kelly. **Official Scorer:** David Humphrey.
Stadium Name (year opened): Nelson W. Wolff Municipal Stadium (1994). **Location:** From I-10, I-35 or I-37, take U.S. 90 West to Callaghan Road exit, stadium is on right. **Standard Game Times:** 7:05 p.m., Sun. 6:05.
Visiting Club Hotel: Unavailable.

SHREVEPORT
Captains

Office Address: 2901 Pershing Blvd., Shreveport, LA 71109. **Mailing Address:** P.O. Box 3448, Shreveport, LA 71133. **Telephone:** (318) 636-5555. **FAX:** (318) 636-5670. **E-Mail Address:** captains@shreve.net. **Website:** www.shreveportcaptains.com

Affiliation (first year): San Francisco Giants (1979). **Years in League:** 1895, 1908-10, 1915-32, 1938-42, 1946-57, 1968-.

Ownership, Management
Operated by: Shreveport Baseball, Inc.
Principal Owner/President: Taylor Moore.
General Manager: Daniel Robinson. **Assistant GM/Personnel Director:** Terri Sipes. **Director, Merchandise/Tickets:** Sheila Martin. **Senior Account Executive:** Roxy Dancy. **Director, Food Services:** Joe Parault. **Coordinator, Group Sales:** Kristen Noles. **Director, Stadium Operations:** Steve Bange. **Head Groundskeeper:** Kenny Parr.

Field Staff
Manager: Bill Hayes. **Pitching Coach:** Ross Grimsley. **Trainer:** Donna Papangellin.

Game Information
Radio Announcer: Doug Greenwald. **No. of Games Broadcast:** Home-70, Away-70. **Flagship Station:** KWKH 1130-AM.
PA Announcer: Unavailable. **Official Scorer:** Jim Dawson.
Stadium Name (year opened): Fair Grounds Field (1986). **Location:** Hearne Avenue exit off I-20, left into Louisiana State Fairgrounds. **Standard Game Times:** April-May 7:05 p.m., June-Sept. 7:35; Sat. 7:35; Sun. 6:05.
Visiting Club Hotel: Shoney's Inn-Bossier City, 1836 Old Minden Rd., Bossier City, LA 71111. Telephone: (318) 747-7700.

TULSA
Drillers

Office Address: 4802 E 15th St., Tulsa, OK 74112. **Telephone:** (918)

744-5998. **FAX:** (918) 747-3267. **E-Mail Address:** mail@tulsadrillers.com.
Website: www.tulsadrillers.com.
  Affiliation (first year): Texas Rangers (1977). **Years in League:** 1933-42, 1946-65, 1977-.

Ownership, Management
  Operated by: Tulsa Baseball, Inc.
  Principal Owner/President: Went Hubbard.
  Executive Vice President/General Manager: Chuck Lamson.
Assistant General Manager: Mike Melega. **Bookkeeper:** Cheryll Moore.
Director, Public Relations: Brian Carroll. **Director, Stadium Operations:**
Mark Hilliard. **Head Groundskeeper:** Gary Shepherd. **Assistant
Groundskeeper:** Sean Dooley. **Manager, Promotions/Merchandise:** Joe
Benbow. **Assistant, Promotions/Merchandise:** Nikki Morris. **Director,
Ticket Sales:** Debbie Jones. **Assistant, Ticket Sales:** Chuck Bell.
Manager, Group Sales: Jeff Gladu. **Assistant Manager, Food/Beverage:**
Chad Kramer. **Office Manager:** Belinda Shepherd.

Field Staff
  Manager: Bobby Jones. **Coach:** Moe Hill. **Pitching Coach:** Mark
Brewer. **Trainer:** Mike Quinn.

Game Information
  Radio Announcer: Mark Neely. **No. of Games Broadcast:** Home-70,
Away-70. **Flagship Station:** KQLL 1430-AM.
  PA Announcer: Kirk McAnany. **Official Scorers:** Jeff Brucculeri, Bruce
Howard.
  Stadium Name (year opened): Drillers Stadium (1981). **Location:**
Three miles north of I-44 and 1.5 miles south of I-244 at 15th Street and
Yale Avenue. **Standard Game Times:** 7:35 p.m.; Sun. (April-May) 2:05,
(June-Aug.) 6:05.
  Visiting Club Hotel: Best Western Tradewinds Central, 3141 E Skelly
Dr., Tulsa, OK 74105. Telephone: (918) 749-5561.

WICHITA
Wranglers

  Office Address: 300 S Sycamore, Wichita, KS 67213. **Mailing
Address:** P.O. Box 1420, Wichita, KS 67201. **Telephone:** (316) 267-3372.
FAX: (316) 267-3382. **E-Mail Address:** wranglers@wichitawranglers.com.
Website: www.wichitawranglers.com.
  Affiliation (first year): Kansas City Royals (1995). **Years in League:**
1987-.

Ownership, Management
  Operated by: Wichita Baseball, Inc. **Principal Owner:** Rich Products
Corp. **Chairman:** Robert Rich Sr. **President:** Robert Rich Jr.
  Vice President/General Manager: Steve Shaad. **Assistant
GM/Director, Sponsorships, Advertising and Promotions:** Greg
Kalkwarf. **Assistant GM/Director, Ticket Sales:** Tim Lyons. **Assistant
GM/Chief Financial Officer:** Chris Taylor. **Director, Business
Operations:** Shelly Robbins. **Office Manager/Executive Assistant to VP:**
Mary Luce. **Director, Marketing:** Kyle Richardson. **Manager, Client
Relations/Sponsorships:** Kristin Lynch. **Account Executive:** Kyle Ebers.
Manager, Stadium/Baseball Operations: Kevin Grimsley. **Stadium
Maintenance:** Teressa Hackworth. **Head Groundskeeper:** David
Poppleton. **Coordinator, Group Sales:** Kevin Whitworth. **Account
Executive, Group Sales:** Madeline Hawthorne. **Coordinator, Corporate
Ticket Sales:** Matt Twombly. **Clubhouse Manager:** Scott Lesher.

Field Staff
  Manager: Keith Bodie. **Coach:** Kevin Long. **Pitching Coach:** Steve
Crawford. **Trainer:** Trent Stratton.

Game Information
  Radio Announcer: Unavailable. **No. of Games Broadcast:** Home-70,
Away-70. **Flagship Station:** KQAM 1480-AM.
  PA Announcer: Scott Stocki. **Official Scorer:** Ted Woodward.
  Stadium Name (year opened): Lawrence-Dumont Stadium (1934).
Location: I-35 to Kellogg Avenue West, north on Broadway, west on Lewis.
Standard Game Times: 7 p.m.; Sun. (April-May) 2, (June-August) 6.
  Visiting Club Hotel: Ramada Inn/Wichita, 7335 E Kellogg, Wichita, KS
67207. Telephone: (316) 685-1281.

CALIFORNIALEAGUE

Class A Advanced

Office Address: 2380 S Bascom Ave., Suite 200, Campbell, CA 95008. **Telephone:** (408) 369-8038. **FAX:** (408) 369-1409. **E-Mail Address:** cabaseball@aol.com. **Website:** www.californialeague.com.

Years League Active: 1941-1942, 1946-.

President/Treasurer: Joe Gagliardi.

Vice President: Harry Stavrenos (San Jose). **Corporate Secretary:** Bill Weiss.

Directors: Bobby Brett (High Desert), Chris Chen (Modesto), Mike Ellis (Lancaster), Pat Patton (Bakersfield), Tom Seidler (Mudville), Harry Stavrenos (San Jose), Hank Stickney (Rancho Cucamonga), Ken Stickney (Lake Elsinore), Donna Tuttle (San Bernardino), Jim Wadley (Visalia).

Joe Gagliardi

Director, Marketing: Pete Thureson.

League Administrator: Kathleen Kelly.

Director, Umpire Development: John Oldham.

2000 Opening Date: April 6. **Closing Date:** Sept. 3.

Regular Season: 140 games (split schedule).

Division Structure: North—Bakersfield, Modesto, Mudville, San Jose, Visalia. **South**—High Desert, Lake Elsinore, Lancaster, Rancho Cucamonga, San Bernardino.

Playoff Format: Six teams. First-half champions in each division earn first-round bye; second-half champions meet wild card with next best overall record in best-of-3 quarterfinals. Winners meet first-half champions in best-of-5 semifinals. Winners meet in best-of-5 series for league championship.

All-Star Game: June 20 at Kinston, NC (California League vs. Carolina League).

Roster Limit: 25 active. **Player Eligibility Rule:** No more than two players and one player-coach on active list may have more than six years experience.

Brand of Baseball: Rawlings ROM-CAL.

Statistician: Howe Sportsdata, Boston Fish Pier, West Bldg. #1, Suite 302, Boston MA 02210; P.O. Box 5061, San Mateo, CA 94402.

Umpires: Ryan Bleiberg (Simi Valley, CA), John Bullock (North Hollywood, CA), Paul Chandler (Silverdale, WA), Steven Corvi (Peoria, AZ), Stephen Cox (Tulsa, OK), Tyler Hoffman (Qualicum Beach, British Columbia), Scott Letendre (Tempe, AZ), Mark Mauro (San Mateo, CA), Cale Smith (Kirkland, WA), Ray Villeneuve (El Paso, TX).

Stadium Information

Club	Stadium	Dimensions LF	CF	RF	Capacity	'99 Att.
Bakersfield	Sam Lynn Ballpark	328	354	328	4,200	107,747
High Desert	Mavericks	340	401	340	3,808	146,772
Lake Elsinore	The Diamond	330	400	310	7,866	282,533
Lancaster	Lancaster Municipal	350	410	350	4,500	218,479
Modesto	Thurman Field	312	400	319	4,000	133,757
Mudville	Billy Hebert Field	325	392	335	3,500	73,702
R. Cucamonga	Epicenter	335	400	335	6,615	321,682
San Bernardino	The Ranch	330	410	330	5,000	167,437
San Jose	Municipal	340	390	340	4,000	157,598
Visalia	Recreation Park	320	405	320	1,800	65,538

BAKERSFIELD
Blaze

Office Address: 4009 Chester Ave., Bakersfield, CA 93301. Mailing Address: P.O. Box 10031, Bakersfield, CA 93389. Telephone: (661) 322-1363. FAX: (661) 322-6199. E-Mail Address: blaze1@bakersfieldblaze.com. Website: www.bakersfieldblaze.com.

Affiliation: San Francisco Giants (1997). Years In League: 1941-42, 1946-75, 1978-79, 1982-.

Ownership, Management

Principal Owner/President: Pat Patton.

Vice President/General Manager: Jack Patton. Assistant General Manager: Susan Wells. Director, Baseball Operations: Joe Foye. Director, Ballpark Services: Brian Thomas. Director, Stadium Operations: Craig Noren. Head Groundskeeper: Leon Williams. Director, Community Relations: Paul Sheldon. Director, Special Projects: Cricket Whitaker. Clubhouse Operations: Mike Taylor. Office Manager: Seve Niron.

Field Staff

Manager: Lenn Sakata. Pitching Coach: Steve Renko. Trainer: Rob Knepper.

Game Information

Radio Announcers: David Flemming, Mark Roberts. No. of Games Broadcast: Home-70, Away-70. Flagship Station: KGEO 1230-AM.

PA Announcer: Unavailable. Official Scorer: Tim Wheeler.

Stadium Name (year opened): Sam Lynn Ballpark (1941). Location: Highway 99 to California Avenue, east three miles to Chester Avenue, north two miles to stadium. Standard Game Time: 7:15 p.m.

Visiting Club Hotel: Parkway Inn, 2400 Camino Del Rio Court, Bakersfield, CA 93308. Telephone: (661) 327-0681.

HIGH DESERT
Mavericks

Office Address: 12000 Stadium Way, Adelanto, CA 92301. Telephone: (760) 246-6287. FAX: (760) 246-3197. E-Mail Address: mavsinfo@hdmavs.com. Website: www.hdmavs.com.

Affiliation (first year): Arizona Diamondbacks (1997). Years in League: 1991-.

Ownership, Management

Operated by: High Desert Mavericks, Inc.

Principal Owner: Bobby Brett.

General Manager: Rick Janac. Assistant General Manager: Mike Fleming. Director, Ticket Sales: Chris Jones. Director, Broadcasting: Bryan Goldwater. Assistant, Marketing/Public Relations: Stacy Maffei. Account Executive: Burke Nelson. Office Manager: Silvia Watson. Head Groundskeeper: Tino Gonzales. Clubhouse Manager: Mike Weil.

Field Staff

Manager: Scott Coolbaugh. Coach: Rick Schu. Pitching Coach: Mike Parrott. Trainer: Colin Foye.

Game Information

Radio Announcer: Bryan Goldwater. No. of Games Broadcast: Home-70, Away-70. Flagship Station: KROY 1590-AM.

PA Announcer: Unavailable. Official Scorer: Jim Erwin.

Stadium Name (year opened): Mavericks Stadium (1991). Location: I-15 North to Highway 395 to Adelanto Road. Standard Game Times: 7:05 p.m.; Sun. (April-May) 2:05, (June-Aug.) 5:05.

Visiting Club Hotel: Ramada Inn-Victorville, 15494 Palmdale Rd., Victorville, CA 92392. Telephone: (760) 245-6565.

LAKE ELSINORE
Storm

Office Address: 500 Diamond Dr., Lake Elsinore, CA 92530. **Mailing Address:** P.O. Box 535, Lake Elsinore, CA 92531. **Telephone:** (909) 245-4487. **FAX:** (909) 245-0305. **E-Mail Address:** info@stormbaseball.com. **Website:** www.stormbaseball.com.

Affiliation (first year): Anaheim Angels (1994). **Years in League:** 1994-.

Ownership, Management

Operated by: Mandalay Sports Entertainment.

Principal Owner: Ken Stickney. **Chairman:** Peter Guber. **Vice Chairman:** Paul Schaeffer.

General Manager: Dave Oster. **Assistant General Manager/Director, Marketing:** David Jojala. **Director, Broadcasting:** Sean McCall. **Director, Business Administration:** Yvonne Hunneman. **Director, Community Relations/Game Day Operations:** Matt DeMargel. **Director, Corporate Accounts:** Ira Fertig. **Director, Group Sales:** Mary Stanley. **Director, Stadium Operations:** Bruce Kessman. **Director, Sales:** Arin McCarthy. **Director, Executive Accounts:** Molly Stockwell. **Director, Ticket Operations:** Kathy Mair. **Assistant Ticket Office Manager:** Tom Bougher. **Office Administrator:** Jo Equila. **Assistant Director, Marketing:** Willie Wong. **Assistant Director, Public Relations:** Morgan Dokson. **Assistant Director, Operations:** Luke Schaffer.

Field Staff

Manager: Mario Mendoza. **Coach:** John Orton. **Pitching Coach:** Kernan Ronan. **Trainer:** Adam Nevala.

Game Information

Radio Announcer: Sean McCall. **No. of Games Broadcast:** Home-70, Away-70. **Flagship Station:** KFRG 92.9-FM.

PA Announcer: Joe Martinez. **Official Scorers:** Dennis Bricker, Nelda Bricker.

Stadium Name (year opened): The Diamond (1994). **Location:** From I-15, exit at Diamond Drive, west for one mile to stadium. **Standard Game Times:** 7:05 p.m.; Sun. (first half) 2:05, (second half) 5:05.

Visiting Club Hotel: Lake Elsinore Hotel and Casino, 20930 Malaga St., Lake Elsinore, CA 92530. **Telephone:** (909) 674-3101.

LANCASTER
Jethawks

Office Address: 45116 Valley Central Way, Lancaster, CA 93536. **Telephone:** (661) 726-5400. **FAX:** (661) 726-5406. **E-Mail Address:** ljethawks@qnet.com. **Website:** www.jethawks.com.

Affiliation (first year): Seattle Mariners (1996). **Years in League:** 1996-.

Ownership, Management

Operated by: Clutch Play Baseball, LLC.

Chairman: Horn Chen. **President:** Mike Ellis.

Vice President/Chief Operating Officer: Matt Ellis. **General Manager:** Kevin Younkin. **Assistant General Manager:** Chris Hale. **Director, Finance:** Michele Ellis. **Director, Stadium Operations:** John Laferney. **Director, Merchandising:** Lori Mayle. **Director, Broadcasting/Public Relations:** Dan Hubbard. **Director, Ticket Sales:** Kevin Bolinger. **Manager, Concessions:** Andrew Abaya. **Manager, Group Sales:** Jennifer Ryder.

Field Staff

Manager: Mark Parent. **Coach:** Dana Williams. **Pitching Coach:** Scott Budner. **Trainer:** Troy McIntosh.

Game Information

Radio Announcer: Dan Hubbard. **No. of Games Broadcast:** Home-70, Away-70. **Flagship Stations:** KUTY 1470-AM, KHJ 1380-AM.

PA Announcer: Larry Thornhill. **Official Scorer:** Dave Guenther.

Stadium Name (year opened): Lancaster Municipal Stadium (1996). **Location:** Highway 14 in Lancaster to Avenue I exit, west one block to stadium. **Standard Game Times:** 7:15 p.m.; Sun. 2.

Visiting Club Hotel: Unavailable.

MODESTO
A's

Office Address: 601 Neece Dr., Modesto, CA 95351. **Mailing Address:** P.O. Box 883, Modesto, CA 95353. **Telephone:** (209) 572-4487. **FAX:** (209) 572-4490. **E-Mail Address:** modestoa@aol.com. **Website:** www.modesto athletics.com.

Affiliation (first year): Oakland Athletics (1975). **Years in League:** 1946-64, 1966-.

Ownership, Management

Operated by: Modesto A's Professional Baseball Club, Inc.

Principal Owner/President: Chris Chen.

Vice President, Business Development: Tim Marting.

General Manager: John Katz. **Assistant General Manager, Operations:** Greg Coleman. **Director, Food Services:** Alan Day. **Director, Broadcasting/Media Relations:** Adam Fox. **Director, Sales/Marketing:** Ryan Jamrog. **Director, Community Affairs:** Sara Scheffler. **Office/ Accounting Manager:** Debra Forgnone. **Ticket Manger:** Daniel Plantier. **Clubhouse Operations:** David Tomchuk. **Head Groundskeeper:** Walter Woodley.

Field Staff

Manager: Greg Sparks. **Coach:** Brian McArn. **Pitching Coach:** Glenn Abbott. **Trainer:** Blake Bowers.

Game Information

Radio Announcers: Adam Fox, Steve McElroy. **No. of Games Broadcast:** Home-50, Away-50. **Flagship Station:** KANM 970-AM.

PA Announcer: Scott Preston. **Official Scorer:** Sean Bohannon.

Stadium Name (year opened): John Thurman Field (1952). **Location:** Highway 99 in Southwest Modesto to Tuolomne Boulevard exit, west on Tuolomne for one block to Neece Drive, left for ¼ mile to stadium. **Standard Game Times:** 7:05 p.m.; Sun. (April-June) 1:05, (July-Aug.) 5:05.

Visiting Club Hotel: Vagabond Inn, 1525 McHenry Ave., Modesto, CA 95350. Telephone: (209) 521-6340.

MUDVILLE
Nine

Office Address: Oak Alpine and Sutter Streets, Stockton, CA 95204. **Mailing Address:** 11 S San Joaquin St., 9th Floor, Stockton, CA 95202. **Telephone:** (209) 320-6050. **FAX:** (209) 320-6070. **E-Mail Address:** casey@mudville.com. **Website:** www.mudville.com.

Affiliation (first year): Milwaukee Brewers (1979). **Years in League:** 1941, 1946-72, 1978-.

Ownership, Management

Operated by: Top of the Third, Inc.

Principal Owners: Kevin O'Malley, Tom Seidler.

President: Tom Seidler.

Vice President/General Manager: Kevin O'Malley. **Director, Finance:** Jennifer Whiteley. **Director, Baseball Operations:** Tim McIntosh. **Director, Media/Public Relations:** Phil Elson. **Sales Executives:** Alex Geche, Tom Moccia, Rod Pahati. **Director, Group Sales:** Carly Petersen. **Director, Food Services:** Mark Britton. **Office Manager:** Molly Rogers.

Field Staff

Manager: Barry Moss. **Coach:** George McPherson. **Pitching Coach:** Lonnie Keeter. **Trainer:** Jeff Paxson.

Game Information

Radio Announcers: Phil Elson, Tim McIntosh. **No. of Games Broadcast:** Home-70, Away-70. **Flagship Station:** KJAX 1280-AM.

PA Announcer: Unavailable. **Official Scorer:** Tim Ankorn.

Stadium Name (year opened): Billy Hebert Field (1927). **Location:** From I-5 North, take Pershing Street exit, right on Harding Way, left on California St., right on Alpine St., left on Alvarado into Oak Park, take first left, stadium on right. **Standard Game Times:** 7:09 p.m.; Sun. (April-June) 1:09, (July-August) 6:09.

Visiting Club Hotel: Best Western Stockton Inn, 4219 E Waterloo Rd., Stockton, CA 95215. Telephone: (209) 931-3131.

RANCHO CUCAMONGA
Quakes

Office Address: 8408 Rochester Ave., Rancho Cucamonga, CA 91730.
Mailing Address: P.O. Box 4139, Rancho Cucamonga, CA 91729.
Telephone: (909) 481-5000. **FAX:** (909) 481-5005. **E-Mail Address:**
rcquakes@aol.com. **Website:** www.rcquakes.com.

Affiliation (first year): San Diego Padres (1993). **Years In League:** 1993-.

Ownership, Management

Operated by: Valley Baseball Inc.

Principal Owners: Jack Cooley, Mark Harmon, Hank Stickney.

Chairman: Hank Stickney.

General Manager: Pat Filippone. **Assistant General Manager:** Gerry McKearney. **Director, Finance:** Larry Collins. **Head Groundskeeper:** Rex Whitney. **Director, Media/Public Relations:** Davidia Benavidez. **Director, Corporate Sales:** James Keyston. **Director, Marketing:** Cindy Eritano. **Director, Community Relations:** Heather Williams. **Director, Ticket Sales:** Andrew Stuebner. **Director, Group Sales:** Linda Rathfon. **Ticket Representatives:** Chris Bitters, Marty Haber, Joel Malcore, Andy Molina, Jan Selasky. **Receptionists:** Cristina Fittante, Kara Fotia.

Field Staff

Manager: Tom LeVasseur. **Coach:** Eric Bullock. **Pitching Coach:** Mike Harkey. **Trainer:** Jason Haeussinger.

Game Information

Radio Announcer: Rob Buska. **No. of Games Broadcast:** Home-70, Away-70. **Flagship Station:** Unavailable.

PA Announcer: Dennis Bullock. **Official Scorer:** Larry Kavanaugh.

Stadium Name (year opened): The Epicenter (1993). **Location:** I-10 to I-15 North, exit at Foothill Boulevard, left on Foothill, left on Rochester to stadium. **Standard Game Times:** 7:15 p.m.; Sun. (first half) 2:15, (second half) 6:15.

Visiting Club Hotel: Best Western Heritage Inn, 8179 Spruce Ave., Rancho Cucamonga, CA 91730. Telephone: (909) 466-1111.

SAN BERNARDINO
Stampede

Office Address: 280 South E St., San Bernardino, CA 92401.
Telephone: (909) 888-9922. **FAX:** (909) 888-5251. **E-Mail Address:**
staff@stampedebaseball.com. **Website:** www.stampedebaseball.com.

Affiliation (first year): Los Angeles Dodgers (1995). **Years in League:** 1941, 1987-.

Ownership, Management

Operated by: Stampede Professional Baseball.

Principal Owners: David Elmore, Donna Tuttle.

President: Donna Tuttle. **Chief Financial Officer:** Gayla Anhaeuser.

Vice President/General Manager: Derek Leistra. **Assistant General Manager:** Paul Stiritz. **Director, Media/Public Relations:** Randy Miller. **Director, Broadcasting:** Mike Saeger. **Director, Ticket Sales:** Robert Acevedo. **Assistant Ticket Manager:** Catherine Allison. **Manager, Group Sales:** Leslie Madril. **Clubhouse Operations:** Mike Unruh. **Account Executives:** Ed Armenta, Matt Daly, Jorge Gonzalez, Mark Reinhill, Brian Stetsko. **Head Groundskeeper:** Al Meyers.

Field Staff

Manager: Dino Ebel. **Coach:** Jack Clark. **Pitching Coach:** Shawn Barton. **Trainer:** Robert Picard.

Game Information

Radio Announcer: Mike Saeger. **No. of Games Broadcast:** Home-70, Away-70. **Flagship Station:** Unavailable.

PA Announcer: J.J. Gould. **Official Scorer:** Steve Imbryani.

Stadium Name (year opened): The Ranch (1996). **Location:** From south, I-215 to 2nd Street exit, east on 2nd, right on G Street. From north, I-215 to 3rd Street exit, left on Rialto, right on G Street. **Standard Game Times:** 7:05 p.m.; Sun. (first half) 2:05, (second half) 5:05.

Visiting Club Hotel: Radisson Hotel, 295 North E St., San Bernardino, CA 92401. Telephone: (909) 381-6181.

SAN JOSE
Giants

Office Address: 588 E Alma Ave., San Jose, CA 95112. Mailing Address: P.O. Box 21727, San Jose, CA 95151. Telephone: (408) 297-1435. FAX: (408) 297-1453. E-Mail Address: sanjose_giants@mind-spring.com. Website: www.sjgiants.com.

Affiliation (first year): San Francisco Giants (1988). Years in League: 1942, 1947-58, 1962-76, 1979-.

Ownership, Management
Operated by: Progress Sports Management.
Principal Owners: Heidi Cox, Richard Beahrs.
President: Harry Stavrenos.
General Manager: Mark Wilson. Assistant General Manager: Steve Fields. Director, Stadium Operations: Rick Tracy. Director, Media/Public Relations: Mike McCarroll. Director, Operations: Dave Moudry. Director, Sales: Linda Pereira. Director, Guest Services: Zach Walter.

Field Staff
Manager: Keith Comstock. Pitching Coach: Bert Bradley. Trainer: Rene Velesquez.

Game Information
Radio Announcer: Unavailable. No. of Games Broadcast: Unavailable. Flagship Station: KSJS 90.5-FM.
PA Announcers: Jim Chapman, Brian Burkett. Official Scorer: John Pletsch.
Stadium Name (year opened): Municipal Stadium (1942). Location: From I-280, 10th Street exit to Alma, left on Alma, stadium on right. From U.S. 101, Tully Road exit to Senter, right on Senter, left on Alma, stadium on left. Standard Game Times: 7 p.m.; Sat. 5; Sun. (first half) 1, (second half) 5.
Visiting Club Hotel: Wyndham Hotel, 1350 N First St., San Jose, CA 95112. Telephone: (408) 453-6200.

VISALIA
Oaks

Office Address: 440 N Giddings Ave., Visalia, CA 93291. Mailing Address: P.O. Box 48, Visalia, CA 93279. Telephone: (559) 625-0480. FAX: (559) 739-7732. E-Mail Address: visoak@aol.com. Website: www.visaliaoaks.com.

Affiliation: Oakland Athletics (1997). Years in League: 1946-62, 1968-75, 1977-.

Ownership, Management
Operated by: California League.
President: Jim Wadley.
General Manager: Andrew Bettencourt. Assistant General Manager: Todd Doten. Director, Media/Public Relations: Harry Kargenian. Director, Ticket Sales: Kathy Elick. Head Groundskeeper: Darren Holt. Director, Stadium Operations: Peter Thompson.

Field Staff
Manager: Juan Navarrete. Coach: Steve Hosey. Pitching Coach: Jim Bennett. Trainer: Jeff Collins.

Game Information
Radio Announcer: Unavailable. No. of Games Broadcast: Home-70, Away-70. Flagship Station: KTIP 1450-AM.
PA Announcer/Official Scorer: Harry Kargenian.
Stadium Name (year opened): Recreation Park (1946). Location: From Highway 99, take 198 East to Mooney Boulevard exit, left on Giddings Avenue. Standard Game Times: 7:05 p.m.; Sun. (April-May 7) 2:05, (May 28-Sept.) 6:05.
Visiting Club Hotel: Holiday Inn, 9000 West Airport Dr., Visalia, CA 93277. Telephone: (559) 651-5000.

CAROLINALEAGUE

Class A Advanced

Office Address: 1806 Pembroke Rd., Greensboro, NC 27408. **Mailing Address:** P.O. Box 9503, Greensboro, NC 27429. **Telephone:** (336) 691-9030. **FAX:** (336) 691-9070.

E-Mail Address: office@carolinaleague. com. **Website:** www.carolinaleague.com.

Years League Active: 1945-.

President/Treasurer: John Hopkins.

Vice Presidents: Kelvin Bowles (Salem), Calvin Falwell (Lynchburg). **Corporate Secretary:** Matt Minker (Wilmington).

Directors: Don Beaver (Winston-Salem), Kelvin Bowles (Salem), Calvin Falwell (Lynchburg), George Habel (Myrtle Beach), North Johnson (Kinston), Peter Kirk (Frederick), Matt Minker (Wilmington), Art Silber (Potomac).

John Hopkins

Administrative Assistants: Michael Albrecht, Marnee Larkins.

2000 Opening Date: April 6. **Closing Date:** Sept. 3.

Regular Season: 140 games (split schedule).

Division Structure: North—Frederick, Lynchburg, Potomac, Wilmington. **South**—Kinston, Myrtle Beach, Salem, Winston-Salem.

Playoff Format: First-half division champions play second-half division champions in best-of-3 series. Winners meet in best-of-5 series for Mills Cup.

All-Star Game: June 20 at Kinston, NC (Carolina League vs. California League).

Roster Limit: 25 active. **Player Eligibility Rule:** No age limit. No more than two players and one player coach on active list may have six or more years of prior minor league service.

Brand of Baseball: Rawlings.

Statistician: Howe Sportsdata, Boston Fish Pier, West Bldg. #1, Suite 302, Boston MA 02210.

Umpires: Scot Chamberlain (Strawberry Plains, TN), Greg Chittenden (Springfield, MO), Peter Cicarelli (East Rutherford, NJ), Duston Dellinger (Mooresville, NC), David Falkavage (Stevens Point, WI), Scott Kennedy (Frankfort, KY), Ed Rogers (Thomson, GA), Ryan West (Arvada, CO).

Stadium Information

Club	Stadium	LF	CF	RF	Capacity	'99 Att.
Frederick	Harry Grove	325	400	325	5,400	313,603
Kinston	Grainger	335	390	335	4,200	124,010
Lynchburg	Hutchinson	325	390	325	4,000	110,937
Myrtle Beach	Coastal Federal	325	405	328	4,181	232,619
Potomac	Pfitzner	315	400	315	6,000	209,168
Salem	Salem Memorial	325	401	325	6,300	206,012
Wilmington	Frawley	325	400	325	5,600	321,143
Winston-Salem	Ernie Shore	325	400	325	6,280	134,764

FREDERICK
Keys

Office Address: 6201 New Design Rd., Frederick, MD 21703. **Mailing Address:** P.O. Box 3169, Frederick, MD 21705. **Telephone:** (301) 662-0013. **FAX:** (301) 662-0018. **E-Mail Address:** frederickkeys@erols.com. **Website:** www.frederickkeys.com.

Affiliation (first year): Baltimore Orioles (1989). **Years in League:** 1989-.

Ownership, Management
Operated by: Maryland Baseball, LLC.

Principal Owners: John Daskalakis, Peter Kirk, Frank Perdue, Hugh Schindel, Pete Simmons.

Chairman/President: Peter Kirk.

General Manager: Joe Pinto. **Assistant General Manager:** Gina Stepoulos. **Director, Stadium Operations:** Dave Wisner. **Director, Public Relations:** Heather Clabaugh. **Manager, Promotions:** Hannah Brook. **Director, Group Sales:** Paul Dever. **Assistant Director, Group Sales:** Laura Springer. **Group Sales Representative:** Melissa Marineau. **Assistant Director, Ticket Operations:** Jennifer Martenot. **Account Executives:** Shaun O'Neal, Ernie Stepoulos, Jimmy Sweet, Pam Wilson. **Director, Marketing:** Mark Zeigler. **Bookkeeper:** Tami Hetrick. **Head Groundskeeper:** Tommy Long. **Director, Food Services:** Mike Brulatour.

Field Staff
Manager: Dave Machemer. **Coach:** Bien Figueroa. **Pitching Coach:** Larry Jaster. **Trainer:** P.J. Mainville.

Game Information
Radio Announcer: Bob Socci. **No. of Games Broadcast:** Home-70, Away-70. **Flagship Station:** WXTR 820-AM.

PA Announcer: Rick McCauslin. **Official Scorer:** George Richardson.

Stadium Name (year opened): Harry Grove Stadium (1990). **Location:** From I-70, take exit 54 (Market Street), left at light. From I-270, take exit 31A (Market Street/Route 85) for two miles, stadium on left. **Standard Game Times:** 7:05 p.m.; Sun. 1:05.

Visiting Club Hotel: Comfort Inn, 420 Prospect Blvd., Frederick, MD 21701. Telephone: (301) 695-6200.

KINSTON
Indians

Office Address: 400 E Grainger Ave., Kinston, NC 28501. **Mailing Address:** P.O. Box 3542, Kinston, NC 28502. **Telephone:** (252) 527-9111. **FAX:** (252) 527-2328. **E-Mail Address:** info@kinstonindians.com. **Website:** www.kinstonindians.com.

Affiliation (first year): Cleveland Indians (1987). **Years in League:** 1956-57, 1962-74, 1978-.

Ownership, Management
Operated by: Slugger Partners, LP.

Principal Owners: Cam McRae, North Johnson.

Chairman: Cam McRae. **President/General Manager:** North Johnson. **Assistant General Manager:** John Purvis. **Director, Food Services:** Rita Spence. **Head Groundskeeper:** Tommy Walston. **Group Sales Assistants:** Brian Knapp, Keith Mitchell. **Clubhouse Operations:** Robert Smeraldo. **Office Manager:** Shari Massengill.

Field Staff
Manager: Brad Komminsk. **Coach:** Luis Rivera. **Pitching Coach:** Steve Lyons. **Trainer:** Teddy Blackwell.

Game Information
Radio Announcer: Robert Portnoy. **No. of Games Broadcast:** Home-70, Away-70. **Flagship Station:** WRNS 960-AM.

PA Announcer: Jeff Diamond. **Official Scorers:** Karl Grant, Keith Spence.

Stadium Name (year opened): Grainger Stadium (1949). **Location:** From west, take U.S. 70 Business (Vernon Avenue), left on East Street; from east take U.S. 70 W, right on Highway 58, right on Vernon Avenue, right on East Street. **Standard Game Times:** 7 p.m.; Sun. 2, 7.

Visiting Club Hotel: Hampton Inn, Hwy. 70 Bypass, Kinston NC 28504. Telephone: (252) 523-1500.

LYNCHBURG
Hillcats

Office Address: 3180 Fort Ave., Lynchburg, VA 24501. **Mailing Address:** P.O. Box 10213, Lynchburg, VA 24506. **Telephone:** (804) 528-1144. **FAX:** (804) 846-0768. **E-Mail Address:** hillcatsbb @aol.com. **Website:** www.lynchburg-hillcats.com.

Affiliation (first year): Pittsburgh Pirates (1995). **Years in League:** 1966-.

Ownership, Management
Operated by: Lynchburg Baseball Corp.
President: Calvin Falwell.
General Manager: Paul Sunwall. **Assistant General Manager:** Ronnie Roberts. **Director, Sales/Field Supervisor:** Darren Johnson. **Director, Broadcasting:** Matt Provence. **Director, Group Sales:** Bill Papierniak. **Office Manager:** Karen East.

Field Staff
Manager: Tracy Woodson. **Coach:** Tony Beasley. **Pitching Coach:** Scott Lovekamp. **Trainer:** David Sentfen.

Game Information
Radio Announcer: Matt Provence. **No. of Games Broadcast:** Home-70, Away-70. **Flagship Station:** WBRG 1050-AM.
PA Announcer: Chuck Young. **Official Scorers:** Malcolm Haley, Chuck Young.
Stadium Name (year opened): Merritt Hutchinson Stadium (1940). **Location:** U.S. 29 South to City Stadium (exit 6); U.S. 29 North to Lynchburg College/City Stadium (exit 4). **Standard Game Times:** 7:05 p.m.; Sun. 2:05.
Visiting Club Hotel: Best Western, 2815 Candlers Mountain Rd., Lynchburg, VA 24502. Telephone: (804) 237-2986.

MYRTLE BEACH
Pelicans

Office Address: 1251 21st Ave. N, Myrtle Beach, SC 29577. **Telephone:** (843) 918-6002. **FAX:** (843) 918-6001. **E-Mail Address:** info@myrtlebeachpelicans.com. **Website:** www.myrtlebeachpelicans.com.
Affiliation (first year): Atlanta Braves (1999). **Years in League:** 1999-.

Ownership, Management
Operated by: Capitol Broadcasting Company.
Principal Owner: Jim Goodmon. **Division Vice President:** George Habel. **VP/Legal Counsel:** Mike Hill.
General Manager: Steve Malliet. **Assistant GM/Director, Sales and Marketing:** Matt Harris. **Assistant GM/Director, Ticket Sales:** Gary Saunders. **Accounting Manager:** Anne Frishmuth. **Director, Stadium Operations:** Andrew Stewart. **Director, Media/Community Relations:** Bryan Dolgin. **Account Representatives:** Kelly Harvey-Sufka, Leann Rothrock. **Director, Promotions/Merchandising:** Dave Frost. **Director, Group Sales:** Jennifer Violand. **Manager, Group Sales:** Angela Hughes. **Director, Client Relations:** Melissa McGrath. **Clubhouse Operations:** Gerald Bass. **Box Office Manager:** Scott Tanfield. **Head Groundskeeper:** Bill Butler. **Office Manager:** Ody Perez.

Field Staff
Manager: Brian Snitker. **Coach:** Sixto Lezcano. **Pitching Coach:** Bruce Dal Canton. **Trainer:** Mike Graus.

Game Information
Radio Announcers: Garry Griffith, Bryan Dolgin. **No. of Games Broadcast:** Home-70, Away-70. **Flagship Station:** WRNN 94.5-FM.
PA Announcer: Matt Harris. **Official Scorer:** Mike McDonald.
Stadium Name (year opened): Coastal Federal Field (1999). **Location:** Highway 17 bypass to 21st Avenue North, ½ mile to stadium. **Standard Game Times:** 7:05 p.m.; Sun. (April-May) 4:05.

Visiting Club Hotel: Hampton Inn-48th Avenue, 4709 N Kings Hwy., Myrtle Beach, SC 29577. Telephone: (843) 449-5231.

POTOMAC
Cannons

Office Address: 7 County Complex Ct., Woodbridge, VA 22192. **Mailing Address:** P.O. Box 2148, Woodbridge, VA 22193. **Telephone:** (703) 590-2311. **FAX:** (703) 590-5716. **E-Mail Address:** cannonswin@aol.com. **Website:** www.potomaccannons.com.

Affiliation (first year): St. Louis Cardinals (1997). **Years in League:** 1978-.

Ownership, Management
Operated by: Prince William Professional Baseball Club, Inc.

Principal Owner: Art Silber. **Chairman:** John Allen. **Vice President:** Lani Silber.

General Manager: Dean Sisco. **Assistant GM:** Max Baker. **Director, Media/Public Relations:** Mike Antonellis. **Director, Community Relations:** Rich Arnold. **Director, Marketing:** Dave Schwartz. **Director, Ticket Sales:** Bobby Holland. **Director, Group Sales:** Tim Phillips. **Director, Food Services:** Tim Tierney. **Account Representative:** Don Wallace. **Head Groundskeeper:** Mike Lundy.

Field Staff
Manager: Joe Cunningham. **Coach:** Glen Brummer. **Pitching Coach:** Mark Grater. **Trainer:** Unavailable.

Game Information
Radio Announcer: Mike Antonellis. **No. of Games Broadcast:** Home-70, Away-70. **Flagship Station:** WKCW 1420-AM.

PA Announcer: Unavailable. **Official Scorers:** John Oravec, Dave Vincent.

Stadium Name (year opened): G. Richard Pfitzner Stadium (1984). **Location:** From I-95, take exit 158B and continue on Prince William Parkway for 5 miles, right into County Complex Court. **Standard Game Times:** 7:30 p.m.; Sat. 7; Sun. (April-June) 1:30, (July-Sept.) 6.

Visiting Club Hotel: Days Inn Potomac Mills, 14619 Potomac Mills Rd., Woodbridge, VA 22192. Telephone: (703) 494-4433.

SALEM
Avalanche

Office Address: 1004 Texas St., Salem, VA 24153. **Mailing Address:** P.O. Box 842, Salem, VA 24153. **Telephone:** (540) 389-3333. **FAX:** (540) 389-9710. **E-Mail Address:** info@salemavalanche.com. **Website:** www.salemavalanche.com.

Affiliation (first year): Colorado Rockies (1995). **Years in League:** 1968-.

Ownership, Management
Operated by: Salem Professional Baseball Club, Inc.

Principal Owner/President: Kelvin Bowles.

General Manager: Joe Preseren. **Assistant GM, Sales/Marketing:** Christian Carlson. **Assistant GM, Stadium Operations:** Stan Macko. **Director, Media/Community Relations:** Bernadette Vielhaber. **Director, Group Sales:** Tim Schuster. **Director, Merchandising:** Page Griffin. **Head Groundskeeper:** Mark Bragunier. **Director, Food Services:** Todd Lange.

Field Staff
Manager: Alan Cockrell. **Coach:** Joe Marchese. **Pitching Coach:** Bob McClure. **Trainer:** Jeremy Moeller.

Game Information
Radio Announcer: Unavailable. **No. of Games Broadcast:** Home-70, Away-70. **Flagship Stations:** WGMN 1240-AM, WVGM 1320-AM.

PA Announcer: Bruce Reynolds. **Official Scorer:** Brian Hoffman.

Stadium Name (year opened): Salem Memorial Baseball Stadium (1995). **Location:** I-81 to exit 141 (Route 419), follow signs to Salem Civic Center Complex. **Standard Game Times:** 7 p.m.; Sun. (April-June) 2, (July-Aug.) 5.

Visiting Club Hotel: Days Inn-Airport, 8118 Plantation Rd., Roanoke, VA 24019. Telephone: (540) 366-0341.

WILMINGTON
Blue Rocks

Office Address: 801 S Madison St., Wilmington, DE 19801. Telephone: (302) 888-2015. FAX: (302) 888-2032. E-Mail Address: info@bluerocks.com. Website: www.bluerocks.com.

Affiliation (first year): Kansas City Royals (1993). Years in League: 1993-.

Ownership, Management

Operated by: Wilmington Blue Rocks, LP.

President: Matt Minker. Vice President: Tom Palmer.

General Manager: Chris Kemple. Director, Finance: Craig Bailey. Director, Stadium Operations: Andrew Layman. Head Groundskeeper: Steve Gold. Director, Broadcasting/Media Relations: Mark Nasser. Assistant, Broadcasting/Media Relations: Jim Tocco. Director, Sales/Marketing: Doug Stewart. Assistant Director, Marketing: Tripp Baum. Marketing Assistant: Justin Agialoro. Director, Community Relations: Chris Parise. Assistant Director, Community Relations: James Moore. Director, Publications/Promotions: Jim Beck. Director, Ticket Operations/Group Sales: Marla Chalfie. Director, Merchandising: Paul Siegworth. Home Clubhouse: Ben Fonseca. Office Manager: Holly Jones. Ticket Office Manager: Jared Forma.

Field Staff

Manager: Jeff Garber. Coach: Steve Balboni. Pitching Coach: Larry Carter. Trainer: Chad Spaulding.

Game Information

Radio Announcers: Mark Nasser, Jim Tocco. No. of Games Broadcast: Home-70, Away-70. Flagship Station: WJBR 1290-AM.

PA Announcer: John McAdams. Official Scorers: Mike Brint, E.J. Casey, Dick Shute.

Stadium Name (year opened): Judy Johnson Field at Daniel S. Frawley Stadium (1993). Location: I-95 North to Maryland Ave. (exit 6), right onto Maryland Ave., right on Read Street, right on South Madison Street to ballpark; I-95 South to Maryland Ave. (exit 6), left at Martin Luther King Blvd., right on South Madison Street. Standard Game Times: 7:05 p.m.; Sat. (April-May) 2:05; Sun. 2:05.

Visiting Club Hotel: Quality Inn-Skyways, 147 N DuPont Hwy., New Castle, DE 19720. Telephone: (302) 328-6666.

WINSTON-SALEM
Warthogs

Office Address: 401 Deacon Blvd., Winston-Salem, NC 27105. Mailing Address: P.O. Box 4488, Winston-Salem, NC 27115. Telephone: (336) 759-2233. FAX: (336) 759-2042. E-Mail Address: warthogs@warthogs.com. Website: www.warthogs.com.

Affiliation (first year): Chicago White Sox (1997). Years in League: 1945-.

Ownership, Management

Operated by: Beaver Sports, Inc.

Principal Owner/President: Don Beaver.

General Manager: Peter Fisch. Assistant General Manager: Brian Harper. Special Assistant to GM: David Beal. Director, Broadcast/Media Relations: Tom Hart. Director, Community Relations: Holli Herren. Director, Group Sales: Ryan Manuel. Director, Merchandising: Dan Williams.

Field Staff

Manager: Brian Dayett. Coach: Daryl Boston. Pitching Coach: Juan Nieves. Trainer: Joe Geck.

Game Information

Radio Announcer: Tom Hart. No. of Games Broadcast: Home-70, Away-70. Flagship Station: WIFM 100.9-FM.

PA Announcer: Unavailable. Official Scorers: Chris Capo, Adam Tillery.

Stadium Name (year opened): Ernie Shore Field (1956). Location: I-40 Business to Cherry Street exit, north through downtown, right on Deacon Boulevard, park on left. Standard Game Times: 7:15 p.m.; Sun. 2:05.

Visiting Club Hotel: Best Western, 1680 Westbrook Plaza Dr., Winston-Salem, NC 27101. Telephone: (336) 714-3000.

FLORIDA STATE LEAGUE

Class A Advanced

Street Address: 103 E Orange Ave., Daytona Beach, FL 32114. **Mailing Address:** P.O. Box 349, Daytona Beach, FL 32115. **Telephone:** (904) 252-7479. **FAX:** (904) 252-7495. **E-Mail Address:** bball-league@mindspring.com.

Years League Active: 1919-1927, 1936-1941, 1946-.

President/Treasurer: Chuck Murphy.

Vice Presidents: Ken Carson (Dunedin), Jordan Kobritz (Daytona).

Corporate Secretary: David Hood.

Directors: Sammy Arena (Tampa), Ken Carson (Dunedin), Andy Dunn (Brevard County), Tony Flores (St. Petersburg), Marvin Goldklang (Fort Myers), Grant Griesser (Vero Beach), Jordan Kobritz (Daytona), Matt LaBranche (Charlotte), Dave

Chuck Murphy

Miller (Lakeland), Tim Purpura (Kissimmee), Kent Qualls (Sarasota), Rob Rabenecker (Jupiter), Paul Taglieri (St. Lucie), John Timberlake (Clearwater).

Office Secretary: Peggy Catigano.

2000 Opening Date: April 6. **Closing Date:** Sept. 3.

Regular Season: 140 games (split schedule).

Division Structure: East—Brevard County, Daytona, Jupiter, Kissimmee, St. Lucie, Vero Beach. **West**—Charlotte, Clearwater, Dunedin, Fort Myers, Lakeland, St. Petersburg, Sarasota, Tampa.

Playoff Format: First-half division champions play second-half champions in best-of-3 series. Winners meet in best-of-5 series for league championship.

All-Star Game: June 17 at Jupiter.

Roster Limit: 25. **Player Eligibility Rule:** No age limit. No more than two players and one player-coach on active list may have six or more years of prior minor league service.

Brand of Baseball: Rawlings.

Statistician: Howe Sportsdata, Boston Fish Pier, West Bldg. #1, Suite 302, Boston, MA 02210.

Umpires: Frank Coffland (San Antonio, TX), Bradley Cole (Sioux City, IA), Dan Cricks (Rockledge, FL), Chad Fairchild (Bradenton, FL), Bryce Fielder (Swisher, IA), Brian Hale (Trussville, AL), Chris Hubler (Dysart, IA), Steve Metheny (Irondale, AL), Trey Nelson (Lincoln, NE), Todd Parker (Hugo, OK), Dan Payne (San Jose, CA), Travis Reininger (Brighton, CO), David Riley (Indianapolis, IN), Chad Sexton (St. Petersburg, FL).

Stadium Information

Club	Stadium	Dimensions			Capacity	'99 Att.
		LF	CF	RF		
Brevard	Space Coast	340	404	340	7,500	115,145
Charlotte	Charlotte County	340	410	340	5,424	42,119
Clearwater	Jack Russell Memorial	330	400	330	6,917	70,147
Daytona	Jackie Robinson Ballpark	317	400	325	4,000	62,491
Dunedin	Dunedin	335	400	315	6,106	51,819
Fort Myers	Hammond	330	405	330	7,500	108,074
Jupiter	Roger Dean	330	400	325	6,871	105,037
Kissimmee	Osceola County	330	410	330	5,200	33,789
Lakeland	Joker Marchant	340	420	340	7,100	36,092
St. Lucie	Thomas J. White	338	410	338	7,500	40,928
St. Petersburg	Al Lang	330	400	330	7,004	82,631
Sarasota	Ed Smith	340	400	340	7,500	51,148
Tampa	Legends Field	318	408	314	10,386	91,603
Vero Beach	Holman	340	400	340	6,500	50,838

BREVARD COUNTY
Manatees

Office Address: 5800 Stadium Pkwy., Melbourne, FL 32940. **Telephone:** (321) 633-9200. **FAX:** (321) 633-9210. **E-Mail Address:** marlins@metrolink.net. **Website:** bcmanatees.com.

Affiliation (first year): Florida Marlins (1994). **Years in League:** 1994-.

Ownership, Management
Operated by: Florida Marlins of Brevard, Ltd.
Principal Owner: John Henry.
Director, Operations: Andy Dunn. **President, Brevard Concessions:** Roy Lake. **Facility Engineer:** Jack Haberthier. **Head Groundskeeper:** Doug Lopas. **Manager, Corporate Sales:** Jeff Kuenzli. **Manager, Ticket/Public Relations:** Pat Herman. **Manager, Group Sales:** Trey Fraser. **Assistant Facility Engineer:** Kevin Seidell.

Field Staff
Manager: Dave Huppert. **Coach:** Frank Cacciatore. **Pitching Coach:** Euclides Rojas. **Trainer:** Ruben Barrera.

Game Information
Radio: None.
PA Announcer: Scott Terry. **Official Scorer:** Ron Jernick.
Stadium Name (year opened): Space Coast Stadium (1994). **Location:** I-95 North to Wickham Road (exit 73), left on Wickham, right on Lake Andrew Drive, left onto Judge Fran Jamison Way, right on Stadium Parkway; I-95 South to Fiske Boulevard (exit 74), left on Fiske, follow Fiske/Stadium Parkway. **Standard Game Times:** 7:05 p.m., Sun. 1:35.
Visiting Club Hotel: Melbourne Airport Hilton, 200 Rialto Pl., Melbourne, FL 32901. Telephone: (321) 768-0200.

CHARLOTTE
Rangers

Office Address: 2300 El Jobean Rd., Port Charlotte, FL 33948. **Telephone:** (941) 625-9500. **FAX:** (941) 624-5168. **E-Mail Address:** rangers@charlotterangers.com. **Website:** www.charlotterangers.com.

Affiliation (first year): Texas Rangers (1987). **Years in League:** 1987-.

Ownership, Management
Operated by: Southwest Sports Group.
Principal Owner: Thomas Hicks.
General Manager: Matt LaBranche. **Director, Stadium Operations/Food Services:** Chris Easom. **Head Groundskeeper:** Tom Vida. **Director, Promotions:** Carl Benson. **Director, Ticket Sales:** Jessica Halperin. **Office Manager:** Tina Buonaiuto.

Field Staff
Manager: James Byrd. **Coach:** Edgar Caceres. **Pitching Coach:** Aris Tirado. **Trainer:** Brian Ball.

Game Information
Radio: None.
PA Announcer: Kenny Rodman. **Official Scorer:** Peter Dulk.
Stadium Name (year opened): Charlotte County Stadium (1987). **Location:** I-75 South to exit 32, follow Toledo Blade Blvd. west for seven miles to stop sign at SR 776, right on 776 for one mile. **Standard Game Times:** 6:30 p.m.; Sun. 2.
Visiting Club Hotel: Days Inn-Murdock, 1941 Tamiami Trail, Murdock, FL 33948. Telephone: (941) 627-8900.

CLEARWATER
Phillies

Office Address: 800 Phillies Drive, Clearwater, FL 33755. **Mailing Address:** P.O. Box 10336, Clearwater, FL 33757. **Telephone:** (727) 441-8638. **FAX:** (727) 447-3924. **Website:** www.clearwaterphillies.com.

Affiliation (first year): Philadelphia Phillies (1985). **Years in League:** 1985-.

Ownership, Management

Operated by: The Philadelphia Phillies.

Chairman: Bill Giles. **President:** David Montgomery.

Director, Florida Operations: John Timberlake. **Assistant Director, Florida Operations:** Lee McDaniel. **Business Manager, Florida Operations:** Dianne Gonzalez. **General Manager:** John Cook. **Director, Marketing:** Dan McDonough. **Director, Media/Public Relations:** Jason Adams. **Director, Merchandising:** Kerri Leeman. **Director, Community Relations:** Amy Koffel. **Office Manager:** De De Angelillis. **Head Groundskeeper:** Opie Cheek. **Clubhouse Operations:** Cliff Armbruster.

Field Staff

Manager: Ken Oberkfell. **Coach:** Al LeBoeuf. **Pitching Coach:** Warren Brusstar. **Trainer:** Craig Strobel.

Game Information

Radio: None.

PA Announcer: Don Gucklan. **Official Scorer:** Unavailable.

Stadium Name (year opened): Jack Russell Memorial Stadium (1955). **Location:** U.S. 19 North to Drew Street, west to Greenwood Avenue, north to Seminole, right to park. **Standard Game Times:** 7:05 p.m., Sun. 5:05.

Visiting Club Hotel: Econo Lodge, 21252 U.S. 19 North, Clearwater, FL 33765. Telephone: (727) 796-3165.

DAYTONA
Cubs

Office Address: 105 E Orange Ave., Daytona Beach, FL 32114. **Mailing Address:** P.O. Box 15080, Daytona Beach, FL 32115. **Telephone:** (904) 257-3172. **FAX:** (904) 257-3382.

Affiliation (first year): Chicago Cubs (1993). **Years in League:** 1920-24, 1928, 1936-41, 1946-73, 1977-87, 1993-.

Ownership, Management

Operated by: Florida Professional Sports, Inc.

Principal Owner/President: Jordan Kobritz.

General Manager: Debbie Kobritz. **Account Representative:** Mark McNerney. **Clubhouse Operations:** Rick Currey. **Administrative Assistant:** Kim Davis.

Field Staff

Manager: Richie Zisk. **Coach:** Joey Cora. **Pitching Coach:** Tom Pratt. **Trainer:** Alan Morales.

Game Information

Radio: None.

PA Announcer: Cliff Olos. **Official Scorer:** Lyle Fox.

Stadium Name (year opened): Jackie Robinson Ballpark (1930). **Location:** From I-95, take International Speedway Boulevard exit (Route 92), east to Beach Street, south to Orange Avenue, east to ballpark; From A1A North/South, take Orange Avenue west to ballpark. **Standard Game Times:** 7 p.m.; Sun. 1.

Visiting Club Hotel: Howard Johnson Plaza/Harbour Beach Resort, 701 S Atlantic Ave., Daytona Beach, FL 32118. Telephone: (904) 258-8522.

DUNEDIN
Blue Jays

Office Address: 373 Douglas Ave., Dunedin, FL 34698. **Mailing Address:** P.O. Box 957, Dunedin, FL 34697. **Telephone:** (727) 733-9302. **FAX:** (727) 734-7661. **E-Mail Address:** dunedin@bluejays.ca. **Website:** www.bluejays.ca/dunedin.

Affiliation (first year): Toronto Blue Jays (1987). **Years in League:** 1978-79, 1987-.

Ownership, Management

Operated by: Toronto Blue Jays.

Director, Florida Operations: Ken Carson. **General Manager:** Ed Vonnes. **Head Groundskeeper:** Steve Perry. **Director, Community Relations:** Carrie Short. **Director, Promotions:** Nick Neubauer. **Clubhouse Operations:** Mickey McGee. **Office Manager:** Pat Smith. **Administrative Assistant:** Ann Carson.

Field Staff
Manager: Marty Pevey. **Coach:** Dennis Holmberg. **Pitching Coach:** Scott Breeden. **Trainer:** Jay Inouye.

Game Information
Radio: None.

PA Announcers: Matt Carson, Ed Groth. **Official Scorer:** Larry Weiderecht.

Stadium Name (year opened): Dunedin Stadium (1990). **Location:** From I-275, north on Highway 19, left on Sunset Point Road for 4½ miles, right on Douglas Avenue, stadium is ½ mile on right. **Standard Game Times:** 7 p.m.; Sun. 5.

Visiting Club Hotel: Red Roof Inn, 32000 U.S. Hwy. 19 N, Palm Harbor, FL 34684. Telephone: (727) 786-2529.

FORT MYERS
Miracle

Office Address: 14400 Six Mile Cypress Pkwy., Fort Myers, FL 33912. **Telephone:** (941) 768-4210. **FAX:** (941) 768-4211. **E-Mail Address:** miracle@miraclebaseball.com. **Website:** www.miraclebaseball.com.

Affiliation: Minnesota Twins (1993). **Years in League:** 1926, 1978-87, 1992-.

Ownership, Management
Operated by: Greater Miami Baseball Club, LP.

Principal Owner: Marvin Goldklang. **President:** Mike Veeck.

General Manager: Derek Sharrer. **Assistant General Manager:** David Burke. **Director, Business Operations:** Suzanne Reaves. **Director, Stadium Operations:** Jody Clarke. **Head Groundskeeper:** Keith Blasingem. **Director, Media/Public Relations:** Mark Weaver. **Director, Sales/Marketing:** Linda McNabb. **Senior Account Representative:** Neil Packanik. **Account Representatives:** Seth Petree, Pete Swan. **Director, Community Relations:** Lou Slack. **Director, Promotions/Ticket Sales:** Andrew Seymour. **Manager, Corporate/Hospitality Sales:** Terry Olman.

Field Staff
Manager: Jose Marzan. **Coach:** Riccardo Ingram. **Pitching Coach:** Eric Rasmussen. **Trainer:** Larry Bennese.

Game Information
Radio Announcer: Mark Weaver. **No. of Games Broadcast:** Home-30, Away-70. **Flagship Station:** WTLQ 1200-AM.

PA Announcer: Ted Fitzgeorge. **Official Scorer:** Benn Norton.

Stadium Name (year opened): William H. Hammond Stadium (1991). **Location:** Exit 21 off I-75, west on Daniels Parkway, left on Six Mile Cypress Parkway. **Standard Game Times:** 7:05 p.m.; Sun. 4:05.

Visiting Club Hotel: Wellesley Inn and Suites, 4400 Ford St. Extension, Fort Myers, FL 33909. Telephone: (941) 278-3949.

JUPITER
Hammerheads

Office Address: 4751 Main St., Jupiter, FL 33458. **Mailing Address:** P.O. Box 8929, Jupiter, FL 33468. **Telephone:** (561) 775-1818. **FAX:** (561) 691-6886. **Website:** www.rogerdeanstadium.com.

Affiliation (first year): Montreal Expos (1969). **Years in League:** 1998-.

Ownership, Management
Operated by: Montreal Expos Professional Baseball.

Chairman: Jacques Menard. **President:** Jeffrey Loria.

General Manager: Rob Rabenecker. **Executive Assistant to GM:** Carole Ray Dixon. **Manager, Field Operations:** Cindy Unger. **Director, Operations:** Brian Barnes. **Director, Marketing:** Jennifer Chalhub. **Hammerhead Operations Manager:** Todd Pund. **Controller:** David Resnick. **Director, Sales/Marketing:** Scott Brown. **Account Representatives:** Rob Lougee, Juan Rodriguez, Sami Strauss, Rick Tickner. **Director, Merchandising:** Ashley Brown. **Office Manager:** Kathy Spangler.

Field Staff
Manager: Luis Dorante. **Coach:** Mike Felder. **Pitching Coach:** Ace Adams. **Trainer:** Carl Scheiner.

Game Information

Radio: None.

PA Announcer: Dick Sanford. **Official Scorer:** Jim Turner.

Stadium Name (year opened): Roger Dean Stadium (1998). **Location:** Exit 58 on I-95, east on Donald Ross Road for ¼ mile. **Standard Game Times:** 7:05 p.m., Sun. 2:05.

Visiting Club Hotel: Wellesley Inn, 34 Fisherman's Wharf, Jupiter, FL 33477. Telephone: (561) 575-7201.

KISSIMMEE
Cobras

Office Address: 1000 Bill Beck Blvd., Kissimmee, FL 34744. **Mailing Address:** P.O. Box 422229, Kissimmee, FL 34742. **Telephone:** (407) 933-5500. **FAX:** (407) 847-6237. **E-Mail Address:** barnes@kua.net. **Website:** www.kissimmeecobras.com.

Affiliation (first year): Houston Astros (1985). **Years in League:** 1985-.

Ownership, Management

Operated by: Houston Astros Baseball.

Chairman: Drayton McLane. **President:** Tal Smith.

General Manager: Jay Edmiston. **Assistant General Manager:** David Barnes. **Director, Stadium Operations:** Don Miers. **Head Grounds-keeper:** Rick Raasch. **Director, Food Services:** Jason Marsh. **Clubhouse Operations:** Matt Bass. **Office Manager:** Olga Torres.

Field Staff

Manager: Manny Acta. **Coach:** Ivan DeJesus. **Pitching Coach:** Jack Billingham. **Trainer:** Terry Shoemaker.

Game Information

Radio: None.

PA Announcer: Unavailable. **Official Scorer:** Greg Kaye.

Stadium Name (year opened): Osceola County Stadium (1985). **Location:** From Florida Turnpike South, take exit 244, west on U.S. 192, right on Bill Beck Boulevard; From Florida Turnpike North, take exit 242, west on U.S. 192, right on Bill Beck Blvd.; From I-4, take exit onto 192 East for 12 miles, stadium on left; From 17-92 South, take U.S. 192, left for three miles. **Standard Game Times:** 7:05 p.m.; Sun. 2:05.

Visiting Club Hotel: Stadium Inn and Suites, 2039 E Irlo Bronson Hwy., Kissimmee, FL 34744. Telephone: (407) 846-7814.

LAKELAND
Tigers

Office Address: 2125 N Lake Ave., Lakeland, FL 33805. **Mailing Address:** P.O. Box 90187, Lakeland, FL 33804. **Telephone:** (863) 688-7911. **FAX:** (863) 688-9589. **E-Mail Address:** ltigers@lakelandtigers.com. **Website:** www.lakelandtigers.com.

Affiliation (first year): Detroit Tigers (1967). **Years in League:** 1919-26, 1953-55, 1960, 1962-64, 1967-.

Ownership, Management

Operated by: Detroit Tigers.

Principal Owner: Mike Ilitch. **President:** John McHale Jr.

General Manager: Unavailable. **Director, Sales/Media Relations:** Zach Burek. **Director, Group Sales:** Rob Fredericks. **Director, Merchandising/Concessions:** Kay LaLonde. **Director, Marketing/Community Relations:** Patti Sarano. **Ticket Operations:** Jason Elias. **Clubhouse Operations:** Dan Price. **Head Groundskeeper:** Larry Glass.

Field Staff

Manager: Skeeter Barnes. **Coach:** Basilio Cabrera. **Pitching Coach:** Joe Boever. **Trainer:** Matt Rankin.

Game Information

Radio: None.

PA Announcer: Wayne Koehler. **Official Scorer:** Sandy Shaw.

Stadium Name (year opened): Joker Marchant Stadium (1966). **Location:** Exit 19 on I-4 to Lakeland Hills Blvd., left 1½ miles. **Standard Game Times:** 6 p.m.; Sun. 1.

Visiting Club Hotel: Unavailable.

ST. LUCIE
Mets

Office Address: 525 NW Peacock Blvd., Port St. Lucie, FL 34986.
Telephone: (561) 871-2100. **FAX:** (561) 878-9802. **Website:** www.lets-go-mets.com.
Affiliation (first year): New York Mets (1988). **Years in League:** 1988-.

Ownership, Management
Operated by: Sterling/Doubleday Enterprises, LP.
General Manager: Paul Taglieri. **Director, Sales:** Traer Van Allen.
Director, Marketing: Ari Skalet. **Director, Ticket Operations:** Ben Eversole. **Office Assistant:** JoAnne Colenzo.

Field Staff
Manager: Dave Engle. **Coach:** Roger LaFrancois. **Pitching Coach:** Buzz Capra. **Trainer:** Eric Montague.

Game Information
Radio: None.
PA Announcer: Phil Scott. **Official Scorer:** Unavailable.
Stadium Name (year opened): Thomas J. White Stadium (1988). **Location:** Exit 63C (St. Lucie West Boulevard) off I-95, east ½ mile, left on NW Peacock Boulevard. **Standard Game Times:** 7 p.m., Sun. 2.
Visiting Club Hotel: Holiday Inn, 10120 S Federal Hwy., Port St. Lucie, FL 34952. Telephone: (561) 337-2200.

ST. PETERSBURG
Devil Rays

Office Address: 180 Second Ave. SE, St. Petersburg, FL 33701.
Mailing Address: P.O. Box 12557, St. Petersburg, FL 33733. **Telephone:** (727) 825-3284. **FAX:** (727) 825-3122. **E-Mail Address:** rays@stpetedevilrays.com. **Website:** www.stpetedevilrays.com.
Affiliation (first year): Tampa Bay Devil Rays (1997). **Years In League:** 1920-28, 1955-.

Ownership, Management
Operated by: Tampa Bay Devil Rays, Ltd.
Principal Owner/President: Vince Naimoli.
General Manager: Tony Flores. **Director, Stadium Operations:** Adrian Moore. **Director, Media/Public Relations:** Jarrod Wronski.

Field Staff
Manager: Julio Garcia. **Coach:** Mike Compton. **Pitching Coach:** Bryan Kelly. **Trainer:** Jeff Stay.

Game Information
Radio: None.
PA Announcer: Jarrod Wronski. **Official Scorer:** Geoff Vandal.
Stadium Name (year opened): Florida Power Park/Al Lang Field (1977). **Location:** I-275 to exit 9, left on First Street South to Second Avenue South, stadium on right. **Standard Game Times:** 7:05 p.m., Sun. 5.
Visiting Club Hotel: Days Inn, 2595 54th Ave. N, St. Petersburg, FL 33701. Telephone: (727) 522-3191.

SARASOTA
Red Sox

Office Address: 2700 12th St., Sarasota, FL 34237. **Mailing Address:** P.O. Box 2816, Sarasota, FL 34230. **Telephone:** (941) 365-4460. **FAX:** (941) 365-4217.
Affiliation (first year): Boston Red Sox (1994). **Years in League:** 1927, 1961-65, 1989-.

Ownership, Management
Operated by: Red Sox of Florida, Inc.
Principal Owner: Boston Red Sox.
Interim General Manager: Todd Stephenson. **Director, Sales/Marketing:** Mike Lewis.

Field Staff
Manager: Ron Johnson. **Coach:** Ino Guerrero. **Pitching Coach:** Larry Pierson. **Trainer:** Stan Skolfield.

Game Information
Radio: None.

PA Announcer: Joe McCurro. **Official Scorer:** Bob Comiskey.

Stadium Name (year opened): Ed Smith Stadium (1989). **Location:** I-75 to exit 39, three miles west to Tuttle Avenue, right on Tuttle ½ mile to 12th Street, stadium on left. **Standard Game Times:** 7:05 p.m., Sun. (April-May) 2:05, (June-Sept.) 5:05.

Visiting Club Hotel: Hampton Inn, 5000 N Tamiami Trail, Sarasota, FL 34234. Telephone: (941) 351-7734.

TAMPA
Yankees

Office Address: One Steinbrenner Dr., Tampa, FL 33614. **Telephone:** (813) 875-7753. **FAX:** (813) 673-3174. **E-Mail Address:** tyank1@aol.com.

Affiliation (first year): New York Yankees (1994). **Years in League:** 1919-27, 1957-1988, 1994-.

Ownership, Management
Operated by: New York Yankees, LP.

Principal Owner: George Steinbrenner.

General Manager: Sammy Arena. **Assistant GM:** Eddie Robinson III. **Director, Stadium Operations:** Dean Holbert. **Director, Sales/Marketing:** Howard Grosswirth. **Account Representative:** Heath Hardin. **Director, Ticket Sales:** Vance Smith. **Head Groundskeeper:** Gary Lackey.

Field Staff
Manager: Tom Nieto. **Coach:** Unavailable. **Pitching Coach:** Rich Monteleone. **Trainer:** Unavailable.

Game Information
Radio: None.

PA Announcer: Ed McCloskey. **Official Scorer:** J.J. Pizzio.

Stadium Name (year opened): Legends Field (1996). **Location:** I-275 to Martin Luther King, west on Martin Luther King to Dale Mabry. **Standard Game Times:** 7 p.m., Sun. 1.

Visiting Club Hotel: Holiday Inn Express, 4732 N Dale Mabry Hwy., Tampa, FL 33614. Telephone: (813) 877-6061.

VERO BEACH
Dodgers

Office Address: 4101 26th St., Vero Beach, FL 32960. **Mailing Address:** P.O. Box 2887, Vero Beach, FL 32961. **Telephone:** (561) 569-4900. **FAX:** (561) 567-0819. **E-Mail Address:** dodgers@vero.com. **Website:** www.vero.com/dodgers.

Affiliation (first year): Los Angeles Dodgers (1980). **Years in League:** 1980-.

Ownership, Management
Operated by: Los Angeles Dodgers.

General Manager: Grant Griesser. **Assistant General Manager:** Nicole Turner. **Head Groundskeeper:** John Yencho. **Director, Ticket Sales:** Louise Boissy. **Director, Group Sales/Special Projects:** Trevor Gooby. **Director, Merchandising:** Kathy Bond.

Field Staff
Manager: John Shoemaker. **Coach:** Tony Harris. **Pitching Coach:** Marty Reed. **Trainer:** Unavailable.

Game Information
Radio Announcer: Bob DeCourcey. **No. of Games Broadcast:** Home-70, Away-70. **Flagship Station:** WTTB 1490-AM.

PA Announcer: Unavailable. **Official Scorer:** Randy Phillips.

Stadium Name (year opened): Holman Stadium (1953). **Location:** Exit I-95 to Route 60 East, left on 43rd Avenue, right on Aviation Boulevard. **Standard Game Times:** 7 p.m.; Sun. 2.

Visiting Club Hotel: Vero Beach Inn, 4700 North A1A, Vero Beach, FL 32963. Telephone: (561) 231-1600.

MIDWESTLEAGUE

Class A

Office Address: 1118 Cranston Rd., Beloit, WI 53511. **Mailing Address:** P.O. Box 936, Beloit, WI 53512. **Telephone:** (608) 364-1188. **FAX:** (608) 364-1913. **E-Mail Address:** midwest@inwave.com.

Years League Active: 1947-.

President/Treasurer: George Spelius.

Vice President: Ed Larson. **Legal Counsel/Secretary:** Richard Nussbaum.

Directors: Andrew Appleby (Fort Wayne), Lew Chamberlin (West Michigan), George Chaney (Clinton), William Collins III (Michigan), Dennis Conerton (Beloit), Tom Dickson (Lansing), Kevin Krause (Quad City), Wally Krouse (Cedar Rapids), Alan Levin (South Bend), Hank Stickney (Dayton), Larry Trucco (Wisconsin), Rocky Vonachen (Peoria), Dave Walker (Burlington), Mike Woleben (Kane County).

George Spelius

League Administrator: Stephanie Gray.

2000 Opening Date: April 6. **Closing Date:** Sept. 4.

Regular Season: 140 games (split schedule).

Division Structure: East—Dayton, Fort Wayne, Lansing, Michigan, South Bend, West Michigan. West—Beloit, Burlington, Cedar Rapids, Clinton, Kane County, Peoria, Quad City, Wisconsin.

Playoff Format: Eight teams qualify. First-half and second-half division champions, and wild-card teams, meet in best-of-3 quarterfinal series. Winners meet in best-of-3 series for divisional championship. Division champions meet in best-of-5 final for league championship.

All-Star Game: June 20 at Geneva, IL (Kane County).

Roster Limit: 25 active. **Player Eligibility Rule:** No age limit. No more than two players and one player-coach on active list may have more than five years experience.

Brand of Baseball: Rawlings ROM-MID.

Statistician: Howe Sportsdata, Boston Fish Pier, West Bldg. #1, Suite 302, Boston MA 02210.

Umpires: Peter Durfee (Tucson, AZ), Jimmy Forbis (Lawrence, KS), Cameron Keller (Hastings, NE), Tony Klubertanz (Sun Prairie, WI), Scott McClellan (Fort Wayne, IN), John McMasters (Tacoma, WA), Troy Penrod (Salem, OR), Tony Prater (Portland, OR), Tim Strike (Anchorage, AK), Kevin Sweeney (Rio Rancho, NM), Bill Van Raaphorst (El Cajon, CA), Garrett Watson (Reno, NV), Darin Williams (Beebe, AR), John Woods (Phoenix, AZ).

Stadium Information

Club	Stadium	LF	CF	RF	Capacity	'99 Att.
Beloit	Pohlman Field	325	380	325	3,501	54,689
Burlington	Community Field	338	403	315	3,502	66,178
Cedar Rapids	Veterans Memorial	325	385	325	6,000	127,612
Clinton	Riverview	335	390	325	2,500	61,485
Dayton*	Fifth Third Field	320	400	320	7,230	63,705
Fort Wayne	Memorial	330	400	330	6,516	201,395
Kane County	Philip B. Elfstrom	335	400	335	7,400	451,145
Lansing	Oldsmobile Park	305	412	305	11,000	462,515
Michigan	C.O. Brown	323	401	336	6,600	108,033
Peoria	Pete Vonachen	335	383	335	5,200	150,254
Quad City	John O'Donnell	340	390	340	5,200	145,734
South Bend	Coveleski Regional	336	405	336	5,000	200,518
West Michigan	Old Kent Park	327	402	327	10,900	457,350
Wisconsin	Fox Cities	325	405	325	5,500	223,814

Dimensions shown in the LF / CF / RF columns.

* Club operated in Rockford, Ill., in 1999

BELOIT
Snappers

Office Address: 2301 Skyline Dr., Beloit, WI 53511. **Mailing Address:** P.O. Box 855, Beloit, WI 53512. **Telephone:** (608) 362-2272. **FAX:** (608) 362-0418. **E-Mail Address:** snappy@snappersbaseball.com. **Website:** www.snappersbaseball.com.

Affiliation (first year): Milwaukee Brewers (1982). **Years in League:** 1982-.

Ownership, Management
Operated by: Beloit Professional Baseball Association, Inc.
Chairman: Dennis Conerton. **President:** Marcy Olsen.
General Manager: Bruce Keiter. **Assistant General Manager:** Brent Wheeler. **Director, Community Relations/Promotions:** Dave Costello. **Director, Group Sales/Merchandising:** Rebecca Braun. **Director, Food/Beverage Services:** Bob Preston. **Director, Ticket Operations:** Brian Schackow. **Office Manager:** Stephanie Lake.

Field Staff
Manager: Don Money. **Coach:** Rich Morales. **Pitching Coach:** R.C. Lichtenstein. **Trainer:** Greg Barajas.

Game Information
Radio Announcer: Michael Scott. **No. of Games Broadcast:** Home-70. **Flagship Station:** WGEZ 1490-AM.
PA Announcer: Unavailable. **Official Scorer:** Steve Clark.
Stadium Name (year opened): Pohlman Field (1982). **Location:** I-90 to exit 185-A, right at Cranston Road for 1½ miles. I-43 to Wisconsin 81 to Cranston Road, right at Cranston for 1½ miles. **Standard Game Times:** 7 p.m., (April-May) 6; Sat. 6; Sun. 2.
Visiting Club Hotel: Comfort Inn, 2786 Milwaukee Rd., Beloit, WI 53511. Telephone: (608) 362-2666.

BURLINGTON
Bees

Office Address: 2712 Mt. Pleasant St., Burlington, IA 52601. **Mailing Address:** P.O. Box 824, Burlington, IA 52601. **Telephone:** (319) 754-5705. **FAX:** (319) 754-5882. **E-Mail Address:** staff@gobees.com. **Website:** www.gobees.com.

Affiliation (first year): Chicago White Sox (1999). **Years in League:** 1962-.

Ownership, Management
Operated by: Burlington Baseball Association, Inc.
President: Dave Walker.
General Manager: Chuck Brockett. **Assistant General Manager:** Cliff Wiley. **Head Groundskeeper:** Todd VanScoy. **Director, Media/Public Relations:** Randy Wehofer. **Director, Food Services:** Joe Moulin. **Office Manager:** Danise Barton.

Field Staff
Manager: Jerry Terrell. **Coach:** Greg Ritchie. **Pitching Coach:** J.R. Perdew. **Trainer:** Josh Fallin.

Game Information
Radio Announcer: Randy Wehofer. **No. of Games Broadcast:** Home-70, Away-70. **Flagship Station:** KBUR 1490-AM.
PA Announcer: Jeff Sands. **Official Scorer:** Scott Logas.
Stadium Name (year opened): Community Field (1947). **Location:** From U.S. 34, take U.S. 61 North to Mt. Pleasant Street, east ⅛ mile. **Standard Game Times:** 7:05 p.m.; Sat. (April-May) 6:05; Sun. (April-May) 2:05, (June-Sept.) 6:05.
Visiting Club Hotel: Pzazz Best Western, 3001 Winegard Dr., Burlington, IA 52601. Telephone: (319) 753-2223.

CEDAR RAPIDS
Kernels

Office Address: 950 Rockford Rd. SW, Cedar Rapids, IA 52404.

Mailing Address: P.O. Box 2001, Cedar Rapids, IA 52406. **Telephone:** (319) 363-3887. **FAX:** (319) 363-5631. **E-Mail Address:** kernels@kernels.com. **Website:** www.kernels.com.

Affiliation (first year): Anaheim Angels (1993). **Years in League:** 1962-.

Ownership, Management

Operated by: Cedar Rapids Baseball Club, Inc.
President: Wally Krouse.
General Manager: Jack Roeder. **Director, Operations/Merchandising:** Nancy Cram. **Head Groundskeeper:** Bud Curran. **Director, Media/Community Relations:** Kyle Tadman. **Director, Group Sales/Gameday Operations:** Kelly Davis. **Director, Broadcasting:** John Rodgers.

Field Staff

Manager: Mitch Seoane. **Coach:** Tyrone Boykin. **Pitching Coach:** Randy Kramer. **Trainer:** Alfonso Flores.

Game Information

Radio Announcer: John Rodgers. **No. of Games Broadcast:** Home-70, Away-70. **Flagship Station:** KCRG 1600-AM.
PA Announcer: Dale Brodt. **Official Scorer:** Andy Pantini.
Stadium Name (year opened): Veterans Memorial Stadium (1949). **Location:** I-380 to Wilson Ave. exit, west to Rockford Road, right one mile to corner of 8th Ave. and 15th Street SW. **Standard Game Times:** 7 p.m.; Sun. 2.
Visiting Club Hotel: Best Western Village Inn, 100 F Ave. NW, Cedar Rapids, IA 52405. Telephone: (319) 366-5323.

CLINTON
LumberKings

Office Address: Riverview Stadium, Sixth Avenue North and First Avenue, Clinton, IA 52732. **Mailing Address:** P.O. Box 1295, Clinton, IA 52733. **Telephone:** (319) 242-0727. **FAX:** (319) 242-1433. **E-Mail Address:** lkingn@clinton.net. **Website:** www.clinton.net/~lkings.

Affiliation (first year): Cincinnati Reds (1999). **Years in League:** 1956-.

Ownership, Management

Operated by: Clinton Baseball Club, Inc.
Chairman: Don Roode. **President:** George Chaney.
General Manager: Ted Tornow. **Assistant General Manager:** Ben Giancola.

Field Staff

Manager: Jay Sorg. **Coach:** Greg Grall. **Pitching Coach:** Derek Botelho. **Trainer:** Chris Lapole.

Game Information

Radio Announcer: Jeff Palermo. **No. of Games Broadcast:** Home-70, Away-70. **Flagship Station:** KCLN 1390-AM.
PA Announcer: Morty Kriner. **Official Scorer:** Unavailable.
Stadium Name (year opened): Riverview Stadium (1937). **Location:** Highway 30 East to Sixth Avenue North, right on Sixth, cross railroad tracks, stadium on right. **Standard Game Times:** 7 p.m.; Sun. 2.
Visiting Club Hotel: Ramada Inn, 1522 Lincoln Way, Clinton, IA 52732. Telephone: (319) 243-8841.

DAYTON
Dragons

Office Address: 220 N Patterson Blvd., Dayton, OH 45402. **Mailing Address:** P.O. Box 2107, Dayton, OH 45401. **Telephone:** (937) 228-2287. **FAX:** (937) 228-2284. **E-Mail Address:** email@daytondragons.com. **Website:** www.daytondragons.com.

Affiliation (first year): Cincinnati Reds (2000). **Years in League:** 2000-.

Ownership, Management

Operated by: Dayton Professional Baseball Club, LLC.
Owner: Archie Griffin. **Chief Executive Officer:** Hank Stickney. **Managing Director:** Ken Stickney. **Chairman:** Peter Gruber. **Vice Chairman:** Paul Schaeffer.
President: Robert Murphy. **Vice President:** Eric Deutsch. **VP, Baseball/Stadium Operations:** Gary Mayse. **VP, Sales/Marketing:** Kevin

Rochlitz. **Manager, Communications:** Brad Eaton. **Managers, Corporate Marketing:** Jeff Forthofer, Eric Hostetter, Dale Lacy, Deron Marchant, Jeff Stewart, Ryan Von Sossan. **Managers, Marketing:** Chip Hurt, Courtney Wendeln. **Senior Ticket Agent:** Sally Ledford. **Box Office Managers:** Damon Swenson, James Trzeciak. **Manager, Operations:** Joe Eaglowski. **Group Sales:** Brian Brinck. **Office Administrator:** Leslie Stuck. **Administrative Assistant:** Debi Leputa. **Office Support:** Cherry Klenke. **Receptionist:** Caroline Wilson.

Field Staff
Manager: Fred Benavides. **Coach:** Brian Conley. **Pitching Coach:** Don Alexander. **Trainer:** Randy Brackney.

Game Information
Radio Announcer: Unavailable. **No. of Games Broadcast:** Home-70, Away-70. **Flagship Station:** Unavailable.
PA Announcer: Unavailable. **Official Scorer:** Unavailable.
Stadium Name (year opened): Fifth Third Field (2000). **Location:** I-75 South to downtown Dayton, left at First Street; I-75 North, right at First Street exit. **Standard Game Times:** 7 p.m.; Sun. 2.
Visiting Club Hotel: Fairfield Inn-Dayton North, 6960 Miller Lane, Dayton, OH 45414. Telephone: (937) 898-1120.

FORT WAYNE
Wizards

Office Address: 1616 E. Coliseum Blvd., Fort Wayne, IN 46805. **Telephone:** (219) 482-6400. **FAX:** (219) 471-4678. **E-Mail Address:** info@wizardsbaseball.com. **Website:** www.wizardsbaseball.com.
Affiliation (first year): San Diego Padres (1999). **Years in League:** 1993-.

Ownership, Management
Operated by: General Sports and Entertainment.
Managing Member: Andrew Appleby. **Managing General Partner:** Alan Levin. **President/General Manager:** Bill Larsen. **Assistant GM/Business Operations:** Carl Steeg. **Assistant GM/Sales and Marketing:** Mike Nutter. **Assistant GM/Ticket and Group Sales:** David Lorenz. **Director, Media/Community Relations:** Jackie Miller. **Account Representatives:** Chris Foos, Eric Leach, Jared Parcell, Ricki Schlabach, Tim Seaton, Chris Watson. **Director, Promotions:** Ryan Shoener. **Director, Merchandise:** Deb Steeg. **Office Manager:** Lisa Lorenz.

Field Staff
Manager: Craig Colbert. **Coach:** Brian Giles. **Pitching Coach:** Darren Balsley. **Trainer:** Brian Komprood.

Game Information
Radio Announcer: Unavailable. **No. of Games Broadcast:** Home-70, Away-70. **Flagship Station:** WHWD 1380-AM.
PA Announcer: Unavailable. **Official Scorers:** Mark Lazzer, Rich Tavierne.
Stadium Name (year opened): Memorial Stadium (1993). **Location:** Exit 112A (Coldwater Road) off I-69 to Coliseum Boulevard, left on Coliseum to stadium. **Standard Game Times:** 7 p.m.; Sat. 6; Sun. 2.
Visiting Club Hotel: Unavailable.

KANE COUNTY
Cougars

Office Address: 34W002 Cherry Lane, Geneva, IL 60134. **Telephone:** (630) 232-8811. **FAX:** (630) 232-8815. **E-Mail Address:** info@kcougars @aol.com. **Website:** www.kccougars.com.
Affiliation (first year): Florida Marlins (1993). **Years in League:** 1991-.

Ownership, Management
Operated by: Cougars Baseball Partners/American Sports Enterprises, Inc. **President:** Mike Woleben. **Vice President:** Mike Murtaugh.
General Manager: Jeff Sedivy. **Assistant General Manager:** Curtis Haug. **Business Manager:** Mary Almlie. **Director, Media Relations/Advertising:** Marty Cusack. **Director, Promotions:** Jeff Ney. **Personnel Manager:** Patti Savage. **Coordinators, Group Sales:** Amy Mason, Sue

Schlinger. **Coordinator, Season Tickets:** Jennifer Plesa. **Ticket Office:** Jill Lundin, Kelle Renniger. **Office Manager/Receptionist:** Carol Huppert. **Assistant Business Manager:** Doug Czurylo. **Account Executives:** Bill Baker, Brett Bartemeyer, John Knechtges, Jason Ovitt. **Design/Graphics:** Emmet Broderick, Todd Koenitz. **Community Relations/Donations:** Kate Dzierzanowski. **Facilities Management:** Mike Fik, Mike Kurns. **Director, Concessions:** Rich Essegian. **Clubhouse:** Jose Torres. **Head Groundskeeper:** Sarah Martin. **Head of Security:** Dan Klinkhammer.

Field Staff
Manager: Russ Morman. **Coach:** Matt Winters. **Pitching Coach:** Jeff Andrews. **Trainer:** Alan Diamond.

Game Information
Radio Announcer: Scott Franzke. **No. of Games Broadcast:** Home-70, Away-70. **Flagship Station:** WKKD 95.9-FM.
PA Announcer: Kevin Sullivan. **Official Scorer:** Ray Nemec.
Stadium Name (year opened): Philip B. Elfstrom Stadium (1991). **Location:** From east or west, I-88 (East-West Tollway) to Farnsworth Road North exit, 5 miles north to Cherry Lane; from north, Route 59 South to Route 64 (North Avenue), west to Kirk Road, south past Route 38 to Cherry Lane; from northwest, I-90 to Randall Road South exit, south to Fabyan Parkway, east to Kirk Road, north to Cherry Lane. **Standard Game Times:** 7 p.m., Sat. 6, Sun. 2.
Visiting Club Hotel: Travelodge, 1617 Naperville Rd., Naperville, IL 60563. Telephone: (630) 505-0200.

Office Address: 505 E Michigan Ave., Lansing MI 48912. **Telephone:** (517) 485-4500. **FAX:** (517) 485-4518. **E-Mail Address:** lugnuts@tcimet.net. **Website:** www.lansinglugnuts.com.
Affiliation (first year): Chicago Cubs (1999). **Years In League:** 1996-.

Ownership, Management
Operated by: Take Me Out to the Ballgame, LLC
Principal Owners: Tom Dickson, Sherrie Myers.
Assistant GM, Operations: Greg Rauch. **Assistant GM, Marketing:** Linda Frederickson. **Vice President, Sales:** Jeff Calhoun. **Director, Customer Service/Public Relations:** Darla Bowen. **Director, Finance/Human Resources:** Kimberly Hengesbach. **Director, Operations:** Rich Zizek. **Head Groundskeeper:** Eric Corey. **Operations Manager:** Jeremy Knuckman. **Marketing Manager:** David Prout. **Sponsorship Service Manager:** Megan Frazer. **Ticket Manager:** Chris Troub. **Retail Manager:** Melissa VanBuren. **Corporate Account Executives:** Brandon Bissell, Tony Olds. **Group Sales Representatives:** Steve Bennecke, David Dossin, Joe Pfeiffer. **Sponsorship Service Representatives:** Jennifer Darga, Maggie Maier. **Sales Assistant:** Michael Bonetti. **Coordinator, Operations:** Seth VanHoven. **General Manager, Concessions:** Randy Brubaker. **Office Manager, Concessions:** Christine Strukel.

Field Staff
Manager: Steve McFarland. **Coach:** Pat Listach. **Pitching Coach:** Stan Kyles. **Trainer:** Unavailable.

Game Information
Radio Announcer: Scott Moore. **No. of Games Broadcast:** Home-70, Away-70. **Flagship Station:** WJIM 1240-AM.
PA Announcer: Unavailable. **Official Scorer:** Mike Clark.
Stadium Name (year opened): Oldsmobile Park (1996). **Location:** I-96 East/West to U.S. 496, exit at Larch Street. **Standard Game Times:** 7:05 p.m.; (April-May) 6:05; Sun. 2:05.
Visiting Club Hotel: Holiday Inn South, 6820 S Cedar St., Lansing, MI 48911. Telephone: (517) 694-8123, (800) 338-8123.

Office Address: 1392 Capital Ave. NE, Battle Creek, MI 49017. **Telephone:** (616) 660-2287. **FAX:** (616) 660-2288. **E-Mail Address:** battlecats@net-link.net. **Website:** www.michiganbattlecats.com.

Affiliation (first year): Houston Astros (1999). **Years in League:** 1995-.

Ownership, Management
Operated by: American Baseball Capital II, Inc.
Principal Owner/Chairman: William Collins III. **President:** William Collins Jr.
General Manager: Jerry Burkot. **Assistant General Manager:** Kim Godek. **Controller:** T.J. Egan. **Director, Stadium Operations:** Len Matthews. **Corporate Sales:** Deb Hornaday, Larry Utterback. **Ticket/Group Sales:** David Darkey. **Director, Community Relations/Merchandise:** Lindsay Gardner. **Assistant Head Groundskeeper:** Willis Vaughn. **Assistant, Stadium Operations:** Kyle Lewis.

Field Staff
Manager: Al Pedrique. **Coach:** John Massarelli. **Pitching Coach:** Charley Taylor. **Trainer:** Shawn Moffitt.

Game Information
Radio Announcers: Ken Ervin, Terry Newton. **No. of Games Broadcast:** Home-70, Away-70. **Flagship Station:** WBCK 930-AM.
PA Announcers: Roy LaFountain, John Patrick. **Official Scorer:** Robin Hartman.
Stadium Name (year opened): C.O. Brown Stadium (1990). **Location:** I-94 to exit 98B (downtown), to Capital Avenue and continue five miles east to stadium. **Standard Game Times:** 7 p.m., (April-May) 6:30; Sat (April-May) 2; Sun. 2.
Visiting Club Hotel: Battle Creek Inn, 5050 Beckley Rd., Battle Creek, MI 49015. Telephone: (616) 979-1100.

PEORIA
Chiefs

Office Address: 1524 W Nebraska Ave., Peoria, IL 61604. **Telephone:** (309) 688-1622. **FAX:** (309) 686-4516. **E-Mail Address:** team@chiefs net.com. **Website:** www.chiefsnet.com.
Affiliation (first year): St. Louis Cardinals (1995). **Years in League:** 1983-.

Ownership, Management
Operated by: Peoria Chiefs Community Baseball Club, LLC.
Chairman: Pete Vonachen.
President/General Manager: Rocky Vonachen. **Assistant GM, Marketing/Promotions:** Michael Baird. **Assistant GM, Operations:** Mark Vonachen. **Director, Ticket Sales:** John Beintema. **Manager, Group Sales:** Jennifer Blackorby. **Director, Broadcasting/Media Relations:** Ed Beach. **Office Manager:** Barbara Lindberg. **Head Groundskeeper:** Ryan Middleton. **Group Sales Representatives:** Ryan Sivori, Aaron Rowe, Jeff Wieland. **Receptionist:** Karen Patterson.

Field Staff
Manager: Tom Lawless. **Coach:** Todd Steverson. **Pitching Coach:** Sid Monge. **Trainer:** Drew McCarthy.

Game Information
Radio Announcer: Ed Beach. **No. of Games Broadcast:** Unavailable. **Flagship Station:** WTAZ 1350-AM.
PA Announcer: Jason Skinner. **Official Scorer:** Kevin Capie.
Stadium Name (year opened): Pete Vonachen Stadium (1984). **Location:** I-74 to exit 91B (University Street North), left on Nebraska Avenue, left to ballpark. **Standard Game Times:** 7 p.m., (April-May) 6:30; Sun. 2.
Visiting Club Hotel: Holiday Inn City Centre, 500 Hamilton Blvd., Peoria, IL 61602. Telephone: (309) 674-2500.

QUAD CITY
River Bandits

Office Address: 209 S Gaines St., Davenport, IA 52802. **Mailing Address:** P.O. Box 3496, Davenport, IA 52808. **Telephone:** (319) 324-2032. **FAX:** (319) 324-3109. **E-Mail Address:** bandit@riverbandits.com. **Website:** www.riverbandits.com.
Affiliation (first year): Minnesota Twins (1999). **Years in League:** 1960-.

Ownership, Management

Operated by: Seventh Inning Stretch, LLC.
Principal Owner/President: Kevin Krause.
Vice President/General Manager: Tim Bawmann. Assistant GM/Director, Sales: Dave Ziedelis. VP, Concessions: Brian Eggers. Director, Group Sales/Merchandising: Brad Lott. Director, Ticket Operations: Neil Birdsall. Director, Public Relations: Michael Gorrasi. Assistant Director, Group Sales: Jason Penning. Director, Broadcasting: Neil Solondz. Office Manager: Michelle Calabresse. Administrative Assistants: Scott Althoff, Melissa Muehler, Danielle Smalec. Head Groundskeeper: Tony Huntley.

Field Staff

Manager: Stan Cliburn. Coach: Floyd Rayford. Pitching Coach: Gary Lucas. Trainer: Tony Leo.

Game Information

Radio Announcer: Neil Solondz. No. of Games Broadcast: Home-70, Away-70. Flagship Station: WKBF 1270-AM.
PA Announcer: Darren Pietra. Official Scorer: Michael Gorrasi.
Stadium Name (year opened): John O'Donnell Stadium (1931). Location: From I-74, take State Street exit, left into River Drive, left on Gaines Street; From I-80, take Harrison Street exit, right onto River Drive, left on South Gaines. Standard Game Times: 7 p.m.; Mon., Wed.-Fri. (April-May) 6; Tue. 3; Sun. (April-May) 2, (June-Sept.) 4.
Visiting Club Hotel: Blackhawk Hotel, 200 E Third St., Davenport, IA 52081. Telephone: (319) 323-2711.

SOUTH BEND
Silver Hawks

Office Address: 501 W South St., South Bend, IN 46601. Mailing Address: P.O. Box 4218, South Bend, IN 46634. Telephone: (219) 235-9988. FAX: (219) 235-9950. E-Mail Address: hawks@silverhawks.com. Website: www.silverhawks.com.
Affiliation (first year): Arizona Diamondbacks (1997). Years in League: 1988-.

Ownership, Management

Operated by: Palisades Baseball, Ltd.
Principal Owner: Alan Levin. Vice President: Erik Haag. Director, Finance: Andy Zmudzinski. VP, Sales: Keith Hallal. Administrative Assistant: Althea Horne.
General Manager: Mike Foss. Director, Group Sales: Mark Gordon. Assistant Director, Group Sales: Deb Petersen. Account Executive, Group Sales: Corey Brandobura. Director, Marketing/Promotions: Paul Flindall. Director, Corporate/Media Relations: George Gentithes. Director, Ticket Operations: Mike Wiseman. Assistant Director, Finance: Ellen Chadwick. Office Manager: Eric Kazmierzak. Head Groundskeeper: Joel Reinebold.

Field Staff

Manager: Dave Jorn. Coaches: Rodney Lofton, Jim Reinebold. Pitching Coach: Royal Clayton. Trainer: Matt Veader.

Game Information

Radio Announcer: Unavailable. No. of Games Broadcast: Home-70, Away-70. Flagship Station: WHVQ 92.1-FM.
PA Announcer: Unavailable. Official Scorer: Unavailable.
Stadium Name (year opened): Stanley Coveleski Regional Stadium (1988). Location: I-80/90 toll road to exit 77, take U.S. 31/33 south to South Bend, to downtown (Main Street), to Western Avenue, right on Western, left on Taylor. Standard Game Times: 7 p.m.; Sat. (April-May) 2; Sun. 2.
Visiting Club Hotel: Ramada Inn, 52890 U.S. 31/33 N, South Bend, IN 46637. Telephone: (219) 272-5220.

WEST MICHIGAN
Whitecaps

Office Address: 4500 W River Dr., Comstock Park, MI 49321. Mailing Address: P.O. Box 428, Comstock Park, MI 49321. Telephone: (616) 784-

4131. **FAX:** (616) 784-4911. **E-Mail Address:** playball@whitecaps-base ball.com. **Website:** www.whitecaps-baseball.com.

Affiliation (first year): Detroit Tigers (1997). **Years in League:** 1994-.

Ownership, Management

Operated by: Whitecaps Professional Baseball Corp.

Principal Owners: Dennis Baxter, Lew Chamberlin.

Chief Executive Officer/Managing Partner: Lew Chamberlin.

President/General Manager: Scott Lane. **VP, Sales/Marketing:** John Guthrie. **VP, Operations:** Jim Jarecki. **Director, Public Relations/Merchandising:** Lori Clark. **Director, Sales:** Dan Morrison. **Director, Accounting:** Marc Waite. **Ticket Manager:** Bruce Radley. **Manager, Group Sales:** Alanna Kuhn. **Manager, Operations:** Matt Costello. **Manager, Community Relations:** Anjie Coplin. **Manager, Gameday Promotions:** Rob Bolton. **Manager, Human Resources:** Ellen Chamberlin. **Head Groundskeeper:** Raechal Sager. **Manager, Facility Maintenance:** Fred Mowery. **Group Sales Representatives:** Tobias Cortese, Jeremy Plain, Clifton Young. **Media Relations Assistant:** Joel Koch. **Promotions/Sales Assistant:** Jami Dock. **Facility Maintenance Assistant:** Brian Hammond. **Ticket Sales Assistant:** Mickey Graham. **Ticket Sales Intern:** Craig Gregonis. **Receptionist:** Trina Sicard.

Field Staff

Manager: Bruce Fields. **Coach:** Brian Saltzgaber. **Pitching Coach:** Joe Georger. **Trainer:** Bryan Goike.

Game Information

Radio Announcers: Rick Berkey, Rob Sanford. **No. of Games Broadcast:** Home-70, Away-70. **Flagship Station:** WOOD 1300-AM.

PA Announcer: Unavailable. **Official Scorers:** Mike Dean, Don Thomas.

Stadium Name (year opened): Old Kent Park (1994). **Location:** U.S. 131 North from Grand Rapids to exit 91 (West River Drive). **Standard Game Times:** 7 p.m., (April-May) 6:35; Sat. (April-May) 2; Sun. 2.

Visiting Club Hotel: Days Inn-Downtown, 310 Pearl St. NW, Grand Rapids, MI 49504. Telephone: (616) 235-7611.

WISCONSIN
Timber Rattlers

Office Address: 2400 N Casaloma Dr., Appleton, WI 54915. **Mailing Address:** P.O. Box 7464, Appleton, WI 54912. **Telephone:** (920) 733-4152. **FAX:** (920) 733-8032. **E-Mail Address:** rattlers@timberrattlers.com. **Website:** www.timberrattlers.com.

Affiliation (first year): Seattle Mariners (1993). **Years in League:** 1962-.

Ownership, Management

Operated by: Appleton Baseball Club, Inc.

Chairman: Kevin Doyle. **President:** Larry Trucco.

Manager, Baseball Operations: Rob Zerjau. **Controller:** Cathy Spanbauer. **Head Groundskeeper:** Greg Hofer. **Director, Media/Public Relations:** Becky Batley. **Corporate Sales Representatives:** Jay Olson, Tracy Thompson. **Director, Promotions/Merchandising:** Brian Schalk. **Director, Ticket Sales:** Jay Finnerty. **Group Sales Managers:** Aaron Osborne, Matt Venz, Jason Wahlers. **Marketing Assistant:** Erin Mulhern. **Office Manager:** Mary Robinson.

Field Staff

Manager: Gary Thurman. **Coach:** Scott Steinmann. **Pitching Coach:** Rafael Chaves. **Trainer:** Jeff Carr.

Game Information

Radio Announcer: Chris Mehring. **No. of Games Broadcast:** Home-70, Away-70. **Flagship Station:** WJOK 1050-AM.

PA Announcer: Unavailable. **Official Scorer:** Doug Hahn.

Stadium Name (year opened): Fox Cities Stadium (1995). **Location:** Highway 41 to Wisconsin Avenue exit, west to Casaloma Drive, right on Casaloma, stadium ½ mile on right. **Standard Game Times:** 7:05 p.m., (April-May) 6:35; Sun. 1:05.

Visiting Club Hotel: Unavailable.

SOUTH ATLANTIC LEAGUE

Class A

Office Address: 504 Crescent Hill, Kings Mountain, NC 28086. **Mailing Address:** P.O. Box 38, Kings Mountain, NC 28086. **Telephone:** (704) 739-3466. **FAX:** (704) 739-1974. **E-Mail Address:** sal@shelby.net. **Website:** www.southatlanticleague.com.

Years League Active: 1948-1952, 1960-.

President/Secretary-Treasurer: John Moss.

Vice Presidents: Winston Blenckstone (Hagerstown), Ron McKee (Asheville).

Directors: Don Beaver (Hickory), Winston Blenckstone (Hagerstown), Chuck Boggs (Charleston, WV), Rob Cohen (Capital City), Joseph Finley (Cape Fear), Marv Goldklang (Charleston, SC), Larry Hedrick (Piedmont), Bill Lee (Greensboro), Ron McKee (Asheville), Chip Moore (Macon), Martha

John Moss

Morrow (Columbus), Michael Savit (Augusta), Ken Silver (Savannah), Pete Simmons (Delmarva).

Administrative Assistant: Elaine Moss. **Assistant to President:** Bryan Olson.

2000 Opening Date: April 6. **Closing Date:** Sept. 4.

Regular Season: 142 games (split schedule).

Division Structure: North—Cape Fear, Charleston WV, Delmarva, Greensboro, Hagerstown, Hickory, Piedmont. **South**—Asheville, Augusta, Capital City, Charleston SC, Columbus, Macon, Savannah.

Playoff Format: First-half and second-half division champions meet in best-of-3 semifinal series. Winners advance to best-of-5 series for league championship.

All-Star Game: June 20 at Charleston, SC.

Roster Limit: 25 active. **Player Eligibility Rule:** No age limit. No more than two players and one player-coach on active list may have more than five years of experience.

Brand of Baseball: Rawlings.

Statistician: Howe Sportsdata, Boston Fish Pier, West Bldg. #1, Suite 302, Boston, MA 02210.

Umpires: Tyler Bolick (Roswell, GA), Scott Charlton (Guelph, Ontario), Stephen Cheek (Columbus, GA), Ben Clanton (Nesbit, MS), Craig Funaro (East Haven, CT), Raymond Gregson (River Ridge, LA), Rusty Griffin (Gillsville, GA), Adrian Johnson (Houston, TX), Joe Johnson (Pennsville, NJ), Bryon Martin (Henderson, KY), Peter Masterson (Middleburg, FL), Brian Phillips (West Palm Beach, FL), Joshua Rees (Sheboygan, WI), James Roebuck (Connelly Springs, NC).

Stadium Information

Club	Stadium	LF	CF	RF	Capacity	'99 Att.
Asheville	McCormick Field	328	402	300	4,000	137,836
Augusta	Lake Olmstead	330	400	330	4,322	156,685
Cape Fear	J.P. Riddle	330	400	330	4,200	72,856
Capital City	Capital City	330	395	320	6,000	133,273
Charleston, SC	Riley Ballpark	306	386	336	5,800	238,184
Charleston, WV	Watt Powell Park	340	406	330	4,500	92,738
Columbus	Golden Park	330	415	330	5,000	104,153
Delmarva	Perdue	309	402	309	5,200	296,004
Greensboro	War Memorial	327	401	327	7,500	156,270
Hagerstown	Municipal	335	400	330	4,600	105,380
Hickory	L.P. Frans	330	401	330	5,062	188,531
Macon	Luther Williams	338	402	338	3,806	115,897
Piedmont	Fieldcrest Cannon	330	400	310	4,700	119,637
Savannah	Grayson	290	410	310	8,000	132,017

ASHEVILLE
Tourists

Office Address: McCormick Field, 30 Buchanan Pl., Asheville, NC 28801. **Mailing Address:** P.O. Box 1556, Asheville, NC 28802. **Telephone:** (828) 258-0428. **FAX:** (828) 258-0320. **E-Mail Address:** touristsbb@mind-spring.com. **Website:** www.theashevilletourists.com.

Affiliation (first year): Colorado Rockies (1994). **Years in League:** 1976-.

Ownership, Management
Operated by: Asheville Tourists Baseball, Inc.
Principal Owners: Peter Kern, Ron McKee.
President: Peter Kern.
General Manager: Ron McKee. **Assistant General Managers:** Dave Meyer, Chris Smith. **Director, Business Operations:** Carolyn McKee. **Director, Stadium Operations:** Larry Hawkins. **Director, Tickets/Merchandising:** Margarita Turner. **Director, Group Sales:** Hope Ballew. **Head Groundskeeper:** Patrick Schrimplin.

Field Staff
Manager: Joe Mikulik. **Coach:** Javier Gonzalez. **Pitching Coach:** Tom Edens. **Trainer:** Beau Clay.

Game Information
Radio: None.
PA Announcer: Rick Diggler. **Official Scorers:** Wilt Browning, Mike Gore.
Stadium Name (year opened): McCormick Field (1992). **Location:** I-240 to Charlotte Street South exit, south one mile on Charlotte, left on McCormick Place. **Standard Game Times:** 7 p.m., Sun. 2.
Visiting Club Hotel: Holiday Inn East, 1450 Tunnel Rd., Asheville, NC 28805. Telephone: (828) 298-5611.

AUGUSTA
Greenjackets

Office Address: 78 Milledge Rd., Augusta, GA 30904. **Mailing Address:** P.O. Box 3746, Augusta, GA 30904. **Telephone:** (706) 736-7889. **FAX:** (706) 736-1122. **E-Mail Address:** grnsox@aol.com. **Website:** www.green jackets.net.

Affiliation (first year): Boston Red Sox (1999). **Years in League:** 1988-.

Ownership, Management
Operated by: H.W.S. Baseball, LLC.
Principal Owners: Michael Savitt, Jeffrey Savitt.
President: Michael Savitt.
General Manager: Chris Scheuer. **Assistant General Managers:** Tony DaSilveira, David Van Lenten. **Business Manager:** Jennifer Cogan. **Director, Ticket Sales:** Eric Berge. **Director, Promotions:** Scotty McDuffy. **Head Groundskeeper:** John Packer. **Administrative Assistants:** Jennifer Johnson, Dominic O'Marshall.

Field Staff
Manager: Mike Boulanger. **Coach:** Victor Rodriguez. **Pitching Coach:** Bob Kipper. **Trainer:** Bill Coffey.

Game Information
Radio: None.
PA Announcer: Torye Hurst. **Official Scorers:** Steve Cain, Rob Mueller.
Stadium Name (year opened): Lake Olmstead Stadium (1995). **Location:** I-20 to exit 65 (Washington Road), east to Broad Street, exit left on Milledge Road, stadium on right. **Standard Game Times:** 7:05 p.m; Sun. 2:30.
Visiting Club Hotel: Holiday Inn-West, 1075 Stevens Creek Rd., Augusta, GA 30907. Telephone: (706) 738-8811.

CAPE FEAR
Crocs

Office Address: 2823 Legion Rd., Fayetteville, NC 28306. Mailing Address: P.O Box 64939, Fayetteville, NC 28306. Telephone: (910) 424-6500. FAX: (910) 424-4325. E-Mail Address: salcrocs@aol.com. Website: www.capefearcrocs.com.

Affiliation (first year): Montreal Expos (1997). Years in League: 1987-.

Ownership, Management
Operated by: American Baseball Company, LLC.

Principal Owners: Joseph Caruso, Joseph Finley, Joseph Plumeri, Craig Stein.

General Manager: Brad Taylor. Director, Media/Military Special Events: Buck Rogers. Director, Ticket/Merchandise Operations: Scott Zapko. Director, Merchandise: Yvette Taylor. Operations/Group Sales: Matt Gregor.

Field Staff
Manager: Bill Masse. Coach: Johnny Rodriguez. Pitching Coach: Tom Signore. Trainer: Unavailable.

Game Information
Radio: None.

PA Announcer: Gary Parks. Official Scorer: Mike Colbert.

Stadium Name (year opened): J.P. Riddle Stadium (1987). Location: From I-95, take exit 46 (NC Highway 87) North, left at exit 100 (East Mountain Drive), left at Legion Road. Standard Game Times: 7:05 p.m., Sun. (April-May) 2:05, (June-Aug.) 5:05.

Visiting Club Hotel: Econo Lodge, 1952 Cedar Creek Rd., Fayetteville, NC 28306. Telephone: (910) 433-2100.

Lakewood Baseball Club
(Location of Cape Fear franchise, 2001)

Office Address: 725 Airport Road, Suite 6A, Lakewood, NJ 08701. Telephone: (732) 901-7000. FAX: (732) 901-0067. E-Mail Address: info@lakewoodprobaseball.com. Website: www.lakewoodprobaseball.com.

General Manager: Geoff Brown. Assistant GM, Operations: John Clark.

CAPITAL CITY
Bombers

Office Address: 301 S Assembly St., Columbia, SC 29201. Mailing Address: P.O. Box 7845, Columbia, SC 29202. Telephone: (803) 256-4110. FAX: (803) 256-4338. E-Mail Address: info@bomberball.com. Website: www.bomberball.com.

Affiliation (first year): New York Mets (1983). Years in League: 1983-.

Ownership, Management
Operated by: Capital City Professional Baseball, LLC.

Principal Owner/President: Rob Cohen. Executive Vice President: Marsha Colten.

General Manager: Tim Swain. Assistant GM, Media/Operations: Mark Bryant. Assistant GM, Ticket Operations: Doug Gehlken. Director, Stadium Operations/Head Groundskeeper: Bob Hook. Corporate Sales Manager: Flynn Bowie. Associate Director, Sales: Len Jackson. Director, Ticket Sales: Mike Madden. Director, Group Sales: Brian Kenna. Group Sales Executives: Jesse Reese, Jeremy Wells. Grounds Assistant: Mark Brinkley.

Field Staff
Manager: John Stephenson. Coach: Donovan Mitchell. Pitching Coach: Doug Simons. Trainer: Brian Chicklo.

Game Information
Radio: Unavailable.

PA Announcer: John Avery. Official Scorer: Julian Gibbons.

Stadium Name (year opened): Capital City Stadium (1991). Location: I-26 East to Columbia, Elmwood Avenue to Assembly Street, right on Assembly for four miles; I-77 South to Columbia, exit at State Road 277 (Bull Street), right on Elmwood, left on Assembly. Standard Game Times: 7:05 p.m., Sun. 2:05.

Visiting Club Hotel: Travelodge, 2210 Bush River Rd., Columbia, SC 29210. Telephone: (803) 798-9665.

CHARLESTON, S.C.
RiverDogs

RIVERDOGS

Office Address: 360 Fishburne Ave., Charleston, SC 29403. **Mailing Address:** P.O. Box 20849, Charleston, SC 29413. **Telephone:** (843) 723-7241. **FAX:** (843) 723-2641. **E-Mail Address:** dogsrus@awod.com. **Website:** www.riverdogs.com.

Affiliation (first year): Tampa Bay Devil Rays (1997). **Years in League:** 1973-78, 1980-.

Ownership, Management

Operated by: South Carolina Baseball Club, LP.

Principal Owner: Marv Goldklang. **Chairman:** Bill Murray. **President:** Mike Veeck.

Vice President/General Manager: Mark Schuster. **Assistant GM:** Dave Echols. **Business Manager:** Sharon Evans. **Director, Broadcast Sales:** Jim Lucas. **Senior Account Representative:** Jason Bauer. **Director, Community Relations:** Bridget McClung. **Director, Promotions:** Samantha Startt. **Ticket Manager:** Steve Jette. **Director, Food Services:** John Schumacher. **Media Relations:** David Raymond. **Assistant, Media Relations:** Joe Block. **Office Manager:** Mary Jane MacInnes.

Field Staff

Manager: Charlie Montoyo. **Coach:** Dwight Smith. **Pitching Coach:** Milt Hill. **Trainer:** Matt Lucero.

Game Information

Radio Announcers: David Raymond, Jim Tocco. **No. of Games Broadcast:** Home-71, Away-71. **Flagship Station:** WQNT 1450-AM.

PA Announcer: Unavailable. **Official Scorer:** Tony Ciuffo.

Stadium Name (year opened): Joseph P. Riley Jr. Ballpark (1997). **Location:** From U.S. 17, take Lockwood Drive North, right on Fishburne Street. **Standard Game Times:** 7:05 p.m.; Sun. (April-May) 2:05, (June-Aug.) 5:05.

Visiting Club Hotel: Howard Johnson River Front, Highway 17, Charleston, SC 29403. Telephone: (843) 722-4000.

CHARLESTON, W.VA.
Alley Cats

Office Address: 3403 MacCorkle Ave. SE, Charleston, WV 25304. **Mailing Address:** P.O. Box 4669, Charleston, WV 25364. **Telephone:** (304) 344-2287. **FAX:** (304) 344-0083. **E-Mail Address:** team@charlestonalley-cats.com. **Website:** www.charlestonalleycats.com.

Affiliation (first year): Kansas City Royals (1999). **Years in League:** 1987-.

Ownership, Management

Operated by: Wheelers Baseball, LP.

Principal Owners: Dave Houchins, Andy Paterno.

General Manager: Tim Bordner. **Office Manager:** Lisa Spoor. **Director, Media/Public Relations:** Dan Loney. **Director, Stadium Operations:** Pat Day. **Director, Concessions:** Jamie Ball. **Director, Promotions:** Shannon Hans. **Assistant Director, Concessions:** Brian Ferek. **Assistant Director, Merchandising:** Kirstie Mahoney. **Clubhouse Operations:** Mike Spencer. **Head Groundskeeper:** Bob Hartman.

Field Staff

Manager: Joe Szekely. **Coach:** Terry Bradshaw. **Pitching Coach:** Jaime Garcia. **Trainer:** Joe Bishop.

Game Information

Radio Announcer: Dan Loney. **No. of Games Broadcast:** Home-71, Away-71. **Flagship Station:** WQBE 950-AM.

PA Announcer: Unavailable. **Official Scorer:** Unavailable.

Stadium Name (year opened): Watt Powell Park (1949). **Location:** From north/west, I-64/77 to exit 98 (35th Street Bridge), cross bridge, ballpark is at MacCorkle; From south/east, I-64/77 to exit 95 (MacCorkle Avenue), take MacCorkle Avenue West ramp (Route 61 North), stadium is

2½ miles on left. **Standard Game Times:** 7:15 p.m.; Sun. 2:15.
Visiting Club Hotel: TraveLodge of Dunbar, 1007 Dunbar Ave., Dunbar, WV 25064. Telephone: (304) 768-1000.

COLUMBUS
RedStixx

Office Address: 100 Fourth St., Columbus, GA 31901. **Mailing Address:** P.O. Box 1886, Columbus, GA 31902. **Telephone:** (706) 571-8866. **FAX:** (706) 571-9107. **E-Mail Address:** info@redstixx.com. **Website:** www.redstixx.com.
Affiliation (first year): Cleveland Indians (1991). **Years in League:** 1991-.

Ownership, Management
Operated by: Columbus RedStixx and Professional Baseball, Inc.
Principal Owner/President: Martha Morrow.
General Manager: Bob Flannery. **Vice President:** Jim White. **Director, Media/Community Relations:** Melea Hames. **Director, Sales/Marketing:** Mike Weisbart. **Director, Group Sales:** Bill Levy. **Director, Concessions:** John Evans. **Head Groundskeeper:** Mike Heidinger. **Office Manager:** Rosemary Johnson.

Field Staff
Manager: Ricky Gutierrez. **Coach:** Lou Frazier. **Pitching Coach:** Sam Militello. **Trainer:** Todd Tomczyk.

Game Information
Radio Announcer: Unavailable. **No. of Games Broadcast:** Home-71. **Flagship Station:** WDAK 540-AM.
PA Announcer: Steve Thiele. **Official Scorer:** Kathy Gierer.
Stadium Name (year opened): Golden Park (1951). **Location:** I-185 South to exit 1 (Victory Drive), west to Fourth Street (Veterans Parkway), in South Commons Complex on left. **Standard Game Times:** 7:15 p.m.; Sun. (April-June) 2:15.
Visiting Club Hotel: Holiday Inn North, 2800 Manchester Expy., Columbus, GA 31904. Telephone: (706) 324-0231.

DELMARVA
Shorebirds

Office Address: 6400 Hobbs Rd., Salisbury, MD 21804. **Mailing Address:** P.O. Box 1557, Salisbury, MD 21802. **Telephone:** (410) 219-3112. **FAX:** (410) 219-9164. **Website:** www.theshorebirds.com.
Affiliation (first year): Baltimore Orioles (1997). **Years in League:** 1996-.

Ownership, Management
Operated by: Maryland Baseball, LLC.
Principal Owners: John Daskalakis, Peter Kirk, Frank Perdue, Hugh Schindel, Pete Simmons.
Chairman: Peter Kirk. **President:** Pete Simmons.
General Manager: Jim Terrill. **Assistant GM:** Doug George. **Assistant GM/Special Projects:** Kathy Clemmer. **Controller:** Brad Ehnat. **Director, Stadium Operations:** Steve McCormick. **Head Groundskeeper:** Josh Ingle. **Director, Media/Public Relations:** Justin Decremer. **Director, Marketing:** Chad Prior. **Account Representatives:** Chris Fielding, Chris Ouellet, Charlie Shahan. **Director, Community Relations:** Ralph Murray. **Accounting Manager:** Gail Potts. **Ticket Manager:** Jeff Garner. **Director, Group Sales:** Brenda Ferguson. **Director, Merchandising:** Petra Keith. **Director, Food Services:** Amy Geppi. **Group Sales Representatives:** Greg McBride, John Perdue, Stephanie West. **Office Manager:** Joyce Young. **Group Sales Intern:** Bill Kennedy.

Field Staff
Manager: Joe Ferguson. **Coach:** Bobby Rodriguez. **Pitching Coach:** Dave Schuler. **Trainer:** Mark Shires.

Game Information
Radio Announcer: Shane Griffin. **No. of Games Broadcast:** Home-71, Away-71. **Flagship Station:** WSBL 98.1-FM.
PA Announcer: C.R. Hook. **Official Scorer:** Barry Grim.

Stadium Name (year opened): Arthur W. Perdue Stadium (1996). **Location:** From U.S. 50 East, right on Hobbs Road; From U.S. 50 West, left on Hobbs Road. **Standard Game Times:** 7:05 p.m., Sun. (April-June) 1:05.

Visiting Club Hotel: Ramada Inn and Convention Center, 300 S Salisbury Blvd., Salisbury, MD 21801. Telephone: (410) 546-4400.

GREENSBORO
Bats

Office Address: 510 Yanceyville St., Greensboro, NC 27405. **Telephone:** (336) 333-2287. **FAX:** (336) 273-7350. **E-Mail Address:** the bats@bellsouth.net. **Website:** www.greensborobats.com.

Affiliation (first year): New York Yankees (1990). **Years in League:** 1979-.

Ownership, Management
Operated by: Greensboro Baseball, LLC.
Principal Owners: Cooper Brantley, Bill Lee, Jim Melvin, Pat Pittard, Len White.
President: Bill Blackwell.
General Manager: John Frey. **Assistant GM, Concessions:** Mike Lieberman. **Director, Business Operations:** Jennifer Leung. **Director, Stadium Operations/Head Groundskeeper:** Jake Holloway. **Director, Promotions/Media Relations:** Tim Clever. **Director, Group Sales:** Chris Bates. **Office Manager:** Natalie Ward. **Operations Intern:** Chris Ward.

Field Staff
Manager: Stan Hough. **Coach:** Tony Perezchica. **Pitching Coach:** Gary Lavelle. **Trainer:** Unavailable.

Game Information
Radio: Unavailable.
PA Announcer: Jim Scott. **Official Scorer:** Joe Cristy.
Stadium Name (year opened): War Memorial Stadium (1926). **Location:** I-40/I-85 to Highway 29, north to Lee Street, west to Bennett Avenue, right on Bennett. **Standard Game Times:** 7 p.m., Sun. 2.

Visiting Club Hotel: TraveLodge, 2112 W Meadowview Rd., Greensboro, NC 27403. Telephone: (336) 292-2020.

HAGERSTOWN
Suns

Office Address: 274 E Memorial Blvd., Hagerstown, MD 21740. **Mailing Address:** P.O. Box 230, Hagerstown, MD 21741. **Telephone:** (301) 791-6266. **FAX:** (301) 791-6066. **E-Mail Address:** info@hagerstownsuns.com. **Website:** www.hagerstownsuns.com.

Affiliation (first year): Toronto Blue Jays (1993). **Years in League:** 1993-.

Ownership, Management
Operated by: Norwin Corporation.
Principal Owner/President: Winston Blenckstone.
General Manager: David Blenckstone. **Director, Business Operations:** Carol Gehr. **Director, Broadcasting/Media Relations:** Karl Schalk. **Assistant GM/Director, Sales and Marketing:** Mike Heckman. **Assistant GM/Director, Stadium Operations:** Henry Porter. **Head Groundskeeper:** Mike Showe.

Field Staff
Manager: Rolando Pino. **Coach:** Ken Landreaux. **Pitching Coach:** Hector Berrios. **Trainer:** Mike Frostad.

Game Information
Radio Announcer: Karl Schalk. **No. of Games Broadcast:** Home-71, Away-71. **Flagship Station:** WHAG 1410-AM.
PA Announcer: Rick Reeder. **Official Scorers:** Jan Marcus, Mike Treadwell.
Stadium Name (year opened): Municipal Stadium (1931). **Location:** Exit 32B (U.S. 40 West) on I-70 West, left at Eastern Blvd.; Exit 6A (U.S. 40 East) on I-81 South, right at Cleveland Ave. **Standard Game Times:** 7:05 p.m.; Mon. 6:05; Sun. (April-June) 2:05; (July-Sept.) 5:05.
Visiting Club Hotel: Ramada Inn and Convention Center, 901 Dual Hwy., Hagerstown, MD 21740. Telephone: (301) 733-5100.

HICKORY
Crawdads

Office Address: 2500 Clement Blvd. NW, Hickory, NC 28601. Mailing Address: P.O. Box 1268, Hickory, NC 28603. Telephone: (828) 322-3000. FAX: (828) 322-6137. E-Mail Address: crawdad@abts.net. Website: www.hickorycrawdads.com.

Affiliation (first year): Pittsburgh Pirates (1999). Years in League: 1952, 1960, 1993-.

Ownership, Management
Operated by: Hickory Baseball, Inc.
Principal Owners: Don Beaver, Luther Beaver, Charles Young.
President: Don Beaver.
General Manager: David Haas. Assistant General Manager: Heidi Kemery. Ticket Manager: Vance Spinks. Director, Community Relations: Erin Hagerty. Office Manager: Jeanna Homesley. Director, Broadcasting/Media Relations: Canio Costanzo. Account Representatives: Patrick Heavner, Lisa Howell, Jonas Peters.

Field Staff
Manager: Jay Loviglio. Coach: Greg Briley. Pitching Coach: Blaine Beatty. Trainer: Jason Jadgchew.

Game Information
Radio Announcer: Canio Costanzo. No. of Games Broadcast: Home-71, Away-71. Flagship Station: WMNC 92.1-FM.
PA Announcers: JuJu Phillips, Steve Fisher. Official Scorers: Mike MacEachern, Gary Olinger.
Stadium Name (year opened): L.P. Frans Stadium (1993). Location: I-40 to exit 123 (Lenoir North), 321 North to Clement Blvd., left for ½ mile. Standard Game Times: 7 p.m.; Sun. (April-May) 2, (June-Aug.) 6.
Visiting Club Hotel: Red Roof Inn, 1184 Lenoir Rhyne Blvd., Hickory, NC 28602. Telephone: (828) 323-1500.

MACON
Braves

Office Address: Luther Williams Field, Seventh Street, Macon, GA 31201. Mailing Address: P.O. Box 4525, Macon, GA 31208. Telephone: (912) 745-8943. FAX: (912) 743-5559. E-Mail Address: maconbraves @mindspring.com. Website: www.mbraves.com.

Affiliation (first year): Atlanta Braves (1991). Years in League: 1980-87, 1991-.

Ownership, Management
Operated by: Atlanta National League Baseball Club, Inc.
Principal Owner: Ted Turner. President: Stan Kasten.
General Manager: Michael Dunn. Director, Stadium Operations: Terry Morgan. Head Groundskeeper: George Stephens. Director, Sales/Marketing: Jim Tessmer. Director, Ticket Sales: Kristie Hancock. Director, Special Projects: Mike Miskavech.

Field Staff
Manager: Jeff Treadway. Coach: Tommy Gregg. Pitching Coach: Kent Willis. Trainer: Justin Sharpe.

Game Information
Radio Announcers: Kevin Coulombe, Bobby Pope. No. of Games Broadcast: Home-20. Flagship Station: WMAC 940-AM.
PA Announcer: Jimmy Jones. Official Scorer: Kevin Coulombe.
Stadium Name (year opened): Luther Williams Field (1929). Location: Exit 4 off I-16, across Otis Redding Bridge to Riverside Drive, follow signs to Central City Park. Standard Game Times: 7 p.m., Sun. 2.
Visiting Club Hotel: Comfort Inn North, 2690 Riverside Dr., Macon, GA 31204. Telephone: (912) 746-8855.

PIEDMONT
Boll Weevils

Office Address: 2888 Moose Rd., Kannapolis, NC 28083. Mailing Address: P.O. Box 64, Kannapolis, NC 28082. Telephone: (704) 932-3267. FAX: (704) 938-7040. E-Mail Address: bollweevils@ctc.net. Website: www.bollweevils.com.

Affiliation (first year): Philadelphia Phillies (1995). Years in League: 1995-.

Ownership, Management
Operated by: Iredell Trading Co.

Principal Owners: Larry Hedrick, Sue Hedrick.

Vice President/General Manager: Todd Parnell. Assistant GM/Director, Baseball Operations: Eric Allman. Director, Stadium Operations/Head Groundskeeper: Jaime Pruitt. Director, Promotions/Public Relations: Randy Long. Director, Ticket Sales: Tim Mueller. Director, Merchandising: Eric Allman. Director, Food Services: Jason Wichern. Bookkeeper: Deb Hall. Stadium Operations Assistants: Chris Canaday, Dutch Morgan. Group Sales/Promotions Assistants: Tracy Snelbaker, Nathaniel Wilks.

Field Staff
Manager: Greg Legg. Coach: Jerry Martin. Pitching Coach: Rod Nichols. Trainer: Paul Gabrielson.

Game Information
Radio: None.

PA Announcer: Unavailable. Official Scorer: Matt Kastel.

Stadium Name (year opened): Fieldcrest Cannon Stadium (1995). Location: Exit 63 on I-85, west on Lane Street to Stadium Drive. Standard Game Times: 7:05 p.m.; (April-May) 6:35 p.m.; Sun. 2:05.

Visiting Club Hotel: Rodeway Inn, 321 Bendix Dr., Salisbury, NC 28146. Telephone: (704) 633-5961.

SAVANNAH
Sand Gnats

Office Address: 1401 E Victory Dr., Savannah, GA 31404. Mailing Address: P.O. Box 3783, Savannah, GA 31414. Telephone: (912) 351-9150. FAX: (912) 352-9722. E-Mail Address: savgnats@aol.com. Website: www.sandgnats.com.

Affiliation (first year): Texas Rangers (1998). Years in League: 1984-.

Ownership, Management
Operated by: Savannah Professional Baseball Club, Inc.

Principal Owner/President: Ken Silver.

General Manager: Nick Brown. Assistant GM/Director, Food Services: Brad Haynes. Assistant GM: Mitch Mann. Director, Media/Ticket Sales: Brian Becknell. Director, Promotions/Merchandising: Todd Antonopoulos. Director, Business Operations: Deleah Garcia.

Field Staff
Manager: Paul Carey. Pitching Coach: Fred Dabney. Trainer: Unavailable.

Game Information
Radio: None.

PA Announcer: Unavailable. Official Scorer: Marcus Holland.

Stadium Name (year opened): Grayson Stadium (1941). Location: I-16 to 37th Street exit, left on 37th, right on Abercorn Street, left on Victory Drive; I-95 to exit 16 (Savannah/Pembroke), east on 204, right on Victory Drive, stadium is on right in Daffin Park. Standard Game Times: 7:15 p.m; Sun. 2.

Visiting Club Hotel: Country Hearth Inn, 301 Governor Treutlen Rd., Pooler, GA 31322. Telephone: (912) 748-6464.

NEW YORK-PENN LEAGUE

Short-Season Class A

Mailing Address: 1629 Oneida St., Utica, NY 13501. **Telephone:** (315) 733-8036. **FAX:** (315) 797-7403. **E-Mail Address:** nypenn@dreamscape.com.

Years League Active: 1939-.

President: Bob Julian.

Vice President: Sam Nader (Oneonta).

Treasurer: Bill Gladstone (Pittsfield). **Corporate Secretary:** Tony Torre (New Jersey).

Directors: Steve Cohen (Brooklyn), Rob Fowler (Utica), Joshua Getzler (Staten Island), Bill Gladstone (Pittsfield), Barry Gordon (New Jersey), Alan Levin (Mahoning Valley), Paul Marriott (Batavia), Sam Nader (Oneonta), Ray Pecor (Vermont), Leo Pinckney (Auburn), Paul Velte (Williamsport), Skip Weisman (Hudson Valley), Drew Weber (Lowell), David Wellenzohn (Jamestown).

Bob Julian

Administrative Assistant: Robert Ingalls.

2000 Opening Date: June 20. **Closing Date:** Sept. 6.

Regular Season: 76 games.

Division Structure: McNamara—Brooklyn, Hudson Valley, Lowell, New Jersey, Pittsfield, Staten Island, Vermont. **Pinckney-Stedler**—Auburn, Batavia, Jamestown, Mahoning Valley, Utica, Oneonta, Williamsport.

Playoff Format: Division champions and two wild-card teams meet in best-of-3 semifinals. Winners meet in best-of-3 series for league championship.

All-Star Game: None.

Roster Limit: 30 active, but only 25 may be in uniform and eligible to play in any given game. **Player Eligibility Rule:** No more than four players who are 23 or older. No more than three players on active list may have four or more years of prior service.

Brand of Baseball: Rawlings.

Statistician: Howe Sportsdata, Boston Fish Pier, West Bldg. #1, Suite 302, Boston MA 02210.

Umpires: Michael Belin (Niagara Falls, NY), Bill Davis (Marion, OH), Justin Durkin (Youngstown, OH), Rodney Galloway (Webster, TX), Robert Healey (Cranston, RI), Darren Hyman (Moline, IL), Tony Inzero (Hamden, CT), Michael Johnson (Birmingham, MI), Ben Lindquist (Jamestown, NY), Jason Markley (Hastings, MI), Karreem Mebane (Hamden, CT), Erik Stahlbusch (Grand Rapids, MI), Jason Venzon (Salinas, CA), Andrew Vincent (Simsbury, CT).

Stadium Information

Club	Stadium	Dimensions			Capacity	'99 Att.
		LF	CF	RF		
Auburn	Falcon Park	330	400	330	2,500	57,933
Batavia	Dwyer	325	400	325	2,600	39,357
Brooklyn*	McCallen Field	340	390	340	1,000	46,905
Hudson Valley	Dutchess	325	400	325	4,320	161,678
Jamestown	Diethrick Park	335	410	353	4,200	62,428
Lowell	Lelacheur Park	337	400	301	5,000	180,077
Mahoning Valley	Cafaro Field	335	405	335	6,000	203,073
New Jersey	Skylands Park	330	392	330	4,356	135,802
Oneonta	Damaschke Field	352	406	350	4,200	51,047
Pittsfield	Wahconah Park	334	374	333	4,500	80,131
Staten Island	Staten Island	325	400	325	4,500	117,765
Utica	Donovan	324	400	324	4,000	64,468
Vermont	Centennial Field	330	405	323	4,000	112,842
Williamsport	Bowman Field	345	405	350	4,200	57,548

* Club operated in St. Catharines in 1999

AUBURN
Doubledays

Office Address: 130 N Division St., Auburn, NY 13021. **Telephone:** (315) 255-2489. **FAX:** (315) 255-2675. **E-Mail Address:** ddays@auburn doubledays.com. **Website:** www.auburndoubledays.com.

Affiliation (first year): Houston Astros (1982). **Years in League:** 1958-80, 1982-.

Ownership, Management
Operated by: Auburn Community Baseball, Inc.
Chairman: Tom Ganey. **President:** Leo Pinckney.
General Manager: Dan Mahoney. **Assistant General Manager:** Dave Hoffman. **Head Groundskeeper:** Rich Wild.

Field Staff
Manager: Unavailable. **Coach:** Jorge Orta. **Pitching Coach:** Bill Ballou. **Trainer:** Jamey Snodgrass.

Game Information
Radio Announcer: Unavailable. **No of Games Broadcast:** Away-38. **Flagship Station:** WDWN 89.1-FM
PA Announcer: Unavailable. **Official Scorer:** Unavailable.
Stadium Name (year opened): Falcon Park (1995). **Location:** I-90 to exit 40, south on Route 34 to Route 5. **Standard Game Times:** 7 p.m., Sun. 6.
Visiting Club Hotel: Days Inn, 37 William St., Auburn, NY 13021. Telephone: (315) 252-7567.

BATAVIA
Muckdogs

Office Address: Dwyer Stadium, 299 Bank St., Batavia, NY 14020. **Telephone:** (716) 343-5454. **FAX:** (716) 343-5620. **E-Mail Address:** brrc@muckdogs.com. **Website:** www.muckdogs.com.

Affiliation (first year): Philadelphia Phillies (1988). **Years in League:** 1939-53, 1957-59, 1961-.

Ownership, Management
Operated by: Genesee County Baseball Club.
President: Larry Roth.
General Manager: Paul Marriott. **Assistant General Manager:** Jon Blumenthal. **Director, Business Operations:** Melissa Meeder. **Head Groundskeeper:** John Goodfellow. **Director, Media/Public Relations:** Adam Gerstenhaber. **Director, Community Relations:** Linda Crook. **Director, Ticket Sales:** Ryan Liddell. **Clubhouse Operations:** Tony Pecora.

Field Staff
Manager: Frank Klebe. **Coach:** Alberto Fana. **Pitching Coach:** Ken Westray. **Trainer:** Brian Cammarota.

Game Information
Radio Announcer: Adam Gerstenhaber. **No. of Games Broadcast:** Away-38. **Flagship Station:** WBSU 89.1-FM.
PA Announcer/Official Scorer: Wayne Fuller.
Stadium Name (year opened): Dwyer Stadium (1996). **Location:** I-90 to exit 48, left on Route 98 South, left on Richmond Avenue, left on Bank Street. **Standard Game Times:** 7:05 p.m.; Sun. 2:05.
Visiting Club Hotel: Days Inn of Batavia, 200 Oak St., Batavia, NY 14020. Telephone: (716) 343-1440.

BROOKLYN

Mailing Address: 123-01 Roosevelt Ave., Flushing, NY 11368. **Telephone:** (718) 803-4023. **FAX:** (718) 507-6395. **E-Mail Address:** scohe@nymets.com.

Affiliation (first year): Toronto Blue Jays (1986). **Years in League:**

2000-.

Ownership, Management
Operated by: Sterling Doubleday Enterprises, LP.
Chairman: Nelson Doubleday. **President:** Fred Wilpon.
General Manager: Steve Cohen.

Field Staff
Manager: Eddie Rodriguez. **Coach:** Unavailable. **Pitching Coach:** Jim Rooney. **Trainer:** Unavailable.

Game Information
Radio: None.
PA Announcer: Unavailable. **Official Scorer:** Unavailable.
Stadium Name (year opened): McCallen Field (1962). **Location:** From Brooklyn, take Belt Parkway East to Van Wyck Expressway North, exit at Main Street, proceed to Grand Central Parkway Service Road, left at Utopia Parkway to St. John's University; from New York, take Queens Midtown Tunnel to Long Island Expressway to Utopia Parkway Exit, south on Utopia Parkway to Union Turnpike to St. John's University. **Standard Game Times:** Unavailable.
Visiting Club Hotel: Unavailable.

HUDSON VALLEY
Renegades

Office Address: Dutchess Stadium, Route 9D, Wappingers Falls, NY 12590. **Mailing Address:** P.O. Box 661, Fishkill, NY 12524. **Telephone:** (914) 838-0094. **FAX:** (914) 838-0014. **E-Mail Address:** info@hvrene gades.com. **Website:** www.hvrenogadco.com.
Affiliation (first year): Tampa Bay Devil Rays (1996). **Years in League:** 1994-.

Ownership, Management
Operated by: Keystone Professional Baseball Club, Inc.
Principal Owner: Marv Goldklang. **President:** Skip Weisman
Vice President/General Manager: Steve Gliner. **Assistant GM/Director, Corporate Sales and Merchandising:** Kathy Butcko. **Director, Stadium Operations/Promotions:** Elmer LeSuer. **Director, Ticket Operations:** Sally Berry. **Director, Business Operations:** Jennifer Vitale. **Coordinator, Customer Service:** Kristina Desiderio. **Head Groundskeeper:** Tom Hubmaster. **Director, Food Services:** Joe Ausanio. **Assistant Director, Ticket Operations:** Bonnie Johnson. **Coordinator, Media/Public Relations:** Ryan Leone. **Administrative Assistant, Tickets:** Derek Sharp. **Administrative Assistant, Concessions:** Adam Lipp. **Clubhouse Manager:** Eric Rassin.

Field Staff
Manager: Dave Silvestri. **Coach:** Ramon Ortiz. **Pitching Coach:** John Duffy. **Trainer:** Dan Plante.

Game Information
Radio Announcer: Rick Schultz. **No. of Games Broadcast:** Home-38, Away-38. **Flagship Stations:** WBNR 1260-AM, WLNA 1420-AM.
PA Announcer: Rick Zolzer. **Official Scorer:** Bob Beretta.
Stadium Name (year opened): Dutchess Stadium (1994). **Location:** I-84 to exit 11 (Route 9D North), north 1 mile to stadium. **Standard Game Times:** 7:15 p.m., Sun. 5:15.
Visiting Club Hotel: Wellesley Inn, 2477 Route 9, Fishkill, NY 12524. Telephone: (914) 896-4995.

JAMESTOWN
Jammers

Office Address: 485 Falconer St., Jamestown, NY 14702. **Mailing Address:** P.O. Box 638, Jamestown, NY 14702. **Telephone:** (716) 664-0915. **FAX:** (716) 664-4175. **E-Mail Address:** jjammers@alltel.net.
Affiliation (first year): Atlanta Braves (1999). **Years in League:** 1939-57, 1961-73, 1977-.

Ownership, Management
Operated by: Rich Baseball Operations.

Principal Owner/President: Robert Rich Jr. **Chairman:** Robert Rich Sr. **General Manager:** David Wellenzohn. **Assistant General Manager:** Norma Marvell. **Head Groundskeeper:** Tom Casler. **Director, Sales/Marketing:** Kelly Johnson. **Director, Food Services:** Rich Ruggerio. **Assistant to GM:** James Comerford.

Field Staff
Manager: Jim Saul. **Coach:** Manny Jimenez. **Pitching Coach:** Jerry Nyman. **Trainer:** Anthony Medina.

Game Information
Radio Announcer: Unavailable. **No. of Games Broadcast:** Home-38, Away-19. **Flagship Station:** WKSN 1340-AM.

PA Announcer: James Payne. **Official Scorer:** Jim Riggs.

Stadium Name (year opened): Russell Diethrick Park (1941). **Location:** From I-90, south on Route 60, left on Buffalo Street, left on Falconer Street. **Standard Game Times:** 7:05 p.m.; Sun. 6:05.

Visiting Club Hotel: Red Roof Inn, 1980 E Main St., Falconer, NY 14733. Telephone: (716) 665-3670.

LOWELL
Spinners

Office Address: 450 Aiken St., Lowell, MA 01854. **Telephone:** (978) 459-2255. **FAX:** (978) 459-1674. **E-Mail Address:** generalinfo@lowellspinners.com. **Website:** www.lowellspinners.com.

Affiliation (first year): Boston Red Sox (1996). **Years in League:** 1996-.

Ownership, Management
Operated by: Diamond Action, Inc.
President: Drew Weber.

General Manager: Shawn Smith. **Assistant General Manager:** Brian Lindsay. **Controller:** Priscilla Harbour. **Director, Stadium Operations:** Dan Beaulieu. **Director, Corporate Sales:** John Egan. **Director, Public Relations/Promotions:** Steve MacDonald. **Director, Merchandising:** Joann Weber. **Director, Ticket Operations:** Mike Biagini. **Director, Group Sales:** Jeff Tagliaferro. **Operations Director:** Alyssa Cuozzo. **Head Groundskeeper:** Rick Walker.

Field Staff
Manager: Arnie Beyeler. **Coach:** Steve Alonzo. **Pitching Coach:** Dave Tomlin. **Trainer:** Keith Johnson.

Game Information
Radio Announcers: Bob Ellis, Chaz Scoggins. **No. of Games Broadcast:** Home-38, Away-38. **Flagship Station:** WCCM 800-AM.

PA Announcer: George Brown. **Official Scorers:** Eric McDowell, Jim Seavey.

Stadium Name (year opened): Edward LeLacheur Park (1998). **Location:** From Routes 495 and 3, take exit 35C (Lowell Connector), follow connector to exit 5B (Thorndike Street) onto Dutton Street, past city hall, left onto Father Morrissette Boulevard, right on Aiken Street. **Standard Game Times:** 7:05 p.m.; Sun. 5:05.

Visiting Club Hotel: Doubletree Inn, 50 Warren St., Lowell, MA 01852. Telephone: (978) 452-1200.

MAHONING VALLEY
Scrappers

Office Address: 111 Eastwood Mall Blvd., Niles, OH 44446. **Mailing Address:** P.O. Box 1357, Niles, OH 44446. **Telephone:** (330) 505-0000. **FAX:** (330) 505-9696. **E-Mail Address:** mvscrappers@cboss.com. **Website:** www.mvscrappers.com.

Affiliation (first year): Cleveland Indians (1999). **Years in League:** 1999-.

Ownership, Management
Operated by: Palisades Baseball, Ltd.

Managing General Partner: Alan Levin. **Executive Vice President:** Erik Haag. **Director, Finance:** Andy Zmudzinski. **Vice President, Sales:** Keith Hallal.

General Manager: Andy Milovich. **Assistant General Manager:** Dave

Smith. **Director, Stadium Operations:** Matt Duncan. **Director, Ticket Operations:** Joe Fanto. **Director, Group Sales:** Brian Heller. **Accountant:** Mary Crites. **Director, Promotions/Marketing:** Jeff Snodgrass. **Director, Concessions:** Tim Arseneau. **Office Manager:** Stephany Dann.

Field Staff
Manager: Ted Kubiak. **Coach:** Willie Aviles. **Pitching Coach:** Terry Clark. **Trainer:** Lee Slagle.

Game Information
Radio Announcer: John Batcho. **No. of Games Broadcast:** Home-38, Away-38. **Flagship Station:** WBBW 1240-AM.

PA Announcer: Chad Krispinsky. **Official Scorer:** Rocco Gasparro.

Stadium Name (year opened): Cafaro Field (1999). **Location:** I-80 to 11 North to 82 West to 46 South, stadium located behind Eastwood Mall. **Standard Game Times:** 7 p.m., Sun. 2.

Visiting Club Hotel: Days Inn, 1300 Youngstown-Warren Rd., Niles, OH 44446. Telephone: (330) 544-1301.

NEW JERSEY
Cardinals

Office Address: 94 Championship Pl., Suite 2, Augusta, NJ 07822. **Telephone:** (973) 579-7500. **FAX:** (973) 579-7502. **E-Mail Address:** office@njcards.com. **Website:** www.njcards.com.

Affiliation (first year): St. Louis Cardinals (1994). **Years in League:** 1994-.

Ownership, Management
Operated by: Minor League Heroes, LP.

Chairman: Barry Gordon. **President:** Marc Klee.

Vice President/General Manager: Tony Torre. **Assistant GM:** Herm Sorchar. **Head Groundskeeper:** Ralph Naife. **Director, Marketing:** Bob Commentucci. **Director, Sales:** Bob Mischler. **Director, Ticket Sales:** Bob Lord. **Director, Group Sales:** Matt Millet. **Director, Merchandising:** Sweets Wilson. **Office Manager:** Anna Condon. **Bookkeeper:** Janet Olczewski.

Field Staff
Manager: Jeff Shireman. **Pitching Coach:** Gary Buckels. **Trainer:** R.J. Romero.

Game Information
Radio Announcers: Joel Konya, Phil Pepe. **No. of Games Broadcast:** Home-38. **Flagship Stations:** WNNJ 1360-AM, WHCY 106.3-FM.

PA Announcer: Unavailable. **Official Scorer:** Ken Hand.

Stadium Name (year opened): Skylands Park (1994). **Location:** I-80 to exit 34B (Route 15 North) to Route 565 East; I-84 to Route 6 (Matamoras) to Route 206 North to Route 565 East. **Standard Game Times:** 7:15 p.m.; Sat. 5; Sun. 1.

Visiting Club Hotel: Best Western at Hunt's Landing, 120 Routes 6 and 209, Matamoras, PA 18336. Telephone: (800) 308-2378.

ONEONTA
Tigers

Office Address: 95 River St., Oneonta, NY 13820. **Telephone:** (607) 432-6326. **FAX:** (607) 432-1965. **E-Mail Address:** naderas@telenet.net.

Affiliation (first year): Detroit Tigers (1999). **Years in League:** 1966-.

Ownership, Management
Operated by: Oneonta Athletic Corp., Inc.

President/General Manager: Sam Nader. **Director, Business/Stadium Operations:** John Nader. **Controller:** Sidney Levine. **Head Groundskeeper:** Ted Christman. **Director, Media/Public Relations:** Alice O'Conner. **Director, Marketing/Merchandising:** Suzanne Longo. **Director, Special Projects:** Mark Nader. **Director, Ticket Sales:** Bob Zeh. **Director, Food Services:** Brad Zeh.

Field Staff
Manager: Kevin Bradshaw. **Coach:** Liliano Castro. **Pitching Coach:** Bill Monbouquette. **Trainer:** Ed Halbur.

Game Information

Radio: None.

PA Announcer: Doug Decker. **Official Scorer:** Dave Bishop.

Stadium Name (year opened): Damaschke Field (1940). **Location:** Exit 15 off I-88. **Standard Game Times:** 7 p.m., Sun. 6.

Visiting Club Hotels: Town House Motor Inn, 318 Main St., Oneonta, NY 13820. Telephone: (607) 432-1313; Oasis Motor Inn, 366 Chestnut St., Oneonta, NY 13820. Telephone: (607) 432-6041.

PITTSFIELD
Mets

Office Address: 105 Wahconah St., Pittsfield, MA 01201. **Mailing Address:** P.O. Box 328, Pittsfield, MA 01202. **Telephone:** (413) 499-6387. **FAX:** (413) 443-7144. **E-Mail Address:** pittmets@berkshire.net. **Website:** www.pittsfieldmets.com.

Affiliation (first year): New York Mets (1989). **Years in League:** 1989-.

Ownership, Management

Operated by: National Pastime Corporation.

Principal Owners: Martin Barr, John Burton, William Gladstone, Richard Murphy, Alfred Roberts, Stephen Siegel.

President: William Gladstone.

General Manager: Richard Murphy. **Director, Business Operations:** Jason Mancivalano. **Director, Media/Public Relations:** Rick Stohr.

Field Staff

Manager: Tony Tijerina. **Coach:** Ken Berry. **Pitching Coach:** Bob Stanley. **Trainer:** Jason Wulf.

Game Information

Radio Announcer: Bob Shade. **No. of Games Broadcast:** Home-38, Away-38. **Flagship Station:** WBRK 101.7-FM.

PA Announcer: Dave Curran. **Official Scorer:** Unavailable.

Stadium Name (year opened): Wahconah Park (1919). **Location:** From east, Mass Pike exit 2 to Route 7 North to Pittsfield, right on North Street, left on Wahconah Street; From west, Route 295E to 41 North to 20E into Pittsfield, left on Route 7, right on North Street, left on Wahconah. **Standard Game Times:** 7 p.m.; Sun. 6.

Visiting Club Hotel: Holiday Inn of the Berkshires, 40 Main St., North Adams, MA 01247. Telephone: (413) 663-6500.

STATEN ISLAND
Yankees

Office Address: 2025 Richmond Ave., Suite 212, Staten Island, NY 10314. **Telephone:** (718) 698-9265. **FAX:** (718) 698-9291. **E-Mail Address:** siyanks@siyanks.com. **Website:** www.siyanks.com.

Affiliation (first year): New York Yankees (1999). **Years in League:** 1999-.

Ownership, Management

Operated by: Staten Island Major League Holdings, LLC.

Principal Owners: Josh Getzler, Phyllis Getzler, Stan Getzler.

Chairman: Stan Getzler. **President:** Henry Steinbrenner. **Chief Operating Officer:** Josh Getzler.

General Manager: Jeff Dumas. **Special Assistant to GM:** Jane Rogers. **Bookkeeper:** Ruth Rizzo. **Director, Public Relations/Broadcasting:** Steve Lenox. **Director, Stadium Operations:** Pete Pullara. **Head Groundskeeper:** Sean Mantucca. **Director, Marketing/Promotions:** Matt Kanarick. **Director, Ticket Sales:** John Davison. **Director, Concessions/Merchandise:** Jennifer Fontanez. **Director, Group Sales:** Kimberly Powers.

Field Staff

Manager: Joe Arnold. **Coach:** Kevin Higgins. **Pitching Coach:** Neil Allen. **Trainer:** E.J. Amo.

Game Information

Radio Announcer: Steve Lenox. **No. of Games Broadcast:** Home-38, Away-38. **Flagship Station:** Unavailable.

PA Announcer: Matt Kanarick. **Official Scorer:** Richard Senzeo.

Stadium Name: College of Staten Island Field. **Location:** Staten Island Expressway (I-278) to exit 10 (Victory Boulevard). **Standard Game Times:** 7 p.m.

Visiting Club Hotel: The Navy Lodge, Bldg. 408, N Path Road, Staten Island, NY 10305. Telephone: (718) 442-0413.

UTICA
Blue Sox

Office Address: 1700 Sunset Ave., Utica, NY 13502. **Mailing Address:** P.O. Box 751, Utica, NY 13503. **Telephone:** (315) 738-0999. **FAX:** (315) 738-0992. **Website:** www.uticabluesox.com.

Affiliation (first year): Florida Marlins (1996). **Years in League:** 1977-.

Ownership, Management
Operated by: Utica Baseball Club, Ltd.
Principal Owner/President: Bob Fowler.
General Manager: Rob Fowler. **Assistant General Manager:** Jim Griffiths. **Head Groundskeeper:** Bob Cunningham. **Clubhouse Operations:** Bob Perry.

Field Staff
Manager: Jon Deeble. **Coach:** Joe Aversa. **Pitching Coach:** Bill Sizemore. **Trainer:** Unavailable.

Game Information
Radio: None.
PA Announcer: Dominick Ciocono. **Official Scorer:** John Horne.
Stadium Name (year opened): Donovan Stadium (1976). **Location:** New York State Thruway to exit 31 (Genesee Street), south to Burrstone Road, right to stadium. **Standard Game Time:** 7 p.m.

Visiting Club Hotel: Ramada Inn, Oneida County Airport, Oriskany, NY 13424. Telephone: (315) 736-3377.

VERMONT
Expos

Office Address: 1 Main St., Box 4, Winooski, VT 05404. **Telephone:** (802) 655-4200. **FAX:** (802) 655-5660. **E-Mail Address:** vtexpos@togeth er.net. **Website:** www.vermontexpos.com

Affiliation (first year): Montreal Expos (1994). **Years in League:** 1994-.

Ownership, Management
Operated by: Vermont Expos, Inc.
Principal Owner/President: Ray Pecor.
General Manager: Kyle Bostwick. **Assistant General Manager:** C.J Knudsen. **Director, Business Operations:** Monica Lalime. **Controller:** Mia Ouellette. **Director, Stadium Operations:** Jim O'Brien. **Head Groundskeeper:** Lee Keller. **Director, Public Relations:** Marie Heikkinen. **Director, Media Relations:** Paul Stanfield. **Director, Sales/Marketing:** Chris Corley. **Director, Ticket Sales:** Mike Simpson. **Director, Food Services:** Steve Bernard. **Director, Special Projects:** Onnie Mathews. **Clubhouse Operations:** Phil Schelzo. **Quality Control:** Ron Citorik.

Field Staff
Manager: Tim Leiper. **Coach:** Keke Ayo. **Pitching Coach:** Gil Lopez. **Trainer:** Liam Frawley.

Game Information
Radio Announcer: George Commo. **No. of Games Broadcast:** Home-25, Away-25. **Flagship Station:** WKDR 1390-AM.
PA Announcer: Rich Haskell. **Official Scorer:** Ev Smith.
Stadium Name (year opened): Centennial Field (1922). **Location:** I-89 to exit 14W, right on East Avenue for one mile, right at Colchester Avenue. **Standard Game Times:** 7:05 p.m., Sun. 5:05.

Visiting Club Hotel: Best Western Windjammer Inn and Conference Center, 1076 Williston Rd., South Burlington, VT 05403. Telephone: (802) 863-1125.

WILLIAMSPORT
Crosscutters

Office Address: Bowman Field, 1700 W Fourth St., Williamsport, PA 17701. **Mailing Address:** P.O. Box 3173, Williamsport, PA 17701. **Telephone:** (570) 326-3389. **FAX:** (570) 326-3494. **E-Mail Address:** xcut ters@aol.com. **Website:** www.crosscutters.com.

Affiliation (first year): Pittsburgh Pirates (1999). **Years in League:** 1968-72, 1994-.

Ownership, Management
Operated by: Geneva Cubs Baseball, Inc.
Principal Owners: Mike Roulan, Paul Velte.
President: Paul Velte.
General Manager: Doug Estes. **Director, Marketing/Public Relations:** Gabe Sinicropi.

Field Staff
Manager: Curtis Wilkerson. **Coach:** Eric Chavez. **Pitching Coach:** Miguel Bonilla. **Trainer:** Jose Ministral.

Game Information
Radio Announcer: Unavailable. **No. of Games Broadcast:** Away-30. **Flagship Station:** WMYL 95.5-FM.

PA Announcer: Unavailable. **Official Scorer:** Kenny Myers.

Stadium Name (year opened): Bowman Field (1923). **Location:** From south, Route 15 to Maynard Street, right on Maynard, left on Fourth Street for one mile; From north, Route 15 to Fourth Street, left on Fourth. **Standard Game Time:** 7:05 p.m.

Visiting Club Hotel: Holiday Inn, 1840 E Third St., Williamsport, PA 17701. Telephone: (570) 326-1981.

NORTHWEST LEAGUE

Short-Season Class A

Office Address: 910 Main Street, Suite 351, Boise, ID 83712. **Mailing Address:** P.O. Box 1645, Boise, ID 83701. **Telephone:** (208) 429-1511. **FAX:** (208) 429-1525. **E-Mail Address:** bobrichmond@worldnet.att.net.

Years League Active: 1901-1922, 1937-1942, 1946-.

President/Treasurer: Bob Richmond.

Vice President: Bill Pereira (Boise).

Corporate Secretary: Jerry Walker (Salem-Keizer).

Directors: Bob Beban (Eugene), Bobby Brett (Spokane), Jack Cain (Portland), Mike Ellis (Yakima), Fred Herrmann (Vancouver), Bill Pereira (Boise), Mark Sperandio (Everett), Jerry Walker (Salem-Keizer).

Bob Richmond

Administrative Assistant: Rob Richmond.

2000 Opening Date: June 20. **Closing Date:** Sept. 6.

Regular Season: 76 games.

Division Structure: North—Boise, Everett, Spokane, Yakima. **South**—Eugene, Portland, Salem-Keizer, Vancouver.

Playoff Format: Division winners play best-of-5 series for league championship.

All-Star Game: None.

Roster Limit: 30 active, 35 under control. **Player Eligibility Rule:** No more than four players 23 or older. No more than three players on active list may have four or more years of prior service.

Brand of Baseball: Rawlings.

Statistician: Howe Sportsdata, Boston Fish Pier, West Bldg. #1, Suite 302, Boston MA 02210.

Umpires: Kevin Causey (Springdale, AR), Carl Coles (Chino, CA), Andy Hergesheimer (Seattle, WA), Ryan Houchen (Canyon Country, CA), Michael Muchlinski (Ephrata, WA), Shawn Rakos (Pacific, WA), Joe Stegner (Boise, ID), Kevin Walker (Walla Walla, WA).

Stadium Information

Club	Stadium	Dimensions			Capacity	'99 Att.
		LF	CF	RF		
Boise	Memorial	335	405	335	4,500	132,885
Eugene	Civic	335	400	328	6,800	122,500
Everett	Everett Memorial	330	395	330	3,682	103,455
Portland	Civic	308	407	348	23,150	206,136
Salem-Keizer	Volcanoes	325	400	325	4,100	124,627
Spokane	Seafirst	335	398	335	7,162	187,315
Vancouver*	Nat Bailey	335	395	335	6,500	69,495
Yakima	Yakima County	295	406	295	3,000	74,977

*Club operated in Medford, Ore., in 1999

BOISE
Hawks

Office Address: 5600 Glenwood Dr., Boise, ID 83714. **Telephone:** (208) 322-5000. **FAX:** (208) 322-7432. **E-Mail Address:** rcbrach@rmci.net. **Website:** www.boisehawks.com.

Affiliation (first year): Anaheim Angels (1989). **Years in League:** 1975-76, 1978, 1985-.

Ownership, Management
Operated by: Boise Hawks Baseball Club, Inc.
Principal Owner: Bill Pereira.
Chairman: Bill Campbell. **President:** Cord Pereira.
General Manager: Ryan Brach. **Controller:** Lee Ryan. **Director, Media/Public Relations:** Jack Carnefix. **Head Groundskeeper:** Boyd Mauer. **Coordinator, Marketing:** Jennifer Bonham. **Director, Ticketing:** Jeremy Hawks. **Director, Group Sales:** Bryan Newton. **Ticket Account Executive:** Torin Oberlindacher. **Group Ticket Account Executive:** David Lileks. **VP, Sales/Marketing:** Eric Trapp. **VP/General Manager:** Edward Moore. **Art Director:** Craig Sarton. **Creative Director:** Michael Reagan. **Director, Media:** Jodie Hochwart.

Field Staff
Manager: Tom Kotchman. **Coach:** Todd Claus. **Pitching Coach:** Zeke Zimmerman. **Trainer:** Unavailable.

Game Information
Radio Announcer: Rob Simpson. **No. of Games Broadcast:** Home-38, Away-38. **Flagship Station:** KTIK 1340-AM.
PA Announcer: Greg Culver. **Official Scorer:** Dan Ward.
Stadium Name (year opened): Memorial Stadium (1989). **Location:** I-84 to Cole Road, north to Western Idaho Fairgrounds. **Standard Game Times:** 7:05 p.m.; Sun. 6:05.
Visiting Club Hotel: Holiday Inn, 3300 Vista Ave., Boise, ID 83705. Telephone: (208) 344-8365.

EUGENE
Emeralds

Office Address: 2077 Willamette St., Eugene, OR 97405. **Mailing Address:** P.O. Box 5566, Eugene, OR 97405. **Telephone:** (541) 342-5367. **FAX:** (541) 342-6089. **E-Mail Address:** ems@go-ems.com. **Website:** www.go-ems.com.

Affiliation (first year): Chicago Cubs (1999). **Years in League:** 1955-68, 1974-.

Ownership, Management
Operated by: Elmore Sports Group, Ltd.
Principal Owner: David Elmore.
President/General Manager: Bob Beban. **Assistant General Manager:** Mark Ruckwardt. **Business Manager:** Eileen Beban. **Director, Marketing/Media Relations:** Bryan Beban. **Director, Tickets:** Brian Rogers. **Director, Special Events:** Geoff Norman. **Facilities Director:** David Puente.

Field Staff
Manager: Danny Sheaffer. **Coach:** Tom Beyers. **Pitching Coach:** Mike Anderson. **Trainer:** Unavailable.

Game Information
Radio Announcer: Ray Martin. **No. of Games Broadcast:** Home-38, Away-38. **Flagship Station:** KPNW 1120-AM.
PA Announcer: Unavailable. **Official Scorer:** Unavailable.
Stadium Name (year opened): Civic Stadium (1938). **Location:** From I-5, take I-105 to Exit 2, stay left and follow to downtown, cross over Ferry Street Bridge to Eighth Avenue, left on Pearl Street, south to 20th Avenue. **Standard Game Times:** 7:05 p.m; Sun. 6:05.
Visiting Club Hotel: Doubletree Inn, 3280 Gateway Rd., Springfield, OR 97477. Telephone: (541) 726-8181.

EVERETT
Aquasox

Office Address: 3802 Broadway, Everett, WA 98201. Telephone: (425) 258-3673. FAX: (425) 258-3675. E-Mail Address: aquasox@aquasox. com. Website: www.aquasox.com.

Affiliation (first year): Seattle Mariners (1995). Years in League: 1984-.

Ownership, Management
Operated by: Farm Club Sports, Inc.
President: Mark Sperandio.
General Manager: Robb Stanton. Director, Sales/Marketing: Brian Sloan. Director, Ballpark Operations: Gary Farwell. Director, Ticket Services: Jackson Hutton. Director, Ticket Sales: Pat Dillon. Director, Community Relations: Sydney Swenson. Marketing Assistant: David Roberts.

Field Staff
Manager: Terry Pollreisz. Coaches: Andy Bottin, Darrin Garner. Pitching Coach: Marcos Garcia. Trainer: Spyder Webb.

Game Information
Radio Announcer: Pat Dillon. No. of Games Broadcast: Home-38, Away-38. Flagship Station: KSER 90.7-FM.
PA Announcer: Tom Lafferty. Official Scorer: Pat Castro.
Stadium Name (year opened): Everett Memorial Stadium (1984). Location: I-5, exit 192. Standard Game Times: 7:05 p.m.; Sat.-Sun. 6:05.
Visiting Club Hotel: Best Western Cascadia Inn, 2800 Pacific Ave., Everett, WA 98201. Telephone: (425) 258-4141.

PORTLAND
Rockies

Office Address: 1844 SW Morrison, Portland, OR 97205. Mailing Address: P.O. Box 998, Portland, OR 97207. Telephone: (503) 223-2837. FAX: (503) 223-2948. E-Mail Address: rockies@teleport.com. Website: www.portlandrockies.com.

Affiliation (first year): Colorado Rockies (1995). Years in League: 1973-77, 1995-.

Ownership, Management
Operated by: Portland Baseball, Inc.
Principal Owners: Jack Cain, Mary Cain. President: Jack Cain.
General Manager: Mark Helminiak. Director, Merchandising: Bob Cain. Sales Manager: Kevin Robinson. Coordinator, Group Sales: J.D. Bigelow. Marketing Assistant: Katy Kurtz. Account Executives: Matt Brubaker, Greg Herbst, Kevin Herbst, Dick Johnson, Bruce McFarland, Derek Milholland, Jeff Robbins, Tom Shepherd.

Field Staff
Manager: Billy White. Coach: Stu Cole. Pitching Coach: Richard Palacios. Trainer: Unavailable.

Game Information
Radio Announcers: Rich Burk, Mike O'Brien. No. of Games Broadcast: Home-38, Away-38. Flagship Station: 1520-AM.
PA Announcer: Bob Akamian. Official Scorers: Chuck Charnquist, John Hiltsenteger.
Stadium Name (year opened): Civic Stadium (1926). Location: I-405 to West Burnside exit, SW 20th Street to stadium. Standard Game Times: 7:05 p.m.; Sun. 2:05.
Visiting Club Hotel: Unavailable.

SALEM-KEIZER
Volcanoes

Street Address: 6700 Field of Dreams Way NE, Keizer, OR 97307. Mailing Address: P.O. Box 20936, Keizer, OR 97307. Telephone: (503) 390-2225. FAX: (503) 390-2227. E-Mail Address: probasebal@aol.com.

Website: www.volcanoesbaseball.com.

Affiliation (first year): San Francisco Giants (1997). **Years in League:** 1997-.

Ownership, Management

Operated By: Sports Enterprises, Inc.

Principal Owners: Jerry Walker, Bill Tucker.

President/General Manager: Jerry Walker.

Manager, Corporate Sales/Director, Promotions: Lisa Walker. **Director, Business Operations:** Rick Nelson. **Director, Stadium Operations:** Michael McCleary. **Head Groundskeeper:** Scott Bigham. **Director, Sales/Media Relations:** Pat Lafferty. **Director, Community Relations:** Jay Lynch. **Director, Ticket/Group Sales:** Michael Jermain. **Director, Merchandising:** Kim Jubie. **Marketing:** Aaron Reynolds. **Director, Food Services:** Carol Unruh. **Facility Management:** Lois Holeman, Nate Holeman.

Field Staff

Manager: Fred Stanley. **Coach:** Bert Hunter. **Pitching Coach:** Trevor Wilson. **Trainer:** Mark Gruesbeck.

Game Information

Radio Announcer: Pat Lafferty. **No. of Games Broadcast:** Home-38, Away-38. **Flagship Station:** KYKN 1430-AM.

PA Announcer: Jay Lynch. **Official Scorer:** Dawn Hills.

Stadium Name (year opened): Volcanoes Stadium (1997). **Location:** I-5 at exit 260 (Chemawa Road), west one block to Radiant Drive, north six blocks to stadium. **Standard Game Time:** 7:05 p.m.

Visiting Club Hotel: Ramada Inn, 200 Commercial St. SE, Salem, OR 97301. Telephone: (503) 363-4123.

Office Address: 602 N Havana, Spokane, WA 99202. **Mailing Address:** P.O. Box 4758, Spokane, WA 99202. **Telephone:** (509) 535-2922. **FAX:** (509) 534-5368. **E-Mail Address:** mail@spokaneindiansbaseball.com. **Website:** www.spokaneindiansbaseball.com.

Affiliation (first year): Kansas City Royals (1995). **Years in League:** 1972, 1983-.

Ownership, Management

Operated by: Longball, Inc.

Principal Owners: Bobby Brett, George Brett, J.B. Brett, Ken Brett.

President: Andrew Billig.

Vice President/General Manager: Paul Barbeau. **VP, Sponsorships:** Otto Klein. **Assistant GM, Tickets:** Brent Miles. **Director, Season Ticket Sales:** Grant Riddle. **Director, Group Ticket Sales:** Jonathan Goldstein. **Executive Administrative Assistant:** Barbara Klante. **Controller:** Carol Dell. **Director, Operations:** Chad Smith. **Marketing Assistant:** Michael Lindskog. **Promotions Assistant:** Jana Suko. **Account Executives:** Jimmy Lake, Brian Powell. **Manager, Concessions:** Denny Fore. **Head Groundskeeper:** Anthony Lee. **Assistant Director, Stadium Operations:** Larry Blumer.

Field Staff

Manager: Tom Poquette. **Coach:** Unavailable. **Pitching Coach:** Randy Smith. **Trainer:** Ken Forth.

Game Information

Radio Announcer: Bob Robertson. **No. of Games Broadcast:** Home-38, Away-38. **Flagship Station:** KKPL 630-AM.

PA Announcer: Unavailable. **Official Scorer:** Unavailable.

Stadium Name (year opened): The Stadium at Spokane County Fair & Expo Center (1958). **Location:** I-90 to Havana exit, follow directions to fairgrounds.

Standard Game Times: 7:05 p.m.; Sun. 6:05.

Visiting Club Hotel: Budget Inn, 110 E Fourth Ave., Spokane, WA 99202. Telephone: (509) 838-6101.

VANCOUVER
Canadians

Office Address: 4601 Ontario St., Vancouver, British Columbia V5V 3H4. Telephone: (604) 872-5232. FAX: (604) 872-1714. E-Mail Address: staff@canadiansbaseball.com. Website: www.canadiansbaseball.com.

Affiliation (first year): Oakland Athletics (2000). Years in League: 2000-.

Ownership, Management
Operated by: National Sports Organization, Inc.
Principal Owners: Dwain Cross, Fred Herrmann, Bud Kaufman.
President: Fred Herrmann.
General Manager: Dan Kilgras. Assistant General Manager: Jamie Brown. Controller: Kate Hicks. Head Groundskeeper: Richard Steinmuller. Director, Media/Public Relations: Steve Hoem. Account Representative: Alan Crossley. Office Manager: Carol Miner. Group/Ticket Sales: Stephen Hopkins.

Field Staff
Manager: Dave Joppie. Coach: Billy Owens. Pitching Coach: Unavailable. Trainer: Unavailable.

Game Information
Radio: None
PA Announcer: Unavailable. Official Scorer: Unavailable.
Stadium Name (year opened): Nat Bailey Stadium (1952). Location: From downtown, take Cambie Street Bridge, left on East 33rd Street, left on Clancy Loriinger Way, right to stadium; From south, take Highway 99 to Oak Street, right on 41st Avenue, left on Ontario. Standard Game Times: 7:05 p.m.; Sun. 1:30.
Visiting Club Hotel: Delta Pacific Resort Hotel, 10251 St. Edwards Dr., Richmond, British Columbia V6X 2M9. Telephone: (604) 278-9611.

YAKIMA
Bears

Office Address: 810 W Nob Hill Blvd., Yakima, WA 98902. Mailing Address: P.O. Box 483, Yakima, WA 98907. Telephone: (509) 457-5151. FAX: (509) 457-9909. E-Mail Address: yakimabearsbaseball@hotmail.com.

Affiliation (first year): Los Angeles Dodgers (1990). Years in League: 1955-66, 1990-.

Management
General Manager: Bob Romero. Director, Stadium Operations: Gerry Sayler. Director, Sales/Food Services: Trevor Vander Veen. Office Manager: Louis Adams. Head Groundskeeper: Bob Garretson. Clubhouse Operations: Paul Romero. Administrative Assistants: Bobbi Chandler, Billy Gerchick.

Field Staff
Manager: Butch Hughes. Coach: Damon Farmar. Pitching Coach: Fred Corral. Trainer: Unavailable.

Game Information
Radio Announcer: Joe Dominey. No. of Games Broadcast: Home-38, Away-38. Flagship Station: KMWX 1460-AM.
PA Announcer: Todd Lyons. Official Scorers: Doug Evans, Gene Evans.
Stadium Name (year opened): Yakima County Stadium (1993). Location: I-82 to exit 34 (Nob Hill Boulevard), west to Fair Avenue, right on Fair, right on Pacific Avenue. Standard Game Times: 7:05 p.m.; Sun. 6:05.
Visiting Club Hotel: Best Western Ahtanum Inn, 2408 Rudkin Rd., Union Gap, WA 98903. Telephone: (509) 248-9700.

APPALACHIAN LEAGUE

Rookie Advanced Classification

Mailing Address: 283 Deerchase Circle, Statesville, NC 28625. **Telephone:** (704) 873-5300. **FAX:** (704) 873-4333. **E-Mail Address:** applylg@i-america.net.

Years League Active: 1921-25, 1937-55, 1957-.

President/Treasurer: Lee Landers. **Corporate Secretary:** Dan Moushon (Burlington).

Directors: Dick Balderson (Danville), Jim Duquette (Kingsport), Tom Foley (Princeton), Neal Huntington (Burlington), Len Johnston (Bluefield), Mike Jorgensen (Johnson City), Reid Nichols (Pulaski), Tim Purpura (Martinsville), Jim Rantz (Elizabethton), Ken Williams (Bristol).

Lee Landers

League Administrator: Bobbi Landers.

2000 Opening Date: June 23. **Closing Date:** Sept. 1.

Regular Season: 68 games.

Division Structure: East—Bluefield, Burlington, Danville, Martinsville, Princeton. **West**—Bristol, Elizabethton, Johnson City, Kingsport, Pulaski.

Playoff Format: Division winners meet in best-of-3 series for league championship.

All-Star Game: None.

Roster Limit: 30 active. **Player Eligibility Rule:** No more than 12 players who are 21 or older; no more than two of the 12 may be 23 or older; no more than two years of prior service.

Brand of Baseball: Rawlings.

Statistician: Howe Sportsdata, Boston Fish Pier, West Bldg. #1, Suite 302, Boston, MA 02210.

Umpires: Glenn Cale (Lakeland, FL), Alex Campbell (Dallas, TX), Brandon Cooper (Louisville, KY), Blake Estes (Houston, TX), G.G. Fernandez (Miami, FL), Chad Galloway (Roanoke, AL), Chris Keffer (Richmond, VA), James Pearson (Mansfield, LA), Nate Provance (St. Ann, MO), Anthony Wilder (Shelbyville, KY).

Stadium Information

Club	Stadium	LF	CF	RF	Capacity	'99 Att.
Bluefield	Bowen Field	335	365	335	2,250	32,392
Bristol	DeVault Memorial	325	400	310	2,000	22,194
Burlington	Burlington Athletic	335	410	335	3,000	43,718
Danville	Dan Daniel Memorial	330	400	330	2,588	57,044
Elizabethton	Joe O'Brien Field	335	414	326	1,500	11,823
Johnson City	Howard Johnson	320	410	320	2,500	15,193
Kingsport	Hunter Wright	330	410	330	2,500	55,457
Martinsville	Hooker Field	330	402	330	3,200	43,309
Princeton	Hunnicutt Field	330	396	330	1,950	33,017
Pulaski	Calfee Park	335	405	310	2,500	16,370

The *Dimensions* column header spans LF, CF, and RF.

BLUEFIELD
Orioles

Office Address: 2003 Stadium Dr., Bluefield, WV 24701. **Mailing Address:** P.O. Box 356, Bluefield, WV 24701. **Telephone:** (540) 326-1326. **FAX:** (540) 326-1318.

Affiliation (first year): Baltimore Orioles (1958). **Years in League:** 1946-55, 1957-.

Ownership, Management
Operated by: Bluefield Baseball Club, Inc.
Director: Don Buford (Baltimore Orioles).
President/General Manager: George McGonagle. **Director, Business Operations:** Chandra Bostic. **Controller:** Charles Peters. **Director, Special Projects:** Tuillio Ramella.

Field Staff
Manager: Duffy Dyer. **Coaches:** Len Johnston, Gary Kendall. **Pitching Coach:** Bob Lacey. **Trainer:** Tobyn Jurging.

Game Information
Radio Announcer: Larry McKay. **No. of Games Broadcast:** Home-20, Away-20. **Flagship Station:** WHIS 1440-AM.
PA Announcer: Chuck Raven. **Official Scorer:** Will Prewitt.
Stadium Name (year opened): Bowen Field (1939). **Location:** I-77 to Bluefield exit, Route 290 to Route 460 West, right onto Leatherwood Lane, left at first light, past Chevron station and turn right, stadium ¼ mile on left. **Standard Game Times:** 7 p.m., Sun. 6.
Visiting Club Hotel: Ramada Inn-East River, 3175 E Cumberland Rd., Bluefield, WV 24701. Telephone: (304) 325-5421.

BRISTOL
Sox

Office Address: 1501 Euclid Ave., Bristol, VA 24201. **Mailing Address:** P.O. Box 1434, Bristol, VA 24203. **Telephone:** (540) 645-7275. **FAX:** (540) 669-7686. **E-Mail Address:** bwsox@3wave.com. **Website:** www.3wave.com/brisox.

Affiliation (first year): Chicago White Sox (1995). **Years in League:** 1921-25, 1940-55, 1969-.

Ownership, Management
Operated by: Bristol Baseball, Inc.
Director: Ken Williams (Chicago White Sox).
President: Boyce Cox. **General Manager:** Robert Childress.

Field Staff
Manager: R.J. Reynolds. **Coach:** Orsino Hill. **Pitching Coach:** Sean Snedeker. **Trainer:** Chris Goroscis.

Game Information
Radio: None.
PA Announcer: Boyce Cox. **Official Scorer:** Allen Shepherd.
Stadium Name (year opened): DeVault Memorial Stadium (1969). **Location:** I-81 to exit 3 onto Commonwealth Ave., right on Euclid Ave. for ½ mile. **Standard Game Time:** 7 p.m.
Visiting Club Hotel: Ramada Inn, 2122 Euclid Ave., Bristol, VA 24201. Telephone: (540) 669-7171.

BURLINGTON
Indians

Office Address: 1450 Graham St., Burlington, NC 27217. **Mailing Address:** P.O. Box 1143, Burlington, NC 27217. **Telephone:** (336) 222-0223. **FAX:** (336) 226-2498. **E-Mail Address:** bindians@aol.com.

Affiliation (first year): Cleveland Indians (1986). **Years in League:** 1986-.

Ownership, Management
Operated by: Burlington Baseball Club, Inc.
Director: Neal Huntington (Cleveland Indians).
President: Miles Wolff. **Vice President:** Dan Moushon.
General Manager: Mike Edwards. **Assistant General Manager:** Ben Wittkowski.

Field Staff
Manager: David Turgeon. **Coach:** Jack Mull. **Pitching Coach:** Tony Arnold. **Trainer:** Michael Salazar.

Game Information
Radio Announcer: Bill Czaja. **No. of Games Broadcast:** Home-34, Away-34. **Flagship Station:** WBAG 1150-AM.
PA Announcer: Byron Tucker. **Official Scorer:** Unavailable.
Stadium Name (year opened): Burlington Athletic Stadium (1960). **Location:** I-40/85 to exit 145, north on Route 100 (Maple Avenue) for 1½ miles, right on Mebane Street for 1½ miles, right on Beaumont, left on Graham. **Standard Game Time:** 7 p.m.
Visiting Club Hotel: Holiday Inn-Outlet Center, 2444 Maple Ave., Burlington, NC 27215. Telephone: (336) 229-5203.

DANVILLE
Braves

Office Address: Dan Daniel Memorial Park, 302 River Park Dr., Danville, VA 24540. **Mailing Address:** P.O. Box 3637, Danville, VA 24543. **Telephone:** (804) 791-3346. **FAX:** (804) 791-3347. **E-Mail Address:** dbraves@gamewood.net. **Website:** www.danvillebraves.com.
Affiliation (first year): Atlanta Braves (1993). **Years in League:** 1993-.

Ownership, Management
Operated by: Danville Braves, Inc.
Director: Dick Balderson (Atlanta Braves).
President/General Manager: Tim Cahill.

Field Staff
Manager: J.J. Cannon. **Coach:** Edinson Renteria. **Pitching Coach:** Bill Champion. **Trainer:** Unavailable.

Game Information
Radio: None.
PA Announcer: Unavailable. **Official Scorers:** Danny Miller, Dave Pavoro.
Stadium Name (first year): Dan Daniel Memorial Park (1993). **Location:** U.S. 58 to Rivermont Road, follow signs to park; U.S. 29 bypass to Dan Daniel Park exit (U.S. 58 East), to Rivermont Road, follow signs. **Standard Game Time:** 7 p.m.
Visiting Club Hotel: Innkeeper-West, 3020 Riverside Dr., Danville, VA 24541. Telephone: (804) 799-1202.

ELIZABETHTON
Twins

Office Address: 208 N Holly Lane, Elizabethton, TN 37643. **Mailing Address:** 136 S Sycamore St., Elizabethton, TN 37643. **Telephone:** (423) 547-6440. **FAX:** (423) 547-6442. **E-Mail Address:** twins@preferred.com.
Affiliation (first year): Minnesota Twins (1974). **Years in League:** 1937-42, 1945-51, 1974-.

Ownership, Management
Operated by: City of Elizabethton.
Director: Jim Rantz (Minnesota Twins).
President: Harold Mains.
General Manager: Mike Mains. **Assistant GM:** Lisa Story. **Head Groundskeeper:** Willie Church. **Director, Sales/Marketing:** Shelley Cornett. **Director, Promotions:** Jim Jones. **Director, Ticket Sales:** Jane Crow. **Director, Group Sales:** Harold Ray. **Director, Merchandising:** Linda Church. **Director, Food Services:** Jane Hardin. **Clubhouse Operations:** David McQueen.

Field Staff
Manager: Jeff Carter. **Coach:** Ray Smith. **Pitching Coach:** Jim Shellenback. **Trainer:** Corey Andrews.

Game Information
Radio Announcer: Frank Santore. **No. of Games Broadcast:** Home-35, Away-6. **Flagship Station:** WBEJ 1240-AM.

PA Announcer: Tom Banks. **Official Scorer:** Bill Crow.

Stadium Name (year opened): Joe O'Brien Field (1974). **Location:** I-81 to I-181, exit at Highway 321/67, left at Holly Lane. **Standard Game Time:** 7 p.m.

Visiting Club Hotel: Days Inn, 505 W Elk Ave., Elizabethton, TN 37643. Telephone: (423) 543-3344.

JOHNSON CITY
Cardinals

Office Address: 111 Legion St., Johnson City, TN 37601. **Mailing Address:** P.O. Box 179, Johnson City, TN 37605. **Telephone:** (423) 461-4866. **FAX:** (423) 461-4864. **E-Mail Address:** jccardinals@worldnetatt.net. **Website:** www.freeyellow.com/members2/jccardinals/.

Affiliation (first year): St. Louis Cardinals (1975). **Years in League:** 1921-24, 1937-55, 1957-61, 1964-.

Ownership, Management
Operated By: City of Johnson City.

Director: Mike Jorgensen (St. Louis Cardinals).

Interim General Manager: Mary Ann Marsh. **Clubhouse Operations:** Carl Black. **Groundskeeper:** Michael Whitson.

Field Staff
Manager: Luis Melendez. **Pitching Coach:** Elias Sosa. **Trainer:** Unavailable.

Game Information
Radio: None.

PA Announcer: Unavailable. **Official Scorer:** Unavailable.

Stadium Name (year opened): Howard Johnson Field (1956). **Location:** I-181 to exit 32, left on East Main, right on Legion Street. **Standard Game Time:** 7 p.m.

Visiting Club Hotel: Holiday Inn, 101 W Springbrook Dr., Johnson City, TN 37601. Telephone: (423) 282-4611.

KINGSPORT
Mets

Office Address: 433 E Center St., Kingsport, TN 37662. **Mailing Address:** P.O. Box 1128, Kingsport, TN 37662. **Telephone:** (423) 378-3744. **FAX:** (423) 392-8538. **E-Mail Address:** kingsportmets@aol.com. **Website:** www.kmets.com.

Affiliation (first year): New York Mets (1980). **Years in League:** 1921-25, 1938-52, 1957, 1960-63, 1969-82, 1984-.

Ownership, Management
Operated by: S&H Baseball, LLC.

Director: Jim Duquette (New York Mets).

President: Rick Spivey. **Vice President:** Steve Harville.

General Manager: Myra McEntire.

Field Staff
Manager: Edgar Alfonzo. **Coach:** Juan Lopez. **Pitching Coach:** Unavailable. **Trainer:** Miles Rush.

Game Information
Radio Announcer: Tom Taylor. **No. of Games Broadcast:** Home-34, Away-34. **Flagship Station:** WKIN 1320-AM.

PA Announcer: Don Spivey. **Official Scorer:** Eddie Durham.

Stadium Name (year opened): Hunter Wright Stadium (1995). **Location:** I-81 to I-181 North, exit 11E (Stone Drive), left on West Stone Drive (U.S. 11W) for 1½ miles, right on Granby Road for ½ mile. **Standard Game Time:** 7 p.m.

Visiting Club Hotel: Ramada Inn, 2005 Lamasa Dr., Kingsport, TN 37660. Telephone: (423) 245-0271.

MARTINSVILLE
Astros

Office Address: Hooker Field, 450 Commonwealth Blvd., Martinsville, VA 24112. **Mailing Address:** P.O. Box 3614, Martinsville, VA 24115. **Telephone:** (540) 666-2000. **FAX:** (540) 666-2139. **E-Mail Address:** mastros@kimbanet.com.

Affiliation (first year): Houston Astros (1999). **Years in League:** 1988-.

Ownership, Management
Operated by: Houston Astros Baseball Club.
Director: Tim Purpura (Houston Astros).
General Manager: Carper Cole. **Assistant General Manager:** Jennifer Grundy. **Head Groundskeeper:** Sammy Pickeral. **Clubhouse Operations:** Troy Wells.

Field Staff
Manager: Brad Wellman. **Coach:** Scott Makarewicz. **Pitching Coach:** Stan Boroski. **Trainer:** Kevin Eichorn.

Game Information
Radio Announcer: Unavailable. **No. of Games Broadcast:** Home-34. **Flagship Station:** WHEE 1370-AM.
PA Announcer: Unavailable. **Official Scorer:** Unavailable.
Stadium Name (year opened): Hooker Field (1988). **Location:** U.S. 220 Business to Commonwealth Boulevard, east for three miles; U.S. 58 to Chatham Heights Road, north two blocks, stadium is at intersection of Commonwealth and Chatham Heights. **Standard Game Time:** 7 p.m.
Visiting Club Hotel: Dutch Inn, 2360 Virginia Ave., Collinsville, VA 24078. Telephone: (540) 647-3721.

PRINCETON
Devil Rays

Office Address: Hunnicutt Field, Old Bluefield Road, Princeton, WV 24740. **Mailing Address:** P.O. Box 5646, Princeton, WV 24740. **Telephone:** (304) 487-2000. **FAX:** (304) 487-8762. **E-Mail Address:** devilrays@inetone.net. **Website:** www.inetone.net/devilrays.

Affiliation (first year): Tampa Bay Devil Rays (1997). **Years in League:** 1988-.

Ownership, Management
Operated by: Princeton Baseball Association, Inc.
Director: Tom Foley (Tampa Bay Devil Rays).
President: Dewey Russell.
General Manager: Jim Holland. **Director, Stadium Operations:** Mick Bayle. **Head Groundskeeper:** Frankie Bailey. **Account Representative:** Paul Lambert. **Clubhouse Operations:** Tommy Thomason. **Executive Administrative Assistant:** Daniella Hatfield. **Website Coodinator:** Samantha Craig.

Field Staff
Manager: Edwin Rodriguez. **Coach:** Jamie Nelson. **Pitching Coach:** Unavailable. **Trainer:** Chris Tomashoff.

Game Information
Radio: None.
PA Announcer: Melanie Roth. **Official Scorer:** Dick Daisey.
Stadium Name (year opened): Hunnicutt Field (1988). **Location:** Exit 9 off I-77, U.S. 460 West to downtown exit, left on Stafford Drive, stadium located behind Mercer County Technical Education Center. **Standard Game Times:** 7 p.m.
Visiting Club Hotel: Days Inn, I-77 and Ambrose Lane, Princeton, WV 24740. Telephone: (304) 425-8100.

PULASKI
Rangers

Office Address: 700 S Washington Ave., Pulaski, VA 24301. **Mailing**

Address: P.O. Box 676, Pulaski, VA 24301. **Telephone:** (540) 980-1070, 674-2756. **FAX:** (540) 994-0847, 674-0611. **E-Mail Address:** hnicely@ swva.net. **Website:** www.pulaskirangers.com.

Affiliation (first year): Texas Rangers (1997). **Years in League:** 1946-50, 1952-55, 1957-58, 1969-77, 1982-92, 1997-.

Ownership, Management

Operated by: Pulaski Baseball, Inc.

Principal Owners: Wayne Carpenter, Tom Compton, Dave Edmonds, Hi Nicely, Rick Mansell.

Director: Reid Nichols (Texas Rangers).

President: Tom Compton.

General Manager: Chad Brisco. **Director, Stadium Operations:** Dave Hart. **Director, Sales/Promotions:** Tom Wallace. **Director, Ticket Sales:** Rick Mansell. **Head Groundskeeper:** Don Newman. **Assistant Grounds-keeper:** Gary Martin.

Field Staff

Manager: Bruce Crabbe. **Coach:** Unavailable. **Trainer:** Unavailable.

Game Information

Radio: None.

PA Announcer: Unavailable. **Official Scorer:** Unavailable.

Stadium Name (year opened): Calfee Park (1935). **Location:** I-81 to exit 89 (Route 11), north to Pulaski, right on Pierce Avenue. **Standard Game Time:** 7 p.m.

Visiting Club Hotel: Unavailable.

PIONEERLEAGUE

Rookie Advanced Classification

Office Address: 812 W 30th Ave., Spokane, WA 99203. **Mailing Address:** P.O. Box 2564, Spokane, WA 99220. **Telephone:** (509) 456-7615. **FAX:** (509) 456-0136. **E-Mail Address:** baseball@ior.com. **Website:** www.pioneerleague.com.

Years League Active: 1939-42, 1946-.

President/Secretary-Treasurer: Jim McCurdy.

Vice President: Mike Ellis (Missoula).

Directors: Dave Baggott (Ogden), Mike Ellis (Missoula), Larry Geske (Great Falls), Kevin Greene (Idaho Falls), Rob Owens (Helena), Kevin Haughian (Butte), Bob Wilson (Billings), D.G. Elmore (Medicine Hat).

Jim McCurdy

Administrative Assistant: Teryl Mac-Donald.

2000 Opening Date: June 16. **Closing Date:** Sept. 3.

Regular Season: 76 games (split schedule).

Division Structure: North—Great Falls, Helena, Medicine Hat, Missoula. **South—**Billings, Butte, Idaho Falls, Ogden.

Playoff Format: First-half division winners play second-half division winners in best-of-3 series. Winners meet in best-of-3 series for league championship.

All-Star Game: None.

Roster Limit: 30 active. **Player Eligibility Rule:** No more than 17 players 21 and older, provided that no more than three are 23 or older. No player on active list may have more than three years of prior service.

Brand of Baseball: Rawlings.

Statistician: Howe Sportsdata, Boston Fish Pier, West Bldg. #1, Suite 302, Boston, MA 02210.

Umpires: Tim Cordill (Kansas City, KS), Bill Dishman (Coweta, OK), Chris Hamburg (Troutdale, OR), Noel Harthcock (Sherwood, AR), Maria Papageorgiou (Rock Island, IL), Todd Tichenor (Holcomb, KS), Andrew Wendel (San Marcos, TX).

Stadium Information

Club	Stadium	LF	CF	RF	Capacity	'99 Att.
Billings	Cobb Field	335	405	325	4,200	92,147
Butte	Alumni Coliseum	335	450	355	1,500	20,119
Great Falls	Legion Park	335	414	335	3,800	87,867
Helena	Kindrick Field	335	400	325	2,010	25,979
Idaho Falls	McDermott Field	340	400	350	2,928	64,134
Medicine Hat	Athletic Park	350	380	350	3,000	26,852
Missoula	Lindborg-Cregg	330	410	330	2,200	56,099
Ogden	Lindquist Field	335	396	334	5,000	81,345

BILLINGS
Mustangs

Office Address: Cobb Field, 901 N 27th St., Billings, MT 59103. **Mailing Address:** P.O. Box 1553, Billings, MT 59103. **Telephone:** (406) 252-1241. **FAX:** (406) 252-2968. **E-Mail Address:** mustangs@billingsmustangs.net. **Website:** www.billingsmustangs.com.

Affiliation (first year): Cincinnati Reds (1974). **Years in League:** 1948-63, 1969-.

Ownership, Management
Operated by: Billings Pioneer Baseball Club, Inc.
Chairman: Ron May.
President/General Manager: Bob Wilson. **Assistant General Manager:** Gary Roller. **Head Groundskeeper:** Dale Graves. **Director, Broadcasting:** Scott Lauer. **Clubhouse Operations:** Allen Reynolds.

Field Staff
Manager: Russ Nixon. **Coaches:** Brian Wilson, Robbie Williams. **Pitching Coach:** Tod Powor. **Trainer:** Steve Baumann.

Game Information
Radio Announcer: Scott Lauer. **No. of Games Broadcast:** Home-38, Away-38. **Flagship Station:** KCTR 970-AM.
PA Announcer: Unavailable. **Official Scorer:** Jack Skinner
Stadium Name (year opened): Cobb Field (1948). **Location:** I-90 to 27th Street North exit, north to Ninth Avenue North. **Standard Game Times:** 7 p.m., Sun. 6.
Visiting Club Hotel: Rimrock Inn, 1203 N 27th St., Billings, MT 59101. Telephone: (406) 252-7107.

BUTTE
Copper Kings

Office Address: 1300 W Park Street, Butte, MT 59701. **Mailing Address:** P.O. Box 888, Butte, MT 59703. **Telephone:** (406) 723-8206. **FAX:** (406) 723-9148. **E-Mail Address:** copkings@montana.com. **Website:** www.copperkings.com.

Affiliation (first year): Anaheim Angels (1997). **Years in League:** 1978-85, 1987-.

Ownership, Management
Operated by: NMFS, LLC.
Principal Owner/Chairman: Kevin Haughian.
President/General Manager: Brent Boznanski. **Vice President/Assistant GM:** Kristie Schmitt. **Director, Operations:** Kirk Fuhringer.

Field Staff
Manager: Joe Urso. **Coach:** Jose Monzon. **Pitching Coach:** Mike Butcher. **Trainer:** Unavailable.

Game Information
Radio Announcer: Unavailable. **No. of Games Broadcast:** Home-38, Away-38. **Flagship Station:** KXTL 1370-AM.
PA Announcer: Unavailable. **Official Scorer:** Unavailable.
Stadium Name (year opened): Alumni Coliseum (1962). **Location:** I-90 to Montana Street exit, north to Park Street, west to stadium (on Montana Tech campus). **Standard Game Times:** 7:05 p.m., Sun. 2:05.
Visiting Club Hotel: Comfort Inn, 2777 Harrison Ave., Butte, MT 59701. Telephone: (406) 494-8850.

GREAT FALLS
Dodgers

Office Address: 12 Third St. NW, Great Falls, MT 59404. **Mailing Address:** P.O. Box 1621, Great Falls, MT 59403. **Telephone:** (406) 452-5311. **FAX:** (406) 454-0811. **E-Mail Address:** dodgers@sofast.net. **Website:** www.mcn.net/~dodgers.

Affiliation (first year): Los Angeles Dodgers (1984). **Years in League:** 1948-63, 1969-.

Ownership, Management
Operated by: Great Falls Baseball Club, Inc.
President: Larry Geske.
General Manager: Jim Keough. **Head Groundskeeper:** Bob Pinski.
Office Manager: Ginger Robbins. **Clubhouse Operations:** Kenny Roach.

Field Staff
Manager: Juan Bustabad. **Coach:** Quinn Mack. **Pitching Coach:** Greg Gohr. **Trainer:** Chris Hiatt.

Game Information
Radio Announcer: Ryan Kilbane. **No. of Games Broadcast:** Away-38.
Flagship Station: KEIN 1310-AM.
PA Announcer: Ryan Kilbane. **Official Scorer:** Tim Paul.
Stadium Name (year opened): Legion Park (1956). **Location:** From I-15, take 10th Ave. South (exit 281) for four miles to 26th Street, left to 8th Ave. North, left to 25th Street North, right to ballpark. **Standard Game Times:** 7 p.m., Sun. 4.
Visiting Club Hotel: Midtown Hotel, 526 Second Ave. N, Great Falls, MT 59401. Telephone: (406) 453-2411.

HELENA
Brewers

Office Address: 1103 N Main, Helena, MT 59601. **Mailing Address:** P.O. Box 4606, Helena, MT 59604. **Telephone:** (406) 449-7616. **FAX:** (406) 449-6979. **E-Mail Address:** helbrewers@aol.com. **Website:** www.helena brewers.com.
Affiliation (first year): Milwaukee Brewers (1985). **Years in League:** 1978-.

Ownership, Management
Operated by: Never Say Never, Inc.
Principal Owners: Rob Owens, Linda Gach Ray.
Chairman: Linda Gach Ray. **President:** Rob Owens.
General Manager: Kyle Fisher. **Director, Stadium Operations:** Brian Goetz. **Account Representative/Director, Food Services:** Matt Medina.

Field Staff
Manager: Dan Norman. **Coach:** Frank Kremblas. **Pitching Coach:** Gilbert Rondon. **Trainer:** Matt Rosler.

Game Information
Radio Announcer: Dan Peterson. **No. of Games Broadcast:** Home-38, Away-38. **Flagship Station:** KBLL 1240-AM.
PA Announcer: Unavailable. **Official Scorer:** Dan Peterson.
Stadium Name (year opened): Kindrick Legion Field (1939). **Location:** Cedar Street exit off I-15, west to Main Street, left at Memorial Park. **Standard Game Time:** 7:05 p.m.
Visiting Club Hotel: Super 8, 2201 11th Ave., Helena, MT 59601. Telephone: (406) 443-2450

IDAHO FALLS
Padres

Office Address: 568 W Elva, Idaho Falls, ID 83402. **Mailing Address:** P.O. Box 2183, Idaho Falls, ID 83403. **Telephone:** (208) 522-8363. **FAX:** (208) 522-9858. **E-Mail Address:** padres@ifpadres.com. **Website:** www.ifpadres.com.
Affiliation (first year): San Diego Padres (1995). **Years in League:** 1940-42, 1946-.

Ownership, Management
Operated by: The Elmore Group.
Principal Owner: David Elmore.
President/General Manager: Kevin Greene. **Assistant GM, Merchandise/Operations:** Marcus Loyola. **Director, Public Relations:** Michael James. **Media Relations/Sales:** Gabe Ross. **Head Groundskeeper:** Craig Evans.

Field Staff

Manager: Don Werner. **Coach:** Jake Molina. **Pitching Coach:** Darryl Milne. **Trainer:** Will Sinon.

Game Information

Radio Announcers: John Balginy, Adam Epstein, Jim Garshow. **No. of Games Broadcast:** Home-38, Away-38. **Flagship Station:** KUPI 980-AM.
PA Announcer: Kelly Beckstead. **Official Scorer:** John Balginy.
Stadium Name (year opened): McDermott Field (1976). **Location:** I-15 to West Broadway exit, left onto Memorial Drive, right on Mound Avenue, ¼ mile to stadium. **Standard Game Times:** 7:15 p.m., Sun. 5.
Visiting Club Hotel: Days Inn, 700 Lindsay Blvd., Idaho Falls, ID 83402. Telephone: (888) 522-2910.

MEDICINE HAT
Blue Jays

Office Address: 1 Birch St. SE, Medicine Hat, Alberta T1A 0A5. **Mailing Address:** P.O. Box 465, Medicine Hat, Alberta T1A 2G2. **Telephone:** (403) 526-0404. **FAX:** (403) 504-2670.
Affiliation (first year): Toronto Blue Jays (1978). **Years in League:** 1977-.

Ownership, Management

Operated by: Medicine Hat Professional Baseball.
Principal Owner: D.G. Elmore.
President/General Manager: Paul Fetz. **Assistant GM:** Jason MacAskill.

Field Staff

Manager: Paul Elliott. **Coach:** Geovany Miranda. **Pitching Coach:** Dane Johnson. **Trainer:** Schad Richea.

Game Information

Radio: None.
PA Announcer: Unavailable. **Official Scorer:** Unavailable.
Stadium Name (year opened): Athletic Park (1977). **Location:** First Street SW exit off Trans Canada Highway, left on River Road. **Standard Game Time:** 7:05 p.m.
Visiting Club Hotel: Unavailable.

MISSOULA
Osprey

Office Address: 137 E Main St., Missoula, MT 59802. **Telephone:** (406) 543-3300. **FAX:** (406) 543-9463. **E-Mail Address:** generalmgr@missoulaosprey.com. **Website:** www.missoulaosprey.com.
Affiliation (first year): Arizona Diamondbacks (1999). **Years in League:** 1956-60, 1999-.

Ownership, Management

Operated by: Mountain Baseball, LLC
Chairman: Horn Chen. **President:** Mike Ellis.
General Manager: Shelly Poitras. **Assistant GM:** Trent Dlugosh. **Account Executive:** Jared Amoss.

Field Staff

Manager: Chip Hale. **Coach:** Aurelio Rodriguez. **Pitching Coach:** James Keller. **Trainer:** Unavailable.

Game Information

Radio Announcer: Unavailable. **No. of Games Broadcast:** Home-38, Away-38. **Flagship Station:** KGRZ 1450-AM.
PA Announcer: Unavailable. **Official Scorer:** Unavailable.
Stadium Name (year opened): Lindborg-Cregg Field (1999). **Location:** I-90 to Reserve Street exit, south on Reserve, right on Spurgin Road, left on Tower Road, stadium on left. **Standard Game Times:** 7:05 p.m., Sun. 2:05.
Visiting Club Hotel: Unavailable.

OGDEN
Raptors

Office Address: 2330 Lincoln Ave., Ogden, UT 84401. **Telephone:** (801) 393-2400. **FAX:** (801) 393-2473. **E-Mail Address:** homerun@ogden-raptors.com. **Website:** www.ogden-raptors.com.

Affiliation (first year): Milwaukee Brewers (1996). **Years in League:** 1939-42, 1946-55, 1966-74, 1994-.

Ownership, Management

Operated by: Ogden Professional Baseball, Inc.
Principal Owners: Dave Baggott, John Lindquist.
Chairman/President: Dave Baggott.
General Manager: John Stein. **Assistant General Manager:** Jill Steenburg. **Head Groundskeeper:** Ken Kopinski. **Director, Merchandising:** Geri Kopinski.

Field Staff

Manager: Ed Sedar. **Coach:** Jorge Brito. **Pitching Coach:** Steve Cline. **Trainer:** Keith Sayers.

Game Information

Radio Announcer: Ron Potesta. **No. of Games Broadcast:** Home-38, Away-38. **Flagship Station:** Unavailable.
PA Announcer: Pete Diamond. **Official Scorer:** Unavailable.
Stadium Name (year opened): Lindquist Field (1997). **Location:** I-15 North to 21st Street exit, east to Lincoln Avenue, south three blocks to park. **Standard Game Times:** 7 p.m.; Sun. 1:30.
Visiting Club Hotel: Days Inn of Ogden, 3306 Washington Blvd., Odgen, UT 84401. Telephone: (801) 399-5671.

ARIZONALEAGUE

Rookie Classification

Mailing Address: P.O. Box 1645, Boise, ID 83701. **Telephone:** (208) 428-1511. **FAX:** (208) 429-1525.

Years League Active: 1988-.
President/Treasurer: Bob Richmond.
Vice President: Tommy Jones (Diamondbacks). **Corporate Secretary:** Ted Polakowski (Athletics).
Administrative Assistant: Rob Richmond.
2000 Opening Date: June 23. **Closing Date:** Aug. 30. **Game Times:** 10 a.m.; night games 7 p.m.
Division Structure: North—Athletics, Cubs, Giants, Mariners, Padres. **South**—Diamondbacks, Mexico All-Stars, Rockies, White Sox.

Bob Richmond

Regular Season: 56 games.
Playoff Format: Division champions meet in one-game championship.
All-Star Game: None.
Roster Limit: 30 active, 35 under control. **Player Eligibility Rule:** No more than eight players 20 or older, and no more than two players 21 or older. At least 10 pitchers. No more than two years of prior service, excluding Rookie leagues outside the United States and Canada.
Brand of Baseball: Rawlings.
Statistician: Howe Sportsdata, Boston Fish Pier, West Bldg. #1, Suite 302, Boston, MA 02210.

Clubs	Playing Site	Manager
Athletics	Papago Park Sports Complex, Phoenix	John Kuehl
Cubs	Fitch Park, Mesa	Carmelo Martinez
Diamondbacks	Kino Baseball Complex, Tucson	Bob Mariano
Giants	Scottsdale Stadium, Scottsdale	Unavailable
Mariners	Peoria Sports Complex, Peoria	Omer Munoz
Mexico All-Stars	Kino Baseball Complex, Tucson	Unavailable
Padres	Peoria Sports Complex, Peoria	Howard Bushong
Rockies	Hi Corbett Field, Tucson	P.J. Carey
White Sox	Tucson Electric Park, Tucson	Jerry Hairston

GULFCOASTLEAGUE

Rookie Classification

Mailing Address: 1503 Clower Creek Dr., Suite H-262, Sarasota, FL 34231. **Telephone:** (941) 966-6407. **FAX:** (941) 966-6872.

Years League Active: 1964-.
President/Secretary-Treasurer: Tom Saffell.
First Vice President: Steve Noworyta (Phillies). **Second Vice President:** Jim Rantz (Twins).
Administrative Assistant: Bill Ventolo.
2000 Opening/Closing Dates: Unavailable.
Regular Season: 60 games.
Division Structure: Unavailable.
Playoff Format: Unavailable.
All-Star Game: None.

Tom Saffell

Roster Limit: 30 active. **Player Eligibility Rule:** No more than eight players 20 or older, and no more than two players 21 or older. Limit of four players of any age who were eligible but passed over in the 2000 draft. No more than two years of prior service, excluding Rookie leagues outside the United States and Canada.

Brand of Baseball: Rawlings.
Statistician: Howe Sportsdata, Boston Fish Pier, West Bldg. #1, Suite 302, Boston, MA 02210.

Clubs	Playing Site	Manager
Braves	Disney's Wide World of Sports, Orlando	Rick Albert
Expos	Roger Dean Stadium, Jupiter	Steve Phillips
Marlins	Carl Barger Baseball Complex, Melbourne	Kevin Boles
Orioles	Twin Lakes Park, Sarasota	Jesus Alfaro
Phillies	Carpenter Complex, Clearwater	Ramon Aviles
Pirates	Pirate City Complex, Bradenton	Woody Huyke
Rangers	Charlotte County Stadium, Port Charlotte	Al Newman
Reds	Ed Smith Stadium, Sarasota	Luis Quinones
Red Sox	Red Sox minor league complex, Fort Myers	John Sanders
Royals	Baseball City Sports Complex	Ron Karkovice
Tigers	Tigertown, Lakeland	Gary Green
Twins	Lee County Stadium, Fort Myers	Darryl Kennedy
Yankees	Yankee Complex, Tampa	Derek Shelton

MINOR LEAGUE SCHEDULES

CLASS AAA

International League

Buffalo

APRIL
12-13-14 .... Ottawa
15-16-16-17 .... Scranton
24-25-26 .... Pawtucket
28-29-30 .... Rochester

MAY
9-10-11-12 .... Norfolk
13-14-15-16 .. Columbus
18-19 .... Syracuse
30-31 .... Toledo

JUNE
1-2 .... Toledo
3-4-5-6 .... Indianapolis
16-17-18-19 ... Charlotte
20-21-22-23 ...... Durham

JULY
2-3 .... Scranton
4-5 .... Ottawa
6-7 .... Syracuse
8-9-10 .... Rochester
17-18-19-20 ... Richmond
28-29-30-31 .... Louisville

AUGUST
1-2 .... Pawtucket
3-4 .... Syracuse
5-6 .... Scranton
18-19-20 .... Ottawa
25-26-27 .... Pawtucket

SEPTEMBER
1-2 ....Syracuse
3-4 .... Rochester

Charlotte

APRIL
12-13 .... Toledo
14-15-16-17 .. Columbus
25-26-27-28 .... Norfolk
29-30 .... Richmond

MAY
13-14-14-15 .... Louisville
23-24-25 .... Richmond
28-29 .... Durham

JUNE
3-4-5-6 .... Rochester
8-9-10-11 ...... Pawtucket
20-21-22-23 . Indianapolis
24-25-26-27 .... Buffalo
30 .... Norfolk

JULY
1....................... Norfolk
4 .... Durham
13-14-15-16 ... Syracuse
17-18-19-20 .... Scranton
24-25 .... Louisville
28-29-30-31 .... Toledo

AUGUST
5-6-7-8 .... Ottawa
9 .... Durham
10-11 .... Norfolk
15-16 .... Columbus
21-22 .... Indianapolis
23-24 .... Durham
25-26-27 .... Richmond

SEPTEMBER
2-3 .... Durham

Columbus

APRIL
6-7 .... Durham

8-9-10-11 .... Charlotte
20-21 .... Louisville
22-22-24-25 . Indianapolis
26-27 .... Toledo

MAY
5-6-7-8 .... Pawtucket
9-10-11-12 .... Rochester
22-23-24-25 ... Syracuse
26-27-28-29 .... Buffalo

JUNE
7-8-9 .... Norfolk
10-11 .... Richmond
20-21-22-23 .... Scranton
24-25-26-27 ...... Ottawa
30 .... Louisville

JULY
1 .... Louisville
3-4 .... Toledo
13-14-15-16..... Durham
18-19-20 .... Norfolk

AUGUST
3-4 .... Toledo
5-6-7-8 .... Richmond
10-11 .... Indianapolis
17-18 .... Charlotte
19-20-21-22... Louisville
29-30............. Indianapolis
31 .... Toledo

SEPTEMBER
1 .... Toledo

Durham

APRIL
12-13............. Columbus
14-15-16-17....... Toledo
24-25-26-27-28 ..... Rich.
29-30 .... Norfolk

MAY
9-10-11-12 . Indianapolis
13-14-14-15 .... Scranton
17-18 .... Louisville
26-27 .... Charlotte
30-31 .... Norfolk

JUNE
8-9-10-11 ...... Rochester
12-13-14-15 .. Pawtucket
28-29-30 .... Buffalo

JULY
1 .... Buffalo
2-3 .... Charlotte
5-6 .... Louisville
7-8-9-10 .... Columbus
17-18-19-20 ... Syracuse
21-22-23 .... Charlotte
26-27 .... Toledo
28-29-30 .... Richmond

AUGUST
10-11-12-13 .... Ottawa
14-15 .... Louisville
17-18 .... Indianapolis
25-26-27-28 ..... Norfolk

SEPTEMBER
4 .... Charlotte

Indianapolis

APRIL
12-13-14 .... Richmond
15-16-17-18 .... Norfolk
28-29-30 .... Toledo

MAY
1-2-3 .... Columbus

4-5-6-7 .... Louisville
13-14-15-16 ...... Ottawa
17-18 .... Charlotte
19-20-21 .... Durham
30-31 .... Scranton

JUNE
1-2 .... Scranton
12-13-14-15 .... Buffalo
16-17-18-19 ... Syracuse
28-29-30 .... Pawtucket

JULY
1 .... Pawtucket
4 .... Louisville
5-6 .... Norfolk
7-8-9-10 .... Charlotte
17-18-19-20 .. Rochester
21-22-23 .... Columbus

AUGUST
2-3-4 .... Durham
12-13 .... Toledo
14-15-16 .... Richmond
23-24 .... Columbus
25-26-27 .... Toledo
31 .... Louisville

SEPTEMBER
1-2 .... Louisville

Louisville

APRIL
12-13-14 .... Norfolk
15-16-17-18 .. Richmond
26 .... Indianapolis
28-29-30 .... Columbus

MAY
1-2-3 .... Toledo
9-10-11-12 .... Ottawa
19-20-21 .... Charlotte
22-23-24-25... Durham

JUNE
3-4-5-6 .... Scranton
8-9-10-11............ Buffalo
20-21-22-23 ... Syracuse
24-25-26-27 .. Pawtucket
28-29 .... Columbus

JULY
2-3 .... Indianapolis
13-14-15-16 .. Rochester
17-18 .... Toledo
21-22-23 .... Norfolk

AUGUST
2-3-4 .... Charlotte
5-6 .... Durham
7-8-9 .... Indianapolis
17-18.............. Richmond
25-26-27 .... Columbus
28-29-30 .... Toledo

SEPTEMBER
3-4.................. Indianapolis

Norfolk

APRIL
6-7-8-9............ Louisville
10-11 .... Indianapolis
19-20-21 .... Charlotte
22-23 .... Durham

MAY
1-2-3-4 .... Buffalo
5-6-7-8 .... Syracuse
22-23-24-25 .. Pawtucket
26-27-28-29 .... Ottawa

JUNE
1-2 .... Durham
3-4 .... Richmond
13-14-15 .... Columbus
21-22-23 .... Richmond
24-25-26-27 . Indianapolis
28-29 .... Charlotte

JULY
2 .... Richmond
13-14-15-16 .... Toledo
24-25 .... Toledo
26-27 .... Louisville
28-29-30-31 . Rochester

AUGUST
12-13-14 .... Columbus
15-16-17-18 .... Toledo
19-20-21-22 .. Durham
30-31 .... Charlotte

SEPTEMBER
1 .... Charlotte
2-3 .... Richmond

Ottawa
APRIL
6-7-8-9 .... Buffalo
10-11 .... Pawtucket
18-19 .... Scranton
20-21-22-23 ... Syracuse

MAY
1-2-3-4 .... Durham
5-6-7-8 .... Charlotte
18-19-20-21 ...... Scranton
22-23-24 .... Rochester

JUNE
3-4-5-6 .... Columbus
8-9-10-11 ... Indianapolis
16-17-18-19 .... Louisville
28-29-30 .... Toledo

JULY
1 .... Toledo
2-3 .... Rochester
13-14-15-16 .. Richmond
17-18-19-20 .. Pawtucket
28-29-30-31 .... Scranton

AUGUST
1-2 .... Syracuse
3-4 .... Pawtucket
14-15-16-17 ...... Buffalo
25-26-27 .... Rochester
28-29 .... Scranton

SEPTEMBER
3-4 .... Syracuse

Pawtucket
APRIL
6-7-8-9 .... Syracuse
15-16 .... Rochester
18-19 .... Buffalo
27-28-29-30 .... Ottawa

MAY
2-3-4 .... Scranton
13-14-15-16 .. Richmond
18-19-20-21 .... Toledo
30-31 .... Charlotte

JUNE
1-2 .... Charlotte
3-4-5-6 .... Durham
15-17-18-19 ...... Norfolk
20-21-22-23 .. Rochester

JULY
2-3 .... Syracuse
8-9-10 .... Scranton
13-14-15-16 ...... Buffalo
24-25-26-27 . Indianapolis
28-29-30-31 .. Columbus

AUGUST
8-9 .... Buffalo
10-11-12-13 ... Louisville
19-20 .... Scranton

JUNE
21-22-23-24 .... Ottawa
28-29 .... Syracuse
30-31 .... Rochester

Richmond
APRIL
6-7-8-9 ...... Indianapolis
10-11 .... Louisville
20-21 .... Durham
22-23 .... Charlotte

MAY
1-2-3-4 .... Syracuse
5-6-7-8 .... Buffalo
18-19-20-21 ...... Scranton
26-27-28-29 .. Pawtucket
30-31 .... Ottawa

JUNE
1-2 .... Ottawa
5-6 .... Norfolk
13-14-15 .... Toledo
16-17-18-19 .. Columbus
20 .... Norfolk

JULY
3-4 .... Norfolk
5-6 .... Columbus
7-8-8-9 .... Louisville
21-22-23 .... Toledo
24-25-25 .... Durham
26-27 .... Charlotte

AUGUST
1-2-3-4 .... Rochester
12-13 .... Charlotte
19-20 .... Indianapolis
23-24 .... Norfolk
28-29 .... Charlotte
30-31 .... Durham

SEPTEMBER
1 .... Durham
4 .... Norfolk

Rochester
APRIL
8-9 .... Scranton
10-11 .... Buffalo
13-14 .... Scranton
18 .... Syracuse
21-22-23 .... Pawtucket
27 .... Syracuse

MAY
1-2-3-4 .... Charlotte
13-14-15-16 .... Toledo
18-19-20-21 .. Columbus
26-27-28-29 . Indianapolis
30-31 .... Louisville

JUNE
1-2 .... Louisville
12-13-14-15 ...... Ottawa
16-17-18-19 ...... Durham
24-25-26-27 .. Richmond
28-29 .... Scranton

JULY
4-5 .... Syracuse
6-7 .... Ottawa
21-22-23 .... Pawtucket
24-25-26-27 ...... Buffalo

AUGUST
5-6-7-8 .... Norfolk
10-11 .... Syracuse
15-16 .... Pawtucket
17-18 .... Scranton
19-20 .... Syracuse
28-29 .... Buffalo

SEPTEMBER
1-2 .... Ottawa

Scranton/W-B
APRIL
6-7 .... Rochester
10-11 .... Syracuse
21-22-23 .... Buffalo

APRIL
24-25-26 .... Ottawa
MAY
5-6-7-8 .... Durham
9-10-11-12 .... Richmond
22-23-24-25 . Indianapolis
26-27-28-29 .... Louisville

JUNE
8-9-10-11 .... Syracuse
12-13-14-15 .... Charlotte
24-25-26-27 .... Toledo
30 .... Rochester

JULY
1-1 .... Rochester
4-5-6-7 .... Pawtucket
21-22-23 .... Ottawa
24-25-26-27 .. Columbus

AUGUST
1-2-3-4 .... Norfolk
10-11 .... Buffalo
12-13-14 .... Rochester
15-16 .... Syracuse
22-23-24 .... Buffalo
30-31 .... Ottawa

SEPTEMBER
1-2-3-4 .... Pawtucket

Syracuse
APRIL
12-13-14 .... Pawtucket
15-16 .... Ottawa
19 .... Rochester
24-25-26 .... Rochester
28-29-30 .... Scranton

MAY
9-10-11-12 ...... Charlotte
13-14-15-16 .... Norfolk
20 .... Buffalo
30 31 .... Columbus

JUNE
1-2 .... Columbus
3-4-5-6 .... Toledo
12-13-14-15 ... Louisville
24-25-26-27 .... Durham
28-29-30 .... Richmond

JULY
1 .... Richmond
8-9 .... Ottawa
21-22-23 .... Buffalo
24-25-26-27 .... Ottawa
28-29-30-31 . Indianapolis

AUGUST
5-6-7 .... Pawtucket
8-9 .... Scranton
12-13 .... Buffalo
17-18 .... Pawtucket
21-22-23-24 .. Rochester
25-26-27 .... Scranton
30-31 .... Buffalo

Toledo
APRIL
6-7 .... Charlotte
8-9-10-11 .... Durham
18-19 .... Columbus
20-21 .... Indianapolis
22-23-24-25 ... Louisville

MAY
5-6-7-8 .... Rochester
9-10-11-12 .... Pawtucket
22-23-24-25 ...... Buffalo
26-27-28-29 ... Syracuse

JUNE
7-8-9 .... Richmond
10-11 .... Norfolk
16-17-18-19 .... Scranton
20-21-22-23 .... Ottawa

JULY
2 .... Columbus
5-6 .... Charlotte

7-8-9-10 .... Norfolk
13-14-15-16 . Indianapolis
19-20 .... Louisville
AUGUST
1-2 .... Columbus

5-6 .... Indianapolis
7-8 .... Durham
9-10-11 .... Richmond
19-20 .... Charlotte
23-24 .... Louisville

SEPTEMBER
2-3-4 .... Columbus

Pacific Coast League

Albuquerque
APRIL
14-15-16-17 .. Oklahoma
18-19-20-21 .. Edmonton
27-28-29-30 . Sacramento
MAY
2-3-4-5 .... Fresno
6-7-8-9-10 . Colo. Springs
19-20-21-22 ...... Omaha
23-24-25-26 ...... Calgary
JUNE
1-2-3-4 ..... Colo. Springs
9-10-11-12 ...... Memphis
13-14-15-16 .. Oklahoma
22-23-24-25 .... Nashville
JULY
4-5-6 .... New Orleans
13-14-15-16 .... Iowa
17-18-19-20 ...... Memphis
30-31 .... New Orleans
AUGUST
1-2 .... New Orleans
3-4-5-6 .... Omaha
7-8-9-10 .... Iowa
19-20-21-22 .... Nashville

Calgary
APRIL
6-7-8-9 .... Las Vegas
10-11-12-13 .... Tucson
22-23-24-25 .. Edmonton
MAY
2-3-4-5 .... Memphis
6-7-8-9 .... Nashville
16-17-18 .... Tucson
19-20-21-22 . Las Vegas
JUNE
1-2-3-4 .... Salt Lake
14-15-16 .... Omaha
17-18-19-20 .... Iowa
26-27-28-29 ...... Fresno
30 .... Sacramento
JULY
1-2-3 .... Sacramento
17-18-19-20 ... Salt Lake
21-22-23-24 ...... Fresno
AUGUST
3-4-5-6 .... Tacoma
11-12-13-14 . Sacramento
19-20-21-22 ...... Tacoma
24-25-26-27 .. Edmonton

Colo. Springs
APRIL
14-15-16-17 .. Edmonton
18-19-20-21 .. Oklahoma
27-28-29-30 ...... Fresno
MAY
2-3-4-5 .... Sacramento
19-20-21-22 .... Nashville
23-24-25-26 .... Iowa
27-28-29-30 .... N.O.
JUNE
5-6-7-8 .... Omaha
9-10-11-12 ...... Nashville
17-18-19-20 . Albuquerque
22-23-24-25 .... Memphis
JULY
4-5-6 .... Calgary
13-14-15-16 ..... Memphis

17-18-19-20-21 ...... N.O.
30-31 .... Omaha
AUGUST
1-2 .... Omaha
7-8-9-10 .... Oklahoma
24-25-26-27 . Albuquerque
28-29-30-31 .... Iowa

Edmonton
APRIL
7-8-9 .... Tucson
10-11-12 ...... Las Vegas
27-28-29-30 ...... Tacoma
MAY
2-3-4-5 .... Nashville
6-7-8-9 .... Memphis
19-20-20-21-22 .. Tucson
23-24-25-25-26 ...... L.V.
JUNE
1-2-3-4 .... Tacoma
13-14-15-16 .... Iowa
17-18-19-20 ...... Omaha
26-27-28-29 .... Sac.
30 .... Fresno
JULY
1-2-3 .... Fresno
13-14-15-16 ... Salt Lake
26-27-28-29 ...... Fresno
30-31 .... Sacramento
AUGUST
1-2 .... Sacramento
15-16-17-18 ...... Calgary
28-29-30-31 ... Salt Lake
SEPTEMBER
1-2-3-4 .... Calgary

Fresno
APRIL
6-7-8-9 .... Sacramento
14-15-16-17 ...... Calgary
18-19-20-21 ...... Tacoma
22-23-23-24 .... L.V.
MAY
10-11-12-13-14 ..... Edm.
15-16-17-18 ... Salt Lake
JUNE
1-2-4-4 .... Tucson
5-6-7-8 .... Edmonton
9-10-11-12 .... Calgary
22-23-24-25 .... Tucson
JULY
4-5-6 .... Las Vegas
13-14-15-16 . Sacramento
17-18-19-20 .... Nashville
30-31 .... Iowa
AUGUST
1-2 .... Iowa
3-4-5-6 .... Salt Lake
11-12-13-14 ..... Memphis
15-16-17-18 ...... Omaha
24-25-26-27 ...... Tacoma

Iowa
APRIL
6-7-8-9 .... Memphis
10-11-12-13 .... Nashville
22-23-24-25 .. Colo. Spr.
MAY
2-3-4-5 .... Oklahoma
6-7-8-9-10 . New Orleans
19-20-21-22 .... Memphis

27-28-29-30-31 .... Nash.
JUNE
5-6-7-8 ...... Albuquerque
9-10-11-12 .... Omaha
22-23-24-25 .... N.O.
JULY
4-5-6 .... Tucson
7-8-9 .... Colo. Springs
17-18-19-20 ...... Tacoma
21-22-23-24 ...... Omaha
AUGUST
3-4-5-6 .... Oklahoma
11-12-13-14 .. Las Vegas
19-20-21-22 ... Salt Lake
SEPTEMBER
1-2-3-4 ...... Albuquerque

Las Vegas
APRIL
14-15-16-17 .... N.O.
18-19-20-21 ... Salt Lake
26-27-28-29-30 ...... Cal.
MAY
2-3-4-5 .... Tucson
15-16-17-18 ...... Tacoma
27-28-29-30 .... Fresno
JUNE
9-10-11-12 .... Tucson
13-14-15-16 .. Colo. Spr.
26-27-28-29 . Albuquerque
30 .... Salt Lake
JULY
1-2-3 .... Salt Lake
7-8-9 .... Calgary
17-18-19-20. Sacramento
21-22-23-24 ...... Tacoma
AUGUST
3-4-5-6 .... Edmonton
15-16-17-18 .. Oklahoma
19-20-21-22.. Edmonton
28-29-30-31 ...... Fresno
SEPTEMBER
1-2-3-4 .... Sacramento

Memphis
APRIL
14-15-16-17 .... Iowa
18-19-20-21 ...... Omaha
27-28-29-30 .... N.O.
MAY
11-12-13-14. Albuquerque
15-16-17-18. Colo. Springs
23-24-25-26 .. Oklahoma
27-28-29-30 ...... Omaha
JUNE
5-6-7-8 .... Las Vegas
14-15-16-17 ...... Tacoma
18-19-20-21 ... Salt Lake
30 .... Iowa
JULY
1-2-3 .... Iowa
7-8-9 .... Nashville
21-22-23-24-25.. Tucson
26-27-28-29 .. Oklahoma
AUGUST
3-4-5-6 .... New Orleans
15-16-17-18. Albuquerque
19-20-21-22 .. Colo. Spr.
24-25-26-27 .... Nashville

Nashville

APRIL
14-15-16-17....... Omaha
18-19-20-21 .... Iowa
27-28-29-30 .. Oklahoma

MAY
11-12-13-14 Colo. Springs
15-16-17-18. Albuquerque
23-24-25-26 .... N.O.

JUNE
1-2-3-4 .... Las Vegas
5-6-7-8............. Tucson
14-15-16-17 ... Salt Lake
18-19-20-21 ...... Tacoma
26-27-28-29 .... Memphis
30 .... Omaha

JULY
1-2-3 .... Omaha
13-14-15-16 .. Oklahoma
30-31 .... Memphis

AUGUST
1-2 .... Memphis
3-4-5-6..... Colo. Springs
15-16-17-18......... Iowa
28-29-30-31. Albuquerque

SEPTEMBER
1-2-3-4 ..... New Orleans

New Orleans

APRIL
6-7-8-9...... Colo. Springs
10-11-12-13. Albuquerque
22-23-24-25 .... Nashville

MAY
2-3-4-5............. Omaha
15 16 17 18.......... Iowa
19-20-21-22.. Oklahoma

JUNE
1-2-3-4 .... Memphis
14 15 16 16 .... Fresno
17-18-19-20. Sacramento
30.................. Oklahoma

JULY
1-2-3 .... Oklahoma
13-14-15-16...... Omaha
22-23-24-25 .. Edmonton
26-27-28 29 ..... Calgary

AUGUST
7-8-9-10 .... Nashville
11-12-13-14.. Memphis
15-16-17-18 .. Colo. Spr.
24-25-26-27 .... Iowa
28-29-30-31 ... Memphis

Oklahoma

APRIL
6-7-8-9 ...... Albuquerque
10-11-12-13... Colo. Spr.
22-23-24-25-26 .. Memphis

MAY
6-7-8-9.............. Omaha
11-12-13-14 .... Iowa
27-28-29-30. Albuquerque

JUNE
1-2-3-4 .... Sacramento
17-18-19-20-21 .. Fresno
26-27-28-29........... Iowa

JULY
4-5-6 .... Nashville
7-8-9.... New Orleans
18-19-20-21 .. Edmonton

22-23-24-25 .. Colo. Spr.
30-31 .... Calgary

AUGUST
1-2 .... Calgary
11-12-13-14 .... New Orleans
19-20-21-22. New Orleans
28-29-30-31....... Omaha

SEPTEMBER
1-2-3-4.......... Memphis

Omaha

APRIL
6-7-8-9 .... Nashville
10-11-12-13 .... Memphis
22-23-24-25-26 .... Alb.
28-29-30 .... Iowa

MAY
1 .... Iowa
11-12-13-14 .... N.O.
15-16-17-18 .. Oklahoma
23-24-25-26 ...... Tacoma

JUNE
1-2-3-4 .... Iowa
22-23-24-25 .. Oklahoma
26-27-28-29 .... N.O.

JULY
4-5-6 .... Memphis
7-8-9 .... Albuquerque
17-18-19-20 .... Tucson
25-26-27-28-29 .... Nash.

AUGUST
7-8-9-10 .... Las Vegas
11-12-13-14 ... Colo. Spr.
24-25-26-27 ... Salt Lake

SEPTEMBER
1-2-3-4..... Colo. Springs

Sacramento

APRIL
18-19-20-21 ...... Calgary

MAY
6 7 8 9 .... Fresno
15-16-17-18 .. Edmonton
19-20-21-22 .... Fresno
27-28-29-30-31. Tacoma

JUNE
5-6-7-8 .... Calgary
9-10-11-12 .... Edmonton
22-23-24-25 .. Las Vegas

JULY
4-5-6 .... Tacoma
7-8-9 .... Salt Lake
21-22-23-24 ..... Nashville
26-27-28-29........... Iowa

AUGUST
3-4-5-6 .... Tucson
7-8-9-10 .... Memphis
15-16-17-18 ... Salt Lake
19-20-21-22....... Omaha
24-25-26-27 . Las Vegas
28-29-30-31 .... Tucson

Salt Lake

APRIL
10-11-12-13 .... Fresno
14-15-16-17 .. Sacramento
22-23-24-25-26 .. Sacra.
27-28-29-30.... Tucson

MAY
2-3-4-5 .... Tacoma
11-12-13-14... Las Vegas

22-23-24-25 .. Colo. Spr.
30-31 .... Calgary

AUGUST
1-2 .... Calgary
11-12-13-14.. New Orleans
19-20-21-22. New Orleans
28-29-30-31.... Omaha

SEPTEMBER
1-2-3-4............ Memphis

23-24-25-26 .... Fresno
27-28-29-30-31 . Edmonton

JUNE
5-6-7-8 ..... New Orleans
9-10-11-12 ... Oklahoma
22-23-24-25 ..... Calgary
26-27-28-29 .. Colo. Spr.

JULY
4-5-6 .... Edmonton
21-22-23-24. Albuquerque
26-27-28-29 . Las Vegas

AUGUST
7-8-9-10 .... Calgary
11-12-13-14 .... Tucson

SEPTEMBER
1-2-3-4............... Tacoma

Tacoma

APRIL
6-7-8-9 .... Salt Lake
10-11-12-13 .. Sacramento
22-23-24-25....... Tucson

MAY
6-7-8-9-10 .... Las Vegas
11-12-13-14.. Sacramento
19-20-21-22 .. Salt Lake

JUNE
5-6-7-8 .... Oklahoma
9-10-11-12.. New Orleans
22-23-24-25 .. Edmonton
30 .... Colo. Springs

JULY
1-2-3 .... Colo. Springs
7-8-9 .... Fresno
13-14-15-16 ...... Calgary
26-27-28-29. Albuquerque
30-31 .... Las Vegas

AUGUST
1-2 .... Las Vegas
7-8-9-10 .... Fresno
11-12-13-14 .. Edmonton
15-16-17-18....... Tucson
28-29-30-31 ...... Calgary

Tucson

APRIL
14-15-16-17 ...... Tacoma
18-19-20-21 .... N. O.

MAY
6-7-8-9 .... Salt Lake
12-13-13-14 ...... Calgary
23-24-25-26.. Sacramento
27-28-29-30-31. Calgary

JUNE
13-14-15-16.. Sacramento
17-18-19-20 . Las Vegas
26-27-28-29 ..... Tacoma
30 .... Albuquerque

JULY
1-2-3 .... Albuquerque
7-8-9 .... Edmonton
13-14-15-16 . Las Vegas
26-27-28-29 .. Colo. Spr.
30-31 .... Salt Lake

AUGUST
1-2.................. Salt Lake
7-8-9-10 .... Edmonton
19-20-21-22 ...... Fresno
24-25-26-27 .. Oklahoma

SEPTEMBER
1-2-3-4 .... Fresno

CLASSAA

Eastern League

Akron

APRIL
7-8-9 .... Erie
10-11-12-13 .... Bowie
17-18-19-20 ..... Reading
21-22-23 .... Altoona

MAY
1-2-3 .... Harrisburg
12-13-14 .... Portland
23-24-25 ..... New Britain
26-27-28-29 ...... Trenton

JUNE
6-7-8 .... Bowie
9-10-11 .... Harrisburg
16-17-18 .... Altoona
19-20-21 .... Erie
26-27-28-29 ...... Altoona
30 .... Erie

JULY
1-2-3 .... Erie
13-14-15-16 . Binghamton
26-27-28 .... Norwich

AUGUST
1-2-3-4 .... New Haven
5-6-7 .... Bowie
11-12-13 .... Reading
25-26-27-28 .. Harrisburg
29-30-31 .... Reading

Altoona

APRIL
7-8-9 .... Harrisburg
14-15-16 .... Reading
17-18-19-20 .... Bowie
27-28-29-30 .... Erie

MAY
8-9-10 .... Akron
16-16-17 .... Norwich
19-20-21 ..... New Britain
26-27-28-29 . Binghamton
30-31 .... Portland

JUNE
1-2 .... Portland
6-7-8 .... Erie
9-10-11 .... Reading
19-20-21-22 .... Harris.

JULY
4-5-6-7 .... Reading
8-9-10 .... Bowie
18-19-20 ...... New Haven
21-22-23-24 ...... Trenton

AUGUST
5-6-7 .... Erie
15-16-17 .... Akron
18-19-20 .... Harrisburg
29-30-31 .... Bowie

SEPTEMBER
1-2-3-4 .... Akron

Binghamton

APRIL
7-8-9 .... Norwich
10-11-12 .... Trenton
21-22-23 .... Portland
24-25-26-27 ..... Norwich

MAY
5-6-7 .... New Britain
15-16-17 .... Akron
18-19-20-21 .... Erie
22-23-24-25 .... Bowie

JUNE
3-4-5 .... Norwich
9-10-11 ...... New Haven
15-16-17-18 ...... Portland
19-20-21-22 . New Britain
30 ....Trenton

JULY
1-2-3 .... Trenton
8-9-10 .... New Haven
21-22-23 .... Harrisburg
29-30-31 .... Altoona

AUGUST
1-2-3-4 .... Reading
8-9-10 .... Trenton
18-19-20 .... Portland
29-30-31 ..... New Britain

SEPTEMBER
1-2-3-4 .... New Haven

Bowie

APRIL
7-8-9 .... Reading
21-22-23 .... Harrisburg
27-28-29-30 .... Akron

MAY
1-2-3 .... Erie
4-5-6-7 .... Altoona
15-16-17 ..... New Haven
18-19-20-21 ...... Trenton

JUNE
3-4-5 .... Reading
13-14-15 .... Altoona
19-20-21-22 ...... Reading
23-24-25 .... Akron
27-28-29 ...... Harrisburg

JULY
4-5-6-7 .... Erie
17-18-19 .... Binghamton
21-22-23-24 ...... Norwich
29-30-31 .... Portland

AUGUST
1-2-3-4 ..... New Britain
11-12-13 .... Altoona
14-15-16-17.. Harrisburg
22-23-24 .... Akron
25-26-27 .... Erie

Erie

APRIL
10-11-12-13 .... Altoona
14-15-16 .... Bowie
24-25-26 .... Akron

MAY
4-5-6-7 .... Harrisburg
9-10 .... Reading
15-16-17 .... Portland
26-27-28-29 .... N.B.
31 .... Trenton

JUNE
1-2 .... Trenton
3-4-5 .... Akron
9-10-11-12 .... Bowie
23-24-25 .... Altoona
26-27-28-29 ...... Reading

JULY
8-9-10 .... Harrisburg
17-18-19-20 ...... Norwich
21-22-23-24 New Haven
26-27-28 .... Binghamton

JUNE
3-4-5 .... Norwich
9-10-11 .... New Haven
15-16-17-18 ...... Portland
19-20-21-22 . New Britain
30 ....Trenton

JULY
1-2-3 .... Trenton
8-9-10 .... New Haven
21-22-23 .... Harrisburg
29-30-31 .... Altoona

AUGUST
1-2-3-4 .... Reading
8-9-10 .... Trenton
18-19-20 .... Portland
29-30-31 ..... New Britain

SEPTEMBER
1-2-3-4 .... New Haven

Harrisburg

APRIL
14-15-16 .... Akron
17-18-19-20 .... Erie
24-25-26 .... Altoona
28-29-30 .... Reading

MAY
8-9-10 .... Bowie
11-12-13-14 . Binghamton
18-19-20-21 .... Portland
31 .... Norwich

JUNE
1-2 .... Norwich
3-4-5 .... Altoona
12 .... Reading
13-14-15 .... Erie
16-17-18 .... Bowie
30 .... Altoona

JULY
1-2-3 .... Altoona
4-5-6-7 .... Akron
13-14-15-16 New Britain
18-19-20 .... Trenton
29-30-31 ..... New Haven

AUGUST
5-6-7 .... Reading
8-9-10 .... Akron
22-23-24 .... Reading
29-30-31 .... Erie

SEPTEMBER
1-2-3-4 .... Bowie

New Britain

APRIL
7-8-9 .... Portland
17-18-19-20 .... Bing.
28-29-30 .... Norwich

MAY
1-2-3-4 .... Trenton
8-9-10 .... New Haven
11-12-13-14 ...... Reading
15-16-17 .... Harrisburg
31 .... Bowie

JUNE
1-2 .... Bowie
3-4-5 .... Portland
9-10-11 .... Trenton
12-13-14 .... Binghamton
26-27-28-29 .... N.H.
30 .... Norwich

JULY
1-2-3 .... Norwich
8-9-10 .... Trenton
17-18-19-20 .... Akron
25-26-27-28 ...... Altoona
29-30-31 .... Erie

AUGUST
5-6-7 .... Binghamton
11-12-13 ...... New Haven
22-23-24 .... Norwich
25-26-27-28 ..... Portland

New Haven

APRIL
10-11-12 .... Portland
13-14-15-16.. Binghamton
21-22-23 ..... New Britain
24-25-26 .... Trenton

MAY
1-2-3 .... Binghamton
12-13-14 .... Erie
22-23-24-25 ...... Altoona
26-27-28-29 .... Harr.
31 .... Akron

JUNE
1-2 .... Akron
12-13-14-15 .... Norwich
16-17-18 ..... New Britain
23-24-25 .... Binghamton
30 .... Portland

JULY
1-2-3 .... Portland
13-14-15-16 .... Bowie
26-27-28 .... Reading

AUGUST
5-6-7 .... Norwich
8-9-10 .... Portland
15-16-17 .... Trenton
18-19-20-21.. New Britain
25-26-27-28 .... Trenton
29-30-31 .... Norwich

Norwich

APRIL
10-11-12-13. New Britain
17-18-19-20. New Haven
21-22-23 .... Trenton

MAY
1-2-3-4 .... Portland
5-6-7 .... New Haven
12-13-14 .... Bowie
18-19-20-21 .... Akron
22-23-24 .... Erie

JUNE
6-7-8 .... New Britain
9-10-11 .... Portland
20-21-22 ..... New Haven
23-24-25 .... Portland
26-27-28-29 .... Trenton

JULY
4-5-6-7 .... Binghamton

13-14-15-16 ...... Altoona
29-30-31 .... Reading

AUGUST
1-2-3-4 .... Harrisburg
8-9-10 ...... New Britain
15-16-17 ...... Binghamton
18-19-20 .... Trenton
25-26-27 ...... Binghamton

Portland

APRIL
14-15-16 .... Norwich
24-25-26 ..... New Britain
27-28-29-30. New Haven

MAY
5-6-7 .... Trenton
8-9-10 .... Binghamton
23-24-25 .... Reading
26-27-28-29 .... Bowie

JUNE
6-7-8 .... New Haven
19-20-21-22 ..... Trenton
26-27-28 ...... Binghamton

JULY
4-5-6-7 .... New Britain
8-9-10 .... Norwich
13-14-15-16 .... Erie
21-22-23-24 .... Akron
26-27-28 .... Harrisburg

AUGUST
2-3-4 .... Altoona
5-6-7 .... Trenton
11-12-13-14.. Binghamton
15-16-17 ..... New Britain
22-23-24 ..... New Haven

SEPTEMBER
1-2-3-4 .... Norwich

Reading

APRIL
10-11-12-13 . Harrisburg
21-22-23 .... Erie
24-25-26 .... Bowie

MAY
1-2-3 .... Altoona
4-5-6-7 .... Akron
15-16-17 .... Trenton
18-19-20-21 New Haven
26-27-28-29 ...... Norwich

31 .... Binghamton

JUNE
1-2 .... Binghamton
6-7-8 .... Harrisburg
13-14-15 .... Akron
16-17-18 .... Erie
23-24-25 ...... Harrisburg
30 .... Bowie

JULY
1-2-3 .... Bowie
8-9-10 .... Akron
17-18-19-20 ..... Portland
21-22-23 ..... New Britain

AUGUST
8-9-10 .... Altoona
14-15-16-17 .... Erie
18-19-20 .... Bowie
25-26-27-28 .... Altoona

Trenton

APRIL
7-8-9 .... New Haven
14-15-16 ..... New Britain
17-18-19-20 .... Portland
28-29-30 .. Binghamton

MAY
8-9-10 .... Norwich
12-13-14 .... Altoona
22-23-24-25 Harrisburg

JUNE
3-4-5 .... New Haven
6-7-8 .... Binghamton
12-13-14 .... Portland
16-17-18 .... Norwich
23-24-25 .... New Britain

JULY
4-5-6-7 .... New Haven
13-14-15-16 .... Reading
26-27-28 .... Bowie
29-30-31 .... Akron

AUGUST
1-2-3-4 .... Erie
11-12-13-14 .... Norwich
21-22-23-24 .... Bing.
29-30-31 .... Portland

SEPTEMBER
1-2-3-4 .... New Britain

Southern League

Birmingham

APRIL
14-15-16-17 .... Mobile
22-23-24-25 .... Hunt.
30 .... Greenville

MAY
1-2-3 .... Greenville
5-6-7-8 .... West Tenn
13-14-15 .... Carolina
22-23-24-25 .... W.T.
26-27-28-29 .... Hunt.
30-31 .... Mobile

JUNE
6-7 .... Tennessee
10-11-12-13 .... Mobile
21-22-23-24 .... Orlando
30 .... Tennessee

JULY
1 .... Tennessee
4-5 .... Mobile
13-14-15-16 ... Huntsville
22-23 .... Mobile
25-26-27-28 .... Jack.
29-30-31 ...... West Tenn

AUGUST
1 .... West Tenn
11-12-13-14.. West Tenn
24-25-26-27 .... Chat.
28-29-30-31 .... Hunt.

Carolina

APRIL
14-15-16-17 .. Tennessee
18-19-20-21 . West Tenn
26-27-28-29 .... Jack.
30 .... Orlando

MAY
1-2-3 .... Orlando
18-19-20-21 . Greenville
22-23-24-25...... Orlando

JUNE
1-2-3-4 .... Tennessee
12-13 .... Tennessee
14-15-16-17 .... Mobile
21-22 .... Tennessee
25-26-27-28 .... Hunt.

JULY
4-5-6 .... Greenville
7-8-9-10 ..... Birmingham

17-18-19-20 .... Jack.
21-22-23-24......... Tenn.

AUGUST
2-3-4-5 .... Orlando
11-12-13-14 ...... Chatta.
29-30-31 .... Greenville

SEPTEMBER
1-2-3-4 .... Tennessee

Chattanooga

APRIL
10-11-12-13 .... Birm.
14-15-16-17 . West Tenn
22-23-24-25 .... Carolina

MAY
5-6-7-8 .... Mobile
9-10-11-12 .... Birm.
18-19-20-21 ...... Orlando
22-23-24-25 .... Hunt.
28-29 .... Greenville

JUNE
2-3 .... West Tenn
10-11-12-13 .... Jack.
14-15-16-17 .... Birm.
21-22 .... Huntsville

JULY
4-5-7-8 .... Tennessee
13-14-15-16 .... Mobile
25-26-27-28 .... Mobile
29-30-31 .... Jacksonville
AUGUST
1 .... Jacksonville
4-5 .... Greenville
6-7 .... Huntsville
16-17-18-19 .... Birm.
22-23 .... West Tenn
30-31 .... Tennessee

Greenville
APRIL
6-7-8-9 .... Tennessee
10-11-12-13 ...... Carolina
22-23-24-25 .... Mobile
26-27-28-29 ...... Orlando
MAY
9-10-11-12 .... West Tenn
13-14-15-16 .... Jack.
26-27 .... Chattanooga
30-31 .... Carolina
JUNE
1-2-3-3 ...... Jacksonville
10-11-12-13 ...... Orlando
30 .... Carolina
JULY
1-2-3 .... Carolina
7-8-9-10 ..... Jacksonville
17-18-19-20 .... Tenn.
21-22-22-23 ... Huntsville
29-30-31 .... Carolina
AUGUST
1 .... Carolina
2-3 .... Chattanooga
7-8-9-10 ..... Birmingham
24-25-26-27 .... Jack.
SEPTEMBER
1-2-3-4 .... Orlando

Huntsville
APRIL
6-7-8-9 ...... Chattanooga
14-15-16-17 .. Greenville
26-27-28-29 .... Tenn.
30 .... Chattanooga
MAY
1-2-3 .... Chattanooga
13-14-15-16 .... Mobile
18-19-20-21 .... Birm.
30-31 .... West Tenn
JUNE
6-7-8-9 .... Carolina
10-11-12-13 .. West Tenn
23-24 .... Chattanooga
30 .... West Tenn
JULY
1-2-3 .... West Tenn
7-8-9-10 .... Orlando
17-18-19-20 ...... Chatta.
27-28 .... West Tenn
29-30-31 .... Mobile
AUGUST
1 .... Mobile
2-3 .... Mobile
8-9 .... Chattanooga
11-12-13-14 .... Jack.
20-21-22-23 .... Birm.

SEPTEMBER
1-2-3-4 .... Mobile

Jacksonville
APRIL
6-7-8-9 .... Carolina
10-11-12-13 ...... Tenn.
18-19-20-21 .... Birm.
24-25 .... Orlando
MAY
5-6-7-8 .... Carolina
9-10-11-12 ..... Huntsville
17-18-19-20 ...... Tenn.
22-23 .... Carolina
26-27-28-29 ...... Carolina
JUNE
15-16-17-18 .. Greenville
21-22 .... Mobile
30 .... Orlando
JULY
1-2-3 .... Orlando
13-14-15-16 . West Tenn
21-22-23-24 ...... Orlando
AUGUST
2-3-4-5 .... Tennessee
6-7-8-9 .... Greenville
16-17-18-19 .. Greenville
20-21-22-23 ...... Orlando
SEPTEMBER
1-2-3-4 ...... Chattanooga

Mobile
APRIL
6-7-8-9 .... Birmingham
10-11-12-13 ...... Orlando
18-19-20-21 ... Huntsville
26-27-28-29 .... Chatta.
MAY
9-10-11-12 ... Tennessee
18-19-20-21 . West Tenn
24-25 .... Jacksonville
JUNE
1-2-3-4 .... Huntsville
6-7-8-9 ...... Chattanooga
23-24 .... Jacksonville
26-27-28-29 .... Green.
30 .... Chattanooga
JULY
1-2-3 .... Chattanooga
6-7-8-9 .... West Tenn
17-18-19-20-21 .... Birm.
AUGUST
2-3-4-5-6 .... Birmingham
16-17-18-19 ... Huntsville
20-21-22-23 ...... Carolina
28-29-30-31 . West Tenn

Orlando
APRIL
14-15-16-17 Jacksonville
19-20-21 .... Greenville
22-23 .... Jacksonville
MAY
5-6-7-8 .... Huntsville
9-10-11-12 .... Carolina
13-14-15-16 . Tennessee
30-31 .... Jacksonville
JUNE
1-2-3-4 .... Birmingham
5-6-7-8-9 .... Greenville
26-27-28-29 .... Chatta.

JULY
4-5 .... Jacksonville
13-14-15-16 ..... Carolina
17-18-19-20 . West Tenn
25-26-27-28 .. Greenville
AUGUST
6-7-8-9 .... Tennessee
11-12-13-14 .. Greenville
16-17-18-19 ...... Carolina
24-25-26-27 ...... Mobile
28-29-30-31 .... Jack.

Tennessee
APRIL
20-21 .... Chattanooga
22-23-24-25 . West Tenn
30 .... Jacksonville
MAY
1-2-3 .... Jacksonville
4-5-6-7 .... Greenville
22-23-24-25 .. Greenville
26-27-28-29 ...... Orlando
30-31 .... Chattanooga
JUNE
8-9 .... Birmingham
10-11 .... Carolina
14-15-16-17 ...... Orlando
18-19 .... Chattanooga
23-24 .... Carolina
25-26-27-28 Jacksonville
JULY
2-3 .... Birmingham
9-10 .... Chattanooga
13-14-15-16 .. Greenville
25-26-27-28 ...... Carolina
29-30-31 .... Orlando
AUGUST
1 .... Orlando
11-12-13-14 ...... Mobile
20-21-22-23 .. Greenville
24-25-26-27 ... Huntsville
28-29 .... Chattanooga

West Tenn
APRIL
6-7-8-9 .... Orlando
10-11-12-13 ... Huntsville
26-27-28-29 .... Birm.
30 .... Mobile
MAY
1-2-3 .... Mobile
13-14-15-16 . Chattanooga
26-27-28-29 .... Mobile
JUNE
4-5 .... Chattanooga
6-7-8-9 .... Jacksonville
15-16-17-18 ... Huntsville
21-22-23-24 .. Greenville
25-26-27-28 .... Birm.
JULY
4-5 .... Huntsville
21-22-23-24 ...... Chatta.
25-26 .... Huntsville
AUGUST
4-5 .... Huntsville
7-8-9-10 .... Mobile
16-17-18-19 . Tennessee
20-21 .... Chattanooga
24-25-26-27 ..... Carolina
SEPTEMBER
1-2-3-4 .... Birmingham

Texas League

Arkansas

APRIL
16-17-18-19........ Wichita
20-21-22-22........... Tulsa

MAY
4-5-6-7............ Midland
8-9-10-11.......... El Paso
16-17-18-19. Shreveport
20-20-21-22........ Wichita

JUNE
2-3-4-5....... San Antonio
6-7-8-9...... Round Rock
26-27-28-29........ San Ant.
30............. Round Rock

JULY
1-1-3............ Round Rock
8-8-10-11.............. Tulsa
13-14-15-15. Shreveport
29-29-31........... Wichita

AUGUST
1................. Wichita
3-4-5-5........ Shreveport
7-8-9-10-11-12..... Tulsa
23-24-25-26...... Midland
27-28-29-30..... El Paso

El Paso

APRIL
6-7-8-9-10-11......... R.R.
12-13-14-15..... San Ant.
25-26-27-28. Shreveport
29-30............ Arkansas

MAY
1-2............. Arkansas
12-13-14-15. San Antonio
16-17-18-19...... Midland
28-29-30-31 Round Rock

JUNE
2-3-4-5................ Tulsa
6-7-8-9............. Wichita
25-27-28-29....... Wichita
30..................... Tulsa

JULY
1-2-3................. Tulsa
8-9-10-11.... Round Rock
13-14-15-16...... Midland
29-30-31.... San Antonio

AUGUST
1............... San Antonio
13-15-16-18. Shreveport
18-19-20-21..... Arkansas
31................. Midland

SEPTEMBER
1-2-3.............. Midland

Midland

APRIL
6-7-8-9-10-11... San Ant.
12-13-14-15. Round Rock
25-26-27-28... Arkansas
29-30.......... Shreveport

MAY
1-2............ Shreveport
12-13-14-15. Round Rock
20-21-22-23..... San Ant.
24-25-26-27..... El Paso

JUNE
2-3-4-5................ Wichita
6-7-8-9.............. Tulsa
26-27-28-29......... Tulsa
30..................... Wichita

JULY
1-2-3................ Wichita
8-8-10-11 ... San Antonio
25-26-27-28...... El Paso
29-30-31.............. Round Rock

AUGUST
1................. Round Rock
3-4-5-5........ Shreveport
14-15-16-17...... Arkansas
18-19-20-21. Shreveport

Round Rock

APRIL
16-17-18-19......... El Paso
20-21-22-23..... Midland

MAY
4-5-6-7................ Tulsa
8-9-10-11............ Wichita
20-21-22-23...... El Paso
24-25-26-27..... San Ant.

JUNE
10-11-12-13. Shreveport
14-15-16-17.... Arkansas
21-22-23-24.... Midland

JULY
4-5-6-7................ Midland
17-18-19-20.... Arkansas
21-22-23-24. Shreveport
25-26-27-28..... San Ant.

AUGUST
3-4-5-6........ San Antonio
7-8-9-10-11-12... El Paso
23-24-25-26........ Tulsa
27-28-29-30....... Wichita

San Antonio

APRIL
16-17-18-19...... Midland
20-21-22-23...... El Paso

MAY
4-5-6-7............... Wichita
8-9-10-11.............. Tulsa
16-17-18-19. Round Rock
29-30-31........... Midland

JUNE
1................. Midland
10-11-12-13.... Arkansas
14-15-16-17. Shreveport
21-22-23-24.... El Paso

JULY
4-5-6-7................ El Paso
13-14-15-16. Round Rock
17-18-19-20. Shreveport
21-22-23-24.... Arkansas

AUGUST
7-8-9-10-11-12.. Midland
23-24-25-26....... Wichita
27-28-29-30....... Tulsa
31.............Round Rock

SEPTEMBER
1-2-3.......... Round Rock

Shreveport

APRIL
16-17-18-19.......... Tulsa
20-21-21-22...... Wichita

MAY
4-5-6-7............. El Paso
8-9-10-11.......... Midland
20-20-21-23.......... Tulsa
24-25-26-27.... Arkansas

JUNE
2-3-4-5...... Round Rock
6-7-8-9...... San Antonio
26-27-28-29........... R.R.
30............. San Antonio

JULY
1-2-3......... San Antonio
8-9-10-11........... Wichita
25-26-27-28.... Arkansas
29-30-31.............. Tulsa

AUGUST
1.................... Tulsa
7-8-9-10-11-12..... Wich.
23-24-25-26...... El Paso
27-28-29-30.... Midland
31................. Arkansas

SEPTEMBER
1-2-3............ Arkansas

Tulsa

APRIL
6-7-8-9-10-11...... Shrev.
12-13-14-15.... Arkansas
25-26-27-28........... R.R.
29-30....... San Antonio

MAY
1-2......... San Antonio
12-13-14-15.... Arkansas
16-17-18-19...... Wichita
29-30-31...... Shreveport

JUNE
1................. Shreveport
10-11-12-13.... El Paso
14-15-16-17...... Midland
21-22-23-24.. Shreveport

JULY
4-5-6-7............ Arkansas
13-14-15-16........ Wichita
17-18-19-20..... El Paso
21-22-23-24...... Midland

AUGUST
3-4-5-6............... Wichita
14-15-16-17............ R.R.
18-19-20-21..... San Ant.

Wichita

APRIL
6-7-8-9-10-11 . Arkansas
12-13-14-15 Shreveport
25-26-27-28..... San Ant.
29-30......... Round Rock

MAY
1-2........... Round Rock
12-13-14-15. Shreveport
25-26-27-28.......... Tulsa
29-30-31........ Arkansas

JUNE
1................. Arkansas
10-11-12-13...... Midland
14-15-16-17...... El Paso
21-22-23-24.... Arkansas

JULY
4-5-6-7......... Shreveport
17-18-19-20..... Midland
21-22-23-24...... El Paso
25-26-27-28.......... Tulsa

AUGUST
15-15-16-17...... San Ant.
18-19-20-21. Round Rock
31...................... Tulsa

SEPTEMBER
1-2-3.................... Tulsa

CLASS A

California League

Bakersfield

APRIL
6-7-8 .... Lancaster
9-10-11 .... Lake Elsinore
20-21-22-23-24 .... S.J.
26-27-28-29-30 . Mudville

MAY
10-11-12 .... San Bern.
13-14-15 .... Visalia
23-24-25 ... High Desert
26-27-28 .... R. Cuca.

JUNE
10 .... Visalia
11-12-13-14 ..... Modesto
15-16 .... Visalia
28-29-30 .... R. Cuca.

JULY
4-5-6 .... Visalia
7-8-9 .... San Bern.
11 .... Visalia
18-19-20-21-22 . Mudville
23-24-25 .... Modesto
30-31 .... Lancaster

AUGUST
1 .... Lancaster
2-3-4 .... San Jose
5-6 .... Modesto
11-12-13 .. Lake Elsinore
27 .... Visalia
30-31 .... High Desert

SEPTEMBER
1 .... High Desert
2-3 .... San Jose

High Desert

APRIL
6-7-8 .... Visalia
9-10-11 ...... San Jose
23-24-25 .. Lake Elsinore
27-28-29-30 .. San Bern.

MAY
1-2-3 .... Mudville
7-8-9 .... Bakersfield
17-18-19 .... Modesto
20-21-22 ...... Lancaster
29 .... San Bernardino
30 .... R. Cucamonga

JUNE
1 .... Lancaster
4-5 .... Lake Elsinore
9 .... R. Cucamonga
14 .... Lancaster
16-17-18 .... R. Cuca.
22-23-24 ..... Bakersfield
25 .... Lake Elsinore
28-29-30 .... Modesto

JULY
3 .... Lancaster
4-5-6 .... Mudville
7 .... Lancaster
10-11 .... R. Cuca.
15-17-18 .. Lake Elsinore
23-24-25 .... San Jose
27-28-29 .... Visalia

AUGUST
5-6-7-8-9 ...... San Bern.
13 .... Lancaster
19-20 .... R. Cuca.
24 .... Lancaster
25 .... R. Cucamonga

26 .... Lancaster

SEPTEMBER
2 .... Lake Elsinore

Lake Elsinore

APRIL
6-7 .... R. Cucamonga
12-13-14 .... San Bern.
15-16 .... High Desert
17-18-19 .... R. Cuca.
27-28-29 .... Modesto

MAY
1-2 .... San Bernardino
4-5-6 .... Mudville
17-18-19 ...... Bakersfield
20-21-22 ...... San Jose
23-24 .... Lancaster
30-31 .... Visalia

JUNE
1 .... Visalia
6-7-8 .... High Desert
9-10-11 .... Lancaster
22 .... Lancaster
26-27 .... High Desert

JULY
7-8-9 .... Mudville
16 .... High Desert
19-20-21-22 ... San Jose
23-24-25 .... Visalia

AUGUST
2-3 .... R. Cucamonga
7-8 .... Modesto
10 .... R. Cucamonga
15 .... San Bernardino
16 .... R. Cucamonga
17 .... San Bernardino
18 .... High Desert
20 .... Lancaster
21-22-23 ...... Bakersfield
25 .... Lancaster
26 .... R. Cucamonga
28-29-30 .... San Bern.
31 .... Lancaster

SEPTEMBER
1 .... Lancaster
3 .... High Desert

Lancaster

APRIL
12-13-14 .... Mudville
15-16 ...... R. Cucamonga
17-18-19 ...... San Jose
23-24-25 .... Visalia
27-28-29 .. R. Cucamonga
30 .... Lake Elsinore

MAY
1-2-3 .... Bakersfield
4-5 .... High Desert
13-14-15 .... San Bern.
18-19 .... San Bern.
26-27 .... High Desert

JUNE
4-5-6 .... Modesto
7-8 .... R. Cucamonga
12 .... Lake Elsinore
15 .... High Desert
16-17-18 .. Lake Elsinore
23-24 .... Lake Elsinore
25-26-27 .... Visalia

JULY

1-2 .... High Desert
4-5-6 .... Modesto
8-9 .... High Desert
10-11 ...... Lake Elsinore
19 .... San Bernardino
22 .... San Bernardino
23-24-25 .... Mudville

AUGUST
2-3-4 .... San Bern.
5-6-7 .... San Jose
8-9-10 .... Bakersfield
11-12-15-18 ..... R. Cuca.
19 .... Lake Elsinore
27 .... High Desert

Modesto

APRIL
8 .... Mudville
9-10-11 .... Lancaster
17-18-19 ... High Desert
20-21-22 .... Visalia
23 .... Mudville

MAY
6 .... San Jose
7-8-9 .... San Bern.
10-11-12 .. Lake Elsinore
13-14-15 .... R. Cuca.
20-21-22 .... Mudville
24-25-26-27 ... San Jose
30-31 .... Bakersfield

JUNE
1-2-3 .... Bakersfield
17-18 .... Visalia

JULY
1-2-3 ...... Rancho Cuca.
11-12 .... San Jose
13-14-15-16-17 . Bakers.
27-28-29 .... Lancaster
30-31 .... Lake Elsinore

AUGUST
1 .... Lake Elsinore
2-3-4 .... High Desert
10-11-12-13-13 ... Visalia
17-18-19 .... Mudville
21-22-23 ...... San Jose
25-26-27 .... San Bern.
29-30 .... Mudville

Mudville

APRIL
6-7 .... Modesto
15-16 .... San Bern.
17-18 .... Bakersfield
19 .... Visalia
20-21-22 .... High Desert
24 .... Modesto

MAY
7-8-9 ..... R. Cucamonga
10-11-12 .... Lancaster
13-13-14 .. Lake Elsinore
17-18-19 .... Visalia
29 .... Bakersfield
31 .... San Jose

JUNE
1 .... San Jose
4-5 .... San Jose
7 .... Modesto
12 .... San Jose
14 .... Visalia
15 .... San Bernardino

16 .... Modesto
17-18 .... Bakersfield
22-23-24 ...... Modesto
JULY
1-2-3 .... Bakersfield
10-11 .... San Bern.
13-14-15 .... Lancaster
16-17 .... Visalia
27-28-29... R. Cucamonga
30-31 .... R. Cucamonga
AUGUST
1 .... R. Cucamonga
11-12 .... San Jose
15-16 .... Modesto
20 .... Bakersfield
21-22-23 .... High Desert
24 .... San Bernardino
25-26-27 .... San Jose
31 .... Visalia
SEPTEMBER
1-2 .... Visalia

R. Cucamonga
APRIL
8 .... Lake Elsinore
9-10-11 .... Mudville
12-13-14 .... High Desert
20-21-22....... Lancaster
30 .... Modesto
MAY
1-2 .... Modesto
3 .... Lake Elsinore
4-5-6 .... Bakersfield
17-18-19 ...... San Jose
20-21-22 .... Visalia
24 .... San Bernardino
25 .... Lake Elsinore
31 .... High Desert
JUNE
1 .... San Bernardino
2-3 .... Lake Elsinore
4-5-6 .... San Bern.
10 .... High Desert
22-23-24 .... Visalia
25-26-27 ..... Bakersfield
JULY
4-5-6 .... San Jose
7-8-9 .... Modesto
12-13-14 .... High Desert
15-16-18 ...... San Bern.
19 .... High Desert
20-21 .... Lancaster
22 .... High Desert
AUGUST
4-5-6 .... Lake Elsinore
7-8-9 .... Mudville
17-18 .... Lancaster

24 .... Lake Elsinore
27 .... Lake Elsinore
28-29-30 .... Lancaster
SEPTEMBER
1-2 .... San Bernardino

San Bernardino
APRIL
6-7-8 .... San Jose
9-10-11 .... Visalia
20-21-22.. Lake Elsinore
23-24-25 .... R. Cuca.
MAY
3-4-5 .... Modesto
6 .... High Desert
17 .... Lancaster
20-21-22 ...... Bakersfield
23 .... R. Cucamonga
25 .... Lancaster
26-27 .... Lake Elsinore
28-30 .... Lancaster
JUNE
2-3 .... High Desert
8-9-10 .... Mudville
11-12 .... High Desert
13 .... Lancaster
14 .... R. Cucamonga
22-23-24 ...... San Jose
25-26-27 .... Modesto
28-29-30 .... Mudville
JULY
4-5-6 .... Lake Elsinore
13-14 .... Lake Elsinore
20-21 .... High Desert
23-24-25 .... R. Cuca.
27-28-29 ...... Bakersfield
AUGUST
10-11-12 .... High Desert
13 .... R. Cucamonga
16 .... Lancaster
18-19-20 .... Visalia
21-22-23 ...... Lancaster
31 .... R. Cucamonga
SEPTEMBER
3 .... Lancaster

San Jose
APRIL
12-13-14-15-16. Bakers.
26 .... Modesto
27-28-29-30 ...... Visalia
MAY
7-8-9 .... Lancaster
10-11-12 .... R. Cuca.
13-14-15 .... High Desert
28-29 .... Modesto
30 .... Mudville

JUNE
2-3 .... Mudville
6 .... Mudville
8-9-10 .... Modesto
11 .... Mudville
13-14-15 .. Lake Elsinore
16-17-18 ...... San Bern.
25-26-27 .... Mudville
28-29-30.. Lake Elsinore
JULY
1-2-3 .... San Bern.
13-14-15 .... Visalia
16-17-18 ...... Lancaster
27-28-29 .... R. Cuca.
30-31 .... High Desert
AUGUST
1 .... High Desert
10 .... Mudville
13 .... Mudville
15-16-17-18-19. Bakers.
20-24-28 .... Modesto
29-30 .... Visalia
31 .... Modesto
SEPTEMBER
1 .... Modesto

Visalia
APRIL
12-13-14-15-16. Modesto
17-18-18 .... San Bern.
MAY
1-2-3-4-5 .... San Jose
6 .... Lancaster
7-8-9 .... Lake Elsinore
10-11-12 ..... High Desert
24-25-26-27-28 ..... Mud.
JUNE
2-3 .... Lancaster
4-5-7-8-9 ..... Bakersfield
11-12-13 .... R. Cuca.
28-29-30 .... Lancaster
JULY
1-2-3 .... Lake Elsinore
7-8-9 .... San Jose
10 .... Bakersfield
18-19-20-21-22. Modesto
30-31 .... San Bern.
AUGUST
1 .... San Bernardino
2-3-4-5-6 ...... Mudville
7 .... Bakersfield
8 .... San Jose
15-16 .... High Desert
21-22-23.. R. Cucamonga
24-25-26 ..... Bakersfield
SEPTEMBER
3 .... Modesto

Carolina League

Frederick
APRIL
10-11-12 .... Kinston
13-14-15-16 .... W-S
24-25-26-27 .... Potomac
28-29-30 ...... Lynchburg
MAY
8-9-10 .... Wilmington
18-19-20-21 .... M.B.
22-23-24 .... Salem
JUNE
1-2-3-4 .... Kinston
5-6-7 ...... Myrtle Beach
15-16-17-18.. Lynchburg
30 .... Winston-Salem
JULY
1-2 .... Winston-Salem
3-4-5 .... Salem

Kinston
APRIL
13-14-15-16 .... Potomac
17-18-19 .... Frederick
28-29-30 .... M.B.
MAY
2-3-4 .... Salem
5-6-7 ..... Winston-Salem

11-12-13 .... Potomac
14-15-16 ...... Wilmington
24-25-26 ...... Lynchburg
27-28-29-30 .... Wilm.
AUGUST
4-5-6 .... Kinston
8-9-10 ...... Myrtle Beach
18-19-20 .... Potomac
21-22-23-24 ...... Salem
25-26-27 .... W-S

15-16-17 ...... Lynchburg
19-20-21 ...... Wilmington
26-27-28 .... Potomac
JUNE
5-6-7 ...... Winston-Salem
9-10-11-12 ...... Frederick
22-23-24-25 .... M.B.
26-27-28 ...... Wilmington
30 .... Salem
JULY
1-2 .... Salem
7-8-9 .... Lynchburg
17-18-19 .... Frederick
20-21-22-23 .... W-S
24-25-26-27 ...... Salem
AUGUST
7-8-9-10 ...... Wilmington
11-12-13-14.. Lynchburg
22-23-24 .... M.B.

25-26-27 .... Potomac

Lynchburg

APRIL
13-14-15-16.. Wilmington
17-18-19 .. Myrtle Beach
24-25-26-27 ...... Kinston
MAY
5-6-7 .... Frederick
9-10-11 .... Potomac
18-19-20-21 .....Salem
22-23-24 .... W-S
29-30-31........ Frederick
JUNE
5-6-7 .... Wilmington
8-9-10 .... Salem
26-27-28 .... W-S
29-30 .... Potomac
JULY
1-2 .... Potomac
3-4-5 .... Myrtle Beach
14-15-16 .... Kinston
17-18-19 .... Potomac
20-21-22 .... Wilmington
27-28-29-30 ...... M.B.
AUGUST
4-5-6 .... Salem
7-8-9-10 .... W-S
18-19-20 .... Kinston
31 .... Frederick
SEPTEMBER
1-2-3.............. Frederick

Myrtle Beach

APRIL
6-7-8-9........ Lynchburg
10-11-12 .... Potomac
20-21-22-23 .... Frederick
25-26-27 ..... Wilmington
MAY
5-6-7 .... Salem
8-9-10-11 .... W-S
22-23-24......... Kinston
29-30-31 .... Potomac
JUNE
2-3-4 ..... Winston-Salem
13-14 .... Frederick
15-16-17-18 ...... Kinston
29-30 .... Wilmington
JULY
1-2 .... Wilmington
10-11-12 ...... Lynchburg
14-15-16 .... Salem
20-21-22-23 ... Frederick
31 .... Potomac
AUGUST
1-2-3 .... Potomac
4-5-6...... Wilmington
15-16-17 ...... Lynchburg
18-19-20................ W-S

Potomac

APRIL
6-7-8-9 .... Kinston
17-18-19-20 .... Salem
21-22-23 ...... Lynchburg
MAY
2-3-4.......... Frederick
12-13-14 .. Myrtle Beach
18-19-20-21 .... W-S
22-23-24...... Wilmington
JUNE
2-3-4 .... Lynchburg
12-13-14 .... Kinston
15-16-17-18 .... Wilm.
26-27-28 .... Frederick
JULY
3-4-5.............. Kinston
6-7-8-9 .. Myrtle Beach
11-12.. Winston-Salem
24-25-26 .. Myrtle Beach
28-29-30 .... Kinston
AUGUST
7-8-9 .... Salem
11-12-13-14 ..... Frederick
21-22-23-24.. Lynchburg
28-29-30 .... W-S
SEPTEMBER
1-2-3 .... Wilmington

Salem

APRIL
10-11-12 ...... Lynchburg
13-14-15-16 .... M.B.
25-26-27...... W-S
28-29-30...... Wilmington
MAY
8-9-10.......... Kinston
12-13-14 .... Frederick
15-16-17 .... Potomac
25-26-27-28.. Lynchburg
JUNE
1-2-3-4 .... Wilmington
5-6-7 .... Potomac
15-16-17-18 .... W-S
22-23-24-25 .... Frederick
26-27-28 .... M.B.
JULY
10-11-12-13...... Kinston
17-18-19...... Wilmington
20-21-22-23 ...... Potomac
AUGUST
1-2-3............ Frederick
11-12-13............ W-S
15-16-17........ Kinston
25-26-27 .. Myrtle Beach

Wilmington

APRIL
6-7-8-9 .... Frederick
17-18-19.......... W-S
21-22-23 .... Salem
MAY
1-2-3-4 .... Lynchburg
5-6-7 .... Potomac
11-12-13-14...... Kinston
15-16-17 .. Myrtle Beach
26-27-28......... Frederick
29-30-31........ Kinston
JUNE
8-9-10-11.. Myrtle Beach
12-13-14 .... Lynchburg
22-23-24-25 .... Potomac
JULY
6-7-8-9 .... Salem
10-11-12-13........... W-S
24-25-26............. W-S
31 .... Kinston
AUGUST
1-2 .... Kinston
11-12-13.. Myrtle Beach
15-16-17 .... Potomac
18-19-20 .... Salem
25-26-27 ...... Lynchburg
28-29-30 .... Frederick

Winston-Salem

APRIL
6-7-8-9 .... Salem
10-11-12 ...... Wilmington
20-21-22-23 ...... Kinston
28-29-30 .... Potomac
MAY
1-2-3 ...... Myrtle Beach
12-13-14 .... Lynchburg
15-16-17........ Frederick
25-26-27-28 .... M.B.
29-30-31 .... Salem
JUNE
8-9-10-11 .... Potomac
13-14........... Kinston
22-23-24-25.. Lynchburg
JULY
3-4-5........... Wilmington
6-7-8-9 .... Frederick
17-18-19 .. Myrtle Beach
28-29-30 .... Salem
AUGUST
1-2-3............. Lynchburg
4-5-6 .... Potomac
15-16-17........ Frederick
21-22-23-24 .... Wilm.
31 .... Kinston
SEPTEMBER
1-2-3.................. Kinston

Florida State League

Brevard County

APRIL
6-7 .... Jupiter
16-17-18-19 .... Lakeland
22-23 .... Jupiter
24-25-26-27 .... Sarasota
28..................... St. Lucie
MAY
1..................... St. Lucie
11-12-13-14 .... Charlotte
17-18 .... Daytona
19-20-21-22 . Fort Myers
25 .... Kissimmee
27-28.............. St. Lucie
30 .... Vero Beach

JUNE
2-3 .... Vero Beach
8 .... Kissimmee
10-11................ Daytona
12-13-19-20. Kissimmee
24 .... Vero Beach
28-29-30 St. Petersburg
JULY
1 .... St. Petersburg
12-13-14-15 ..... Dunedin
16-17-18-19 .. Clearwater
26-27 .... Vero Beach
31...................... Daytona
AUGUST
1 .... Daytona
2-3 .... Jupiter

4-5 .... Vero Beach
9-10 .... Kissimmee
11-12 .... Jupiter
14-15-16-17........ Tampa
29-30........... St. Lucie
SEPTEMBER
2-3 .... Daytona

Charlotte

APRIL
7.................... Fort Myers
12-13-14-15.... Jupiter
16-17-18-19 ... St. Lucie
21-22 .... Sarasota
MAY
3-4-5-6........ Vero Beach

10 .... Lakeland
15-16` .... Dunedin
23-24 .... Fort Myers
25-26 ..... St. Petersburg
28 .... Fort Myers
30-31-31 .... Tampa

JUNE
1 .... Tampa
2-3 .... Clearwater
6-7 .... Dunedin
8 .... Fort Myers
10 .... Lakeland
14-15-23-24 .... Sarasota

JULY
3-4 .... Tampa
7-8-9-10 .... Brevard
20 .... Fort Myers
22-23 .... Lakeland
24-25 .... Fort Myers
26-27-28-29 . Kissimmee
31 .... Sarasota

AUGUST
1 .... Sarasota
7-8-9-10 . St. Petersburg
14-15 .... Clearwater
18-19 .... Dunedin
21-22-23-24 . Daytona
29-30 .... Clearwater

SEPTEMBER
2-3 .... Lakeland

Clearwater

APRIL
7 .... St. Petersburg
8-9-10-11 .... Daytona
12-13-14-15 . St. Petersburg
21-22-23 St. Petersburg

MAY
3-4 .... Fort Myers
7-8 .... Charlotte
9 .... Tampa
11-12 .... Dunedin
13-13 .... Tampa
17-18 .... Charlotte
19-20-21-22. Kissimmee
27-28 .... Lakeland

JUNE
4-5 .... Sarasota
8-9 .... Dunedin
14 .... Lakeland
15 .... Tampa
19-20 .... Dunedin
21-22 .... Charlotte
27 .... St. Petersburg
28-29 .... Tampa

JULY
12-13-14-15 Vero Beach
20-21-22-23 .... St. Lucie
25-26-27 .... Lakeland
28-29 .... Tampa

AUGUST
1 .... St. Petersburg
2-3 .... Dunedin
9-10-16-17 ..... Sarasota
18-19-21-22 . Fort Myers
25-26-27-28.. Jupiter

Daytona

APRIL
7 .... Kissimmee
16-17-18-19 .... Sarasota
24-25-26-27 .... Lakeland
28-29-30 .... Lakeland

MAY
1 .... Lakeland
11-12-13-13 . Fort Myers
15-16 .... Jupiter
19-20-21-22 ... St. Lucie
23-24-25-26 Vero Beach

JUNE
2-3-4-5 ..... Kissimmee
6-7-14-15 .... Brevard
19-20 ..... Vero Beach
21 ....Kissimmee
26-27 .... Brevard

JULY
3-4-5-6 .... Clearwater
7-8-9-10 .... Jupiter
20-21 .... Kissimmee
22-22 ..... Vero Beach
26-27-28-29 ..... Dunedin

AUGUST
2-3-4-5 .. St. Petersburg
14-15-16-17 .... St. Lucie
18-19 .... Brevard
29-30-31 .... Tampa

SEPTEMBER
1 .... Tampa

Dunedin

APRIL
6 .... Lakeland
8-9-10-11 .... Brevard
16-17 .... Tampa
20-21 .... Fort Myers

MAY
3-4-5-6 .... Kissimmee
7-8-9-10 .... Daytona
17-18-20 .... Lakeland
21-22 .... Sarasota
25-26 .... Fort Myers
27 .... Tampa
30-30 .... Clearwater
31 .... St. Petersburg

JUNE
1 .... St. Petersburg
4-5 .... Charlotte
10-11 .... Clearwater
12-13 .... Sarasota
24 .... Tampa

JULY
3-4-5-6 .... St. Lucie
7-8 .... Lakeland
9-10 .... Tampa
20-21-22-23 .... Jupiter
24-25 .... Sarasota

AUGUST
4-5 .... Clearwater
7-8 .... Lakeland
9-10 .... Fort Myers
11-12 ..... St. Petersburg
21-22-23-24 Vero Beach
25-26-27-28... Charlotte
31 .... Clearwater

SEPTEMBER
1 .... Clearwater
2-3 .... St. Petersburg

Fort Myers

APRIL
6 .... Charlotte
8-9 .... Lakeland
12-13 ..... St. Petersburg
16-17-18-19....... Jupiter
22-23 .... Dunedin
24-25-26-27 Vero Beach

MAY
5-6 .... Clearwater
7-8-9-10 .... St. Lucie
15-16 .... Lakeland
17-18 .... Sarasota
27 .... Charlotte
30-30 .... Sarasota
31 .... Clearwater

JUNE
1 .... Clearwater
9 .... Charlotte
10-11 .... Tampa

14-15 ...... St. Petersburg
28-29-30 .... Dunedin

JULY
1 .... Dunedin
3-4-5-6 .... Brevard
7-8 .... Tampa
12-13-14-15 .... Daytona
16-17-18-19 ... St. Pete.
21 .... Charlotte
28-29 .... Lakeland

AUGUST
4-5 .... Charlotte
7-8 .... Tampa
11-12 .... Charlotte
14-15-16-17. Kissimmee
23-24 .... Sarasota

SEPTEMBER
2-3 .... Clearwater

Jupiter

APRIL
8-9-10-11 St. Petersburg
20-21 .... Brevard
24-25-26-27 .... Dunedin
28-29-30 ..... Clearwater

MAY
1 .... Clearwater
11-12-13-14. Kissimmee
10 20 21 22... Tampa
23-24 .... Brevard
30-30-31 .... Daytona

JUNE
1 .... Daytona
4-5.................... St. Lucie
6-7-8-9 .. Vero Beach
10 .... St. Lucie
21-22 .... Brevard
23-24 .... St. Lucie

JULY
3-4-5-6 .... Sarasota
12-13-14-15 . Lakeland
16-17-18-19... Charlotte
28-29 ..... Vero Beach

AUGUST
1 .... St. Lucie
4-5.................. Kissimmee
7-8-9-10 .... Daytona
14-15 ..... Vero Beach
18-19 .... St. Lucie
29-30-31 ..... Fort Myers

SEPTEMBER
1 .... Fort Myers
2-3 .... Kissimmee

Kissimmee

APRIL
6...................... Daytona
8-9-10-11 .... Charlotte
12-13-14-15 .... Sarasota
24-25-26-27 .... Lakeland
28-29-30 ..... Fort Myers

MAY
1 .... Fort Myers
9-10 .... Vero Beach
15-16 .... Brevard
17-18 .... Jupiter
23-24 .... St. Lucie
26 .... Brevard
27-28 .... Daytona

JUNE
1 .... Vero Beach
6-7 .... St. Lucie
9 .... Brevard
10 .... Vero Beach
14-15 .... Jupiter
22-23-24 .... Daytona
28-29-30 .... Jupiter

JULY
1 .... Jupiter

FLORIDA STATE LEAGUE 2000 SCHEDULE

5-6 .... Vero Beach
7-8-9-10 .... Clearwater
16-17-18-19 ..... Dunedin
22-23-24-25 ..... Brevard
AUGUST
7-8 .... St. Lucie
11-12................ Daytona
21-22................. St. Lucie
25-26-27-28....... Tampa
29-30-31 St. Petersburg
SEPTEMBER
1 .... St. Petersburg

Lakeland
APRIL
7 .... Dunedin
10-11 .... Fort Myers
12-13-14-15 Vero Beach
20-21-22-23 ... St. Lucie
MAY
3-4-5-6 .... Jupiter
7-8 .... Tampa
9 .... Charlotte
11-12 .... Sarasota
13-13 ..... St. Petersburg
19 .... Dunedin
21-22 .... Charlotte
23-24 .... Clearwater
30-30 .... St. Petersburg
JUNE
4-5 .... Tampa
11 .... Charlotte
12-13 .... Clearwater
15 .... Dunedin
19-20 .... Sarasota
21-22-23 .... Dunedin
24 .... Clearwater
26-27 .... Fort Myers
30 .... Clearwater
JULY
1 .... Clearwater
4-5 .... St. Petersburg
9-10 .... Fort Myers
20-21 .... Tampa
24 .... Clearwater
31 .... Kissimmee
AUGUST
1-2-3 .... Kissimmee
4-5 .... Tampa
11-12 .... Sarasota
16-17 .... Charlotte
21-22-23-24 ..... Brevard
25-26-27-28 ..... Daytona

St. Lucie
APRIL
6 .... Vero Beach
8-9-10-11 .... Tampa
12-13-14-15 ..... Dunedin
24-25-26-27 . Clearwater
29-30 .... Brevard
MAY
11-12 .... Vero Beach
15-16-17-18 St. Petersburg
25-26 .... Jupiter
30-30 .... Kissimmee
31 .... Brevard
JUNE
1 .... Brevard
2-3 .... Jupiter
8-9 .... Daytona
11 .... Jupiter
12-13 .... Daytona
14 .... Vero Beach
19-20 .... Daytona
21-22 .... Vero Beach
26-27 .... Kissimmee
28-29-30 .... Daytona
JULY
1 .... Daytona

12-13-14-15 .... Charlotte
16-17-18-19 ..... Lakeland
28-29 .... Brevard
31 .... Jupiter
AUGUST
2-3-4-5 .... Sarasota
9-10 .... Vero Beach
23-24 .... Kissimmee
25-26-27-28 . Fort Myers
31 .... Brevard
SEPTEMBER
1 .... Brevard

St. Petersburg
APRIL
6 .... Clearwater
14-15 .... Fort Myers
16-17-18-19. Kissimmee
20 .... Clearwater
24-25-26-27 .... Tampa
28 .... Sarasota
30 .... Charlotte
MAY
1 .... Charlotte
3-4-5-6 .... Daytona
7-8-9-10 .... Brevard
23-24 .... Dunedin
27 .... Sarasota
JUNE
2-3 .... Dunedin
4-5 .... Fort Myers
6-7 .... Lakeland
10 .... Sarasota
12-13-19-20 .... Charlotte
22 .... Tampa
23-24 .... Fort Myers
26 .... Clearwater
JULY
2 .... Fort Myers
3-6 .... Lakeland
7-8-9-10 .... St. Lucie
14 .... Tampa
20-21 .... Sarasota
22 .... Fort Myers
24-25-26-27 .... Jupiter
29 .... Sarasota
31 .... Clearwater
AUGUST
14-15 .... Lakeland
16-17 .... Dunedin
18-20 .... Sarasota
23-24 .... Clearwater
25-26-27-28 Vero Beach

Sarasota
APRIL
6 .... Tampa
8-9-10-11 .... Vero Beach
20-23 .... Charlotte
29 .... St. Petersburg
30 .... Tampa
MAY
3-4-5-6 .... St. Lucie
7-8-9-10 .... Jupiter
13-14 .... Dunedin
15-16 .... Clearwater
19-20 .... Charlotte
25-26 .... Clearwater
28 .... St. Petersburg
31 .... Lakeland
JUNE
1-2-3 .... Lakeland
6-7 .... Fort Myers
8-9-11 ... St. Petersburg
21-22 .... Fort Myers
26-27 .... Charlotte
28-29 .... Lakeland
30 .... Tampa
JULY
1 .... Tampa

12-13-14-15.. Kissimmee
16-17-18-19 ..... Daytona
22-23 .... Tampa
26-27 .... Ft. Myers
28 .... St. Petersburg
AUGUST
7-8 .... Clearwater
14-15 .... Dunedin
19-22 ...... St. Petersburg
25-26-27-28 ..... Brevard
29-30 .... Dunedin
31 .... Charlotte
SEPTEMBER
1 .... Charlotte

Tampa
APRIL
7 .... Sarasota
12-13-14-15 ..... Daytona
18-19 .... Dunedin
20-21-22-23 . Kissimmee
28-29 .... Charlotte
MAY
1 .... Sarasota
3-4-5-6 .... Brevard
10 .... Clearwater
11-12 ...... St. Petersburg
23-24 .... Sarasota
25-26 .... Lakeland
28 .... Dunedin
JUNE
2-3 .... Fort Myers
6-7 .... Clearwater
8-9 .... Lakeland
12-13 .... Fort Myers
14 .... Dunedin
19-20 .... Fort Myers
21 .... St. Petersburg
23 .... Clearwater
26-27 .... Dunedin
JULY
5-6 .... Charlotte
12-13-15 St. Petersburg
16-17-18-19 Vero Beach
24-25-26-27 .... St. Lucie
31 .... Dunedin
AUGUST
1 .... Dunedin
2-3 .... Charlotte
9-10 .... Lakeland
11-12 .... Clearwater
18-19 .... Lakeland
21-22-23-24 .... Jupiter
SEPTEMBER
2-3 .... Sarasota

Vero Beach
APRIL
7 .... St. Lucie
16-17-18-19 . Clearwater
20-21-22-23 ..... Daytona
28-29-30 .... Dunedin
MAY
1 .... Dunedin
7-8 .... Kissimmee
13-13 .... St. Lucie
15-16-17-18 ...... Tampa
19-20-21-22 .... St. Pete.
27-28 .... Jupiter
31 .... Kissimmee
JUNE
4-5-5 .... Brevard
11 .... Kissimmee
12-13 .... Jupiter
15 .... St. Lucie
23 .... Brevard
26-27 .... Jupiter
28-29-30 .... Charlotte

246 • BASEBALL AMERICA 2000 DIRECTORY

JULY

1	Charlotte
3-4	Kissimmee
7-8-9-10	Sarasota
20-21	Brevard
24-25	Daytona

| 31 | Fort Myers |

AUGUST

1-2-3	Fort Myers
7-8	Brevard
11-12	St. Lucie
16-17	Jupiter

| 18-19 | Kissimmee |
| 29-30-31 | Lakeland |

SEPTEMBER

| 1 | Lakeland |
| 2-3 | St. Lucie |

Midwest League

Beloit

APRIL

6-7	Wisconsin
10-11	Peoria
18-19-20-21	Cedar Rap.
22-23-24-25	Burlington

MAY

5-6-7-8	Dayton
9-10-11-12	Kane County
18-19-20-21	Fort Wayne
30-31	Quad City

JUNE

1	Quad City
2-3-4-5	South Bend
10-11	Wisconsin
15-16	Peoria
22-23-24-25	Wisconsin
26-27-28-29	West Mich.

JULY

4-5-6	Quad City
17-18-19-20	Michigan
21-22-23-24	Cedar Rap.
28-29-30-31	Peoria

AUGUST

| 10-11-12-13 | Clinton |
| 19-20-21-22 | Lansing |

SEPTEMBER

| 1-2-3-4 | Kane County |

Burlington

APRIL

6-7	Clinton
10-11-12-13	Quad City
14-15-16	Kane County
27-28-29-30	South Bend

MAY

5-6-7-8	Wisconsin
9-10-11-12	Dayton
22-23-24-25	Beloit
26-27-28	Cedar Rapids

JUNE

6-7	Clinton
10-11-12-13	Fort Wayne
15	Cedar Rapids
26-27-28-29	Michigan
30	Lansing

JULY

1-2-3	Lansing
9-10	Cedar Rapids
21-22	Quad City
25-26-27	Kane County

AUGUST

1-2-3-4	Beloit
6-7	Quad City
11-12	Cedar Rapids
19-20-21-22	Peoria
24-25-26-27	Clinton

SEPTEMBER

| 1-2-3-4 | West Mich. |

Cedar Rapids

APRIL

6-7-8-9	Quad City
14-15-16	Peoria
22-23-24-25	Clinton

MAY

| 5-6-7-8 | Michigan |
| 9-10-11-12 | West Mich. |

| 22-23-24-25 | Kane County |
| 29 | Burlington |

JUNE

6-7-8-9	Beloit
10-11-12-13	Lansing
16-17-18	Burlington
26-27-28-29	Fort Wayne

JULY

4-5-6	Peoria
7-8	Burlington
13-14-15-16	Beloit
17-18-19-20	Quad City
28-29-30-31	Wisconsin

AUGUST

5 6 7 8	Clinton
10-13	Burlington
19-20-21-22	South Bend
24-25-26-27	Dayton

Clinton

APRIL

8-9	Burlington
10-11-12-13	Cedar Rapids
18-19-20-21	Kane County
29-30	Quad City

MAY

9-10-11-12	South Bend
18-19-20-21	Peoria
22-23-24-25	Dayton
30-31	Wisconsin

JUNE

1	Wisconsin
2-3	Quad City
8-9	Burlington
15-16-17-18	Fort Wayne
22-23-24-25	Cedar Rapids

JULY

4 5 6	Wisconsin
7-8-9-10	Beloit
21-22-23-24	Peoria
28-29-30-31	Burlington

AUGUST

1-2-3-4	Lansing
15-16-17-18	Kane County
19 20 21 22	Michigan
28-29-30-31	West Mich.

Dayton

APRIL

14-15-16	West Mich.
18-19-20-21	South Bend
27-28-29-30	Cedar Rap.

MAY

1-2-3-4	Fort Wayne
13-14-15-16	Quad City
18-19-20-21	Michigan
26-27-28-29	Wisconsin

JUNE

2-3-4-5	Peoria
6-7-8-9	Lansing
22-23-24-25	West Mich.
26-27-28-29	Clinton

JULY

4-5-6	West Mich.
17-18-19-20	Fort Wayne
21-22-23-24	Lansing
28-29-30-31	South Bend

AUGUST

| 10-11-12-13 | Michigan |

| 15-16-17-18 | Beloit |
| 28-29-30-31 | Burlington |

Fort Wayne

APRIL

10-11-12-13	Lansing
22-23-24-25	Dayton
27-28-29-30	West Mich.

MAY

9-10-11-12	Quad City
13-14-15-16	Cedar Rapids
22-23-24-25	Peoria
30-31	South Bend

JUNE

1	South Bend
2-3-4-5	Michigan
6-7-8-9	Wisconsin
24-25	Lansing

JULY

4-5-6	South Bend
7-8-9-10	Dayton
13-14	Lansing
21-22-23-24	Kane County
28-29-30-31	Michigan

AUGUST

10 11 12 13	West Mich.
15-16-17-18	Burlington
28-29-30-31	Beloit

SEPTEMBER

| 1-2-3-4 | Clinton |

Kane County

APRIL

6-7-8-9	Peoria
12-13	Wisconsin
22-23-24-25	Quad City
27-28	Wisconsin

MAY

5 6 7 8	Fort Wayne
13-14-15-16	Clinton
18-19-20-21	South Bend
26-27-28-29	Beloit
30-31	Burlington

JUNE

1	Burlington
15-16-17-18	Dayton
26-27	Quad City

JULY

4-5-6	Burlington
13-14-15-16	Michigan
17-18-19-20	Clinton
28-29	Quad City

AUGUST

1-2-3-4	Cedar Rapids
5-6-7-8	Beloit
19-20-21-22	West Mich.
24-25-26-27	Lansing
28-29-30-31	Wisconsin

Lansing

APRIL

6-7-8-9	Dayton
14-15-16	Michigan
18-19-20-21	West Mich.

MAY

1-2-3-4	Clinton
13-14-15-16	Beloit
18-19-20-21	Burlington
26-27-28-29	Fort Wayne

JUNE
2-3-4-5 ..... Kane County
15-16-17-18 . South Bend
22-23 .... Fort Wayne
26-27-28-29 .... Peoria
JULY
4-5-6 .... Michigan
15-16 .... Fort Wayne
17-18-19-20 . South Bend
28-29-30-31. West Mich.
AUGUST
10-11-12-13 .. Wisconsin
15-16-17-18 .. Quad City
28-29-30-31 Cedar Rap.
SEPTEMBER
1-2-3-4 .... Dayton

Michigan
APRIL
8-9 .... South Bend
10-11-12-13 .... Dayton
18-19-20-21 Fort Wayne
27-28-29-30 .... Beloit
MAY
1-2-3-4 ..... Kane County
13-14-15-16 .. Burlington
26-27-28-29 . West Mich.
30-31 .... Lansing
JUNE
1 .... Lansing
8-9 .... South Bend
10-11-12-13 .... Clinton
22-23-24-25 .... Peoria
30 .... Dayton
JULY
1-2-3 .... Dayton
9-10 .... West Michigan
21-22-23-24 .. Wisconsin
25-26-27 .... Lansing
AUGUST
1-2-3-4 .... South Bend
5-6-7-8 .... Fort Wayne
15-16 ... West Michigan
24-25-26-27 .. Quad City
SEPTEMBER
1-2-3-4 ...... Cedar Rapids

Peoria
APRIL
12-13 .... Beloit
18-19-20-21 .. Burlington
27-28-29-30 ..... Lansing
MAY
9-10-11-12 ...... Michigan
13-14-15-16 .. Wisconsin
26-27-28-29 .... Clinton
30-31 .... Cedar Rapids
JUNE
1 .... Cedar Rapids
6-7-8-9 ... West Michigan
10-11-12-13 .. Quad City
17-18 .... Beloit
30 .... Beloit

JULY
1-2-3 .... Beloit
7-8-9-10 ... Kane County
13-14-15-16 .. Burlington
25-26-27 . Cedar Rapids
AUGUST
1-2-3-4 .... Dayton
5-6-7-8 .... Wisconsin
12-13 .... Quad City
15-16-17-18 . South Bend
24-25-26-27 .. Fort Wayne
28-29 .... Quad City

Quad City
APRIL
14-15-16 .... Beloit
18-19-20-21 ... Wisconsin
27-28 .... Clinton
MAY
1-2-3-4 .... Peoria
5-6-7-8 .... Lansing
18-19-20-21. Cedar Rapids
22-23-24-25 ..... Michigan
JUNE
4-5 .... Clinton
6-7-8-9 ..... Kane County
15-16-17-18. West Mich.
28-29 .... Kane County
30 .... Fort Wayne
JULY
1-2-3 .... Fort Wayne
7-8-9-10 .... Wisconsin
13-14-15-16 .... Clinton
23-24 .... Burlington
25-26-27 .... Beloit
30-31 .... Kane County
AUGUST
5-8 .... Burlington
10-11 .... Peoria
19-20-21-22 ...... Dayton
30-31 .... Peoria
SEPTEMBER
1-2-3-4 .... South Bend

South Bend
APRIL
6-7 .... Michigan
10-11 ..... West Michigan
14-15-16 ......Fort Wayne
22-23-24-25 ...... Lansing
MAY
1-2-3-4 ..... Cedar Rapids
5-6-7-8 .... Peoria
15-16 ..... West Michigan
22-23-24-25 .. Wisconsin
26-27-28-29 .. Quad City
JUNE
6-7 .... Michigan
10-11-12-13 .... Dayton
22-23-24-25 .. Burlington
30 .... Clinton
JULY
1-2-3 .... Clinton
7-8-9-10 .... Lansing
21-22-23-24. West Mich.

25-26-27 ..... Fort Wayne
AUGUST
5-6-7-8 .... Dayton
10-11-12-13 .. Kane County
24-25-26-27 .... Beloit
28-29-30-31 .... Michigan

West Michigan
APRIL
6-7-8-9 ... West Michigan
12-13 .... South Bend
22-23-24-25 ... Michigan
MAY
1-2-3-4 .... Beloit
5-6-7-8 .... Clinton
13-14 .... South Bend
22-23-24-25 ..... Lansing
30-31 .... Dayton
JUNE
1 .... Dayton
2-3-4-5 .... Burlington
10-11-12-13 .. Kane County
22-23-24-25 .. Quad City
30 .... Cedar Rapids
JULY
1-2-3 .... Cedar Rapids
7-8 .... Michigan
13-14-15-16 .. South Bend
17-18-19-20 .... Peoria
25-26-27 .... Dayton
AUGUST
1-2-3-4 ...... Fort Wayne
5-6-7-8 .... Lansing
17-18 .... Michigan
24-25-26-27 .. Wisconsin

Wisconsin
APRIL
8-9 .... Beloit
10-11 .... Kane County
14-15-16 .... Clinton
22-23-24-25 .... Peoria
29-30 .... Kane County
MAY
1-2-3-4 .... Burlington
9-10-11-12 .... Lansing
18-19-20-21. West Mich.
JUNE
2-3-4-5 .... Cedar Rapids
12-13 .... Beloit
15-16-17-18 .... Michigan
26-27-28-29.. South Bend
30 .... Kane County
JULY
1-2-3 .... Kane County
13-14-15-16 .... Dayton
17-18-19-20 .. Burlington
25-26-27 .... Clinton
AUGUST
1-2-3-4 .... Quad City
15-16-17-18. Cedar Rapids
19-20-21-22.. Fort Wayne
SEPTEMBER
1-2-3-4 .... Peoria

South Atlantic League

Asheville
APRIL
6-7-8-9 .... Piedmont
10-11-12-13.. Hagerstown
18-19-20-21 ... Char., SC
MAY
1-2-3-4 .... Capital City
6-7-8 .... Hickory
18-19-20-21 .. Char., WV
26-27-28-29 .... Macon
30-31 .... Columbus

JUNE
1-2 .... Columbus
6-7-8-9 .... Augusta
26-27-28-29 . Cape Fear
30 .... Capital City
JULY
1-2 .... Capital City
7-8-9-10 ..... Capital City
13 .... Hickory
18-19-20-21 ... Delmarva
22-23-24-25 .... G'boro

31 .... Savannah
AUGUST
1-2-3 .... Savannah
4-5-6-7 .... Macon
15-16-17-18 .. Columbus
24-25-26-27 ... Char., SC

Augusta
APRIL
14-15-16-17 .. Savannah
22-23-24-25 .... Asheville

27-28-29-30 . Cape Fear

MAY
5-6-7-8 .... Char., WV
9-10-11-12 .... Columbus
17-18-19-20 .. Delmarva
22-23-24-25........ G'boro

JUNE
3-4-5 .... Capital City
15-16-17-18...... Macon
22-23-24-25 ... Piedmont
30................... Piedmont

JULY
1-2................ Piedmont
6 .... Capital City
7-8-9-10..........Macon
22-23-24-25 .. Savannah
31 .... Char., SC

AUGUST
1-2-3............. Char., SC
8-9-10-11 .... Columbus
15-16-17-18 . Hagerstown
19-20-21-22 .... Asheville

SEPTEMBER
1-2-3-4 .... Hickory

Cape Fear
APRIL
10-11-12-13 ... Delmarva
18-19-20-21 ...... Macon
22-23-24-25...... G'boro

MAY
5-6-7-8 ...... Hagerstown
13-14-15-16 .... Columbus
17-18-19-20 ...... Hickory
26-27-28-29 Capital City

JUNE
3-4-5 .... Char., WV
6-7................... Hickory
10-11-12-13 .... Asheville
22-23-24-25 ... Delmarva

JULY
3-4-5-6 .... Char., WV
7-8-9-10 ...... Savannah
18-19............... Hickory
26-27-28-29 ..... Augusta

AUGUST
4-5-6-7 ...... Hagerstown
8-9-10-11 ..... Char., SC
23-24-25-26..... G'boro
28-29-30-31 ... Piedmont

Capital City
APRIL
6-7-8-9 .... Char., SC
14-15-16-17 ..... Hickory
24-25............. Columbus
26-27-28-29 ... Piedmont

MAY
9-10-11-12 .... Savannah
18-19-20-21 . Greensboro
22-23-24-25 .... Asheville
30-31 .... Augusta

JUNE
1-2................... Augusta
10-11-12-13 ... Delmarva
26-27-28-29. Hagerstown

JULY
3-4-5................ Augusta
12-13............... Augusta
18-19-20-21 ... Char., SC
22-23-24-25 ...... Macon
28-29............ Columbus
31 .... Char., WV

AUGUST
1-2-3 .... Char., WV
12-13............... Augusta
15-16-17-18 . Cape Fear
28-29-30-31 .... Asheville

Charleston, SC
APRIL
10-11-12-13...... Augusta
14-15-16-17 .... Columbus
27-28-29-30 ..... Asheville

MAY
1-2-3-4 .... Hagerstown
9-10-11-12 .... Macon
22-23-24-25 . Cape Fear
30-31 .... Greensboro

JUNE
1-2 .... Greensboro
3-4 .... Savannah
6-7-8-9 ...... Capital City
15-16 .... Savannah
30 .... Macon

JULY
1-2 .... Macon
7-8-9-10 .... Delmarva
12-13............. Savannah
14-15-16-17 ...... Augusta
27-28-29-30 ...... Hickory

AUGUST
4-5-6-7 .... Piedmont
12-13............. Savannah
15-16-17-18 . Char., WV
19-20-21-22 Capital City
28-29-30-31 ... Columbus

Charleston, WV
APRIL
14-15-16-17 . Cape Fear
22-23-24-25........ Macon

MAY
1-2-3-4 .... Delmarva
9-10-11-12........ Hickory
13-14-15-16 Capital City
22-23-24-25 . Savannah
26-27-28-29 . Hagerstown

JUNE
6-7-8-9 .... Piedmont
10-11-12-13 ... Char., SC
22-23-24-25 ... Asheville
30 .... Hagerstown

JULY
1-2 .... Hagerstown
12-13............. Piedmont
14-15-16-17 . Greensboro
22-23-24-25 . Cape Fear

AUGUST
4-5-6-7 .... Hickory
8-9-10-11 ...... Delmarva
12-13............. Piedmont
24-25-26-27 ... Columbus
28-29-30-31 ...... Augusta

Columbus
APRIL
6-7-8-9 .... Char., WV
10-11-12-13 Capital City
18-19-20-21 ...... Augusta
22-22 .... Capital City

MAY
1-2 .... Macon
5-6-7-8 .... Savannah
17-18-19-20 . Hagerstown
22-23-24-25 ... Piedmont
26-27-28-29... Char., SC

JUNE
3-4 ....Macon
10-11-12-13..... Hickory
26-27-28-29 ..... Augusta
30 .... Savannah

JULY
1-1................. Savannah
12-13 .... Macon

14-15-16-17 . Cape Fear
22-23-24-25... Char., SC
26-27 .... Capital City

AUGUST
4-5-6-7 ...... Greensboro
12-13 .... Macon
19-20-21-22 .. Delmarva

SEPTEMBER
1-2-3-4 .... Asheville

Delmarva
APRIL
14-15-16-17 ... Piedmont
18-19......... Greensboro
22-23-24-25... Char., SC
26-27-28-29 ... Columbus

MAY
5-6-7-8 ...... Greensboro
9-10-11-12.... Cape Fear
22-23-24-25...... Macon
30-31 .... Char., WV

JUNE
1-2 .... Char., WV
6-7-8-9 ...... Hagerstown
15-16-17-18 ....Asheville
26-27-28-29.. Char., WV
30 ....Cape Fear

JULY
1-2 ....Cape Fear
12-13.......... Hagerstown
14-15-16-17 ...... Hickory
22-23-24-25 ... Piedmont
26-27 .... Greensboro

AUGUST
4-5-6-7 .... Capital City
12-13.......... Hagerstown
24-25-26-27 ..... Augusta
28-29-30-31 . Savannah

Greensboro
APRIL
6-7-8-9 .... Cape Fear
10-11 .... Hickory
20-21 .... Delmarva
27-28-29-30 .. Char., WV

MAY
1-2 .... Hickory
9-10-11-12 .... Asheville
13-14-15-16 . Hagerstown
26-27-28-29 ... Piedmont

JUNE
6-7-8-9 .... Macon
15-16-17-18 .. Columbus
26-27-28-29... Char., SC
30 .... Hickory

JULY
1-2 .... Hickory
12-13........... Cape Fear
18-19-20-21 ..... Augusta
28-29 .... Delmarva
31 .... Piedmont

AUGUST
1-2-3 .... Piedmont
8-9-10-11 ... Capital City
12-13........... Cape Fear
15-16-17-18 .. Savannah
28-29-30-31 . Hagerstown

SEPTEMBER
1-2-3-4 .... Char., WV

Hagerstown
APRIL
14-15-16-17 . Greensboro
18-19-20-21 .. Char., WV
26-27-28-29 .. Savannah

MAY
9-10-11-12 .... Piedmont
22-23-24-25 ...... Hickory
30-31 .... Cape Fear

JUNE
1-2.................. Cape Fear
3-4-5 .... Delmarva
10-11-12-13 ..... Augusta
15-16-17-18 Capital City
22-23-24-25... Char., SC

JULY
3-4-5-6 .... Greensboro
7-8-9-10 .... Columbus
14-15-16-17 .... Asheville
27-28-29-30 .. Char., WV
31.................. Delmarva

AUGUST
1-2-3 .... Delmarva
8-9-10-11 .... Hickory
24-25-26-27....... Macon

SEPTEMBER
1-2-3-4 .... Cape Fear

Hickory

APRIL
6-7-8-9 .... Augusta
12-13......... Greensboro
20-21............. Piedmont
22-23-24-25 .. Savannah

MAY
3-4 .... Greensboro
5...................... Asheville
13-14-15-16... Char., SC
26-27-28-29 ... Delmarva
30-31............. Piedmont

JUNE
3-4-5 .... Asheville
8-9............... Cape Fear
15-16-17-18.. Char., WV
22-23-24-25 Capital City
28.................. Piedmont

JULY
3-4-5-6 .... Delmarva
7-8-9-10 .... Char., WV
12................... Asheville
20-21 .... Cape Fear
22-23-24-25 . Hagerstown
31 .... Columbus

AUGUST
1-2-3 .... Columbus
12-13 .... Asheville
15-16-18 .... Piedmont
19-20-21-22....... G'boro
28-29-30-31 .... Macon

Macon

APRIL
6-7-8-9 .... Hagerstown
14-15-16-17 .... Asheville
27-28-29-30 ...... Hickory

MAY
3-4-4 .... Columbus
5-6-7-8 .... Capital City
13-14-15-16 .... Augusta
17-18-19-20.. Char., SC
30-31 .... Savannah

JUNE
1-2.................. Savannah
10-11-12-13 ... Peidmont
22-23-24-25 .. Greensboro
26-27-28-29 .. Savannah

JULY
3-4-5-6 .... Asheville
14-15-16-17. Capital City
18-19-20-21 .. Columbus
31 .... Cape Fear

AUGUST
1-2-3.............. Cape Fear
15-16-17-18 ... Delmarva
19-20-21-22 .. Char., WV

SEPTEMBER
1-2-3-4 .... Char., SC

Piedmont

APRIL
10-11-12-13 .. Char., WV
18-19................. Hickory
22-23-24-25 . Hagerstown

MAY
1-2-3-4 .... Augusta
5-6-7-8 .... Char., SC
13-14-15-16 ... Delmarva

18-19-20-21 .. Savannah
JUNE
1-2.................... Hickory
3-4-5........... Greensboro
15-16-17-18 .. Cape Fear
26-27-29........... Hickory

JULY
3-4-5-6 .... Columbus
7-8-9-10 ..... Greensboro
18-19-20-21 . Hagerstown
27-28-29-30 .... Asheville

AUGUST
8-9-10-11........... Macon
17 .... Hickory
19-20-21-22 . Cape Fear
23-24-25-26 Capital City

SEPTEMBER
1-2-3-4 .... Delmarva

Savannah

APRIL
6-7-8-9 .... Delmarva
10-11-12-13....... Macon
18-19-20-21 Capital City

MAY
1-2-3-4 .... Cape Fear
13-14-15-16 ... Asheville
26-27-28-29 ..... Augusta

JUNE
5 .... Char., SC
6-7-8-9 .... Columbus
10-11-12-13 ....
Greensboro
17-18 .... Char., SC
22-23-24-25 .. Columbus

JULY
3-4-5-6........... Char., SC
14-15-16-17 ... Piedmont
18-19-20-21 .. Char., WV
26-27-28-29........Macon

AUGUST
4-5-6-7 .... Augusta
8-9-10-11 .... Asheville
19-20-21-22 . Hagerstown

SHORTSEASON

CLASS A

New York-Penn League

Auburn

JUNE
22-23 .... Williamsport
28-29...... Hudson Valley
30...................... Vermont

JULY
1 .... Vermont
6-7-8-9 .... Jamestown
13-14 ...... New Jersey
19-20 ...... Staten Island
21 .... Oneonta
23 .... Utica
25 .... Batavia
29-30 .... Mah. Valley
31 .... Williamsport

AUGUST
1 .... WIlliamsport
3 .... Oneonta
7.......................... Utica
9-10 .... Mah. Valley
11-12.................... Lowell
15........................ Utica
17 .... Batavia
19-20 .... Oneonta
21-22 .... Pittsfield
29-30 .... Batavia

SEPTEMBER
1 .... Utica
3-4 .... Brooklyn

Batavia

JUNE
20-21 .... Mah. Valley
22-23 .... New Jersey

JULY
4...................... Jamestown
6-7-8-9............. Oneonta
12 .... Jamestown
17-18............... Brooklyn
19-20 .... Pittsfield
26....................... Auburn
29-30 .... Vermont

AUGUST
2-3 .... Hudson Valley
4-5 .... Mah. Valley
9-10-11-12 .... Utica
18........................ Auburn
19-20 .... Williamsport
21-22.................. Lowell
25-26 .... Jamestown
28-31 .... Auburn

SEPTEMBER
1-2 .... Williamsport
5-6............. Staten Island

Brooklyn

JUNE
21-23...Hudson Valley
24-25............... Batavia
26-27 .... Auburn
30............. Staten Island

JULY
2 .... Staten Island
8-9........................ Utica
11-12 .... Mah. Valley
15-16...........Williamsport
21-22............. Jamestown
23-25 .... Hudson Valley
31........................ Lowell

AUGUST
1-2-3 .... Lowell
6.................. Staten Island
11-12-13-14 ...... Vermont
16 .... Staten Island
17 .... New Jersey
21-23........... New Jersey
25-26-27-28...... Pittsfield
30-31 .... Oneonta

SEPTEMBER
1 .... New Jersey

Hudson Valley

JUNE
20-22............. Brooklyn
24............ Staten Island
26-27 ... Williamsport
30.......................... Utica

JULY
1 .... Utica
2-3 .... Mah. Valley
4-5 .... Lowell
15-16 .... Auburn
17 .... Staten Island
19-20 .... Vermont
24-26 .... Brooklyn
27-29........... New Jersey
31 .... Batavia

AUGUST
1 .... Batavia
6-7................... Oneonta
9-10-11-12 ...... Pittsfield
17-18................. Lowell
19-20........Jamestown
22 .... Staten Island
23-24 .... Vermont
26 .... Staten Island
27 .... New Jersey
31 .... New Jersey

Jamestown

JUNE
20-21 .... Auburn
28-29........ Staten Island
30 .... Oneonta

JULY
1 .... Oneonta
2-3 .... Vermont
5-11 .... Batavia
13-14.................. Lowell
17-18 ...... New Jersey
19-20 .... Brooklyn
23-24 .... Mah. Valley
25-26-27-28 .... Utica

AUGUST
4-5 .... Auburn
8-9 .... Williamsport
11-12 .... Oneonta
13-14..... Hudson Valley
30-31 .... Pittsfield

SEPTEMBER
1-2 .... Mah. Valley
3-4 .... Batavia
5-6 .... Williamsport

Lowell

JUNE
20-21-22-23..... Pittsfield
24-25........... Jamestown

JULY
2-3 .... New Jersey
6-7-8-9 ... Hudson Valley
17-18 .... Auburn
19-20 .... New Jersey
27-28 .... Mah. Valley
29-30...................... Utica

AUGUST
4-5 .... Staten Island
6-7-8-9 .... Vermont
19-20 .... Brooklyn
23-24 .... Batavia
25-26 .... Williamsport
27-28 .... Staten Island

SEPTEMBER
3-4 .... Oneonta
5-6............. Brooklyn

Mahoning Valley

JUNE
22-23-24-25 ...... Utica
26-27 .... Staten Island

JULY
4-5 .... Brooklyn
6-7-8-9 ... Williamsport
17-18-19-20..... Oneonta
21-22 .... Pittsfield
31 .... Jamestown

AUGUST
1-2-3 .... Jamestown
6-7 .... Batavia
11-12 .... New Jersey
13-14................. Batavia
15-16.................. Lowell
23-24-25-26 .... Auburn
27-28 .... Vermont

SEPTEMBER
5-6.......... Hudson Valley

New Jersey

JUNE
26-27-28-29 ...... Lowell
30 .... Mah. Valley

JULY
1 .... Mah. Valley
4-5........................ Utica
6-7-8-9 .... Pittsfield
15-16........... Jamestown
21-22............. Batavia
23-24 .... Williamsport
28-30...... Hudson Valley
31 .... Oneonta

AUGUST
1 .... Oneonta
10-14........ Staten Island
15-16 .... Vermont
18.................... Brooklyn
19................. Staten Island
22-24 .... Brooklyn
25-26 .... Vermont
28-30...... Hudson Valley

SEPTEMBER
2 .... Brooklyn
4 .... Staten Island
5-6 .... Auburn

Oneonta

JUNE
20-21 .... Williamsport

22-23........... Jamestown
28-29.......... Mah. Valley
JULY
2-3.................... Batavia
4-5................... Vermont
11-12.......... New Jersey
15-16................ Lowell
22...................... Auburn
23-24............... Pittsfield
25-26.......... Mah. Valley
27-28................ Auburn
AUGUST
2......................... Auburn
4-5.......... Hudson Valley
9-10.............. Brooklyn
13........................ Utica
15-16................ Batavia
21-22...... Williamsport
23-24........... Jamestown
26-28.................. Utica
SEPTEMBER
1-2............ Staten Island
6............................ Utica

Pittsfield
JUNE
24-25................ Oneonta
26-27................. Batavia
30........................ Lowell
JULY
1......................... Lowell
2-3........................ Utica
4-5.......... Staten Island
13-14........ Mah. Valley
15-16-17-18..... Vermont
25-26................. Lowell
27-28-29-30.... Brooklyn
AUGUST
4-5-6-7....... New Jersey
13-14................ Auburn
15-16........... Jamestown
17-18........ Staten Island
23-24........ Williamsport
SEPTEMBER
1-2-3-4 ... Hudson Valley

Staten Island
JUNE
20-21-22-23..... Vermont

25........... Hudson Valley
JULY
1-3................. Brooklyn
11-12.................. Auburn
13-14................ Oneonta
15-16.......... Mah. Valley
18............ Hudson Valley
21-22-23-24........ Lowell
27-28.................. Batavia
29-30............ Jamestown
31...................... Pittsfield
AUGUST
1-2-3................. Pittsfield
7...................... Brooklyn
9................... New Jersey
11-12...... Williamsport
13.................. New Jersey
15.................... Brooklyn
20.................. New Jersey
21............ Hudson Valley
23-24.................. Utica
25........... Hudson Valley
SEPTEMBER
3.................. New Jersey

Utica
JUNE
20-21.......... New Jersey
26-27........... Jamestown
28-29............. Pittsfield
JULY
6-7................. Brooklyn
11-12................. Lowell
13-14-15-16...... Batavia
21-22...... Hudson Valley
24...................... Auburn
31...................... Vermont
AUGUST
1...................... Vermont
2-3-4-5....... Williamsport
6...................... Auburn
14.................... Oneonta
16..................... Auburn
17-18-19-20 Mah. Valley
21-22........... Jamestown
25-27............... Oneonta
30-31........ Staten Island
SEPTEMBER
2.......................... Auburn

5...................... Oneonta

Vermont
JUNE
24-25................ Auburn
26-27................ Oneonta
28-29.............. Brooklyn
JULY
6-7-8-9..... Staten Island
11-12-13-14 Hud. Valley
21-22.......... Williamsport
23-24................ Batavia
25-26.......... New Jersey
AUGUST
2-3............... New Jersey
4-5................... Brooklyn
17-18........... Jamestown
19-20................ Pittsfield
21-22.......... Mah. Valley
30-31.................. Lowell
SEPTEMBER
1-2...................... Lowell
3-4........................ Utica
5-6.................... Pittsfield

Williamsport
JUNE
24-25.......... New Jersey
28-29-30......... Batavia
JULY
1......................... Batavia
2-3-4-5............. Auburn
11-12................ Pittsfield
13-14.............. Brooklyn
17-18-19-20........ Utica
25-26........ Staten Island
27-28................ Vermont
29-30.............. Oneonta
AUGUST
6-7................ Jamestown
13-14.................. Lowell
15-16...... Hudson Valley
17-18................ Oneonta
27-28............. Jamestown
30-31.......... Mah. Valley
SEPTEMBER
3-4 .... Mah. Valley

Northwest League

Boise
JUNE
20-21 .... Portland
25-26-27-28-29 ... Salem
JULY
3-4-5 .... Yakima
12-13-14 .... Portland
26-27-28-29-30. Eugene
AUGUST
3-4-5 .... Spokane
9-10-11 .... Yakima
12-13-14-15-16 ..... Van.
29-30-31 .... Spokane
SEPTEMBER
1-2-3-4-5-6 .... Everett

Eugene
JUNE
25-26-27-28-29 .. Yakima
JULY
3-4-5 .... Vancouver
12-13-14-15-16 .. Spokane
20-21-22-23-24 .. Everett
31 .... Portland
AUGUST
1-2 .... Portland

3-4-5 .... Vancouver
9-10-11 .... Salem
18-19-20-21-22 .... Boise
26-27-28 .... Salem
SEPTEMBER
4-5-6 .... Portland

Everett
JUNE
25-26-27-28-29 Portland
JULY
3-4-5 .... Spokane
12-13-14-15-16 ..... Salem
17-18-19 .... Yakima
26-27-28-29-30 ...... Van.
AUGUST
3-4-5 .... Yakima
9-10-11 .... Spokane
12-13-14-15-16. Eugene
23-24-25-26-27-28 .. Boise

Portland
JUNE
22-23-24 .... Boise
JULY
3-4-5 .... Salem
6-7-8-9-10 .... Everett

15-16 .... Boise
17-18-19 .... Eugene
26-27-28-29-30 .. Spokane
AUGUST
3-4-5 .... Salem
9-10-11 .... Vancouver
12-13-14-15-16 ... Yakima
23-24-25 .... Eugene
29-30-31 .... Vancouver

Salem
JUNE
20-21-22-23-24 .. Everett
30 .... Eugene
JULY
1-2 .... Eugene
6-7-8-9-10 .... Boise
17-18-19 .... Vancouver
26-27-28-29-30 .. Yakima
AUGUST
6-7-8 .... Portland
12-13-14-15-16 .. Spokane
23-24-25 .... Vancouver
29-30-31 .... Eugene
SEPTEMBER
1-2-3 .... Portland

Spokane

JUNE
20-21-22-23-24.. Eugene
30......................... Boise

JULY
1-2 .... Boise
6-7-8-9-10 .... Vancouver
17-18-19.............. Boise
20-21-22-23-24.... Salem
31 .... Everett

AUGUST
1-2 .... Everett
6-7-8 .... Everett
18-19-20-21-22 Portland
23-24-25 .... Yakima

SEPTEMBER
1-2-3 .... Yakima

Vancouver

JUNE
25-26-27-28-29.. Spokane
30.................... Portland

JULY
1-2 .... Portland
12-13-14-15-16.. Yakima
20-21-22-23-24 .... Boise
31 .... Salem

AUGUST
1-2 .... Salem
6-7-8 .... Boise
18-19-20-21-22.. Everett
26-27-28 .... Portland

SEPTEMBER
1-2-3 .... Eugene
4-5-6 .... Salem

Yakima

JUNE
20-21-22-23-24 ...... Van.
30................... Everett

JULY
1-2 .... Everett
6-7-8-9-10 .... Eugene
20-21-22-23-24 Portland
31 .... Boise

AUGUST
1-2 .... Boise
6-7-8 .... Boise
18-19-20-21-22 ... Salem
26-27-28 .... Spokane
29-30-31 .... Everett

SEPTEMBER
4-5-6 .... Spokane

ROOKIE LEAGUES

Appalachian League

Bluefield

JUNE
24 .... Martinsville
25-26 .... Pulaski

JULY
2-3-4 .... Elizabethton
6 .... Pulaski
10-12............. Princeton
14-15-16... Johnson City
17-18-19.......... Burlington
26-27-28.............. Bristol
29-30-31...... Martinsville

AUGUST
5-6-7 .... Princeton
15-16-17 ...... Kingsport
21-22-23 .... Danville
25-26 .... Pulaski
31 .... Danville

SEPTEMBER
1 .... Danville

Bristol

JUNE
24.................... Kingsport
27-28 .... Elizabethton
29-30 .... Johnson City

JULY
5-6-7 .... Martinsville
8-9-10 .... Burlington
20-21-22.......... Bluefield
23-24-25 .... Danville
30-31 .... Kingsport

AUGUST
5 .... Kingsport
8-9-10 .... Elizabethton
11 .... Johnson City
15-16-17 ...... Princeton
18-19-20 .... Pulaski
27-28 .... Johnson City
31 .... Kingsport

SEPTEMBER
1 .... Kingsport

Burlington

JUNE
23 .... Pulaski
27-28 .... Martinsville
29-30 .... Elizabethton

JULY
1 .... Elizabethton
2-3-4 .... Princeton
12-13 .... Danville
14-15-16............. Bristol
23-24-25...... Martinsville
26-27-28 .... Pulaski

AUGUST
5-6-7.................. Danville
8-9-10 .... Bluefield
21-22-23.. Johnson City
24-25-26 .... Kingsport
29-30 .... Princeton

Danville

JUNE
24.................... Princeton
27-28 .... Bluefield
29-30 .... Pulaski

JULY
1 .... Pulaski
2-3-4 .... Bristol
14-15-16..... Martinsville
20-21-22 .... Kingsport
29-30-31 .... Elizabethton

AUGUST
2-3-4 .... Princeton
11-12-13 .... Bluefield
18-19-20 .... Burlington
24-25-26... Johnson City
27-28 .... Burlington
29-30 .... Martinsville

Elizabethton

JUNE
23 .... Johnson City
25-26 .... Kingsport

JULY
5-6-7 .... Princeton
8-9-10 .... Danville
14-15-16 ...... Kingsport
17-18-19............. Bristol
26-27-28... Johnson City

AUGUST
2-3-4 .... Bluefield
5-6-7 .... Pulaski
15-16-17 ...... Burlington
18-19-20..... Martinsville
29-30 .... Bristol
31 .... Johnson City

SEPTEMBER
1 .... Johnson City

Johnson City

JUNE
24 .... Elizabethton
25-26 .... Bristol

JULY
1 .... Bristol
5-6-7 .... Danville
8-9-10.......... Martinsville
12-13 .... Elizabethton
20-21-22.... Elizabethton
23-24-25 .... Princeton

Kingsport

JUNE
23 .... Bristol
27-28 .... Johnson City

JULY
5-6-7 .... Burlington
8-9-10 .... Pulaski
12-13 .... Bristol
17-18-19 .... Johnson City
23-24-25 .... Bluefield
29-30-31 .... Danville
29 .... Bristol

AUGUST
6-7 .... Bristol
8-9-10 .... Martinsville
11-12-13 ...... Elizabethton
18-19-20 ...... Princeton
27-28 .... Elizabethton

Martinsville

JUNE
23 .... Bluefield
25-26 .... Danville
29-30 .... Bluefield

JULY
1 .... Bluefield
2-3-4 .... Kingsport
12-13 .... Pulaski
17-18-19 .... Pulaski
20-21-22 .... Princeton

AUGUST
2-3-4 .... Burlington
5-6-7........ Johnson City
15-16-17....... Danville
21-22-23.... Elizabethton
24-25-26............ Bristol
31 ....Burlington

SEPTEMBER
1 .... Burlington

Princeton

JUNE
23 .... Danville
25-26 .... Burlington
29-30.............. Kingsport

JULY
1 .... Kingsport
8-9-13.............. Bluefield
17-18-19........... Danville

29-30-31 .... Burlington

AUGUST
2-3-4 .... Kingsport
12-13 .... Bristol
15-16-17 .... Pulaski
19-19-20......... Bluefield
29-30 .... Kingsport

26-27-28...... Martinsville
29-30-31 .... Pulaski

AUGUST

8-9-10....... Johnson City
11-12-13......... Burlington
21-22-23............ Bristol
24-25-26 ...... Elizabethton
27-28 .... Bluefield
31 .... Pulaski

SEPTEMBER

1 .... Pulaski

Pulaski

JUNE

24................... Burlington
27-28............. Princeton

JULY

2-3-4......... Johnson City
5-7 .... Bluefield
14-15-16 .... Princeton
20-21-22 ...... Burlington
23-24-25.... Elizabethton

AUGUST

2-3-4.................... Bristol
8-9-10.............. Danville
11-12-13...... Martinsville
21-22-23....... Kingsport
24 .... Bluefield
27-28......... Martinsville
29-30.............. Bluefield

Pioneer League

Billings

JUNE

16-17-18-19. Idaho Falls
20-21-22.... Great Falls
29-30 .... Butte

JULY

4-5-6-7.............. Ogden
8-9-10............ Missoula
15-16 .... Butte
26-27-28 .... Helena
30-31 .... Idaho Falls

AUGUST

1-8-9............ Idaho Falls
10-11................. Butte
12-13-14 .. Medicine Hat
24-25 .... Ogden
28-29-30 .... Butte

SEPTEMBER

2-3 .... Ogden

Butte

JUNE

16-17-18-19....... Ogden
20-21-22 .. Medicine Hat

JULY

1-2-3 .... Billings
6-7 .... Idaho Falls
12-13-14 .... Helena
17-18 .... Billings
19-20-21 .... Ogden
22-23 .... Idaho Falls
27-28-29 ...... Great Falls

AUGUST

2-3 .... Billings
4-5-6-7...... Idaho Falls
18-19-20 .... Missoula
22-23 .... Billings
26-27 .... Ogden

Great Falls

JUNE

16-17.............. Missoula
18-19 .... Helena
27-28-29 .... Missoula

JULY

2-3 .... Helena
4-5........... Medicine Hat
8-9-10 .... Butte
12-13-14 ...... Idaho Falls
21-22-23 .. Medicine Hat

AUGUST

2-3 .... Helena
8-9................. Missoula
10-11 ..... Medicine Hat
15-16-17 .... Ogden
18-19-20 .... Billings
22-23.............. Missoula
26-27....... Medicine Hat

SEPTEMBER

2-3 .... Helena

Helena

JUNE

16-17....... Medicine Hat
20-21-22 .... Ogden
23-24-25 .... Billings
27-28-29 .. Medicine Hat

JULY

6-7 .... Missoula
15-16 .... Great Falls
21-22-23 .... Missoula
24-25 .... Great Falls

AUGUST

4-5 .... Great Falls
6-7 .... Missoula
12-13-14 .... Butte
15-16-17...... Idaho Falls
22-23-24-25.... Med. Hat
26-27.............. Missoula
31 .... Great Falls

SEPTEMBER

1 ....Great Falls

Idaho Falls

JUNE

23-24-25 .. Medicine Hat
27-28 .... Billings

JULY

1-2-3 ....Ogden
4-5 .... Butte
8-9-10 .... Helena
17-18 .... Ogden
19-20-21 .... Billings
24-25 .... Butte
26-27-28 .... Missoula

AUGUST

2-3-10-11 .... Ogden
12-13-14...... Great Falls
24-25 .... Butte
26-27-31 .... Billings

SEPTEMBER

1....................... Billings
2-3 .... Butte

Medicine Hat

JUNE

18-19.............. Missoula
30...................... Helena

JULY

1...................... Helena
2-3.................. Missoula
6-7 .... Great Falls
8-9-10................ Ogden
12-13-14 .... Billings
17-18 .... Helena
19-20 .... Great Falls

30-31 .... Helena

AUGUST

1...................... Helena
2-3............... Missoula
6-7 .... Great Falls
8-9 .... Helena
15-16-17 .... Butte
18-19-20 ...... Idaho Falls
28-29-30 ...... Great Falls
31 .... Missoula

SEPTEMBER

1 ....Missoula

Missoula

JUNE

20-21-22...... Idaho Falls
23-24-25 .... Butte
30 .... Great Falls

JULY

1 .... Great Falls
4-5 .... Helena
15-16........ Medicine Hat
17-18 .... Great Falls
19-20 .... Helena
24-25........ Medicine Hat
30-31 .... Great Falls

AUGUST

1 .... Great Falls
4-5 .... Medicine Hat
10-11................. Helena
12-13-14........... Ogden
15-16-17 .... Billings
24-25 .... Great Falls
28-29-30 .... Helena

SEPTEMBER

2-3............ Medicine Hat

Ogden

JUNE

23-24-25 ..... Great Falls
27-28 .... Butte
29-30 .... Idaho Falls

JULY

12-13-14 ...... Missoula
15-16 .... Idaho Falls
22-23-24-25 .... Billings
26-27-28 .. Medicine Hat
30-31 ....Butte

AUGUST

1........................ Butte
4-5-6-7 .... Billings
8-9 .... Butte
18-19-20 .... Helena
22-23 .... Idaho Falls
28-29-30 ...... Idaho Falls
31............................ Butte

SEPTEMBER

1...........................Butte

INDEPENDENT LEAGUES

1999 STANDINGS

ATLANTIC LEAGUE

	W	L	PCT	GB		W	L	PCT	GB
*Bridgeport	78	42	.650	—	Newark	55	64	.462	22½
Atlantic City	61	58	.513	16½	Lehigh Valley	52	67	.437	25½
*Somerset	60	60	.500	18	Nashua	52	67	.437	25½

PLAYOFFS: Finals (best-of-5)—Bridgeport def. Somerset 3-0.

FRONTIER LEAGUE

EAST	W	L	PCT	GB	WEST	W	L	PCT	GB
London	54	30	.643	—	Evansville	43	41	.512	—
Chillicothe	45	38	.542	8½	Dubois County	42	42	.500	1
Johnstown	43	41	.512	11	Cook County	41	43	.488	2
Richmond	40	43	.482	13½	Springfield	39	45	.464	4
Canton	33	51	.393	21	River City	39	45	.464	4

PLAYOFFS: Semifinals (best-of-3)—London def. Johnstown 2-0 and Chillicothe def. Evansville 2-1. **Finals** (best-of-3)—London def. Chillicothe 2-0.

NORTHERN LEAGUE

CENTRAL DIVISION

EAST	W	L	PCT	GB	WEST	W	L	PCT	GB
**Schaumburg	44	42	.512	—	*Sioux City	51	34	.600	—
St. Paul	38	47	.447	5½	Fargo-Moorhead	50	35	.588	1
Madison	37	47	.440	6	*Winnipeg	48	38	.558	3½
Duluth-Superior	35	49	.417	8	Sioux Falls	37	48	.435	14

PLAYOFFS: First Round (best-of-5)—Winnipeg def. Sioux City 3-0 and Fargo-Moorhead def. Schaumburg 3-0. **Semifinals** (best-of-5)—Winnipeg def. Fargo-Moorhead 3-0. **Finals** (best-of-5)—Albany-Colonie def. Winnipeg 3-1.

EASTERN DIVISION

NORTH	W	L	PCT	GB	SOUTH	W	L	PCT	GB
*Albany-Colonie	45	41	.523	—	*Allentown	47	39	.547	—
*Adirondack	43	43	.500	2	*New Jersey	45	40	.529	1½
Quebec	43	43	.500	2	Elmira	43	42	.506	3½
Massachusetts	41	45	.477	4	Waterbury	36	50	.419	11

PLAYOFFS: First Round (best-of-5)—New Jersey def. Allentown 3-0 and Albany-Colonie def. Adirondack 3-2. **Semifinals** (best-of-5)—Albany-Colonie def. New Jersey 3-1. **Finals** (best-of-5)—Albany-Colonie def. Winnipeg 3-1.

TEXAS-LOUISIANA LEAGUE

	W	L	PCT	GB		W	L	PCT	GB
Amarillo	63	21	.750	—	Ozark Mountain	32	50	.390	30
Alexandria	48	36	.571	15	Bayou	32	51	.386	30½
Abilene	46	38	.548	17	Greenville	26	58	.310	37
Rio Grande Valley	45	38	.542	17½					

PLAYOFFS: Semifinals (best-of-3)—Amarillo def. Rio Grande Valley 2-1 and Alexandria def. Abilene 2-1. **Finals** (best-of-5)—Amarillo def. Alexandria 3-0.

WESTERN LEAGUE

	W	L	PCT	GB		W	L	PCT	GB
Chico	63	27	.700	—	Reno	41	49	.456	22
Tri-City	48	42	.533	15	Zion	41	49	.456	22
Sonoma County	41	49	.456	22	Sacramento	36	54	.400	27

PLAYOFFS: Semifinals (best-of-5)—Chico def. Reno 3-2 and Tri-City def. Sonoma County 3-0. **Finals** (best-of-5)—Tri-City def. Chico 3-1.

*Split-season champion

ATLANTIC LEAGUE

Mailing Address: 31 Turner Lane, West Chester, PA 19380. **Telephone**: (610) 696-8662. **FAX**: (610) 696-8667. **E-Mail Address**: atllge@aol.com. **Website**: www.atlanticleague.com.

Year Founded: 1998.
Chief Executive Officer: Frank Boulton.
Executive Director: Joe Klein. Assistant to Executive Director: Ben Fonseca.
Vice Presidents: Rick Cerone, Mickey Herbert.
2000 Opening Date: April 28. Closing Date: Sept. 25.
Regular Season: 140 games (split schedule).
Division Structure: North—Bridgeport, Lehigh Valley, Long Island, Nashua. South—Atlantic City, Maryland, Newark, Somerset.
Playoff Format: First-half division winners meet second-half winners in best-of-3 series. Winners meet in best-of-5 final for league championship.
All-Star Game: July 12 at Somerset.
Roster Limit: 25. Eligibility Rule: No restrictions.
Brand of Baseball: Rawlings.
Statistician: Howe Sportsdata, Boston Fish Pier, West Bldg. #1, Suite 302, Boston, MA 02210.

ATLANTIC CITY
Surf

Office Address: 545 N Albany Ave., Atlantic City, NJ 08401. **Telephone**: (609) 344-8873. **FAX**: (609) 344-7010. **E-Mail Address**: surf@acsurf.com. **Website**: www.acsurf.com.
Operated by: Atlantic City Surf Professional Baseball Club, Inc.
Principal Owners: Frank Boulton, Tony Rosenthal.
President/General Manager: Ken Shepard. Assistant General Manager: Mario Perrucci. Director, Stadium Operations: Todd Garrison. Director, Media Relations/Broadcasting: Cheri Bungard. Director, Ticket Sales: Brian Beck. Director, Group Sales: John Kiphorn. Director, Merchandising: Scott Eafrati. Director, Promotions: Joe Harrington. Director, Sales/Special Projects: Jeff Kleeman. Clubhouse Operations: Tom Whaley. Office Manager: Patty MacLuckie.
Manager: Bobby Helms. Coach: Unavailable.

Game Information
Radio Announcer: Chuck Betson. No. of Games Broadcast: Unavailable. Flagship Station: Unavailable.
PA Announcer: Kevin Casey. Official Scorer: Unavailable.
Stadium Name (year opened): The Sandcastle (1998). Location: Atlantic City Expressway to exit 2, east on Routes 40/322. Standard Game Times: 7:05 p.m.; Sun. (April-June) 2:05, (July-Sept.) 4:05.
Visiting Club Hotel: Comfort Inn North, 539 Absecon Blvd., Absecon, N.J. 08201. Telephone: (609) 641-7272.

BRIDGEPORT
Bluefish

Office Address: 500 Main St., Bridgeport, CT 06604. **Telephone**: (203) 345-4800. **FAX**: (203) 345-4830. **E-Mail Address**: sschoenfeld@bridgeportbluefish.com **Website**: www.bridgeportbluefish.com.
Operated by: Bridgeport Bluefish Professional Baseball Club, LLC.
Principal Owner: Mickey Herbert.
General Manager: Charlie Dowd. Assistant General Manager: John Brandt. Director, Public/Media Relations: Steve Schoenfeld. Advertising Sales Account Executive: John Harris. Office Manager: Diane Coniglio. Director, Concessions: Rick DelVecchio. Director, Promotions: Rachael DiLauro. Director, Community Relations: John Farrell. Director, Ticketing: Bill Renick. Controller: Tony Scott. Director, Merchandising: Jay Zammiello. Director, Group Sales: Doug LeBlanc. Assistant Director, Group Sales: Jessica Sousa. Head Groundskeeper: Rick Capecelatro.
Manager: Willie Upshaw. Coaches: Mel Wearing, Dave Osteen. Trainer: Unavailable.

Game Information

Radio Announcer: Jeff Holtz. **No. of Games Broadcast:** 20. **Flagship Station:** WICC 600-AM.

PA Announcer: Bill Jensen. **Official Scorer:** Unavailable.

Stadium Name (year opened): The Ballpark at Harbor Yard (1998). **Location:** I-95 to exit 27, Route 8 to exit 1. **Standard Game Times:** 7:05 p.m., (April-May, Sept.) 6:35; Sun. 1:05.

Visiting Club Hotel: Holiday Inn Bridgeport, 1070 Main St., Bridgeport, CT 06604. Telephone: (203) 334-1234.

LEHIGH VALLEY
Black Diamonds

(Information for 2000 is tentative)

Office Address: 800 Cedarville Rd., Easton, PA 18042. **Mailing Address:** P.O. Box 4000, Easton, PA 18043. **Telephone:** (610) 250-2273. **FAX:** (610) 250-6552.

Operated by: Lehigh Valley Professional Sports Clubs, Inc.

Principal Owner: Tom Flaherty. **Chief Executive Officer:** Dilip Petigara. **Manager:** Unavailable. **Pitching Coach:** Unavailable.

Game Information

Radio: Unavailable.

Stadium Name: Lehigh Valley Multi-Purpose Sport Complex. **Standard Game Times:** 7:05 p.m., Sun. 1:35.

LONG ISLAND
Ducks

Mailing Address: Courthouse Drive, Central Islip, NY 11722. **Telephone:** (516) 756-4625. **FAX:** (516) 756-1654. **E-Mail Address:** ducksli@aol.com. **Website:** www.liducks.com.

Operated by: Long Island Ducks Professional Baseball.

Principal Owner/Chief Executive Officer: Frank Boulton.

General Manager: Matt O'Brien. **Director, Operations:** Dean Rivera. **Director, Marketing:** Kristin Beernink. **Director, Group Sales:** Doug Cohen. **Manager, Media Relations:** Frank Pokorney. **Manager, Community Relations:** Chris Lombardo. **Manager, Ticket Sales:** Scott Robertson. **Office Manager:** Gerry Anderson.

Manager/Director, Player Procurement: Bud Harrelson. **Coaches:** Paul Gibson, Joe Pignatano. **Trainer:** Unavailable.

Game Information

Radio: Unavailable.

PA Announcer: Unavailable. **Official Scorer:** Joe Donnelly.

Stadium Name (year opened): Suffolk County Sports Park (2000). **Location:** Southern State Parkway east to Carleton Avenue North (exit 43 south), right onto Courthouse Drive, stadium behind federal courthouse complex. **Standard Game Times:** 7:05 p.m., Sat.-Sun. 2:05.

Visiting Club Hotel: Huntington Hilton, 598 Broad Hollow Rd., Melville, NY 11747. Telephone: (516) 845-1000.

MARYLAND

(Information for 2000 is tentative)

Office Address: 200 N Philadelphia Blvd., Suite B, Aberdeen, MD 21001. **Mailing Address:** P.O. Box 1177 Aberdeen, MD 21001. **Telephone:** (301) 805-6000. **FAX:** (301) 805-6008.

Operated by: Aberdeen Professional Baseball Club, Inc.

General Manager: Keith Lupton. **Assistant General Manager:** Doug Augis. **Director, Media Relations:** Charlie Vascellaro. **Director, Special Projects:** D'Anne Spangler.

Director, Baseball Operations: Bill Ripken.

Game Information

Radio: Unavailable.

PA Announcer: Jim McMahon. **Official Scorer:** Unavailable.

Stadium Name: Thomas Run Field at Harford Community College. Location: Six miles west of I-95 on Route 22. Standard Game Times: 7:05 p.m., Sun. 1:05.

NASHUA
Pride

Office Address: 100 Main St., Suite 1, Nashua, NH 03060. Telephone: (603) 883-2255. FAX: (603) 883-0880. E-Mail Address: prideball@aol.com. Website: www.nashua.com.
Operated by: Nashua Pride Professional Baseball, LLC.
Principal Owner/President: Chris English.
General Manager: Billy Johnson. Assistant to General Manager: Heather Evans. Manager, Community Relations: Kim Anastasiou. Manager, Operations: Todd Marlin. Manager, Merchandise: Jason LaBossiere. Manager, Ticketing: Chris Arres. General Manager, Food Services: Jim Patterson. Clubhouse Operations: Fernando Ybarra. Head Groundskeeper: George Toma.
Manager: Butch Hobson. Coach: Unavailable.

Game Information
Radio Announcer: Unavailable. No. of Games Broadcast: Home-70, Away-70. Flagship Station: Unavailable.
PA Announcer: Ken Cail. Official Scorer: Unavailable.
Stadium Name (year opened): Holman Stadium (1937). Location: Route 3 to exit 7E (Amherst Street), one mile on left. Standard Game Times: Mon.-Tue. 6:35; Wed.-Sat. 7:05; Sun. 6:05.
Visiting Club Hotel: Unavailable.

NEWARK
Bears

Office Address: 450 Broad St., Newark, NJ 07102. Telephone: (973) 848-1000. FAX: (973) 621-0095. Website: www.newarkbears.com
Operated by: Newark Bears, Inc.
Principal Owner/President: Rick Cerone.
General Manager: Kevin Reynolds. Assistant General Manager: Adam Lorber. Business Manager: Roger Concalvez. Director, Sales: Damon Thornton. Director, Merchandising: Jeof Vita. Director, Stadium Operations: J.G. Robilotti. Director, Media Relations: Dave Popkin. Director, Community Relations: Jim Monaghan. Account Representative: Greg Aroneo. Director, Promotions/Video Production: Nicole Paradiso. Director, Ticket Sales: Dave Shipitofsky. Director, Group Sales: Kecia Tillman. Manager, Marketing: Matt DeSantis. Coordinator, Sales/Publications: Tammy Lennox. Coordinator, Sales: Matt DeFazio. Coordinator, Group Sales: Erica Levenson. Office Manager: Kelly Carthens. Head Groundskeeper: Anthony Mariano.
Manager: Tom O'Malley. Coach: Tony Ferreira. Trainer: John DeSimini.

Game Information
Radio Announcer: Dave Popkin. No. of Games Broadcast: Home-70, Away-70. Flagship Station: WSOU 89.5-FM.
PA Announcer: Unavailable. Official Scorer: Unavailable.
Stadium Name (year opened): Riverfront Stadium (1999). Location: New Jersey Parkway North/South to exit 145 (280 East), to exit 15; New Jersey Turnpike North/South to 280 West to exit 15A. Standard Game Times: 7:05 p.m., (April-June) 6:35; Sat. 6:05; Sun. 1:35.
Visiting Club Hotel: Howard Johnson at Newark International Airport, 20 Frontage Rd., Newark, NJ 07114. Telephone: (973) 344-1500.

SOMERSET
Patriots

Office Address: One Patriots Park, Bridgewater, NJ 08807. Telephone: (908) 252-0700. FAX: (908) 252-0776. Website: www.somersetpatriots.com.
Operated by: Somerset Patriots Baseball Club, LLC.
Principal Owners: Steven Kalafer, Michael Kalafer, Jack Cust, Byron Brisby. Chairman: Steven Kalafer. President: Michael Kalafer.

Vice President/General Manager: David Gasaway. **Assistant GM/Stadium Operations**: Chris Bryan. **Assistant GM/Sales**: Patrick McVerry. **Controller**: Wayne Seguin. **Head Groundskeeper**: Ray Cipperly. **Director, Media Relations**: Marc Russinoff. **Director, Sales**: David Marek. **Account Representatives**: Dane Lyle, Rob Lukachyk, Marc Skowronek. **Director, Community Relations**: Rich Reitman. **Director, Ticket Sales**: Rob Patton. **Director, Group Sales**: Brendan Fairfield. **Director, Merchandising**: Arlene Saraco.

Manager: Sparky Lyle. **Coaches**: Unavailable. **Trainer**: Paul Kolody. **Director, Player Procurement**: Jim Frey.

Game Information

Radio Announcer: David Schultz. **No. of Games Broadcast:** Home-74, Away-66. **Flagship Station:** WCTC 1450-AM.

PA Announcers: Paul Spychala, Jim Gano. **Official Scorer:** John Nolan.

Stadium Name (year opened): Somerset Ballpark (1999). **Location:** Route 287 North to exit 13B/Route 287 South to exit 13 (Somerville Route 28 West); at second light take jughandle on right and cross over Route 28 to Chimney Rock Road to Foothill Road. **Standard Game Times:** 7:05; Sun., 2:05.

Visiting Club Hotel: Somerset Ramada, 60 Cottontail Lane, Somerset, NJ 08873. Telephone: (732) 560-9880.

FRONTIER LEAGUE

Office Address: 45 N 4th St., Zanesville, OH 43701. **Mailing Address**: P.O. Box 2662, Zanesville, OH 43702. **Telephone**: (740) 452-7400. **FAX**: (740) 452-2999. **E-Mail Address**: klee@y-city.net. **Website**: www.frontier-league.com.

Year Founded: 1993.

Commissioner: Bill Lee. **President**: Chris Hanners (Chillicothe). **Vice President**: Duke Ward (Richmond). **Corporate Secretary/Treasurer**: Bob Wolfe.

Directors: David Arch (Cook County), Heath Brown (Dubois County), Chris Hanners (Chillicothe), Charles Jacey (Evansville), John Kuhn (London), Kevin Rhomberg (Canton), Rich Sauget (Gateway), Tom Sullivan (Johnstown), John Wallenstein (Springfield), Duke Ward (Richmond), Ken Wilson (River City).

Administrative Assistant: Kathy Lee.

2000 Opening Date: May 31. **Closing Date**: Aug. 29.

Regular Season: 84 games.

Division Structure: **East**—Canton, Chillicothe, Johnstown, London, Richmond. **West**—Cook County, Dubois County, Evansville, River City, Springfield. **2001 Expansion Franchise:** Gateway Grizzlies, 1405 Nickell St., Sauget, IL 62206. Telephone: (618) 632-0100.

Playoff Format: Division winners plus next two highest finishers meet in best-of-3 semifinals. Winners meet in best-of-5 series for league championship.

All-Star Game: July 12 at O'Fallon, MO (River City).

Roster Limit: 24. **Eligibility Rule**: Minimum of 10 first-year players; maximum of seven players with one year professional experience; maximum of two players with two years of experience and maximum of three players with three or more years of experience. No player may be 27 prior to May 31.

Brand of Baseball: Wilson.

Statistician: Howe Sportsdata, Boston Fish Pier, West Bldg. #1, Suite 302, Boston, MA 02210.

CANTON
Crocodiles

Office Address: 2501 Allen Ave. SE, Canton, OH 44707. **Telephone**: (330) 455-2255. **FAX**: (330) 454-4835. **E-Mail Address**: crocodiles@tusco.net.

Operated by: Canton Frontier League Baseball, LLC.

General Manager: Kevin Rhomberg. **Assistant General Manager**: Carl Crowl. **Director, Sales**: Richard Schaedler. **Head Groundskeeper**: Kevan Lindsey.

Manager: Dan Massarelli. **Coaches**: Joe Charboneau, Doc Schaedler. **Trainer**: Unavailable.

Game Information
Radio: None.
PA Announcer: Unavailable. **Official Scorer:** Unavailable.
Stadium Name (year opened): Thurman Munson Memorial Stadium (1989). **Location:** I-77 to exit 103, left on Mill Road, left on Allen Ave. **Standard Game Times:** 7:05 p.m., Sun. 6:05.
Visiting Club Hotel: Red Roof Inn, 5353 Inn Circle Ct. NW, Canton, OH 44720. Telephone: (330) 499-1970.

CHILLICOTHE
Paints

Office Address: 59 N Paint St., Chillicothe, OH 45601. **Telephone:** (740) 773-8326. **FAX:** (740) 773-8338. **E-Mail Address:** paints@bright.net. **Website:** www.chillicothepaints.com.
Operated by: Chillicothe Paints Professional Baseball Association, Inc.
Principal Owner: Chris Hanners. **President:** Shirley Bandy.
General Manager: Bryan Wickline. **Director, Stadium Operations:** Ralph Moore. **Stadium Superintendent:** Jim Miner. **Director, Finance:** Maleine Davis. **Office Manager:** Aaron Lemaster. **Director, Sales/Marketing:** John Wend. **Director, Tickets/Group Sales:** Spencer Bradley. **Director, Merchandise:** Logan Hanners. **Director, Souvenirs/Concessions:** Patrick Davidson. **Head Groundskeeper:** Noah Hanners.
Manager/Director, Baseball Operations: Roger Hanners. **Coaches:** Steve Dawes, Marty Dunn, Jamie Keefe. **Trainer:** Scott Kaser.

Game Information
Radio Announcer: Kevin Rouch. **No. of Games Broadcast:** Away-42. **Flagship Station:** WXIZ 100.9-FM.
PA Announcer: John Wend. **Official Scorer:** Aaron Lemaster.
Stadium Name (year opened): V.A. Memorial Stadium (1954). **Location:** Route 23 to Route 35, west on Route 35, north on Route 104. **Standard Game Times:** 7:05 p.m., Sun. 6:05.
Visiting Club Hotel: Days Inn of Chillicothe, 1250 N Bridge St., Chillicothe, OH 45601. Telephone: (740) 775-7000.

COOK COUNTY
Cheetahs

Office Address: 4545 Midlothian Turnpike, Crestwood, IL 60445. **Telephone:** (708) 489-2255. **FAX:** (708) 489-2999. **Website:** www.cookcocheetahs.com.
Operated by: Cheetah Professional Sports II, LLC.
Chairman: David Arch. **President:** Leon Steinberg.
General Manager: Gerald Clarke. **Assistant General Managers:** Steve Arch, Larry Millar. **Chief Operating Officer:** Frank McGuinn. **Head Groundskeeper:** Marty Pellicore. **Director, Ticket Sales:** Dave Fitzgerald.
Manager: Ron LeFlore. **Coaches:** Carlos May, Milt Pappas, Scott Spero, Doug Wellenreiter. **Trainers:** Rob Lacey, Lorie Worjanowski.

Game Information
Radio: Unavailable.
PA Announcer: Unavailable. **Official Scorer:** Ray Nemec.
Stadium Name (year opened): Hawkinson Ford Field (1999). **Location:** I-294 to Cicero Ave. exit (Route 50), south for 1.5 miles, left at Midlothian Turnpike, right on Kenton Ave. **Standard Game Times:** 7 p.m., Sun. 5.
Visiting Club Hotel: Georgio's Comfort Inn, 8800 W 159th St., Orland Park, IL 60462. Telephone: (708) 403-1100.

DUBOIS COUNTY
Dragons

Office Address: 426 E Fourth St., Huntingburg, IN 47542. **Mailing Address:** P.O. Box 301, Huntingburg, IN 47542. **Telephone:** (812) 683-4405. **FAX:** (812) 683-4299. **E-Mail Address:** dragons@psci.net. **Website:** www.dragonsbaseball.com.
Operated by: Dragons Baseball, LLC.

General Manager: Heath Brown. **Controller**: Ken Craig. **Marketing Representative**: Brad Rane. **Office Manager**: Kelly Livesay. **Head Groundskeeper**: Jim Gunselman.

Manager: Tim Wallace. **Coaches**: Brian Nichols, Mike Samuels.

Game Information

Radio: Unavailable.

PA Announcer: Scott Sollman. **Official Scorer:** Aaron Hartje.

Stadium Name (year opened): Huntingburg League Stadium (1996). **Location:** I-64 to U.S. 231 North, right onto First Street. **Standard Game Times:** 7:05 p.m., Sun. 5:05.

Visiting Club Hotel: Best Western Dutchman Inn, 406 E 22nd St., Huntingburg, IN 47542. Telephone: (812) 683-2334.

EVANSVILLE
Otters

Office Address: 1701 N Main St., Evansville, IN 47711. **Telephone**: (812) 435-8686. **FAX**: (812) 435-8688. **E-Mail Address**: ottersbb@evansville.net. **Website**: www.otters.evansville.net.

Operated by: Old Time Sports I, LLC.

President: Charles Jacey.

Executive Vice President/Chief Operating Officer: Curt Jacey.

VP/General Manager: Jim Miller. **VP/Sales, Marketing**: Jack Tracz. **Assistant General Manager**: Pam Miller. **Director, Operations**: Steve Tahsler. **Director, Tickets/Corporate Development**: Don Campbell. **Personnel Manager**: Angie Embrey.

Manager/Director, Baseball Operations: Greg Tagert. **Coaches**: Mike Kass, Jeff Leystra, J.R. Seymour. **Trainer**: Jim Miller.

Game Information

Radio Announcer: Denny Cotton. **No. of Games Broadcast:** Home-42, Away-42. **Flagship Station:** WVHI 1330-AM.

PA Announcer: Ron Johnson. **Official Scorer:** Glen Agler.

Stadium Name (year opened): Bosse Field (1915). **Location:** U.S. 41 to Diamond Ave. West, left at Heidelbach Ave. **Standard Game Times:** 7:05 p.m., Sun. 6:05.

Visiting Club Hotel: Unavailable.

JOHNSTOWN
Johnnies

Office Address: 345 Main St., Johnstown, PA 15901. **Telephone**: (814) 536-8326. **FAX**: (814) 539-0056. **E-Mail Address**: gmpas@johnniesbaseball.com. **Website**: www.johnniesbaseball.com.

Operated by: Johnstown Professional Baseball, Inc.

President/Director, Player Procurement:: Tom Sullivan.

General Manager: Patty Sladki. **Director, Media/Public Relations**: Don McIsaac. **Director, Community Relations**: Ed Zimmerman. **Director, Ticket Sales**: Courtney Brydon. **Director, Merchandising**: Chastity Wills. **Director, Food Services**: Mike Philibin. **Director, Stadium Operations**: Mike Hudak. **Head Groundskeeper**: Greg Avramis.

Manager: Mike Moore. **Coaches**: Bill Mashing, Kirk Taylor. **Trainer**: Derek Repucci.

Game Information

Radio Announcer: Unavailable. **No. of Games Broadcast:** Home-42, Away-42. **Flagship Station:** WCRO 1230-AM.

PA Announcer: Unavailable. **Official Scorer:** Unavailable.

Stadium Name (year opened): Point Stadium (1923). **Location:** Route 56 in downtown Johnstown. **Standard Game Times:** 7:05 p.m., Sun. 6:05.

Visiting Club Hotel: Holiday Inn Downtown, 250 Market St., Johnstown, PA 15901. Telephone: (814) 535-7777.

LONDON
Werewolves

Office Address: Labatt Park, 25 Wilson Ave., London, Ontario N6H 1X2.

Telephone: (519) 679-7337. **FAX**: (519) 679-5713. **E-Mail Address**: lon
donbaseball@lon.imag.net. **Website**: www.londonwerewolves.com.
  Operated by: London Professional Baseball, LLC.
  Principal Owners: James Kuhn, John Kuhn.
  President/General Manager: John Kuhn. **Assistant General Manager**:
Todd Merton. **Director, Stadium Operations**: Matty O'Matthew. **Director,
Media/Public Relations**: Kris Dinel. **Director, Sales/Marketing**: Darrell
Bradbury. **Director, Community Relations**: Wayne Urbshott. **Director,
Promotions**: Warren Vaughn. **Head Groundskeeper**: Mike Regan.
Director, Special Projects: Stan Wilcox. **Clubhouse Operations**: John
Delainey, Brian Regan, Andrew Rosser.
  Manager: Andy McCauley. **Coach**: Bruce Gray. **Director, Player
Procurement**: Don Leppert. **Trainer**: Scott Crich.

Game Information
  Radio: Unavailable.
  PA Announcer: Tony Clifton. **Official Scorer**: Jason Rozon.
  Stadium Name (year opened): Labatt Memorial Park (1866). **Location**:
Highway 401 to Wellington Road, north to downtown, left on Queens Ave.
over Thames River. **Standard Game Times**: 7:05 p.m., Sun. 5:05.
  Visiting Club Hotel: Super 8, 636 York St., London, Ontario N5W 2S7.
Telephone: (519) 433-8161.

  Mailing Address: 201 NW 13th St., Richmond, IN 47374. **Telephone**:
(765) 935-7529. **FAX**: (765) 962-7047. **E-Mail Address**: roosters@info
com.com. **Website**: www.richmondroosters.com
  Operated by: Richmond Baseball, LLC.
  General Manager: Deanna Beaman. **Director, Business Operations**:
Duke Ward. **Head Groundskeeper**: Cindy Blunk. **Clubhouse Operations**:
John Mann. **Office Manager**: Becky Andrews.
  Manager: John Cate. **Coaches**: Brad Finken, Woody Sorrell. **Trainer**:
Unavailable.

Game Information
  Radio Announcer: Gary Kitchel. **No. of Games Broadcast**: Home-42,
Away-42. **Flagship Station**: WHON 930-AM.
  PA Announcer: Unavailable. **Official Scorer**: Dave Knight.
  Stadium Name (year opened): McBride Stadium (1936). **Location**: I-70
to Williamsburg Pike (exit 149A), right on West Main Street, right on NW
13th Street. **Standard Game Times**: 6:30 p.m.; Sun. 2:30.
  Visiting Club Hotel: Ramada Inn, 4700 E National Rd., Richmond, IN
47374. Telephone: (765) 962-5551.

  Office Address: T.R. Hughes Ballpark, 900 Ozzie Smith Dr., O'Fallon,
MO 63366. **Mailing Address**: P.O. Box 662, O'Fallon, MO 63366.
Telephone: (636) 240-2287. **FAX**: (636) 240-7313. **E-Mail Address**: pat
daly@rivercityrascals.com. **Website**: www.rivercityrascals.com.
  Operated by: Missouri River Baseball, LLC.
  Managing Partner: Ken Wilson.
  General Manager: Patrick Daly. **Assistant General Manager**: Matt
Jones. **Director, Sales/Marketing**: Keith Lucier. **Director, Merchandising**:
Bobby Rhoden. **Director, Public Relations**: Danelle DeGroodt. **Director,
Ticket Sales/Operations**: Steve Chanez. **Director, Stadium Operations**:
Tony Funderburg. **Director, Broadcasting/Media Relations**: Mike Carver.
Director, Business Operations: Jeri Binsbacher. **Administrative Assis-
tant**: Roy Tippett. **Head Groundskeeper**: Mark Cantrall.
  Manager: Neil Fiala. **Coaches**: Randy Martz, Dick Schofield. **Trainer**:
Unavailable.

Game Information
  Radio Announcer: Mike Carver. **No. of Games Broadcast**: Home-42,
Away-42. **Flagship Station**: KFNS 100.7-FM.
  PA Announcer: Ken Webb. **Official Scorer**: Dick Buchanan.
  Stadium Name (year opened): T.R. Hughes Ballpark (1999). **Location**:
I-70 to K and M exits, right on Tom Ginnever Ave. **Standard Game Times**:

7:05 p.m., Sun. 6:05.

Visiting Club Hotel: Holiday Inn Select, St. Peters/St. Charles, 4221 South Outer Rd., St. Peters, MO 63376. Telephone: (636) 928-2927.

SPRINGFIELD
Capitals

Office Address: 1351 N Grand Ave. East, Springfield, IL 62702. **Telephone**: (217) 525-5500. **FAX**: (217) 525-5508. **E-Mail Address**: baseball@springfieldcapitals.com **Website**: www.springfieldcapitals.com.

Operated by: Springfield Capitals Professional Baseball, LLC.

General Manager: John Wallenstein. **Director, Business Operations**: Todd Fulk. **Head Groundskeeper**: Larry Rockford. **Account Representative**: Brent Zampier. **Director, Food Service**: Lanny Higgins. **Director, Baseball Operations**: Jim Belz.

Manager: Unavailable. **Coach**: Don Herron. **Trainer**: Unavailable.

Game Information

Radio Announcer: Steve Shannon. **No. of Games Broadcast:** Home-20, Away-20. **Flagship Station:** WFMB 1450-AM.

PA Announcer: Paul MacDonna. **Official Scorer:** Bob Shankland.

Stadium Name (year opened): Lanphier Park (1928). **Location:** I-55 to Clearlake exit, west into Springfield, right on North Grand Ave. **Standard Game Times:** 7:05 p.m., Sun. 4:05.

Visiting Club Hotel: Unavailable.

NORTHERNLEAGUE

CENTRAL DIVISION

Office Address: 524 S Duke St., Durham, NC 27701. **Mailing Address**: P.O. Box 1282, Durham, NC 27702. **Telephone**: (919) 956-8150. **FAX**: (919) 683-2693. **E-Mail Address**: northernlg@earthlink.net. **Website**: www.northernleague.com.

Year Founded: 1993.

Commissioner: Miles Wolff. **President:** Dan Moushon.

Directors: Rich Ehrenreich (Schaumburg), Marv Goldklang (St. Paul), Sam Katz (Winnipeg), Ed Nottle (Sioux City), Harry Stavrenos (Duluth-Superior), Bill Terlecky (Madison), Bruce Thom (Fargo-Moorhead), Mike Veeck (Sioux Falls).

Supervisor, Umpires: Butch Fisher.

2000 Opening Date: May 26. **Closing Date:** Sept. 1.

Regular Season: 86 games (split schedule).

Division Structure: East—Duluth-Superior, Madison, St. Paul, Schaumburg. West—Fargo-Moorhead, Sioux City, Sioux Falls, Winnipeg.

All-Star Game: Aug. 1 at Little Falls, NJ (New Jersey/Eastern Division).

Playoff Format: First-half division winners (East, West, North, South) play second-half division winners in best-of-5 series. Winners meet in best-of-5 division championship series. Winners meet in best-of-5 series for league championship.

Roster Limit: 22. **Eligibility Rule:** Minimum of five first-year players; maximum of four veterans (at least four years of professional service).

Brand of Baseball: Rawlings.

Statistician: Howe Sportsdata, Boston Fish Pier, West Bldg. #1, Suite 302, Boston, MA 02210.

DULUTH-SUPERIOR
Dukes

Office Address: 207 W Superior St., Suite 206, Duluth, MN 55802. **Mailing Address**: P.O. Box 205, Duluth, MN 55801. **Telephone**: (218) 727-4525. **FAX**: (218) 727-4533. **E-Mail Address**: hitnrun@dsdukes.com. **Website**: www.dsdukes.com.

Operated By: Dukes Baseball, Inc.

Principal Owners: Harry Stavrenos, Ted Cushmore. **General Manager**: George Stavrenos. **Coordinator, Community**

Relations: Jennifer Bahl. **Head Groundskeeper:** Ray Adameak. **Clubhouse Operations:** Jimmy Telin. **Team Physician:** Dr. David Webb. **Manager/Coaches:** Unavailable. **Director, Scouting:** Harry Stavrenos.

Game Information
Radio Announcer: Unavailable. **No. of Games Broadcast:** Home-43, Away-43. **Flagship Station:** WDSM 710-AM.

PA Announcer: Jeff Papas. **Official Scorer:** Unavailable.

Stadium Name (year opened): Wade Stadium (1941). **Location:** I-35 to 40 Ave. West, right on Grand Ave., right on 34th Ave. **Standard Game Times:** 7:05 p.m., Sun. 2:05.

Visiting Club Hotel: Black Bear Hotel, 1789 Hwy. 210, Carlton MN 55718. **Telephone:** (218) 878-7400.

FARGO-MOORHEAD
Redhawks

Office Address: 1515 15th Ave. N Fargo, ND 58102. **Mailing Address:** P.O. Box 5258, Fargo, ND 58105. **Telephone:** (701) 235-6161. **FAX:** (701) 297-9247. **E-Mail Address:** redhawks@fmredhawks.com. **Website:** www.fmredhawks.com.

Operated by: Fargo Baseball, LLC.

President: Bruce Thom.

Vice President/General Manager: Tim Flakoll. **Assistant General Manager:** Lee Schwartz. **Director, Media Relations:** Josh Buchholz. **Director, Promotions:** Kris Packer. **Assistant Director, Promotions:** Josh Krueger. **Senior Accountant:** Sue Wild. **Assistant Accountant:** Brian Heim. **Director, Ticket Sales:** Paula Cihla. **Director, Stadium Operations/Head Groundskeeper:** Blair Tweet. **Director, Food Services:** Nathan Flom. **Receptionist:** Jenny Vangerud.

Manager/Director, Player Procurement: Doug Simunic. **Pitching Coach/Assistant Director, Player Procurement:** Jeff Bittiger. **Trainer:** Jeff Bjerke.

Game Information
Radio Announcer: Jack Michaels. **No. of Games Broadcast:** Home-43, Away-43. **Flagship Station:** KVOX 1280-AM.

PA Announcer: Merrill Piepkorn. **Official Scorer:** Hob Olson.

Stadium Name (year opened): Newman Outdoor Field (1996). **Location:** I-29 North to exit 67, right on 19th Ave North, right on Albrecht Blvd. **Standard Game Times:** 7:05 p.m., Sun. 2:05.

Visiting Club Hotel: Comfort Inn West, 3825 9th Ave. SW, Fargo, ND 58103. Telephone: (701) 282-9596.

MADISON
Black Wolf

Office Address: 2920 N Sherman Ave., Madison, WI 53704. **Telephone:** (608) 244-5666. **FAX:** (608) 244-6996. **E-Mail Address:** madwolf@mad wolf.com. **Website:** www.madwolf.com.

Operated by: Madison Baseball, LLC.

Chairman: Patrick Sweeney. **President/General Manager:** Bill Terlecky.

Director, Media/Public Relations: John LaRue. **Controller:** George Kiehl. **Director, Ticket Sales:** Amanda Law. **Director, Group Sales:** Anje Van Roo. **Director, Food Services:** Paul Ross. **Director, Special Projects:** Aaron Lawry. **Head Groundskeeper:** Ken Smith.

Manager/Director, Player Procurement: Al Gallagher. **Coaches:** Stan Evans, Bronson Heflin, Bob Wagner. **Trainer:** Justin Byers.

Game Information
PA Announcer: Unavailable. **Official Scorer:** Unavailable.

Stadium Name (year opened): Warner Park (1984). **Location:** I-90 north to Hwy. 30, exit onto Northport Dr., left on Sherman Ave.; I-90 South to Hwy. 151 south, exit onto Aberg Ave. to Northport Drive, left on Sherman Ave. **Standard Game Times:** 7 p.m., Sun., 1:30.

Visiting Club Hotel: Econolodge, 4726 E Washington Ave., Madison, WI 53704. Telephone: (608) 241-4171.

ST. PAUL
Saints

Office Address: 1771 Energy Park Dr., St. Paul, MN 55108. **Telephone**: (651) 644-3517. **FAX**: (651) 644-1627. **E-Mail Address**: funsgood@spsaints.com. **Website**: www.spsaints.com.

Operated by: St. Paul Saints Baseball Club, Inc.

Principal Owners: Marvin Goldklang, Mike Veeck, Bill Murray, Van Schley.

Chairman: Marvin Goldklang. **President**: Mike Veeck.

Vice President/General Manager: Bill Fanning. **Director, Operations**: Bill Fisher. **Director, Media/Public Relations**: Anthony LaPanta. **Director, Sales**: Bob St. Pierre. **Director, Group Sales**: Elizabeth Adams. **Director, Promotions**: Tom Brock. **Director, Merchandising**: Jason Lonstein. **Directors, Food Services**: Steve Marso, John Marso. **Manager, Tickets**: Ryan Kuhn. **Controller**: Wayne Engel. **Office Manager**: Kelly Komppa. **Director, Stadium Operations**: Bob Klepperich. **Bookkeeper**: Missy Ekern. **Head Groundskeeper**: Connie Rudolph.

Manager/Director, Player Procurement: Marty Scott. **Coaches**: Ray Korn, Wayne Terwilliger. **Trainer**: Chris Strickland.

Game Information

Radio Announcers: Jim Lucas, Don Wardlow. **No. of Games Broadcast:** Home-43, Away-43. **Flagship Station:** Unavailable.

PA Announcer: Eric Webster. **Official Scorer:** Chuck Manka.

Stadium Name (year opened): Midway Stadium (1982). **Location:** From I-94, take Snelling Ave. exit, north on Snelling, west onto Energy Park Drive. **Standard Game Times:** 7:05 p.m., Sun. 1:05.

Visiting Club Hotel: Ramada Inn, 2540 N Cleveland Ave., St. Paul, MN 55108. Telephone: (651) 636-4567.

SCHAUMBURG
Flyers

Office Address: 1999 S Springinsguth Rd., Schaumburg, IL 60168. **Mailing Address**: P.O. Box 68905, Schaumburg, IL 60168. **Telephone**: (877) 691-2255. **FAX**: (847) 891-6441. **E-Mail Address**: info@flyersbaseball.com. **Website**: www.flyersbaseball.com.

Operated by: Schaumburg Professional Baseball, LLC.

Principal Owner: Richard Ehrenreich.

Vice President/General Manager: John Dittrich. **Assistant General Manager**: Rick Rungaitis. **Director, Stadium Operations**: Matt Yob. **Director, Media Relations**: Matt McLaughlin. **Director, Publications**: Brian Hertel. **Account Representative**: David Neeson. **Manager, Business/Tickets**: Lois Dittrich. **Manager, Group Sales**: Brett Fata. **Director, Merchandising**: Michelle Arrigo. **Administrative Assistant**: Jenny Dittrich. **Receptionist**: Christina Mirovsky. **Head Groundskeeper**: Steve Erickson.

Manager: Ron Kittle. **Pitching Coach**: Greg Hibbard. **Coach/Director, Baseball Operations**: Peter Caliendo. **Trainer**: John Sarna.

Game Information

Radio Announcer: Eric Collins. **No. of Games Broadcast:** Home-43, Away-43. **Flagship Station:** WAVR 930-AM.

PA Announcer: Mark Gizel. **Official Scorer:** Marc Grossman.

Stadium Name (year opened): Alexian Field (1999). **Location:** From north, take Roselle Road to Elgin-O'Hare Expressway, west on expressway to Irving Park Road, left on Springinsguth. From south, take U.S. 20 (Lake Street) to Elgin-O'Hare Expressway, east on expressway, right on Springinsguth Road. **Standard Game Times:** 7:20 p.m.; Sat. 6:20; Sun. 1:20.

Visiting Club Hotel: AmeriSuites, 2750 Greenspoint Parkway, Hoffman Estates, IL 60195. Telephone: (847) 839-1800.

SIOUX CITY
Explorers

Office Address: 3400 Line Dr., Sioux City, IA 51106. **Telephone**: (712) 277-9467. **FAX**: (712) 277-9406. **E-Mail Address**: info@xsbaseball.com.

Website: www.xsbaseball.com.

Operated by: Sioux City Explorers Baseball Club, LLC.

Principal Owner/President: Ed Nottle.

Vice President/General Manager: Tim Utrup. Controller: Donna Mather. Director, Sales/Marketing: Kevin Farlow. Director, Ticket Sales: Pat Tilmon.

Manager: Ed Nottle. Coaches: Jay Kirkpatrick, Pat Tilmon. Trainer: Mike Wright.

Game Information

Radio Announcer: Todd Jamison. No. of Games Broadcast: Home-43, Away-43. Flagship Station: KSCJ 1360-AM.

PA Announcer: Unavailable. Official Scorer: Randy Kascht.

Stadium Name (year opened): Lewis & Clark Park (1993). Location: I-29 to Singing Hills North, right on Line Drive. Standard Game Times: 7:05 p.m., Sun. 6:05.

Visiting Club Hotel: Best Western, 130 Nebraska St., Sioux City, IA 51101. Telephone: (712) 277-1550.

SIOUX FALLS
Canaries

Office Address: 1001 N West Ave., Sioux Falls, SD 57104. Mailing Address: P.O. Box 84412, Sioux Falls, SD 57118. Telephone: (605) 333-0179. FAX: (605) 333-0139. E-Mail Address: canaries@iw.net. Website: www.canariesbaseball.com.

Operated By: Sioux Falls Canaries Professional Baseball Club, LLC.

Principal Owner: Ben Zuraw. Chairman: Marvin Goldklang. President: Mike Veeck.

General Manager: Ripper Hatch. Assistant General Manager: Larry McKenney. Director, Business Operations: Brad Seymour. Director, Communications: Chris Metz. Director, Sales: Matt Brown. Director, Promotions: Joe Wagoner. Director, Concessions/Merchandise: Scott Hannion. Ticket Manager/Group Sales Coordinator: Gretchen Sagmoe. Ticket Sales Representatives: Jason Carlin, Brian Hennke. Group Sales Representative: Greg Ringle.

Manager/Director, Player Personnel: Doc Edwards. Coaches: Unavailable. Trainer: Unavailable.

Game Information

Radio Announcer: Kris Atteberry. No. of Games Broadcast: Home-43, Away-43. Flagship Station: WSN 1230-AM.

PA Announcer: Dan Christopherson. Official Scorer: Troy King.

Stadium Name (year opened): Sioux Falls Stadium (1964). Location: I-29 to Russell St., south one mile, right on West Ave. Standard Game Times: 7:05 p.m., Sun. 2:05, 6:05.

Visiting Club Hotel: Brimark Inn, 3200 W Russell St., Sioux Falls, SD 57107. Telephone: (605) 332-2000.

WINNIPEG
Goldeyes

Office Address: One Portage Ave. East, Winnipeg, Manitoba R3B 3N3. Telephone: (204) 982-2273. FAX: (204) 982-2274. E-Mail Address: goldeyes@goldeyes.com. Website: www.goldeyes.com.

Operated by: Winnipeg Goldeyes Baseball Club, Inc.

Principal Owner/President: Sam Katz.

General Manager: John Hindle. Vice President, Ticket Sales: Andrew Collier. Director, Marketing: Dan Chase. Director, Communications: Jonathan Green. Director, Promotions: Barb McTavish. Director, Group Sales: Lorraine Maciboric. Vice President, Sales: Robert Zyluk. Account Representatives: Trevor Franzmann, Regan Katz, Dave Loat, Dennis McLean, Tracy Smith. Director, Merchandising: Tracy Nanka. Bookkeeper: Judy Jemson. Head Groundskeeper: Don Ferguson.

Manager/Director, Player Procurement: Hal Lanier. Coach: Scott Neiles. Trainer: Patrick Smith.

Game Information

Radio Announcer: Paul Edmonds. No. of Games Broadcast: 60. Flagship Station: CJOB 680-AM.

PA Announcer: Ron Arnst. Official Scorer: Steve Eitzen.

Stadium Name (year opened): CanWest Global Park (1999). **Location:** Pembina Highway (Route 75), east on River Ave., north on Main Street, east on Water Ave. **Standard Game Times:** 7:05 p.m., Sun. 1:35.

Visiting Club Hotel: Ramada Marlborough, 331 Smith St., Winnipeg, Manitoba R3B 2G9. Telephone: (204) 942-6411.

EASTERN DIVISION

Office Address: 1308 Davos Pointe, Woodridge, NY 12789. **Telephone:** (914) 436-0411. **FAX:** (914) 436-6864. **E-Mail Address:** info@northern league.com. **Website:** www.northernleague.com.

Executive Director: Mike McGuire.

Division Structure: North—Adirondack, Albany-Colonie, Quebec, Waterbury. South—Allentown, Catskill, Elmira, New Jersey.

Directors: Steve Ervin (Elmira), Charlie Jacey (Adirondack), Peter Karoly (Allentown), Greg Lockhard (New Jersey), Van Schley (Catskill), Tom Sullivan (Albany-Colonie), Bob Wirz (Waterbury), Miles Wolff (Quebec)

Supervisor, Umpires: George Cox.

Administrative Assistant: Corinne McGuire.

ADIRONDACK
Lumberjacks

Office Address: 175 Dix Ave., Glens Falls, NY 12801. **Telephone:** (518) 743-9618. **FAX:** (518) 743-9721. **E-Mail Address:** baseball@superior.net. **Website:** www.adirondacklumberjacks.com.

Operated by: Old Time Sports, LLC.

Principal Owner: Charles Jacey.

General Manager: Curt Jacey. **Controller:** Andrea Johnson. **Director, Sales/Marketing:** Dave VanDeWater. **Director, Food Services:** Sue Didio. **Director, Group Sales:** Jeff Liddle. **Head Groundskeeper:** Butch Levack.

Manager: Les Lancaster. **Coaches:** Unavailable. **Trainer:** Donny Woods. **Director, Player Procurement:** Nick Belmonte.

Game Information

Radio Announcer: Ken Lechese, Brian Donelly. **No. of Games Broadcast:** Home-43, Away-6. **Flagship Station:** WWSC 1450-AM.

PA Announcer: Dave VanDeWater. **Official Scorer:** Butch Race.

Stadium Name (year opened): East Field (1980). **Location:** I-87 to exit 19, right onto Quaker Road for 5 miles, right on Dix Ave. **Standard Game Times:** 7 p.m., Sun. 5.

Visiting Club Hotel: Sleep Inn, Route 9, Queensbury, NY 12804. Telephone: Unavailable.

ALBANY-COLONIE
Diamond Dogs

Office Address: Heritage Park, 780 Watervliet-Shaker Rd., Albany, NY 12211. **Telephone:** (518) 869-9234. **FAX:** (518) 869-5291. **E-Mail Address:** acdogs@acmenet.net. **Website:** www.diamonddogs.com.

Operated by: Diamond Dogs Sports, Inc.

President: Tom Sullivan.

Vice President/General Manager: Charlie Voelker. **Assistant General Manager:** Kevin Forrester. **Director, Sales/Marketing:** Jeff Finnegan. **Head Groundskeeper:** Dave Hildenbrandt. **Director, Merchandising:** Erinn McNeil. **Director, Group Sales:** Robert Totaro. **Office Manager:** Sue De Rocco.

Manager/Director, Player Procurement: Mike Marshall. **Pitching Coach:** Raphael Valdez.

Game Information

Radio Announcers: Rip Rowan, Jacob Van Ryan. **No. of Games Broadcast:** Home-43, Away-43. **Flagship Station:** Unavailable.

PA Announcer: Unavailable. **Official Scorer:** Unavailable.

Stadium Name (year opened): Heritage Park (1983). **Location:** I-87 North to exit 4, stay left toward airport, left on Route 155. **Standard Game Times:** 7:05 p.m., Sun. 2:05.

Visiting Club Hotel: Unavailable.

ALLENTOWN
Ambassadors

Office Address: 1511-1525 Hamilton St., Allentown, PA 18102. **Telephone**: (610) 437-6800. **FAX**: (610) 437-6804. **E-Mail Address**: info@ambassadorbaseball.com. **Website**: www.ambassadorbaseball.com.

Operated by: Allentown Ambassadors Professional Baseball Team, Inc.

Principal Owners: Peter Karoly, Lauren Angstadt.

General Manager: Dean Gyorgy. **Director, Sales/Marketing**: Andy Berg. **Special Assistant to GM**: Russ Ardolina. **Director, Community Relations**: Carol Hecht. **Account Representatives**: Kevin Rogers, Matthew Seperka. **Conroller**: Blake Balmer.

Manager/Director, Player Procurement: Joe Calfapietra. **Coaches**: Tom Donahue, Denton Lackatosh.

Game Information

Radio: Unavailable.

PA Announcer: Unavailable. **Official Scorer:** Jim Marshall.

Stadium Name (year opened): Bicentennial Park (1930). **Location:** I-78 to Lehigh Street, north on Lehigh for 2 miles toward downtown. **Standard Game Times:** 7:05 p.m., Sun. 5:05.

Visiting Club Hotel: Unavailable.

CATSKILL
Cougars

Mailing Address: P.O. Box 394, Mountaindale, NY 12763. **Telephone**: (914) 436-4386. **FAX**: (914) 436-9129. **E-Mail Address**: info@cougars baseball.com. **Website**: www.cougarsbaseball.com.

Principal Owners: Van Schley, Mike Veeck, Bill Murray.

Chairman: Van Schley. **President:** Michael McGuire.

General Manager: Jay Bulduuoi. **Assistant General Manager:** Corinne McGuire.

Manager: Dan Shwam. **Coach:** Mike Juhl.

Game Information

Radio: None.

PA Announcer: Unavailable. **Official Scorer:** Unavailable.

Stadium Name (year opened): Baxter Field (1996). **Location:** Route 17 to exit 109, left on Wurtsboro Road, right on New Road for 7.4 miles. **Standard Game Times:** 7:05 p.m..

Visiting Club Hotel: Unavailable.

ELMIRA
Pioneers

Office Address: 546 Luce St., Elmira, NY 14904. **Telephone**: (607) 734-1270. **FAX**: (607) 734-0891. **E-Mail Address**: pioneers@elmirapioneers.com. **Website**: www.elmirapioneers.com.

Operated by: Elmira Baseball, LLC.

President: John Ervin.

General Manager: Ric Sisler. **Assistant General Manager**: Matt Hufnagel. **Director, Business Operations**: Steve Ervin. **Director, Sales/Marketing**: Jennifer Booth. **Head Groundskeeper:** Dale Storch.

Manager: Jon Debus. **Coaches**: Unavailable. **Director, Player Procurement**: Jeff Kunion.

Game Information

Radio Announcer: Unavailable. **No. of Games Broadcast:** Home-32. **Flagship Station:** WWLZ 820-AM.

PA Announcer: Mike Stobel. **Official Scorer:** Tom Yoder.

Stadium Name (year opened): Dunn Field (1939). **Location:** I-86 (Route 17) to exit 56, left onto Judson Street, right onto Water Street, left onto Madison Street, left onto Maple Ave., left onto Luce. **Standard Game Times:** 7:05 p.m., Sun. 5:05.

Visiting Club Hotel: Holiday Inn Elmira-Riverview, 760 E Water, Elmira, NY 14901. Telephone: (607) 734-4211.

NEW JERSEY
Jackals

Office Address: One Hall Dr., Little Falls, NJ 07424. **Telephone**: (973) 746-7434. **FAX**: (973) 655-8021. **E-Mail Address**: njjackals@aol.com. **Website**: www.jackals.com.

Operated by: Floyd Hall Enterprises, LLC.

Principal Owner/Chairman: Floyd Hall. **President**: Greg Lockard.

General Manager: Leo Kirk. **Director, Business Operations**: Jennifer Fertig. **Director, Media/Public Relations**: Jim Cerny. **Head Grounds-keeper**: Larry Castoro. **Director, Sales/Marketing**: Kenneth Yudman. **Director, Ticket Sales**: Elisabeth Unley. **Office Manager**: Joy Robbins. **Clubhouse Operations**: Justin Petite.

Manager: Kash Beauchamp. **Coach**: Vance Lovelace. **Trainer**: Unavailable.

Game Information

Radio Announcers: Jim Cerny, Kevin Burkehardt. **No. of Games Broadcast:** Home-42, Away-42. **Flagship Station:** WMTR.

PA Announcer: George Ruthauser. **Official Scorer:** Al Langer.

Stadium Name (year opened): Yogi Berra Stadium (1998). **Location:** Route 80 or Garden State Parkway to Route 46, take Valley Road exit to Montclair State Universtiy. **Standard Game Times:** 7:10 p.m., Sun. 6:10.

Visiting Club Hotel: Mountain Inn, 156 Route 46, Rockaway, NJ 07866. Telephone: (973) 627-8310.

QUEBEC
Les Capitales

Office Address: 100 Rue du Cardinal Maurice-Roy, Quebec City, Quebec G1K 8Z1. **Telephone**: (418) 521-2255. **FAX**: (418) 521-2266. **E-Mail Address**: webmaster@capitalesdequebec.com. **Website**: www.capitalesdequebec.com.

Principal Owners: Miles Wolff, Lorne Michaels, Joe Helyar.

President: Miles Wolff.

General Manager: Nicolas Lobbe. **Assistant General Manager**: Jeff Cote. **Director, Business Operations**: Remi Bolduc. **Director, Stadium Operations**: Jean Gagnon. **Director, Media/Public Relations**: Alain Garon. **Director, Sales/Marketing**: Leo St. Jacques. **Director, Ticket Sales**: Josee Metivier. **Director, Promotions**: Steve Poirier.

Manager: Jay Ward. **Coaches**: Stephane Bedard, Jim Boynewicz.

Game Information

Radio: None.

PA Announcer: Unavailable. **Official Scorer:** Unavailable.

Stadium Name (year opened): Stade de Quebec (1939). **Location:** Highway 40 to Highway 173 (Centre-Ville) exit, 2 miles to Parc Victoria. **Standard Game Times:** 7:05 p.m., Sun. 2:05.

Visiting Club Hotel: Confortel L'Hotel, 6500 Blvd. Hamel, Ancienne Lorette, Quebec G2E 2J1. Telephone: (418) 877-4777.

WATERBURY
Spirit

Office Address: 1200 Watertown Ave., Waterbury, CT 06708. **Telephone**: (203) 419-0393. **FAX**: (203) 419-0396. **E-Mail Address**: info@waterburyspirit.com. **Website**: www.waterburyspirit.com.

Operated by: WC Sports, LLC.

Chairman: David Carpenter. **President/Chief Operating Officer**: Bob Wirz.

Business Manager: Kevin Walsh. **Assistant GM/Director, Marketing**: Terry Cole. **Director, Baseball Operations**: George Tsamis. **Controller**: Ginny Kozlowski. **Director, Food Services**: Joe Caiazzo. **Office Manager**: Jennifer Lucas. **Clubhouse Manager**: Walter Brackett.

Manager/Director, Player Procurement: George Tsamis. **Coach**: Jackie Hernandez. **Trainer**: Unavailable.

Game Information

Radio Announcer: Stu Paul. **No. of Games Broadcast:** Unavailable. **Flagship Station:** WATR 1320-AM.

PA Announcer: Chuck Petruccione. **Official Scorer:** Steve Feldman.

Stadium Name (year opened): Municipal Stadium (1930). **Location:** Route 8 North to exit 35, left onto Watertown Ave.; Route 8 South to exit 36, right onto Watertown Ave. **Standard Game Times:** 7:05 p.m., Sun. 5:05.

Visiting Club Hotel: Unavailable.

TEXAS-LOUISIANALEAGUE

Mailing Address: 800 E Campbell, Suite 108, Richardson, TX 75081. **Telephone:** (214) 575-5800. **FAX:** (214) 570-0319. **E-Mail Address:** txproball@aol.com. **Website:** www.txproball.com.

Year Founded: 1994.

Operated by: Texas Professional Baseball, LLC.

Principal Owner: Horn Chen. **President:** Byron Pierce. **Director, Media Relations:** Bruce Unrue.

2000 Opening Date: May 4. **Closing Date:** Aug. 31.

Regular Season: 112 games.

All-Star Game: July 12 at Ozark, MO.

Playoff Format: Top four teams meet in best-of-5 series. Winners meet in best-of-7 series for league championship.

Roster Limit: 22. **Player Eligibility Rule:** Minimum of three players with no previous professional experience, maximum of three veterans with more than four experience.

Brand of Baseball: Rawlings.

Statistician: Howe Sportsdata, Boston Fish Pier, West Bldg. #1, Suite 302, Boston, MA 02210.

ALEXANDRIA
Aces

Office Address: 1 Babe Ruth Dr., Alexandria, LA 71301. **Mailing Address:** P.O. Box 6005, Alexandria, LA 71307. **Telephone:** (318) 473-2237. **FAX:** (318) 473-2229. **E-Mail Address:** acesbaseball@centurytel.net.

General Manager: Craig Brasfield. **Assistant General Manager:** Chet Carey. **Director, Business Operations/Merchandising:** Carrie Brasfield. **Director, Stadium Operations:** Jodie White. **Head Groundskeeper/Clubhouse Operations:** John Hickman. **Director, Media/Public Relations:** Ryan Sachs. **Director, Ticket/Group Sales:** Amy Desselle. **Director, Food Services:** Fred Eloi. **Director, Special Projects:** Ricky Doyle. **Visiting Clubhouse Manager:** John Chambers.

Manager: John O'Brien. **Trainer:** Mike Palumbo.

Game Information

Radio Announcers: Lyn Rollins, Ryan Sachs. **No. of Games Broadcast:** Home-56, Away-56. **Flagship Station:** KOUZ 89.9-FM.

PA Announcer: Rich Dupree. **Official Scorer:** Jim Smilie.

Stadium Name (year opened): Bringhurst Field (1933). **Location:** One mile east of Alexandria Mall on 165 Business (Masonic Drive), left onto Babe Ruth Drive. **Standard Game Time:** 6:35 p.m.

Visiting Club Hotel: MacArthur Inn, 2211 N MacArthur Dr., Alexandria, LA 71301. Telephone: (318) 443-2561.

AMARILLO
Dillas

Mailing Address: P.O. Box 31241, Amarillo, TX 79120. **Telephone:** (806) 342-3455. **FAX:** (806) 374-2269. **Website:** www.dillas.com.

General Manager: Unavailable. **Assistant General Manager:** Daren Brown. **Director, Promotions/Community Relations:** Cindy Withrow. **Office Manager:** Jamie Wynn. **Director, Ticket Sales:** Richard Duffendack. **Clubhouse Operations:** George Escamilla.

Manager: Daren Brown. **Coach:** Lonnie Maclin.

Game Information

Radio Announcer: Brett Quintyne. **No. of Games Broadcast:** Home-60, Away-52. **Flagship Station:** KPUR 1440-AM.

PA Announcer: Joe Frank Wheeler. **Official Scorer:** Chris Moore.

Stadium Name: Potter County Memorial. **Location:** I-40 to Grand Ave. North exit, left at 3rd Ave. **Standard Game Times:** 7:05 p.m., Sun. 5:05.

Visiting Club Hotel: Radisson Inn-Airport, 7909 East I-40, Amarillo, TX, 79118. Telephone: (806) 373-3303.

GREENVILLE
Bluesmen

Mailing Address: 1040 S Raceway Rd., Greenville, MS 38701. **Telephone:** (662) 335-2583. **FAX:** (662) 335-7742. **E-Mail Address:** bluesmen@tecinfo.com. **Website:** www.tecinfo.com/~bluesmen.

Operated by: Greenville Bluesmen Professional Baseball Club, LLC.

President/General Manager: Bill Hood. **Director, Media Relations:** Heather Williams.

Manager: Chris Cassels. **Coaches:** Chris Bryant, Mack Gower.

Game Information

Radio Announcer: Chuck Early. **No. of Games Broadcast:** Home-56, Away-56. **Flagship Station:** WNIX 1330-AM.

PA Announcers: Ray Hamilton, Heather Williams. **Official Scorer:** Morris Morrow.

Stadium Name (year opened): Legion Field (1971). **Location:** South on Raceway Road off Highway 82. **Standard Game Times:** 7:05 p.m., Sun. 6:05.

Visiting Club Hotel: Ramada Inn, 2700 Hwy. 82 East, Greenville, MS. Telephone: (662) 332-4411.

JACKSON
DiamondKats

Mailing Address: 1200 Lakeland Dr., Jackson, MS 39216. **Telephone:** (601) 362-2540. **FAX:** (601) 362-8020.

Interim General Manager: Tim Bennett. **Director, Media/Public Relations:** Andrew Aguilar. **Director, Group Sales/Promotions:** Richard Deaton. **Director, Stadium Operations:** Paul Cofer. **Office Manager:** Usana Tillman.

Manager: Steve Dillard. **Coaches:** Unavailable.

Game Information

Radio Announcer: Andrew Aguilar. **No. of Games Broadcast:** Home-56, Away-56. **Flagship Station:** Unavailable.

PA Announcer: Unavailable. **Official Scorer:** Unavailable.

Stadium Name (year opened): Smith-Wills Stadium (1975). **Location:** I-55 North to exit 98B, go right for ½ mile; I-55 South to exit 98B, go left for ¾ mile. **Standard Game Times:** 7 p.m., Sat. 6.

Visiting Club Hotel: Unavailable.

LAFAYETTE
Bayou Bullfrogs

Mailing Address: 801 W Congress St., Lafayette, LA 70501. **Telephone:** (337) 233-0998. **FAX:** (337) 237-3539.

General Manager: Anthony DeVincenzo. **Director, Ticket/Group Sales:** Trey White. **Director, Stadium Operations:** Nick Domingue. **Office Manager:** Carolyn Tate.

Manager: John Harris. **Coach:** Ron Guidry.

Game Information

Radio: None.

PA Announcer: Chuck Childress. **Official Scorer:** Unavailable.

Stadium Name (year opened): Tigue Moore Field (1979). **Location:** I-10 to Ambassador Caffery Road exit, to Bertrand Road, 3 miles to stadium. **Standard Game Times:** 6:35 p.m.

Visiting Club Hotel: Unavailable.

OZARK MOUNTAIN
Ducks

Office Address: 5245 N 17th St., Ozark, MO 65721. Mailing Address: P.O. Box 1472, Ozark, MO 65721. Telephone: (417) 581-2868. FAX: (417) 581-8342. E-Mail Address: info@ozarkducksbaseball.com. Website: www.ozarkducksbaseball.com.

General Manager: Brad Eldridge. Director, Business Operations: Todd Rahr. Director, Stadium Operations: Brock Phipps. Director, Community Relations: Jim Metcalf. Director, Sales/Marketing: Matt Puccio. Account Representative: Byron Pierce Jr. Director, Ticket Sales: Andrew Thomas. Director, Merchandising: Misty Tharp. Director, Group Sales: Dustin Robertson. Director, Special Projects: Sherri Eldridge. Clubhouse Operations: Mike Reagan. Office Manager: Carolina George.

Manager: Barry Jones. Coach: Mike Smith. Trainer: Gary Turbak.

Game Information

Radio Announcers: Art Hains, Tom Ladd, Jim Metcalf. No. of Games Broadcast: Home-60, Away-52. Flagship Station: KWTO 98.7-FM.

PA Announcer: Trevor Worley. Official Scorer: Tim Tourville.

Stadium Name (year opened): Price Cutter Park (1999). Location: Highway 65 to CC&J exit, right onto 17th Street, follow signs to stadium. Standard Game Times: 7:05 p.m.; Sun. 2:05, 6:05.

Visiting Club Hotel: Clarion Hotel, 3333 S Glenstone Ave., Springfield, MO 65804. Telephone: (417) 883-6550.

RIO GRANDE VALLEY
WhiteWings

Mailing Address: 1216 Fair Park Blvd., Harlingen, TX 78550. Telephone: (956) 412-9464. FAX: (956) 412-9479. E-Mail Address: homerun@rgvwhitewings.com. Website: www.rgvwhitewings.com.

General Manager: Mike Babcock. Director, Stadium Operations: John Cannon. Head Groundskeeper: Omar Benavides. Director, Sales/Marketing: Clay Stanton. Office Manager: Marilyn Farley.

Manager: Eddie Dennis.

Game Information

Radio: None.

PA Announcer: Unavailable. Official Scorer: Unavailable.

Stadium Name (year opened): Harlingen Stadium (1951). Location: Expressway 83 to Lewis Lane exit, stadium is behind auditorium. Standard Game Times: 7:05 p.m., Sun. 6:05.

Visiting Club Hotel: Best Western, Expressway 83 and Stuart Place Road, Harlingen, TX 78550. Telephone: (956) 425-7070.

SAN ANGELO
Colts

Mailing Address: 3427 Johnson St., San Angelo, TX 76904. Telephone: (915) 942-6587. FAX: (915) 947-9480. E-Mail Address: colts@wcc.net. Website: www.sanangelocolts.com.

Operated by: San Angelo Colts Baseball Club, LLC.

President/General Manager: Harlan Bruha. Assistant General Manager: D.R. Smith. Director, Business Operations: Paula Dowler. Director, Media/Public Relations: Tom Nurre. Office Manager: Kathleen Quanz.

Manager: Dan Madsen. Pitching Coach: David Pierce. Trainer: Joe Briley.

Game Information

Radio Announcer: Tom Nurre. No. of Games Broadcast: Home-56, Away-56. Flagship Station: KKSA 1260-AM.

PA Announcer: Unavailable. Official Scorer: Unavailable.

Stadium Name (year opened): Colts Stadium (2000). Location: From north/south, take U.S. 87 to Knickerbocker Road, west to stadium; From east/west, take U.S. 67 to U.S. 87 South, to Knickerbocker Road, west to stadium. Standard Game Time: 7:05 p.m.

Visiting Club Hotel: Quality Inn, 4205 S Bryant Blvd., San Angelo, TX 76903. Telephone: (915) 653-6966.

WESTERNLEAGUE

Office Address: 426 Broadway, Suite 204, Chico, CA 95928. Mailing Address: PO Box 386, Chico CA 95927. Telephone: (530) 897-6125. FAX: (530) 897-6124. E-Mail Address: office@westernbaseball.com. Website: www.westernbaseball.com.

Year Founded: 1995.
President: Bob Linscheid. Director, Marketing: Margaret Schmidt. Administrative Assistant: Sarah Brawn. Chief Umpire: Daniel Perugini.
2000 Opening Date: May 19. Closing Date: Sept. 3.
Regular Season: 90 games.
Division Structure: North—Chico, Feather River, Solano, Tri-City. South—Sonoma County, Valley, Yuma, Zion.
Playoff Format: Top two teams in each division meet in best-of-5 series. Winners meet in best-of-5 series for league championship.
All-Star Game: July 10 at Chico.
Roster Limit: 22. Player Eligibility Rule: Minimum of four first-year professionals, maximum of eight with five or more years of professional service.
Brand of Baseball: Wilson.
Statistician: Howe Sportsdata, Boston Fish Pier, West Bldg. #1, Suite 302, Boston, MA 02210.

CHICO
Heat

Street Address: 250 Vallombrosa Ave., Suite 200, Chico, CA 95926. Telephone: (530) 343-4328. FAX: (530) 894-1799. E-Mail Address: information@chicoheat.com. Website: www.chicoheat.com.
Operated by: Chico Heat Baseball Club, LLC.
Principal Owner/President: Steve Nettleton.
General Manager: Brian Ceccon. Controller: Allan Guidi. Director, Sales/Promotions: Jeff Kragel. Director, Media Relations/Group Sales: Rory Miller. Director, Ticket Sales: Eric Tillmanns. Director, Merchandising: Chris Holen. Director, Food Services: Bob Pinocchio.
Manager: Charley Kerfeld. Coaches: Jon Fuller, Jeff Pico. Trainer: Ernie Vega. Directors, Player Procurement: Brian Ceccon, Charley Kerfeld.

Game Information
Radio Announcers: Rory Miller, Mike Baca. No. of Games Broadcast: Home-45, Away-45. Flagship Station: KPAY 1290-AM.
PA Announcer: Gordon Rowndtree. Official Scorer: Unavailable.
Stadium Name (year opened): Nettleton Stadium (1952). Location: From Highway 99, west at East First Ave., left onto Warner Street, right onto College Drive. Standard Game Times: 7:05 p.m., Sun. 6:05
Visiting Club Hotel: Holiday Inn, 685 Manzanita Ct., Chico, CA 95926. Telephone: (530) 345-2491.

FEATHER RIVER
Mudcats

Office Address: 903 B St., Marysville, CA 95901. Mailing Address: P.O. Box C, Marysville, CA 95901. Telephone: (530) 741-3600. FAX: (530) 741-3087.
Operated By: Feather River Baseball, LLC.
President: Scott Mendonsa.
General Manager: Joe Cates. Assistant General Manager: Scott Blackwood. Director, Media Relations: Amy Phillips. Head Groundskeeper: Mike Pimentel. Office Manager: Kristina Haynes.
Manager: Rex Gonzalez. Coach: Mike Joekel.

Game Information
Radio Announcer: Unavailable. No. of Games Broadcast: Home-45, Away-45. Flagship Station: Unavailable.
PA Announcer: Unavailable. Official Scorer: Unavailable.
Stadium Name (year opened): Bryant Field (2000). Location: Highway 99 North off I-5, to Highway 70, right on 9th Street, left on B Street. Standard Game Times: 7:05 p.m.

Visiting Club Hotel: TraveLodge, 721 10th St., Marysville, CA 95901. Telephone: (530) 742-8586.

SOLANO
Steelheads

Office Address: 1021 Helen Power Dr., Suite P300, Vacaville, CA 95687. Telephone: (707) 452-7400. FAX: (707) 452-7410. E-Mail Address: info@steelheadsbaseball.com. Website: www.steelheadsbaseball.com.
Operated By: Solano Steelheads, LLC.
Principal Owner/General Manager: Bruce Portner. Assistant General Manager: Matt Thomas. Director, Sales/Marketing: Patrick Cassidy. Director, Promotions: Jamie Baumgarten.
Manager: Bo Dodson. Coaches: Scott Stover, Gary Wilson.

Game Information
Radio Announcer: Unavailable. No. of Games Broadcast: Home-42, Away-19. Flagship Station: KATD 990-AM.
PA Announcer: Unavailable. Official Scorer: Bill Jones.
Stadium Name (year opened): Nut Tree Stadium (2000). Location: I-80 East to Allison Road exit, left back over freeway, right on East Monte Vista Ave.; I-80 West to East Monte Vista Ave., right to stadium. Standard Game Times: 7:05 p.m., Sun. 4:05.
Visiting Club Hotel: Microtel Inn and Suites, 1480 Ary Lane, Dixon, CA 95620. Telephone: (707) 693-0606.

SONOMA COUNTY
Crushers

Office Address: 5900 Labath Ave., Rohnert Park, CA 94928. Telephone: (707) 588-8300. FAX: (707) 588-8721. Website: www.crush erabaseball.com
Operated by: Sonoma County Professional Baseball, Inc.
President/General Manager: Robert Fletcher. Director, Business Operations: Susan Fletcher. Director, Stadium Operations: Steve Fraire. Director, Sales/Marketing: Kevin Wolski.
Manager: Jeffrey Leonard. Coach: Dolf Hes.

Game Information
Radio Announcer: Roxy Bernstein. No. of Games Broadcast: Home-45, Away-45. Flagship Station: KBBF 89.1 FM.
PA Announcer: Jeremy Logan. Official Scorer: Tom Stillman.
Stadium Name (year opened): Rohnert Park Stadium (1981). Location: Route 101, west on Rohnert Park Expressway, right on Labath Ave. Standard Game Times: 7:05 p.m.; Wed., Sun. 1:35; Sat. 5:05.
Visiting Club Hotel: Unavailable.

TRI-CITY
Posse

Office Address: 6200 Burden Rd., Pasco, WA 99301. Telephone: (509) 547-6773. FAX: (509) 547-4008. E-Mail Address: posse@tcposse.com. Website: www.tcposse.com.
Operated By: Tri-City Posse Baseball, Inc.
President/General Manager: John Montero. Assistant General Manager: Rich Buel. Office Manager: Rick Marple. Head Groundskeeper: Gordi Frantti.
Manager: Wally Backman. Coaches: Chris Catanoso, Floyd Youmans. Trainer: Leo Combs.

Game Information
Radio Announcer: Rich Buel. No. of Games Broadcast: Home-45, Away-45. Flagship Station: KALE 960-AM.
PA Announcer: Unavailable. Official Scorer: Unavailable.
Stadium Name (year opened): Posse Stadium (1995). Location: I-84 to Road 68, right on Burden Road. Standard Game Times: 7:05 p.m., Sun. 5:05.
Visiting Club Hotel: Pasco Red Lion, 1668 20th Ave, Pasco, WA 99301. Telephone: (509) 547-0701.

VALLEY
Vipers

Office Address: 3906 N Scottsdale Rd., Scottsdale, AZ 85250.
Telephone: (480) 663-8100. **FAX**: (480) 663-0101. **E-Mail Address**: val
leyvipers@earthlink.net. **Website**: www.valleyvipers.com.
Operated by: Valley Vipers Professional Baseball, LLC.
President: James Goldsmith.
General Manager: George King. **Director, Stadium Operations**: Dana
Braccia. **Controller**: Robert Chia. **Director, Merchandising**: Mort
Bloomberg.
Manager: Bob Welch. **Coach**: Guy Sularz. **Director, Player Development**: George King.

Game Information
Radio Announcer: Dave Tunell. **No. of Games Broadcast**: Home-45,
Away-45. **Flagship Station**: 960-AM.
PA Announcer: Unavailable. **Official Scorer**: Unavailable.
Stadium Name (year opened): Scottsdale Stadium (1992). **Location**:
Northeast corner of Civic Center Blvd. and Osborn Road. **Standard Game
Time**: 6:45 p.m..
Visiting Club Hotel: Fairfield Inn, 5101 N Scottsdale Rd., Scottsdale, AZ
85250. Telephone: (480) 945-4392.

YUMA
Bullfrogs

Office Address: 204 S Madison Ave, Yuma, AZ 85364. **Telephone**:
(520) 782-3536. **FAX**: (520) 782-3911. **E-Mail Address**: lynn@yuma
frogs.com. **Website**: www.yumafrogs.com.
Operated by: Family Baseball of Yuma.
Principal Owners: Pete Dunn, Donna Dunn.
General Manager: Dave McDowell. **Director, Sales/Marketing**: Joe
Henderson. **Office Manager**: Lynn Fazz. **Director, Group Sales**: Pete
Cicero. **Director, Merchandising**: Andrew Guidi.
Manager: Bill Plummer. **Coaches**: Terrel Hansen, Chris White.

Game Information
Radio Announcer: Unavailable. **No. of Games Broadcast**: Home-45,
Away-45. **Flagship Station**: KBLU 560-AM.
PA Announcer: Unavailable. **Official Scorer**: Unavailable.
Stadium Name (year opened): Desert Sun Stadium (1973). **Location**: I-8
to 16th Street West exit, south on Avenue A. **Standard Game Time**: 7:30 p.m..
Visiting Club Hotel: Unavailable.

ZION
Pioneerzz

Office Address: 1240 E 100 South, Suite 16B, St. George, UT 84790.
Telephone: (435) 656-9000. **FAX**: (435) 628-8389. **Website**: www.zion pio-
neerzz.com.
Operated by: Shugart Corporation.
Principal Owner: Dennis Narlinger.
President/General Manager: Pat Elster. **Director, Sales/Stadium
Operations**: Debbie Waggoner. **Controller**: Steve Alvey. **Director, Ticket
Sales**: Andy Romney. **Office Manager**: Lena Burton.
Manager: Mike Littlewood. **Coach**: Randy Wilstead. **Trainer**: Ken Hurt.

Game Information
Radio Announcer: Larry Jewel. **No. of Games Broadcast**: Home-45,
Away-45. **Flagship Station**: Total Sports 1450-AM.
PA Announcer: Ed Rodgers. **Official Scorer**: Unavailable.
Stadium Name (year opened): Bruce Hurst Field (1994). **Location**: I-
15 to exit 6, east on St. George Blvd., south on 700 East, west on 600
South. **Standard Game Times**: 7:05 p.m..
Visiting Club Hotel: St. Redd's Oasis Resort, 897 W Mesquite Blvd,
Mesquite, NV 89027. Telephone: (702) 346-5232.

INDEPENDENT SCHEDULES

Atlantic League

Atlantic City

MAY
2-3-4.............. Maryland
5-6-7 .... Bridgeport
10-11 .... Maryland
15-16-17-18 .... Nashua
19-20-21 ..... Long Island
29-30-31 .... Newark

JUNE
1 .... Newark
2-3-4 .... Somerset
12-13-14 .. Lehigh Valley
19-20-21-22.. Maryland
26-27-28 .... Maryland
30 .... Bridgeport

JULY
1-2 .... Bridgeport
3-4-5 .... Nashua
6-7-8 .... Long Island
9-10 .... Maryland
17-18-19 .... Newark
24-25-26-27 .... L.I.
28-29-30 .... Somerset

AUGUST
2-3-4 .... Lehigh Valley
11-12-13 .... Maryland
14-15-16-17.. Bridgeport
25-26-27 .... Nashua

SEPTEMBER
8-9-10 .... Newark
18-19-20-21 ... Somerset
22-23-24-25....... Lehigh

Bridgeport

APRIL
28-29-30 .... Somerset

MAY
8-9-10-11 .... Lehigh
12-13-14..... Atlantic City
15-16-17-18 ...... Newark
26-27-28 .... Maryland

JUNE
6-7-8 .... Nashua
9-10-11 .... Long Island
12-13-14......... Maryland
15-16-17-18 .. Somerset
23-24-24-25........... A.C.
26-27-28 .. Lehigh Valley

JULY
14-15-16 .... Maryland
24-25-26-27 ...... Nashua
28-29-30-31 .... L.I.

AUGUST
2-3-4 .... Maryland
5-6-7 .... Somerset
8-9-10 .... Newark
18-19-20 .. Lehigh Valley
22-23-24..... Atlantic City

SEPTEMBER
1-2-3 .... Newark
4-5-6-7............ Maryland
15-16-17 .... Nashua
19-20-21 ...... Long Island

Lehigh Valley

APRIL
28-29-30 .... Maryland

MAY
2-3-4 .... Bridgeport

5-6-7 .... Maryland
12-13-14 .... Nashua
15-16-17-18 Long Island
19-20-21 .... Somerset
26-27-28..... Atlantic City

JUNE
2-3-4 .... Newark
15-16-17-18.... Maryland
19-20-21-22.. Bridgeport
23-24-25 ....Maryland
29-30 .... Nashua

JULY
1-2 .... Nashua
3-4-5 .... Long Island
14-15-16 .... Atlantic City
24-25-26-27 .. Somerset
28-29-30 .... Newark

AUGUST
11-12-13 .... Bridgeport
14-15-16-17.... Maryland
22-23-24 .... Nashua
25-26-27 ..... Long Island

SEPTEMBER
4-5-6-7 ...... Atlantic City
11-12-13-14 ...... Newark
15-16-17 .... Somerset

Long Island

APRIL
28-29-30 .... Nashua

MAY
8-9-10-11 .... Newark
12-13-14......... Maryland
22-23-24-25........ Lehigh
29-30-31 .... Maryland

JUNE
1 .... Maryland
2-3-4 .... Bridgeport
6-7-8 .... Atlantic City
12-13-14 .... Somerset
15-16-17-18 ...... Nashua
26-27-28 .... Newark
29-30 .... Maryland

JULY
1-2 .... Maryland
14-15-16 .... Somerset
17-18-19 .... Maryland
20-21-22-23.. Bridgeport

AUGUST
5-6-6 .... Nashua
8-9-10 ...... Lehigh Valley
18-19-20 .... Newark
21-22-23 .... Maryland
28-29-30-31 .... A.C.

SEPTEMBER
1-2-3 .... Lehigh Valley
5-6-7 .... Somerset
11-12-13 .... Bridgeport
15-16-17.... Atlantic City

Maryland

MAY
15-16-17-18 ... Somerset

JULY
20-21-22-23 ...... Nashua

AUGUST
5-6-7 .... Lehigh Valley
8-9-10 .... Somerset
18-19-20.... Atlantic City
28-29-30-31 ...... Newark

SEPTEMBER
8-9-10 ..... Long Island
12-13-14 .... Nashua
22-23-24-25.. Bridgeport

Nashua

MAY
5-6-7 .... Long Island
8-9-10-11 .... Somerset
19-20-21 ...... Bridgeport
22-23-24-25......... A.C.
29-30-31 .. Lehigh Valley

JUNE
1.............. Lehigh Valley
2-3-4 .... Maryland
9-10-11 .... Maryland
12-13-14 .... Newark
19-20-21 .... Somerset
23-24-25 ..... Long Island

JULY
6-7-8 .... Bridgeport
14-15-16 .... Newark
17-18-19 .. Lehigh Valley
28-29-30 .... Maryland

AUGUST
8-9-10......... Atlantic City
14-15-16-17 Long Island
18-19-20 .... Somerset
28-29-30-31.. Bridgeport

SEPTEMBER
1-2-0......... Atlantic City
8-9-10 ...... Lehigh Valley
18-19-20-21... Maryland
22-23-24-25 ...... Newark

Newark

APRIL
28-29-30.... Atlantic City

MAY
2-3-4 .... Long Island
12-13-14 .... Somerset
19-20-21 .... Maryland
22-23-24-25.. Bridgeport
26-27-28 .... Nashua

JUNE
6-7-8 .... Maryland
9-10-11 ..... Lehigh Valley
15-16-17-18.......... A.C.
19-20-21-22 Long Island
29-30 .... Somerset

JULY
1-2 .... Somerset
3-4-5 .... Bridgeport
6-7-8 .... Maryland
20-21-22-23...... Lehigh
24-25-26-27.... Maryland

AUGUST
2-3-4 .... Nashua
5-6-7 .... Atlantic City
11-12-13 ..... Long Island
22-23-24 .... Somerset
25-26-27 ...... Bridgeport

SEPTEMBER
4-5-6-7 .... Nashua
15-16-17........ Maryland
19-20-21 .. Lehigh Valley

Somerset

MAY
1-2-3-4 .... Nashua

5-6-7 .... Newark
22-23-24-25.... Maryland
26-27-28 ..... Long Island
29-30-31 .... Bridgeport
JUNE
1 .... Bridgeport
7-8 .... Lehigh Valley
9-10-11 ...... Atlantic City
23-24-25 .... Newark

26-27-28 .... Nashua
JULY
3-4-5 .... Maryland
6-7-8-9 ..... Lehigh Valley
17-18-19 ...... Bridgeport
20-21-22-23 ...... A.C.
AUGUST
1-2-3-4 .... Long Island

11-12-13 .... Nashua
14-15-16-17 ..... Newark
25-26-27 .... Maryland
28-29-30-31........ Lehigh
SEPTEMBER
1-2-3 .... Maryland
8-9-10 .... Bridgeport
12-13-14 ..... Atlantic City
22-23-24-25 Long Island

Frontier League

Canton
JUNE
3-4-5 .... Evansville
6-7-8 .... Johnstown
16-17-18 .... River City
19-20-21 ... Cook County
29-30............. Richmond
JULY
1 .... Richmond
5-6-7 .... Chillicothe
8-9-10 .... London
20-21-22 ...... Evansville
23-24-25 ...... Johnstown
AUGUST
2-3-4 ...... Springfield
8-9-10 .... Chillicothe
11-12-13......... River City
18-19-20 Dubois County
27-28-29........... London

Chillicothe
MAY
31 .... Canton
JUNE
1-2 .... Canton
6-7-8 .... Richmond
13-14-15 .... Springfield
16-17-18 .... Evansville
22-23-24... Cook County
29-30............ Johnstown
JULY
1 .... Johnstown
8-9-10........... Springfield
14-15-16 .... London
23-24-25............ London
29-30-31............ Canton
AUGUST
2-3-4 ...... Dubois County
11-12-13......... Johnstown
18-19-20 ...... River City
27-28-29 .... Richmond

Cook County
MAY
31 .... Springfield
JUNE
1-2................. Springfield
6-7-8.................. London
16-17-18....... Johnstown
25-26-27 .... Richmond
JULY
2-3-4 .... River City
8-9-10 .... Evansville
14-15-16 Dubois County
20-21-22....... River City
23-24-25 Dubois County
29-30-31............ London
AUGUST
5-6-7 .... Canton
15-16-17 .... Chillicothe
21-22-23 ...... Evansville
27-28-29 .... Springfield

Dubois County
JUNE
3-4-5............. Springfield

9-10-11 ..... Cook County
16-17-18............. London
19-20-21 ..... Chillicothe
25-26-27............ Canton
29-30............. Evansville
JULY
1 .... Evansville
5-6-7 .... Johnstown
8-9-10........... River City
17-18-19 ...... Johnstown
29-30-31 ...... Evansville
AUGUST
8-9-10 .... Cook County
15-16-17 ...... Richmond
21-22-23 .... River City
24-25-26....... Springfield

Evansville
JUNE
6-7-8.... Dubois County
12-13-14... Cook County
22-23-24 ...... Johnstown
25-26-27 .... London
JULY
2-3-4 .... Canton
14-15-16 ...... Springfield
17-18-19........ River City
23-24-25........ Springfield
26-27-28 ...... Cook County
AUGUST
5-6-7 .... Chillicothe
11-12-13 Dubois County
18-19-20 .... Richmond
24-25-26 .... Canton
27-28-29 .... River City

Johnstown
MAY
31 .... Dubois County
JUNE
1-2 .... Dubois County
3-4-5 .... Richmond
9-10-11 .... Chillicothe
13-14-15........... London
19-20-21 ...... River City
25-26-27....... Springfield
JULY
2-3-4 .... London
14-15-16 .... Canton
20-21-22 ...... Chillicothe
29-30-31 .... Richmond
AUGUST
15-16-17 ...... Evansville
18-19-20...... Cook County
21-22-23 .... Canton
27-28-29 Dubois County

London
JUNE
3-4-5 .... Chillicothe
9-10-11 .... Canton
19-20-21 ...... Springfield
22-23-24 .... River City
29-30 ...... Cook County
JULY
1 .... Cook County
5-6-7 .... Richmond

17-18-19 .... Canton
26-27-28 ...... Johnstown
AUGUST
2-3-4 .... Evansville
8-9-10 .... Johnstown
11-12-13....... Cook County
15-16-17 Dubois County
21-22-23 .... Richmond
24-25-26 ...... Chillicothe

Richmond
MAY
31 .... London
JUNE
1-2 .... London
9-10-11 .... River City
13-14-15 .... Canton
19-20-21 ...... Evansville
22-23-24 Dubois County
JULY
2-3-4 .... Chillicothe
8-9-10 .... Johnstown
17-18-19 ...... Chillicothe
20-21-22.............. London
26-27-28 .... Canton
AUGUST
2-3-4 .... Cook County
8-9-10 .... River City
15-16-17 .... Springfield
24-25-26 ...... Johnstown

River City
MAY
31 .... Evansville
JUNE
3-4-5........ Cook County
13-14-15 Dubois County
25-26-27 ...... Chillicothe
29-30 .... Springfield
JULY
1 .... Springfield
5-6-7 .... Evansville
14-15-16 .... Richmond
23-24-25 .... Richmond
26-27-28 Dubois County
AUGUST
2-3-4 .... Johnstown
5-6-7............... London
11-12-13....... Springfield
15-16-17 .... Canton
24-25-26...... Cook County

Springfield
JUNE
6-7-8 .... River City
9-10-11........ Evansville
16-17-18 .... Richmond
22-23-24 .... Canton
JULY
2-3-4..... Dubois County
5-6-7........... Cook County
17-18-19... Cook County
20-21-22 Dubois County
26-27-28 .... Chillicothe
29-30-31 .... River City

Northern League

CENTRAL DIVISION

Duluth
MAY
26-27-28 ... Schaumburg
29-30-31 .... Madison
JUNE
5-6-7 .... St. Paul
9-10-11 .... Winnipeg
19-20-21 .... Sioux City
30......................... Fargo
JULY
1-2 .... Fargo
3-4-5 .... Sioux Falls
14-15-16 .... Sioux Falls
18-19-20 .... Sioux City
28-29-30 .... St. Paul
AUGUST
7 .... St. Paul
8-9-10 .... Schaumburg
11-12-13 .... Madison
18-19-20 .... Fargo
21-22-23 .... Winnipeg

Fargo-Moorhead
MAY
29-30-31 ...... Sioux Falls
JUNE
2-3-4 .... Duluth
9-10-11 .... St. Paul
13-14-15 ... Schaumburg
22-23-24-25 ... Winnipeg
JULY
4-5-6 .... Madison
7-8-9 .... Sioux City
14-15-16 .... Madison
18-19-20 ... Schaumburg
28-29-30........ Winnipeg
AUGUST
8-9-10 .... Sioux City
11-12-13 ...... Sioux Falls
22-23-24 .... St. Paul
25-26-27 .... Duluth

Madison
JUNE
1-2-3 .... St. Paul
6-7-8 .... Schaumburg
16-17-18 .... Fargo
19-20-21 ...... Sioux Falls
27-28-29 ...... Sioux City
30 .... Winnipeg
JULY
1-2 .... Winnipeg
10-11-12 .... Duluth
17-18-19........ Winnipeg
21-22-23 .... Fargo
28-29-30 ... Schaumburg
AUGUST
8-9-10 .... St. Paul

18-19-20 ...... Sioux City
22-23-24 ..... Sioux Falls
29-30-31 .... Duluth
SEPTEMBER
1.......................... Duluth

St. Paul
MAY
26-27-28 .... Madison
JUNE
8...................... Duluth
12-13-14........ Winnipeg
18 .... Sioux City
23-24-25 .... Duluth
26 .... Sioux City
27-28-29 .... Fargo
JULY
5...................... Sioux City
6-7-8 .... Sioux Falls
10-11-12 ... Schaumburg
21-22-23 ...... Sioux City
25-26-27 .... Madison
AUGUST
2-3-4 .... Sioux Falls
5-6 .... Duluth
15-16-17 .... Fargo
18-19-20........ Winnipeg
29-30-31 ... Schaumburg
SEPTEMBER
1................ Schaumburg

Schaumburg
MAY
29-30-31 .... St. Paul
JUNE
2-3-4 .... Sioux City
9-10-11 ...... Sioux Falls
19-20-21 .... Fargo
22-23-24-25 ..... Madison
JULY
3-4-5 .... Winnipeg
7-8-9 .... Duluth
14-15-16........ Winnipeg
24-25-26 .... Fargo
AUGUST
2-3-4 .... Duluth
5-6-7 .... Sioux Falls
11-12-13 .... St. Paul
15-16-17 ...... Sioux City
25-26-27 .... Madison

Sioux City
MAY
26-27-28 .... Fargo
30-31 .... Winnipeg
JUNE
1 .... Winnipeg
9-10-11 .... Madison

13-14-15 .... Duluth
16 .... St. Paul
22-23-24-25. Sioux Falls
30............... Schaumburg
JULY
1-2 .... Schaumburg
3-4 .... St. Paul
14-15-16 .... St. Paul
24-25-26 .... Duluth
AUGUST
2-3-4 .... Fargo
5-6-7 .... Madison
11-12-13 .... Winnipeg
21-22-23 ... Schaumburg
25-26-27 ..... Sioux Falls

Sioux Falls
JUNE
2-3-4............... Winnipeg
6-7-8 .... Sioux City
12-13-14 .... Madison
16-17-18 .... Duluth
27-28-29 ... Schaumburg
30 .... St. Paul
JULY
1-2 .... St. Paul
10-11-12 .... Fargo
17-18-19 .... St. Paul
21-22-23 .... Duluth
28-29-30 ...... Sioux City
AUGUST
8-9-10 .... Winnipeg
14-15-16 .... Madison
18-19-20 ... Schaumburg
29-30-31 .... Fargo
SEPTEMBER
1......................... Fargo

Winnipeg
MAY
26-27-28 ...... Sioux Falls
JUNE
6-7-8 .... Fargo
16-17-18 ... Schaumburg
19-20-21 .... St. Paul
26-27-28 .... Duluth
JULY
7-8-9 .... Madison
10-11-12........ Sioux City
21-22-23 ... Schaumburg
24-25-26 ...... Sioux Falls
AUGUST
2-3-4 .... Madison
5-6-7 .... Fargo
15-16-17 .... Duluth
25-26-27 .... St. Paul
29-30-31   Sioux City
SEPTEMBER
1 .... Sioux City

EASTERN DIVISION

Adirondack
MAY
26-27-28 .... Allentown
29-30-31 ..... New Jersey
JUNE
9-10-11 .... Elmira
19-20-21............. Albany
22-23-24-25...... Quebec
30 .... Catskill

JULY
1-2 .... Catskill
3-4-5 .... Waterbury
14-15-16 .... Elmira
24-25-26 .... Allentown
AUGUST
2-3-4 .... Waterbury
5-6-7 .... Albany
11-12-13 .... Quebec

15-16-17 .... Catskill
25-26-27 .... New Jersey

Albany
MAY
26-27-28 .... Catskill
30-31 .... Elmira
JUNE
1 .... Elmira
9-10-11 .... New Jersey

13-14-15...... Adirondack
22-23-24-25 .. Waterbury
30.................. Allentown
JULY
1-2 .... Allentown
3-4-5 .... Quebec
14-15-16 .... Quebec
17-18-19...... New Jersey
28-29-30..... Adirondack
AUGUST
8-9-10........ Allentown
11-12-13 .... Waterbury
18-19-20 .... Catskill
21-22-23 .... Elmira

Allentown
MAY
30-31 .... Quebec
JUNE
1 .... Quebec
2-3-4 .... Albany
9-10-11 .... Waterbury
19-20-21 .... Catskill
22-23-24-25 ... Elmira
JULY
6-7-8 .... Adirondack
10-11-12..... New Jersey
14-15-16 .... Catskill
18-19-20 ...... Waterbury
28-29-30..... New Jersey
AUGUST
2-3-4............. Albany
11-12-13........ Elmira
18-19-20 .... Quebec
21-22-23 ...... Adirondack

Catskill
MAY
30-31 .... Waterbury
JUNE
1.................. Waterbury
2-3-4.......... Adirondack
9-10-11 .... Quebec
13-14-15 .... Allentown
22-23-24-25 .... New Jersey
JULY
3-4-5 .... Elmira
7-8-9................. Albany
18-19-20...... Adirondack

21-22-23 .... Albany
29-30 .... Elmira
AUGUST
6 .... New Jersey
8-9-10 .... Quebec
13 .... New Jersey
22-23-24 ...... Waterbury
25-26-27 .... Allentown
29 .... Elmira

Elmira
MAY
26-27-28 ...... Waterbury
JUNE
6-7-8 .... Albany
12-13-14 .... Quebec
16-17-18 .... Allentown
27-28-29 ..... Adirondack
JULY
7-8-9 .... New Jersey
10-11-12 ...... Catskill
21-22-23 ..... Adirondack
25-26-27 .... Quebec
28 .... Catskill
AUGUST
2-3-4........ New Jersey
5-6-7........... Allentown
15-16-17........ Albany
25-26-27 ...... Waterbury
30-31 .... Catskill
SEPTEMBER
1 .... Catskill

New Jersey
JUNE
2-3-4 .... Quebec
5-6-7 .... Adirondack
16-17-18 .... Catskill
19-20-21 ...... Waterbury
27-28-29........ Albany
30 .... Elmira
JULY
1-2 .... Elmira
3-4-5 .... Allentown
21-22-23 .... Waterbury
25-26-27 .... Albany
AUGUST
5-7 .... Catskill
8-9-10 .... Elmira
11-12 .... Catskill

18-19-20...... Adirondack
21-22-23 .... Quebec
29-30-31 .... Allentown
SEPTEMBER
1 .... Allentown

Quebec
MAY
26-27-28..... New Jersey
JUNE
6-7-8 .... Allentown
16-17-18............. Albany
19-20-21 .... Elmira
27-28-29 .... Catskill
JULY
7-8-9 .... Waterbury
10-11-12 .... Adirondack
17-18-19 ...... Elmira
21-22-23 .... Allentown
AUGUST
2-3-4 .... Catskill
5-6-7 .... Waterbury
15-16-17..... New Jersey
25-26-27 .... Albany
29-30-31 .... Adirondack
SEPTEMBER
1 .... Adirondack

Waterbury
JUNE
2-3-4 .... Elmira
6-7-8 .... Catskill
12-13-14..... New Jersey
16-17-18..... Adirondack
27-28-29 .... Allentown
30 .... Quebec
JULY
1-2 .... Quebec
10-11-12 .... Albany
14-15-16 ..... New Jersey
25-26-27 .... Catskill
28-29-30 .... Quebec
AUGUST
8-9-10.......... Adirondack
15-16-17 .... Allentown
18-19-20 .... Elmira
29-39-31 .... Albany
SEPTEMBER
1 .... Albany

Texas-Louisiana League

Alexandria
MAY
4-5-5-6-7..... San Angelo
15-16.............. Greenville
18-19-19 .... Ozark
20-21-22-23 ..... Jackson
JUNE
2-3 .... Greenville
7-8-9-9-10.. Rio Grande
11-12-13-14 ...... Amarillo
17-18................. Greenville
29-30 .... Ozark
JULY
1 .... Ozark
14-14-15-16 ...... Amarillo
17-18-19 ..... Rio Grande
AUGUST
3-4-5-6 .... Jackson
8-9-10-11 .... Lafayette
20-21-22..... San Angelo
24-25-26-27.... Lafayette
31 .... Greenville
SEPTEMBER
1 .... Greenville

2-3 .... Ozark

Amarillo
MAY
4-5-6-7 .... Rio Grande
9-10-11-12 .. San Angelo
13-14-15-16.... Lafayette
18-19 .... San Angelo
29-30-31 ...... Alexandria
JUNE
1 .... Alexandria
2-3-4-5.......... Lafayette
7-8-9-10........... Ozark
15-16-17-18.... Lafayette
24-25 .... San Angelo
28-29-30 .... Jackson
JULY
1 .... Jackson
2-3-4-5 .... Greenville
26-27-28-29.. Alexandria
AUGUST
4-5-6-7 .... Ozark
16-17-18-19 ..... Jackson
20-21-22-23 .. Greenville
29-30-31 ..... Rio Grande

SEPTEMBER
1 .... Rio Grande

Greenville
MAY
4-5-6-7 .... Jackson
9-10-11-12...... Lafayette
13-14 .... Alexandria
29-30................ Jackson
JUNE
4-5 .... Alexandria
7-8-9-10 ..... San Angelo
15-16 .... Alexandria
24-25-26-27 Rio Grande
28-29-30......... Lafayette
JULY
1 .... Lafayette
13-14-15-16......... Ozark
17-18-19-20 San Angelo
23-24................ Jackson
30-31 .... Amarillo
AUGUST
1-2 .... Amarillo
8-9-10-11 .... Amarillo
12-13-14-15 Rio Grande

Jackson

MAY
9-10-11-12.... Alexandria
13-14-15-16......... Ozark
18-19.............. Greenville
25-26-27-28...... Amarillo
31.................. Greenville

JUNE
1.................... Greenville
2-3-4-5........ San Angelo
20-21-22-23 Rio Grande
24-25-26-27... Alexandria

JULY
6-7-8-9............ Amarillo
13-14-15-16.... Lafayette
17-18-19-20...... Ozark
21-22............. Greenville

AUGUST
8-9-10-11 .... Rio Grande
25-26-27-28 San Angelo
29-30-31........... Lafayette

SEPTEMBER
1 .... Lafayette
2-3................ Greenville

Lafayette

MAY
18-19...... Rio Grande
20-21-22-23......... Ozark

JUNE
7-8-9-10.......... Jackson
11-12-13-14 .. Greenville
20-21-22-23.. Alexandria

JULY
6-7-8-9........ San Angelo
17-18-19-20..... Amarillo

30-31................ Jackson

AUGUST
1-2................... Jackson
3-4-5-6.......... Greenville
12-13-14-15.. Alexandria
16-17-18-19 San Angelo
20-21-22-23 Rio Grande

SEPTEMBER
2-3............. Rio Grande

Ozark

MAY
4-5-6-7............ Lafayette
9-10-11-12.. Alexandria
25-26-27-28.. Alexandria
29-30-31..... San Angelo

JUNE
1................. San Angelo
2-3-4-5....... Rio Grande
20-21-22-23... Amarillo
24-25-26-27.... Lafayette

JULY
2-3-4-5............ Jackson
6-7-8-9........... Amarillo
21-22-23-24.... Lafayette
26-27-28-29 .. Greenville

AUGUST
12-13-14-15...... Amarillo
16-17-18-19 .. Greenville
20-21-22-23 ..... Amarillo
29-30-31 ..... San Angelo

SEPTEMBER
1 .... San Angelo

Rio Grande

MAY
20-21-22-23..... Amarillo
25-26-27-28 .. Greenville
30-30-31....... Lafayette

JUNE
1 .... Lafayette
11-12-13-14 ..... Jackson
15-16-17-18......... Ozark
28-29-30 ..... San Angelo

JULY
1 .... San Angelo
2-3-4-5............ Greenville
6-7-8-9 .... Greenville
21-22-23-24.. Alexandria
26-27-28-29 ..... Jackson

AUGUST
1-2-2-3................ Ozark
4-5-6-7......... San Angelo
16-17-18-19.. Alexandria
25-26-27-28...... Amarillo

San Angelo

MAY
13-14-15-16 Rio Grande
20-21-22-23 .. Greenville
25-26-27-28.... Lafayette

JUNE
11-12-13-14 ...... Ozark
15-16-17-18 ..... Jackson
20-21-22-23 .. Greenville
26-27............. Amarillo

JULY
2-3-4-5.......... Alexandria
13-14-15-16 Rio Grande
21-22-23-24..... Amarillo
26-27-28-29... Lafayette
30-31 .... Alexandria

AUGUST
1-2 .... Alexandria
8-9-10-11 .... Ozark
12-13-14-15 .... Jackson

SEPTEMBER
2-3.................. Amarillo

Western League

Chico

MAY
23-24-25.. Feather River
26-27-28 .... Yuma
30-31.................. Solano

JUNE
1...................... Solano
13-14-15 .... Sonoma
16-17-18................ Zion
27-28-29 .... Tri-City

JULY
1-2-3 .... Valley
7-8-9 .... Tri-City
21-22-23 .... Tri-City
24-25-26 .... Solano

AUGUST
4-5-6 .... Chico
7-8-9...................... Zion
14-15-16 .... Yuma
18-19-20 .... Valley
29-30-31 .... Sonoma

Solano

MAY
26-27-28.. Feather River

JUNE
2-3-4 .... Tri-City
5-6-7 .... Yuma
9-10-11 .... Zion
23-24-25 .... Sonoma
27-28-29 .... Valley

JULY
4-5-6 .... Chico
14-15-16 .... Valley
21-22-23 .... Chico
28-29-30 .... Tri-City

AUGUST
1-2-3 .... Sonoma
11-12-13.. Feather River
14-15-16............. Valley
21-22-23.. Feather River
25-26-27 .... Yuma

Feather River

MAY
19-20-21 .... Solano
30-31 .... Tri-City

JUNE
1........................ Tri-City
2-3-4 .... Chico
13-14-15 .... Yuma
16-17-18 .... Valley
19-20-21 .... Zion

JULY
1-2-3 .... Sonoma
7-8-9 .... Solano
21-22-23 .... Tri-City
24-25-26 .... Solano

Sonoma County

MAY
26-27-28................ Zion
29-30-31 .... Valley

JUNE
5-6-7........ Feather River
16-17-18 .... Solano
19-20-21 .... Chico
27-28-29 .... Yuma

JULY
4-5-6 .... Tri-City
7-8-9...................... Zion
18-19-20 .... Solano
21-22-23 .... Yuma

AUGUST
4-5-6 .... Valley
7-8-9 .... Chico
18-19-20................ Zion
21-22-23 .... Tri-City

SEPTEMBER
1-2-3....... Feather River

Tri-City

MAY
19-20-21 .... Chico
22-23-24 .... Yuma

JUNE
5-6-7...................... Zion
9-10-11 .... Sonoma
20-21-22 .... Valley
23-24-25.. Feather River

JULY
1-2-3 .... Solano

14-15-16 .... Sonoma
17-18-19 .... Valley
AUGUST
1-2-3....... Feather River
4-5-6...................... Zion
15-16-17 .... Chico
18-19-20 .... Yuma
28-29-30 .... Solano
SEPTEMBER
1-2-3 .... Chico

Valley
MAY
22-23-24 .... Sonoma
26-27-28 .... Tri-City
JUNE
6-7-8 .... Chico
9-10-11 .... Feather River
13-14-15 .... Solano
23-24-25 .... Yuma
JULY
4-5-6...................... Zion
7-8-9 .... Yuma
21-22-23................. Zion
31 .... Yuma
AUGUST
1-2.................... Yuma

8-9-10 .... Solano
11-12-13 .... Tri-City
15-16-17 .... Sonoma
25-26-27.. Feather River
28-29-30 .... Chico

Yuma
MAY
19-20-21 .... Sonoma
29-30-31................. Zion
JUNE
2-3-4 .... Valley
9-10-11................. Chico
16-17-18 .... Tri-City
19-20-21 .... Solano
JULY
4-5-6....... Feather River
14-15-16 .... Chico
17-18-19.. Feather River
24-25-26 .... Valley
28-29-30 .... Sonoma
AUGUST
4-5-6 .... Solano
8-9-10 .... Tri-City
21-22-23................. Zion
SEPTEMBER
1-2-3 .... Valley

Zion
MAY
18-19-20 .... Valley
22-23-24 .... Solano
JUNE
1-2-3 .... Sonoma
12-13-14 .... Tri-City
22-23-24 .... Chico
27-28-29.. Feather River
30 .... Yuma
JULY
1-3...................... Yuma
13-14-15.. Feather River
17-18-19 .... Chico
24-25-26 .... Sonoma
27-28-29 .... Valley
AUGUST
10-11-12 .... Sonoma
24-25-26 .... Tri-City
28-29-30 .... Yuma
31...................... Solano
SEPTEMBER
1-2...................... Solano

FOREIGN LEAGUES

1999 STANDINGS

MEXICAN LEAGUE

Triple-A Classification

CENTRAL	W	L	PCT	GB		SOUTH	W	L	PCT	GB
Mexico City Tigers	75	38	.664	—		Cancun	63	57	.525	—
Mexico City Reds	74	43	.632	3		Tabasco	63	57	.525	—
Cordoba	51	66	.436	26		Yucatan	60	56	.517	1
Oaxaca	49	70	.412	29		Campeche	58	60	.492	4
Aguascalientes	47	74	.388	33		Veracruz	50	69	.420	12½

NORTH	W	L	PCT	GB			W	L	PCT	GB
Saltillo	74	45	.622	—		Two Laredos	53	65	.449	20½
Monclova	71	46	.607	1		Union Laguna	50	69	.420	24
Monterrey	64	54	.542	9½		Reynosa	42	75	.359	31

PLAYOFFS (all series best-of-7): **Quarterfinals**—Mexico City Reds def. Monterrey 4-1; Mexico City Tigers def. Tabasco 4-3; Monclova def. Cancun 4-0; Saltillo def. Campeche 4-2. **Semifinals**—Mexico City Reds def. Saltillo 4-3; Mexico City Tigers def. Monclova 4-2. **Finals**—Mexico City Reds def. Mexico City Tigers 4-2.

JAPAN LEAGUES

CENTRAL	W	L	PCT	GB		PACIFIC	W	L	PCT	GB
Chunichi	81	54	.600	—		Fukuoka	78	54	.591	—
Yomiuri	75	60	.556	6		Seibu	75	59	.560	4
Yokohama	71	64	.526	10		Orix	68	65	.511	10½
Yakult	66	69	.489	15		Chiba Lotte	63	70	.474	15½
Hiroshima	57	78	.422	24		Nippon	60	73	.451	18½
Hanshin	55	80	.407	26		Kintetsu	54	77	.412	23½

PLAYOFFS: Finals (best-of-7)—Fukuoka def. Chunichi 4-1.

TAIWAN LEAGUES

CPBL	W	L	PCT	GB			W	L	PCT	GB
China Trust	60	29	.674	—		Brother	39	52	.429	22
President	56	37	.601	6		Mercury	37	53	.411	23
Weichuan	49	39	.557	10		Sinon	30	61	.330	31

PLAYOFFS: Semifinals (best-of-3)— Weichuan def. President 2-1. **Finals** (best-of-7)—Weichuan def. China Trust 4-1.

TAIWAN MAJOR	W	L	PCT	GB			W	L	PCT	GB
Taipei	48	33	.593	—		Chiayi	40	42	.488	8½
Taichung	40	42	.488	8½		Kaohsiung	36	47	.434	13

PLAYOFFS: Semifinals (best-of-3)—Taichung def. Chiayi 2-1. **Finals** (best-of-7)—Taichung def. Taipei 4-2.

KOREAN BASEBALL ORGANIZATION

DREAM	W	L	PCT	GB		SAMSUNG	W	L	PCT	GB
Doosan	76	51	.598	—		Samsung	73	57	.562	—
Lotte	75	52	.591	1		Hanwha	72	58	.554	1
Hyundai	68	59	.535	8		LG Twins	61	70	.466	12½
Haitai	60	69	.465	17		Ssangbangwool	28	97	.224	42½

PLAYOFFS: Finals (best-of-7)—Hanwha def. Lotte 4-1.

DOMINICAN SUMMER LEAGUE

Rookie Classification

S.D. EAST	W	L	PCT	GB		S.D. EAST	W	L	PCT	GB
Mets I	53	20	.726	—		Devil Rays	55	17	.764	—
Tigers	52	21	.712	1		Athletics West	53	18	.746	1½
Brewers	45	26	.634	7		Yankees	41	28	.594	12½
Mariners	41	30	.577	11		Pirates	34	36	.486	20
Diamondbacks	41	30	.577	11		Reds	32	40	.444	23
Dodgers I	31	38	.449	20		Cubs	32	40	.444	23
Expos	29	42	.408	23		Twins/Co-op	29	43	.403	26
Marlins	27	44	.380	25		Mets II/Co-op	28	43	.394	26½
Cardinals	25	47	.347	27½		Padres	27	45	.375	28
Athletics East	12	58	.171	39½		Rangers	24	45	.348	29½

SAN PEDRO	W	L	PCT	GB			W	L	PCT	GB
Dodgers II	52	18	.743	—		Red Sox	30	40	.429	22
Astros	47	23	.671	5		Blue Jays	26	43	.377	25½
Angels	44	25	.638	7½		Braves	21	49	.300	31
Orioles	38	31	.551	13½		Giants	19	48	.284	31½

CIBAO	W	L	PCT	GB			W	L	PCT	GB
Phillies	47	20	.701	—		Royals	26	42	.382	21½
Indians	40	28	.588	7½		Rockies	23	44	.343	24
White Sox	32	34	.485	14½						

PLAYOFFS: Semifinals (best-of-3)—Phillies def. Devil Rays 2-1; Mets I def. Dodgers II 2-0. **Finals** (best-of-5)—Phillies def. Mets I 3-2.

VENEZUELAN SUMMER LEAGUE

Rookie Classification

	W	L	PCT	GB		BARQUISIMETO	W	L	PCT	GB
Cagua	32	24	.569	—		Chino Canonico	39	19	.672	—
La Victoria	33	26	.558	½		San Felipe	32	25	.561	6½
Ciudad Alianza	29	26	.526	2½		Chivacoa	26	31	.456	12½
La Pradera	28	30	.483	5		Cabudare	19	41	.317	21
San Joaquin	27	32	.458	6½						
Univ. of Carabobo	24	35	.407	9½						

ITALY

	W	L	PCT	GB			W	L	PCT	GB
Rimini	40	8	.833	—		Caserta	23	25	.479	17
Nettuno	31	17	.646	9		Modena	19	29	.396	21
Grosseto	29	19	.604	11		San Marino	14	34	.292	26
Parma	29	19	.604	11		Collecchio	8	40	.167	32
Bologna	23	25	.479	17						

HOLLAND

	W	L	PCT	GB			W	L	PCT	GB
Neptunus	38	7	.844	—		Sparta/Feyenoord	24	21	.533	14
Kinheim	31	14	.689	7		ADO	21	24	.467	17
HCAW	29	16	.644	9		RCH	13	32	.289	25
Hoofddorp Pioniers	27	16	.622	10		Tilburg	7	36	.178	30
Amsterdam Expos	27	18	.600	11		Twins	6	39	.133	32

MEXICAN LEAGUE

Class AAA

NOTE: The Mexican League is a member of the National Association of Professional Baseball Leagues and has a Triple-A classification. However, its member clubs operate largely independent of the 30 major league teams, and for that reason the league is listed in the international and winter league section.

Mailing Address: Angel Pola No. 16, Col. Periodista, CP 11220, Mexico, D.F. **Telephone:** 011-525-557-10-07, 011-525-557-14-08. **FAX:** 011-525-395-24-54. **E-Mail Address:** lmb@lmb.com.mx. **Website:** www.lmb.com.mx.

Years League Active: 1955-.

President: Jose Orozco Topete. **Vice Presidents:** Gustavo Ricalde Duran, Cuauhtemoc Rodriguez Meza. **Commissioner:** Felizardo Gastelum. **Director, Operations:** Nestor Alva Brito.

2000 Opening Date: April 5. **Closing Date:** Aug. 24.

Regular Season: 122 games.

Division Structure: Central—Cordoba, Mexico City Red Devils, Mexico City Tigers, Oaxaca, Puebla. **North**—Laredo, Monclova, Monterrey, Reynosa, Saltillo, Union Laguna. **South**—Campeche, Cancun, Tabasco, Veracruz, Yucatan.

Playoff Format: Three-tier playoffs involving top two teams in each zone, plus two wild-card teams. Two finalists meet in best-of-7 series for league championship.

All-Star Game: Mexican League vs. Texas League—June 18 at El Paso, Texas; June 20 at Monterrey.

Roster Limit: 25. **Roster Limit, Imports:** 5.

Statistician: Ana Luisa Perea Talarico, Angel Pola No. 16, Col. Periodista, CP 11220, Mexico, D.F.

CAMPECHE PIRATES

Office Address: Unidad Deportiva 20 de Noviembre, Local 4, CP 24000, Campeche, Campeche. **Telephone:** (981) 6-60-71. **FAX:** (981) 6-38-07. **E-Mail Address:** piratasc@prodigy.net.mx.

President: Javier Espejo. **General Manager:** Socorro Morales.

Manager: Marco Antonio Vazquez.

CANCUN LOBSTERMEN

Office Address: Av. Kabah, Super Manzana 31, Lote 25, Manzana 6 Col. Altos, CP 77500, Cancun, Quintana Roo. **Telephone:** (98) 87-40-11. **FAX:** (98) 87-40-14.

President: Miguel Marzuca Medina. **General Manager:** Ruben Herrera.

Manager: Francisco Baeza.

CORDOBA COFFEEGROWERS

Office Adress: Av. 1, Esq. Calle 24 S/N, CP 94500, Cordoba, Veracruz. **Telephone:** (271) 6-54-11, 6-55-35, 6-55-70.

Presidents: Jose Antonio Mansur Galan, Jean Paul Mansur Beltran. **General Manager:** Antelmo Hernandez Quirasco.

Manager: Eduardo Diaz.

OWLS OF THE TWO LAREDOS

Office Address: Av. Degollado #235-G, Col. Independencia, CP 88020, Nuevo Laredo, Tamaulipas. **Telephone:** (87) 12-22-99. **FAX:** (87) 12-07-36. **E-Mail Address:** tecolotes@ globalpc.net. **Website:** www.t2l.com.mx.

President: Martin Reyes Madrigal. **General Manager:** Felipe Garcia.

Manager: Armando Cabrera.

MEXICO CITY RED DEVILS

Office Address: Av. Cuauhtemoc No. 451-101, Col. Narvarte, CP 03020, Mexico, D.F. **Telephone:** (56) 39-87-22. **FAX:** (56) 39-97-22.

Co-Presidents: Roberto Mansur Galan, Alfredo Harp Heluy. **General Manager:** Pedro Mayorquin Aguilar.

Manager: Unavailable.

MEXICO CITY TIGERS

Office Address: Tuxpan No. 45-A, 5o. Piso, Col. Roma Sur, CP 06760, Mexico, D.F. **Telephone:** (90) 55-84-02-16. **FAX:** (90) 55-84-02-49. **E-Mail Address:** tigres@tigrescapitalinos.com.mx. **Website:** www.tigrescapitalinos.com.mx.

President: Cuauhtemoc Rodriguez. **General Manager:** Alfonso Lopez.

Manager: Dan Firova.

MONCLOVA STEELERS

Office Address: Cuauhtemoc #1002, Col. Ciudad Deportiva, CP 25750,

Monclova, Coahuila. **Telephone:** (86) 34-21-72. **FAX:** (86) 34-21-76. **E-Mail Address:** acereros@gen.com.mx.
President: Alonso Ancira Gonzalez. **General Manager:** Carlos de la Garza Barajas.
Manager: Unavailable.

MONTERREY SULTANS
Office Address: Av. Manuel L. Barragan S/N, Estadio Monterrey, CP 64460, Monterrey, Nuevo Leon. **Telephone:** (8) 351-86-34, 351-02-09, 351-91-86. **FAX:** (8) 351-94-87.
President: Jose Garcia. **General Manager:** Roberto Magdelano Ramirez.
Manager: Joe Almaraz.

OAXACA WARRIORS
Office Address: Privada del Chopo No. 105, Fraccionamiento El Chopo, CP 68050, Oaxaca, Oaxaca. **Telephone:** (9) 5-15-55-22. **FAX:** (9) 5-15-49-66. **E-Mail Address:** guerreros@infosel.net.mex. **Website:** www.guerreros.com.mx.
President: Vicente Perez Avella. **General Manager:** Guillermo Velazquez.
Manager: Nelson Barrera.

PUEBLA PARROTS
Office Address: Calz. Zaragoza S/N, Estadio Hermanos Serdan, Unidad Deportiva 5 de Mayo, CP 72220, Puebla, Puebla. **Telephone:** (2) 222-21-16. **FAX:** (2) 222-21-17.
President: Ricardo Henaine Mezher. **General Manager:** Samuel Lozano Molina.
Manager: Enrique Reyes.

REYNOSA BRONCOS
Office Address: Blvd. Hidalgo Km 102, Col. Privada Adolfo Lopez Mateos, CP 88650, Reynosa, Tamaulipas. **Telephone:** (89) 25 28 08. 24 17-50. **FAX:** (89) 24-26-95. **E-Mail Address:** broncos1@prodigynet.mx.
President: Carlos Torres. **General Manager:** Leonardo Clayton Rodriguez.
Manager: Guadalupe Lopez.

SALTILLO SARAPE MAKERS
Office Address: Blvd. Nazario S Ortiz Garza S/N, Col. Ciudad Deportiva, CP 25280, Saltillo, Coahuila. **Telephone:** (8) 416-94-55, 416-97-55. **FAX:** (8) 439-05-50. **Website:** www.saraperos.com.mx.
President: Juan Lopez. **General Manager:** Jaime Blancarte Pimentel.
Manager: Houston Jimenez.

TABASCO CATTLEMEN
Office Address: Explanada de la Ciudad Deportiva, Parque de Beisbol Centenario del 27 de Febrero, Col. Atasta de Serra, CP 86100, Villahermosa, Tabasco. **Telephone:** (93) 52-27-86. **FAX:** (93) 52-27-87. **E-Mail Address:** colmecas@tabasco.podernet.com.mx. **Website:** www.tabasco.gob.mx/olmecas/bien.htm.
President: Angel Melo. **General Manager:** Juan Antonio Balmaceda.
Manager: Javier Martinez.

UNION LAGUNA COTTON PICKERS
Office Address: Juan Gutemberg S/N, Col. Zona Centro, Estadio de la Revolucion, CP 27000, Torreon, Coahuila. **Telephone:** (17) 17-43-35. **FAX:** (17) 18-55-15. **E-Mail Address:** unionlaguna@hotmail.com. **Website:** www.coah1.telmex.net.
President: Javier Cavazos Gomez. **General Manager:** Moises Camacho.
Manager: Pompeyo Davalillo.

VERACRUZ EAGLES
Office Address: Av. Jacarandas S/N Esq. Espana, Fraccionamiento Virginia, CP 94294, Boca del Rio, Veracruz. **Telephone:** (2) 9-35-50-04. **FAX:** (2) 9-35-50-08.
President: Antonio Chedraui Mafud. **General Manager:** Rafael Duran.
Manager: Unavailable.

YUCATAN LIONS
Office Address: Calle 50 #406-B, Entre 35 Y37, Col. Jesus Carranza, CP 97109, Merida, Yucatan. **Telephone:** (99) 26-30-22. **FAX:** (99) 26-36-31.
President: Gustavo Ricalde Duran. **General Manager:** Jose Rivero Ancona.
Manager: Francisco Estrada.

MEXICAN ACADEMY

Rookie Classification
Mailing Address: Angel Pola No. 16 Col. Periodista, CP 11220, Mexico, D.F. **Telephone:** 011-525-557-10-07, 011-525-557-14-08. **FAX:** 011-525-395-24-54.
Years Active: 1997-.
Commissioner: Unavailable.

JAPANESELEAGUES

Mailing Address: Imperial Tower, 14F, 1-1-1 Uchisaiwai-cho, Chiyoda-ku, Tokyo 100-0011. Telephone: 03-3502-0022. FAX: 03-3502-0140.
Commissioner: Hiromori Kawashima.
Executive Secretary: Yoshiaki Kanai. Executive Director, General Affairs/Public Relations: Kazuo Hasegawa. Executive Director, Baseball Operations: Masaru Madate. Assistant Director, International Affairs: Nobuhisa "Nobby" Ito.
Japan Series: Best-of-7 series between Central and Pacific League champions, begins Oct. 21 at home of Central League club.
All-Star Series: July 22 at Tokyo Dome; July 23 at Green Stadium, Kobe; July 25 at Nagasaki Stadium.
Roster Limit: 70 per organization (one major league club, one minor league club). Major league club is permitted to register 28 players at a time, though only 25 may be available for each game. Roster Limit, Imports: 4 (2 position players, 2 pitchers) in majors; unlimited in minors.

CENTRAL LEAGUE

Mailing Address: Asahi Bldg. 3F, 6-6-7 Ginza, Chuo-ku, Tokyo 104-0061. Telephone: 03-3572-1673. FAX: 03-3571-4545.
Years League Active: 1950-.
President: Sumiko Takahara.
Secretary General: Ryoichi Shibusawa. Planning Department: Masaaki Nagino. Public Relations: Hideo Okoshi.
2000 Opening Date: March 31. Closing Date: Sept. 28.
Regular Season: 135 games.
Playoff Format: None.

CHUNICHI DRAGONS
Mailing Address: Chunichi Bldg. 6F, 4-1-1 Sakae, Naka-ku, Nagoya 460-0008. Telephone: 052-252-5226. FAX: 052-263-7696.
Chairman: Hirohiko Oshima. President: Tsuyoshi Sato. General Manager: Osamu Ito. Field Manager: Senichi Hoshino.
1999 Attendance: 2,541,000.
2000 Foreign Players: Mel Bunch, Dan Carlson, Leo Gomez, Lu Jiangang (China), Jeong Bum Lee (Korea), Dave Nilsson, Tsao Ching Yang (Taiwan).

HANSHIN TIGERS
Mailing Address: 1-47 Koshien-cho, Nishinomiya-shi, Hyogo-ken 663-8152. Telephone: 0798-46-1515. FAX: 0798-40-0934.
Chairman: Shunjiro Kuma. President: Yorihiro Takada. General Manager: Katsuyoshi Nozaki. Field Manager: Katsuya Nomura.
1999 Attendance: 2,601,000.
2000 Foreign Players: Howard Battle, Greg Hansell, Kurt Miller, Rafael Ramirez, Tony Tarasco.

HIROSHIMA TOYO CARP
Mailing Address: 5-25 Motomachi, Naka-ku, Hiroshima 730-8508. Telephone: 082-221-2040. FAX: 082-228-5013.
Chairman: Kohei Matsuda. General Manager: Katsutoshi Kamidoi. Field Manager: Mitsuo Tatsukawa.
1999 Attendance: 1,066,500.
2000 Foreign Players: Jeff Ball, Angel Brito, Chris Cumberland, Eddy Diaz, Nate Minchey, Reinoso Pascual, Sal Urso.

YAKULT SWALLOWS
Mailing Address: Shimbashi MCV Bldg. 5F, 5-13-5 Shimbashi, Minato-ku, Tokyo 105-0004. Telephone: 03-5470-8915. FAX: 03-5470-8916.
Chairman: Naomi Matsuzono. President/General Manager: Itaru Taguchi. Field Manager: Tsutomu Wakamatsu.
1999 Attendance: 1,716,000.
2000 Foreign Players: Jason Jacome, Don Lemon, Torey Lovullo, Daniel Matsumoto (Brazil), Rodrigo Miyamoto (Brazil), Roberto Petagine, Leonardo Sato (Brazil).

YOKOHAMA BAYSTARS
Mailing Address: Kannai Arai Bldg, 7F, 1-8 Onoe-cho, Naka-ku, Yokohama 231-0015. Telephone: 045-681-0811. FAX: 045-661-2500.
Chairman: Keijiro Nakabe. President: Takashi Ohori. General Manager: Yoshio Noguchi. Field Manager: Hiroshi Gondo.
1999 Attendance: 1,770,000.
2000 Foreign Players: Rafael Betancourt, Lou Merloni, Bobby Rose.

YOMIURI GIANTS

Mailing Address: Takebashi 3-3 Bldg., 3-3 Kanda Nishiki-cho, Chiyoda-ku, Tokyo 101-8462. **Telephone:** 03-3295-7711. **FAX:** 03-3295-7708.

Chairman: Tsuneo Watanabe. **General Manager:** Hiroyuki Yamamuro. **Field Manager:** Shigeo Nagashima.

1999 Attendance: 3,645,000.

2000 Foreign Players: Chong Min Chul (Korea), Balvino Galvez, Domingo Martinez, Darrell May, Cho Sung Min (Korea).

PACIFIC LEAGUE

Mailing Address: Asahi Bldg. 9F, 6-6-7 Ginza, Chuo-ku, Tokyo 104-0061. **Telephone:** 03-3573-1551. **FAX:** 03-3572-5843.

Years League Active: 1950-.

President: Kazuo Harano. **Secretary General:** Shigeru Murata. **Administration Department:** Katsuhisa Matsuzaki.

2000 Opening Date: April 1. **Closing Date:** Oct. 7.

Regular Season: 135 games.

Playoff Format: None.

CHIBA LOTTE MARINES

Mailing Address: WBG Marive West 26F, 2-6 Nakase, Mihama-ku, Chiba-shi, Chiba-ken 261-7125. **Telephone:** 043-297-2101. **FAX:** 043-297-2181.

Chairman: Takeo Shigemitsu. **General Manager:** Setsuo Goto.

Field Manager: Koji Yamamoto.

1999 Attendance: 1,070,000.

2000 Foreign Players: Jeff Barry, Frank Bolick, Brian Warren.

FUKUOKA DAIEI HAWKS

Mailing Address: Fukuoka Dome 6F, 2-2-2 Jigyohama, Chuo-ku, Fukuoka 810-0065. **Telephone:** 092-844-1189. **FAX:** 092-844-4600.

Chairman of the Board: Isao Nakauchi. **President:** Tadashi Nakauchi. **General Manager:** Takuzo Ueda. **Field Manager:** Sadaharu Oh.

1999 Attendance: 2,390,000.

2000 Foreign Players: Rod Pedraza, Melvin Nieves, Brady Raggio, Matt Randall.

NIPPON HAM FIGHTERS

Mailing Address: Roppongi Denki Bldg. 6F, 6-1-20 Roppongi, Minato-ku, Tokyo 106-0032. **Telephone:** 03-3403-9131. **FAX:** 03-3403-9143.

Chairman: Yoshinori Okoso. **President/General Manager:** Takeshi Kojima. **Field Manager:** Yasunori Oshima.

1999 Attendance: 1,416,000.

2000 Foreign Players: Micah Franklin, Carlos Mirabel, Sherman Obando, Kevin Ohme, Rafael Orellano, Nigel Wilson, Shannon Withem.

ORIX BLUE WAVE

Mailing Address: Sumitomo Kaijo Kobe Bldg., 2F, 1-1-18 Sakae-machi Dori, Chuo-ku, Kobe 650-0023. **Telephone:** 078-333-0065. **FAX:** 078-333-0048.

Chairman: Yoshihiko Miyauchi. **President:** Yutaka Okazoe. **General Manager:** Steve Ino. **Field Manager:** Akira Ogi.

1999 Attendance: 1,206,000.

2000 Foreign Players: George Arias, Willie Banks, Orlando Merced, Troy Neel, Carlos Pulido, Roger Hansen (coach).

OSAKA KINTETSU BUFFALOES

Mailing Address: Midosuji Grand Bldg. 5F, 2-2-3 Namba, Chuo-ku, Osaka 542-0076.

Telephone: 06-6212-9744. **FAX:** 06-6212-6834.

Chairman: Shigeichiro Kanamori. **President:** Kenzo Fujii. **General Manager:** Isami Okamoto. **Field Manager:** Masataka Nashida.

1999 Attendance: 1,155,000.

2000 Foreign Players: Andy Abad, Phil Clark, Narciso Elvira, Tuffy Rhodes, Brad Tweedlie, Bob Wolcott.

SEIBU LIONS

Mailing Address: 2135 Kami-Yamaguchi, Tokorozawa-shi, Saitama-ken 359-1189. **Telephone:** 042-924-1155. **FAX:** 042-928-1919.

Chairman: Yoshiaki Tsutsumi. **President/General Manager:** Kenji Ono. **Field Manager:** Osamu Higashio.

1999 Attendance: 1,834,000.

2000 Foreign Players: Tony Fernandez, Reggie Jefferson, Hsu Ming-chieh (Taiwan), Corey Paul.

OTHER LEAGUES

DOMINICAN REPUBLIC

DOMINICAN SUMMER LEAGUE
Member, National Association
Rookie Classification

Mailing Address: Calle Segundo No. 14, Reparto Antilla, Santo Domingo, Dominican Republic. **Telephone:** (809) 563-3233. **FAX:** (809) 532-3619, 563-2455.

Years League Active: 1985-.

President: Freddy Jana. **Administrative Assistant:** Orlando Diaz.

2000 Member Clubs, Division Structure (tentative): **Santo Domingo East**—Athletics East, Brewers, Cardinals, Diamondbacks, Dodgers, Expos, Mariners, Marlins, Tigers, Twins. **Santo Domingo West**—Athletics West, Cubs, Devil Rays, Mets I, Padres, Pirates, Rangers, Reds, Twins, Yankees. **San Pedro de Macoris**—Angels, Astros, Blue Jays, Braves, Dodgers II, Giants, Orioles, Red Sox. **Cibao**—Indians, Mets II, Phillies, Rockies, Royals, White Sox.

2000 Opening Date: June 1 (tentative). **Closing Date:** Aug. 30 (tentative).

Regular Season: 72 games.

Playoff Format: Four division winners meet in best-of-3 series. Winners meet in best-of-5 series for league championship.

Roster Limit: 30 active. **Player Eligibility Rule:** No more than eight players 20 or older and no more than two players 21 or older. At least 10 players must be pitchers. No more than two years of prior service, excluding Rookie leagues outside the U.S. and Canada.

VENEZUELA

VENEZUELAN SUMMER LEAGUE
Member, National Association
Rookie Classification

Mailing Address: CC Caribbean Plaza Mogulo 8, P.A. Local 173, Valencia, Carabobo, Venezuela. **Telephone:** 011-58-41-24-0321 or 0980. **FAX:** 011-58-41-24-0705.

Years League Active: 1997-.

Administrator: Saul Gonzalez. **Coordinator:** Ramon Fereira.

Member Clubs, 2000: Unavailable (12 tentative).

2000 Opening Date: Unavailable. **Closing Date:** Unavailable.

Regular Season: Unavailable.

Playoffs: None.

Roster Limit: 30 active. **Player Eligibility Rule:** No player on active list may have more than three years of minor league service. Open to players from all Latin American Spanish-speaking countries except Mexico, the Dominican Republic and Puerto Rico.

TAIWAN

CHINESE PROFESSIONAL BASEBALL LEAGUE

Mailing Address: 2F, No. 32, Pateh Road, Sec. 3, Taipei, Taiwan. **Telephone:** 886-2-2577-6992. **FAX:** 886-2-2577-2606. **Website:** www.cpbl.com.tw.

Years League Active: 1990-.

Commissioner: T.C. Huang. **Secretary General:** Wayne Lee.

Member Clubs: Brother Elephants (Taipei), China Trust Whales (Chiayi City), President Lions (Tainan), Sinon Bulls (Taichung).

Regular Season: 90 games (split schedule).

2000 Opening Date: March 11. **Closing Date:** Oct. 8.

Import Rule: Two import players may be active and on the field at the same time.

TAIWAN MAJOR LEAGUE

Mailing Address: 5F, No. 214, Tunhua North Rd., Taipei, Taiwan. **Telephone:** 886-2-2545-9566. **FAX:** 886-2-2514-0802. **Website:** www.naluwan.com.tw.

Years League Active: 1997-.

President: Felix S.T. Chen. **General Manager:** Joey Chen. **Secretary General:** Dean Yuan.

Member Clubs: Chia-nan Luka, Kao-ping Fala, Taichung Agan, Taipei Gida.

Regular Season: 84 games.

2000 Opening Date: March 25. **Closing Date:** Oct. 8.
Import Rule: Four (two on field at one time).

SOUTH KOREA

KOREA BASEBALL ORGANIZATION

Mailing Address: The Hall of Baseball, 946-16 Dogok-Dong, Kangnam-Ku, Seoul, South Korea. **Telephone:** (82) 2-3461-7887. **FAX:** (82) 2-3462-7800/7860.

Years League Active: 1982-.

Commissioner: Yong Oh Park. **Secretary General:** Young Eun Choi. **Manager, International Affairs/Public Relations:** Sang-Hyun Lee. **Assistant Manager:** Smiley Kim.

2000 Opening Date: Unavailable. **Closing Date:** Unavailable.

Regular Season: 132 games.

Division Structure: Dream League—Doosan, Haitai, Hyundai, Lotte. **Magic League**—Hanhwa, LG, Samsung, Ssangbangwool.

Korean Series: Four teams meet in best-of-7 semifinal series. Winners meet in best-of-7 series for league championship.

Roster Limit: 25 active through Aug. 31, when rosters expand to 30. **Imports:** 2 active.

DOOSAN BEARS

Mailing Address: Chamsil Baseball Stadium, Chamsil-1 Dong, Songpa-Ku, Seoul, Korea. **Telephone:** 2-2401-777. **FAX:** 2-2401-788.

General Manager: Kun Koo Kang.

HAITAI TIGERS

Mailing Address: 622 Lim-Dong, Puk-Ku, Kwangju, Korea. **Telephone:** 62-525-1950. **FAX:** 62-525-5350.

General Manager: Yoon Bum Choi.

HANHWA EAGLES

Mailing Address: 22-1 Young-Jeon-Dong, Daejeon, Korea. **Telephone:** 42-631-6331-3. **FAX:** 42-632-2929.

General Manager: Kyung Yon Hwang.

HYUNDAI UNICORNS

Mailing Address: 1128-10 Hyundai Building, 12th Floor, Kuwol-Dong, Namdong Ku, Inchon, Korea. **Telephone:** 32-433-7979. **FAX:** 32-435-3108. **General Manager:** Yong Hwi Kim.

LG TWINS

Mailing Address: 891 LG Young Dong Building, 10th Floor, Dae-Chi-Dong, Kangnam-Ku, Seoul, Korea. **Telephone:** 2-3459-5345. **FAX:** 2-3459-5354.

General Manager: Jong Jun Choi.

LOTTE GIANTS

Mailing Address: 930 Sajik-Dong Dongrae-Ku, Pusan, Korea. **Telephone:** 51-505-7422-3. **FAX:** 51-506-0090.

General Manager: Chul Hwa Lee.

SAMSUNG LIONS

Mailing Address: 184-3 Sunhwari, Jinliangeup, Kyungsan, Kyung-Buk, Korea. **Telephone:** 53-859-3111-3. **FAX:** 53-859-3117.

General Manager: Jong Man Kim.

SSANGBANGWOOL RAIDERS

Mailing Address: 1-1220 Dokjin-Dong 1GA, Dokjin-Ku, Jeonju, Korea. **Telephone:** 652-275-2014/5. **FAX:** 652-275-2113.

General Manager: Eun Su Yoo.

OTHER LEAGUES

HOLLAND

Mailing Address: Royal Dutch Baseball/Softball Federation, P.O. Box 60, NL-2080 AB, Sant Poort, Zuid, Holland 5202250. **Telephone:** (31-23) 5390-244. **FAX:** (31-23) 5385-922.

President: T.T. Gieskens. **Media Relations:** Mieke Van den Kerkhof.

ITALY

Mailing Address: Italian Baseball Federation, Viale Tiziano 74, 00196 Rome, Italy. **Telephone:** (011-39-6) 36858130. **FAX:** (011-39-6) 36858201. **President:** Aldo Notari. **General Secretary:** Dino Rossi.

WINTER LEAGUES

1999-00 STANDINGS

CARIBBEAN WORLD SERIES

	W	L	Pct.	GB		W	L	Pct.	GB
Puerto Rico	6	0	1.000	—	Venezuela	1	5	.167	5
Dominican Republic	4	2	.667	2	Mexico	1	5	.167	5

DOMINICAN LEAGUE

	W	L	Pct.	GB		W	L	Pct.	GB
Aguilas	30	18	.625	—	Estrellas	23	25	.479	7
Escogido	27	20	.574	2½	Pollos	16	31	.340	13½
Licey	23	25	.479	7					

Round-Robin	W	L	Pct.	GB		W	L	Pct.	GB
Estrellas	10	8	.556	—	Licey	8	10	.444	2
Aguilas	10	8	.556	—	Escogido	8	10	.444	2

PLAYOFFS: Finals (best-of-7)—Aguilas def. Estrellas 4-3.

MEXICAN PACIFIC LEAGUE

	W	L	Pct.	GB		W	L	Pct.	GB
*Mazatlan	40	28	.588	—	Culiacan	37	31	.544	3
Navojoa	39	28	.582	½	Los Mochis	29	39	.426	11
Hermosillo	38	29	.567	1½	Guasave	25	43	.368	15
*Mexicali	38	30	.559	2	Obregon	25	43	.368	15

*Split season champion

PLAYOFFS: Quarterfinals (best-of-7)—Culiacan def. Mazatlan 4-1; Hermosillo def. Mexicali 4-3; Navojoa def. Los Mochis 4-1. **Semifinals** (best-of-7)—Hermosillo def. Culiacan 4-3; Navojoa def. Mexicali 4-3. **Finals** (best-of-7)—Navojoa def. Hermosillo 4-0.

PUERTO RICAN LEAGUE

	W	L	Pct.	GB		W	L	Pct.	GB
Mayaguez	27	23	.540	—	Caguas	26	25	.510	1½
Santurce	26	23	.531	½	Bayamon	24	25	.490	2½
Ponce	26	24	.520	1	San Juan	20	29	.408	6½

PLAYOFFS: Semifinals (best-of-7)—Mayaguez def. Caguas 4-1; Santurce def. Ponce 4-2. **Finals** (best-of-9)—Santurce def. Mayaguez 5-2.

VENEZUELAN LEAGUE

EAST	W	L	Pct.	GB	WEST	W	L	Pct.	GB
Oriente	32	25	.561	—	Occidente	36	26	.581	—
Magallanes	31	31	.500	3½	Lara	34	26	.567	1
La Guaira	25	33	.431	7½	Zulia	35	27	.565	1
Caracas	20	42	.323	14½	Aragua	29	32	.475	6½

Round-Robin	W	L	Pct.	GB		W	L	Pct.	GB
Zulia	10	6	.625	—	Occidente	9	8	.529	1½
Magallanes	10	7	.588	½	Lara	7	9	.438	3
					Oriente	5	11	.313	5

PLAYOFFS: Finals (best-of-7)—Zulia def. Magallanes 4-1.

ARIZONA FALL LEAGUE

EAST	W	L	Pct.	GB	WEST	W	L	Pct.	GB
Mesa	31	13	.705	—	Peoria	17	27	.386	—
Scottsdale	25	19	.568	6	Maryvale	17	27	.386	—
Phoenix	25	19	.568	6	Grand Canyon	17	27	.386	—

PLAYOFFS: Finals (best-of-3)—Mesa def. Maryvale 2-0.

INTERNATIONAL BASEBALL LEAGUE AUSTRALIA

	W	L	Pct.	GB		W	L	Pct.	GB
Victorian	11	6	.647	—	Queensland	8	9	.471	3
Western	10	7	.588	1	Southern	7	10	.412	4
Country NSW	9	8	.529	2	NSW Storm	6	11	.353	5

CALIFORNIA FALL LEAGUE

	W	L	Pct.	GB		W	L	Pct.	GB
Lancaster	26	16	.619	—	Lake Elsinore	21	21	.500	5
San Bernardino	22	20	.524	4	Rancho Cucamonga	15	27	.357	11

PLAYOFFS: Lancaster def. San Bernardino 2-1.

WINTERBASEBALL

Mailing Address: Frank Feliz Miranda No. 1 Naco, Santo Domingo, Dominican Republic. **Telephone:** (809) 562-4737, 562-4715. **FAX:** (809) 565-4654.

Commissioner: Juan Fco. Puello Herrera.

Member Leagues: Dominican Republic, Mexican Pacific, Puerto Rican, Venezuelan.

2001 Caribbean Series: Feb. 2-7 at Culiacan, Mexico.

DOMINICAN LEAGUE

Office Address: Ave. Lopez de Vega, Suite 46, Altos Enz. Piantini, Santo Domingo, Dominican Republic. **Mailing Address:** Apartado Postal 1246, Santo Domingo, Dominican Republic. **Telephone:** (809) 476-0080. **FAX:** (809) 476-0084.

Years League Active: 1951-.

President: Dr. Manuel Antun Batlle. **Vice President:** Eduardo Antun Batlle. **Administrative Assistant:** Fitzgerald Astacio.

1999-2000 Opening Date: Oct. 27. **Closing Date:** Dec 30.

Regular Season: 48 games.

Playoff Format: Top four teams meet in 18 game round-robin. Two teams advance to best-of-7 series for league championship. Winner advances to Caribbean World Series.

Roster Limit: 30. **Roster Limit, Imports:** 7.

AGUILAS CIBAENAS

Office Address: Estadio Cibao, Avenida Imbert, Santiago, Dom. Rep. **Mailing Address:** EPS B-225, P.O. Box 02-5360, Miami, FL 33102. **Telephone:** (809) 575-4310, 575-1810. **FAX:** (809) 575-0865.

President: Winston Llenas. **General Manager:** Reynaldo Bisono.

1999-2000 Manager: Tony Pena.

AZUACAREROS DEL ESTE
(Did not operate in 1999-2000)

Mailing Address: Apartado Postal 145, La Romana, Dom. Rep. **Telephone:** (809) 556-6188. **FAX:** (809) 550-1550.

President: Arturo Gil. **General Manager:** Pablo Peguero.

ESCOGIDO LIONS

Office Address: Estadio Quisqueya, Ens. la Fe, Santo Domingo, Dom. Rep. **Mailing Address:** P.O. Box 1287, Santo Domingo, Dom. Rep. **Telephone:** (809) 565-1910. **FAX:** (809) 567-7643. **Website:** www.escogido.com.do.

President: Daniel Aquino Mendez. **General Manager:** Mario Soto.

1999-2000 Manager: Dave Miley.

ESTRELLAS ORIENTALES

Office Address: Avenida Lopez de Vega No. 46, Altos, Enz. Piantini, Santo Domingo, Dom. Rep. **Telephone:** (809) 476-0080. **FAX:** (809) 476-0084.

President: Eduardo Antun. **General Manager:** Junior Noboa.

1999-2000 Manager: Alfredo Griffin.

LICEY TIGERS

Mailing Address: Estadio Quisqueya, Santo Domingo, Dom. Rep. **Telephone:** (809) 567-3090. **FAX:** (809) 542-7714. **Website:** www.licey.com.

President: Miguel Heded. **General Manager:** Rafael Landestoy.

1999-2000 Managers: Ron Washington, Teddy Martinez, Elvio Jimenez.

POLLOS DEL NORDESTE

Office Address: Estadio Julian Javier, San Francisco de Macoris, Dom. Rep. **Mailing Address:** EPS No. F-1447, P.O. Box 02-5301, Miami, FL 33102. **Telephone:** (809) 588-8882. **FAX:** (809) 588-8733.

President: Julio Hazim. **General Manager:** Ramon Naranjo.

1999-2000 Manager: Miguel Dilone.

MEXICAN PACIFIC LEAGUE

Mailing Address: Pesqueira y Allende 401-R, Sur Altos, Navojoa, Sonora, Mexico. **Telephone:** (52-642) 2-31-00. **FAX:** (52-642) 2-72-50. **E-**

Mail Address: ligadelpacifico@imparcial.com.mx. **Website:** www.ligadel pacifico.com.mx.

Years League Active: 1958-.

President: Dr. Arturo Leon Lerma. **General Manager:** Obiel Denis Gonzalez.

1999-2000 Opening Date: Oct. 13. **Closing Date:** Dec. 30.

Regular Season: 68 games.

Playoff Format: Six teams advance to best-of-7 quarterfinals. Three winners and losing team with best record advance to best-of-7 semifinals. Winners meet in best-of-7 series for league championship. Winner advances to Caribbean World Series.

Roster Limit: 30. **Roster Limit, Imports:** 5.

CULIACAN TOMATO GROWERS

Street Address: Av. Alvaro Obregon 348 Sur, CP 80200, Culiacan, Sinaloa, Mexico. **Telephone:** (67) 12-24-46. **FAX:** (67) 13-33-69.

President: Juan Manuel Ley Lopez. **General Manager:** Jaime Blancarte.

1999-2000 Manager: Houston Jimenez.

GUASAVE COTTONEERS

Mailing Address: Ave. Obregon No. 43, Guasave, Sinaloa, Mexico. **Telephone:** (687) 2-29-98. **FAX:** (687) 2-14-31.

President: Carlos Chavez. **General Manager:** Sebastian Sandoval.

1999-2000 Manager: Aurelio Rodriguez.

HERMOSILLO ORANGE GROWERS

Mailing Address: Blvd. Navarrete No. 309, Esq. Torreon y Atenas, Hermosillo, Sonora, Mexico. **Telephone:** (62) 60-69-32, 60-69-33. **FAX:** (62) 60-69-31.

President: Enrique Mazon Rubio. **General Manager:** Marco Antonio Manzo.

1999-2000 Manager: Tim Johnson.

LOS MOCHIS SUGARCANE GROWERS

Mailing Address: Madero No. 116 Oreiente, CP 81200, Los Mochis, Sinaloa, Mexico. **Telephone:** (68) 12-86-02. **FAX:** (68) 12-67-40.

President: Mario Lopez Valdez. **General Manager:** Antonio Castro Chavez.

1999-2000 Manager: Shane Turner.

MAZATLAN DEER

Mailing Address: Gutierrez Najera No. 821, Col. Montuosa, Mazatlan, Sinaloa, Mexico. **Telephone:** (98) 81-17-10. **FAX:** (98) 81-17-11.

President: Hermilo Diaz Bringas. **General Manager:** Alejandro Vega.

1999-2000 Manager: Raul Cano.

MEXICALI EAGLES

Mailing Address: Calzada Cuauhtemoc S/N, Las Fuentes, Mexicali, Baja California. **Telephone:** (65) 67-00-40, 67-00-10. **FAX:** (65) 67-00-95.

President: Alberto Murillo. **General Manager:** Leonardo Ovies.

1999-2000 Manager: Paquin Estrada.

NAVOJOA MAYOS

Mailing Address: Allende No. 208, Despacho 2, CP 85800, Novojoa, Sonora, Mexico. **Telephone:** (642) 2-14-33, 2-37-64. **FAX:** (642) 2-89-97.

President: Victor Cuevas Garibay. **General Manager:** Lauro Villalobos.

1999-2000 Manager: Lorenzo Bundy.

OBREGON YAQUIS

Mailing Address: Yucatan y Nainari No. 294, Edificio C. Depto. 11, Ciudad Obregon, Sonora, Mexico. **Telephone:** (64) 13-77-66. **FAX:** (64) 14-11-56.

President: Luis Felipe Garcia DeLeon. **General Manager:** Luis Carlos Joffroy.

1999-2000 Manager: Marco Antonio Vazquez.

PUERTO RICAN LEAGUE

Mailing Address: P.O. Box 1852, Hato Rey, PR 00919. **Telephone:** (787) 765-6285, 765-7285. **FAX:** (787) 767-3028.

Years League Active: 1938-.

President: Ramon Arce. **Executive Director/Administrator:** Benny Agosto.

1999-2000 Opening Date: Nov. 3. **Closing Date:** Jan. 10.

Regular Season: 50 games.

Playoff Format: Top four teams meet in best-of-7 semifinal series. Winners meet in best-of-9 series for league championship. Winner advances to Caribbean World Series.

Roster Limit: 26. **Roster Limit, Imports:** 9.

BAYAMON VAQUEROS
Office Address: Road #2, Juan Ramon Loubriel Stadium, Bayamon, PR. **Mailing Address:** Unavailable. **Telephone/FAX:** Unavailable.
President: Josue Vega.
General Manager/1999-2000 Manager: Frankie Thon.

CAGUAS CRIOLLOS
Mailing Address: P.O. Box 1415, Caguas, PR 00726. **Telephone:** (787) 258-2222. **FAX:** (787) 743-0545.
General Manager: Joey Cora.
1999-2000 Manager: Adalberto Pena.

MAYAGUEZ INDIANS
Mailing Address: 3089 Marina Station, Mayaguez, PR 00681.
Telephone: (787) 834-6111, 834-5211. **FAX:** (787) 834-7480.
President/General Manager: Luis Ivan Mendez.
1999-2000 Manager: Al Newman.

PONCE LIONS
Mailing Address: P.O. Box 7444, Ponce, PR 00732. **Telephone:** (787) 848-0050. **FAX:** (787) 848-8884.
President: Antonio Munoz Jr. **General Manager:** Ramon Conde.
1999-2000 Manager: Carlos Lezcano.

SAN JUAN SENATORS
Office Address: Estadio Hiram Bithorn, Roosevelt Avenue, Hato Rey, PR 00927. **Mailing Address:** P.O. Box 366246, San Juan, PR 00936.
Telephone: (787) 754-1300. **FAX:** (787) 763-2217.
President: Benjamin Rivera. **General Manager:** Sandy Alomar Sr.
1999-2000 Manager: Jerry Morales.

SANTURCE CRABBERS
Mailing Address: P.O. Box 1077, Hato Rey, PR 00919. **Telephone:** (787) 274-0240, 274-0241. **FAX:** (787) 765-0410.
President: Reinaldo Paniagua. **General Manager:** Hector Otero.
1999-2000 Manager: Mako Oliveras.

VENEZUELAN LEAGUE

Mailing Address: Avenida Casanova, Centro Comercial El Recreo, Torre Sur, Piso 3, Oficinas 36-37, Caracas, Venezuela. **Telephone:** (011-58-2) 761-2750, 761-4817. **FAX:** (011-58-2) 761-7661.
Years League Active: 1946-.
President: Efrain Munoz. **General Manager:** Domingo Alvarez.
Division Structure: East—Caracas, La Guaira, Magallanes, Oriente. **West**—Aragua, Lara, Pastora, Zulia.
1999-2000 Opening Date: Oct. 12. **Closing Date:** Dec. 30.
Regular Season: 62 games.
Playoff Format: Top two teams in each division, plus a wild-card team, meet in 16-game round-robin series. Top two finishers meet in a best-of-7 series for league championship. Winner advances to Caribbean World Series.
Roster Limit: 26. **Roster Limit, Imports:** 7.

ARAGUA TIGERS
Mailing Address: Estadio Jose Perez Colmenares, Calle Campo Elias, Barrio Democratico, Maracay, Aragua, Venezuela. **Telephone:** (58-043) 54-4632. **FAX:** (58-43) 53-8655. **E-Mail Address:** tigres@telcel.net.ve.
President/General Manager: Jose Pages.
1999-2000 Managers: Alfredo Ortiz, Rodolfo Hernandez.

CARACAS LIONS
Mailing Address: Av. Francisco de Miranda, Centro Seguros La Paz, Piso 4, La California, Municipio Sucre, Caracas, Venezuela 1070.
Telephone: (582) 238-7733. **FAX:** (582) 238-0691.
President: Pablo Morales. **Vice President/General Manger:** Oscar Prieto.
1999-2000 Managers: John Stearns, Manny Acta.

LA GUAIRA SHARKS
Mailing Address: Primera Avenida, Urbanizacion Miramar, Detras del Periferico de Pariata, Maiquetia, Vargas, Venezuela. **Telephone:** (58-31) 25-579. **FAX:** (58-31) 23-116.
President/General Manager: Unavailable.
1999-2000 Manager: Luis Salazar.

LARA CARDINALS
Mailing Address: Av. Rotaria, Estadio Antonio Herrera, Barquisimeto, Venezuela 3001. **Telephone:** (58-51) 42-3132 or 4543. **FAX:** (58-51) 42-1921. **E-Mail Address:** cardenal@cardenales.org. **Website:** www.cardenales.org.

President: Adolfo Alvarez. **General Manager:** Humberto Oropeza. **1999-2000 Manager:** Omar Malave.

MAGALLANES NAVIGATORS

Mailing Address: Centro Comercial Caribbean Plaza, Modulo 8, Local 173, Valencia, Carabobo, Venezuela. **Telephone:** (58-041) 24-0321 or 0980. **FAX:** (58-041) 24-0705.

President: Juan Jose Avila.
1999-2000 Manager: Phil Regan.

OCCIDENTE PASTORA

Mailing Address: Estadio Bachiller Julio Hernandez Molina, Avenida Romulo Gallegos, Aruare, Venezuela. **Telephone:** (055) 22-2945. **FAX:** (055) 21-8595.

President: Enrique Finol. **General Manager:** Carlos Jimenez.
1999-2000 Manager: Luis Dorante.

ORIENTE CARIBBEANS

Mailing Address: Avenida Estadium Alfonso Carrasquel, Oficina del Equipo de Caribes de Oriente, Centro Comercial Novocentro, Piso 2, Local 2-4, Puerto la Cruz, Anzoategui, Venezuela. **Telephone:** (081) 66-2536 or 66-7054. **FAX:** (081) 66-7054.

President: Gioconda de Marquez. **Vice President:** Pablo Ruggeri.
1999-2000 Manager: Al Pedrique.

ZULIA EAGLES

Mailing Address: Avenida 8, Urb. Santa Rita, Edificio Las Carolinas, Local M-10, Maracaibo, Zulia, Venezuela. **Telephone:** (58-061) 97-9834 or 97-9839. **FAX:** (58-061) 98-0210.

President: Lucas Rincon. **Vice President/General Manager:** Luis Rodolfo Machado Silva.
1999-2000 Manager: Marc Bombard.

OTHER WINTER LEAGUES

ARIZONA FALL LEAGUE

Mailing Address: 10201 S 51st St., Suite 230, Phoenix, AZ 85044. **Telephone:** (480) 496-6700. **FAX:** (480) 496-6384. **E Mail Address:** afl@majorleaguebaseball.com. **Website:** www.majorleaguebaseball.com/arizona.

Years League Active: 1992-.
Operated by: Major League Baseball.
Executive Vice President: Steve Cobb. **Administrative Assistant:** Joan McGrath.
Division Structure: East—Mesa, Phoenix, Scottsdale; **West**—Grand Canyon, Maryvale, Peoria.
2000 Opening Date: Oct. 4. **Closing Date:** Nov. 19.
Regular Season: 52 games.
Playoff Format: Division champions meet in best-of-3 series for league championship.
Roster Limit: 30. Players with less than one year of major league service are eligible.

GRAND CANYON RAFTERS

Mailing Address: See league address.
Working Agreement: Baltimore Orioles, Boston Red Sox, New York Yankees, Tampa Bay Devil Rays, Toronto Blue Jays.
1999 Manager: Tom Nieto (Yankees).

MARYVALE SAGUAROS

Mailing Address: See league address.
Working Agreements: Chicago Cubs, Cincinnati Reds, Houston Astros, Milwaukee Brewers, Pittsburgh Pirates.
1999 Manager: Bob Melvin (Brewers).

MESA SOLAR SOX

Mailing Address: See league address.
Working Agreements: Atlanta Braves, Florida Marlins, Montreal Expos, New York Mets, Philadelphia Phillies.
1999 Manager: Chris Cron (White Sox).

PEORIA JAVELINAS

Mailing Address: See league address.
Working Agreements: Anaheim Angels, Oakland Athletics, St. Louis Cardinals, Seattle Mariners, Texas Rangers.
1999 Manager: Brad Mills (Phillies).

PHOENIX DESERT DOGS

Mailing Address: See league address.
Working Agreements: Chicago White Sox, Cleveland Indians, Detroit

Tigers, Kansas City Royals, Minnesota Twins.
  1999 Manager: John Mizerock (Royals).
SCOTTSDALE SCORPIONS
  Mailing Address: See league address.
  Working Agreements: Arizona Diamondbacks, Colorado Rockies, Los Angeles Dodgers, San Diego Padres, San Francisco Giants.
  1999 Manager: Eddie Murray (Orioles).

INTERNATIONAL BASEBALL LEAGUE AUSTRALIA

  Office Address: 112 Barry Parade, Fortitude Valley, Queensland 4006 Australia. **Mailing Address:** P.O. Box 552, Fortitude Valley, Queensland 4006 Australia. **Telephone:** (011-61-7) 3832-0043. **FAX:** (011-61-7) 3832-4884. **E-Mail Address:** info@ibla.com.au. **Website:** www.ibla.com.au.
  Principal Owner/Chairman: David Nilsson. **Chief Executive Officer:** Glen Partridge. **Baseball Operations:** Peter Wood. **Media Communications:** Toni Bush.
  Member Clubs, 1999-2000: North—Country New South Wales, New South Wales Storm, Queensland Rams. **South**—South Australian Bite, Victorian Aces, Western Heelers.
  1999-2000 Opening Date: Dec. 3. **Closing Date:** Jan. 23.
  Regular Season: 17 games.
  Playoff Format: Top two teams in each division meet in best-of-3 semi-finals; winners meet in best-of-3 series for league championship.

COLLEGE BASEBALL

COLLEGEBASEBALL

NATIONAL COLLEGIATE ATHLETIC ASSOCIATION

Mailing Address: P.O. Box 6222, Indianapolis, IN 46206. **Telephone:** (317) 917-6222. **FAX:** (317) 917-6826, 917-6857. **E-Mail Addresses:** dpoppe@ncaa.org, jimwright@ncaa.org, jpainter@ncaa.org. **Websites:** www.ncaa.org, www.ncaabaseball.com.

President: Cedric Dempsey. **Director, Championships:** Dennis Poppe. **Contact, College World Series:** Jim Wright. **Contact, Statistics:** John Painter.

Chairman, Division I Baseball Committee: Dick Rockwell (athletic director, LeMoyne). **Division I Baseball Committee:** Mitch Barnhart (athletic director, Oregon State), Jay Bergman (baseball coach, Central Florida), Joe Durant (baseball coach, Florida A&M), John Easterbrook (athletic director, Cal State Fullerton), Paul Fernandes (associate athletic director, Columbia), Wally Groff (athletic director, Texas A&M), Tom Jurich (athletic director, Louisville), Bob Todd (baseball coach, Ohio State).

Chairman, Division II Baseball Committee: Mark Ekeland (baseball coach, South Dakota State). **Chairman, Division III Baseball Committee:** Gary Rundles (baseball coach, Carson-Newman College).

2001 National Convention: Jan. 6-7 at Lake Buena Vista, FL.

2000 Championship Tournaments
NCAA Division I

54th College World Series	Omaha, NE, June 9-17
Super Regionals (16)	Campus sites, June 2-4
Regionals (8)	Campus sites, May 26-28

NCAA Division II

33rd World Series	Montgomery, AL, May 27-June 3
Regionals (8)	Campus sites, May 18-20

NCAA Division III

25th World Series	Salem, VA, May 26-30
Regionals (8)	Campus sites, May 17-21

NATIONAL ASSOCIATION OF INTERCOLLEGIATE ATHLETICS

Mailing Address: 6120 S Yale Ave., Suite 1450, Tulsa, OK 74136. **Telephone:** (918) 494-8828. **FAX:** (918) 494-8841.

Chief Executive Officer: Steve Baker. **Director, Championship Events:** Natalie Cronkhite. **Baseball Event Coordinator:** Mark Chiarucci.

2000 Championship Tournament

NAIA World Series	Lewiston, ID, May 26-June 2

NATIONAL JUNIOR COLLEGE ATHLETIC ASSOCIATION

Mailing Address: P.O. Box 7305, Colorado Springs, CO 80933. **Telephone:** (719) 590-9788. **FAX:** (719) 590-7324.

Executive Director: George Killian. **Director, Division I Baseball Tournament:** Sam Suplizio. **Director, Division II Tournament:** John Daigle. **Director, Division III Tournament:** Bob Pacer.

2000 Championship Tournaments
Division I

World Series	Grand Junction, CO, May 27-June 3

Division II

World Series	Millington, TN, May 27-June 3

Division III

World Series	Batavia, NY, May 20-26

CALIFORNIA COMMUNITY COLLEGE COMMISSION ON ATHLETICS

Mailing Address: 2017 O St., Sacramento, CA 95814. **Telephone:** (916) 444-1600. **FAX:** (916) 444-2616. **Website:** www.coasports.org.

Commissioner of Athletics: Joanne Fortunato. **Associate Commissioner of Athletics:** Stuart Van Horn. **Sports Information Director:** Jack Shinar.

2000 Championship Tournament

State Championship	Fresno City College, May 27-29

AMERICAN BASEBALL COACHES ASSOCIATION

Office Address: 108 S University Ave., Suite 3, Mount Pleasant, MI 48858. **Telephone:** (517) 775-3300. **FAX:** (517) 775-3600. **E-Mail Address:** abca@abca.org. **Website:** www.abca.org.

Executive Director: Dave Keilitz. **Assistant to Executive Director:** Betty Rulong. **Administrative Assistant:** Nick Phillips.

Chairman: Carroll Land (Point Loma Nazarene, CA). **President:** Keith Madison (University of Kentucky).

2001 National Convention: Jan. 4-7 at Nashville (Opryland Hotel).

AMERICA EAST CONFERENCE

Mailing Address: 10 High St., Suite 860, Boston, MA 02110. **Telephone:** (617) 695-6369. **FAX:** (617) 695-6385. **E-Mail Address:** bourque@ameri caeast.com. **Website:** www.americaeast.com.

Baseball Members (First Year): Delaware (1992), Drexel (1992), Hartford (1990), Hofstra (1995), Maine (1990), Northeastern (1990), Towson (1996), Vermont (1990).

Assistant Commissioner/Communications: Matt Bourque.

2000 Tournament: Four teams, double-elimination. May 18-20 at Frawley Stadium, Wilmington, DE.

ATLANTIC COAST CONFERENCE

Office Address: 4512 Weybridge Lane, Greensboro, NC 27407. **Mailing Address:** P.O. Drawer ACC, Greensboro, NC 27417. **Telephone:** (336) 851-6062. **FAX:** (336) 854-8797. **E-Mail Address:** amoore@theacc.org. **Website:** www.theacc.com.

Baseball Members (First Year): Clemson (1953), Duke (1953), Florida State (1992), Georgia Tech (1980), Maryland (1953), North Carolina (1953), North Carolina State (1953), Virginia (1955), Wake Forest (1953).

Assistant Director, Media Relations: Amy Moore.

2000 Tournament: Nine teams, double-elimination. May 16-21 at Knights Stadium, Fort Mill, SC.

ATLANTIC-10 CONFERENCE

Mailing Address: 2 Penn Center Plaza, Suite 1410, Philadelphia, PA 19102. **Telephone:** (215) 751-0500. **FAX:** (215) 751-0770. **E-Mail Address:** web site@atlantic10.org. **Website:** www.atlantic10.org.

Baseball Members (First Year): East—Fordham (1996), Massachusetts (1977), Rhode Island (1981), St. Bonaventure (1980), St. Joseph's (1983), Temple (1983). **West**—Dayton (1996), Duquesne (1977), George Washington (1977), LaSalle (1996), Virginia Tech (1996), Xavier (1996).

Director, Communications: Ray Cella.

2000 Tournament: Four teams, double-elimination. May 18-20 at Boyertown, PA.

BIG EAST CONFERENCE

Mailing Address: 56 Exchange Terrace, Providence, RI 02903. **Telephone:** (401) 272-9108. **FAX:** (401) 751-8540. **E-Mail Address:** rcarolla@bigeast.org. **Website:** www.bigeast.org

Baseball Members (First Year): Boston College (1985), Connecticut (1985), Georgetown (1985), Notre Dame (1996), Pittsburgh (1985), Rutgers (1996), St. John's (1985), Seton Hall (1985), Villanova (1985), West Virginia (1996)

Assistant Director, Communications: Rob Carolla.

2000 Tournament: Six teams, double-elimination. May 17-20 at Somerset Ballpark, Bridgewater, NJ.

BIG SOUTH CONFERENCE

Mailing Address: 6428 Bannington Dr., Suite A, Charlotte, NC 28226. **Telephone:** (704) 341-7990. **FAX:** (704) 341-7991. **E-Mail Address:** drewd@bigsouth.org. **Website:** www.bigsouthsports.com.

Baseball Members (First Year): Charleston Southern (1983), Coastal Carolina (1983), Elon (1999), High Point (1999), Liberty (1991), UNC Asheville (1985), Radford (1983), Winthrop (1983).

Director, Public Relations: Drew Dickerson.

2000 Tournament: Four teams, double-elimination. May 20-23 at Conway, SC (Coastal Carolina College).

BIG TEN CONFERENCE

Mailing Address: 1500 W Higgins Rd., Park Ridge, IL 60068. **Telephone:** (847) 696-1010. **FAX:** (847) 696-1110. **E-Mail Address:** ljuscik@bigten.org. **Website:** www.bigten.org.

Baseball Members (First Year): Illinois (1896), Indiana (1906), Iowa (1906), Michigan (1896), Michigan State (1950), Minnesota (1906), Northwestern (1898), Ohio State (1913), Penn State (1992), Purdue (1906).

Associate Director, Communications: Lisa Juscik.

2000 Tournament: Four teams, double-elimination. May 18-21 at regular season champion.

BIG 12 CONFERENCE

Mailing Address: 2201 Stemmons Freeway, 28th Floor, Dallas, TX 75207. **Telephone:** (214) 742-1212. **FAX:** (214) 753-0145. **E-Mail Address:** bo@big12sports.com. **Website:** www.big12sports.com.

Baseball Members (First Year): Baylor (1997), Iowa State (1997), Kansas (1997), Kansas State (1997), Missouri (1997), Nebraska (1997), Oklahoma (1997), Oklahoma State (1997), Texas (1997), Texas A&M (1997), Texas Tech (1997).

Director, Media Relations: Bo Carter.

2000 Tournament: Eight teams, double-elimination. May 17-21 at Southwestern Bell Bricktown Ballpark, Oklahoma City, OK.

BIG WEST CONFERENCE

Mailing Address: 2 Corporate Park, Suite 206, Irvine, CA 92606. **Telephone:** (949) 261-2525. **FAX:** (949) 261-2528. **E-Mail Address:** mvillamor@bigwest.org. **Website:** www.bigwest.org.

Baseball Members (First Year): Cal Poly San Luis Obispo (1997), UC Santa Barbara (1970), Cal State Fullerton (1975), Long Beach State (1970), Nevada (1993), New Mexico State (1992), Pacific (1972), Sacramento State (1997).

Assistant Director, Information: Mike Villamor.

2000 Tournament: None.

COLONIAL ATHLETIC ASSOCIATION

Mailing Address: 8625 Patterson Ave., Richmond, VA 23229. **Telephone:** (804) 754-1616. **FAX:** (804) 754-1830. **E-Mail Address:** svehorn@caasports.com. **Website:** www.caasports.com.

Baseball Members (First Year): East Carolina (1986), George Mason (1986), James Madison (1986), UNC Wilmington (1986), Old Dominion (1992), Richmond (1986), Virginia Commonwealth (1996), William & Mary (1985).

Sports Information Director: Steve Vehorn.

2000 Tournament: Eight teams, double-elimination. May 16-21 at Coy Tillet Field, Manteo, NC.

CONFERENCE USA

Mailing Address: 35 E Wacker Dr., Suite 650, Chicago, IL 60601. **Telephone:** (312) 553-0483. **FAX:** (312) 553-0495. **E-Mail Address:** rdanderson@c-usa.org. **Website:** www.c-usa.org.

Baseball Members (First Year): Alabama-Birmingham (1996), Cincinnati (1996), Houston (1997), Louisville (1996), Memphis (1996), UNC Charlotte (1996), Saint Louis (1996), South Florida (1996), Southern Mississippi (1996), Tulane (1996).

Director, Information Services: Russell Anderson.

2000 Tournament: Eight teams, double-elimination. May 17-21 at St. Petersburg, FL.

IVY LEAGUE

Mailing Address: 330 Alexander Rd., Princeton, NJ 08544. **Telephone:** (609) 258-6426. **FAX:** (609) 258-1690. **E-Mail Address:** ivygroup@princeton.edu. **Website:** www.ivyleaguesports.com.

Baseball Members (First Year): Rolfe—Brown (1948), Dartmouth (1930), Harvard (1948), Yale (1930). **Gehrig**—Columbia (1930), Cornell (1930), Pennsylvania (1930), Princeton (1930).

Assistant, Public Information: Jennifer Enke.

2000 Tournament: Best-of-3 series between division champions. May 6-7 at Gehrig Division champion.

METRO ATLANTIC ATHLETIC CONFERENCE

Mailing Address: 1090 Amboy Ave., Edison, NJ 08837. **Telephone:** (732) 225-0202. **FAX:** (732) 225-5440. **E-Mail Address:** catherine.hughes@maac.org. **Website:** www.maac.org.

Baseball Members (First Year): North—Canisius (1990), LeMoyne (1990), Marist (1998), Niagara (1990), Siena (1990). **South**—Fairfield (1982), Iona (1982), Manhattan (1982), Rider (1998), St. Peter's (1982).

Director, Media Relations: Catherine Hughes.

2000 Tournament: Four teams, double-elimination. May 18-20 at Dutchess Stadium, Fishkill, NY.

MID-AMERICAN CONFERENCE

Mailing Address: 24 Public Square, 15th Floor, Cleveland, OH 44113. **Telephone:** (216) 566-4622. **FAX:** (216) 858-9622. **E-Mail Address:** bmcgowan@midamconf.com. **Website:** www.midamconf.com.

Baseball Members (First Year): East—Akron (1992), Bowling Green State (1952), Kent (1951), Marshall (1997), Miami (1947), Ohio (1946). **West**—Ball State (1973), Central Michigan (1971), Eastern Michigan (1971), Northern Illinois (1997), Toledo (1950), Western Michigan (1947).

Assistant Commissioner, Communications: Brian McGowan.

2000 Tournament: Six teams (three from each division), double-elimination. May 17-20 at site of team with best conference winning percentage.

MID-CONTINENT CONFERENCE

Mailing Address: 340 W Butterfield Rd., Suite 3-D, Elmhurst, IL 60126. **Telephone:** (630) 516-0661. **FAX:** (630) 516-0673. **E-Mail Address:** nsmidcon@aol.com. **Website:** www.mid-con.com.

Baseball Members (First Year): Chicago State (1994), Indiana-Purdue (1999), Oakland (2000), Oral Roberts (1998), Southern Utah (2000), Valparaiso (1983), Western Illinois (1982), Youngstown State (1992).

Director, Media Relations: Nancy Smith.

2000 Tournament: Six teams, double-elimination. May 17-21 at Tulsa, OK (Oral Roberts University).

MID-EASTERN ATHLETIC CONFERENCE

Mailing Address: 102 N Elm St., Suite 401, P.O. Box 21205, Greensboro, NC 27420. **Telephone:** (336) 275-9961. **FAX:** (336) 275-9964. **E-Mail Address:** meac@nr.infi.net. **Website:** www.meacsports.com.

Baseball Members (First Year): North—Coppin State (1985), Delaware State (1970), Howard (1970), Maryland-Eastern Shore (1970). **South**—Bethune-Cookman (1979), Florida A&M (1979), Norfolk State (1998), North Carolina A&T (1970).

Assistant Commissioner, Media Relations: Bradford Evans. **Baseball Contact:** Mitchell Jennings.

2000 Tournament: Eight teams, double-elimination. April 28-30 at Daytona Beach, FL (Bethune-Cookman College).

MIDWESTERN COLLEGIATE CONFERENCE

Mailing Address: 201 S Capitol Ave., Suite 500, Indianapolis, IN 46225. **Telephone:** (317) 237-5604. **FAX:** (317) 237-5620. **E-Mail Address:** jlehman@mccnet.org. **Website:** www.mccsportsnet.com.

Baseball Members (First Year): Butler (1979), Cleveland State (1994), Detroit (1980), Illinois-Chicago (1994), Wisconsin-Milwaukee (1994), Wright State (1994).

Assistant Commissioner: Josh Lehman.

2000 Tournament: Six teams, double-elimination. May 18-21 at Dayton, OH (Wright State University).

MISSOURI VALLEY CONFERENCE

Mailing Address: 1000 Union Station, Suite 105, St. Louis, MO 63103. **Telephone:** (314) 421-0339. **FAX:** (314) 421-3505. **E-Mail Address:** smontooth@mvc.org. **Website:** www.mvc.org.

Baseball Members (First Year): Bradley (1955), Creighton (1976), Evansville (1994), Illinois State (1980), Indiana State (1976), Northern Iowa (1991), Southern Illinois (1974), Southwest Missouri State (1990), Wichita State (1945).

Assistant Director, Media Relations: Stacey Montooth.

2000 Tournament: Six teams, double-elimination. May 17-20 at Wichita, KS (Wichita State University).

MOUNTAIN WEST CONFERENCE

Mailing Address: P.O. Box 35670, Colorado Springs, CO 80935. **Telephone:** (719) 533-9500/9511. **FAX:** (719) 533-9512. **E-Mail Address:** jhedlund@mountainwestconf.com. **Website:** www.mountainwestconf.com.

Baseball Members (First Year): Air Force (2000), Brigham Young (2000), Nevada-Las Vegas (2000), New Mexico (2000), San Diego State (2000), Utah (2000).

Assistant Director, Media Relations: Javan Hedlund.

2000 Tournament: Six teams, double-elimination. May 17-20 at Las Vegas (University of Nevada-Las Vegas).

NORTHEAST CONFERENCE

Mailing Address: 220 Old New Brunswick Rd., Piscataway, NJ 08854. **Telephone:** (732) 562-0877. **FAX:** (732) 562-8838. **E-Mail Address:** rratner@northeastconference.org. **Website:** www.northeastconference.org.

Baseball Members (First Year): North—Central Connecticut State (1999), Long Island (1981), Quinnipiac (1999), Sacred Heart (2000), St. Francis, N.Y. (1981). **South**—Fairleigh Dickinson (1981), Maryland-Baltimore County (1999), Monmouth (1985), Mount St. Mary's (1989), Wagner (1981).

Assistant Commissioner: Ron Ratner.

2000 Tournament: Four teams, double-elimination. May 12-14 at The Sandcastle, Atlantic City, N.J.

OHIO VALLEY CONFERENCE

Mailing Address: 278 Franklin Rd., Suite 103, Brentwood, TN 37027. **Telephone:** (615) 371-1698. **FAX:** (615) 371-1788. **E-Mail Address:** rwashburn@ovc.org. **Website:** www.ovcsports.com.

Baseball Members (First Year): Austin Peay State (1962), Eastern Illinois (1996), Eastern Kentucky (1948), Middle Tennessee State (1952), Morehead State (1948), Murray State (1948), Southeast Missouri State (1991), Tennessee-Martin (1992), Tennessee Tech (1949).

Assistant Commissioner: Rob Washburn.

2000 Tournament: Six teams, double-elimination. May 18-20 at site of highest seeded team with lights.

PACIFIC-10 CONFERENCE

Mailing Address: 800 S Broadway, Suite 400, Walnut Creek, CA 94596. **Telephone:** (925) 932-4411. **FAX:** (925) 932-4601. **E-Mail Address:** gniemi@pac-10.org. **Website:** www.pac-10.org.

Baseball Members (First Year): Arizona (1979), Arizona State (1979), California (1916), UCLA (1928), Oregon State (1916), Southern California (1922), Stanford (1917), Washington (1916), Washington State (1917).

Public Relations Intern: Gavin Niemi.

2000 Tournament: None.

PATRIOT LEAGUE

Mailing Address: 3897 Adler Pl., Suite 310, Bethlehem, PA 18017. **Telephone:** (610) 691-2414. **FAX:** (610) 691-8414. **E-Mail Address:** cgartley@patriotleague.org. **Website:** www.patriotleague.org.

Baseball Members (First Year): Army (1993), Bucknell (1991), Holy Cross (1991), Lafayette (1991), Lehigh (1991), Navy (1993).

Assistant Executive Director, Communications: Chris Gartley.

2000 Tournament: Top three teams; No. 2 plays No. 3 in one-game playoff. Winner faces No. 1 team in best-of-3 series at No. 1 seed, dates unavailable.

SOUTHEASTERN CONFERENCE

Mailing Address: 2201 Richard Arrington Blvd. N, Birmingham, AL 35203. **Telephone:** (205) 458-3000. **FAX:** (205) 458-3030. **E-Mail Address:** twilson@sec.org. **Website:** www.secsports.com.

Baseball Members (First Year): East—Florida (1933), Georgia (1933), Kentucky (1933), South Carolina (1992), Tennessee (1933), Vanderbilt (1933). **West**—Alabama (1933), Arkansas (1992), Auburn (1933), Louisiana State

(1933), Mississippi (1933), Mississippi State (1933).

Assistant Director, Media Relations: Tammy Wilson.

2000 Tournament: Eight teams, modified double-elimination. May 17-21 at Hoover Metropolitan Stadium, Birmingham, AL.

SOUTHERN CONFERENCE

Mailing Address: One West Pack Square, Suite 1508, Asheville, NC 28801. **Telephone:** (828) 255-7872. **FAX:** (828) 251-5006. **E-Mail Address:** sshutt@socon.org. **Website:** www.soconsports.com.

Baseball Members (First Year): Appalachian State (1971), Charleston (1998), The Citadel (1936), Davidson (1991), East Tennessee State (1978), Furman (1936), Georgia Southern (1991), UNC Greensboro (1997), Virginia Military Institute (1924), Western Carolina (1976), Wofford (1997).

Director, Public Affairs: Steve Shutt.

2000 Tournament: Eight teams, double-elimination. May 17-21 at Charleston, SC (The Citadel).

SOUTHLAND CONFERENCE

Mailing Address: 8150 N Central Expy., Suite 930, Dallas, TX 75206. **Telephone:** (214) 750-7522. **FAX:** (214) 750-8077. **E-Mail Address:** cgrubbs@southland.org. **Website:** www.southland.org.

Baseball Members (First Year): Lamar (1999), Louisiana-Monroe (1983), McNeese State (1973), Nicholls State (1992), Northwestern State (1988), Sam Houston State (1988), Southeastern Louisiana (1998), Southwest Texas State (1988), Texas-Arlington (1964), Texas-San Antonio (1992).

Baseball Intern: Chad Grubbs.

2000 Tournament: Six teams, double-elimination. May 17-20 at Monroe, LA (University of Louisiana-Monroe).

SOUTHWESTERN ATHLETIC CONFERENCE

Mailing Address: A.G. Gaston Building, 1527 Fifth Ave. North, Birmingham, AL 35204. **Telephone:** (205) 320-0263 . **FAX:** (205) 297-9820. **E-Mail Address:** lhardy@swac.org. **Website:** www.swac.org.

Baseball Members (First Year): East—Alabama A&M (2000), Alabama State (1982), Alcorn State (1962), Jackson State (1958), Mississippi Valley State (1968). **West**—Arkansas-Pine Bluff (1999), Grambling State (1958), Prairie View A&M (1920), Southern (1934), Texas Southern (1954).

Associate Commissioner: Lonza Hardy Jr.

2000 Tournament: Six teams, double-elimination. May 4-7 at Jackson, MS (Jackson State University).

SUN BELT CONFERENCE

Mailing Address: One Galleria Blvd., Suite 2115, Metairie, LA 70001. **Telephone:** (504) 834-6600, ext. 11. **FAX:** (504) 834-6806. **E-Mail Address:** der amus@sunbeltsports.org. **Website:** www.sunbeltsports.org.

Baseball Members (First Year): Arkansas-Little Rock (1991), Arkansas State (1991), Florida International (1999), Louisiana-Lafayette (1991), Louisiana Tech (1991), New Orleans (1976), South Alabama (1976), Western Kentucky (1982).

Director, Service Bureau: Kevin DeRamus.

2000 Tournament: Eight teams, double-elimination. May 16-20 at Eddie Stanky Field, Mobile, AL.

TRANS AMERICA ATHLETIC CONFERENCE

Mailing Address: The Commons, 3370 Vineville Ave., Suite 108-B, Macon, GA 31204. **Telephone:** (912) 474-3394. **FAX:** (912) 474-4272. **E-Mail Address:** taac@taac.org. **Website:** www.taac.org.

Baseball Members (First Year): Campbell (1994), Central Florida (1992), Florida Atlantic (1993), Georgia State (1983), Jacksonville (1999), Jacksonville State (1996), Mercer (1978), Samford (1978), Stetson (1985), Troy State (1998).

Assistant Commissioner: Tom Snyder.

2000 Tournament: Six teams, double-elimination. May 17-20 at Brest Field, Jacksonville, FL.

WEST COAST CONFERENCE

Mailing Address: 1200 Bayhill Dr., Suite 302, San Bruno, CA 94066. **Telephone:** (650) 873-8622. **FAX:** (650) 873-7846. **E-Mail Address:** dott@west coast.org. **Website:** www.wccsports.com.

Baseball Members (First Year): Coast—Gonzaga (1996), Loyola Marymount (1968), San Francisco (1968), Santa Clara (1968). **West**—Pepperdine (1968), Portland (1996), San Diego (1979), Saint Mary's (1968).

Assistant Commissioner: Don Ott.

2000 Tournament: Division champions meet in best-of-3 series, May 20-21, site unavailable.

WESTERN ATHLETIC CONFERENCE

Mailing Address: 9250 East Costilla Ave., Suite 300, Englewood, CO 80112. **Telephone:** (303) 799-9221. **FAX:** (303) 799-3888. **E-Mail Address:** wac@wac.org. **Website:** www.wac.org.

Baseball Members (First Year): Fresno State (1992), Hawaii (1978), Hawaii-Hilo (2000), Rice (1996), San Jose State (1996), Texas Christian (1996).

Senior Associate Commissioner: Jeff Hurd. **Director, Sports Information:** Dave Chaffin.

2000 Tournament: None.

CALIFORNIA COLLEGIATE ATHLETIC ASSOCIATION

Mailing Address: 800 S Broadway, Suite 102, Walnut Creek, CA 94596. **Telephone:** (925) 472-8299. **FAX:** (925) 472-8887. **E-Mail Address:** jlang@goc caa.org. **Website:** www.goccaa.org.

Baseball Members: UC Davis, UC Riverside, Cal Poly Pomona, Cal State Chico, Cal State Dominguez Hills, Cal State Los Angeles, Cal State San Bernardino, Cal State Stanislaus, Grand Canyon, San Francisco State, Sonoma State.

CAROLINAS-VIRGINIA
INTERCOLLEGIATE ATHLETIC CONFERENCE

Mailing Address: 26 Club Dr., Thomasville, NC 27360. **Telephone:** (336) 884-0482. **FAX:** (336) 884-0315. **E-Mail Address:** cvac@northstate.net. **Website:** www.cvac.net.

Baseball Members: Anderson, Barton, Belmont Abbey, Coker, Erskine, Limestone, Longwood, Mount Olive, Pfeiffer.

CENTRAL INTERCOLLEGIATE ATHLETIC ASSOCIATION

Mailing Address: 303 Butler Farm Rd., Suite 102, Hampton, VA 23666. **Telephone:** (757) 865-0071. **FAX:** (757) 865-8436. **E-Mail:** ciaaoffice@aol.com. **Website:** www.theciaa.com.

Baseball Members: Bowie State, Elizabeth City State, Saint Augustine's, Saint Paul's, Shaw, Virginia State.

GREAT LAKES INTERCOLLEGIATE ATHLETIC CONFERENCE

Mailing Address: 3250 W Big Beaver, Suite 300, Troy, MI 48084. **Telephone:** (248) 649-2036. **FAX:** (248) 649-6847. **E-Mail Address:** tomjb@tir.com. **Website:** www.gliac.org.

Baseball Members: Ashland, Findlay, Gannon, Grand Valley State, Hillsdale, Mercyhurst, Northwood, Saginaw Valley State, Wayne State (Mich.), Westminster (Pa.).

GREAT LAKES VALLEY CONFERENCE

Mailing Address: Pan Am Plaza, Suite 560, 201 S Capitol Ave., Indianapolis, IN 46225. **Telephone:** (317) 237-5636. **FAX:** (317) 237-5632. **E-Mail:** cmglvc@aol.com. **Website:** www.siue.edu/athletic/gluchome.html.

Baseball Members: Bellarmine, IU/PU-Fort Wayne, Indianapolis, Kentucky Wesleyan, Lewis, Missouri-Saint Louis, Northern Kentucky, Quincy, Saint Joseph's, Southern Illinois-Edwardsville, Southern Indiana, Wisconsin-Parkside.

GULF SOUTH CONFERENCE

Mailing Address: 4 Office Park Circle, Suite 218, Birmingham, AL 25223. **Telephone:** (205) 870-9750. **FAX:** (205) 870 4723. **E Mail Address:** ming berg@ix.netcom.com. **Website:** www.gulfsouthconference.org.

Baseball Members: Alabama-Huntsville, Arkansas-Monticello, Arkansas Tech, Central Arkansas, Christian Brothers, Delta State, Henderson State, Lincoln Memorial, Montovallo, North Alabama, Southern Arkansas, Valdosta State, West Alabama, West Florida, West Georgia.

HEART OF TEXAS CONFERENCE

Mailing Address: 527 Dale, Waco, TX 76706. **Telephone:** (254) 662-6472. **FAX:** (254) 662-6627.

Baseball Members: Concordia-Austin, Incarnate Word, Saint Edward's, Saint Mary's, Texas Lutheran, Texas Wesleyan.

LONE STAR CONFERENCE

Mailing Address: 1221 W Campbell Rd. No. 217, Richardson, TX 75080. **Telephone:** (972) 234-0033. **FAX:** (972) 234-4110. **E-Mail:** tinderj@lonestarcon ference.org. **Website:** www.lonestarconference.org.

Baseball Members: Abilene Christian, Cameron, Central Oklahoma, East Central, Eastern New Mexico, Harding, Northeastern State, Ouachita Baptist, Southeastern Oklahoma, Southwestern Oklahoma, Tarleton State, Texas A&M-Kingsville, West Texas A&M.

MID-AMERICA INTERCOLLEGIATE ATHLETICS ASSOCIATION

Mailing Address: 10551 Barkley, Suite 501, Overland Park, KS 66212. **Telephone:** (913) 341-3839. **FAX:** (913) 341-2995. **E-Mail Address:** miaasid@aol.com. **Website:** http://members.aol.com/miaasid.

Baseball Members: Central Missouri State, Emporia State, Missouri-Rolla, Missouri Southern State, Missouri Western State, Northwest Missouri State, Pittsburg State, Southwest Baptist, Truman State, Washburn.

NEW ENGLAND COLLEGIATE CONFERENCE

Mailing Address: Moore Fieldhouse, Sports Information, 125 Wintergreen Ave., New Haven, CT 06515. **Telephone:** (203) 392-6004. **FAX:** (203) 392-6967.

Baseball Members: Binghamton, Bridgeport, Felician, Franklin Pierce, Massachusetts-Lowell, New Hampshire College, New Haven, Southern Connecticut State, Teikyo Post.

NEW YORK COLLEGIATE ATHLETIC CONFERENCE

Mailing Address: 3031 Arrowhead Lane, Norristown, PA 19401. **Telephone:** (610) 825-5068. **FAX:** (610) 825-3676.

Baseball Members: Adelphi, Concordia (N.Y.), Dowling, Mercy, Molloy, New Jersey Institute of Technology, Philadelphia Textile, Queens, Saint Rose.

NORTH CENTRAL INTERCOLLEGIATE ATHLETIC CONFERENCE

Mailing Address: 2400 N Louise, Ramkota Inn, Sioux Falls, SD 57107. **Telephone:** (605) 338-0907. **FAX:** (605) 373-9018. **E-Mail Address:** nccinfo@inst.augie.edu. **Website:** http://inst.augie.edu/~ncc.

Baseball Members: Augustana (S.D.), Minnesota State-Mankato, Morningside, Nebraska-Omaha, North Dakota, North Dakota State, Northern Colorado, St. Cloud State, South Dakota, South Dakota State.

NORTHEAST-10 CONFERENCE

Mailing Address: 16 Belmont St., South Easton, MA 02375. **Telephone:** (508) 230-9844. **FAX:** (508) 230-9845. **E-Mail:** jharper@northeast10.org. **Website:** www.northeast10.org.

Baseball Members: American International, Assumption, Bentley, Bryant, Merrimack, Saint Anselm, Saint Michael's, Stonehill.

NORTHERN SUN INTERCOLLEGIATE CONFERENCE

Mailing Address: 1901 University Ave. SE, Suite 310-F, Minneapolis, MN 55414. **Telephone:** (612) 626-7681. **FAX:** (612) 626-7682. **Website:** www.northernsun.org.

Baseball Members: Bemidji State, Concordia (Minn.), Minnesota-Crookston, Minnesota-Duluth, Minnesota-Morris, Northern State, Southwest State, Wayne State (Neb.), Winona State.

Sports Information Director: Kevin Kurtt.

PEACH BELT ATHLETIC CONFERENCE

Mailing Address: P.O. Box 204890, Augusta, GA 30917. **Telephone:** (706) 860-8499. **FAX:** (706) 650-8113. **E-Mail Address:** mediarelations@peachbelt.com. **Website:** www.peachbelt.com.

Baseball Members: Armstrong Atlantic State, Augusta State, Columbus State, Francis Marion, Georgia College, Kennesaw State, Lander, UNC Pembroke, North Florida, South Carolina-Aiken, South Carolina-Spartanburg.

PENNSYLVANIA STATE ATHLETIC CONFERENCE

Mailing Address: 306 Annex Building, Susquehanna Ave., Lock Haven, PA 17745. **Telephone:** (570) 893-2780. **FAX:** (570) 893-2206. **E-Mail Address:** wadair@eagle.lhup.edu. **Website:** www.lhup.edu/psac.

Baseball Members: Bloomsburg, California (Pa.), Cheyney, Clarion, East Stroudsburg, Edinboro, Indiana (Pa.), Kutztown, Lock Haven, Mansfield, Millersville, Shippensburg, Slippery Rock, West Chester.

ROCKY MOUNTAIN ATHLETIC CONFERENCE

Mailing Address: Copper Building, Suite B, 1631 Mesa Ave., Colorado Springs, CO 80906. **Telephone:** (719) 471-4936. **FAX:** (719) 471-0088. **E-Mail Address:** ccole@rmi.net. **Website:** www.rmacsports.org.

Baseball Members: Colorado School of Mines, Fort Hays State, Mesa State, Metro State, Nebraska-Kearney, New Mexico Highlands, Regis, Southern Colorado.

Assistant Commissioner, Media Relations: Chris Cole.

SOUTH ATLANTIC CONFERENCE

Mailing Address: Gateway Plaza, Suite 130, 226 N Park Dr., Rock Hill, SC 29730. **Telephone:** (803) 981-5240. **FAX:** (803) 981-9444. **E-Mail Address:** thesac@rhtc.net. **Website:** www.thesac.com.

Baseball Members: Carson-Newman, Catawba, Gardner-Webb, Lenoir-Rhyne, Mars Hill, Newberry, Presbyterian, Tusculum, Wingate.

Assistant to Commissioner: Lauren Massey.

SOUTHERN INTERCOLLEGIATE ATHLETIC CONFERENCE

Mailing Address: Harris Tower, 233 Peachtree St. NE, Suite 301, Atlanta, GA 30303. **Telephone:** (404) 659-3380. **FAX:** (404) 659-7422.

Baseball Members: Albany State (Ga.), Kentucky State, Lane, LeMoyne-Owen, Miles, Paine, Savannah State, Tuskegee.

SUNSHINE STATE CONFERENCE

Mailing Address: 7061 Grand National Dr., Suite 138, Orlando, FL 32819. **Telephone:** (407) 248-8460. **FAX:** (407) 248-8325. **E-Mail Address:** walt_riddle@yahoo.com. **Website:** www.rollins.edu/athletics/ssc.

Baseball Members: Barry, Eckerd, Florida Southern, Florida Tech, Lynn, Rollins, Saint Leo, Tampa.

WEST VIRGINIA INTERCOLLEGIATE ATHLETIC CONFERENCE

Mailing Address: 1422 Main St., Princeton, WV 24740. **Telephone:** (304) 487-6298. **FAX:** (304) 487-6299. **E-Mail Address:** wviac2@citilink.net. **Website:** www.wviac.org.

Baseball Members: Alderson-Broaddus, Bluefield State, Charleston (W.Va.), Concord, Davis & Elkins, Fairmont State, Ohio Valley, Salem-Teikyo, Shepherd, West Liberty State, West Virginia State, West Virginia Tech, West Virginia Wesleyan.

*Recruiting coordinator

AIR FORCE ACADEMY Falcons

Conference: Mountain West.
Mailing Address: 2169 Field House Dr., Suite 111, USAF Academy, CO 80840.
Head Coach: Reed Peters. **Assistant Coaches:** Bobby Applegate, *Mike Saks. **Telephone:** (719) 333-7898. ■ **Baseball SID:** Dave Toller. **Telephone:** (719) 333-2313. **FAX:** (719) 333-3798.
Home Field: Falcon Field. **Seating Capacity:** 1,000. **Outfield Dimensions:** LF—349, CF—400, RF—316. **Press Box Telephone:** (719) 333-3472.

AKRON Zips

Conference: Mid-American (East).
Mailing Address: 176 JAR Arena, Akron, OH 44325.
Head Coach: Dave Fross. **Assistant Coaches:** *Tim Berenyi, Dan Massarelli. **Telephone:** (330) 972-7277. ■ **Baseball SID:** Josh Harris. **Telephone:** (330) 972-7468. **FAX:** (330) 374-8844.
Home Field: Lee Jackson Field. **Seating Capacity:** 2,500. **Outfield Dimensions:** LF—330, CF—400, RF—330. **Press Box Telephone:** (330) 972-8896.

ALABAMA Crimson Tide

Conference: Southeastern (West).
Mailing Address: P.O. Box 870391, Tuscaloosa, AL 35487.
Head Coach: Jim Wells. **Assistant Coaches:** Todd Butler, *Mitch Gaspard, Jim Gatewood. **Telephone:** (205) 348-4029. ■ **Baseball SID:** Barry Allen. **Telephone:** (205) 348-6084. **FAX:** (205) 348-8840/8841.
Home Field: Sewell-Thomas Stadium. **Seating Capacity:** 6,400. **Outfield Dimensions:** LF—325, CF—400, RF—325. **Press Box Telephone:** (205) 348-4927.

ALABAMA-BIRMINGHAM Blazers

Conference: Conference USA.
Mailing Address: 617 13th St. S, Birmingham, AL 35294.
Head Coach: Larry Giangrosso. **Assistant Coaches:** *Lee Hall, Frank Walton. **Telephone:** (205) 934-5181. ■ **Baseball SID:** Chris Pika. **Telephone:** (205) 934-0722. **FAX:** (205) 934-7505.
Home Field: Jerry D. Young Memorial Field. **Seating Capacity:** 1,000. **Outfield Dimensions:** LF—337, CF—390, RF—330. **Press Box Telephone:** (205) 934-0200.

ALABAMA A&M Bulldogs

Conference: Southwestern Athletic (East).
Mailing Address: P.O. 1597, Normal, AL 35762.
Head Coach: Thomas Wesley. **Telephone:** (256) 858-4004. ■ **Baseball SID:** Ashley Balch. **Telephone:** (256) 858-4005. **FAX:** (256) 858-4003.

ALABAMA STATE Hornets

Conference: Southwestern Athletic (East).
Mailing Address: 915 S. Jackson St., Montgomery, AL 36104.
Head Coach: Larry Watkins. **Telephone:** (334) 229-4228. ■ **Baseball SID:** Kevin Manns. **Telephone:** (334) 229-4511. **FAX:** (334) 262-2971.

ALBANY Great Danes

Conference: Independent.
Mailing Address: PE 331, 1400 Washington Ave., Albany, NY 12222.
Head Coach: Jon Mueller. **Assistant Coaches:** Mike Lilac, Rich Wurster. **Telephone:** (518) 442-3014. ■ **Baseball SID:** Josh White. **Telephone:** (518) 442-3072. **FAX:** (518) 518-442-3139.

ALCORN STATE Braves

Conference: Southwestern Athletic (East).
Mailing Address: 1000 ASU Drive, No. 510, Alcorn State, MS 39096.
Head Coach: Willie McGowan. **Assistant Coach:** David Robinson. **Telephone:** (601) 877-6279. ■ **Baseball SID:** Peter Forest. **Telephone:** (601) 877-6466. **FAX:** (601) 877-3821.

APPALACHIAN STATE Mountaineers

Conference: Southern.
Mailing Address: Owens Fieldhouse, Boone, NC 28608.
Head Coach: Troy Huestess. **Assistant Coaches:** Jeremy Livengood, Stony Wine. **Telephone:** (828) 262-6097. ■ **Baseball SID:** Bill Dyer. **Telephone:** (828) 262-2268. **FAX:** (828) 262-6106.

ARIZONA Wildcats

Conference: Pacific-10.
Mailing Address: P.O. Box 210096, Tucson, AZ 85721.
Head Coach: Jerry Stitt. **Assistant Coaches:** Tod Brown, *Bill Kinneberg, Victor Solis. **Telephone:** (520) 621-4102. ■ **Baseball SID:** David Hardee. **Telephone:** (520) 621-0914. **FAX:** (520) 621-2681.
Home Field: Frank Sancet Field. **Seating Capacity:** 6,700. **Outfield Dimensions:** LF—360, CF—400, RF—360. **Press Box Telephone:** (520) 621-4440.

ARIZONA STATE Sun Devils

Conference: Pacific-10.
Mailing Address: ICA Bldg., Fifth Floor, Tempe, AZ 85287.
Head Coach: Pat Murphy. **Assistant Coaches:** Mike Rooney, *Jay Sferra. **Telephone:** (480) 965-3677. ■ **Baseball SID:** Aimee Dombroski. **Telephone:** (480) 965-6592. **FAX:** (480) 965-5408.
Home Field: Packard Stadium. **Seating Capacity:** 4,000. **Outfield Dimensions:** LF—340, CF—395, RF—340. **Press Box Telephone:** (480) 965-1509.

ARKANSAS Razorbacks

Conference: Southeastern (West).
Mailing Address: P.O. Box 7777, Fayetteville, AR 72702.
Head Coach: Norm DeBriyn. **Assistant Coaches:** Doug Clark, *Tim Montez. **Telephone:** (501) 575-3655. ■ **Baseball SID:** Chris Williams. **Telephone:** (501) 575-2751. **FAX:** (501) 575-7481.
Home Field: Baum Stadium. **Seating Capacity:** 3,300. **Outfield Dimensions:** LF—320, CF—400, RF—320. **Press Box Telephone:** (501) 444-0031.

ARKANSAS-LITTLE ROCK Trojans

Conference: Sun Belt.
Mailing Address: 2801 University, Little Rock, AR 72204.
Head Coach: Brian Rhees. **Assistant Coaches:** Mark Coca, *Karl Kuhn. **Telephone:** (501) 663-8095. ■ **Baseball SID:** Leigh Ann Gullett. **Telephone:** (501) 569-3077. **FAX:** (501) 569-3030.

ARKANSAS-PINE BLUFF Golden Lions

Conference: Southwestern Athletic (West).
Mailing Address: N University, Pine Bluff, AR 71601.
Head Coach: Elbert Bennett. **Assistant Coach:** *George Howard. **Telephone:** (870) 543-8284. ■ **Baseball SID:** Carl Whimper. **Telephone:** (870) 543-8683. **FAX:** (870) 543-8114.

ARKANSAS STATE Indians

Conference: Sun Belt.
Mailing Address: P.O. Box 1000, State University, AR 72467.
Head Coach: Bill Bethea. **Assistant Coaches:** David Kenley, *Earl Wheeler. **Telephone:** (870) 972-2700. ■ **Baseball SID:** Scott Costello. **Telephone:** (870) 972-2541. **FAX:** (870) 972-3367.
Home Field: Tomlinson Stadium/Kell Field. **Seating Capacity:** 1,000. **Outfield Dimensions:** LF—335, CF—400, RF—335. **Press Box Telephone:** (870) 972-3383.

ARMY Cadets

Conference: Patriot.
Mailing Address: 639 Howard Road, West Point, NY 10996.
Head Coach: Dan Roberts. **Assistant Coach:** Joe Sottolano. **Telephone:** (914) 938-3712. ■ **Baseball SID:** Bob Beretta. **Telephone:** (914) 938-3308. **FAX:** (914) 446-2556.

AUBURN Tigers

Conference: Southeastern (West).
Mailing Address: P.O. Box 351, Auburn, AL 36830.
Head Coach: Hal Baird. **Assistant Coaches:** *Steve Renfroe, Tom Slater. **Telephone:** (334) 844-4975. ■ **Baseball SID:** Kirk Sampson. **Telephone:** (334) 844-9800. **FAX:** (334) 844-9803.
Home Field: Hitchcock Field at Plainsman Park. **Seating Capacity:** 3,186. **Outfield Dimensions:** LF—315, CF—385, RF—331. **Press Box Telephone:** (334) 844-4138.

AUSTIN PEAY STATE Governors

Conference: Ohio Valley.
Mailing Address: P.O. Box 4515, Clarksville, TN 37044.
Head Coach: Gary McClure. **Assistant Coaches:** *Brian Hetland, Larry Owens. **Telephone:** (931) 221-6266. ■ **Baseball SID:** Cody Bush. **Telephone:** (931) 221-7561. **FAX:** (931) 221-7562.

BALL STATE Cardinals

Conference: Mid-American (West).
Mailing Address: HP 120, Ball State U., Muncie, IN 47306.
Head Coach: Rich Maloney. **Assistant Coaches:** *Matt Husted, Chris Kessick, John Lowery. **Telephone:** (765) 285-8932. ■ **Baseball SID:** Bob Moore. **Telephone:** (765) 285-8242. **FAX:** (765) 285-8929.
Home Field: Ball Diamond. **Seating Capacity:** 1,700. **Outfield Dimensions:** LF—330, CF—400, RF—330. **Press Box Telephone:** (765) 285-8932.

BAYLOR Bears

Conference: Big 12.
Mailing Address: 150 Bear Run, Waco, TX 76711.
Head Coach: Steve Smith. **Assistant Coaches:** Chris Berry, Steve Johnigan, *Mitch Thompson. **Telephone:** (254) 710-3097. ■ **Baseball SID:** Amy Townsend. **Telephone:** (254) 710-3043. **FAX:** (254) 710-1369.
Home Field: Ferrell Field at Baylor Ballpark. **Seating Capacity:** 5,000.

Outfield Dimensions: LF—330, CF—400, RF—330. **Press Box Telephone:** (254) 754-5546.

BELMONT Bruins

Conference: Independent.

Mailing Address: 1900 Belmont Blvd., Nashville, TN 37212.

Head Coach: Dave Jarvis. **Assistant Coaches:** *Chris Moodelmog, Dave Whitten. **Telephone:** (615) 460-6166. ■ **Baseball SID:** Matt Wilson. **Telephone:** (615) 460-6698. **FAX:** (615) 460-5584.

BETHUNE-COOKMAN Wildcats

Conference: Mid-Eastern Athletic (South).

Mailing Address: 640 Dr. Mary McLeod Bethune Blvd., Daytona Beach, FL 32114.

Head Coach: Mervyl Melendez. **Assistant Coaches:** Willie Brown, Eddy Hidalgo, *Tim Touma. **Telephone:** (904) 255-1401, ext. 349. ■ **Baseball SID:** Charles Jackson. **Telephone:** (904) 258-7921. **FAX:** (904) 253-4231.

BOSTON COLLEGE Eagles

Conference: Big East.

Mailing Address: 140 Commonwealth Ave., Conte Forum, Chestnut Hill, MA 02467.

Head Coach: Peter Hughes. **Assistant Coaches:** Rob Carpentier, Pat Mason, *Brian Sankey. **Telephone:** (617) 552-3092. ■ **Baseball SID:** Kara McGillicuddy. **Telephone:** (617) 552-1188. **FAX:** (617) 552-4903.

Home Field: Eddie Pellagrini/ Shea Field. **Seating Capacity:** 1,000. **Outfield Dimensions:** LF—340, CF—400, RF—320. **Press Box Telephone:** None.

BOWLING GREEN STATE Falcons

Conference: Mid-American (East).

Mailing Address: Perry Stadium East, Bowling Green, OH 43403.

Head Coach: Danny Schmitz. **Assistant Coaches:** L.J. Archambeau, Tod Brown. **Telephone:** (419) 372-7065. ■ **Baseball SID:** Jeff Weiss. **Telephone:** (419) 372-7077. **FAX:** (419) 372-6015.

BRADLEY Braves

Conference: Missouri Valley.

Mailing Address: 1501 W Bradley Ave., Peoria, IL 61625.

Head Coach: Dewey Kalmer. **Assistant Coaches:** John Dyke, *John Young. **Telephone:** (309) 677-2684. ■ **Baseball SID:** Bobby Parker. **Telephone:** (309) 677-2624. **FAX:** (309) 677-2626.

Home Field: Pete Vonachen Stadium at Meinen Field. **Seating Capacity:** 6,500. **Outfield Dimensions:** LF—000, CF—383, RF—330. **Press Box Telephone:** (309) 688-2653.

BRIGHAM YOUNG Cougars

Conference: Mountain West.

Mailing Address: 54 SFH, Provo, UT 84602.

Head Coach: Vance Law. **Assistant Coach:** *Dave Eldredge. **Telephone:** (801) 378-5049. ■ **Baseball SID:** Ralph Zobell. **Telephone:** (801) 378-9759. **FAX:** (801) 378-3520.

Home Field: Cougar Field. **Seating Capacity:** 3,000. **Outfield Dimensions:** LF—345, CF—390, RF—345. **Press Box Telephone:** (801) 378-4041.

BROWN Bears

Conference: Ivy League (Rolfe).

Mailing Address: Pizzitola Center, Box 1932, Providence, RI 02912.

Head Coach: Marek Drabinski. **Assistant Coaches:** *Brett Borretti, John Koning. **Telephone:** (401) 863-3090. ■ **Baseball SID:** Julie Bettencourt. **Telephone:** (401) 863-2219. **FAX:** (401) 863-1436.

BUCKNELL Bison

Conference: Patriot.

Mailing Address: Moore Ave., Lewisburg, PA 17837.

Head Coach: Gene Depew. **Assistant Coaches:** *Mike Anders, Brian Hoyt. **Telephone:** (570) 577-3593. ■ **Baseball SID:** Todd Newcomb. **Telephone:** (570) 577-1227. **FAX:** (570) 577-1660.

BUFFALO Bisons

Conference: Independent.

Mailing Address: P.O. Box 605000, Buffalo, NY 14260.

Head Coach: Bill Breene. **Assistant Coaches:** Dave Borsuk, Ron Torgalski. **Telephone:** (716) 645-6808. ■ **Baseball SID:** Paul Vecchio. **Telephone:** (716) 645-6311. **FAX:** (716) 645-6840.

BUTLER Bulldogs

Conference: Midwestern Collegiate.

Mailing Address: 4600 Sunset Ave., Indianapolis, IN 46208.

Head Coach: Steve Farley. **Assistant Coaches:** *Ryan O'Donovan, Matt Tyner. **Telephone:** (317) 940-9721. ■ **Baseball SID:** Tony Hamilton. **Telephone:** (317) 940-9994. **FAX:** (317) 940-9808.

C.W. POST Pioneers

Conference: Independent.

Mailing Address: 720 Northern Blvd., Brookville, NY 11548.

Head Coach: Dick Vining. **Assistant Coaches:** Dan Mascia, Pete Timmes.

Telephone: (516) 299-2938. ■ Baseball SID: Brad Sullivan. Telephone: (516) 299-4156. FAX: (516) 299-3155.

CALIFORNIA Golden Bears

Conference: Pacific-10.
Mailing Address: Haas Pavilion, Berkeley, CA 94720.
Head Coach: Dave Esquer. Assistant Coaches: *Dan Hubbs, David Lawn. Telephone: (510) 643-6006. ■ Baseball SID: Scott Ball. Telephone: (510) 643-1741. FAX: (510) 643-7778.
Home Field: Evans Diamond. Seating Capacity: 4,000. Outfield Dimensions: LF—320, CF—395, RF—320. Press Box Telephone: (510) 642-3098.

UCLA Bruins

Conference: Pacific-10.
Mailing Address: P.O. Box 24044, Los Angeles, CA 90024.
Head Coach: Gary Adams. Assistant Coaches: *Vince Beringhele, Rob Hinds, Tim Leary. Telephone: (310) 794-8210. ■ Baseball SID: Travis King/Erin Rowley. Telephone: (310) 206-8075. FAX: (310) 825-8664.
Home Field: Jackie Robinson Stadium. Seating Capacity: 1,250. Outfield Dimensions: LF—330, CF—390, RF—330. Press Box Telephone: (310) 794-8213.

UC SANTA BARBARA Gauchos

Conference: Big West.
Mailing Address: Robertson Gym, Santa Barbara, CA 93106.
Head Coach: Bob Brontsema. Assistant Coach: *Tom Myers. Telephone: (805) 893-3690. ■ Baseball SID: Danny Harris. Telephone: (805) 893-3428. FAX: (805) 893-4537.
Home Field: Caesar Uyesaka Stadium. Seating Capacity: 1,000. Outfield Dimensions: LF—335, CF—400, RF—335. Press Box Telephone: (805) 893-4671/8079.

CAL POLY SAN LUIS OBISPO Mustangs

Conference: Big West.
Mailing Address: One Grand Ave., San Luis Obispo, CA 93407.
Head Coach: Ritch Price. Assistant Coaches: Todd Coburn, Ryan Graves, *Mike Oakland. Telephone: (805) 756-6367. ■ Baseball SID: Bobby Jezyk. Telephone: (805) 756-6531. FAX: (805) 756-2650.
Home Field: San Luis Obispo Stadium. Seating Capacity: 1,500. Outfield Dimensions: LF—333, CF—410, RF—333. Press Box Telephone: (805) 756-7812.

CAL STATE FULLERTON Titans

Conference: Big West.
Mailing Address: 800 N State College Blvd., PE 133C, Fullerton, CA 92834.
Head Coach: George Horton. Assistant Coaches: *Dave Serrano, Rick Vanderhook, Tim Wallach. Telephone: (714) 278-3789. ■ Baseball SID: Mike Greenlee. Telephone: (714) 278-3970. FAX: (714) 278-3141.
Home Field: Titan Field. Seating Capacity: 4,000. Outfield Dimensions: LF—330, CF—400, RF—330. Press Box Telephone: (714) 278-5327.

CAL STATE NORTHRIDGE Matadors

Conference: Independent.
Mailing Address: 18111 Nordhoff St., Northridge, CA 91330.
Head Coach: Mike Batesole. Assistant Coaches: *Steve Gossett, Grant Hohman. Telephone: (818) 677-7055. ■ Baseball SID: Aaron Meier. Telephone: (818) 677-3243. FAX: (818) 677-4762.
Home Field: Matador Field. Seating Capacity: 1,200. Outfield Dimensions: LF—325, CF—400, RF—325. Press Box Telephone: (818) 677-4293.

CAMPBELL Fighting Camels

Conference: Trans America Athletic.
Mailing Address: P.O. Box 10, Buies Creek, NC 27506.
Head Coach: Chip Smith. Assistant Coaches: Jeff Bock, *Randy Hood, Billy Race. Telephone: (910) 893-1354. ■ Baseball SID: Stan Cole. Telephone: (910) 893-1331. FAX: (910) 893-1330.

CANISIUS Golden Griffins

Conference: Metro Atlantic (North).
Mailing Address: 2001 Main St., Buffalo, NY 14208.
Head Coach: Don Colpoys. Assistant Coaches: Joe Caggiano, Ray Hennessy. Telephone: (716) 888-3672. ■ Baseball SID: John Maddock. Telephone: (716) 888-2977. FAX: (716) 888-2980.

CENTENARY Gents

Conference: Trans America Athletic.
Mailing Address: P.O. Box 41188, Shreveport, LA 71134.
Head Coach: Ed McCann. Assistant Coaches: Kyle Guerry, Aaron Wicklund. Telephone: (318) 869-5095. ■ Baseball SID: Patrick Netherton. Telephone: (318) 869-5092. FAX: (318) 869-5145.

CENTRAL CONNECTICUT STATE Blue Devils

Conference: Northeast.
Mailing Address: 1615 Stanley St., New Britain, CT 06050.
Head Coach: Charlie Hickey. Assistant Coaches: Brian Edge, *Jonathan

Knot. **Telephone:** (860) 832-3074. ■ **Baseball SID:** John Jordan. **Telephone:** (860) 832-3059. **FAX:** (860) 832-3084.

CENTRAL FLORIDA Golden Knights
Conference: Trans America Athletic.
Mailing Address: P.O. Box 163555, Orlando, FL 32816.
Head Coach: Jay Bergman. **Assistant Coaches:** Craig Cozart, *Greg Frady. **Telephone:** (407) 823-0140. ■ **Baseball SID:** Allyn Ross. **Telephone:** (407) 823-0994. **FAX:** (407) 823-5266.
Home Field: Jay Bergman Field. **Seating Capacity:** 1,600. **Outfield Dimensions:** LF—325, CF—400, RF—325. **Press Box Telephone:** Unavailable.

CENTRAL MICHIGAN Chippewas
Conference: Mid-American (West).
Mailing Address: Rose Center, Mount Pleasant, MI 48859.
Head Coach: Judd Folske. **Assistant Coaches:** *Steve Jaksa, Rick Smith. **Telephone:** (517) 774-6670. ■ **Baseball SID:** Fred Stabley Jr. **Telephone:** (517) 774-3277. **FAX:** (517) 774-7324.
Home Field: Theunissen Stadium. **Seating Capacity:** 4,100. **Outfield Dimensions:** LF—325, CF—395, RF—325. **Press Box Telephone:** (517) 774-3579/3594.

CHARLESTON Cougars
Conference: Southern.
Mailing Address: 30 George St., Charleston, SC 29424.
Head Coach: John Pawlowski. **Assistant Coach:** Scott Foxhall. **Telephone:** (843) 953-5916. ■ **Baseball SID:** Tony Ciuffo. **Telephone:** (843) 953-5465. **FAX:** (843) 953-6534.

CHARLESTON SOUTHERN Buccaneers
Conference: Big South.
Mailing Address: P.O. Box 118087, Charleston, SC 29423.
Head Coach: Gary Murphy. **Assistant Coaches:** Jeb Bauer, Chris Gibson, *Dirk Thomas. **Telephone:** (843) 863-7591. ■ **Baseball SID:** Ken Gerlinger. **Telephone:** (843) 863-7688. **FAX:** (843) 863-7676.

CHICAGO STATE Cougars
Conference: Mid-Continent.
Mailing Address: 9501 S. King Dr., Chicago, IL 60628.
Head Coach: Kevin McCray. **Assistant Coaches:** *John Drahos, Terrence Jackson. **Telephone:** (773) 995-3659. ■ **Baseball SID:** Frank Walker. **Telephone:** (773) 995-2217. **FAX:** (773) 995-5779.

CINCINNATI Bearcats
Conference: Conference USA.
Mailing Address: P.O. Box 210021, Cincinnati, OH 45221.
Head Coach: Brian Cleary. **Assistant Coaches:** Dustin Lepper, Brad Meador. **Telephone:** (513) 556-0566. ■ **Baseball SID:** Jeremy Hartigan. **Telephone:** (513) 556-5191. **FAX:** (513) 556-0619.
Home Field: Johnny Bench Field. **Seating Capacity:** 500. **Outfield Dimensions:** LF—327, CF—385, RF—330. **Press Box Telephone:** (513) 556-0818.

THE CITADEL Bulldogs
Conference: Southern.
Mailing Address: 171 Moultrie St., Charleston, SC 29409.
Head Coach: Fred Jordan. **Assistant Coaches:** Chris Lemonis, *Dan McDonnell, Gregg Mucerino. **Telephone:** (843) 953-5285. ■ **Baseball SID:** Geoff Wiswell. **Telephone:** (843) 953-5120. **FAX:** (843) 953-5058.
Home Field: Joseph P. Riley Park (6,000). **Outfield Dimensions:** LF—305, CF—398, RF—337. **Press Box Telephone:** (843) 965-4151.

CLEMSON Tigers
Conference: Atlantic Coast.
Mailing Address: 100 Perimeter Rd., Clemson, SC 29634.
Head Coach: Jack Leggett. **Assistant Coaches:** *Tim Corbin, Hank King, Kevin O'Sullivan. **Telephone:** (864) 656-1947. ■ **Baseball SID:** Brian Hennessy. **Telephone:** (864) 656-2114. **FAX:** (864) 656-0299.
Home Field: Tiger Field. **Seating Capacity:** 5,000. **Outfield Dimensions:** LF—328, CF—400, RF—338. **Press Box Telephone:** (864) 656-7731.

CLEVELAND STATE Vikings
Conference: Midwestern Collegiate.
Mailing Address: 2000 Prospect Ave., Cleveland, OH 44115.
Head Coach: Jay Murphy. **Assistant Coaches:** Ben Boka, Dave Sprochi. **Telephone:** (216) 687-4822. ■ **Baseball SID:** Alan Ashby. **Telephone:** (216) 687-5288. **FAX:** (216) 523-7257.

COASTAL CAROLINA Chanticleers
Conference: Big South.
Mailing Address: P.O. Box 261954, Conway, SC 29526.
Head Coach: Gary Gilmore. **Assistant Coaches:** *Bill Jarman, Matt Schilling, Mac Smith. **Telephone:** (843) 349-2816. ■ **Baseball SID:** Matt Hogue. **Telephone:** (843) 349-2809. **FAX:** (843) 349-2819.

COLUMBIA Lions

Conference: Ivy League (Gehrig).
Mailing Address: 3030 Broadway, ML 1930, New York, NY 10027.
Head Coach: Mikio Aoki. **Assistant Coaches:** Grisha Davida, Chris Neill. **Telephone:** (212) 854-7772. ■ **Baseball SID:** Heather Croze. **Telephone:** (212) 854-2534. **FAX:** (212) 854-8168.

CONNECTICUT Huskies

Conference: Big East.
Mailing Address: U-78, 2111 Hillside Road, Storrs, CT 06269.
Head Coach: Andy Baylock. **Assistant Coaches:** Jerry LaPenta, *Jim Penders. **Telephone:** (860) 486-2458. ■ **Baseball SID:** Al Butler. **Telephone:** (860) 486-3531. **FAX:** (860) 486-5085.
Home Field: J.O. Christian Field. **Seating Capacity:** 2,500. **Outfield Dimensions:** LF—340, CF—405, RF—340. **Press Box Telephone:** None.

COPPIN STATE Eagles

Conference: Mid-Eastern Athletic (North).
Mailing Address: 2500 West North Ave., Baltimore, MD 21216.
Head Coach: Paul Blair. **Assistant Coach:** Andy Grebroski. **Telephone:** (410) 383-5686. ■ **Baseball SID:** Matt Burton. **Telephone:** (410) 383-5981. **FAX:** (410) 383-2511.

CORNELL Big Red

Conference: Ivy League (Rolfe).
Mailing Address: Teagle Hall, Campus Road, Ithaca, NY 14853.
Head Coach: Tom Ford. **Assistant Coach:** Scott Marsh. **Telephone:** (607) 255-6604. ■ **Baseball SID:** Laura Stange. **Telephone:** (607) 255-5627. **FAX:** (607) 255-9791.

CREIGHTON Blue Jays

Conference: Missouri Valley.
Mailing Address: 2500 California Plaza, Omaha, NE 68178.
Head Coach: Jack Dahm. **Assistant Coaches:** Bill Olson, *Ed Servais. **Telephone:** (402) 280-5545. ■ **Baseball SID:** Abby Dillon. **Telephone:** (402) 280-5544. **FAX:** (402) 280-2495.
Home Field: Creighton Sports Complex. **Seating Capacity:** 1,500. **Outfield Dimensions:** LF—330, CF—405, RF—330. **Press Box Telephone:** Unavailable.

DARTMOUTH Big Green

Conference: Ivy League (Rolfe).
Mailing Address: 1083 Alumni Gym, Hanover, NH 03755.
Head Coach: Bob Whalen. **Assistant Coach:** *Tony Baldwin. **Telephone:** (603) 646-2477. ■ **Baseball SID:** Adam Catalano. **Telephone:** (603) 646-2468. **FAX:** (603) 646-1286.

DAVIDSON Wildcats

Conference: Southern.
Mailing Address: P.O. Box 1750, Davidson, NC 28036.
Head Coach: Dick Cooke. **Assistant Coaches:** Rick Hurni, *Damon Towe. **Telephone:** (704) 892-2368. ■ **Baseball SID:** Rick Bender. **Telephone:** (704) 892-2123. **FAX:** (704) 892-2636.

DAYTON Flyers

Conference: Atlantic-10 (West).
Mailing Address: Box 1238, 300 College Park, Dayton, OH 45469.
Head Coach: Tony Vittorio. **Assistant Coaches:** Clint Albert, Terry Bell. **Telephone:** (937) 229-4456. ■ **Baseball SID:** Doug Hauschild. **Telephone:** (937) 229-4390. **FAX:** (937) 229-4461.

DELAWARE Fightin' Blue Hens

Conference: America East.
Mailing Address: 631 S College Ave., Newark, DE 19716.
Head Coach: Bob Hannah. **Assistant Coaches:** Chris Dillon, Dan Hammer, *Jim Sherman. **Telephone:** (302) 831-8596. ■ **Baseball SID:** Kevin Linton. **Telephone:** (302) 831-2186. **FAX:** (302) 831-8653.

DELAWARE STATE Hornets

Conference: Mid-Eastern Athletic (North).
Mailing Address: 1200 N DuPont Hwy., Dover, DE 19901.
Head Coach: Tripp Keister. **Assistant Coaches:** *J.P. Blandin, Tom Hinkle. **Telephone:** (302) 857-6035. ■ **Baseball SID:** Dennis Jones. **Telephone:** (302) 857-6065. **FAX:** (302) 857-6069.

DETROIT Titans

Conference: Midwestern Collegiate.
Mailing Address: P.O. Box 19900, Detroit, MI 48219.
Head Coach: Bob Miller. **Assistant Coach:** Lee Bjerke. **Telephone:** (313) 993-1725. ■ **Baseball SID:** Chris Meese. **Telephone:** (313) 993-1745. **FAX:** (313) 993-1765.

DREXEL Dragons

Conference: America East.
Mailing Address: 3141 Chestnut St., Philadelphia, PA 19104.
Head Coach: Don Maines. **Assistant Coaches:** *Chris Calciano, Jarrod

Hogue. **Telephone:** (215) 895-1782. ■ **Baseball SID:** Chris Beckett. **Telephone:** (215) 895-1570. **FAX:** (215) 895-2038.

DUKE Blue Devils
Conference: Atlantic Coast.
Mailing Address: Box 90555, Cameron Indoor Stadium, Durham, NC 27708.
Head Coach: Bill Hillier. **Assistant Coaches:** *Eric Filipek, Bill Hillier Jr., Jason White. **Telephone:** (919) 684-2358. ■ **Baseball SID:** Greg Hotchkiss. **Telephone:** (919) 684-2633. **FAX:** (919) 684-2489.
Home Field: Jack Coombs Stadium. **Seating Capacity:** 3,000. **Outfield Dimensions:** LF—330, CF—405, RF—335. **Press Box Telephone:** Unavailable.

DUQUESNE Dukes
Conference: Atlantic-10 (West).
Mailing Address: A.J. Palumbo Center, 600 Forbes Ave., Pittsburgh, PA 15282.
Head Coach: Mike Wilson. **Assistant Coaches:** *Joe Hill, Jay Stoner. **Telephone:** (412) 396-5245. ■ **Baseball SID:** George Nieman. **Telephone:** (412) 396-5376. **FAX:** (412) 396-6210.

EAST CAROLINA Pirates
Conference: Colonial Athletic.
Mailing Address: Ward Sports Medicine Bldg., Greenville, NC 27858.
Head Coach: Keith LeClair. **Assistant Coaches:** Tommy Eason, *Kevin McMullan, George Whitfield. **Telephone:** (252) 328-4604. ■ **Baseball SID:** Jerry Trickie. **Telephone:** (252) 328-4522. **FAX:** (252) 328-4528.

EAST TENNESSEE STATE Buccaneers
Conference: Southern.
Mailing Address: P.O. Box 70641, Johnson City, TN 37614.
Head Coach: Tony Skole. **Assistant Coaches:** Nate Goulet, Dave Shelton. **Telephone:** (423) 439-4496. ■ **Baseball SID:** Simon Gray. **Telephone:** (423) 439-5263. **FAX:** (423) 439-6138.

EASTERN ILLINOIS Panthers
Conference: Ohio Valley.
Mailing Address: Lantz Gym, Charleston, IL 61920.
Head Coach: Jim Schmitz. **Assistant Coaches:** Matt Buczkowski, Chris Hall. **Telephone:** (217) 581-2522. ■ **Baseball SID:** Pat Osterman. **Telephone:** (217) 581-6408. **FAX:** (217) 581-6434.

EASTERN KENTUCKY Colonels
Conference: Ohio Valley.
Mailing Address: 521 Lancaster Ave., Richmond, KY 40475.
Head Coach: Jim Ward. **Assistant Coaches:** Jerry Edwards, David Signs, *Jason Stein **Telephone:** (606) 622-2120. ■ **Baseball SID:** Karl Park. **Telephone:** (606) 622-1253. **FAX:** (606) 622-1230.

EASTERN MICHIGAN Eagles
Conference: Mid-American (West).
Mailing Address: Room 307, Convocation Center, Ypsilanti, MI 48197.
Head Coach: Roger Coryell. **Assistant Coaches:** Terry Bigham, Jake Boss, Chris Prozorowicz, Greg Ryan. **Telephone:** (734) 487-1985. ■ **Baseball SID:** Matt Fancett. **Telephone:** (734) 487-0318. **FAX:** (734) 485-3840.
Home Field: Oestrike Stadium. **Seating Capacity:** 2,500. **Outfield Dimensions:** LF—330, CF—390, RF—330. **Press Box Telephone:** (734) 484-1396.

ELON Fightin' Christians
Conference: Big South.
Mailing Address: Campus Box 2500, Elon College, NC 27244.
Head Coach: Mike Kennedy. **Assistant Coaches:** *Brendan Dougherty, Greg Starbuck. **Telephone:** (336) 584-2520. ■ **Baseball SID:** Tom Machamer. **Telephone:** (336) 538-2420. **FAX:** (336) 538-2686.

EVANSVILLE Purple Aces
Conference: Missouri Valley.
Mailing Address: 1800 Lincoln Ave., Evansville, IN 47722.
Head Coach: Jim Brownlee. **Assistant Coaches:** Ryan Barrett, Jeremy Brown, *Tim Brownlee. **Telephone:** (812) 479-2760. ■ **Baseball SID:** Jeff Williams. **Telephone:** (812) 488-1152. **FAX:** (812) 479-2090.

FAIRFIELD Stags
Conference: Metro Atlantic (South).
Mailing Address: 1073 N Benson Rd., Fairfield, CT 06430.
Head Coach: John Slosar. **Assistant Coaches:** Drew Brown, *Sean Martin, Dennis Whalen. **Telephone:** (203) 254-4000, ext. 2605. ■ **Baseball SID:** Drew Brown. **Telephone:** (203) 254-4000, ext. 2878. **FAX:** (203) 254-4117.

FAIRLEIGH DICKINSON Knights
Conference: Northeast.
Mailing Address: Temple Avenue, Rothman Center, Hackensack, NJ 07601.
Head Coach: Dennis Sasso. **Assistant Coaches:** Jerry DeFabbia, Mike Mongiello. **Telephone:** (201) 692-2245. ■ **Baseball SID:** Bob Rothwell. **Telephone:** (201) 692-2204. **FAX:** (201) 692-9361.

FLORIDA Gators

Conference: Southeastern (East).
Mailing Address: P.O. Box 14485, Gainesville, FL 32604.
Head Coach: Andy Lopez. **Assistant Coaches:** *John Humenik, Steve Kling, Mark Wasikowski. **Telephone:** (352) 375-4683, ext. 4457. ■ **Baseball SID:** Steve Shaff. **Telephone:** (352) 375-4683, ext. 6130. **FAX:** (352) 375-4809.
Home Field: McKethan Stadium at Perry Field. **Seating Capacity:** 5,000. **Outfield Dimensions:** LF—329, CF—400, RF—325. **Press Box Telephone:** (352) 375-4683, ext. 4355/4356.

FLORIDA A&M Rattlers

Conference: Mid-Eastern Athletic (South).
Mailing Address: Room 205, Gaither Athletic Center, Tallahassee, FL 32307.
Head Coach: Joe Durant. **Assistant Coaches:** Willie Brown, Brett Richardson. **Telephone:** (850) 599-3203. ■ **Baseball SID:** Alvin Hollins. **Telephone:** (850) 599-3200. **FAX:** (850) 599-3206.

FLORIDA ATLANTIC Owls

Conference: Trans America Athletic.
Mailing Address: 777 Glades Rd., Boca Raton, FL 33431.
Head Coach: Kevin Cooney. **Assistant Coaches:** Bob Deutchman, Jim Lyttle, *John McCormack. **Telephone:** (561) 297-3956. ■ **Baseball SID:** Katrina McCormack. **Telephone:** (561) 297-3163. **FAX:** (561) 297-2996.

FLORIDA INTERNATIONAL Golden Panthers

Conference: Sun Belt.
Mailing Address: 11200 SW 8 St., Golden Panther Arena, Miami, FL 33199.
Head Coach: Danny Price. **Assistant Coaches:** Marc Calvi, *Rolando Casanova, Jason Vetter. **Telephone:** (305) 348-3166. ■ **Baseball SID:** Rich Kelch. **Telephone:** (305) 348-3164. **FAX:** (305) 348-2963.
Home Field: University Park. **Seating Capacity:** 2,000. **Outfield Dimensions:** LF—325, CF—400, RF—325. **Press Box Telephone:** (305) 554-8694.

FLORIDA STATE Seminoles

Conference: Atlantic Coast.
Mailing Address: P.O. Box 2195, Tallahassee, FL 32316.
Head Coach: Mike Martin. **Assistant Coaches:** Chip Baker, Mike Martin Jr., *Jamey Shouppe. **Telephone:** (850) 644-1073. ■ **Baseball SID:** Jeff Purinton. **Telephone:** (850) 644-0615. **FAX:** (850) 644-3820.
Home Field: Dick Howser Stadium. **Seating Capacity:** 5,000. **Outfield Dimensions:** LF—335, CF—400, RF—325. **Press Box Telephone:** (850) 644-1553.

FORDHAM Rams

Conference: Atlantic-10 (East).
Mailing Address: 441 E Fordham Rd., Bronx, NY 10458.
Head Coach: Dan Gallagher. **Assistant Coaches:** John Ceprini, Tony Mellaci, *Nick Restaino. **Telephone:** (718) 817-4290. ■ **Baseball SID:** Joe DiBari. **Telephone:** (718) 817-4240. **FAX:** (718) 817-4244.

FRESNO STATE Bulldogs

Conference: Western Athletic.
Mailing Address: 5305 N Campus Dr., Room 153, Fresno, CA 93740.
Head Coach: Bob Bennett. **Assistant Coaches:** Steve Pearse, *Mike Rupcich. **Telephone:** (559) 278-2178. ■ **Baseball SID:** Steve Weakland. **Telephone:** (559) 278-2509. **FAX:** (559) 278-4689.
Home Field: Beiden Field. **Seating Capacity:** 6,575. **Outfield Dimensions:** LF—330, CF—400, RF—330. **Press Box Telephone:** (559) 278-7678.

FURMAN Paladins

Conference: Southern.
Mailing Address: 3300 Poinsett Highway, Greenville, SC 29613.
Head Coach: Ron Smith. **Assistant Coaches:** Jeff Massey, Rockie Pitman, Jeff Young. **Telephone:** (864) 294-2146. ■ **Baseball SID:** Kylie Inman. **Telephone:** (864) 294-3062. **FAX:** (864) 294-3061.

GEORGE MASON Patriots

Conference: Colonial Athletic.
Mailing Address: MS 3A5/Baseball Office, 4400 University Dr., Fairfax, VA 22030.
Head Coach: Bill Brown. **Assistant Coaches:** *Joe Raccuia, Gary White. **Telephone:** (703) 993-3282. ■ **Baseball SID:** Ben Trittipoe. **Telephone:** (703) 993-3260. **FAX:** (703) 993-3259.

GEORGE WASHINGTON Colonials

Conference: Atlantic-10 (West).
Mailing Address: 600 22nd St. NW, Washington, DC 20037.
Head Coach: Tom Walter. **Assistant Coach:** Chris Burr. **Telephone:** (202) 994-7399. ■ **Baseball SID:** Greg Licamele. **Telephone:** (202) 994-0339. **FAX:** (202) 994-2713.

GEORGETOWN Hoyas

Conference: Big East.
Mailing Address: McDonough Arena, 37th & O Streets NW, Washington, DC 20057.

Head Coach: Pete Wilk. Assistant Coaches: *Matt Allison, Scott DeGeorge. Telephone: (202) 687-2462. ■ Baseball SID: Carlton White. Telephone: (202) 687-5241. FAX: (202) 687-2491.

Home Field: Georgetown Baseball Diamond. Seating Capacity: 1,000. Outfield Dimensions: LF—301, CF—420, RF—330. Press Box Telephone: None.

GEORGIA Bulldogs

Conference: Southeastern (East).

Mailing Address: P.O. Box 1472, Athens, GA 30603.

Head Coach: Ron Polk. Assistant Coaches: Daron Schoenrock, *David Perno. Telephone: (706) 542-7971. ■ Baseball SID: Christopher Lakos. Telephone: (706) 542-1621. FAX: (706) 542-7993.

Home Field: Foley Field. Seating Capacity: 3,200. Outfield Dimensions: LF—350, CF—410, RF—320. Press Box Telephone: (706) 542-6162/6161.

GEORGIA SOUTHERN Eagles

Conference: Southern.

Mailing Address: P.O. Box 8095, Statesboro, GA 30460.

Head Coach: Rodney Hennon. Assistant Coaches: Seam Teagie. * Mike Tidick. Telephone: (912) 486-7360. ■ Baseball SID: Tom McClellan. Telephone: (912) 681-0352. FAX: (912) 681-0046.

Home Field: J.I. Clements Stadium. Seating Capacity: 1,500. Outfield Dimensions: LF—330, CF—385, RF—330. Press Box Telephone: (912) 681-2508.

GEORGIA STATE Panthers

Conference: Trans America Athletic.

Mailing Address: 1 Park Place South, Suite 840, Atlanta, GA 30303.

Head Coach: Mike Hurst. Assistant Coaches: David Hartley, *Bob Keller, Ryan Lambert. Telephone: (404) 651-1198. ■ Baseball SID: Todd Degree. Telephone: (404) 651-4629. FAX: (404) 651-3204.

GEORGIA TECH Yellow Jackets

Conference: Atlantic Coast.

Mailing Address: 150 Bobby Dodd Way NW, Atlanta, GA 30332.

Head Coach: Danny Hall. Assistant Coaches: Jeff Guy, *Mike Trapasso. Telephone: (404) 894-5471. ■ Baseball SID: Mike Stamus. Telephone: (404) 894-5445. FAX: (404) 894-1248.

Home Field: Russ Chandler Stadium. Seating Capacity: 2,500. Outfield Dimensions: LF—320, CF—400, RF—330. Press Box Telephone: (404) 894-0107.

GONZAGA Bulldogs

Conference: West Coast (Coast).

Mailing Address: East 502 Boone Ave, Spokane, WA 99258.

Head Coach: Steve Hertz. Assistant Coaches: Travis Jewett, *Mark Machtolf. Telephone: (509) 323-4226. ■ Baseball SID: Rich Moser. Telephone: (509) 323-6373. FAX: (509) 323-5730.

GRAMBLING STATE Tigers

Conference: Southwestern Athletic (West).

Mailing Address: P.O. Box 868, Grambling, LA 71245.

Head Coach: Wilbert Ellis. Assistant Coach: James Randall. Telephone: (318) 274-6121. ■ Baseball SID: Stanley Lewis. Telephone: (318) 274-6199. FAX: (318) 274-2761.

HARTFORD Hawks

Conference: America East.

Mailing Address: 200 Bloomfield Ave., West Hartford, CT 06117.

Head Coach: Harvey Shapiro. Assistant Coaches: Bill Gross, John Shea. Telephone: (860) 768-4656. ■ Baseball SID: John Sudsbury. Telephone: (860) 768-4620. FAX: (860) 768-4068.

HARVARD Crimson

Conference: Ivy League (Rolfe).

Mailing Address: Murr Center, 65 N Harvard St., Boston, MA 02163.

Head Coach: Joe Walsh. Assistant Coaches: Gary Donovan, Chip Forrest, Marty Nastasia. Telephone: (617) 495-2629. ■ Baseball SID: Paul McNeeley. Telephone: (617) 495-2206. FAX: (617) 495-2130.

HAWAII Rainbows

Conference: Western Athletic.

Mailing Address: 1337 Lower Campus Dr., Honolulu, HI 96822.

Head Coach: Les Murakami. Assistant Coaches: Carl Furutani, Dave Murakami, Les Nakama. Telephone: (808) 956-6247. ■ Baseball SID: Markus Owens. Telephone: (808) 956-7523. FAX: (808) 956-4470.

Home Field: Rainbow Stadium. Seating Capacity: 4,312. Outfield Dimensions: LF—340, CF—400, RF—340. Press Box Telephone: (808) 956-6253.

HAWAII-HILO Vulcans

Conference: Western Athletic.

Mailing Address: 200 W Kawili St., Hilo, HI 96720.

Head Coach: Joey Estrella. Assistant Coaches: Geoff Hirai, Kallen Miyataki. Telephone: (808) 974-7700. ■ Baseball SID: Kelly Leong. Telephone: (808)

974-7606. **FAX:** (808) 974-7711.

HIGH POINT Panthers
Conference: Big South.
Mailing Address: University Station, Montlieu Ave., High Point, NC 27262.
Head Coach: Jim Speight. **Assistant Coach:** Brian Kemp. **Telephone:** (336) 841-9190. ■ **Baseball SID:** Jamie Joss. **Telephone:** (336) 841-4605. **FAX:** (336) 841-9182.

HOFSTRA Flying Dutchmen
Conference: America East.
Mailing Address: 1000 Hempstead Turnpike, Hempstead, NY 11549.
Head Coach: Reginald Jackson. **Assistant Coaches:** *Patrick Anderson, Anthony Marino. **Telephone:** (516) 463-5065. ■ **Baseball SID:** Jim Sheehan. **Telephone:** (516) 463-6764. **FAX:** (516) 463-5033.

HOLY CROSS Crusaders
Conference: Patriot.
Mailing Address: One College St., Worcester, MA 01610.
Head Coach: Paul Pearl. **Assistant Coaches:** Terrence Butt, Fran O'Brien, Tim Whalen. **Telephone:** (508) 793-3628. ■ **Baseball SID:** John Butman. **Telephone:** (508) 793-2583. **FAX:** (508) 793-2309.

HOUSTON Cougars
Conference: Conference USA.
Mailing Address: 3100 Cullen Rd., Houston, TX 77204.
Head Coach: Rayner Noble. **Assistant Coaches:** Kirk Blount, *Trip Couch, Todd Whitting. **Telephone:** (713) 743-9416. ■ **Baseball SID:** John Sullivan. **Telephone:** (713) 743-9404. **FAX:** (713) 743-9411.
Home Field: Cougar Field. **Seating Capacity:** 4,500. **Outfield Dimensions:** LF—330, CF—390, RF—330. **Press Box Telephone:** (713) 743-0840.

HOWARD Bison
Conference: Mid-Eastern Athletic (North).
Mailing Address: Sixth and Girard Streets NW, Washington, DC 20059.
Head Coach: Jimmy Williams. **Assistant Coach:** Andre Rabouin. **Telephone:** (202) 806-7140. ■ **Baseball SID:** Ed Hill. **Telephone:** (202) 806-7188. **FAX:** (202) 806-9090.

ILLINOIS Fighting Illini
Conference: Big Ten.
Mailing Address: 1700 S Fourth St., Champaign, IL 61820.
Head Coach: Itch Jones. **Assistant Coaches:** *Dan Hartleb, Eric Snider. **Telephone:** (217) 333-8605. ■ **Baseball SID:** Michelle Warner. **Telephone:** (217) 333-1391. **FAX:** (217) 333-5540.
Home Field: Illinois Field. **Seating Capacity:** 2,000. **Outfield Dimensions:** LF—330, CF—400, RF—330. **Press Box Telephone:** (217) 333-1227.

ILLINOIS-CHICAGO Flames
Conference: Midwestern Collegiate.
Mailing Address: 839 W Roosevelt Rd., Flames Athletic Center, Chicago, IL 60608.
Head Coach: Mike Dee. **Assistant Coaches:** J.T. Bruett, Chris Malinoski, *Sean McDermott. **Telephone:** (312) 996-8645. ■ **Baseball SID:** Anne Schoenherr. **Telephone:** (312) 996-5880. **FAX:** (312) 996-5882.

ILLINOIS STATE Redbirds
Conference: Missouri Valley.
Mailing Address: Campus Box 7130, Normal, IL 61790.
Head Coach: Jeff Stewart. **Assistant Coaches:** Tim Johnson, Perry Roth. **Telephone:** (309) 438-5151. ■ **Baseball SID:** Andy Knapick. **Telephone:** (309) 438-3249. **FAX:** (309) 438-5634.

INDIANA Hoosiers
Conference: Big Ten.
Mailing Address: 1001 E 17th St., Assembly Hall, Bloomington, IN 47408.
Head Coach: Bob Morgan. **Assistant Coaches:** *Jeff Calcaterra, Scott Googins. **Telephone:** (812) 855-1680. ■ **Baseball SID:** Jeff Fanter. **Telephone:** (812) 855-9399. **FAX:** (812) 855-9401.
Home Field: Sembower Field. **Seating Capacity:** 3,000. **Outfield Dimensions:** LF—333, CF—380, RF—333. **Press Box Telephone:** (812) 855-4787.

INDIANA-PURDUE Metros
Conference: Mid-Continent.
Mailing Address: 901 W New York St., Suite 105, Indianapolis, IN 46202.
Head Coach: Brian Donohew. **Assistant Coaches:** *Mark Flueckiger, Neil Schaffner. **Telephone:** (317) 278-2657. ■ **Baseball SID:** Kevin Buerge. **Telephone:** (317) 274-2725. **FAX:** (317) 278-2683.

INDIANA STATE Sycamores
Conference: Missouri Valley.
Mailing Address: Fourth and Chestnut St., Terre Haute, IN 47809.
Head Coach: Bob Warn. **Assistant Coaches:** Kevin Bowers, *Mitch Hannahs, Justin Stone. **Telephone:** (812) 237-4051. ■ **Baseball SID:** Kris Kaman. **Telephone:** (812) 237-4073. **FAX:** (812) 237-4157.

Home Field: Sycamore Field. **Seating Capacity:** 1,500. **Outfield Dimensions:** LF—340, CF—402, RF—340. **Press Box Telephone:** (812) 237-4188.

IONA Gaels

Conference: Metro Atlantic (South).
Mailing Address: 715 North Ave., New Rochelle, NY 10801.
Head Coach: Al Zoccolillo. **Assistant Coaches:** *Jerry DeFabbia, Stephan Rapaglia, Jared Smith. **Telephone:** (914) 633-2319. ■ **Baseball SID:** Dave Cagianello. **Telephone:** (914) 633-2334. **FAX:** (914) 633-2072.

IOWA Hawkeyes

Conference: Big Ten.
Mailing Address: 340 Carver-Hawkeye Arena, Iowa City, IA 52242.
Head Coach: Scott Broghamer. **Assistant Coaches:** *Elvis Dominguez, Travis Wyckoff. **Telephone:** (319) 335-9390. ■ **Baseball SID:** Kristy Fick. **Telephone:** (319) 335-9411. **FAX:** (319) 335-9457.
Home Field: Iowa Field. **Seating Capacity:** 3,000. **Outfield Dimensions:** LF—330, CF—400, RF—330. **Press Box Telephone:** (319) 335-9520.

IOWA STATE Cyclones

Conference: Big 12.
Mailing Address: 1820 24th St., Ames, IA 50011.
Head Coach: Lyle Smith. **Assistant Coaches:** Jim Murphy, Tony Trumm. **Telephone:** (515) 294-4201. ■ **Baseball SID:** Mike Green. **Telephone:** (515) 294-3372. **FAX:** (515) 294-0558.
Home Field: Cap Timm Field. **Seating Capacity:** 2,000. **Outfield Dimensions:** LF—330, CF—400, RF—330. **Press Box Telephone:** (515) 294-1640.

JACKSON STATE Tigers

Conference: Southwestern Athletic (East).
Mailing Address: 1400 John R. Lynch St., Jackson, MS 39217.
Head Coach: Robert Braddy. **Assistant Coaches:** Lewis Braddy, *Mark Salter. **Telephone:** (601) 968-2291. ■ **Baseball SID:** Sam Jefferson. **Telephone:** (601) 968-2273. **FAX:** (601) 968-2000.

JACKSONVILLE Dolphins

Conference: Trans America Athletic.
Mailing Address: 2800 University Blvd. North, Jacksonville, FL 32211.
Head Coach: Terry Alexander. **Assistant Coaches:** Joe Fletcher, John Howard, *Bob Shepherd. **Telephone:** (904) 745-7412. ■ **Baseball SID:** Romony Baker. **Telephone:** (904) 745-7402. **FAX:** (904) 745-7179.
Home Field: Brest Field. **Seating Capacity:** 2,300. **Outfield Dimensions:** LF—340, CF—405, RF—340. **Press Box Telephone:** (904) 745-7588.

JACKSONVILLE STATE Gamecocks

Conference: Trans America Athletic.
Mailing Address: 700 Pelham Road N., Jacksonville, AL 36265.
Head Coach: Rudy Abbott. **Assistant Coach:** *Skipper Jones. **Telephone:** (256) 782-5367. ■ **Baseball SID:** Greg Seitz. **Telephone:** (256) 782-5279. **FAX:** (256) 782-5958.

JAMES MADISON Dukes

Conference: Colonial Athletic.
Mailing Address: MSC 2303 Godwin Hall, Harrisonburg, VA 22807.
Head Coach: Spanky McFarland. **Assistant Coaches:** *Chuck Bartlett, Ryan Brownlee, John Milisitz. **Telephone:** (540) 568-6467. ■ **Baseball SID:** Curt Dudley. **Telephone:** (540) 568-6154. **FAX:** (540) 568-3703.
Home Field: Long Field/Mauck Stadium. **Seating Capacity:** 1,200. **Outfield Dimensions:** LF—340, CF—400, RF—320. **Press Box Telephone:** (540) 568-6545.

KANSAS Jayhawks

Conference: Big 12.
Mailing Address: 104 Allen Fieldhouse, Lawrence, KS 66045.
Head Coach: Bobby Randall. **Assistant Coaches:** *Mike Bard, Joe DeMarco, Wilson Kilmer. **Telephone:** (785) 864-7907. ■ **Baseball SID:** Mitch Germann. **Telephone:** (785) 864-3420. **FAX:** (785) 864-7944.
Home Field: Hoglund Ballpark. **Seating Capacity:** 2,500. **Outfield Dimensions:** LF—350, CF—392, RF—350. **Press Box Telephone:** (785) 864-4037.

KANSAS STATE Wildcats

Conference: Big 12.
Mailing Address: 1800 College Ave., Bramlage Coliseum, Suite 144, Manhattan, KS 66502.
Head Coach: Mike Clark. **Assistant Coaches:** *Mike Hensley, Robbie Moen, Darin Vaughan. **Telephone:** (785) 532-5723. ■ **Baseball SID:** Tom Gilbert. **Telephone:** (785) 532-7979. **FAX:** (785) 532-6093.
Home Field: Frank Myers Field. **Seating Capacity:** 2,500. **Outfield Dimensions:** LF—340, CF—400, RF—325. **Press Box Telephone:** (785) 532-6926.

KENT Golden Flashes

Conference: Mid-American (East).

Mailing Address: P.O. Box 5190, Kent, OH 44242.

Head Coach: Rick Rembielak. **Assistant Coaches:** *Greg Beals, Mike Birkbeck. **Telephone:** (330) 672-3696. ■ **Baseball SID:** Heather Brocious. **Telephone:** (330) 672-2110. **FAX:** (330) 672-2112.

Home Field: Gene Michael Field. **Seating Capacity:** 2,000. **Outfield Dimensions:** LF—330, CF—400, RF—330. **Press Box Telephone:** (330) 672-2036.

KENTUCKY Wildcats

Conference: Southeastern (East).

Mailing Address: Memorial Coliseum, Lexington, KY 40506.

Head Coach: Keith Madison. **Assistant Coaches:** Greg Goff, Scott Malone, *Jan Weisberg. **Telephone:** (606) 257-6500. ■ **Baseball SID:** Brad Sutton. **Telephone:** (606) 257-3838. **FAX:** (606) 323-4310.

Home Field: Cliff Hagan Stadium. **Seating Capacity:** 2,500. **Outfield Dimensions:** LF—340, CF—390, RF—310. **Press Box Telephone:** (606) 257-8027.

LAFAYETTE Leopards

Conference: Patriot.

Mailing Address: Kirby Sports Center, Easton, PA 18042.

Head Coach: Joe Kinney. **Assistant Coaches:** Gregg Durrah, Daryl Evans. **Telephone:** (610) 330-5476. ■ **Baseball SID:** Phil Labella. **Telephone:** (610) 330-5122. **FAX:** (610) 330-5519.

LAMAR Cardinals

Conference: Southland.

Mailing Address: Box 10066, Beaumont, TX 77710.

Head Coach: Jim Gilligan. **Assistant Coaches:** Emerick Jagneaux, *Jim Ricklefsen. **Telephone:** (409) 880-8315. ■ **Baseball SID:** Daucey Crizer. **Telephone:** (409) 880-8329. **FAX:** (409) 880-2338.

Home Field: Vincent-Beck Stadium. **Seating Capacity:** 3,500. **Outfield Dimensions:** LF—325, CF—380, RF—325. **Press Box Telephone:** (409) 880-8327.

LA SALLE Explorers

Conference: Atlantic-10 (West).

Mailing Address: Box 805, 1900 W Olney Ave., Philadelphia, PA 19141.

Head Coach: Larry Conti. **Assistant Coaches:** Mark Heineman, Fred Holdsworth. **Telephone:** (215) 951-1995. ■ **Baseball SID:** Keith D'Oria. **Telephone:** (215) 951-1605. **FAX:** (215) 951-1694.

LEHIGH Mountain Hawks

Conference: Patriot.

Mailing Address: 641 Taylor St., Bethlehem, PA 18015.

Head Coach: Sean Leary. **Assistant Coaches:** Gerry Mack, Chris Querns, Andy Pitsilos. **Telephone:** (610) 758-4315. ■ **Baseball SID:** Jim Marshall. **Telephone:** (610) 758-3174. **FAX:** (610) 758-6629.

LE MOYNE Dolphins

Conference: Metro Atlantic (North).

Mailing Address: Springfield Road, Syracuse, NY 13214.

Head Coach: Steve Owens. **Assistant Coaches:** Pete Hoy, Bob Nandin. **Telephone:** (315) 445-4415. ■ **Baseball SID:** Mike Donlin. **Telephone:** (315) 445-4412. **FAX:** (315) 445-4678.

LIBERTY Flames

Conference: Big South.

Mailing Address: 1971 University Blvd., Lynchburg, VA 24502.

Head Coach: Dave Pastors. **Assistant Coaches:** Jeff Edwards, Randy Tomlin, Terry Weaver. **Telephone:** (804) 582-2305. ■ **Baseball SID:** Trevor Price. **Telephone:** (804) 582-2292. **FAX:** (804) 582-2076.

LONG BEACH STATE 49ers

Conference: Big West.

Mailing Address: 1250 Bellflower Blvd., Long Beach, CA 90840.

Head Coach: Dave Snow. **Assistant Coaches:** Don Barbara, *Mike Weathers, Jim Yogi. **Telephone:** (562) 985-0457. ■ **Baseball SID:** Steve Janisch. **Telephone:** (562) 985-7797. **FAX:** (562) 985-8197.

Home Field: Blair Field. **Seating Capacity:** 3,000. **Outfield Dimensions:** LF—348, CF—400, RF—348. **Press Box Telephone:** (562) 433-8605.

LONG ISLAND Blackbirds

Conference: Northeast.

Mailing Address: One University Plaza, Brooklyn, NY 11201.

Head Coach: Frank Giannone. **Assistant Coaches:** Chris Bagley, Mike Ryan. **Telephone:** (718) 488-1538. ■ **Baseball SID:** Chris O'Connor. **Telephone:** (718) 488-1420/1307. **FAX:** (718) 488-3302.

LOUISIANA-LAFAYETTE Ragin' Cajuns

Conference: Sun Belt.

Mailing Address: 201 Reinhardt Dr., Lafayette, LA 70506.

Head Coach: Tony Robichaux. **Assistant Coaches:** Anthony Babineaux, Jason Gonzales, *Wade Simoneaux. **Telephone:** (337) 482-6189. ■ **Baseball SID:** Kent Schaub. **Telephone:** (337) 482-6331. **FAX:** (337) 482-6649.

Home Field: Moore Field. **Seating Capacity:** 3,500. **Outfield Dimensions:**

LF—330, CF—400, RF—330. **Press Box Telephone:** (337) 482-6331.

LOUISIANA-MONROE Indians

Conference: Southland.

Mailing Address: 123 Ewing Coliseum, Monroe, LA 71209.

Head Coach: Smoke Laval. **Assistant Coaches:** Brad Holland, Jim Morrill. **Telephone:** (318) 342-5395. ■ **Baseball SID:** Troy Mitchell. **Telephone:** (318) 342-5463. **FAX:** (318) 342-5464.

LOUISIANA STATE Tigers

Conference: Southeastern (West).

Mailing Address: P.O. Box 25095, Baton Rouge, LA 70894.

Head Coach: Skip Bertman. **Assistant Coaches:** Dan Canevari, Bill Dailey, *Turtle Thomas. **Telephone:** (225) 388-4148. ■ **Baseball SID:** Bill Franques/Dave Steinle. **Telephone:** (225) 388-8226. **FAX:** (225) 388-1861.

Home Field: Alex Box Stadium. **Seating Capacity:** 7,760. **Outfield Dimensions:** LF—330, CF—405, RF—330. **Press Box Telephone:** (225) 388-4149.

LOUISIANA TECH Bulldogs

Conference: Sun Belt.

Mailing Address: P.O. Box 3166 T.S., Ruston, LA 71272.

Head Coach: Jeff Richardson. **Assistant Coaches:** Frank Kellner, Brian Rountree. **Telephone:** (318) 257-4111. ■ **Baseball SID:** Chris Weego. **Telephone:** (318) 257-3144. **FAX:** (318) 257-3757.

LOUISVILLE Cardinals

Conference: Conference USA.

Mailing Address: U. of Louisville Baseball Office at KFEC, Louisville, KY 40292.

Head Coach: Lelo Prado. **Assistant Coaches:** Al Lopez, Erik Mirba, *Brian Mundorf. **Telephone:** (502) 852-0103. ■ **Baseball SID:** Sean Moth. **Telephone:** (502) 852-2159. **FAX:** (502) 852-7401.

Home Field: Cardinal Stadium. **Seating Capacity:** 33,000. **Outfield Dimensions:** LF—360, CF—405, RF—315. **Press Box Telephone:** (502) 367-5000.

LOYOLA MARYMOUNT Lions

Conference: West Coast (Coast) .

Mailing Address: 7900 Loyola Blvd., Los Angeles, CA 90045.

Head Coach: Frank Cruz. **Assistant Coaches:** Jason Gill, Tony Nieto, Kelly Nicholson. **Telephone:** (310) 338-2919. ■ **Baseball SID:** Dan Smith. **Telephone:** (310) 338-7643. **FAX:** (310) 338-2703.

MAINE Black Bears

Conference: America East.

Mailing Address: 5745 Mahaney Clubhouse, Orono, ME 04469.

Head Coach: Paul Kostacopoulos. **Assistant Coaches:** Matt Haney, *Mike McRae. **Telephone:** (207) 581-1090. ■ **Baseball SID:** Joe Roberts. **Telephone:** (207) 581-3596. **FAX:** (207) 581-3297.

Home Field: Mahaney Diamond. **Seating Capacity:** 4,000. **Outfield Dimensions:** LF—325, CF—400, RF—325. **Press Box Telephone:** (207) 581-1049.

MANHATTAN Jaspers

Conference: Metro Atlantic (South).

Mailing Address: Manhattan College Parkway, Riverdale, NY 10471.

Head Coach: Steve Trimper. **Assistant Coaches:** Tim Cookley, *Mike Moran. **Telephone:** (718) 862-7486. ■ **Baseball SID:** Jeff Wyshner. **Telephone:** (718) 862-7228. **FAX:** (718) 862-8020.

MARIST Red Foxes

Conference: Metro Atlantic (North).

Mailing Address: 290 North Rd., Poughkeepsie, NY 12601.

Head Coach: John Szefc. **Assistant Coaches:** Mark Barrow, Jim Tyrrell. **Telephone:** (914) 575-3000, ext. 2570. ■ **Baseball SID:** Jill Skotarczak. **Telephone:** (914) 575-3000 ext. 2322. **FAX:** (914) 471-0466.

MARSHALL Thundering Herd

Conference: Mid-American (East).

Mailing Address: P.O. Box 1360, Huntington, WV 25715.

Head Coach: Dave Piepenbrink. **Assistant Coaches:** Tim Frantz, Matt Harre. **Telephone:** (304) 696-5277. ■ **Baseball SID:** Brian Gunning. **Telephone:** (304) 696-6525. **FAX:** (304) 696-2325.

MARYLAND Terrapins

Conference: Atlantic Coast.

Mailing Address: Room 1112 Cole Field House, Campus Drive, College Park, MD 20742.

Head Coach: Tom Bradley. **Assistant Coaches:** Jim Flack, Brent Flynn, *Kelly Kulina. **Telephone:** (301) 314-7122. ■ **Baseball SID:** David O'Brian. **Telephone:** (301) 314-7068. **FAX:** (301) 314-9094.

Home Field: Shipley Field. **Seating Capacity:** 2,200. **Outfield Dimensions:** LF—320, CF—355, RF—325. **Press Box Telephone:** (301) 314-0379.

MARYLAND-BALTIMORE COUNTY Retrievers

Conference: Northeast.
Mailing Address: 1000 Hilltop Circle, Baltimore, MD 21250.
Head Coach: John Jancuska. **Assistant Coach:** *Bob Mumma. **Telephone:** (410) 455-2239. ■ **Baseball SID:** David Gansell. **Telephone:** (410) 455-2197. **FAX:** (410) 455-3994.

MARYLAND-EASTERN SHORE Hawks

Conference: Mid-Eastern Athletic (North).
Mailing Address: William P. Hytche Athletic Center, UMES, Princess Anne, MD 21853.
Head Coach: Kaye Pinhey. **Telephone:** (410) 651-6539. ■ **Baseball SID:** Romanda Noble. **Telephone:** (410) 651-6499. **FAX:** (410) 651-7600.

MASSACHUSETTS Minutemen

Conference: Atlantic-10 (East).
Mailing Address: 248 Boyden Bldg., Amherst, MA 01003.
Head Coach: Mike Stone. **Assistant Coaches:** Raphael Cerrato, Ernie May. **Telephone:** (413) 545-3120. ■ **Baseball SID:** Charles Bare. **Telephone:** (413) 545-2439. **FAX:** (413) 545-1556.

McNEESE STATE Cowboys

Conference: Southland.
Mailing Address: P.O. Box 92724, Lake Charles, LA 70609.
Head Coach: Mike Bianco. **Assistant Coaches:** Clint Carver, *Chad Clement, Butch Millet. **Telephone:** (318) 475-5484. ■ **Baseball SID:** Louis Bonnette. **Telephone:** (318) 475-5207. **FAX:** (318) 475-5202.

MEMPHIS Tigers

Conference: Conference USA.
Mailing Address: 205 Athletic Office Building, 570 Normal, Memphis, TN 38152.
Head Coach: Jeff Hopkins. **Assistant Coaches:** Rob McDonald, *Eric Page, Mike Poor. **Telephone:** (901) 678-2452. ■ **Baseball SID:** Jason Black. **Telephone:** (901) 678-2337. **FAX:** (901) 678-4134.
Home Field: Nat Buring Stadium. **Seating Capacity:** 2,000. **Outfield Dimensions:** LF—320, CF—380, RF—320. **Press Box Telephone:** (901) 678-2862.

MERCER Bears

Conference: Trans America Athletic.
Mailing Address: 1400 Coleman Ave., Macon, GA 31207.
Head Coach: Barry Myers. **Assistant Coach:** Craig Gibson. **Telephone:** (912) 301-2738. ■ **Baseball SID:** Kevin Coulombe. **Telephone:** (912) 301-2735. **FAX:** (912) 301-5350.

MIAMI Hurricanes

Conference: Independent.
Mailing Address: 5821 San Amaro Dr., Coral Gables, FL 33146.
Head Coach: Jim Morris. **Assistant Coaches:** Lazaro Collazo, *Gino DiMare, Mark Kingston. **Telephone:** (305) 284-4171. ■ **Baseball SID:** Joe Hornstein. **Telephone:** (305) 284-3244. **FAX:** (305) 284-2807.
Home Field: Mark Light Stadium. **Seating Capacity:** 5,000. **Outfield Dimensions:** LF—330, CF—400, RF—330. **Press Box Telephone:** (305) 284-5626.

MIAMI RedHawks

Conference: Mid-American (East).
Mailing Address: 110 Withrow Court, Oxford, OH 45056.
Head Coach: Tracy Smith. **Assistant Coaches:** Tyson Neal, *Dan Simonds. **Telephone:** (513) 529-6631. ■ **Baseball SID:** Burt Lawten. **Telephone:** (513) 529-4327. **FAX:** (513) 529-2337.
Home Field: Stanley G. McKie Field. **Seating Capacity:** 1,500. **Outfield Dimensions:** LF—330, CF—390, RF—330. **Press Box Telephone:** (513) 529-4331.

MICHIGAN Wolverines

Conference: Big Ten.
Mailing Address: 1000 S State St., Ann Arbor, MI 48109.
Head Coach: Geoff Zahn. **Assistant Coaches:** *Chris Harrison, Andy Hood, Matt Hyde. **Telephone:** (734) 647-4550. ■ **Baseball SID:** Jim Schneider. **Telephone:** (734) 763-1381. **FAX:** (734) 647-1188.
Home Field: Ray Fisher Stadium. **Seating Capacity:** 4,000. **Outfield Dimensions:** LF—330, CF—400, RF—330. **Press Box Telephone:** (734) 647-1283.

MICHIGAN STATE Spartans

Conference: Big Ten.
Mailing Address: 304 Jenison Field House, East Lansing, MI 48824.
Head Coach: Ted Mahan. **Assistant Coaches:** Greg Gunderson, Corey Mee. **Telephone:** (517) 355-4486. ■ **Baseball SID:** Ben Dhleger. **Telephone:** (517) 355-5271. **FAX:** (517) 353-9636.
Home Fields (Seating Capacity): Kobs Field (4,000), Oldsmobile Park (6,000). **Outfield Dimensions:** Kobs Field/LF—340, CF—400, RF—301; Oldsmobile Park/LF—330, CF—412, LF—337. **Press Box Telephones:** Kobs Field/(517) 353-

3009; Oldsmobile Park/(517) 485-2616.

MIDDLE TENNESSEE STATE Blue Raiders

Conference: Ohio Valley.

Mailing Address: MTSU Box 90, Murfreesboro, TN 37132.

Head Coach: Steve Peterson. **Assistant Coaches:** *Jim McGuire, Mike McLaury, Justis Scott. **Telephone:** (615) 898-2984. ■ **Baseball SID:** Ryan Simmons. **Telephone:** (615) 904-8209. **FAX:** (615) 898-5626.

MINNESOTA Golden Gophers

Conference: Big Ten.

Mailing Address: 516 15th Ave. SE, Minneapolis, MN 55455.

Head Coach: John Anderson. **Assistant Coaches:** *Rob Fornasiere, Todd Oakes. **Telephone:** (612) 625-4057. ■ **Baseball SID:** Mike Vidnovic. **Telephone:** (612) 625-4345. **FAX:** (612) 625-0359.

Home Fields (Seating Capacity): Siebert Field (2,500), Metrodome (55,000). **Outfield Dimensions:** Siebert Field/LF—330, CF—380, RF—330; Metrodome /LF—343, CF—408, RF—327. **Press Box Telephones:** Siebert Field/(612) 625-4031; Metrodome/(612) 627-4400.

MISSISSIPPI Rebels

Conference: Southeastern (West).

Mailing Address: UMAA-West, University, MS 38877.

Head Coach: Pat Harrison. **Assistant Coaches:** Darby Carmichael, *Keith Kessinger. **Telephone:** (662) 915-7519. ■ **Baseball SID:** Rick Stupak. **Telephone:** (662) 915-7522. **FAX:** (662) 915-7006.

Home Field: Oxford University Stadium. **Seating Capacity:** 3,000. **Outfield Dimensions:** LF—330, CF—400, RF—330. **Press Box Telephone:** (662) 915-7858.

MISSISSIPPI STATE Bulldogs

Conference: Southeastern (West).

Mailing Address: P.O. Box 5327, Starkville, MS 39762.

Head Coach: Pat McMahon. **Assistant Coaches:** Jim Case, Matt Ishee, Tommy Raffo. **Telephone:** (662) 325-3597. ■ **Baseball SID:** Joe Dier. **Telephone:** (002) 325-8040. **FAX:** (662) 325-3654.

Home Field: Dudy Noble Field/Polk-DeMent Stadium. **Seating Capacity:** 15,000. **Outfield Dimensions:** LF—325, CF—390, RF—325. **Press Box Telephone:** (662) 325-3776.

MISSISSIPPI VALLEY STATE Delta Devils

Conference: Southwestern Athletic (East).

Mailing Address: 14000 Highway 82 West, No. 7246, Itta Bena, MS 38941.

Head Coach: Cleotha Wilson. **Telephone:** (662) 254-3398. ■ **Baseball SID:** Chuck Prophet. **Telephone:** (662) 254-3551. **FAX:** (662) 254-3639.

MISSOURI Tigers

Conference: Big 12.

Mailing Address: 600 Stadium Blvd., Columbia, MO 65211.

Head Coach: Tim Jamieson. **Assistant Coaches:** Chal Fanning, Evan Pratte. **Telephone:** (573) 882-0731. ■ **Baseball SID:** Jeremy McNelve. **Telephone:** (573) 882-0711. **FAX:** (573) 882 4720.

Home Field: Simmons Field. **Seating Capacity:** 2,500. **Outfield Dimensions:** LF—340, CF—400, RF—340. **Press Box Telephone:** Unavailable.

MONMOUTH Hawks

Conference: Northeast.

Mailing Address: Cedar Ave., West Long Branch, NJ 07764.

Head Coach: Dean Ehehalt. **Assistant Coaches:** *Jeff Barbalinardo, John Crane. **Telephone:** (732) 263-5186. ■ **Baseball SID:** Ross Blacker. **Telephone:** (732) 263-5180. **FAX:** (732) 571-3535.

MOREHEAD STATE Eagles

Conference: Ohio Valley.

Mailing Address: UPO 1023, Morehead, KY 40351.

Head Coach: John Jarnagin. **Assistant Coaches:** *Matt Barnett, Mitch Dunn, Larry Lipker. **Telephone:** (606) 783-2882. ■ **Baseball SID:** Randy Stacy. **Telephone:** (606) 783-2500. **FAX:** (606) 783-2550.

MOUNT ST. MARY'S Mountaineers

Conference: Northeast.

Mailing Address: Route 15, 16300 Old Emmitsburg Rd., Emmitsburg, MD 21727.

Head Coach: Scott Thomson. **Assistant Coaches:** Trevor Buckley, Steve Thomson. **Telephone:** (301) 447-3806. ■ **Baseball SID:** Eric Kloiber. **Telephone:** (301) 447-5384. **FAX:** (301) 447-5300.

MURRAY STATE Thoroughbreds

Conference: Ohio Valley.

Mailing Address: Athletic Dept., P.O. Box 9, Murray, KY 42071.

Head Coach: Mike Thieke. **Assistant Coach:** *Bart Osborne. **Telephone:** (270) 762-4892. ■ **Baseball SID:** David Snow. **Telephone:** (270) 762-3351. **FAX:** (270) 762-6814.

NAVY Midshipmen

Conference: Patriot.

Mailing Address: 566 Brownson Rd., Annapolis, MD 21403.

Head Coach: Bob MacDonald. **Assistant Coaches:** Todd Butler, Glenn Davis, Chris Murphy. **Telephone:** (410) 293-5571. ■ **Baseball SID:** Justin Kischefsky. **Telephone:** (410) 268-6226. **FAX:** (410) 269-6779.

NEBRASKA Cornhuskers

Conference: Big 12.

Mailing Address: 116 S Stadium, P.O. Box 880123, Lincoln, NE 68588.

Head Coach: Dave Van Horn. **Assistant Coaches:** Mike Anderson, Rob Childress. **Telephone:** (402) 472-2269. ■ **Baseball SID:** Aaron Babcock. **Telephone:** (402) 472-2263. **FAX:** (402) 472-2005.

Home Field: Buck Beltzer Stadium. **Seating Capacity:** 1,500. **Outfield Dimensions:** LF—330, CF—400, RF—330. **Press Box Telephone:** (402) 472-9171.

NEVADA Wolf Pack

Conference: Big West.

Mailing Address: Baseball Office, Legacy Hall, Suite 232, Reno, NV 89557.

Head Coach: Gary Powers. **Assistant Coaches:** Gary McNamara, *Stan Stolte. **Telephone:** (775) 784-6900, ext. 252. ■ **Baseball SID:** Zen Mocarski. **Telephone:** (775) 784-6900, ext. 244. **FAX:** (775) 784-4386.

Home Field: Peccole Park. **Seating Capacity:** 1,914. **Outfield Dimensions:** LF—340, CF—401, RF—340. **Press Box Telephone:** (775) 784-1585.

NEVADA-LAS VEGAS Rebels

Conference: Mountain West.

Mailing Address: 4505 Maryland Pkwy., Las Vegas, NV 89154.

Head Coach: Rod Soesbe. **Assistant Coaches:** Jim Pace, Mel Stottlemyre Jr. **Telephone:** (702) 895-3499. ■ **Baseball SID:** Jim Gemma. **Telephone:** (702) 895-3995. **FAX:** (702) 895-0989.

Home Field: Earl E. Wilson Stadium. **Seating Capacity:** 3,000. **Outfield Dimensions:** LF—335, CF—400, RF—335. **Press Box Telephone:** (702) 895-1595.

NEW MEXICO Lobos

Conference: Mountain West.

Mailing Address: 1414 University Blvd., Albuquerque, NM 87122.

Head Coach: Rich Alday. **Assistant Coaches:** Ryan Beggs, *Mark Martinez, Pat Shine. **Telephone:** (505) 925-5720. ■ **Baseball SID:** Bryan Satter. **Telephone:** (505) 925-5528. **FAX:** (505) 925-5529.

Home Field: Lobo Field. **Seating Capacity:** 500. **Outfield Dimensions:** LF—337, CF—412, RF—337. **Press Box Telephone:** (505) 925-5722.

NEW MEXICO STATE Aggies

Conference: Big West.

Mailing Address: Pan American Center West Side, Las Cruces, NM 88003.

Head Coach: Rocky Ward. **Assistant Coaches:** Patrick Reid, Gary Silva, *Gary Ward. **Telephone:** (505) 646-5813. ■ **Baseball SID:** Thomas Dick. **Telephone:** (505) 646-3929. **FAX:** (505) 646-2425.

Home Field: Presley Askew Field. **Seating Capacity:** 1,000. **Outfield Dimensions:** LF—330, CF—400, RF—340. **Press Box Telephone:** Unavailable.

NEW ORLEANS Privateers

Conference: Sun Belt.

Mailing Address: 6801 Franklin Ave., New Orleans, LA 70148.

Head Coach: Randy Bush. **Assistant Coaches:** Brady Benoit, Kenny Bonura, Trey Guillot, Wally Whitehurst. **Telephone:** (504) 280-7021. ■ **Baseball SID:** Ed Cassiere. **Telephone:** (504) 280-6284. **FAX:** (504) 280-7240.

Home Field: Privateer Park. **Seating Capacity:** 5,225. **Outfield Dimensions:** LF—330, CF—405, RF—330. **Press Box Telephone:** (504) 280-7027.

NEW YORK TECH Bears

Conference: Independent.

Mailing Address: P.O. Box 8000, Old Westbury, NY 11568.

Head Coach: Bob Hirschfield. **Assistant Coaches:** *Bill Asermely, Mike Caulfield, Ray Giannelli. **Telephone:** (516) 686-7513. ■ **Baseball SID:** Dave Geringer. **Telephone:** (516) 686-7504. **FAX:** (516) 626-0750.

NIAGARA Purple Eagles

Conference: Metro Atlantic (North).

Mailing Address: P.O. Box 2009, Niagara University, NY 14109.

Head Coach: Jim Mauro. **Assistant Coaches:** Dan Fontana, Bob Mettler, John Schieber. **Telephone:** (716) 286-8602. ■ **Baseball SID:** Ken Baker. **Telephone:** (716) 286-8582. **FAX:** (716) 286-8551.

NICHOLLS STATE Colonels

Conference: Southland.

Mailing Address: P.O. Box 2032, Thibodaux, LA 70310.

Head Coach: B.D. Parker. **Assistant Coaches:** *Gerald Cassard, Steve Miller. **Telephone:** (504) 448-4808. ■ **Baseball SID:** Jack Duggan. **Telephone:** (504) 448-4282. **FAX:** (504) 448-4924.

NORFOLK STATE Spartans

Conference: Mid-Eastern Athletic (South).

Mailing Address: 700 Park Ave., Norfolk, VA 23504.
Head Coach: Marty Miller. Assistant Coach: Anthony Jones. Telephone: (757) 823-9539. ■ Baseball SID: Glen Mason. Telephone: (757) 823-2628. FAX: (757) 823-2129.

NORTH CAROLINA Tar Heels

Conference: Atlantic Coast.
Mailing Address: P.O. Box 2126, Chapel Hill, NC 27515.
Head Coach: Mike Fox. Assistant Coaches: Scott Forbes, *Chad Holbrook, Roger Williams. Telephone: (919) 962-2351. ■ Baseball SID: David Tinson. Telephone: (919) 962-0084. FAX: (919) 962-0612.
Home Field: Boshamer Stadium. Seating Capacity: 4,500. Outfield Dimensions: LF—335, CF—400, RF—335. Press Box Telephone: (919) 962-3509.

UNC ASHEVILLE Bulldogs

Conference: Big South.
Mailing Address: One University Heights, Justice Center, Asheville, NC 28804.
Head Coach: Mike Roberts. Assistant Coaches: *Justin Cronk, Matt Myers. Telephone: (828) 232-5655. ■ Baseball SID: Mike Gore. Telephone: (828) 251-6923. FAX: (828) 251-6386.

UNC CHARLOTTE 49ers

Conference: Conference USA.
Mailing Address: 9201 University City Blvd., Charlotte, NC 28223.
Head Coach: Loren Hibbs. Assistant Coaches: Greg Brummett, Jason Hill, Gerald Par. Telephone: (704) 547-3935. ■ Baseball SID: Brent Stastny. Telephone: (704) 510-6313. FAX: (704) 547-4918.
Home Field: Tom and Lib Phillips Field. Seating Capacity: 2,000. Outfield Dimensions: LF—335, CF—390, RF—335. Press Box Telephone: (704) 547-3184.

UNC GREENSBORO Spartans

Conference: Southern.
Mailing Address: P.O. Box 26168, Greensboro, NC 27402.
Head Coach: Mike Gaski. Assistant Coaches: *Neil Avent, Matt Faulkner. Telephone: (336) 334-5247. ■ Baseball SID: Jeremy Agor. Telephone: (336) 334-5615. FAX: (336) 334-3182.

UNC WILMINGTON Seahawks

Conference: Colonial Athletic.
Mailing Address: 601 S College Rd., Wilmington, NC 28403.
Head Coach: Mark Scalf. Assistant Coaches: Shohn Doty, Rob Flippo, Brandon Hall. Telephone: (910) 962-3570. ■ Baseball SID: Joe Browning. Telephone: (910) 962-3236. FAX: (910) 962-3002.

NORTH CAROLINA A&T Aggies

Conference: Mid-Eastern Athletic (South).
Mailing Address: 1601 E Market St., Moores Gym, Greensboro, NC 27411.
Head Coach: Keith Shumate. Assistant Coach: Tim Wilson. Telephone: (336) 334-7371. ■ Baseball SID: Donald Ware. Telephone: (336) 334-7141. FAX: (336) 334-7272.

NORTH CAROLINA STATE Wolfpack

Conference: Atlantic Coast.
Mailing Address: P.O. Box 8501, Raleigh, NC 27695.
Head Coach: Elliott Avent. Assistant Coaches: *Billy Best, Todd DeMakes, Mark Fuller. Telephone: (919) 515-3613. ■ Baseball SID: Bruce Winkworth. Telephone: (919) 515-1182. FAX: (919) 515-2898.
Home Field: Doak Field. Seating Capacity: 3,000. Outfield Dimensions: LF—340, CF—400, RF—340. Press Box Telephone: (919) 515-7643.

NORTHEASTERN Huskies

Conference: America East.
Mailing Address: 360 Huntington Ave., Boston, MA 02115.
Head Coach: Neil McPhee. Assistant Coaches: Kevin Gately, Matt Noone. Telephone: (617) 373-2672. ■ Baseball SID: Adam Polgren. Telephone: (617) 373-4154. FAX: (617) 373-3152.

NORTHERN ILLINOIS Huskies

Conference: Mid-American (West).
Mailing Address: 112 Evans Field House, DeKalb, IL 60115.
Head Coach: Dave Schrage. Assistant Coaches: David Seifert, *Randy Wee. Telephone: (815) 753-0147. ■ Baseball SID: Michael Smoose. Telephone: (815) 753-1706. FAX: (815) 753-9540.

NORTHERN IOWA Panthers

Conference: Missouri Valley.
Mailing Address: UNI-Dome NW Upper, Cedar Falls, IA 50614.
Head Coach: Rick Heller. Assistant Coaches: Todd Rima, *Jack Sole, Mike Waller. Telephone: (319) 273-6323. ■ Baseball SID: Robert Anderson. Telephone: (319) 273-2932. FAX: (319) 273-3602.

NORTHWESTERN Wildcats

Conference: Big Ten.

Mailing Address: 1501 Central St., Evanston, IL 60208.

Head Coach: Paul Stevens. Assistant Coaches: *Ron Klein, Tim Stoddard. Telephone: (847) 491-4652. ■ Baseball SID: Mike Mahoney. Telephone: (847) 491-7503. FAX: (847) 491-8818.

Home Field: Rocky Miller Park. Seating Capacity: 1,000. Outfield Dimensions: LF—330, CF—400, RF—330. Press Box Telephone: (847) 491-4200.

NORTHWESTERN STATE Demons

Conference: Southland.

Mailing Address: 112 Prather Coliseum, Natchitoches, LA 71497.

Head Coach: John Cohen. Assistant Coaches: Kyle Crookes, *Sean McCann, Bill Wright. Telephone: (318) 357-4139. ■ Baseball SID: Dustin Eubanks. Telephone: (318) 357-6467. FAX: (318) 357-4515.

NOTRE DAME Fighting Irish

Conference: Big East.

Mailing Address: 112 Joyce Center, Notre Dame, IN 46556.

Head Coach: Paul Mainieri. Assistant Coaches: Dusty Lepper, *Brian O'Connor. Telephone: (219) 631-6366. ■ Baseball SID: Pete LaFleur. Telephone: (219) 631-7516. FAX: (219) 631-7941.

Home Field: Frank Eck Stadium. Seating Capacity: 2,500. Outfield Dimensions: LF—331, CF—401, RF—331. Press Box Telephone: (219) 631-9018.

OAKLAND Bobcats

Conference: Mid-Continent.

Mailing Address: Athletic Center Arena, Rochester, MI 48309.

Head Coach: Mark Avery. Assistant Coach: Andy Fairman. Telephone: (248) 370-4059. ■ Baseball SID: Amy Hirschman. Telephone: (248) 370-4008. FAX: (248) 370-4056.

OHIO Bobcats

Conference: Mid-American (East).

Mailing Address: Convocation Center, Richland Ave., Athens, OH 45701.

Head Coach: Joe Carbone. Assistant Coach: Bill Toadvine. Telephone: (740) 593-1180. ■ Baseball SID: Heather Czeczok. Telephone: (740) 593-1129. FAX: (740) 597-1838.

Home Field: Bob Wren Stadium. Seating Capacity: 4,000. Outfield Dimensions: LF—340, CF—405, RF—340. Press Box Telephone: Unavailable.

OHIO STATE Buckeyes

Conference: Big Ten.

Mailing Address: 124 St. John Arena, 410 Woody Hayes Dr., Columbus, OH 43210.

Head Coach: Bob Todd. Assistant Coaches: Pat Bangston, *Greg Cypret, Brian Mannino. Telephone: (614) 292-1075. ■ Baseball SID: Pat Chun. Telephone: (614) 292-6861. FAX: (614) 292-8547.

Home Field: Bill Davis Stadium. Seating Capacity: 4,450. Outfield Dimensions: LF—330, CF—400, RF—330. Press Box Telephone: (614) 292-0021.

OKLAHOMA Sooners

Conference: Big 12.

Mailing Address: 401 W Imhoff, Norman, OK 73019.

Head Coach: Larry Cochell. Assistant Coaches: Ray Hayward, *Bill Mosiello, Aric Thomas. Telephone: (405) 325-8354. ■ Baseball SID: Danielle Felter. Telephone: (405) 325-4274. FAX: (405) 325-7623.

Home Field: L. Dale Mitchell Park. Seating Capacity: 2,700. Outfield Dimensions: LF—335, CF—411, RF—335. Press Box Telephone: (405) 325-8363.

OKLAHOMA STATE Cowboys

Conference: Big 12.

Mailing Address: 423 Squires Rd., Stillwater, OK 74075.

Head Coach: Tom Holliday. Assistant Coaches: Cory Burton, *John Farrell, Robbie Wine. Telephone: (405) 744-5849. ■ Baseball SID: Thomas Samuel. Telephone: (405) 707-7834. FAX: (405) 743-0256.

Home Field: Allie P. Reynolds Stadium. Seating Capacity: 4,000. Outfield Dimensions: LF—330, CF—400, RF—330. Press Box Telephone: (405) 744-5757.

OLD DOMINION Monarchs

Conference: Colonial Athletic.

Mailing Address: Athletic Administration Bldg., Norfolk, VA 23529.

Head Coach: Tony Guzzo. Assistant Coaches: Tag Montague, Chris Rodriguez, *Terry Rooney. Telephone: (757) 683-4230. ■ Baseball SID: Carol Hudson. Telephone: (757) 683-3372. FAX: (757) 683-3119.

Home Field: Bud Metheny Stadium. Seating Capacity: 2,500. Outfield Dimensions: LF—320, CF—395, RF—320. Press Box Telephone: (757) 683-5036.

ORAL ROBERTS Golden Eagles

Conference: Mid-Continent.

Mailing Address: 7777 S Lewis Ave., Tulsa, OK 74171.
Head Coach: Sunny Galloway. Assistant Coaches: Bob Miller, *Robert Walton. Telephone: (918) 495-7131. ■ Baseball SID: Gary Brown. Telephone: (918) 495-7181. FAX: (918) 495-7142.

OREGON STATE Beavers

Conference: Pacific-10.
Mailing Address: Gill Coliseum, Room 103, Corvallis, OR 97331.
Head Coach: Pat Casey. Assistant Coaches: Gary Henderson, Billy Jones, Dan Spencer. Telephone: (541) 737-2825. ■ Baseball SID: Kip Carlson. Telephone: (541) 737-7472. FAX: (541) 737-3072.
Home Field: Goss Stadium/Coleman Field. Seating Capacity: 2,000. Outfield Dimensions: LF—330, CF—400, RF—330. Press Box Telephone: (541) 737-7475.

PACE Setters

Conference: Independent.
Mailing Address: 861 Bedford Rd., Pleasantville, NY 10570.
Head Coach: Fred Calaicone. Assistant Coach: *Henry Manning. Telephone: (914) 773-3413. ■ Baseball SID: Nick Renda. Telephone: (914) 773-3888. FAX: (914) 773-3441.

PACIFIC Tigers

Conference: Big West.
Mailing Address: 3601 Pacific Ave., Stockton, CA 95211.
Head Coach: Quincey Noble. Assistant Coaches: Joe Moreno, Jim Yanko. Telephone: (209) 946-2709. ■ Baseball SID: Cindy Jensen. Telephone: (209) 946-2479. FAX: (209) 946-2757.
Home Field: Billy Hebert Field. Seating Capacity: 3,500. Outfield Dimensions: LF—325, CF—390, RF—330. Press Box Telephone: Unavailable.

PENNSYLVANIA Quakers

Conference: Ivy League (Gehrig).
Mailing Address: Dunning Center, 33rd St., Philadelphia, PA 19104.
Head Coach: Bob Seddon. Assistant Coaches: Bill Wagner, Dan Young. Telephone: (215) 898-6282. ■ Baseball SID: Carla Shultzberg. Telephone: (215) 898-6128. FAX: (215) 898-1747.

PENN STATE Nittany Lions

Conference: Big Ten.
Mailing Address: 112 Bryce Jordan Center, University Park, PA 16802.
Head Coach: Joe Hindelang. Assistant Coaches: *Randy Ford, Dave Jameson, Jon Ramsey. Telephone: (814) 863-0239. ■ Baseball SID: Cyndi Robinson. Telephone: (814) 865-1757. FAX: (814) 863-3165.
Home Field: Beaver Field. Seating Capacity: 1,000. Outfield Dimensions: LF—350, CF—400, RF—350. Press Box Telephone: (814) 865-2552.

PEPPERDINE Waves

Conference: West Coast (West).
Mailing Address: 24255 Pacific Coast Hwy., Malibu, CA 90263.
Head Coach: Frank Sanchez. Assistant Coaches: *Rick Hirtensteiner, Steve Rodriguez. Telephone: (310) 456-4199. ■ Baseball SID: Al Barba. Telephone: (310) 456-4455. FAX: (310) 456-4322.
Home Field: Eddy D. Field Stadium. Seating Capacity: 2,200. Outfield Dimensions: LF—330, CF—400, RF—330. Press Box Telephone: (310) 456-4598.

PITTSBURGH Panthers

Conference: Big East.
Mailing Address: P.O. Box 7436, Pittsburgh, PA 15213.
Head Coach: Joe Jordano. Assistant Coaches: *Joel Domkowski, Rich Pasquale. Telephone: (412) 648-8208. ■ Baseball SID: Nicole Radu. Telephone: (412) 648-8240. FAX: (412) 648-8248.
Home Field: Trees Field. Seating Capacity: 500. Outfield Dimensions: LF—302, CF—400, RF—328. Press Box Telephone: None.

PORTLAND Pilots

Conference: West Coast (West).
Mailing Address: 5000 N Willamette Blvd., Portland, OR 97203.
Head Coach: Chris Sperry. Assistant Coaches: Ryan Brust, Billy Winters. Telephone: (503) 943-7707. ■ Baseball SID: Loren Wohlgemuth. Telephone: (503) 943-7439. FAX: (503) 943-7242.

PRAIRIE VIEW A&M Panthers

Conference: Southwestern Athletic (West).
Mailing Address: P.O. Box 97, Prairie View, TX 77446.
Head Coach: John Tankersley. Assistant Coach: Raymond Burgess. Telephone: (409) 857-4290. ■ Baseball SID: Harlan Robinson. Telephone: (409) 857-2114. FAX: (409) 857-2395.

PRINCETON Tigers

Conference: Ivy League (Gehrig).
Mailing Address: P.O. Box 71, Jadwin Gym, Princeton, NJ 08544.

Head Coach: Scott Bradley. **Assistant Coaches:** Lloyd Brewer, Matt Golden, Pete Silletti. **Telephone:** (609) 258-5059. ■ **Baseball SID:** Matt Ciciarelli. **Telephone:** (609) 258-5701. **FAX:** (609) 258-2399.

PURDUE Boilermakers

Conference: Big Ten.
Mailing Address: 302C Moll, West Lafayette, IN 47907.
Head Coach: Doug Schreiber. **Assistant Coaches:** Gary Adcock, *Todd Murphy. **Telephone:** (765) 494-3998. ■ **Baseball SID:** Pat Connolly. **Telephone:** (765) 494-3201. **FAX:** (765) 494-5447.
Home Field: Lambert Field. **Seating Capacity:** 1,500. **Outfield Dimensions:** LF—343, CF—400, RF—343. **Press Box Telephone:** (765) 494-1522.

QUINNIPIAC Braves

Conference: Northeast.
Mailing Address: 275 Mount Carmel Ave., Hamden, CT 06518.
Head Coach: Joe Mattei. **Assistant Coaches:** Tim Belcher, Rob Manzo. **Telephone:** (203) 287-3357. ■ **Baseball SID:** Al Carbone. **Telephone:** (203) 281-8625. **FAX:** (203) 281-8716.

RADFORD Highlanders

Conference: Big South.
Mailing Address: P.O. Box 6913, Radford, VA 24142.
Head Coach: Lew Kent. **Assistant Coaches:** *Curtis Brown, Jason Fulmer. **Telephone:** (540) 831-5881. ■ **Baseball SID:** Chris King. **Telephone:** (540) 831-5211. **FAX:** (540) 831-5036.

RHODE ISLAND Rams

Conference: Atlantic-10 (East).
Mailing Address: 3 Keaney Rd., Kingston, RI 02881.
Head Coach: Frank Leoni. **Assistant Coaches:** Jay Krystofolski, *Jim Mason. **Telephone:** (401) 874-4550. ■ **Baseball SID:** Mike Ballweg. **Telephone:** (401) 874-2401. **FAX:** (401) 874-5354.

RICE Owls

Conference: Western Athletic.
Mailing Address: 6100 Main St., MS 548, Houston, TX 77005.
Head Coach: Wayne Graham. **Assistant Coaches:** Chris Feris, *Jon Prather. **Telephone:** (713) 348-6022. ■ **Baseball SID:** Bill Cousins. **Telephone:** (713) 348-5775. **FAX:** (713) 348-6019.
Home Field: Reckling Park. **Seating Capacity:** 5,667. **Outfield Dimensions:** LF—330, CF—400, RF—330. **Press Box Telephone:** (713) 348-4931.

RICHMOND Spiders

Conference: Colonial Athletic.
Mailing Address: Robins Center, Richmond, VA 23173.
Head Coach: Ron Atkins. **Assistant Coaches:** Richard Graham, *Mark McQueen. **Telephone:** (804) 289-8391. ■ **Baseball SID:** Phil Stanton. **Telephone:** (804) 289-8320. **FAX:** (804) 289-8820.

RIDER Broncs

Conference: Metro Atlantic (South).
Mailing Address: 2083 Lawrenceville Road, Lawrenceville, NJ 08648.
Head Coach: Sonny Pittaro. **Assistant Coaches:** Rick Freeman, Jeff Plunkett. **Telephone:** (609) 896-5055. ■ **Baseball SID:** Bud Focht. **Telephone:** (609) 896-5138. **FAX:** (609) 896-0341.

RUTGERS Scarlet Knights

Conference: Big East.
Mailing Address: 83 Rockefeller Rd., Piscataway, NJ 08854.
Head Coach: Fred Hill. **Assistant Coaches:** Tom Baxter, Glen Gardner, Rob Valli. **Telephone:** (732) 445-3553. ■ **Baseball SID:** Pat McBride. **Telephone:** (732) 445-4200. **FAX:** (732) 445-3063.
Home Field: Class of 53 Stadium. **Seating Capacity:** 1,500. **Outfield Dimensions:** LF—330, CF—410, RF—320. **Press Box Telephone:** None.

SACRAMENTO STATE Hornets

Conference: Big West.
Mailing Address: 6000 J St., Sacramento, CA 95819.
Head Coach: John Smith. **Assistant Coaches:** Jim Barr, *Brian Hewitt. **Telephone:** (916) 278-7225. ■ **Baseball SID:** Bil Macriss. **Telephone:** (916) 388-1037. **FAX:** (916) 278-5429.
Home Field: Hornet Field. **Seating Capacity:** 1,500. **Outfield Dimensions:** LF—333, CF—400, RF—333. **Press Box Telephone:** Unavailable.

SACRED HEART Pioneers

Conference: Northeast.
Mailing Address: 5151 Park Ave., Fairfield, CT 06432.
Head Coach: Nick Giaquinto. **Assistant Coaches:** Frank Fedak, *Seth Kaplan. **Telephone:** (203) 365-7632. ■ **Baseball SID:** James Zuhlke. **Telephone:** (203) 396-8125. **FAX:** (203) 371-7889.

ST. BONAVENTURE Bonnies

Conference: Atlantic-10 (East).
Mailing Address: Box G, St. Bonaventure, NY 14778.
Head Coach: Larry Sudbrook. **Assistant Coach:** Matt Burke. **Telephone:**

(716) 375-2641. ■ **Baseball SID:** Geoff Sherman. **Telephone:** (716) 375-2319.
FAX: (716) 375-2383.

ST. FRANCIS Terriers
Conference: Northeast.
Mailing Address: 180 Remsen St., Brooklyn Heights, NY 11201.
Head Coach: Frank Del George. **Assistant Coaches:** Tony Barone, *Mike
Lupiparo. **Telephone:** (718) 489-5365. ■ **Baseball SID:** Jim Hoffman.
Telephone: (718) 489-5489. **FAX:** (718) 797-2140.

ST. JOHN'S Red Storm
Conference: Big East.
Mailing Address: 8000 Utopia Pkwy., Jamaica, NY 11439.
Head Coach: Ed Blankmeyer. **Assistant Coaches:** *Chris Dotolo, Mike
Maerten. **Telephone:** (718) 990-6148. ■ **Baseball SID:** Mike Carey. **Telephone:**
(718) 990-1522. **FAX:** (718) 969-8468.
Home Field: McCallen Field. **Seating Capacity:** 1,000. **Outfield
Dimensions:** LF—340, CF—390, RF—340. **Press Box Telephone:** (718) 990-
6057.

ST. JOSEPH'S Hawks
Conference: Atlantic-10 (East).
Mailing Address: 5600 City Ave., Philadelphia, PA 19131.
Head Coach: Jim Ertel. **Assistant Coaches:** *Ken Krsolovic, Jack Stanczak.
Telephone: (610) 660-1718. ■ **Baseball SID:** Phil Denne. **Telephone:** (610)
660-1730. **FAX:** (610) 660-1724.

SAINT LOUIS Billikens
Conference: Conference USA.
Mailing Address: 3672 W. Pine Mall, St. Louis, MO 63108.
Head Coach: Bob Hughes. **Assistant Coaches:** Dan Nicholson, *Todd
Whaley. **Telephone:** (314) 977-3260. ■ **Baseball SID:** Diana Koval. **Telephone:**
(314) 977-3463. **FAX:** (314) 977-7193.
Home Field: Billiken Sports Center. **Seating Capacity:** 1,000. **Outfield
Dimensions:** LF—330, CF—395, RF—330. **Press Box Telephone:** (314) 977-
3563.

ST. MARY'S Gaels
Conference: West Coast (West).
Mailing Address: 1928 St. Mary's Rd., Moraga, CA 94575.
Head Coach: John Baptista. **Assistant Coaches:** Chris Lanerini, Joe Millette,
*Ted Turkington. **Telephone:** (925) 631-4402. **FAX:** (925) 631-4405. ■ **Baseball SID:** Rich Davi.
Telephone: (925) 631-4402. **FAX:** (925) 631-4405.

ST. PETER'S Peacocks
Conference: Metro Atlantic (South).
Mailing Address: 2641 Kennedy Blvd., Jersey City, NJ 07306.
Head Coach: Dan Olear. **Assistant Coach:** Jerry Koslowski. **Telephone:**
(201) 915-9459. ■ **Baseball SID:** Tim Camp. **Telephone:** (201) 915-9101. **FAX:**
(201) 915-9102.

SAM HOUSTON STATE Bearkats
Conference: Southland.
Mailing Address: P.O. Box 2268, Huntsville, TX 77341.
Head Coach: John Skeelers. **Assistant Coach:** Carlo Gott. **Telephone:**
(409) 294-1731. ■ **Baseball SID:** Paul Ridings. **Telephone:** (409) 294-1764.
FAX: (409) 294-9838.

SAMFORD Bulldogs
Conference: Trans America Athletic.
Mailing Address: 800 Lakeshore Dr., Birmingham, AL 35229.
Head Coach: Tim Parenton. **Assistant Coach:** Todd Buczek. **Telephone:**
(205) 726-2134. ■ **Baseball SID:** Matt Sullivan. **Telephone:** (205) 726-2799.
FAX: (205) 870-2524.

SAN DIEGO Toreros
Conference: West Coast (West).
Mailing Address: 5998 Alcala Park, San Diego, CA 92110.
Head Coach: Rich Hill. **Assistant Coaches:** Chris Cannizzaro, Matt Charles,
*Sean Kenny. **Telephone:** (619) 260-5953. ■ **Baseball SID:** Ted Gosen.
Telephone: (619) 260-4803. **FAX:** (619) 260-2213.

SAN DIEGO STATE Aztecs
Conference: Western Athletic.
Mailing Address: Department of Athletics, San Diego, CA 92182.
Head Coach: Jim Dietz. **Assistant Coaches:** Faruq Daruiel, *Rusty Filter,
Ralph Stewart. **Telephone:** (619) 594-6889. ■ **Baseball SID:** Dave Kuhn.
Telephone: (619) 594-5547. **FAX:** (619) 582-6541.
Home Field: Tony Gwynn Stadium. **Seating Capacity:** 3,000. **Outfield
Dimensions:** LF—340, CF—410, RF—340. **Press Box Telephone:** (619) 594-
4103.

SAN FRANCISCO Dons
Conference: West Coast (Coast).
Mailing Address: Memorial Gym, 2130 Fulton St., San Francisco, CA 94117.
Head Coach: Nino Giarratano. **Assistant Coaches:** *Chad Konishi, Troy

Nakamura, Nate Rodriguez. **Telephone:** (415) 422-2935. ■ **Baseball SID:** Ryan McCrary. **Telephone:** (415) 422-6162. **FAX:** (415) 422-2929.

SAN JOSE STATE Spartans

Conference: Western Athletic.

Mailing Address: One Washington Square, San Jose, CA 95192.

Head Coach: Sam Piraro. **Assistant Coaches:** Juan Batula, Brian Forman, Dean Madsen, *Doug Thurman. **Telephone:** (408) 924-1255. ■ **Baseball SID:** Dave Girrard. **Telephone:** (408) 924-1211. **FAX:** (408) 924-1291.

Home Field: Municipal Stadium. **Seating Capacity:** 5,000. **Outfield Dimensions:** LF—330, CF—400, RF—330. **Press Box Telephone:** (408) 924-7276.

SANTA CLARA Broncos

Conference: West Coast (Coast).

Mailing Address: 500 El Camino Real, Santa Clara, CA 95053.

Head Coach: Mike Cummins. **Assistant Coaches:** *Troy Buckley, Jeff Hipps, Jeff Perry. **Telephone:** (408) 554-4882. ■ **Baseball SID:** Jim Young. **Telephone:** (408) 554-4661. **FAX:** (408) 554-4659.

Home Field: Buck Shaw Stadium. **Seating Capacity:** 6,800. **Outfield Dimensions:** LF—350, CF—400, RF—330. **Press Box Telephone:** None.

SETON HALL Pirates

Conference: Big East.

Mailing Address: 400 S Orange Ave., South Orange, NJ 07079.

Head Coach: Mike Sheppard. **Assistant Coaches:** Phil Cundari, Jim McDermott, *Rob Sheppard. **Telephone:** (973) 761-9557. ■ **Baseball SID:** Brett Swick. **Telephone:** (973) 761-9493. **FAX:** (973) 761-9061.

Home Field: Owen T. Carroll Field. **Seating Capacity:** 1,500. **Outfield Dimensions:** LF—325, CF—400, RF—325. **Press Box Telephone:** None.

SIENA Saints

Conference: Metro Atlantic (North).

Mailing Address: 515 New Loudon Rd., Loudonville, NY 12211.

Head Coach: Tony Rossi. **Assistant Coaches:** Tony Curro, Paul Thompson, Ira Tilton. **Telephone:** (518) 786-5044. ■ **Baseball SID:** Jason Rich. **Telephone:** (518) 783-2411. **FAX:** (518) 783-2992.

SOUTH ALABAMA Jaguars

Conference: Sun Belt.

Mailing Address: 1151 HPELS Bldg., Mobile, AL 36688.

Head Coach: Steve Kittrell. **Assistant Coaches:** Ron Pelletier, Ronnie Powell. **Telephone:** (334) 460-6876. ■ **Baseball SID:** Matt Smith. **Telephone:** (334) 460-7035. **FAX:** (334) 460-7297.

Home Field: Eddie Stanky Field. **Seating Capacity:** 3,500. **Outfield Dimensions:** LF—330, CF—400, RF—330. **Press Box Telephone:** (334) 460-7126.

SOUTH CAROLINA Gamecocks

Conference: Southeastern (East).

Mailing Address: 1300 Rosewood Dr., Columbia, SC 29208.

Head Coach: Ray Tanner. **Assistant Coaches:** Stuart Lake, Jerry Meyers, *Jim Toman. **Telephone:** (803) 777-0116. ■ **Baseball SID:** Chris Poore. **Telephone:** (803) 777-5204. **FAX:** (803) 777-2967.

Home Field: Sarge Frye Field. **Seating Capacity:** 5,000. **Outfield Dimensions:** LF—325, CF—390, RF—320. **Press Box Telephone:** Unavailable.

SOUTH FLORIDA Bulls

Conference: Conference USA.

Mailing Address: 4202 E Fowler Ave., PED 214, Tampa, FL 33620.

Head Coach: Eddie Cardieri. **Assistant Coaches:** Russ McNickle, Bryan Peters. **Telephone:** (813) 974-2504. ■ **Baseball SID:** Fred Huff. **Telephone:** (813) 974-4087. **FAX:** (813) 974-5328.

Home Field: Red McEwen Field. **Seating Capacity:** 1,500. **Outfield Dimensions:** LF—340, CF—400, RF—340. **Press Box Telephone:** (813) 974-3604.

SOUTHEAST MISSOURI STATE Indians

Conference: Ohio Valley.

Mailing Address: One University Plaza, Cape Girardeau, MO 63701.

Head Coach: Mark Hogan. **Assistant Coaches:** Mark Lewis, Scott Southard, Jeremy Tyson. **Telephone:** (573) 651-2645. ■ **Baseball SID:** Jeff Vernetti. **Telephone:** (573) 651-2937. **FAX:** (573) 651-2810.

SOUTHEASTERN LOUISIANA Lions

Conference: Southland.

Mailing Address: SLU Station 10309, Hammond, LA 70402.

Head Coach: Greg Marten. **Assistant Coaches:** Johnny Brechtel, *Mark Gosnell. **Telephone:** (504) 549-2896. ■ **Baseball SID:** Dart Volz. **Telephone:** (504) 549-2142. **FAX:** (504) 549-3495.

SOUTHERN Jaguars

Conference: Southwestern Athletic (West).

Mailing Address: P.O. Box 9942, Baton Rouge, LA 70813.

Head Coach: Roger Cador. **Assistant Coaches:** Arnold Brathwaite, Barret

Rey. **Telephone:** (225) 771-2513. ■ **Baseball SID:** Michael Jones. **Telephone:** (225) 771-2601. **FAX:** (225) 771-2896.

SOUTHERN CALIFORNIA Trojans
Conference: Pacific-10.
Mailing Address: HER-103, Los Angeles, CA 90089.
Head Coach: Mike Gillespie. **Assistant Coaches:** Rob Klein, Andy Nieto, *John Savage. **Telephone:** (213) 740-5762. ■ **Baseball SID:** Tim Tessalone. **Telephone:** (213) 740-8480. **FAX:** (213) 740-7584.
Home Field: Dedeaux Field. **Seating Capacity:** 1,800. **Outfield Dimensions:** LF—335, CF—395, RF—335. **Press Box Telephone:** (213) 748-3449.

SOUTHERN ILLINOIS Salukis
Conference: Missouri Valley.
Mailing Address: 128 Lingle Hall, Carbondale, IL 62901.
Head Coach: Dan Callahan. **Assistant Coaches:** Dan Davis, *Ken Henderson, Carl Kochan. **Telephone:** (618) 453-2802. ■ **Baseball SID:** Charles Staniszewski. **Telephone:** (618) 453-7236. **FAX:** (618) 453-2648.
Home Field: Abe Martin Field. **Seating Capacity:** 2,000. **Outfield Dimensions:** LF—340, CF—390, RF—340. **Press Box Telephone:** (618) 453-3794.

SOUTHERN MISSISSIPPI Golden Eagles
Conference: Conference USA.
Mailing Address: P.O. Box 5017, Hattiesburg, MS 39406.
Head Coach: Corky Palmer. **Assistant Coaches:** Lane Burroughs, *Dan Wagner. **Telephone:** (601) 266-5017. ■ **Baseball SID:** Michael Williams. **Telephone:** (601) 266 4503. **FAX:** (601) 266-4507.
Home Field: Pete Taylor Park. **Seating Capacity:** 3,200. **Outfield Dimensions:** LF—340, CF—400, RF 340. **Press Box Telephone:** (601) 266-5864.

SOUTHERN UTAH Thunderbirds
Conference: Mid-Continent.
Mailing Address: 351 W Center St., Cedar City, UT 84720.
Interim Head Coach: Kurt Palmer. **Assistant Coach:** Mike Burrows. **Telephone:** (435) 586-7932. ■ **Baseball SID:** Steve Johnson. **Telephone:** (435) 586-7752. **FAX:** (435) 865-8037.

SOUTHWEST MISSOURI STATE Bears
Conference: Missouri Valley.
Mailing Address: 901 S National Ave., Springfield, MO 65804.
Head Coach: Keith Guttin. **Assistant Coaches:** *Paul Evans, Jamie Sheetz, Brent Thomas. **Telephone:** (417) 836-5242. ■ **Baseball SID:** Mark Stillwell. **Telephone:** (417) 836-5402. **FAX:** (417) 836-4868.

SOUTHWEST TEXAS STATE Bobcats
Conference: Southland.
Mailing Address: 601 University, San Marcos, TX 78666.
Head Coach: Ty Harrington. **Assistant Coach:** Marcus Hendry. **Telephone:** (512) 245-3586. ■ **Baseball SID:** Mark Leddy. **Telephone:** (512) 245-2966. **FAX:** (512) 245-2967.

STANFORD Cardinal
Conference: Pacific-10.
Mailing Address: Arrillaga Family Sports Center, Stanford, CA 94305.
Head Coach: Mark Marquess. **Assistant Coaches:** Tom Konls, Mark O'Brien, *Dean Stotz. **Telephone:** (650) 723-4528. ■ **Baseball SID:** Kyle McRae. **Telephone:** (650) 725-2959. **FAX:** (650) 725-2957.
Home Field: Sunken Diamond. **Seating Capacity:** 4,000. **Outfield Dimensions:** LF—335, CF—400, RF—335. **Press Box Telephone:** (650) 723-4629.

STETSON Hatters
Conference: Trans America Athletic.
Mailing Address: 421 N Woodland Blvd., Unit 8359, DeLand, FL 32720.
Head Coach: Pete Dunn. **Assistant Coaches:** Derek Johnson, Larry Jones, *Tom Riginos. **Telephone:** (904) 822-8106. ■ **Baseball SID:** Cris Belvin. **Telephone:** (904) 822-8131. **FAX:** (904) 822-8132.
Home Field: Conrad Park. **Seating Capacity:** 2,500. **Outfield Dimensions:** LF—335, CF—400, RF—335. **Press Box Telephone:** (904) 736-7360.

STONY BROOK Seawolves
Conference: Independent.
Mailing Address: USB Sports Complex, Stony Brook, NY 11794.
Head Coach: Matt Senk. **Assistant Coaches:** Kevin O'Reilly, Gerry Sputo. **Telephone:** (631) 632-9226. ■ **Baseball SID:** Tim Szlosek. **Telephone:** (631) 632-7125. **FAX:** (631) 632-8841.

TEMPLE Owls
Conference: Atlantic-10 (East).
Mailing Address: Vivacqua Hall, P.O. Box 2842, Philadelphia, PA 19122.
Head Coach: Skip Wilson. **Assistant Coaches:** Scott Lewis, Ed Ross, Steve Young. **Telephone:** (215) 204-7447. ■ **Baseball SID:** Jon Fuller. **Telephone:** (215) 204-7445. **FAX:** (215) 204-7499.

TENNESSEE Volunteers

Conference: Southeastern (East).

Mailing Address: P.O. Box 15016, Knoxville, TN 37901.

Head Coach: Rod Delmonico. **Assistant Coaches:** *Randy Mazey, Larry Simcox. **Telephone:** (865) 974-2057. ■ **Baseball SID:** Jeff Muir. **Telephone:** (865) 974-1212. **FAX:** (865) 974-1269.

Home Field: Lindsey Nelson Stadium. **Seating Capacity:** 4,500. **Outfield Dimensions:** LF—335, CF—404, RF—330. **Press Box Telephone:** (865) 974-3376.

TENNESSEE-MARTIN Skyhawks

Conference: Ohio Valley.

Mailing Address: 1037 Elam Center, Martin, TN 38238.

Head Coach: Victor "Bubba" Cates. **Assistant Coach:** David Hogue. **Telephone:** (901) 587-7337. ■ **Baseball SID:** Lee Wilmot. **Telephone:** (901) 587-7632. **FAX:** (901) 587-7962.

TENNESSEE TECH Golden Eagles

Conference: Ohio Valley.

Mailing Address: P.O. Box 5057, Cookeville, TN 38505.

Head Coach: Mike Maack. **Assistant Coaches:** Mike Anderson, *Donley Canary, Brent Chaffin. **Telephone:** (931) 372-3925. ■ **Baseball SID:** Buddy Pearson. **Telephone:** (931) 372-3293. **FAX:** (931) 372-6139.

TEXAS Longhorns

Conference: Big 12.

Mailing Address: P.O. Box 7399, Austin, TX 78713.

Head Coach: Augie Garrido. **Assistant Coaches:** Frank Anderson, *Tommy Harmon, Rob Penders. **Telephone:** (512) 471-5732. ■ **Baseball SID:** Mike Forcucci. **Telephone:** (512) 471-6039. **FAX:** (512) 471-6040.

Home Field: Disch-Falk Field. **Seating Capacity:** 6,649. **Outfield Dimensions:** LF—340, CF—400, RF—325. **Press Box Telephone:** (512) 471-1146.

TEXAS-ARLINGTON Mavericks

Conference: Southland.

Mailing Address: P.O. Box 19079, Arlington, TX 76019.

Head Coach: Clay Gould. **Assistant Coaches:** Tony Conkle, *Jeff Curtis. **Telephone:** (817) 272-5709. ■ **Baseball SID:** Steve Weller. **Telephone:** (817) 272-2542. **FAX:** (817) 272-5037

Home Field: Allan Saxe Stadium. **Seating Capacity:** 1,200. **Outfield Dimensions:** LF—330, CF—400, RF—330. **Press Box Telephone:** (817) 460-3522.

TEXAS-PAN AMERICAN Broncs

Conference: Independent.

Mailing Address: 1201 W University Dr., Edinburg, TX 78539.

Head Coach: Reggi Tredaway. **Assistant Coaches:** *Mike Brown, Johnny Johnson. **Telephone:** (956) 381-2225. ■ **Baseball SID:** Rusty Whittemore. **Telephone:** (956) 381-2240. **FAX:** (956) 381-2398.

TEXAS-SAN ANTONIO Roadrunners

Conference: Southland.

Mailing Address: 6900 NW Loop 1604, San Antonio, TX 78249.

Head Coach: Mickey Lashley. **Assistant Coaches:** Kevin Brooks, Chip Durham, Preston Rogers. **Telephone:** (210) 458-4805. ■ **Baseball SID:** Rick Nixon. **Telephone:** (210) 458-4551. **FAX:** (210) 458-4569.

TEXAS A&M Aggies

Conference: Big 12.

Mailing Address: Athletic Dept., P.O. Box 30017, College Station, TX 77842.

Head Coach: Mark Johnson. **Assistant Coaches:** David Coleman, *Jim Lawler. **Telephone:** (409) 845-1991. ■ **Baseball SID:** Chuck Glenewinkel. **Telephone:** (409) 845-4810. **FAX:** (409) 862-1618.

Home Field: Olsen Field. **Seating Capacity:** 7,600. **Outfield Dimensions:** LF—330, CF—400, RF—330. **Press Box Telephone:** (409) 845-4810.

TEXAS CHRISTIAN Horned Frogs

Conference: Western Athletic.

Mailing Address: TCU Box 297600, Fort Worth, TX 76129.

Head Coach: Lance Brown. **Assistant Coaches:** Barry Takahashi, *Donnie Watson. **Telephone:** (817) 257-7985. ■ **Baseball SID:** Trey Carmichael. **Telephone:** (817) 257-7969. **FAX:** (817) 257-7964.

Home Field: TCU Diamond. **Seating Capacity:** 1,500. **Outfield Dimensions:** LF—330, CF—390, RF—320. **Press Box Telephone:** (817) 257-7966.

TEXAS SOUTHERN Tigers

Conference: Southwestern Athletic (West).

Mailing Address: 3100 Cleburne Ave., Houston, TX 77004.

Head Coach: Candy Robinson. **Assistant Coaches:** Arthur Jenkins, Ken Mack, *Brian White. **Telephone:** (713) 313-7993. ■ **Baseball SID:** William McCoy. **Telephone:** (713) 313-7270. **FAX:** (713) 313-1045.

TEXAS TECH Red Raiders

Conference: Big 12.

Mailing Address: P.O. Box 43021, Lubbock, TX 79409.

Head Coach: Larry Hays. **Assistant Coaches:** *Greg Evans, Daren Hays, Britt Smith. **Telephone:** (806) 742-3355. ■ **Baseball SID:** Greg Greenwell. **Telephone:** (806) 742-2770. **FAX:** (806) 742-1970.

Home Field: Dan Law Field. **Seating Capacity:** 5,614. **Outfield Dimensions:** LF—330, CF—405, RF—330. **Press Box Telephone:** (806) 742-3688.

TOLEDO Rockets

Conference: Mid-American (West).

Mailing Address: 2801 W Bancroft St., Toledo, OH 43606.

Head Coach: Joe Kruzel. **Assistant Coaches:** *Joe Kruzel, Steve Parrill. **Telephone:** (419) 530-2526. ■ **Baseball SID:** Paul Helgren. **Telephone:** (419) 530-3790. **FAX:** (419) 530-3795.

TOWSON Tigers

Conference: America East.

Mailing Address: 8000 York Rd., Towson, MD 21252.

Head Coach: Mike Gottlieb. **Assistant Coaches:** Peter Buck, Joe Palmer, Dusty Reynolds. **Telephone:** (410) 830-3775. ■ **Baseball SID:** Dan O'Connell. **Telephone:** (410) 830-2232. **FAX:** (410) 830-3861.

TROY STATE Trojans

Conference: Trans America Athletic.

Mailing Address: Davis Field House, Troy, AL 36082.

Head Coach: John Mayotte. **Assistant Coaches:** Jerry Martinez, *Rod McWhorter. **Telephone:** (334) 670-3489. ■ **Baseball SID:** Erick Pennington. **Telephone:** (334) 670-3605. **FAX:** (334) 670 3724.

TULANE Green Wave

Conference: Conference USA.

Mailing Address: Wilson Center, Ben Weiner Dr., New Orleans, LA 70118.

Head Coach: Rick Jones. **Assistant Coaches:** Buddy Gouldsmith, *Jim Schlossnagle. **Telephone:** (504) 862-8239. ■ **Baseball SID:** Krisden Wunsch. **Telephone:** (504) 865-5506. **FAX:** (504) 865-5512.

Home Field: Turchin Stadium. **Seating Capacity:** 5,000. **Outfield Dimensions:** LF—325, CF—400, RF—325. **Press Box Telephone:** (504) 862-8224/8226.

UTAH Utes

Conference: Mountain West.

Mailing Address: 1825 E. South Campus, Salt Lake City, UT 84112.

Head Coach: Tim Esmay. **Assistant Coaches:** Todd Delnoce, John Flores. **Telephone:** (801) 581-3526. ■ **Baseball SID:** Whitney Vernieuw. **Telephone:** (801) 581-3511. **FAX:** (801) 581-4358.

Home Field: Franklin Covey Field. **Seating Capacity:** 12,000. **Outfield Dimensions:** LF—345, CF—420, RF—315. **Press Box Telephone:** (801) 464-0008.

VALPARAISO Crusaders

Conference: Mid-Continent.

Mailing Address: Athletic Recreation Center, Valparaiso, IN 46383.

Head Coach: Paul Twenge. **Assistant Coach:** John Oloon. **Telephone:** (219) 464-5239. ■ **Baseball SID:** Bill Rogers. **Telephone:** (219) 464-5232. **FAX:** (219) 464-5762.

VANDERBILT Commodores

Conference: Southeastern (East).

Mailing Address: 2601 Jess Neely Dr., Nashville, TN 37212.

Head Coach: Roy Mewbourne. **Assistant Coaches:** John Barlowe, Scott Stricklin. **Telephone:** (615) 322-4122. ■ **Baseball SID:** Kristi Strang. **Telephone:** (615) 322-4121. **FAX:** (615) 343-7064.

Home Field: McGugin Field. **Seating Capacity:** 1,000. **Outfield Dimensions:** LF—328, CF—362, RF—316. **Press Box Telephone:** (615) 320-0436.

VERMONT Catamounts

Conference: America East.

Mailing Address: 226 Patrick Gym, Burlington, VT 05405.

Head Coach: Bill Currier. **Assistant Coaches:** Keith Carter, Scott Jenkins, Len Whitehouse. **Telephone:** (802) 656-7701. ■ **Baseball SID:** Bruce Bosley. **Telephone:** (802) 656-1109. **FAX:** (802) 656-8328.

VILLANOVA Wildcats

Conference: Big East.

Mailing Address: 800 Lancaster Ave., Jake Nevin Field House, Villanova, PA 19085.

Head Coach: George Bennett. **Assistant Coaches:** Doc Kennedy, Lou Soscia. **Telephone:** (610) 519-4529. ■ **Baseball SID:** Dean Kenefick. **Telephone:** (610) 519-4120. **FAX:** (610) 519-7323.

Home Field: McGeehan Field. **Seating Capacity:** 2,000. **Outfield Dimensions:** LF—332, CF—402, RF—332. **Press Box Telephone:** None.

VIRGINIA Cavaliers

Conference: Atlantic Coast.

Mailing Address: P.O. Box 3785, Charlottesville, VA 22903.

Head Coach: Dennis Womack. **Assistant Coaches:** *Steve Heon, Steve Whitmyer. **Telephone:** (804) 982-5775. ■ **Baseball SID:** Adam Jones.

Home Field: Virginia Baseball Field. Seating Capacity: 2,300. Outfield Dimensions: LF—352, CF—408, RF—352. Press Box Telephone: (804) 295-9262.

VIRGINIA COMMONWEALTH Rams

Conference: Colonial Athletic.

Mailing Address: 819 W. Franklin St., Richmond, VA 23284.

Head Coach: Paul Keyes. Assistant Coaches: Chris Finwood, Hank Kraft. Telephone: (804) 828-4820. ■ Baseball SID: Mike May. Telephone: (804) 828-7000. FAX: (804) 828-9428.

VIRGINIA MILITARY INSTITUTE Keydets

Conference: Southern.

Mailing Address: VMI Baseball Office, Lexington, VA 24450.

Head Coach: Scott Gines. Assistant Coaches: Bubba Dorman, *Jeff Kinne. Telephone: (540) 464-7605. ■ Baseball SID: Wade Franner. Telephone: (540) 464-7514. FAX: (540) 464-7583.

VIRGINIA TECH Hokies

Conference: Atlantic-10 (West).

Mailing Address: 364 Jamerson Center, Blacksburg, VA 24061.

Head Coach: Chuck Hartman. Assistant Coaches: Jon Hartness, *Jay Phillips. Telephone: (540) 231-3671. ■ Baseball SID: Dave Smith. Telephone: (540) 231-6726. FAX: (540) 231-6984.

WAGNER Seahawks

Conference: Northeast.

Mailing Address: One Campus Road, Staten Island, NY 10301.

Head Coach: Joe Litterio. Assistant Coaches: Jim Agnello, Joe Aragona. Telephone: (718) 390-3154. ■ Baseball SID: Ben Shove. Telephone: (718) 390-3215. FAX: (718) 390-3347.

WAKE FOREST Demon Deacons

Conference: Atlantic Coast.

Mailing Address: P.O. Box 7426, Winston-Salem, NC 27109.

Head Coach: George Greer. Assistant Coaches: *Bobby Moranda, Mike Rikard. Telephone: (336) 758-5570. ■ Baseball SID: Chris Capo. Telephone: (336) 758-5640. FAX: (336) 758-5140.

Home Field: Hooks Stadium. Seating Capacity: 2,500. Outfield Dimensions: LF—340, CF—400, RF—315. Press Box Telephone: (336) 759-9711.

WASHINGTON Huskies

Conference: Pacific-10.

Mailing Address: Graves Bldg., Box 354070, Seattle, WA 98195.

Head Coach: Ken Knutson. Assistant Coaches: Ed Gustafson, *Joe Ross, Joe Weis. Telephone: (206) 543-9365. ■ Baseball SID: Jeff Bechthold. Telephone: (206) 543-2230. FAX: (206) 543-5000.

Home Field: Husky Ballpark. Seating Capacity: 2,000. Outfield Dimensions: LF—327, CF—395, RF—317. Press Box Telephone: (206) 685-1994.

WASHINGTON STATE Cougars

Conference: Pacific-10.

Mailing Address: P.O. Box 641602, Pullman, WA 99164.

Head Coach: Steve Farrington. Assistant Coaches: *Ken Johnson, Russ Swan, Ray Walker. Telephone: (509) 335-0211. ■ Baseball SID: Jeff Evans. Telephone: (509) 335-2684. FAX: (509) 335-0267.

Home Field: Buck Bailey/Bobo Brayton Field. Seating Capacity: 3,500. Outfield Dimensions: LF—330, CF—400, RF—335. Press Box Telephone: (509) 335-2684.

WEST VIRGINIA Mountaineers

Conference: Big East.

Mailing Address: P.O. Box 0877, Morgantown, WV 26507.

Head Coach: Greg Van Zant. Assistant Coaches: *Bruce Cameron, Mike Hampton, Joe McNamee. Telephone: (304) 293-2308. ■ Baseball SID: John Antonik. Telephone: (304) 293-2821. FAX: (304) 293-4105.

Home Field: Hawley Field. Seating Capacity: 1,500. Outfield Dimensions: LF—325, CF—390, RF—325. Press Box Telephone: (304) 293-5988.

WESTERN CAROLINA Catamounts

Conference: Southern.

Mailing Address: Ramsey Center, Cullowhee, NC 28723.

Head Coach: Todd Raleigh. Assistant Coaches: Kevin Ellis, *Hank Kraft, Jeff Sziksai. Telephone: (828) 227-2021. ■ Baseball SID: Jody Jones. Telephone: (828) 227-7171. FAX: (828) 227-7688.

Home Field: Hennon Stadium. Seating Capacity: 1,500. Outfield Dimensions: LF—325, CF—390, RF—325. Press Box Telephone: (828) 227-7020.

WESTERN ILLINOIS Leathernecks

Conference: Mid-Continent.

Mailing Address: 204 Western Hall, 1 University Circle, Macomb, IL 61455.

Head Coach: Kim Johnson. Assistant Coaches: Deon Dittmar, Dan Duffy, *Harry Torgerson. Telephone: (309) 298-1521. ■ Baseball SID: Scot Lafek. Telephone: (309) 298-1133. FAX: (309) 298-2060.

WESTERN KENTUCKY Hilltoppers

Conference: Sun Belt.
Mailing Address: One Big Red Way, Bowling Green, KY 42101.
Head Coach: Joel Murrie. **Assistant Coaches:** Clyde Keller, Dan Mosier.
Telephone: (270) 745-6023. ■ **Baseball SID:** Michael Finch. **Telephone:** (270) 745-4298. **FAX:** (270) 745-3444.

WESTERN MICHIGAN Broncos

Conference: Mid-American (West).
Mailing Address: 218 Read Field House, Kalamazoo, MI 49008.
Head Coach: Fred Decker. **Assistant Coaches:** Scott Demetral, *Ken Jones.
Telephone: (616) 387-8149. ■ **Baseball SID:** Geoff Brown. **Telephone:** (616) 387-4123. **FAX:** (616) 387-4139.
Home Field: Hyames Field. **Seating Capacity:** 4,000. **Outfield Dimensions:** LF—325, CF—390, RF—340. **Press Box Telephone:** Unavailable.

WICHITA STATE Shockers

Conference: Missouri Valley.
Mailing Address: 1845 Fairmount St., Campus Box 18, Wichita, KS 67260.
Head Coach: Gene Stephenson. **Assistant Coaches:** *Brent Kemnitz, Jim Thomas. **Telephone:** (316) 978-3636. ■ **Baseball SID:** Darren Nelson. **Telephone:** (316) 978-3265. **FAX:** (316) 978-3336.
Home Field: Tyler Field-Eck Stadium. **Seating Capacity:** 7,808. **Outfield Dimensions:** LF—330, CF—390, RF—330. **Press Box Telephone:** (316) 978-3390.

WILLIAM & MARY Tribe

Conference: Colonial Athletic.
Mailing Address: P.O. Box 399, Williamsburg, VA 23187.
Head Coach: Jim Farr. **Assistant Coaches:** *Marlin Ikenberry, Ryan Wheeler.
Telephone: (757) 221-3399. ■ **Baseball SID:** Phil Hess. **Telephone:** (757) 221-3368. **FAX:** (757) 221-3412.

WINTHROP Eagles

Conference: Big South.
Mailing Address: Winthrop Coliseum, Rock Hill, SC 29733.
Head Coach: Joe Hudak. **Assistant Coaches:** *Mike McGuire, Jason Murray, Tim Perry. **Telephone:** (803) 323-2129, ext. 6235. ■ **Baseball SID:** Brett Redden. **Telephone:** (803) 323-2129, ext. 6248. **FAX:** (803) 323-2433.

WISCONSIN-MILWAUKEE Panthers

Conference: Midwestern Collegiate.
Mailing Address: P.O. Box 413, Milwaukee, WI 53201.
Head Coach: Jerry Augustine. **Assistant Coaches:** *Scott Doffek, Todd Frohwirth. **Telephone:** (414) 229-5670. ■ **Baseball SID:** Chad Krueger. **Telephone:** (414) 229-4593. **FAX:** (414) 229-6759.

WOFFORD Terriers

Conference: Southern.
Mailing Address: 429 N Church St., Spartanburg, SC 29303.
Head Coach: Steve Traylor. **Assistant Coaches:** Spencer Graham, Scott Jackson. **Telephone:** (864) 597-4126. ■ **Baseball SID:** Bill English. **Telephone:** (864) 597-4093. **FAX:** (864) 597-4129.

WRIGHT STATE Raiders

Conference: Midwestern Collegiate.
Mailing Address: 3640 Colonel Glenn Highway, Dayton, OH 45435.
Head Coach: Ron Nischwitz. **Assistant Coaches:** Dan Bassler, Bo Bilinski.
Telephone: (937) 775-2771. ■ **Baseball SID:** Shawn Adkins. **Telephone:** (937) 775-3666. **FAX:** (937) 775-2818.

XAVIER Musketeers

Conference: Atlantic-10 (West).
Mailing Address: 3800 Victory Pkwy., Cincinnati, OH 45207.
Head Coach: John Morrey. **Assistant Coaches:** Clint Albert, *Joe Regruth.
Telephone: (513) 745-2890. ■ **Baseball SID:** Amber Scott. **Telephone:** (513) 745-2058. **FAX:** (513) 745-2825.

YALE Bulldogs

Conference: Ivy League (Rolfe).
Mailing Address: P.O. Box 208216, New Haven, CT 06520.
Head Coach: John Stuper. **Assistant Coaches:** Dick Jeynes, Dan Scarpa.
Telephone: (203) 432-1466. ■ **Baseball SID:** Rebecka McKinney. **Telephone:** (203) 432-1448. **FAX:** (203) 432-1454.

YOUNGSTOWN STATE Penguins

Conference: Mid-Continent.
Mailing Address: One University Plaza, Youngstown, OH 44555.
Head Coach: Mike Florak. **Assistant Coaches:** *Dan Stricko, Dennis Vince.
Telephone: (330) 742-3485. ■ **Baseball SID:** Rocco Gasparro. **Telephone:** (330) 742-3192. **FAX:** (330) 742-3191.

AMATEUR BASEBALL

INTERNATIONAL

INTERNATIONAL OLYMPIC COMMITTEE
Mailing Address: Chateau de Vidy, 1007 Lausanne, Switzerland.
Telephone: 41-21-621-61-11. **FAX:** 41-21-621-62-16. **Website:** www.olympic.org.
President: Juan Antonio Samaranch. **Director, Communications:** Franklin Servan-Schreiber.

SYDNEY OLYMPIC ORGANIZING COMMITTEE
Street Address: 235 Jones St., Ultimo, New South Wales 2007, Australia. **Mailing Address:** GPO Box 2000, Sydney, New South Wales 2001, Australia. **Telephone:** (61-2) 9297-2000. **FAX:** (61-2) 9297-2020. **Website:** www.sydney.olympic.com.
President: Michael Knight. **Chief Executive Officer:** Sandy Hollway. **General Manager, Media:** Milton Cockburn.
Games of the XXVII Olympiad: Sept. 15-Oct. 1, 2000.

U.S. OLYMPIC COMMITTEE
Mailing Address: One Olympic Plaza, Colorado Springs, CO 80909. **Telephone:** (719) 632-5551. **FAX:** (719) 578-4654.
President: William Hybl. **Executive Director:** Dick Schultz. **Assistant Executive Director, Media/Public Affairs:** Mike Moran.
Games of the XXVII Olympiad: Sept. 15-Oct. 1, 2000, at Sydney, Australia.

GOODWILL GAMES INC.
Office Address: One CNN Center, South Tower, 12th Floor, Atlanta, GA 30348. **Mailing Address:** P.O. Box 10558, Atlanta, GA 30348. **Telephone:** (404) 827-3400. **FAX:** (404) 827-1394.
President: Mike Plant. **Vice President, Sports:** David Raith. **Director, Public Relations:** Jeff Pomeroy.
Goodwill Games, 2001: Dates unavailable, Brisbane, Australia.

INTERNATIONAL BASEBALL FEDERATION
Mailing Address: Avenue de Mon-Repos 24, Case Postale 131, 1000 Lausanne 5, Switzerland. **Telephone:** (41-21) 3188240. **FAX:** (41-21) 3188241. **E-Mail Address:** ibaf@baseball.ch. **Website:** www.baseball.ch.
President: Aldo Notari (Italy). **Secretary General:** John Ostermeyer (Australia). **Executive Director:** Miquel Ortin.

2000 Events
XI World Children's Baseball Fair	Regina, Saskatchewan, Aug. 1-7
XIX AAA World Championship	Edmonton, Alberta, Aug. 3-14
Games of the XXVII Olympiad	Sydney, Australia, Sept. 17-27

INTERNATIONAL SPORTS GROUP
Mailing Address: 142 Shadowood Dr., Pleasant Hill, CA 94523. **Telephone:** (925) 798-4591. **FAX:** (925) 680-1182. **E-Mail Address:** ISGbaseball@aol.com. **Website:** www.intlbaseball.org.
President: Bill Arce. **Secretary/Treasurer:** Jim Jones.

UNIVERSAL BASEBALL
Mailing Address: 2620 Whitehorse-Hamilton Square Rd., Suite 1, Hamilton Square, NJ 08690. **Telephone:** (609) 631-9338. **FAX:** (609) 631-9299. **E-Mail Address:** caseevents@aol.com.
President: Edward O'Mara. **Consultant:** Dick Case.

NATIONAL

USA BASEBALL
Mailing Address, Corporate Headquarters: Hi Corbett Field, 3400 E Camino Campestre, Tucson, AZ 85716. **Telephone:** (520) 327-9700. **FAX:** (520) 327-9221. **E-Mail Address:** usabasebal@aol.com. **Website:** www.usabaseball.com.
Chairman: Cliff Lothery. **President:** Neil Lantz. **Executive Vice President:** Tom Hicks. **Secretary:** Pam Marshall. **Treasurer:** Gale Montgomery. **Executive Officer:** Lindsay Burbage.
Executive Director/Chief Executive Officer: Paul Seiler. **Senior Advisor, National Teams:** Jerry Kindall. **Director, National Teams:** Steve Cohen. **Associate Director, National Teams:** Eric Campbell. **Director, Communications:** Dave Fanucchi. **Associate Directors, Business**

Development: Ray Darwin, David Perkins. **Director, Finance:** Miki Partridge.

National Members: Amateur Athletic Union, American Amateur Baseball Congress, American Baseball Coaches Association, American Legion Baseball, Babe Ruth Baseball, Dixie Baseball, Little League Baseball, National Amateur Baseball Federation, National Association of Intercollegiate Athletics, National Baseball Congress, National Collegiate Athletic Association, National Federation of State High School Athletic Associations, National High School Baseball Coaches Association, National Junior College Athletic Association, Police Athletic League, PONY Baseball, YMCAs of the USA.

2000 Events
Team USA—Professional Level
XXVII Olympic Games .... Sydney, Australia, Sept. 15-Oct. 1

Team USA—Collegiate Level
Team Training Camp... Tucson, AZ, June
Team USA-Japan Exhibition Series................. United States, June-July
USA Red/White/Blue Tour .... United States, July-August

Team USA—Junior Level (18 and under)
Junior National Team Trials .... Tucson, AZ, April
COPABE Junior Pan Am Games .... Veracruz, Mexico, April
USA Junior National Team Trials .... Joplin, MO, July 13-22
IBA World Junior Championship ....Edmonton, Alberta, Aug. 3-14

Team USA—Youth Level (16 and under)
Junior Olympic Championships .... Tucson, AZ, June 16-24
COPABE World Junior Qualifier .... Aruba, July-August

Other Events
U.S. Women's National Championship .... Tucson, AZ, October

AMERICAN BASEBALL FOUNDATION
Mailing Address: 1313 13th St. S, Birmingham, AL 35205. **Telephone:** (205) 558-4235. **FAX:** (205) 918-0800. **E-Mail Address:** ed.ibf5@juno.com.
Executive Director: David Osinski.

BASEBALL CANADA
Mailing Address: 1600 James Naismith Dr., Suite 208, Gloucester, Ontario K1B 5N4. **Telephone:** (613) 748-5606. **FAX:** (613) 748-5767. **E-Mail Address:** info@baseball.ca. **Website:** www.baseball.ca.
Director General: Duncan Grant. **Head Coach:** Greg Hamilton.
Baseball Canada Cup (17 and under): Aug. 24-28, Stonewall, Manitoba.

NATIONAL BASEBALL CONGRESS
Mailing Address: P.O. Box 1420, Wichita, KS 67201. **Telephone:** (316) 267-3372. **FAX:** (316) 267-3382.
Year Founded: 1931.
President: Robert Rich Jr.
Vice President: Steve Shaad. **General Manager/Tournament Director:** Derik Dukes. **Tournament Coordinator:** Stephen Adler. **Stadium Manager:** Kevin Grimsley. **Director, Marketing:** Kyle Richardson.
2000 NBC World Series (non-professional, ex-professional): July 29-Aug. 12, Lawrence Dumont Stadium, Wichita, KS.

ATHLETES IN ACTION
Mailing Address: 3802 Ehrlich Rd., Suite 110, Tampa, FL 33624. **Telephone:** (813) 968-7400. **FAX:** (813) 968-7515. **E-Mail Address:** aiatampa@gate.net. **Website:** www.gate.net/~aiatampa.
Staff: Todd Johnson, Jason Lester, Scott Shepherd.

SUMMERCOLLEGELEAGUES

NATIONAL ALLIANCE OF
COLLEGIATE SUMMER BASEBALL

Mailing Address: 6 Indian Trail, South Harwich, MA 02661. **Telephone:** (508) 432-1774. **FAX:** (508) 432-9766.

Executive Director: Fred Ebbett. **Assistant Executive Director:** Tom Hunton. **Secretary:** Buzzy Levin.

NCAA Sanctioned Leagues: Atlantic Collegiate League, Cape Cod League, Central Illinois Collegiate League, Great Lakes League, New England Collegiate League, Northeastern League, Northwest Collegiate League, Shenandoah Valley League.

ALASKA BASEBALL LEAGUE

Mailing Address: 601 S Main St., Kenai, AK 99611. **Telephone:** (907) 283-7133. **FAX:** (907) 283-3390.

Year Founded: 1974 (reunited, 1998).

President: Dennis Mattingly. **Vice President:** Stan Zaborac. **Publicity Director:** Dick Lobdell

2000 Opening Date: June 8. **Closing Date:** July 26.

Regular Season: 28 league games.

Playoff Format: None. Top two teams advance to National Baseball Congress World Series.

Roster Limit: 22, plus exemption for Alaska residents. **Player Eligibility Rule:** Players with college eligibility, except seniors drafted and unsigned in the 2000 draft.

ALASKA GOLDPANNERS

Mailing Address: P.O. Box 71154, Fairbanks, AK 99707. **Telephone/FAX:** (907) 451-0095. **E-Mail Address:** todd@goldpanners.com. **Website:** www.goldpanners.com.

President: Bill Stroecker. **General Manager:** Don Dennis. **Assistant General Manager:** Todd Dennis. **Head Coach:** Dan Cowgill (Los Angeles CC).

ANCHORAGE BUCS

Mailing Address: P.O. Box 240061, Anchorage, AK 99524. **Telephone:** (907) 561-2827. **FAX:** (907) 561-2920.

President: Eugene Furman. **Executive Director:** Brian Crawford. **General Manager:** Dennis Mattingly. **Head Coach:** John Weber (Santa Ana, Calif., JC).

ANCHORAGE GLACIER PILOTS

Mailing Address: 207 E Northern Lights Blvd., Suite 105, Anchorage, AK 99503. **Telephone:** (907) 274-3627. **FAX:** (907) 274-3628. **Website:** www.glacierpilots.com.

President: Chuck Shelton. **General Manager:** Ron Okerlund. **Head Coach:** Bob Miller (Oral Roberts U.).

HAWAII ISLAND MOVERS

Mailing Address: P.O. Box 17865, Honolulu, HI 96817. **Telephone:** (808) 832-4805. **FAX:** (808) 841-2321.

President/General Manager: Donald Takaki. **Head Coach:** Dave Nakama (San Francisco State U.).

KENAI PENINSULA OILERS

Mailing Address: 601 S Main St., Kenai, AK 99611. **Telephone:** (907) 283-7133. **FAX:** (907) 283-3390. **Website:** www.kenai.net/penoilbb.

President: John Lohrke. **General Manager:** Mike Baxter. **Head Coach:** Gary Adcock (Purdue U.).

MAT-SU MINERS

Mailing Address: P.O. Box 1633, Palmer, AK 99645. **Telephone:** (907) 745-6401. **FAX:** (907) 745-7275.

President: Bill Bartholomew. **General Manager:** Stan Zaborac. **Head Coach:** Robert Meyers (El Camino, Calif., JC).

ATLANTIC COLLEGIATE LEAGUE

Mailing Address: 401 Timber Dr., Berkeley Heights, NJ 07922. **Telephone/FAX:** (908) 464-8042. **E-Mail Address:** acbl@vs-inc.com. **Website:** www.atlanticcbl.org.

Year Founded: 1967.

President: Tom Bonekemper. **Vice President:** Jerry Valonis. **Commissioner:** Robert Pertsas. **Publicity Director:** Ben Smookler.

Member Clubs: Wolff Division—Delaware Valley Gulls (Philadelphia), Jersey Pilots, Quakertown (Pa.) Blazers, Scranton (Pa.) Red Soxx. **Kaiser**

Division—Metro New York Cadets, Nassau (N.Y.) Collegians, Newburgh (N.Y.) Generals, New Jersey Colts (Lyncroft, N.J.).

2000 Opening Date: June 1. **Closing Date:** July 31.

Regular Season: 40 games.

Playoff Format: Top two teams in each division meet in best-of-3 semifinals. Winners meet in one-game championship.

Roster Limit: 23 (college-eligible players only).

CALIFORNIA COASTAL COLLEGIATE LEAGUE

Mailing Address: 4003 Coyote Cir., Clayton, CA 94517. **Telephone/FAX:** (925) 672-9662. **E-Mail Address:** tsdress@aol.com. **Website:** www.leaguelineup.com/cccl.

Year Founded: 1993.

President/Commissioner: Tony Dress. **Assistant Director, Operations:** Christine Wilson.

Member Clubs (all teams located in California): **Northern**—Fresno Barons, San Francisco Seals, San Luis Obispo Blues, Santa Barbara Foresters; **Southern**—North County Waves, San Diego Barona Stars, San Diego Express, San Diego Mavericks.

Playoff Format: Division winners meet for one-game league championship; winner advances to National Baseball Congress World Series.

2000 Opening Date: June 1. **Closing Date:** Aug. 1.

Regular Season: 48 games.

Roster Limit: 33.

CAPE COD LEAGUE

Mailing Address: 7 Nottingham Dr., Yarmouth, MA 02675. **Telephone/FAX:** (508) 996-5004. **E-Mail Address:** capecod@gbweb works.com. **Website:** www.capecodbaseball.com.

Year Founded: 1885.

Commissioner: Bob Stead. **President:** Judy Scarafile. **Deputy Commissioners:** Cathie Nichols, Howard Wayne. **Director, Public Relations:** Missy Ilg-Alaimo.

Vice Presidents: Jim Higgins, Richard Sullivan, Don Tullie.

Division Structure: East—Brewster, Chatham, Harwich, Orleans, Yarmouth-Dennis. **West**—Bourne, Cotuit, Falmouth, Hyannis, Wareham.

2000 Opening Date: June 13. **Closing Date:** Aug. 6.

Regular Season: 44 games.

All-Star Game: July 22 at Brewster.

Playoff Format: Top two teams in each division meet in best-of-3 semifinals. Winners meet in best-of-3 series for league championship.

Roster Limit: 23 (college-eligible players only).

BOURNE BRAVES

Mailing Address: P.O. Box 895, Monument Beach, MA 02553. **Telephone:** (508) 224-9312. **FAX:** (508) 224-7628. **E-Mail Address:** favac@capecod.net. **Website:** www.capecod.com/braves.

President: Cheryl Butts. **General Manager:** Randy Vacchi. **Head Coach:** Mike Rikard (Wake Forest U.).

BREWSTER WHITECAPS

Mailing Address: P.O. Box 2349, Brewster, MA 02631. **Telephone:** (781) 784-7409. **FAX:** (617) 720-7877.

President: Steve Whitehurst. **General Managers:** Phil Edwards, Sol Yas. **Head Coach:** Dave Lawn (U. of California).

CHATHAM A's

Mailing Address: P.O. Box 428, Chatham, MA 02633. **Telephone:** (508) 945-3841. **FAX:** (508) 945-9616. **E-Mail Address:** cthoms@capecod.net.

President: Paul Galop. **General Manager:** Charles Thoms. **Head Coach:** John Schiffner (Plainville, Conn., HS).

COTUIT KETTLEERS

Mailing Address: 77 Spur Lane, Marstons Mills, MA 02648. **Telephone:** (508) 428-3358. **E-Mail Address:** bmurpfcape@aol.com. **Website:** www.capecod.net/kettleers.

President: Ivan Partridge. **General Manager:** Bruce Murphy. **Head Coach:** Mike Coutts.

FALMOUTH COMMODORES

Mailing Address: 33 Wintergreen Rd., Mashpee, MA 02649. **Telephone:** (508) 477-5724. **FAX:** (508) 564-7643. **E-Mail Address:** chuckhs@mediaone.net. **Website:** www.falcommodores.org.

President: Steve Spitz. **General Manager:** Chuck Sturtevant. **Head Coach:** Jeff Trundy (The Gunnery School, Conn.).

HARWICH MARINERS

Mailing Address: 6 Concord Dr., Harwich, MA 02645. **Telephone:** (617)

236-0360. **FAX: (**508) 432-5357

General Manager: Mike DeAnzeris. **Head Coach:** Scott Lawler (North Carolina State U.).

HYANNIS METS

Mailing Address: P.O. Box 852, Hyannis, MA 02601. **Telephone:** (508) 420-0962. **FAX:** (508) 428-8199.

President: Everett Martin. **General Manager:** John Howitt. **Head Coach:** Tom O'Connell.

ORLEANS CARDINALS

Mailing Address: P.O. Box 504, Orleans, MA 02653. **Telephone/FAX:** (508) 255-2237. **Website:** www.c4.net/orleanscardinals/main.html.

President: Mark Hossfeld. **General Managers:** Margo Beaudry, Sue Horton. **Head Coach:** Don Norris (Georgia College).

WAREHAM GATEMEN

Mailing Address: 71 Towhee Rd., Wareham, MA 02571. **Telephone:** (508) 295-3956. **FAX:** (508) 295-8821. **Website:** www.gatemen.org.

President/General Manager: John Wylde. **Head Coach:** Mike Roberts (UNC Asheville).

YARMOUTH-DENNIS RED SOX

Mailing Address: 47 Farm Lane, South Dennis, MA 02660. **Telephone:** (508) 394-9466. **FAX:** (508) 398-2239

General Manager: Jack Martin. **Head Coach:** Scott Pickler (Cypress, Calif., CC).

CENTRAL ILLINOIS COLLEGIATE LEAGUE

Mailing Address: 29 Logan Terrace III, Danville, IL 61832. **Telephone:** (217) 446-6074. **FAX:** (217) 443-8595. **E-Mail Address:** mebtmb19 @soltec.net. **Website:** www.ciclbaseball.com.

Year Founded: 1963.

Commissioner: Tim Bunton. **President:** Duffy Bass. **Administrative Assistants:** Joe Woods, Mike Woods.

Member Clubs (all teams located in Illinois): **East**—Danville Dans, Decatur Blues, Twin City Stars. **West**—Bluff City Bombers, Quincy Gems, Springfield Rifles.

2000 Opening Date: June 6. **Closing Date:** Aug. 4.

Regular Season: 48 games.

All-Star Game: July 14 at Quincy.

Playoff Format: Top two teams in each division meet in double-elimination tournament.

Roster Limit: 23 (college-eligible players only).

CLARK GRIFFITH COLLEGIATE LEAGUE

Mailing Address: 4917 N 30th St., Arlington, VA 22207. **Telephone/FAX:** (703) 536-1729. **E-Mail Address:** cglbaseball@aol.com. **Website:** www.clarkgriffithbaseball.org.

Year Founded: 1945.

President: John Depenbrock. **Vice President:** Frank Fannan. **Administrative Assistant:** Dennis Dwyer. **Director, Publicity:** Ben Trittipoe.

Member Clubs: Arlington (Va.) Senators, Bethesda (Md.) Big Train, Reston (Va.) Hawks, Southern Maryland Battlecats, Vienna (Va.) Mustangs.

2000 Opening Date: June 2. **Closing Date:** Aug. 4.

Regular Season: 40 games (split schedule).

Playoff Format: Top four teams meet in best-of-3 semifinals. Winners meet in best-of-3 series for league championship.

Roster Limit: 27 (players 20 and under).

COASTAL PLAIN LEAGUE

Mailing Address: 4900 Waters Edge Dr., Suite 201, Raleigh, NC 27606. **Telephone:** (919) 852-1960. **FAX:** (919) 852-1973. **Website:** www. coastalplain.com.

Year Founded: 1997.

Chairman/Chief Executive Officer: Jerry Potitt. **President:** Pete Bock. **Director, Operations:** Mark Cryan. **Director, Administration:** Jay Snead. **Administrative Assistant:** Camille Cholerton.

2000 Opening Date: June 1. **Closing Date:** Aug. 9.

Regular Season: 50 games (split schedule).

All-Star Game: July 11 at Wilson.

Playoff Format: First-half winner meets second-half winner in best-of-3 series for league championship.

Roster Limit: 20 (college-eligible players only).

ASHEBORO COPPERHEADS

Mailing Address: P.O. Box 4425, Asheboro, NC 27204. **Telephone:**

(336) 636-5796. **FAX:** (336) 636-5400. **E-Mail Address:** baseball@ashe
boro.com.

President/General Manager: Pat Brown. **Head Coach:** Bill Hillier Jr.
(Duke U.).

DURHAM BRAVES

Mailing Address: P.O. Box 126, Durham, NC 27704. **Telephone/FAX:**
(919) 956-9555.

President: Jim Nelson. **Head Coach:** Josh Sorge (Georgia Tech).

EDENTON STEAMERS

Mailing Address: P.O. Box 86, Edenton, NC 27932. **Telephone:** (252)
482-4080. **FAX:** (252) 482-2337.

General Manager: Tom Howe. **Head Coach:** Stuart Lake (U. of South
Carolina).

FLORENCE REDWOLVES

Mailing Address: P.O. Box 809, Florence, SC 29503. **Telephone:** (843)
629-0700. **FAX:** (843) 629-0703.

General Manager: Bob Flanagan. **Head Coach:** Spencer Graham
(Wofford U.).

OUTER BANKS DAREDEVILS

Mailing Address: P.O. Box 1747, Nags Head, NC 27959. **Telephone:**
(252) 441-4889. **FAX:** (252) 441-3722.

President: Warren Spivey. **Head Coach:** Roger Williams (U. of North
Carolina).

PENINSULA PILOTS

Mailing Address: 1889 W Pembroke Ave., Hampton, VA 23661.
Telephone: (757) 291-1414.

General Manager: Scott Baker. **Head Coach:** Gregg Mucerino (The
Citadel).

PETERSBURG GENERALS

Mailing Address: 1981 Midway Ave., Petersburg, VA 23803.
Telephone: (804) 733-2411. **FAX:** (804) 862-4832.

General Manager: Larry Toombs. **Head Coach:** Aaron Carroll (Chowan,
N.C., College).

THOMASVILLE HI-TOMS

Mailing Address: P.O. Box 3035, Thomasville, NC 27360. **Telephone:**
(336) 476-8667. **FAX:** (336) 472-7198.

General Manager: Mike Jermain. **Head Coach:** Mike Anderson
(Tennessee Tech).

WILMINGTON SHARKS

Mailing Address: P.O. Box 15233, Wilmington, NC 28412. **Telephone:**
(910) 343-5621. **FAX:** (910) 343-8932. **E-Mail Address:** curt@wilmington
sharks.com. **Website:** www.wilmingtonsharks.com.

General Manager: Curt VanDerzee. **Head Coach:** Scott Forbes (U. of
North Carolina).

WILSON TOBS

Mailing Address: P.O. Box 633, Wilson, NC 27894. **Telephone:** (252)
291-8627. **FAX:** (252) 291-1224. **E-Mail Address:** tobs@bbnp.com.
Website: www.tobs.bbnp.com.

General Manager: Chris Allen. **Head Coach:** Jeff Bock (Campbell U.).

EASTERN COLLEGIATE BASEBALL LEAGUE

Mailing Address: 2712 Division St., Easton, PA 18045. **Telephone/FAX:**
(610) 250-7692. **E-Mail Address:** patrick.oconnell6@gte.net.

Year Founded: 2000.

President: Pat O'Connell. **Commissioner:** Howie Bedell. **Vice
President:** Ron Lehr. **Publicity Directors:** Chuck Ciganick, Dick Leidich.

Member Clubs: Delaware River Rapids (Easton, PA), Lancaster County
(Lancaster, PA), Monmouth Hurricanes (Freehold, NJ), Pennsylvanians
(Central, PA).

2000 Opening Date: June 1. **Closing Date:** Aug. 15.

Regular Season: 40 games (split schedule).

All-Star Game: July 14 at Easton.

Playoff Format: First-half champion and second-half champion meet in
best-of-3 series for league championship.

Roster Limit: 23 (college-eligible players only).

GREAT LAKES LEAGUE

Mailing Address: P.O. Box 451, Seville, OH 44273. **Telephone:** (330)
335-6184. **FAX:** (330) 335-8174. **E-Mail Address:** glscl@worldnet.att.net.
Website: www.greatlakesbaseball.home.dhs.org.

Year Founded: 1986.
President: Barry Ruben. Commissioner: Brian Sullivan. Vice President: Rob Piscetta.
Member Clubs: East—Northern Ohio Baseball (Strongville, OH), Sandusky (Ohio) Bay Stars, Stark County Terriers (Canton, OH), Youngstown (Ohio) Express. Central—Columbus (Ohio) All-Americans, Delaware (Ohio) Cows, Grand Lake Mariners (Celina, OH), Lima (Ohio) Locos. West—Lake Erie Monarchs (Carleton, MI), Michigan Panthers (Ypsilanti, MI), Motor City Marauders (Livonia, MI), Summit City Sluggers (Fort Wayne, IN).
2000 Opening Date: June 9. Closing Date: July 29.
Regular Season: 44 games.
All-Star Game: July 30 at Strongville, OH.
Playoff Format: Three division champions and wild-card team meet in best-of-3 semifinals. Winners meet in best-of-3 final for league championship.
Roster Limit: 25 (college-eligible players only).

JAYHAWK LEAGUE

Mailing Address: 5 Adams Pl., Halstead, KS 67056. Telephone/FAX: (316) 755-1285.
Year Founded: 1976.
Commissioner: Bob Considine. President: Don Carlile. Vice President: Laverne Shumacher. Director, Public Relations: Pat Chambers.
2000 Opening Date: June 8. Closing Date: July 18.
Regular Season: 40 games.
Playoff Format: League champion advances to National Baseball Congress World Series
Roster Limit: 25.

EL DORADO BRONCOS
Mailing Address: 865 Fabrique, Wichita, KS 67218. Telephone: (316) 687-2309. FAX: (316) 942-2009. Website: www.eldoradobroncos.com.
President: Jack Howard. General Manager: J.D. Schneider.

ELKHART DUSTERS
Mailing Address: P.O. Box 793, Elkhart, KS 67950. Telephone: (316) 697-2095.
General Manager: Brian Elson.

HAYS LARKS
Mailing Address: 2706 Thunderbird Dr., Hays, KS 67601. Telephone: (785) 625-2137. General Manager: Laverne Shumacher.

LIBERAL BEEJAYS
Mailing Address: P.O. Box 352, Liberal, KS 67901. Telephone: (316) 624-1904.
General Manager: Kim Snell.

NEVADA GRIFFONS
Mailing Address: P.O. Box 601, Nevada, MO 64772. Telephone: (417) 667-8308. FAX: (417) 667-9797.
President: Jack McDonald. General Manager: Pat Chambers.

TOPEKA CAPITOLS
Mailing Address: 2005 SW Sims, Topeka, KS 66604. Telephone: (785) 234-5881.
General Manager: Don Carlile.

NEW ENGLAND COLLEGIATE LEAGUE

Mailing Address: P.O. Box 415, Jamestown, RI 02835. Telephone: (401) 423-9863. FAX: (401) 423-2784. E-Mail Address: thutton@ix.net com.com. Website: www.necbl.org.
Year Founded: 1993.
Commissioner: Thomas Hutton. President: Fay Vincent. Deputy Commissioner: Rich Reimold. Secretary: Rich Rossiter.
Member Clubs: Danbury (Conn.) Westerners, Eastern Tides (Willimantic, CT), Keene (N.H.) Swamp Bats, Manchester (Conn.) Silkworms, Middletown (Conn.) Giants, Mill City All-Americans (Lowell, MA), Rhode Island Gulls (Cranston, RI), Torrington (Conn.) Twisters.
2000 Opening Date: June 4. Closing Date: Aug. 1.
Regular Season: 42 games.
All-Star Game: July 29 at Keene, NH.
Playoff Format: Top four teams meet in best-of-3 series. Winners meet in best-of-5 series for league championship.
Roster Limit: 23 (college-eligible players only).

NORTHEASTERN COLLEGIATE LEAGUE

Mailing Address: 28 Dunbridge Heights, Fairport, NY 14450.

Telephone/FAX: (716) 223-3528.

Year Founded: 1986.

President: Tom Kenney. **Commissioner:** Dave Chamberlain. **Vice President:** Jeff DeLutis.

Member Clubs (all teams located in New York): **East**—Geneva Knights, Hornell Dodgers, Newark Raptors, Wellsville Nitros; **West**—Cortland Apples, Rome Indians, Schenectady Mohawks, Watertown.

2000 Opening Date: June 9. **Closing Date:** Aug. 1.

Regular Season: 42 games.

All-Star Game: July 5 at Rome.

Playoff Format: Top four teams meet in best-of-3 series. Winners meet in one-game final for league championship.

Roster Limit: 24 (college-eligible players only).

NORTHWEST COLLEGIATE BASEBALL LEAGUE

Mailing Address: 23737 SW Pinecone Ave., Sherwood, OR 97140. **Telephone:** (503) 625-4044. **FAX:** (503) 625-0629. **E-Mail Address:** raineyr@sherwood.or.us.

Year Founded: 1992.

Commissioner: Reed Rainey. **Vice President:** Rob Vance.

Member Clubs (all teams located in Oregon): Bucks, Dukes, Lobos, Ports, Stars, Toros.

Roster Limit: 20 (college-eligible players only).

NORTHWOODS LEAGUE

Office Address: 403 E Center St., Rochester, MN 55904. **Mailing Address:** P.O. Box 482, Rochester, MN 55903. **Telephone:** (507) 289-1170. **FAX:** (507) 289-1866. **E-Mail Address:** honkers@rconnect.com. **Website:** www.northwoodsleague.com.

Year Founded: 1994.

Commissioner: George MacDonald Jr. **President:** Dick Radatz Jr. **Vice Presidents:** Bill McKee, John Wendel.

Division Structure: North—Brainerd, Grand Forks, Minot, St. Cloud. **South**—Mankato, Rochester, Waterloo, Wisconsin.

2000 Opening Date: June 2. **Closing Date:** Aug. 8.

Regular Season: 64 games (split schedule).

All-Star Game: Unavailable.

Playoff Format: First-half and second-half division winners meet in best-of-3 series. Winners meet in best-of-3 series for league championship.

Roster Limit: 24 (college-eligible players only).

BRAINERD MIGHTY GULLS

Mailing Address: P.O. Box 122, Brainerd, MN 56401. **Telephone:** (218) 828-8901. **FAX:** (218) 828-8299.

General Manager: Perry Platisha. **Assistant General Manager:** Chuck Carstensen. **Head Coach:** Matt Markovich (Sonoma State, Calif.).

GRAND FORKS CHANNEL CATS

Mailing Address: P.O. Box 14953, Grand Forks, ND 58208. **Telephone:** (701) 780-9500. **FAX:** (701) 780-9520.

General Manager: Dave Schwei. **Head Coach:** Tracy Roles.

MANKATO MASHERS

Mailing Address: 310 Belle Ave., Suite L10, Mankato, MN 56001. **Telephone:** (507) 344-8877. **FAX:** (507) 344-0871.

President: Den Gardner. **General Manager:** Shane Bowyer. **Head Coach:** Brett Lagerblade (Cornell).

MINOT, N.D.

Mailing Address: Unavailable. **Telephone:** (323) 343-3093.

General Manager: Unavailable. **Head Coach:** Cliff Brown (Cal State Los Angeles).

ROCHESTER HONKERS

Office Address: 403 E Center St., Rochester, MN 55904. **Mailing Address:** P.O. Box 482, Rochester, MN 55903. **Telephone:** (507) 289-1170. **FAX:** (507) 289-1866. **Website:** www.rochesterhonkers.com.

General Manager: Dan Litzinger. **Head Coach:** Tom Fleenor (Rollins, Fla., College).

ST. CLOUD RIVER BATS

Mailing Address: P.O. Box 5059, St. Cloud, MN 56302. **Telephone:** (320) 240-9798. **FAX:** (320) 255-5228. **Website:** www.riverbats.com.

President: Joel Sutherland. **General Manager:** Joe Schwei. **Head Coach:** Scott DeGeorge (Georgetown U.).

WATERLOO BUCKS

Mailing Address: P.O. Box 4124, Waterloo, IA 50704. **Telephone:** (319) 232-0500. **FAX:** (319) 232-0700. **Website:** www.waterloobucks.com.

President: Butch Johnson. **General Manager:** Gary Rima. **Head Coach:** Darrell Handelsman (Centenary College).

WISCONSIN WOODCHUCKS

Office Address: 308 Grand Ave., Suite 202, Wausau, WI 54403. **Telephone:** (715) 845-5055. **FAX:** (715) 845-5015. **Website:** www.wood chucks.com.

President: Clark Eckhoff. **General Manager/Head Coach:** Rob Smith.

PACIFIC INTERNATIONAL LEAGUE

Mailing Address: 504 Yale Ave. N, Seattle, WA 98109. **Telephone:** (206) 623-8844. **FAX:** (206) 623-8361. **E-Mail Address:** potter@sea net.com. **Website:** www.leaguelineup.com/pil.

Year Founded: 1988.

President: Mickie Schmith. **Commissioner:** Seth Dawson. **Vice President:** Mark Dow.

Member Clubs: North—Bellingham (Wash.) Bells, Coquitlam (B.C.) Athletics, Everett (Wash.) Merchants, Kelowna (B.C.) Grizzlies, Wenatchee (Wash.) Apple Sox. **South—**Aloha (Ore.) Knights, Bend (Ore.) Elks, Grays Harbor (Wash.) Rain, Ontario Orchard (Ore.) Meadowlarks, Seattle Cruisers, Seattle Performance Radiator Studs.

2000 Opening Date: June 1. **Closing Date:** Aug. 4.

Regular Season: 36 games.

Playoff Format: Division champions meet in best-of-3 series; winner advances to National Baseball Congress World Series.

Roster Limit: 25.

SHENANDOAH VALLEY LEAGUE

Mailing Address: Route 1, Box 189J, Staunton, VA 24401. **Telephone:** (540) 885-8901. **FAX:** (540) 886-2068. **Website:** www.valleyleaguebase ball.com.

Year Founded: 1963.

President: David Biery. **Executive Vice President:** Jim Weissenborn. **Director, Public Relations:** Curt Dudley.

2000 Opening Date: June 2. **Closing Date:** July 24.

Regular Season: 40 games.

All-Star Game: July 9 at Harrisonburg.

Playoff Format: Top four teams meet in best-of-5 semifinal series. Winners meet in best-of-5 series for league championship.

Roster Limit: 25 (college-eligible players only).

FRONT ROYAL CARDINALS

Mailing Address: P.O. Box 995, Front Royal, VA 22630. **Telephone/FAX:** (540) 635-6498.

General Manager: Danny Wood. **President/Assistant General Manager:** Linda Keen. **Head Coach:** Brian Burke (Sherando, Va., HS).

HARRISONBURG TURKS

Mailing Address: 1489 S Main St., Harrisonburg, VA 22801. **Telephone:** (540) 433-0092.

General Manager: Bob Wease. **Head Coach:** Cooper Farris (Mississippi Gulf Coast CC).

NEW MARKET REBELS

Mailing Address: 9184 John Sevier Rd., New Market, VA 22844. **Telephone:** (540) 665-1212.

General Manager: Larry Strawderman. **Head Coach:** Kevin Anderson (George Mason U.).

STAUNTON BRAVES

Mailing Address: P.O. Box 621, Staunton, VA 24402. **Telephone:** (540) 332-9078. **FAX:** (540) 886-7760.

General Manager: Garland Eutsler. **Recruiting Coordinator:** Tom Chrisman. **Head Coach:** Mike Bocock (Harrisonburg, Va., HS).

WAYNESBORO GENERALS

Mailing Address: P.O. Box 2, Stuarts Draft, VA 24477. **Telephone:** (540) 942-2474. **FAX:** (540) 949-0653.

General Manager: Jim Critzer. **Head Coach:** Michael Rudd (Mississippi Gulf Coast CC).

WINCHESTER ROYALS

Mailing Address: P.O. Box 2485, Winchester, VA 22604. **Telephone:** (540) 678-1515.

Recruiting Coordinator: Paul O'Neil. **Head Coach:** Unavailable.

HIGH SCHOOL/YOUTH BASEBALL

HIGHSCHOOLBASEBALL

NATIONAL FEDERATION
OF STATE HIGH SCHOOL ASSOCIATIONS
Mailing Address: P.O. Box 690, Indianapolis, IN 46206. **Telephone:** (317) 972-6900. **FAX:** Unavailable. **Website:** www.nfhsa.org.
Executive Director: Robert Kanaby. **Associate Director:** Fritz McGinness. **Assistant Director/Baseball Rules Editor:** Elliot Hopkins. **Director, Publications/Communications:** Bruce Howard.

NATIONAL HIGH SCHOOL
BASEBALL COACHES ASSOCIATION
Mailing Address: P.O. Box 5128, Bella Vista, AR 72714. **Telephone:** (501) 876-2591. **FAX:** (501) 876-2596.
Executive Director: Jerry Miles. **Administrative Assistant:** Elaine Miles. **President:** David McDonald (Marietta, GA).
2000 National Convention: Dec. 1-3 at Knoxville, TN.

NATIONAL TOURNAMENTS

Postseason
SUNBELT BASEBALL CLASSIC SERIES
Mailing Address: 505 North Blvd., Edmond, OK 73034. **Telephone:** (405) 348-3839.
Chairman: Gordon Morgan. **Director:** John Schwartz.
2000 Series: Seminole, Shawnee and Tecumseh, OK, June 22-26 (8 teams. Arizona, California, Florida, Georgia, Maryland, Ohio, Oklahoma, Texas).

In-Season
FLORIDA SUNSHINE NATIONAL CLASSIC
Mailing Address: Tate High School, Gonzalez, FL 32560. **Telephone:** (850) 968-5755. **E-Mail Address:** tateaggies@aol.com.
Tournament Director: Greg Blackmon.
2000 Tournament: April 17-20 (16 teams).

HORIZON NATIONAL INVITATIONAL
Mailing Address: Horizon High School, 5601 E Groanway Rd., Scottsdale, AZ 85254. **Telephone:** (602) 953-4158.
Tournament Director: Eric Kibler.
2000 Tournament: March 27-30 (12 teams).

LIONS/MIKE MORROW INVITATIONAL
Mailing Address: 1200 Billy Mitchell Dr., Suite A, El Cajon, CA 92020. **Telephone:** (619) 258-2500. **FAX:** (619) 258-1400.
Tournament Organizers: Jim Gordon, Bob Henshaw.
2000 Tournament: April 17-20 (80 teams).

NATIONAL CLASSIC
Mailing Address: El Dorado High School, 1651 N. Valencia Ave., Placentia, CA 92870. **Telephone:** (714) 993-5350, ext. 7602. **FAX:** (714) 777-8127. **E-Mail Address:** inovick@aol.com. **Website:** www.eteamz.com/baseball/eldorado.
Tournament Director: Iran Novick.
2000 Tournament: April 17-20 in Orange County, CA (16 teams).

ORLANDO BASEBALL CLASSIC
Mailing Address: Cypress Creek High School, 1101 Bear Crossing Dr., Orlando, FL 32824. **Telephone:** (407) 852-3472. **FAX:** (407) 850-5160.
Tournament Organizer: George Kirchgassner.
2000 Tournament: March 13-18 at Orlando, FL (16 teams).

SARASOTA BASEBALL CLASSIC
Mailing Address: 2384 Seattle Slew Dr., Sarasota, FL 34240. **Telephone:** (941) 371-3459. **FAX:** (941) 378-5853.
Chairman, Selection Committee: Ed Rincon.
2000 Tournament: April 3-7 at Sarasota, FL.

USA CLASSIC
Mailing Address: 5900 Walnut Grove Rd., Memphis, TN 38120. **Telephone:** (901) 682-7801, ext. 134.
Tournament Organizers: John Daigle, Buster Kelso.
2000 Tournament: April 18-21 at USA Baseball Stadium, Millington, TN (16 teams).

WESTMINSTER NATIONAL CLASSIC
Mailing Address: Westminster Academy, 5601 Federal Hwy., Fort Lauderdale, FL 33308. **Telephone:** (954) 735-1841. **FAX:** (954) 735-1858.
Tournament Director: Rich Hofman.
2000 Tournament: April 4-7 (16 teams).

SHOWCASE**EVENTS**

ALL-AMERICAN BASEBALL TALENT SHOWCASES
Mailing Address: 6 Bicentennial Ct., Erial, NJ 08081. **Telephone:** (609) 627-5283. **FAX:** (609) 627-5330.
National Director: Joe Barth.

AREA CODE GAMES
Mailing Address: P.O. Box 213, Santa Rosa, CA 95402. **Telephone:** (707) 525-0498. **FAX:** (707) 525-0214. **E-Mail Address:** rwilliams@area codebaseball.org. **Website:** www.areacodebaseball.org.
President, Goodwill Series, Inc.: Bob Williams.
2000 Area Code Games: Aug. 6-12, Long Beach, CA (Blair Field).
World Cup XV: Japan and United States, Aug. 29-Sept. 4, Long Beach, CA. **Friendship International Series:** Aug. 8-18, Beijing, China. **Goodwill Series V:** Dec. 17, 2000-Jan. 3, 2001, Adelaide and Brisbane, Australia.

ARIZONA BASEBALL ACADEMY
Mailing Address: 6102 W Maui Lane, Glendale, AZ 85306. **Telephone:** (602) 978-2929. **FAX:** (602) 439-4494.
Academy Director: Ted Heid.
2000 Event: Senior Ball Invitational, Nov. 10-12 at Glendale, AZ.

BASEBALL FACTORY
Office Address: 3290 Pine Orchard Ln., Suite D, Ellicott City, MD 21042. **Telephone:** (800) 641-4487, (410) 418-4904. **FAX:** (410) 418-5434. **E-Mail Address:** info@baseballfactory.com. **Website:** www.base ballfactory.com.
President: Steve Sclafani. **Vice President:** Rob Naddelman.

BEST OF THE WEST SHOWCASE
Mailing Address: 7515 Vista Alegre St. NW, Albuquerque, NM 87120. **Telephone:** (505) 833-0745. **FAX:** (505) 836-1065.
Showcase Organizer: Darrell Carrillo.
2000 Showcase: June 27-29 at Albuquerque, NM (U. of New Mexico/Albuquerque Sports Stadium).

COLLEGE SELECT BASEBALL SHOWCASE
Mailing Address: 345 Buckland Hills Dr., Suite 9123, Manchester, CT 06040. **Telephone:** (800) 782-3672. **Website:** www.collegeselect.org.
National Director: Tom Rizzi.
2000 Showcases: July 1-3 at Norwich, CT (Thomas Dodd Memorial Stadium); Aug. 26-28 at Binghamton, NY (Binghamton Municipal Stadium).

DOYLE BASEBALL SELECT SHOWCASES
Mailing Address: P.O. Box 9156, Winter Haven, FL 33883. **Telephone:** (941) 439-1000. **FAX:** (941) 439-7086.
2000 Fall Classic Showcase: October, Winter Haven, FL.

EAST COAST PROFESSIONAL BASEBALL SHOWCASE
Mailing Address: 601 S College Rd., Wilmington, NC 28403. **Telephone:** (910) 962-3570.
Facility Director: Mark Scalf.
2000 Showcase: Aug. 1-5, Wilmington, NC (UNC Wilmington).

MID-AMERICA FIVE STAR CAMP
Mailing Address: Champions Baseball Academy, 10701 Plantside Dr., Louisville, KY 40299. **Telephone:** (502) 261-9200.
President: John Marshall.
2000 Showcase: July 9-12, Louisville, KY (Louisville Slugger Field).

PACIFIC NORTHWEST CHAMPIONSHIP
Mailing Address: 160 S Pacific Hwy., Woodburn, OR 97370. **Telephone:** (503) 981-5380. **Website:** www.baseballoregon.com.
Tournament Organizer: Roger Amunsen.
2000 Showcase: Aug. 18-20 at Seattle.

PERFECT GAME SHOWCASE
Mailing Address: 1203 Rockford Rd. SW, Cedar Rapids, IA 52404. **Telephone:** (319) 298-2923, (800) 447-9362. **FAX:** (319) 298-2924. **E-mail Address:** jerry@perfectgame.org. **Website:** www.perfectgame.org.
Top Prospects 2000 Pre-Draft Camp: May 8 at Cedar Rapids, IA (Memorial Park). **Lone Star Showdown:** Aug. 15-17 at San Antonio, TX (St. Mary's College). **Fall Wood Bat World Series:** Oct. 27-29, site unavailable. **Perfect Game World Showcase:** Dec. 27-30 at Fort Myers, FL.

PREMIER BASEBALL
Mailing Address: 2411 Teal Ave., Sarasota, FL 34237. **Telephone:** (941) 371-0989. **FAX:** (941) 371-0917.

Camp Directors: John Crumbley, Paul Herfurth, Rich Hofman, Clyde Metcalf.

2000 Showcases: Florida Showcase Camp, May 27-29 at Sarasota, FL; Select Showcase Camp, July 7-9 at Sarasota, FL; Underclassmen Showcase Camp, Dec. 1-3 at Sarasota, FL.

TEAM ONE NATIONAL SHOWCASE

Mailing Address: P.O. Box 8943, Cincinnati, OH 45208. **Telephone/FAX:** (606) 291-4463. **E-Mail Address:** teamonebb@aol.com.

President, Team One Sports: Jeff Spelman. **Assistant Director:** Stan Brzezicki. Telephone: (814) 899-8407. **Director of Scouting:** Anup Sinha. Telephone: (248) 212-8326.

2000 Team One National Showcase: June 22-24, Tempe, AZ (Diablo Stadium, Arizona State).

Regional Showcases: West—June 25-26, Tempe, AZ (Arizona State University); East/Florida—July 21-23, Clemson, SC (Clemson University); Midwest—Aug. 11-13, South Bend, IN (U. of Notre Dame).

TEXAS SCOUTS ASSOCIATION WORKOUT/GAME

Mailing Address: 21718 Bay Palms Dr., Katy, TX 77449. **Telephone:** (281) 463-0665.

Camp Directors: Jim Robinson, Randy Taylor.

2000 Showcase: Aug. 2 at Houston (Enron Field).

TOP 96 INVITATIONAL SHOWCASE

Mailing Address: P.O. Box 5481, Wayland, MA 01778. **Telephone:** (508) 651-0165.

Showcase Organizers: Dave Callum, Doug Henson, Ken Hill.

2000 Showcase: Aug. 11-12 at Lowell, MA.

TOP GUNS SHOWCASE

Mailing Address: 7890 N Franklin Rd., Suite 2, Coeur d'Alene, ID 83815. **Telephone/FAX:** (208) 762-1100.

President: Larry Rook. **Commissioners:** Chuck Brayton, Ron Fraser, Gordon Gillespie, Cliff Gustafson, John Scolinos, John Winkin.

2000 High School National Showcase: June 25-29, Las Vegas, NV (University of Nevada-Las Vegas).

SCOUTING SERVICES

PROSPECTS PLUS

(A Division of Baseball America, Inc.)

Mailing Address: Prospects LLC, P.O. Box 2089, Durham, NC 27702. **Telephone:** (800) 845-2726. **FAX:** (919) 682-2880.

Proprietors: David Rawnsley, Allan Simpson.

YOUTHBASEBALL

ALL AMERICAN AMATEUR
BASEBALL ASSOCIATION (AAABA)

Mailing Address: 331 Parkway Dr., Zanesville, OH 43701. **Telephone:** (740) 453-8531. **FAX:** (740) 453-3978.

Year Founded: 1944.

President: John Austin. **Executive Director:** Bob Wolfe.

2000 National Tournament (21 and under): Aug. 6-12 at Johnstown, PA.

AMATEUR ATHLETIC UNION
OF THE UNITED STATES, INC. (AAU)

Mailing Address: P.O. Box 10000, Lake Buena Vista, FL 32803. **Telephone:** (407) 934-7200. **FAX:** (407) 934-7242.

Year Founded: 1982.

Sport Manager/Baseball: Sheldon Walker.

Age Classifications, National Championships

9 and under	*Orlando, FL, July 14-22
10 and under (46/60 foot)	Des Moines, IA, July 28-Aug. 5
10 and under (48/65 foot)	Des Moines, IA, July 28-Aug. 5
11 and under	*Orlando, FL, July 21-29
12 and under	Burnsville, MN, July 28-Aug. 5
13 and under (54/80 foot)	Sherwood, AR, July 28-Aug. 5
13 and under (60/90 foot)	Kinston, NC, July 28-Aug. 5
14 and under	Sarasota, FL, July 28-Aug. 5
15 and under	Kingsport, TN, July 28-Aug. 5
Junior Olympics (16 and under)	Orlando, FL, July 27-Aug. 5
17 and under	Phoenix, AZ, July 28-Aug. 5
18 and under	*Orlando, FL, July 14-22

National Invitational Championships

11 and under	*Orlando, FL, July 28-Aug. 5
12 and under	*Orlando, FL, July 28-Aug. 5
13 and under (54/80 foot)	Johnson City, TN, July 21-29
13 and under (60/90 foot)	Fort Myers, FL, July 28-Aug. 5
14 and under	*Orlando, FL, July 28-Aug. 5
15 and under	*Orlando, FL, July 21-29
16 and under	Cocoa, FL, July 28-Aug. 5

Other National Championships: High School Age Group, Austin, TX, July 14-22.

*Disney's Wide World of Sports Complex, Lake Buena Vista.

AMERICAN AMATEUR
BASEBALL CONGRESS (AABC)

National Headquarters: 118-119 Redfield Plaza, P.O. Box 467, Marshall, MI 49068. **Telephone:** (616) 781-2002. **FAX:** (616) 781-2060. **E-Mail Address:** aabc@voyager.net. **Website:** www.voyager.net/aabc.

Year Founded: 1935.

President: Joe Cooper.

Age Classifications, World Series

Roberto Clemente (8 and under)	Site unavailable, July 27-30
Willie Mays (10 and under)	Olive Branch, MS, July 27-30
Pee Wee Reese (12 and under)	Toa Baja, PR, Aug. 9-13
Sandy Koufax (14 and under)	Jersey City, NJ, Aug. 3-7
Mickey Mantle (16 and under)	McKinney, TX, Aug. 2-6
Connie Mack (18 and under)	Farmington, NM, Aug. 4-11
Stan Musial (unlimited)	Battle Creek, MI, Aug. 10-13

AMERICAN AMATEUR
YOUTH BASEBALL ALLIANCE

Mailing Address: 12919 Four Winds Farm, St. Louis, MO 63131. **Telephone/FAX:** (573) 518-0319. **E-Mail Address:** clwir28@aol.com. **Website:** www.aayba.com.

President, Baseball Operations: Carroll Wood.

Age Classifications, World Series

10 and under	St. Louis, MO, July 21-29
11 and under	St. Louis, MO, July 7-15
12 and under	St. Louis, MO, July 21-29
13 and under	St. Louis, MO, July 21-29
14 and under (54/80 foot)	St. Louis, MO, July 7-15
14 and under (60/90 foot)	St. Louis, MO, July 21-29

| 15 and under | St. Louis, MO, June 16-24 |
| 16 and under | St. Louis, MO, July 7-15 |

AMERICAN LEGION BASEBALL

National Headquarters: National Americanism Commission, P.O. Box 1055, Indianapolis, IN 46206. **Telephone:** (317) 630-1213. **FAX:** (317) 630-1369. **Website:** www.legion.org.

Year Founded: 1925.

Program Coordinator: Jim Quinlan.

2000 World Series (19 and under): Aug. 18-22 at Alton, IL.

BABE RUTH BASEBALL

International Headquarters: 1770 Brunswick Pike, P.O. Box 5000, Trenton, NJ 08638. **Telephone:** (609) 695-1434. **FAX:** (609) 695-2505. **Website:** www.baberuthleague.org.

Year Founded: 1951.

President/Chief Executive Officer: Ron Tellefsen.

Executive Vice President/Chief Financial Officer: Rosemary Schoellkopf. **Vice President/Marketing:** Joe Smiegocki. **Commissioners:** Robert Faherty, Debra Horn, Joey King.

Age Classifications, World Series

Cal Ripken (11-12)	Mattoon, IL, Aug. 12-19
13-Prep	Jamestown, NY, Aug. 19-26
14	Connersville, IN, Aug. 19-26
13-15	Lebanon, MO, Aug. 19-26
16	Moses Lake, WA, Aug. 12-19
16-18	Concord, NH, Aug. 12-19

CONTINENTAL AMATEUR BASEBALL ASSOCIATION (CABA)

Mailing Address: 82 University St., Westerville, OH 43081. **Telephone:** (740) 382-4620. **FAX:** (614) 899-2103. **Website:** www.cababaseball.com.

Year Founded: 1984.

President: Carl Williams. **Commissioner:** John Mocny. **Franchise Director:** Tanya Wilkinson. **Executive Director:** Roger Tremaine.

Age Classifications, World Series

9 and under	Charles City, IA, July 27-Aug. 7
10 and under	Aurelia, IA, July 27-Aug. 7
11 and under	Tarkio, MO, July 27-Aug. 7
12 and under	Omaha, NE, July 27-Aug. 7
13 and under	Broken Arrow, OK, July 27-Aug. 7
14 and under	Dublin, OH, July 27-Aug. 7
15 and under	Crystal Lake, IL, July 27-Aug. 7
16 and under	Dallas, TX, July 20-31
High school age	Cleveland, OH, July 20-31
18 and under	Homestead, FL, July 27-Aug. 7
College age	Schenectady, NY, July 18-24
Unlimited age	Eau Claire, WI, Aug. 15-21

DIXIE BASEBALL, INC.

Mailing Address: P.O. Box 231536, Montgomery, AL 36123. **Telephone:** (334) 242-8395. **FAX:** (334) 242-0198.

Year Founded: 1956.

Executive Director: P.L. Corley.

Age Classifications, World Series

Dixie Youth (12 and under)	Marshall, TX, Aug. 14-19
Dixie 13	Boaz, AL, Aug. 5-10
Dixie Boys (13-14)	Cleveland, MS, Aug. 5-10
Dixie Pre-Majors (15-16)	Guntersville, AL, July 29-Aug. 3
Dixie Majors (15-18)	Euless, TX, July 29-Aug. 3

DIZZY DEAN BASEBALL, INC.

Mailing Address: 37 Adkinson Dr., Pensacola, FL 32506. **Telephone:** (850) 455-8827.

Year Founded: 1962.

Commissioner: Joedy Bates. **Treasurer/Administrator:** D.B. Stuart.

Age Classifications, World Series

Minor League (9-10)	Oak Grove, MS, July 21-26
Freshman (11-12)	Oak Grove, MS, July 21-26
Sophomore (13-14)	Panama City Beach, FL, July 21-26
Junior (15-16)	Southaven, MS, July 29-Aug. 3
Senior (17-18)	Southaven, MS, July 29-Aug. 3

HAP DUMONT YOUTH BASEBALL

Mailing Address: P.O. Box 17455, Wichita, KS 67217. **Telephone:** (316) 721-1779. **FAX:** (316) 721-8054.

Year Founded: 1974.

National Chairman: Jerry Crowell. **National Vice Chairman:** Jerold Vogt.

Age Classifications, World Series

10 and under	Casper, WY, Aug. 4-9
11 and under	Harrison, AR, Aug. 4-9
12 and under	Cincinnati, OH, Aug. 4-9
13 and under	Russell, KS, Aug. 4-9
14 and under	Brainerd, MN, Aug. 4-9
15 and under	Omaha, NE, Aug. 4-9
16 and under	Gainesville, GA, July 28-Aug. 1
18 and under	Harrison, AR, July 28-Aug. 1

LITTLE LEAGUE BASEBALL, INC.

International Headquarters: P.O. Box 3485, Williamsport, PA 17701. **Telephone:** (570) 326-1921. **FAX:** (570) 326-1074. **Website:** www.little league.org.

Year Founded: 1939.

Chairman: Ted Reich. **Chairman Elect:** Dwight Raiford.

President/Chief Executive Officer: Steve Keener. **Director, Communications:** Dennis Sullivan. **Director, Media Relations:** Lance Van Auken. **Director, Special Projects:** Scott Rosenberg.

Age Classifications, World Series

Little League (11-12)	Williamsport, PA, Aug. 20-26
Junior League (13-14)	Taylor, MI, Aug. 14-19
Senior League (14-16)	Kissimmee, FL, Aug. 12-19
Big League (16-18)	Tucson, AZ, Aug. 6-12

NATIONAL AMATEUR
BASEBALL FEDERATION (NABF)

Mailing Address: P.O. Box 705, Bowie, MD 20715. **Telephone/FAX:** (301) 262-5005. **E-Mail Address:** nabf1914@aol.com. **Website:** www.nabf.com.

Year Founded: 1914.

Executive Director: Charles Blackburn. **Special Events Coordinator, NABF Classics:** Wanda Rutledge.

Age Classifications, World Series

Rookie (10 and under)	Nashville, TN, July 6-9
Freshman (12 and under)	Cincinnati, OH, July 13-16
Sophomore (14 and under)	Dayton, OH, July 20-22
Junior (16 and under)	Northville, MI, July 27-31
High School (17 and under)	Memphis, TN, July 26-29
Senior (18 and under)	Wilmington, DE, Aug. 3-7
College (22 and under)	Dayton, OH, Aug. 10-14
Major (unlimited)	Louisville, KY, Aug. 17-21

NABF Classics (Invitational)

11 and under	Southaven, MS, July 11-15
13 and under	Southaven, MS, July 11-15
14 and under	Memphis, TN, June 29-July 3
15 and under	Daytona Beach, FL, June 26-29
16 and under (East)	Scranton, PA, July 26-31
16 and under (West)	Hopkinsville, KY, July 5-9

NATIONAL ASSOCIATION
OF POLICE ATHLETIC LEAGUES

Mailing Address: 618 U.S. Highway 1, Suite 201, North Palm Beach, FL 33408. **Telephone:** (561) 844-1823. **FAX:** (561) 863-6120. **E-Mail Address:** copnkid1@aol.com. **Website:** www.nationalpal.org.

Year Founded: 1944

Executive Director: Unavailable. **Associate Directors:** Brad Hart, Nerilda Lugo.

Age Classifications, World Series

14 and under	Palm Beach County, FL, July 31-Aug. 5
16 and under	Palm Beach County, FL, July 31-Aug. 5

PONY BASEBALL, INC.

International Headquarters: P.O. Box 225, Washington, PA 15301. **Telephone:** (724) 225-1060. **FAX:** (724) 225-9852. **E-Mail Address:** pony@pulsenet.com. **Website:** www.pony.org.

Year Founded: 1951.

President/Chief Executive Officer: Abraham Key. **Director, Baseball Operations:** Don Clawson.

Age Classifications, World Series

Shetland (5-6)	No National Tournament
Pinto (7-8)	No National Tournament
Mustang (9-10)	Irving, TX, Aug. 2-5
Bronco (11-12)	Monterey, CA, Aug. 3-9
Pony (13-14)	Washington, PA, Aug. 12-19
Colt (15-16)	Lafayette, IN, Aug. 8-15
Palomino (17-18)	Santa Clara, CA, Aug. 11-14

REVIVING BASEBALL IN INNER CITIES (RBI)

Mailing Address: 245 Park Ave., New York, NY 10167. **Telephone:** (212) 931-7897. **FAX:** (212) 949-5695.

Year Founded: 1989.

Founder: John Young. **Vice President, Marketing:** Kathleen Francis. **National Manager:** Thomas Brasuell.

Age Classifications, World Series

Junior Boys (13-15)	*Orlando, FL, Aug. 5-10
Senior Boys (16-18)	*Orlando, FL, Aug. 5-10

*Disney's Wide World of Sports Complex, Lake Buena Vista.

T-BALL USA ASSOCIATION, INC.

Office Address: 2499 Main St., Stratford, CT 06615. **Telephone:** (203) 381-1449. **FAX:** (203) 381-1440. **E-Mail Address:** teeballusa@aol.com. **Website:** www.teeballusa.org.

Year Founded: 1993.

President: Bing Broido. **Executive Vice President:** Lois Richards.

U.S. AMATEUR BASEBALL ASSOCIATION

Mailing Address: 7101 Lake Ballinger Way, Edmonds, WA 98026. **Telephone/FAX:** (425) 776-7130. **E-Mail Address:** usaba@usaba.com. **Website:** www.usaba.com.

Year Founded: 1969.

Executive Director: Al Rutledge.

Age Classifications, World Series

12 and under	Santa Maria, CA, Aug. 11-19
13 and under	Hoquiam, WA, Aug. 3-11
14 and under	South Jordan, UT, Aug. 3-11
15 and under	Site/dates unavailable
16 and under	South Jordan, UT, July 28-Aug. 5
17 and under	Site/dates unavailable
18 and under	Carson City, NV, Aug. 3-11

UNITED STATES SPECIALTY SPORTS ASSOCIATION (USSSA)

National Headquarters: P.O. Box 1998, Petersburg, VA 23805. **Telephone:** (804) 732-4099. **FAX:** (804) 732-1704. **E-Mail Address:** ussahq@aol.com. **Website:** www.usssabaseball.org.

Executive Vice President, Baseball: Rick Fortuna, P.O. Box 1145, Liberty, MO 64069. **Telephone:** (816) 415-2255. **FAX:** (816) 415-2273. **E-Mail Address:** rick@kcsports.org.

Year Founded: (1965)/Baseball (1996).

Age Classifications, World Series

8 and under (Machine pitch)	David City, OK, July 18-23
8 and under (Coach pitch)	Lafayette, LA, July 18-23
9 and under (Major)	Nevada, MO, July 16-23
9 and under (AAA)	Joplin, MO, July 16-23
10 and under (Major)	Ballwin, MO, July 16-23
10 and under (AAA)	Southaven, MS, July 16-23
11 and under (Major)	Omaha, NE, July 16-23
11 and under (AAA)	Overland Park, KS, July 16-23
12 and under (Major)	Atlanta, GA, July 16-23
12 and under (AAA)	Hutchinson, KS, July 16-23
13 and under (Major)	Tulsa, OK, July 16-23
13 and under (AAA)	Broken Arrow, OK, July 16-23
14 and under (Major)	Houston, TX, July 16-23
14 and under (AAA)	Canton, MI, July 16-23
15 and under (Major/AAA)	Winter Haven, FL, July 23-30
16 and under (Major/AAA)	Oklahoma City, OK, July 23-30
18 and under (Major/AAA)	Lakeland, FL, July 23-30

USA JUNIOR OLYMPIC BASEBALL CHAMPIONSHIP

Mailing Address: USA Baseball, 3400 E Camino Campestre, Tucson, AZ 85716. **Telephone:** (520) 327-9700. **FAX:** (520) 327-9221.

Coordinator, Youth Baseball: Ray Darwin.

Age Classifications, Championship

16 and under	Tucson, AZ, June 16-24

YOUTH BASEBALL TOURNAMENT CENTERS

COCOA EXPO SPORTS CENTER

Mailing Address: 500 Friday Rd., Cocoa, FL 32926. **Telephone:** (321) 639-3976. **FAX:** (321) 632-0598. **E-Mail Address:** athleticdirector@cocoa expo.com. **Website:** www.cocoaexpo.com.

Executive Director: Jeff Biddle.

Activities: Spring training program, instructional camps, team training camps, youth tournaments.

2000 Events/Tournaments (ages 10-18): **First Pitch Festival**, May 18-21. **Cocoa Expo Internationale**, June 30-July 6. **Cocoa Expo Summer Classic**, Aug. 7-13. **Cocoa Expo Fall Classic**, Oct. 13-15.

COOPERSTOWN DREAMS PARK

Mailing Address: 101 E Fisher St, 3rd Floor, Salisbury, NC 28144. **Telephone:** (704) 630-0050. **FAX:** (704) 630-0737. **E-Mail Address:** info@cooperstowndreamspark.com. **Website:** www.cooperstowndreams park.com.

Complex Address: Route 28, Cooperstown, NY.

Program Director: Phil Kehr.

Invitational Tournaments (48 teams per week): June 17-23 (10 and under), June 24-30 (12 and under), July 1-7 (12 and under), July 8-14 (12 and under), July 15-21 (12 and under), July 22-28 (12 and under), July 29-Aug. 4 (12 and under), Aug. 5-11 (12 and under), Aug. 12-18 (12 and under), Aug. 19-25 (12 and under).

National Amateur Tournament of Champions: Aug. 26-Sept. 1 (12 and under).

DISNEY'S WIDE WORLD OF SPORTS

Mailing Address: P.O. Box 10000, Lake Buena Vista, FL 32830. **Telephone:** (407) 828-3267. **Website:** www.disneyworldsports.com.

Baseball Program Manager: Kevin Russell. **Baseball Specialist:** Geoff Burkhart. **Program Coordinator, Baseball:** Unavailable.

2000 Events/Tournaments: Sun & Surf Baseball Bash (10 and under, 11, 12, 14, 16), May 26-29. **Salute to Baseball Festival** (10 and under, 11, 12, 14, 16), July 9-15. **Turn Back the Clock Weekend Tournament** (10 and under, 11, 12, 14, 16), Sept. 1-4.

KC SPORTS TOURNAMENTS

Mailing Address: P.O. Box 1145, Liberty, MO 64069. **Telephone:** (816) 415-2255. **FAX:** (816) 415-2273. **E-Mail Address:** don@kcsports.org. **Website:** www.kcsports.org.

Tournament Organizers: Rick Fortuna, Don Smith.

INSTRUCTIONAL SCHOOLS/PRIVATE CAMPS

ALL AMERICAN BASEBALL ACADEMY

Mailing Address: P.O. Box 14595, Long Beach, CA 90803. **Telephone:** (562) 434-7310.

Camp Director: Joe Magno.

THE BASEBALL ACADEMY

Mailing Address: c/o IMG Academies/Bollettieri Sports Academy, 5500 34th St. W, Bradenton, FL 34210. **Telephone:** (941) 727-0303. **FAX:** (941) 727-2962. **Website:** www.zonebaseball.com.

Camp Director: Ken Bolek.

CAL RIPKEN BASEBALL SCHOOL

Mailing Address: 10801 Tony Dr., Suite A, Lutherville, MD 21093. **Telephone:** (800) 486-0850, (410) 823-8467.

CHANDLER BASEBALL CAMP

Office Address: 2000 W Park Rd., Chandler, OK 74834. **Mailing Address:** P.O. Box 395, Chandler, OK 74834. **Telephone:** (405) 258-1720. **Website:** www.chandlerbaseballcamp.com.

Camp Director: Tom Belcher.

BUCKY DENT BASEBALL SCHOOL

Mailing Address: 490 Dotterel Rd., Delray Beach, FL 33444. **Telephone:** (561) 265-0280. **FAX:** (561) 278-6679. **Website:** www.dentbaseball.com.

Vice President: Larry Hoskin.

FROZEN ROPES TRAINING CENTERS

Mailing Address: 31 Jonathan Bourne Dr., Pocasset, MA 02559. **Telephone:** (508) 563-1860. **FAX:** (508) 563-1875. **Website:** www.frozen ropes.com

Corporate Director: Tony Abbatine.

Camp Director: Mike Coutts.

DOYLE BASEBALL SCHOOL

Mailing Address: P.O. Box 9156, Winter Haven, FL 33883. **Telephone:** (941) 439-1000. **FAX:** (941) 439-7086. **Website:** www.doylebaseball.com.

President: Denny Doyle. **Chief Executive Officer:** Blake Doyle. **On-Field Director:** Brian Doyle. **Director, Satellite School:** Rick Siebert.

MICKEY OWEN BASEBALL SCHOOL

Mailing Address: P.O. Box 88, Miller, MO 65707. **Telephone:** (800) 999-8369, (417) 882-2799. **FAX:** (417) 889-6978. **Website:** www.mickey owen.com. **President:** Ken Rizzo. **Director, Marketing:** Mark Daniel. **Camp Director:** Joe Fowler.

NORTH CAROLINA BASEBALL ACADEMY
Mailing Address: 1137 Pleasant Ridge Rd., Greensboro, NC 27409. **Telephone:** (336) 931-1118. **E-Mail Address:** ncba@bellsouth.net. **Website:** www.ncbaseball.com.

Owner/Director: Scott Bankhead. **Assistant Director:** Todd Wilkinson.

NORTHERN VIRGINIA BASEBALL ACADEMY
Mailing Address: P.O. Box 222156, Chantilly, VA 20153. **Telephone:** (703) 222-8837. **FAX:** (703) 222-7350. **Website:** www.nvba.com.

General Manager: Brian Snyder. **Director, Baseball Operations:** Rob Hanne. **Assistant Director, Instruction:** Dan Raley.

PLAYBALL BASEBALL ACADEMY
Mailing Address: P.O. Box 4898, Fort Lauderdale, FL 33338. **Telephone:** (954) 776-6217. **FAX:** (954) 772-4510. **E-Mail Address:** play ball@webtv.net.

SHO-ME BASEBALL CAMP
Mailing Address: 2080 Creekwood, Harrison, AR 72601. **Telephone:** (870) 743-5450.

Camp Director: Phil Wilson.

TEXAS PRIDE BASEBALL ACADEMY
Mailing Address: P.O. Box 890962, Houston, TX 77289. **Telephone:** (281) 990-6031. **FAX:** (713) 871-2024.

Camp Director: Tom Siebert.

SAN DIEGO SCHOOL OF BASEBALL
Mailing Address: P.O. Box 900458, San Diego, CA. **Telephone:** (619) 491-4000. **FAX:** (619) 469-5572.

COLLEGE CAMPS

Almost all of the elite college baseball programs have summer/holiday instructional camps. Please consult the college section, Pages 299-333, for listings.

AGENT DIRECTORY/SERVICE DIRECTORY

AGENTDIRECTORY

ACES, INC.
188 Montague Street
Brooklyn NY 11201
718-237-2900/Fax: 718-522-3906
acesinc2@aol.com

Barry Axelrod, Attorney at Law
2236 Encinitas Boulevard, Suite A
Encinitas CA 92024
760-753-0088/Fax: 760-436-7399

CSMG
847-447-4315/Fax: 847-441-4145

Focus Management, Inc.
Frank A. Blandino
P.O. Box 717
Somerville NJ 08876
908-217-3226/908-281-0550
Fax: 908-281-0596
focusmanagement@rcn.com

Global Sports Consultants, Inc.
Randell Monaco, Esq., Reggie Waller
819 Frankfort Avenue
Huntington Beach CA 92648
800-237-6300/Fax: 714-969-2836
gsportcn@gte.net

Golden Gate - No Limit Sports
Miles McAfee, Ph.D
7677 Oakport Street, Suite 1050
Oakland CA 94621
510-567-1390/Fax: 510-567-1395
Cell: 510-414-062

Golden Sports Management, L.L.C.
Buzz Jordan, Tyler Bain
300 S. Jackson Street, Suite 100
Denver CO 80209
303-398-7038/Fax: 303-398-7051
buzzj@aol.com
www.goldensportsmgmt.com

I.M.G.
Casey Close, Brian Peters, Jeff Berry,
Terry Prince
I.M.G. Center
1360 E. 9th Street, Suite 100
Cleveland OH 44114
216-522-1200/Fax: 216-522-1145

John Boggs & Associates, Inc.
John Boggs, Tony Cabral
5675 Ruffin Road, Suite 350
San Diego CA 92123
858-467-9864/Fax: 858-496-2502
leah@jbasports.com
www.jbasports.com

Northstar Sports Management
Barry Praver
2335 Laurel Lane
Palm Beach Gardens FL 33410
561-775-6313/Fax: 561-775-7633
NorthstarSports@aol.com

Pro Agents, Inc.
David P. Pepe, Billy Martin, Jr.
800-795-3454/Fax: 732-855-6117

Pro-Talent, Inc.
Christopher Fanta, Eduardo Diaz,
Jerry Vainisi
3753 North Western Avenue
Chicago IL 60618
773-583-3411/Fax: 773-583-4277
ProTalentChicago@aol.com

PRO EDGE SPORTS MANAGEMENT
Steve Canter
8871 Wonderland Avenue
Los Angeles CA 90046
323-656-2711/Fax: 323-656-3711

Pro Star Management, Inc.
Joe Bick
250 East Fifth Street, Suite 1500
Cincinnati OH 45202
513-762-7676/Fax: 513-721-4628
prostar@fuse.net

Professional Sports Management Group
Alan Meersand, Jim Schwanke
Main Office:
865 Manhattan Beach Blvd., Ste. 205
Manhattan Beach CA 90266
310-546-3400/Fax: 310-546-4046
meersand@aol.com

Riverfront Sports Management
Brian M. Goldberg
513-721-3111/Fax: 513-721-3077

Sports Management Services, International, Inc.
David Trimble, Warren Hughes, James
Munsey, Jonathan Grossman, Jamie Appel
P.O. Box 17733
Clearwater FL 33762
800-240-2809/Fax: 727-592-9500
smsball@earthlink.com

STRONGHOLD ATHLETIC MANAGEMENT
Ronald J. Antonelli, Joe Speed
120 E. Parrish Street, Suite 300
Durham NC 27701
919-688-6335/Fax: 919-688-3195
Cincinnati Office: 513-607-6104
Fax: 513-755-6157
STRONGHOLD@juno.com

Tanzer Sports Consultants, Inc.
Tommy Tanzer, Steve Alexander,
Jeff Kahn
1567 Aerie Circle
P.O. Box 680340
Park City UT 84068
800-777-7603/Fax: 435-649-6464
tanzrball@aol.com

Thomas A. Connelly, Sports Attorney
4249 E. Smokehouse Trail
Cave Creek AZ 85331
602-549-8251/888-852-8055
Fax: 413-208-2788
tom@sports-lawyer.net
www.sports-lawyer.net

SERVICE DIRECTORY

ACCESSORIES

Frank's Sport Shop
430 East Tremont Avenue
Bronx NY 10457
718-299-5223
Fax: 718-583-1652

Laundry Loops
P.O. Box 5167
Bozeman MT 59717
888-246-5667
Fax: 888-840-6838
laundryloops@avicom.net
www.laundryloops.com

Tuff Toe, Inc.
726 W. Angus Avenue, Suite B
Orange CA 92868
800-888-0802
Fax: 714-997-9594
tufftoe@pacbell.net
tufftoe.com

ACCOUNTANTS

Resnick Amsterdam Leshner P.C.
653 Skippack Pike, Suite 300
Blue Bell PA 19422
215-628-8080
Fax: 215-628-4752
ral@ral-cpa.com
www.ral-cpa.com

Pro Athlete Advisors Co.
800-655-4340

APPAREL

American Promotions of Illinois
3455 Vorce Road
Harbor Springs MI 49740
800-426-8054
Fax: 888-426-8054
amproil@freeway.net
www.americanpromotions.com

Frank's Sport Shop
430 East Tremont Avenue
Bronx NY 10457
718-299-5223
Fax: 718-583-1652

Minor Leagues, Major Dreams
P.O. Box 6098
Anaheim CA 92816
714-939-0939 / 800-345-2421
Fax: 714-939-0655
mlmd@minorleagues.com
www.minorleagues.com

ATHLETIC FIELD CONSTRUCTION

Alpine Services, Inc.
5313 Brookeville Road
Gaithersburg MD 20882
301-963-8833
Fax: 301-963-7901
asi@alpineservices.com
www.alpineservices/asi

BAGS

American Promotions of Illinois
3455 Vorce Road
Harbor Springs MI 49740
800-426-8054
Fax: 888-426-8054
amproil@freeway.net
www.americanpromotions.com

Frank's Sport Shop
430 East Tremont Avenue
Bronx NY 10457
718-299-5223
Fax: 718-583-1652

BASEBALL CARDS

Grandstand Cards
22647 Ventura Boulevard #192
Woodland Hills CA 91364
818-992-5642
Fax: 818-348-9122
gscards@aol.com

Minford Minors
2901 Squirrel Creek Road
Newland NC 28657
828-733-1145
Fax: 828-733-1145
minfomino@skybest.com
www.minfordminors.com

BASEBALLS

American Promotions of Illinois
3455 Vorce Road
Harbor Springs MI 49740
800-426-8054
Fax: 888-426-8054
amproil@freeway.net
www.americanpromotions.com

Fotoball Sports
3738 Ruffin Road
San Diego CA 92123
800-467-9900
Fax: 858-467-9947
info@fotoball.com

Frank's Sport Shop
430 East Tremont Avenue
Bronx NY 10457
718-299-5223
Fax: 718-583-1652

Markwort Sporting Goods Company
4300 Forest Park Avenue
St. Louis MO 63108
314-652-3757
Fax: 314-652-6241
sales@markwort.com
www.markwort.com

Omni Sports Technologies
P.O. Box 751625
Memphis TN 38175
800-529-6664
Fax: 901-366-9446
ostinc@aol.com
www.omnisportstech.com

Phoenix Sports, Inc.
113 Bell Street, Suite 102
Seattle WA 98121
425-742-5688 / 800-776-9229
Fax: 425-742-4383
Fax: 800-776-4422
phoesports@aol.com
www.phoenixsportsinc.com

Vantage Products International
7895 Stage Hills, Suite 105
Bartlett TN 30133
800-244-4457
Fax: 800-321-5882
vpisports@aol.com
vpisports.com

BAGS

Miller Net Company, Inc.
P.O. Box 18787
Memphis TN 38181
901-744-3804
Fax: 901-743-6580
miller@mem.net
home.mem.net/~miller

Omni Sports Technologies
P.O. Box 751625
Memphis TN 38175
800-529-6664
Fax: 901-366-9446
ostinc@aol.com
www.omnisportstech.com

Vantage Products International
7895 Stage Hills, Suite 105
Bartlett TN 38133
800-244-4457
Fax: 800-321-5882
vpisports@aol.com
vpisports.com

BATS

American Promotions of Illinois
3455 Vorce Road
Harbor Springs MI 49740
800-426-8054
Fax: 888-426-8054
amproil@freeway.net
www.americanpromotions.com

Barnstable Bat Co.
40 Pleasant Pines Avenue
Centerville MA 02632
888-549-8046
Fax: 508-362-3983
woodbat@mediaone.net
barnstablebat.com

Brett Bros. Bat Company
East 9514 Montgomery, Bldg. 25
Spokane WA 99206
509-891-6435
Fax: 509-891-4156
info@brettbats.com
www.brettbros.com

Frank's Sport Shop
430 East Tremont Avenue
Bronx NY 10457
718-299-5223
Fax: 718-583-1652

Glomar Enterprises
116 W. Walnut Avenue
Fullerton CA 92832
714-871-5956
Fax: 714-871-5958
www.glomarbats.com

Hoosier Bat Company
4511 Evans
Valparaiso IN 46383
800-228-3787
Fax: 219-465-0877
baseball@netnitco.net
www.hoosierbat.com

Mighty KC Bat Company
3610 Main
Grandview MO 64030
800-417-1047
Fax: 816-763-3124
homey@hitter.net
www.mightykcbats.com

Professional Diamond Clubs, Inc.
Lexington NC
336-248-5537
powerboned@lexcominc.net

Young Bat Company
1449 Ecusta Road
Brevard NC 28715
828-884-8733
Fax: 828-862-3842
youngbatco@citcom.net
www.youngbat.com

BATTING CAGES

Beacon Ballfields
2222 Evergreen Road, Suite 6
Middleton WI 53562
800-747-5985 / 608-824-0068
Fax: 608-836-0724
beacon@ballfields.com
www.ballfields.com

C & H Baseball, Inc.
2215 60th Drive East
Bradenton FL 34203
800-248-5192 / 941-727-1533
Fax: 941-727-0588
chbaseball@earthlink.net

Miller Net Company, Inc.
P.O. Box 18787
Memphis TN 38181
901-744-3804
Fax: 901-743-6580
miller@mem.net
home.mem.net/~miller

National Batting Cages, Inc.
P.O. Box 250
Forest Grove OR 97116-0250
800-547-8800
Fax: 503-357-3727
www.nationalbattingcages.com

Omni Sports Technologies
P.O. Box 751625
Memphis TN 38175
800-529-6664
Fax: 901-366-9446
ostinc@aol.com
www.omnisportstech.com

**Rollaway Batting Cages
by Lanier**
206 S. Three Notch Street
Andalusia AL 36420
800-716-9189
Fax: 334-222-3323
battingcages@alaweb.com
www.alaweb.com/~battingcages

Vantage Products International
7895 Stage Hills, Suite 105
Bartlett TN 38133
800-244-4457
Fax: 800-321-5882
vpisports@aol.com
vpisports.com

BUSINESS DEVELOPMENT

**Resnick Amsterdam
Leshner P.C.**
653 Skippack Pike, Suite 300
Blue Bell PA 19422
215-628-8080
Fax: 215-628-4752
ral@ral-cpa.com
www.ral-cpa.com

CAMPS/SCHOOLS

Cooperstown Baseball Camp
P.O. Box 704
Cooperstown NY 13326
800-726-7314
Fax: 607-293-8131
camp@telenet.net
www.cooperstownbaseball.com

Mickey Owen Baseball School
P.O. Box 88
Miller MO 65707
417-882-2799
Fax: 417-889-6978
mobs@dialus.com
www.mickeyowen.com

"Playball" Baseball Academy
P.O. Box 4898
Fort Lauderdale FL 33338
954-776-6217 / 954-772-4510

**Professional Baseball
Instruction, Inc.**
P.O. Box 109
Franklin Lakes NJ 07417
914-477-2560
Fax: 914-477-3342
doug@baseballclinics.com
www.baseballclinics.com

CAPS/HEADWEAR

**American Promotions of
Illinois**
3455 Vorce Road
Harbor Springs MI 49740
800-426-8054
Fax: 888-426-8054
amproil@freeway.net
www.americanpromotions.com

Frank's Sport Shop
430 East Tremont Avenue
Bronx NY 10457
718-299-5223
Fax: 718-583-1652

Minor Leagues, Major Dreams
P.O. Box 6098
Anaheim CA 92816
714-939-0939 / 800-345-2421
Fax: 714-939-0655
mlmd@minorleagues.com
www.minorleagues.com

Twin City Knitting Company, Inc.
828-464-4830
Fax: 828-465-3209

CHARTS/CARDS

Allegheny Publishing Co.
5346 Castle Rock Road
Roanoke VA 24018-2812
800-733-0543
Fax: 540-989-9676
info@allcoaches.com
www.allcoaches.com

CLEANING–UNIFORMS AND EQUIPMENT

**Eastern Institutional Supply
Company (EISCO)**
1545 Highway 9
Toms River NJ 08755
800-553-4726
Fax: 732-240-3599
brad@eisco1.com
www.eisco1.com

Frank's Sport Shop
430 East Tremont Avenue
Bronx NY 10457
718-299-5223
718-583-1652

Caddy Products
10501 Florida Avenue South
Minneapolis MN 55438
612-828-0030
Fax: 612-829-0166
peter_bergin@mediatechsrc.com

BirdZerk!
P.O. Box 36061
Louisville KY 40233
800-219-0899
502-458-4020
Fax: 502-458-0867
funshows@bellsouth.net
www.birdzerk.com

Carousels USA
P.O. Box 8087
San Antonio TX 78208
210-224-8015
Fax: 210-227-3571

MSE Pro Mascots
2015 Knollwood Road
Roanoke VA 24018
540-774-7157
Fax: 540 772-9548
jjack4hcky@aol.com
www.promascot.com

The King of Sports/Mark Out Productions
Contact: Jon Cudo
15183 SW Walker Road, Suite D
Beaverton OR 97006
503-626-1959
Fax: 978-418-0058
cudo@gameops.com
www.thekingofsports.com

ZOOperstars!
P.O. Box 36061
Louisville KY 40233
800-219-0899
502-458-4020
Fax: 502-458-0867
funshows@bellsouth.net
www.zooperstars.com

The Great Gazebo, Inc.
1512 Meadowbrook
East Lansing MI 48823-2146
800-962-2767
Fax: 517-332-6126
info@greatgazebo.com
www.greatgazebo.com

C & H Baseball, Inc.
2215 60th Drive East
Bradenton FL 34203
800-248-5192
941-727-1533
Fax: 941-727-0588
chbaseball@earthlink.net

Covermaster, Inc.
100 Westmore Drive, 11-D
Rexdale ON M9V 5C3
800-387-5808
Fax: 416-742-6837
info@covermaster.com
www.covermaster.com

Vantage Products International
7895 Stage Hills, Suite 105
Bartlett TN 38133
800-244-4457
Fax: 800-321-5882
vpisports@aol.com
vpisports.com

American Athletic, Inc.
200 American Avenue
Jefferson IA 50129
800-247-3978
Fax: 515-386-4566
thoran@americanathletic.com
www.americanathletic.com

American Athletic, Inc.
200 American Avenue
Jefferson IA 50129
800-247-3978
Fax: 515-386-4566
thoran@americanathletic.com
www.americanathletic.com

C & H Baseball, Inc.
2215 60th Drive East
Bradenton FL 34203
800-248-5192
941-727-1533
Fax: 941-727-0588
chbaseball@earthlink.net

Covermaster, Inc.
100 Westmore Drive, 11-D
Rexdale ON M9V 5C3
800-387-5808
Fax: 416-742-6837
info@covermaster.com
www.covermaster.com

American Promotions of Illinois
3455 Vorce Road
Harbor Springs MI 49740
800-426-8054
Fax: 888-426-8054
amproil@freeway.net
www.americanpromotions.com

Pyrotecnico
800-854-4705
Fax: 724-652-1288

FOOD SERVICE

Concession Solutions
16022 26th Avenue NE
Shoreline WA 98155
206-440-9203
Fax: 206-440-9213
concesssol@aol.com
www.seesystemsdesign.com

KLEMENT Sausage Co.
207 E. Lincoln Avenue
Milwaukee WI 53207
800-558-2330
Fax: 414-744-2438
S.E. Regional Office: 770-474-9414
S.E. Regional Fax: 770-507-1233
www.klements.com

**Sodexho Marriott Services
Concessions & Arena
Management**
90 S. High Street
Dublin OH 43017
614-761-2330
Fax: 614-761-9903
sbaumgartner@sodexhomarriott.com

The Great Gazebo, Inc.
1512 Meadowbrook
East Lansing MI 48823-2146
800-962-2767
Fax: 517-332-6126
info@greatgazebo.com
www.greatgazebo.com

Volume Services America
864-598-8600
Fax: 864-598-8695

GLOVE REPAIR

Henry's BB Club & Glove Repair
719 Moody Street
Waltham MA 02154
781-891-0621

GLOVES

Frank's Sport Shop
430 East Tremont Avenue
Bronx NY 10457
718-299-5223
Fax: 718-583-1652

Guerrero Baseball Gloves
5859 W. Saginaw #269
Lansing MI 48917
800-826-1464
Fax: 517-886-8035

GRAPHIC DESIGN

Low and Inside Creative
P.O. Box 290228
Minneapolis MN 55429
612-797-0777
Fax: 612-767-5510
creative@lowandinside.com
www.lowandinside.com

LAUNDRY STRAPS

Laundry Loops
P.O. Box 5167
Bozeman MT 59717
888-246-5667
Fax: 888-840-6838
laundryloops@avicom.net
www.laundryloops.com

LOGO DESIGN

TradeMark Printing
345 Shoreway Road
San Carlos CA 94070
650-592-9130
Fax: 650-592-2776

MAGNETIC SCHEDULES & PLAYER CARDS

Master Marketing International
1749 S. Naperville Road, Suite 200
Wheaton IL 60187
800-438-3210
630-653-5525
Fax: 630-653-5125
mstrmktg@aol.com
www.magnetpro.com

MASCOT COSTUMES

MSE Pro Mascots
2015 Knollwood Road
Roanoke VA 24018
540-774-7157
Fax: 540-772-9548
jjack4hcky@aol.com
www.promascot.com

MASCOT DOLLS & SOUVENIRS

Market Identity
P.O. Box 3967
Thousand Oaks CA 91359
800-927-8070 ext. 8230
805-579-6066
nbleier@marketidentity.com

MEDIA RELATIONS SERVICES

Sports Systems Services, Inc.
2160 North Central Road, Suite 104
Fort Lee NJ 07024
201-585-9260
Fax: 201-585-3014
chris@sportssystems.com
www.sportssystems.com

MESSAGE CENTERS

Spectrum Scoreboards
800-392-5050
Fax: 713-944-1290

Trans-Lux Sports
1651 North 1000 West
Logan UT 84321
800-543-7904
435-753-2224
Fax: 435-753-2975
sales@trans-luxsports.com
www.trans-luxsports.com

MUGS & SPORT BOTTLES

Whirley Industries, Inc.
618 Fourth Avenue
Warren PA 16365
814-723-7600
800-825-5575
Fax: 814-723-3245
info@whirley.com
www.whirley.com

MUSIC/SOUND EFFECTS

Portland Trail Blazers - Game Ops Commander
1 Center Court, Suite 200
Portland OR 97227
800-346-8037
503-797-9746
Fax: 503-736-5066
john.jackson@ripcity.com
www.gameopscommander.com

Sound Creations
2820 Azalea Place
Nashville TN 37204
615-460-7330
Fax: 615-460-7331
www.clickeffects.com

Stanley Sound Productions
727-442-4971
rush.digitalchainsaw.com/music.html

NATIONAL SHOWCASE EVENTS

Baseball Factory
3290 Pine Orchard Lane, Suite D
Ellicott City MD 21042
800-641-4487
Fax: 410-418-5434
info@baseballfactory.com
www.baseballfactory.com

NETTING/POSTS

C & H Baseball, Inc.
2215 60th Drive East
Bradenton FL 34203
800-248-5192
941-727-1533
Fax: 941-727-0588
chbaseball@earthlink.net

Miller Net Company, Inc.
P.O. Box 18787
Memphis TN 38181
901-744-3804
Fax: 901-743-6580
miller@mem.net
home.mem.net/~miller

Omni Sports Technologies
P.O. Box 751625
Memphis TN 38175
800-529-6664
Fax: 901-366-9446
ostinc@aol.com
www.omnisportstech.com

Vantage Products International
7895 Stage Hills, Suite 105
Bartlett TN 38133
800-244-4457
Fax: 800-321-5882
vpisports@aol.com
vpisports.com

OUTFIELD WALL MURALS

American Athletic, Inc.
200 American Avenue
Jefferson IA 50129
800-247-3978
Fax: 515-386-4566
thoran@americanathletic.com
www.americanathletic.com

PADDING - FIELD/WALL

American Athletic, Inc.
200 American Avenue
Jefferson IA 50129
800-247-3978
Fax: 515-386-4566
thoran@americanathletic.com
www.americanathletic.com

Promats, Inc.
P.O. Box 508
Fort Collins CO 80522
800-678-6287
Fax: 970-482-7740
promats@aol.com
www.promats.com

PHOTOGRAPHY—BASEBALL ACTION

Wagner Photography
Ft. Myers FL
941-277-3100
www.wagnerphotography.com

PITCHING MACHINES

American Athletic, Inc.
200 American Avenue
Jefferson IA 50129
800-247-3978
Fax: 515-386-4566
thoran@americanathletic.com
www.americanathletic.com

C & H Baseball, Inc.
2215 60th Drive East
Bradenton FL 34203
800-248-5192
941-727-1533
Fax: 941-727-0588
chbaseball@earthlink.net

Frank's Sport Shop
430 East Tremont Avenue
Bronx NY 10457
718-299-5223
Fax: 718-583-1652

Miller Net Company, Inc.
P.O. Box 18787
Memphis TN 38181
901-744-3804
Fax: 901-743-6580
miller@mem.net
home.mem.net/~miller

Omni Sports Technologies
P.O. Box 751625
Memphis TN 38175
800-529-6664
Fax: 901-366-9446
ostinc@aol.com
www.omnisportstech.com

Vantage Products International
7895 Stage Hills, Suite 105
Bartlett TN 38133
800-244-4457
Fax: 800-321-5882
vpisports@aol.com
vpisports.com

PLAYING FIELD PRODUCTS

C & H Baseball, Inc.
2215 60th Drive East
Bradenton FL 34203
800-248-5192
941-727-1533
Fax: 941-727-0588
chbaseball@earthlink.net

Covermaster, Inc.
100 Westmore Drive, 11-D
Rexdale ON M9V 5C3
800-387-5808
Fax: 416-742-6837
info@covermaster.com
www.covermaster.com

Diamond Pro
1341 West Mockingbird Lane
Dallas TX 75247
800-228-2987
Fax: 800-640-6735
www.diamondpro.com

Midwest Athletic Surfaces
1125 West State Street
Marshfield WI 54449
715-384-7027
Fax: 715-384-7027
wrngtrkt@commplusis.net
www.commplusis.net/~wrngtrkt

Miller Net Company, Inc.
P.O. Box 18787
Memphis TN 38181
901-744-3804
Fax: 901-743-6580
miller@mem.net
home.mem.net/~miller

Omni Sports Technologies
P.O. Box 751625
Memphis TN 38175
800-529-6664
Fax: 901-366-9446
ostinc@aol.com
www.omnisportstech.com

Partac/Beam Clay
Kelsey Park
Great Meadows NJ 07838-9721
908-637-4191
Fax: 908-637-8421
partac@accessgate.net

Stabilizer Solutions, Inc.
205 S. 28th Street
Phoenix AZ 85034
800-336-2468
Fax: 602-225-5902
lphubbs@stabilizersolutions.com
stabilizersolutions.com

PORTABLE PITCHER'S MOUNDS

American Athletic, Inc.
200 American Avenue
Jefferson IA 50129
800-247-3978
Fax: 515-386-4566
thoran@americanathletic.com
www.americanathletic.com

PRINTING

Low and Inside Creative
P.O. Box 290228
Minneapolis MN 55429
612-797-0777
Fax: 612-767-5510
creative@lowandinside.com
www.lowandinside.com

ProForma Sports
901 E. Mossville Road
Peoria IL 61615
309-579-2324
Fax: 309-579-2591
jkbrooke98@yahoo.com

TradeMark Printing
345 Shoreway Road
San Carlos CA 94070
650-592-9130
Fax: 650-592-2776

PRIZE PROMOTION INSURANCE

GSR - Global Specialty Risk
3838 Oakline Avenue, Suite 200
Dallas TX 75219
800-411-3756
214-526-5050
Fax: 214-526-6050
doug@gsrisk.com
www.gsrisk.com

PROFESSIONAL SERVICES

Diversified Sports Group
Franchise Brokers
800-398-3717

Heery International
999 Peachtree Street NE
Atlanta GA 30367-5401
404-881-9880
Fax: 404-875-1283
mhollema@heery.com
www.heery.com

Independent Scouting Bureau, Inc.
143 Vixen Circle, Suite C
Branson MO 65616
888-741-3206
Fax: 417-337-5282
admin@inscouting.com
www.inscouting.com

American Promotions of Illinois
3455 Vorce Road
Harbor Springs MI 49740
800-426-8054
Fax: 888-426-8054
amproil@freeway.net
www.americanpromotions.com

Fotoball Sports
3738 Ruffin Road
San Diego CA 92123
800-467-9900
Fax: 858-467-9947
info@fotoball.com

Frank's Sport Shop
430 East Tremont Avenue
Bronx NY 10457
718-299-5223
Fax: 718-583-1652

National Pastime - Sport Promotions & Exhibits
P.O. Box 1581
Birmingham MI 48012
248-435-9647
Fax: 248-435-9746
nationalpastimebaseball@yahoo.com
nationalpastime.net

Marketing, Etc.
077-302-8288
404-842-3824
Fax: 404-842-0762

Baker-Dillon Public Relations
P.O. Box 609
Clovis CA 93613
800-570-1262
Fax: 559-325-7195
bdpr@bakerdillonpr.com
www.bakerdillonpr.com

Low and Inside
P.O. Box 290228
Minneapolis MN 55429
612-797-0777
Fax: 612-767-5510
have-a-ball@lowandinside.com
www.lowandinside.com

Frank's Sport Shop
430 East Tremont Avenue
Bronx NY 10457
718-299-5223
Fax: 718-583-1652

Miller Net Company, Inc.
P.O. Box 18787
Memphis TN 38181
901-744-3804
Fax: 901-743-6580
miller@mem.net
home.mem.net/~miller

Omni Sports Technologies
P.O. Box 751625
Memphis TN 38175
800-529-6664
Fax: 901-366-9446
ostinc@aol.com
www.omnisportstech.com

Sport Electronics
312 E. 55th Street
P.O. Box 696
Hinsdale IL 60522
630-920-1808
800-248-4142
Fax: 630-920-1819
radargun@ix.netcom.com
www.radarguns.com

Nevco Scoreboard Company
301 East Harris Avenue
P.O. Box 609
Greenville IL 62246
618-664-0360
Fax: 618-664-0398
nevco@nevcoscoreboards.com
www.nevcoscoreboards.com

Spectrum Scoreboards
800-392-5050
Fax: 713-944-1290

Trans-Lux Sports
1651 North 1000 West
Logan UT 84321
800-543-7904
435-753-2224
Fax: 435-753-2975
sales@trans-luxsports.com
www.trans-luxsports.com

Seating Services Inc.
P.O. Box 4
Angola NY 14006
800-552-9470
Fax: 716-549-9011
Seatingdcc@msn.com
www.seatingservices.com

Southern Bleacher Company
P.O. Box One
Graham TX 76450
800-433-0912
940-549-0733
Fax: 940-549-1365
sobco@wf.net
www.southernbleacher.com

Sturdisteel Company
P.O. Box 2655
Waco TX 76702
800-433-3116
Fax: 254-666-4472
roberts@sturdisteel.com
www.sturdisteel.com

Vantage Products International
7895 Stage Hills, Suite 105
Bartlett TN 38133
800-244-4457
Fax: 800-321-5882
vpisports@aol.com
vpisports.com

SIGNAGE

Action Graphix®
P.O. Box 2337
Jonesboro AR 72401
800-762-9807
870-931-7440
Fax: 870-931-7528
graphix@actiongraphix.com
www.actiongraphix.com

SPORTS MEDICINE

PROSERIES
10826 Venice Blvd., Suite 101
Culver City CA 90232
800-645-7030
Fax: 310-836-9916
pseries@concentric.net
www.proseriesusa.com

SPORTS VISION TRAINING–VECTOGRAM

Stereo Optical Co., Inc.
3539 N. Kenton Avenue
Chicago IL 60641
773-777-2869
Fax: 773-777-4985
sales@stereooptical.com
www.stereooptical.com

STADIUM ARCHITECTS

Design Exchange Architects, Inc.
Polly Drummond Office Park
Bldg. 3, Suite 3205
Newark DE 19711
302-366-1611
Fax: 302-366-1657
tengland@design-exchange.com
www.design-exchange.com

**Devine deFlon Yeager
Architects**
3700 Broadway, Suite 300
Kansas City MO 64111-2506
816-561-2761
Fax: 816-561-9222
slondon@ddyarch.com
www.ddyarch.com

DLR Group Sports
601 West Swann Avenue
Tampa FL 33606
813-254-9811
Fax: 813-254-4230
smeradith@dkrgroup.com
www.dlrgroup.com

Ellerbe Becket
605 West 47th Street, Suite 200
Kansas City, MO 64112
816-561-4443
Fax: 816-561-2863
www.ellerbebecket.com

Heery International
999 Peachtree Street NE
Atlanta GA 30367-5401
404-881-9880
Fax: 404-875-1283
mhollema@heery.com
www.heery.com

HNTB Sports Architecture
1201 Walnut, Suite 700
Kansas City MO 64106
816-472-1201
Fax: 816-472-4060
mdinitto@hntb.com
sports.hntb.com

HOK Sports Facilities Group
323 West 8th Street, Suite 700
Kansas City MO 64105
816-221-1500
Fax: 816-221-1578
www.hok.com/sport

L.D. Astorino & Associates
227 Fort Pitt Boulevard
Pittsburgh PA 15222
412-765-1700
Fax: 412-765-1711
ekinney@ldastorino.com
www.ldastorino.com

TAX/ACCOUNTING

Pro Athlete Advisors Co.
800-655-4340

TICKET SALES

Sport Productions, Inc.
1414 S. Green Road, Suite 107
Cleveland OH 44121
216-291-0100
Fax: 216-297-1076

TICKETS

National Ticket Company
P.O. Box 547
Shamokin PA 17872
800-829-0829
570-672-2900
Fax: 800-829-0888
Fax: 570-672-2999
ticket@nationalticket.com
www.nationalticket.com

Ticketcraft
1390 Jerusalem Avenue
Merrick NY 11566
800-645-4944
Fax: 516-538-6200
donnao@ticketcraft.com
www.ticketcraft.com

Tickets.com
555 Anton Boulevard, 12th Floor
Costa Mesa CA 92626
888-397-3400
Fax: 315-471-2715
sales@tickets.com
brochure.tickets.com

Broach Baseball Tours
704-365-6500
Fax: 704-365-3800
www.broachtours.com

Diamond Travel
1474 East 86th Street
Indianapolis IN 46240
800-ML SCOUT
Fax: 317-843-3910
diamondjwj@aol.com

Sports Travel, Inc.
60 Main Street
P.O. Box 50
Hatfield MA 01038
800-662-4424
Fax: 413-247-5700
info@sportstravelandtours.com
www.sportstravelandtours.com

Dinn Bros. Trophies
221 Interstate Drive
West Springfield MA 01089
800-628-9657
Fax: 800-876-7497
sales@dinntrophy.com
www.dinntrophy.com

Entry Media, Inc.
127 West Fairbanks Avenue #417
Winter Park FL 32789
407-678-4446
Fax: 407-679-3590
entrymedia@worldnet.att.net
www.entrymedia.com

Tickets.com
555 Anton Boulevard, 12th Floor
Costa Mesa CA 92626
888-397-3400
Fax: 315-471-2715
sales@tickets.com
brochure.tickets.com

American Promotions of Illinois
3455 Vorce Road
Harbor Springs MI 49740
800-426-8054
Fax: 888-426-8054
amproil@freeway.net
www.americanpromotions.com

Vantage Products International
7895 Stage Hills, Suite 105
Bartlett TN 38133
800-244-4457
Fax: 800-321-5882
vpisports@aol.com
vpisports.com

ABC's of Pitching
4031 Wild Chapparal Drive
Shingle Springs CA 95682
530-676-BALL(2255)
Fax: 530-676-2257
bosiosportscentral.com

Promats, Inc.
P.O. Box 508
Fort Collins CO 80522
800-678-6287
Fax: 970-482-7740
promats@aol.com
www.promats.com

Mindspring
1430 W. Peachtree St. NW, Ste. 400
Atlanta GA 30309
888-MSPRING
www.mindspring.net

SkilTech
P.O. Box 1007
Bear DE 19701-1007
302-836-4841
Fax: 302-836-3314
info@skiltech.com
www.skiltech.com

**Add your company to the Baseball America
2001 Service Directory.
Call 800-845-2726 for details.**

INDEX

2000DIRECTORYINDEX

MAJOR LEAGUE TEAMS

American League

Page	Club	Phone	FAX
28	Anaheim Angels	714-940-2000	714-940-2001
30	Baltimore Orioles	410-685-9800	410-547-6272
32	Boston Red Sox	617-267-9440	617-375-0944
34	Chicago White Sox	312-674-1000	312-674-5116
36	Cleveland Indians	216-420-4200	216-420-4396
38	Detroit Tigers	313-962-4000	313-471-2138
40	Kansas City Royals	816-921-8000	816-921-1366
42	Minnesota Twins	612-375-1366	612-375-7480
44	New York Yankees	718-293-4300	718-293-8431
46	Oakland Athletics	510-638-4900	510-562-1633
48	Seattle Mariners	206-346-4000	206-346-4400
50	Tampa Bay Devil Rays	727-825-3137	727-825-3111
52	Texas Rangers	817-273-5222	817-273-5206
54	Toronto Blue Jays	416-341-1000	416-341-1250

National League

Page	Club	Phone	FAX
58	Arizona Diamondbacks	602-462-6500	602-462-6599
60	Atlanta Braves	404-522-7630	404-614-1391
62	Chicago Cubs	773-404-2827	773-404-4129
64	Cincinnati Reds	513-421-4510	513-421-7342
66	Colorado Rockies	303-292-0200	303-312-2116
68	Florida Marlins	305-626-7400	305-626-7428
70	Houston Astros	713-259-8000	713-259-5339
72	Los Angeles Dodgers	323-224-1500	323-224-1269
74	Milwaukee Brewers	414-933-4114	414-933-3251
76	Montreal Expos	514-253-3434	514-253-8282
78	New York Mets	718-507-6387	718-565-6395
80	Philadelphia Phillies	215-463-6000	215-389-3050
82	Pittsburgh Pirates	412-323-5000	412-323-5024
84	St. Louis Cardinals	314-421-3060	314-425-0640
86	San Diego Padres	619-881-6500	619-497-5339
88	San Francisco Giants	415-972-2000	415-947-2800

MINOR LEAGUE TEAMS

Page	Club	League	Phone	FAX
155	Akron	Eastern	330-253-5151	330-253-3300
145	Albuquerque	PCL	505-243-1791	505-842-0561
155	Altoona	Eastern	814-943-5400	814-943-9050
169	Arkansas	Texas	501-664-1555	501-664-1834
200	Asheville	SAL	828-258-0428	828-258-0320
208	Auburn	NYP	315-255-2489	315-255-2675
200	Augusta	SAL	706-736-7889	706-736-1122
174	Bakersfield	Cal	661-322-1363	661-322-6199
208	Batavia	NYP	716-343-5454	716-343-5620
192	Beloit	Midwest	608-362-2272	608-362-0418
227	Billings	Pioneer	406-252-1241	406-252-2968
156	Binghamton	Eastern	607-723-6387	607-723-7779
163	Birmingham	Southern	205-988-3200	205-988-9698
221	Bluefield	Appy	540-326-1326	540-326-1318
216	Boise	Northwest	208-322-5000	208-322-7432
156	Bowie	Eastern	301-805-6000	301-805-6008
185	Brevard County	FSL	321-633-9200	321-633-9210
221	Bristol	Appy	540-645-7275	540-669-7686
208	Brooklyn	NYP	718-803-4023	718-507-6395
136	Buffalo	IL	716-846-2000	716-852-6530
192	Burlington, IA	Midwest	319-754-5705	319-754-5882
221	Burlington, NC	Appy	336-222-0223	336-226-2498
227	Butte	Pioneer	406-723-8206	406-723-9148
145	Calgary	PCL	403-284-1111	403-284-4343
201	Cape Fear	SAL	910-424-6500	910-424-4325
201	Capital City	SAL	803-256-4110	803-256-4338
163	Carolina	Southern	919-269-2287	919-269-4910
192	Cedar Rapids	Midwest	319-363-3887	319-363-5631
202	Charleston, SC	SAL	843-723-7241	843-723-2641
202	Charleston, WV	SAL	304-344-2287	304-344-0083
185	Charlotte, FL	FSL	941-625-9500	941-624-5168
136	Charlotte, NC	IL	704-357-8071	704-329-2155
164	Chattanooga	Southern	423-267-2208	423-267-4258

Page	Club	League	Phone	FAX
185	Clearwater	FSL	727-441-8638	727-447-3924
193	Clinton	Midwest	319-242-0727	319-242-1433
146	Colorado Springs	PCL	719-597-1449	719-597-2491
203	Columbus, GA	SAL	706-571-8866	706-571-9107
137	Columbus, OH	IL	614-462-5250	614-462-3271
222	Danville	Appy	804-791-3346	804-791-3347
193	Dayton	Midwest	937-228-2287	937-228-2284
186	Daytona	FSL	904-257-3172	904-257-3382
203	Delmarva	SAL	410-219-3112	410-219-9164
186	Dunedin	FSL	727-733-9302	727-734-7661
137	Durham	IL	919-687-6500	919-687-6560
146	Edmonton	PCL	780-414-4450	780-414-4475
222	Elizabethton	Appy	423-547-6440	423-547-6442
169	El Paso	Texas	915-755-2000	915-757-0671
157	Erie	Eastern	814-456-1300	814-456-7520
216	Eugene	Northwest	541-342-5367	541-342-6089
217	Everett	Northwest	425-258-3673	425-258-3675
187	Fort Myers	FSL	941-768-4210	941-768-4211
194	Fort Wayne	Midwest	219-482-6400	219-471-4678
180	Frederick	Carolina	301-662-0013	301-662-0018
147	Fresno	PCL	559-442-1994	559-264-0795
227	Great Falls	Pioneer	406-452-5311	406-454-0811
204	Greensboro	SAL	336-333-2287	336-273-7350
164	Greenville, SC	Southern	864-299-3456	864-277-7369
204	Hagerstown	SAL	301-791-6266	301-791-6066
157	Harrisburg	Eastern	717-231-4444	717-231-4445
228	Helena	Pioneer	406-449-7616	406-449-6979
205	Hickory	SAL	828-322-3000	828-322-6137
174	High Desert	Cal	760-246-6287	760-246-3197
209	Hudson Valley	NYP	914-838-0094	914-838-0014
165	Huntsville	Southern	256-882-2562	256-880-0801
228	Idaho Falls	Pioneer	208-522-8363	208-522-9858
138	Indianapolis	IL	317-269-3542	317-269-3541
147	Iowa	PCL	515-243-6111	515-243-5152
165	Jacksonville	Southern	904-358-2846	904-358-2845
209	Jamestown	NYP	716-664-0915	716-664-4175
223	Johnson City	Appy	423-461-4866	423-461-4864
187	Jupiter	FSL	561-775-1818	561-691-6886
194	Kane County	Midwest	630-232-8811	630-232-8815
223	Kingsport	Appy	423-378-3744	423-392-8538
180	Kinston	Carolina	252-527-9111	252-527-2328
188	Kissimmee	FSL	407-933-5500	407-847-6237
175	Lake Elsinore	Cal	909-245-4487	909-245-0305
188	Lakeland	FSL	863-688-7911	863-688-9589
201	Lakewood	SAL (2001)	732-901-7000	732-901-3967
175	Lancaster	Cal	661-726-5400	661-726-5406
195	Lansing	Midwest	517-485-4500	517-485-4518
148	Las Vegas	PCL	702-386-7200	702-386-7214
139	Louisville	IL	502-212-2287	502-515-2255
210	Lowell	NYP	978-459-2255	978-459-1674
181	Lynchburg	Carolina	804-528-1144	804-846-0768
205	Macon	SAL	912-745-8943	912-743-5559
210	Mahoning Valley	NYP	330-505-0000	330-505-9696
224	Martinsville	Appy	540-666-2000	540-666-2139
229	Medicine Hat	Pioneer	403-526-0404	403-504-2670
148	Memphis	PCL	901-721-6050	901-721-6017
195	Michigan	Midwest	616-660-2287	616-660-2288
170	Midland	Texas	915-683-4251	915-683-0994
229	Missoula	Pioneer	406-543-3300	406-543-9463
166	Mobile	Southern	334-479-2327	334-476-1147
176	Modesto	Cal	209-572-4487	209-572-4490
176	Mudville	Cal	209-320-6050	209-320-6070
181	Myrtle Beach	Carolina	843-918-6002	843-918-6001
149	Nashville	PCL	615-242-4371	615-256-5684
158	New Britain	Eastern	860-224-8383	860-225-6267
158	New Haven	Eastern	203-782-1666	203-782-3150
211	New Jersey	NYP	973-579-7500	973-579-7502
149	New Orleans	PCL	504-734-5155	504-734-5118
139	Norfolk	IL	757-622-2222	757-624-9090
159	Norwich	Eastern	860-887-7962	860-886-5996
230	Ogden	Pioneer	801-393-2400	801-393-2473
150	Oklahoma	PCL	405-218-1000	405-218-1001
150	Omaha	PCL	402-734-2550	402-734-7166
211	Oneonta	NYP	607-432-6326	607-432-1965
166	Orlando	Southern	407-938-3519	407-938-3442
140	Ottawa	IL	613-747-5969	613-747-0003
140	Pawtucket	IL	401-724-7300	401-724-2140
196	Peoria	Midwest	309-688-1622	309-686-4516
206	Piedmont	SAL	704-932-3267	704-938-7040

Page	Club	League	Phone	FAX
212	Pittsfield	NYP	413-499-6387	413-443-7144
159	Portland, ME	Eastern	207-874-9300	207-780-0317
217	Portland, OR	Northwest	503-223-2837	503-223-2948
182	Potomac	Carolina	703-590-2311	703-590-5716
224	Princeton	Appy	304-487-2000	304-487-8762
224	Pulaski	Appy	540-980-1070	540-994-0847
196	Quad City	Midwest	319-324-2032	319-324-3109
177	Rancho Cuca.	Cal	909-481-5000	909-481-5005
160	Reading	Eastern	610-375-8469	610-373-5868
141	Richmond, VA	IL	804-359-4444	804-359-0731
141	Rochester	IL	716-454-1001	716-454-1056
170	Round Rock	Texas	512-255-2255	512-255-1558
180	St. Lucie	FSL	561-871-2100	561-878-9802
189	St. Petersburg	FSL	727-822-3384	727-895-1556
151	Sacramento	PCL	916-319-4700	916-319-4710
182	Salem	Carolina	540-389-3333	540-389-9710
217	Salem-Keizer	Northwest	503-390-2225	503-390-2227
151	Salt Lake	PCL	801-485-3800	801-485-6818
171	San Antonio	Texas	210-675-7275	210-670-0001
177	San Bernardino	Cal	909-888-9922	909-888-5251
178	San Jose	Cal	408-297-1435	408-297-1453
189	Sarasota	FSL	941-365-4460	941-365-4217
206	Savannah	SAL	912-351-9150	912-352-9722
142	Scranton/W-B	IL	570-969-2255	570-963-6564
171	Shreveport	Texas	318-636-5555	318-636-5670
197	South Bend	Midwest	219-235-9988	219-235-9950
218	Spokane	Northwest	509-535-2922	509-534-5368
212	Staten Island	NYP	718-698-9265	718-698-9291
142	Syracuse	IL	315-474-7833	315-474-2658
152	Tacoma	PCL	253-752-7707	253-752-7135
190	Tampa	FSL	813-875-7753	813-673-3174
167	Tennessee	Southern	423-637-9494	423-523-9913
143	Toledo	IL	419-893-9483	419-893-5847
161	Trenton	Eastern	609-394-3300	609-394-9666
152	Tucson	PCL	520-434-1021	520-889-9477
171	Tulsa	Texas	918-744-5998	918-747-3267
213	Utica	NYP	315-738-0999	315-738-0992
219	Vancouver	NWL	604-872-5232	604-872-1714
213	Vermont	NYP	802-655-4200	802-655-5660
190	Vero Beach	FSL	561-569-4900	561-567-0819
178	Visalia	Cal	559-625-0480	559-739-7732
197	West Michigan	Midwest	616-784-4131	616-784-4911
167	West Tenn	Southern	901-664-2020	901-988-5246
172	Wichita	Texas	316-267-3372	316-267-3382
214	Williamsport	NYP	570-326-3389	570-326-3494
183	Wilmington	Carolina	302-888-2015	302-888-2032
183	Winston-Salem	Carolina	336-759-2233	336-759-2042
198	Wisconsin	Midwest	920-733-4152	920-733-8032
219	Yakima	Northwest	509-457-5151	509-457-9909

Phone and FAX numbers for minor league offices can be found on pages 129.

INDEPENDENT LEAGUE TEAMS

Page	Club	League	Phone	FAX
268	Adirondack	Northern	518-743-9618	518-743-9721
268	Albany-Colonie	Northern	518-869-9234	518-869-5291
271	Alexandria	Texas-La.	318-473-2237	318-473-2229
269	Allentown	Northern	610-437-6800	610-437-6804
271	Amarillo	Texas-La.	806-342-3455	806-374-2269
257	Atlantic City	Atlantic	609-344-8873	609-344-7010
257	Bridgeport	Atlantic	203-345-4800	203-345-4830
260	Canton	Frontier	330-455-2255	330-454-4835
269	Catskill	Northern	914-436-4386	914-436-9129
274	Chico	Western	530-343-4328	530-894-1799
261	Chillicothe	Frontier	740-773-8326	740-773-8338
261	Cook County	Frontier	708-489-2255	708-489-2999
261	Dubois County	Frontier	812-683-4405	812-683-4299
264	Duluth-Superior	Northern	218-727-4525	218-727-4533
269	Elmira	Northern	607-734-1270	607-734-0891
262	Evansville	Frontier	812-435-8686	812-435-8688
265	Fargo-Moorhead	Northern	701-235-6161	701-297-9247
274	Feather River	Western	530-741-3600	530-741-3087
272	Greenville, MS	Texas-La.	662-335-2583	662-335-7742
272	Jackson	Texas-La.	601-362-2545	601-362-8020
262	Johnstown	Frontier	814-536-8326	814-539-0056
272	Lafayette	Texas-La.	337-233-0998	337-237-3539
258	Lehigh Valley	Atlantic	610-250-2273	610-250-6552
262	London	Frontier	519-679-7337	519-679-5713

Page	Club	League	Phone	FAX
258	Long Island	Atlantic	516-756-4625	516-756-1654
265	Madison	Northern	608-244-5666	608-244-6996
258	Maryland	Atlantic	301-805-6000	301-805-6008
259	Nashua	Atlantic	603-883-2255	603-883-0880
270	New Jersey	Northern	973-746-7434	973-655-8021
259	Newark	Atlantic	973-848-1000	973-621-0095
273	Ozark Mountain	Texas-La.	417-581-2868	417-581-8342
270	Quebec	Northern	418-521-2255	418-521-2266
263	Richmond, IN	Frontier	765-935-7529	765-962-7047
273	Rio Grande Valley	Texas-La.	956-412-9464	956-412-9479
263	River City	Frontier	636-240-2287	636-240-7313
266	St. Paul	Northern	651-644-3517	651-644-1627
273	San Angelo	Texas-La.	915-942-6587	915-947-9480
266	Schaumburg	Northern	877-691-2255	847-891-6441
266	Sioux City	Northern	712-277-9467	712-277-9406
267	Sioux Falls	Northern	605-333-0179	605-333-0139
264	Springfield, IL	Frontier	217-525-5500	217-525-5508
275	Solano	Western	707-452-7400	707-452-7410
259	Somerset	Atlantic	908-252-0700	908-252-0776
275	Sonoma County	Western	707-588-8300	707-588-8721
275	Tri-City	Western	509-547-6773	509-547-4008
276	Valley	Western	480-663-8100	480-663-0101
270	Waterbury	Northern	203-419-0393	203-419-0396
267	Winnipeg	Northern	204-982-2273	204-982-2274
276	Yuma	Western	520-782-3536	520-782-3911
276	Zion	Western	435-656-9000	435-628-8389

OTHER ORGANIZATIONS

Page	Organization	Phone	FAX
348	AAABA	740-453-8531	740-453-3978
118	ABC Radio Network Sports	212-456-5185	212-456-5405
117	ABC Sports	212-456-7777	212-456-2877
337	Alaska Baseball League	907-283-7133	907-283-3390
348	Amateur Athletic Union	407-934-7200	407-934-7242
348	American Amateur BB Congress	616-781-2002	616-781-2060
348	American Amateur Youth BB Alliance	573-518-0319	573-518-0319
300	American BB Coaches Assoc.	517-775-3300	517-775-3600
336	American Baseball Foundation	205-558-4235	205-918-0800
27	American League	212-931-7600	212-949-5405
349	American Legion Baseball	317-630-1213	317-630-1369
346	Area Code Games	707-525-0498	707-525-0214
297	Arizona Fall League	480-496-6700	480-496-6384
119	Associated Press	212-621-1630	212-621-1639
127	Assoc. of Prof. BB Players	714-892-9900	714-897-0233
336	Athletes In Action	813-968-7400	813-968-7515
121	Athlon's Baseball	615-327-0747	615-327-1149
337	Atlantic Collegiate League	908-464-8042	908-464-8042
257	Atlantic League	610-696-8662	610-696-8667
349	Babe Ruth Baseball	609-695-1434	609-695-2505
125	Babe Ruth Birthplace/Museum	410-727-1539	410-727-1652
127	Baseball Assistance Team	212-931-7822	212-949-5652
336	Baseball Canada	613-748-5606	613-748-5767
127	Baseball Chapel	609-398-3505	610-586-4538
120	Baseball Digest	847-491-6440	847-491-6203
127	Baseball Family	865-692-9291	865-769-4386
121	Baseball Parent	865-523-1274	865-673-8926
127	Baseball Trade Show	727-822-6937	727-821-5819
119	BB Writers Assoc. of America	631-981-7938	631-585-4669
121	Beckett Publications	972-991-6657	972-991-8930
119	Bloomberg Sports News	609-279-4058	609-279-5870
117	CBS Sports	212-975-5230	212-975-4063
117	CNN/Sports Illustrated	404-878-1600	404-878-0011
118	CTV	416-332-5600	416-332-5629
338	California Coastal Coll. League	925-672-9662	925-672-9662
300	Calif. CC Comm. on Athletics	916-444-1600	916-444-2616
125	Canadian Baseball Hall of Fame	519-284-1838	519-284-1234
119	Canadian Press	416-507-2154	416-507-2074
338	Cape Cod League	508-996-5004	508-996-5004
294	Caribbean BB Confederation	809-562-4737	809-565-4654
339	Central Illinois Collegiate League	217-446-6074	217-443-8595
290	Chinese Pro Baseball League	886-2-2577-6992	886-2-2577-2606
339	Clark Griffith League	703-536-1729	703-536-1729
339	Coastal Plain League	919-852-1960	919-852-1973
120	Collegiate Baseball	520-623-4530	520-624-5501
122	Coman Publishing	919-688-0218	919-682-1532
349	Continental Amateur BB Assoc.	740-382-4620	614-899-2103
122	Diamond Library Publications	203-834-1231	—

Page	Organization	Phone	FAX
349	Dixie Baseball, Inc.	334-242-8395	334-242-0198
349	Dizzy Dean Baseball	850-455-8827	
294	Dominican League	809-476-0080	809-476-0084
290	Dominican Summer League	809-563-3233	809-563-2455
116	ESPN/ESPN2-TV	860-766-2000	860-766-2213
120	ESPN Magazine	212-515-1000	212-515-1290
118	ESPN Radio	860-766-2661	860-766-5523
119	ESPN/SportsTicker	201-309-1200	800-336-0383
346	East Coast Pro Baseball Showcase	910-962-3570	—
340	Eastern Collegiate Baseball League	610-250-7692	610-250-7692
116	Elias Sports Bureau	212-869-1530	212-354-0980
126	Field of Dreams Movie Site	888-875-8404	319-875-7253
128	Fleer/Skybox	856-231-6200	856-727-9460
117	FOX Sports	310-369-6000	310-969-6192
117	FOX Sports Net	310-369-6000	310-969-6122
260	Frontier League	740-452-7400	740-452-2999
117	FX	310-444-8183	310-235-2853
335	Goodwill Games	404-827-3400	404-827-1394
128	Grandstand Cards	818-992-5642	818-348-9122
340	Great Lakes League	330-335-6184	330-335-8174
349	Hap Dumont Youth Baseball	316-721-1779	316-721-8054
125	Harry Wendelstedt Umpire School	904-672-4879	904-672-3212
116	Howe Sportsdata	617-951-0070	617-737-9960
335	International Baseball Federation	41-21-3188240	41-21-3188241
298	Int'l Baseball League Australia	61-7-3832-0043	61-7-3832-4884
120	International Baseball Rundown	630-668-8341	630-510-1154
335	International Olympic Committee	41-21-621-61-11	41-21-621-62-16
335	International Sports Group	925-798-4591	925-680-1182
291	Italian Baseball Federation	39-0-36858130	39-6-36858201
288	Japan League	03-3502-0022	03-3502-0140
341	Jayhawk League	316-755-1285	316-755-1285
125	Jim Evans Academy of Pro. Ump.	512-335-5959	512-335-5411
120	Junior Baseball Magazine	818-710-1234	818-710-1877
291	Korea Baseball Organization	82-2-3461-7887	82-2-3462-7800
122	Krause Publications	715-445-2214	715-445-4087
128	LA Dodgers Adult Baseball Camp	407-569-4900	407-770-2424
350	Little League Baseball, Inc.	570-326-1921	570-326-1074
126	Little League Baseball Museum	670-000-3607	570-326-2267
126	Louisville Slugger Museum	502-588-7228	502-585-1170
26	MLB International	212-931-7500	212-949-5795
127	MLB Players Alumni Association	719-477-1870	719-477-1875
124	MLB Players Association	212-826-0808	212-752-4378
124	MLB Productions	212-931-7900	212-949-5795
25	Major League Baseball	212-931-7800	—
124	Major League Scouting Bureau	909-980-1881	909-980-7794
125	Major League Umpires Assoc.	215-979-3200	215-979-3201
128	Men's Adult Baseball League	631-753-6725	631-753-4031
127	Men's Senior Baseball League	631-753-6725	631-753-4031
286	Mexican League	525-557-10-07	525-395-24-54
294	Mexican Pacific League	52-642-2-3100	52-642-2-7250
129	Minor League Baseball	727-822-6937	727-821-5819
300	NAIA	918-494-8828	918-494-8841
117	NBC Sports	212-664-4444	212-664-3602
300	NCAA	317-917-6222	317-917-6826
300	NJCAA	719-590-9788	719-590-7324
128	National Adult Baseball Assoc.	800-621-6479	303-639-6605
337	Nat'l Alliance of Coll. Summer Ball	508-432-1774	508-432-9766
350	National Amateur Baseball Fed.	301-262-5005	301-262-5005
336	National Baseball Congress	316-267-3372	316-267-3382
126	National Baseball Hall of Fame	607-547-7200	607-547-2044
345	Nat'l Classic HS Tournament	714-993-5350	714-777-8127
119	National Collegiate BB Writers	312-553-0483	312-553-0495
345	Nat'l Fed. of State HS Assoc.	317-972-6900	—
345	Nat'l HS Baseball Coaches Assoc.	501-876-2591	501-876-2596
57	National League	212-339-7700	212-935-5069
126	Negro Leagues Baseball Museum	816-221-1920	816-221-8424
341	New England Collegiate League	401-423-9863	401-423-2784
341	Northeastern Collegiate League	716-223-3528	716-223-3528
264	Northern League (Central Division)	919-956-8150	919-683-2693
268	Northern League (Eastern Division)	914-436-0411	914-436-6864
342	Northwest Collegiate League	503-625-4044	503-625-0629
342	Northwoods League	507-289-1170	507-289-1866
118	One-on-One Sports Radio Network	847-509-1661	847-509-8149
343	Pacific International League	206-623-8844	602-623-8361
128	Pacific Trading Cards	800-551-2002	—
346	Perfect Game Showcase	800-447-9362	319-298-2924
128	Playoff	972-595-1180	972-595-1190
350	Police Athletic Leagues	561-844-1823	561-863-6120

Page	Organization	Phone	FAX
350	PONY Baseball, Inc.	724-225-1060	724-225-9852
125	Pro Baseball Athletic Trainers Soc.	404-875-4000	404-892-8560
127	Pro Baseball Emp. Opportunities	800-842-5618	828-668-4762
125	Pro Baseball Umpire Corp.	727-822-6937	727-821-5819
347	Prospects Plus, LLC	800-845-2726	919-682-2880
295	Puerto Rican League	787-765-6285	787-767-3028
351	RBI	212-931-7897	212-949-5695
128	Randy Hundley's Fantasy Camps	847-991-9595	847-991-9595
128	Roy Hobbs Baseball	888-484-7422	330-923-1967
291	Royal Dutch Baseball Federation	31-23-5390-244	31-23-5385-922
126	SABR	216-575-0500	216-575-0502
124	Scout of the Year Foundation	561-798-5897	—
343	Shenandoah Valley League	540-885-8901	540-886-2068
120	Sport Magazine	212-880-3600	212-229-4838
119	The Sporting News	314-997-7111	314-997-0765
118	Sports Byline USA	415-434-8300	415-391-2569
118	Sportsfan Radio Network	800-895-1022	702-740-4171
120	Sports Illustrated	212-522-1212	212-522-4543
118	The Sports Network	416-494-1212	416-490-7010
121	Spring Training BB Yearbook	919-967-2420	919-967-6294
116	STATS, Inc.	847-677-3322	847-470-9160
121	Street and Smith's Baseball	212-880-8698	212-880-4347
120	Street and Smith's Sports Bus. Jrnl.	704-973-1400	704-973-1401
335	Sydney Olympic Org. Committee	61-2-9297-2000	61-2-9297-2020
351	T-Ball USA Association, Inc.	203-381-1449	203-381-1440
118	TBS	404-827-1700	404-827-1593
290	Taiwan Major League	886-2-2545-9566	886-2-2514-0802
128	Team Best	770-745-3434	770-745-3433
347	Team One National Showcase	606-291-4463	606-291-4463
271	Texas-Louisiana League	214-575-5800	214-570-0319
347	Top Guns Showcase	208-762-1100	208-762-1100
128	Topps	212-376-0300	212-376-0573
121	Total Baseball	914-382-6964	914-382-6037
121	Ultimate Sports Publishing	206-301-9466	206-301-9420
335	Universal Baseball	609-631-9338	609-631-9299
128	Upper Deck	760-929-6500	760-929-6556
351	US Amateur Baseball Association	425-776-7130	425-776-7130
335	USA Baseball	520-327-9700	520-327-9221
351	USSSA	804-732-4099	804-732-1704
335	US Olympic Committee	719-632-5551	719-578-4654
119	USA Today	703-276-3731	703-558-3988
120	USA Today Baseball Weekly	703-558-5630	703-558-4678
296	Venezuelan League	58-2-761-2750	58-2-761-7661
290	Venezuelan Summer League	58-41-24-0321	58-41-24-0705
118	WGN	773-528-2311	773-528-6050
274	Western League	530-897-6125	530-897-6124
125	World Umpires Association	410-329-1999	—